SAMUEL ELBERT

and the Age of

REVOLUTION IN GEORGIA,

1740–1788

MERCER UNIVERSITY PRESS

Endowed by

TOM WATSON BROWN
and
THE WATSON-BROWN FOUNDATION, INC.

SAMUEL ELBERT

and the Age of

REVOLUTION IN GEORGIA,

1740–1788

Clay Ouzts

MERCER UNIVERSITY PRESS
Macon, Georgia

MUP/ 1027

© 2022 by Mercer University Press
Published by Mercer University Press
1501 Mercer University Drive
Macon, Georgia 31207
All rights reserved

26 25 24 23 22   5 4 3 2 1

Books published by Mercer University Press are printed on acid-free paper that meets the requirements of the American National Standard for Information Sciences—Permanence of Paper for Printed Library Materials.

Printed and bound in the United States.

This book is set in ADOBE CASLON PRO.

Cover/jacket design by Burt&Burt.

ISBN   978-0-88146-858-8
Cataloging-in-Publication Data is available from the Library of Congress

*This work is dedicated to my father,
Ronald Claybourn Ouzts (1934–2007),
my mother, Carl Ann Pass Ouzts,
and my children,
Forbes, Addison, Graham, and MacKenzie,
the descendants of Patriots,
and to the memory of Samuel Elbert.*

Contents

Preface: In Search of Samuel Elbert — ix

Acknowledgments — xii

Abbreviations — xxi

1: Parents, Patronage, and Professions: Samuel Elbert's Greening Years — 1

2: "The Bulwark of Our Liberties": Samuel Elbert, the Assembly, and the Voice of the People, 1769–1771 — 28

3: A Devotion to the Duties of Life: Fatherhood, Brotherhood, and Grenadiers, 1771–1773 — 46

4: "That Love for My Country Which Prompted Me": The Americanization of Samuel Elbert — 71

5: "Judged by the Law of Liberty": Samuel Elbert and the Making of a Revolution in Georgia, 1775 — 89

6: "To Do Them Honor": Samuel Elbert and the "Spirit of '76" in Georgia — 113

7: "For God's Sake Let Me Hear from You": Samuel Elbert and the Second Florida Campaign, 1777 — 144

8: "To Save Your Country from Ruin": Samuel Elbert's Western Campaign in the Ceded Lands, 1777 — 172

9: "You Must Imagine What My Feelings Were": Action on the Frederica River and the Third Florida Campaign, 1778 — 199

10: "We Have Lost the Day": The Fall of Savannah — 227

11: "Nothing Less than a Total Rout": The Fall of Augusta and the Battle of Brier Creek — 260

12: "A Day of Reckoning Is Hastening On": The Ordeal of Samuel Elbert, 1779–1781 — 290

13: Land and Laurels: Samuel Elbert and the Consolidation of the Revolution in Georgia, 1781–1784 — 319

14: "Many Irregularities Have Taken Place": Governor Elbert's Trials, Triumphs, and Border Wars, 1785 — 339

15: Rest in Pieces — 372

16: "But All Georgia Will Thy Worth Rehearse": The Meaning of Samuel Elbert — 394

Timeline — 401

Bibliography — 405

Index — 421

Preface

In Search of Samuel Elbert

On Patriot's Day, April 19, 2005, the Marshes of Glynn Chapter of the Georgia Society, Sons of the American Revolution (GSSAR) dedicated a historical marker on St. Simons Island commemorating Samuel Elbert and his 1778 naval victory over a British fleet on the Frederica River. Held at the Fort Frederica National Monument, the dedication included a ceremony by the GSSAR Color Guard, who dressed in period blue uniforms and the typical tri-cornered hats worn by the Continental Army. Many witnessed the event, preceded a day earlier by a two-hour tour on the Frederica River along a portion of the route that Elbert's galleys sailed during the engagement. Everyone present looked forward to a low-country boil and BBQ meal with peach cobbler for dessert after the tour. Later that evening, Virginia Steele Wood, a naval specialist at the Library of Congress and expert on the 1778 battle, spoke at the Coastal Georgia Historical Society quarterly meeting about the significance of Elbert's victory.[1]

The Frederica River ceremony was supposed to be a one-time event, but over the next decade it turned into an annual affair. In 2009, a crowd of more than one hundred people gathered at St. Simons Island's casino to honor Elbert and his capture of British warships. Among the attendees was a delegation of the Samuel Elbert Chapter of the GSSAR from Elbert County in the northeast region of the state near Athens, who laid wreaths, fired honorary muskets, and tolled a bell. Present too were representatives from the National Society of the Daughters of the American Revolution in period costume, who organized the event and respectfully curtseyed before the wreaths as they placed them in their proper positions. After the ceremony, some of the reenactors mingled with the crowd. One handed out toy muskets to children and marched them through a drill. "Put your juice down," one reenactor told a little girl as he gave her a toy musket. For

---

[1] "Patriots Day 2005," *Hornet's Nest*, 12.

several hours, youngsters rolled hoops, played with yo-yos, and participated in colonial games.[2] For many in the audience, it was the first time they had even heard of Elbert.

The accolades heaped upon Elbert continued. In 2006 and 2007, at the Savannah Battlefield Park commemoration of the failed American assault on October 9, 1779, at the Spring Hill Redoubt during the Siege of Savannah, patriotic organizers sold stones representing Patriots killed or wounded during the attack. Anyone could purchase a stone to honor their Revolutionary ancestor for a whopping $1,779. The stones later became part of a reconstructed redoubt close to the original fortification. The Edward Telfair Chapter of the GSSAR spearheaded an effort to get Elbert a stone, although he did not participate in either the siege of Savannah or the epic battle that followed. Norman Hoffman, one of the chief visionaries of the project in the Telfair Chapter, was pleased with the outpouring of financial support for Elbert's stone. "It is the first time the Edward Telfair Chapter has ever gotten anything funded," he said.[3]

Elbert was certainly worthy of the honors bestowed upon him by the GSSAR. Promoted to brigadier general by the end of the Revolution, he was present at nearly every major military engagement in Georgia prior to 1780. Even before that, he was a leading figure among Georgia's revolutionaries and was a prominent member of the Council of Safety that met regularly at Tondee's Tavern in Savannah. He commanded the state's first militia units at the conflict's beginning and was appointed in 1776 as lieutenant colonel (and then colonel) of the 2nd Battalion of Continental troops authorized by Congress. He later commanded the whole Georgia Line. During the war, Elbert participated in two failed campaigns (1777 and 1778) into British-held Florida to capture St. Augustine. He commanded the Georgia Continental troops in Savannah on December 29, 1778, when it fell to the British after a feeble defense. Just over two months later, on March 3, 1779, he was present at the Battle of Brier Creek along the Savannah River below Augusta where he again witnessed the total collapse of the American army and became a prisoner on parole for over two years. After his exchange, he joined General George Washington's Continental Army in Virginia and participated in the epic siege of Yorktown

---

[2] Terry Dickson, "St. Simons Holds War Observance," *Florida Times-Union*, April 19, 2009.

[3] Linda Sickler, "You say you want a revolution?," *Savannah News*, October 2, 2007.

in fall 1781, where General Lord Charles Cornwallis finally surrendered his British army.

During the Revolutionary era, Elbert interacted with several prominent figures, including George Washington and the French commander Gilbert du Motier, Marquis de Lafayette. Elbert later named one of his sons Samuel Emmanuel de la Fayette to honor the Frenchman. He even corresponded once with Philadelphia's esteemed statesman, Benjamin Franklin. In Georgia, he was friends with almost everyone there linked to the Revolution, such as Edward Telfair, George Walton, Archibald Bulloch, John Habersham, Joseph Habersham, Noble Wimberly Jones, and General Lachlan McIntosh, to name only a few.

Elbert's term as Georgia's governor (1785–1786) was likewise characterized by notable achievements, and chief among them was the chartering of Franklin College, later known as the University of Georgia. However, Elbert's year in office was also fraught with challenges, particularly dealing with Georgia's borders. He initiated a diplomatic crisis when he and the Georgia Assembly attempted to create Bourbon County along the banks of the Mississippi on land claimed by both Georgia and Spain. The Treaty of Galphintown, signed with a small delegation of Creeks, and the subsequent running of boundary lines in the disputed Oconee lands touched off a frontier war with the Indians. There was also an ongoing dispute with South Carolina over its boundary with Georgia. The border tensions persisted and were not resolved until after Elbert left office.

Beyond Elbert's Revolutionary War experience and term as governor, he had many links to other aspects of Georgia's history during the eighteenth century. His mother was a passenger on the *Anne* when Oglethorpe founded Georgia in 1733, and his great uncle, William Calvert, another original colonist, became Georgia's first Baptist. Elbert married Elizabeth Rae, the daughter of John Rae, one of Georgia's wealthiest fur traders. Not long after that, Elbert also became involved in the fur trade. His work placed him squarely on the frontier, where he learned the wilderness and developed relationships with Indian leaders. He had a lifelong interest in Masonry. As a grand master of the masonic lodge, he presided over the formal establishment of independent Masonry in Georgia after the Revolution. When he died in 1788, his family buried him in a Native American temple mound a few miles above Savannah on Pipemaker's Creek near its junction with the Savannah River. On that same mound, the Moravians established a school called Irene in 1736 to Christianize Tomochichi's Yamacraw Indians.[4]

In 1790, shortly after he died, the assembly created Elbert County in Northeast Georgia in his honor. The county was part of the original Wilkes County, established in 1777 during the Revolution, which itself lay within the New Purchase obtained by Royal Governor James Wright from the Creeks and Cherokee in 1773. The triangular-shaped county, situated between the forks of the Savannah and Broad Rivers, established Elberton as its county seat in 1803. Though he never stepped foot in what became Elbert County, citizens there have honored him by attaching his name to streets, schools, inns, community organizations, and many other features.

During the Revolution, Georgia produced two brigadier generals in the Continental Army. One was Lachlan McIntosh, who is the subject of a scholarly biography. The other was Samuel Elbert, whose story remains untold. Considering Elbert's achievements, influence, historical significance, and even legacy, it is hard to imagine that there is no modern published study highlighting his life within the larger context of the Revolution. Early histories of the state, beginning with Hugh McCall's two-volume *History of Georgia*, published in 1811, mention Elbert and his role during the conflict. Georgia historian Charles C. Jones Jr. produced the first biographical attempt on Elbert in the 1880s. In 1886, he delivered a keynote address about Elbert to a meeting of the Georgia Historical Society at Hodgson Hall in Savannah. In the following year, he published the address as a short forty-eight-page work titled *The Life and Services of the Honorable Maj. Gen. Samuel Elbert of Georgia*. Jones believed then that the former general and governor would be "enshrined in the annals of Georgia, and his memory will be cherished by all," especially because of his life of virtue and patriotism.[5]

After Jones's biography, nothing else appeared on Elbert until 1951. In that year, Clarice Eulone Purcell successfully defended her unpublished master's thesis at the University of Georgia titled "The Public Career of Samuel Elbert." Sitting on her committee was Georgia's esteemed historian E. Merton Coulter. After Purcell's thesis, studies on Elbert entered a

---

[4] "General Samuel Elbert (1740–1788)," state historical marker, Colonial Park Cemetery, Savannah, GA.

[5] C. C. Jones Jr., *Life and Services of the Honorable Maj. Gen. Samuel Elbert of Georgia*, 42.

second phase of dormancy. Since that time, a few important works on Elbert have appeared in historical journals concerning specific aspects about his Revolutionary experience. In 1980, Gordon B. Smith published an article titled "The Georgia Grenadiers" in the *Georgia Historical Quarterly* that explored the connection between Elbert, the Masonic Lodge in Savannah, and the militia he came to command on the eve of the American Revolution. Nearly a quarter-century later, Virginia Steele Wood's article, "The Georgia Navy's Dramatic Victory," about Elbert's capture of British ships on the Frederica River, appeared in the same journal, coinciding with the dedication of his marker on St. Simons Island in 2005. Other articles about events involving Elbert have appeared. For example, two works on the Battle of Brier Creek (one in 1982 and the other in 2004) offer details about that encounter while exploring Elbert's role in the American defeat.[6] Beyond these few studies, there is little else in the realm of secondary works, scholarly or otherwise, on him.

A variety of archival, microfilm, and printed primary sources were important to this study. Although few, Elbert's personal papers and correspondences are scattered across several manuscript collections in a few archives, like those at the Georgia Historical Society in Savannah, the Hargrett Rare Book and Manuscript Library at the University of Georgia, and the Rubenstein Rare Book and Manuscript Library at Duke University. Most valuable was the "Order Book of Samuel Elbert," covering his years of military service from 1776 until late 1778. A "Letter Book of Governor Samuel Elbert" containing Elbert's personal correspondences with others during his year as governor also exists. There are several links and references to Elbert in printed collections of primary sources, such as the *Colonial Records of Georgia* and *The Revolutionary Records of the State of Georgia*, both edited by Allen Candler, and George White's *Historical Collections of Georgia*. The availability of digital sources, like the Southeastern Native American Documents, 1730–1842, among many others, has made countless documents accessible that were not readily obtainable by earlier scholars.

---

[6] The studies on Brier Creek are David S. Heidler, "The American Defeat at Briar Creek, 3 March 1779," *GHQ* 66/3 (Fall 1982): 317–31, and Joshua B. Howard, "'Things Here Wear Melancholy Appearance': The American Defeat at Brier Creek," *GHQ* 88/4 (Winter 2004): 477–98. See also William Henry, "An Unfortunate Affair: The Battle of Brier Creek and the Aftermath in Georgia," master's thesis, Georgia Southern University, 2012.

Several important secondary works were crucial in this study, and most valuable among them was Kenneth Coleman's *The American Revolution in Georgia*, which guided me through the entire Revolutionary era in the state. The list of other scholarly and insightful studies appearing prominently in this study are too many to name here, but two that I consulted frequently were Harvey Jackson's *Lachlan McIntosh and the Politics of Revolutionary Georgia* and Martha Condray's *The Georgia-Florida Contest in the American Revolution, 1776–1778*.

Despite the primary and secondary sources available for scholarly research, many gaps remain in Elbert's story. Elbert, like most people from his time, was not from a wealthy family and left behind no personal papers or writings to highlight his life before the American Revolution, so little exists about his childhood or early adult years; however, his name appears with more frequency in the documents and newspapers during the late 1760s. Unfortunately, many documents were lost or destroyed during the war or, because of Savannah's historical and accidental fires, consumed in flames. Still, the lack of a rich trove of primary sources impedes a full reckoning of his life and presented the greatest challenge in writing about Elbert. For this reason, I decided to expand the scope of my study and look more broadly at the age of Revolution in Georgia with Elbert as the focus. This work, then, is not a biography of Elbert. Instead, it is a broad overview of the times in which he lived that emphasizes the Revolution and its aftermath through his perspective.

I could easily say that I became interested in Elbert because I am from Elbert County, but that is not how I arrived at my subject. For me, the path to Elbert ran, oddly, through neighboring Oglethorpe County. Shortly after the end of the American Revolution, several Virginia settlers led by George Mathews (a future governor of the state) filtered into "New Georgia's" Broad River valley, which was part of Wilkes County at the time. Among the new arrivals were John Marks; his wife, Lucy Meriwether; and her son, future explorer Meriwether Lewis, who was a young teenager. They constructed a frontier log cabin near our family's property on Millstone Creek, not far from its forks with the Broad River. Lewis remained in the Millstone community for only a few years, but during that time, Indians attacked their small frontier settlement. George R. Gilmer's *Sketches of Some of the First Settlers in Upper Georgia* gives an account of that attack. Gilmer, himself a future Georgia governor, was a descendant of one of the wealthy Virginia families that moved to the Broad River. Much of Gilmer's history came from second-hand information, including the story about the Indian attack on the Millstone community. By Gilmer's reckoning, Cherokee Indians conducted the attack sometimes between 1790 and 1795. He was wrong. According to historian Stephen Ambrose, Lewis was gone from Georgia by 1787, his mother having sent him back to Virginia for a proper education.[7] Furthermore, Georgia's Indian problems at that time did not involve the Cherokee. Instead, the conflicts were with the Creeks and the source of contention was Georgia's claims to the Oconee lands. The Creek Indian attack on the Millstone community referenced by Gilmer took place between 1785 and 1787. The dates are crucial because they fall within the time that Elbert was governor. This incident, then, related back to Elbert and is what originally kindled my interest in him.

The attack on Lewis's frontier home was not isolated as raids occurred all along Georgia's frontier and settlements. My question was "Why?" What prompted the Creeks to strike out against the state in the years following the American Revolution, especially in an area given up by treaty a decade earlier? The answer led me back to Elbert and a series of treaties negotiated with some of the Creek headmen that gave Georgians claim to the lands across the Oconee River. Those treaties, deemed legitimate by Elbert and others, were fraudulent in the eyes of many Creeks. The dispute over the Oconee lands and the subsequent running of boundaries and lines brought to the forefront the opposition of Alexander McGillivray of the Creeks and instigated an Indian war that lasted, off and on, for nearly a decade. The Creek War, then, is the clue I followed that led me to Elbert. Over time, as my research expanded, I went beyond the Indian problems on the frontier to Elbert himself and, from there, to the American Revolution in Georgia and his place in the state's history.

History is a little bit of fact, a little bit of fiction, and a great deal of imagination. In my journey to comprehend Elbert and his times, I have discovered many things, but I have also confronted a host of myths and legends surrounding his life. Did a masonic sign really save his life on the Brier Creek battlefield? Did Indians sent by Loyalists to kill him recognize a second hand signal and embrace him in friendship instead? I have tried to see him, in my mind's eye, as I strolled around the streets and squares of old Savannah, trying to imagine his world and even his appearance. Elbert is almost as elusive now, in terms of places one could visit and see, as he is in the historical documents. Nearly all the places once connected to

---

[7] Gilmer, *Georgians*, 82–83. See also Ambrose, *Undaunted Courage*, 24–25.

him are gone due to fires, modernization, and time. In 1796, a horrible fire that burned most of Savannah turned the original Christ Church, which he attended and where his funeral was held, into a heap of ashes. The original Tondee's Tavern, the cradle of the Revolution in Georgia where Elbert helped to chart the course of his rebellion, was also destroyed in that same conflagration. Rae's Hall Plantation, along Pipemaker's Creek, where Elbert often frequented and visited his wife's family, has long since vanished, as has the Irene Mound where mourners buried him in 1788; it is currently beneath one of the sprawling asphalt parking lots of the Georgia Ports Authority. The few remaining places connected to Elbert are slowly vanishing. The battlefield on Brier Creek in Screven County, where Elbert became a prisoner in 1779, is currently part of the Tuckahoe Wildlife Management Area. Although the site is in near pristine condition, there are plans to run the Palmetto Project gas pipeline from Jacksonville, Florida, to Belton, South Carolina, right through the middle of the battlefield. The whole proposal has unified historians, patriotic organizations like the GSSAR, and even locals into a wall of opposition against the project.[8] Today, the pipeline's fate is still uncertain. There is one certainty, however. If the pipeline is constructed according to present plans, it will destroy the integrity of the Brier Creek Battlefield and endanger one of the last physical links to Elbert that one could see.

Several years ago, in graduate school, one of my history professors emphasized how important it is to get as close as possible to one's historical subject. With the advice of my professor in mind, I visited Elbert's second gravesite in Savannah's Colonial Park Cemetery after spring semester in May 2015. I sat on the ground, near the historical marker, and faced the long, rectangular box covering his remains. For the next hour, I carried on a one-way conversation with him. Based on some of the odd looks I received, I suspect tourists ambling through the graveyard must have thought I was crazy. I ignored them and instead concentrated on my encounter with Elbert. I told him what my intentions were and laid out everything I already knew. I also produced a long list of typed questions (two or three pages) about things I did not know or understand and, one by one, carefully read them off to him. Though it felt good to get everything out in the open, I did not expect any answers. I am eternally grateful that he never replied.

---

[8] For Tondee's Tavern, see "About Tondee's," https://tondees.com/historic-notes.

Acknowledgments

A study of this scope and duration involved many people beyond myself and I am indebted to everyone who aided in this project along the way. That guidance extended beyond the navigation of manuscript collections and digital archives across several libraries and computer networks. It also involved critiques and criticisms of some chapters and a steady stream of encouragement from so many for me to forge ahead and finish the drill, despite the intrusion called "life."

The staff at the University of North Georgia's libraries were extremely helpful (and patient) throughout this process; they got me items on loan and showed me databases and how to search them. Without their assistance, this work would have been much less thorough. I would specifically like to thank Virginia Feher for showing me the Revolutionary War pension database, which became a valuable resource for this study. Angela Megaw showed me other databases, and her patience was remarkable as she rounded up books, documents, and additional things. Emily Thornton was also helpful getting me microfilm and an assortment of other items necessary for the completion of this project. All three of you were just fantastic, and I appreciate your time, patience, and expertise. Thank you. I would also like to thank the staff at regional libraries who also gave their time and knowledge of their collections to help me find sources. I specifically want to thank Jan Burroughs at the Elbert County Public Library. From the moment I met Jan and told her of my project, she was excited to help. Thank you, Jan, for ordering all those rolls of microfilm and books for me on loan. Thank you, too, for your enthusiasm and your willingness to help.

My time at the Georgia Historical Society in Savannah was a joyful experience, not only because of all the history floating around the facility but also because of the dedicated staff who pulled files, manuscripts, and boxes for me from their collections without complaint. They even suggested other sources in their collections for me to examine, many of which I found useful. The staff at Duke's Rubenstein Rare Book and Manuscript Library were just awesome, and I appreciate their help in pulling my endless requests. My week there was memorable, and I hope someday to go back to this unique facility to research another project. I would also like to thank the friendly and excellent staff at the Hargrett Rare Book and Manuscript library at the University of Georgia in Athens. I visited there many times and they were always incredibly helpful and friendly. I thank everyone at Hargrett who helped gather pictures, manuscripts, and other sources in their vast collection for me to use. I especially thank Mary Palmer Linnemann, who spent many hours helping me dig out images for this work.

I have so many friends and colleagues at the University of North Georgia who have been a great inspiration to me both as a scholar and as a teacher. At UNG, the historians have created a group called Works in Progress (WIP) where members submit their chapters, conference papers, and research ideas for others to read and offer criticisms and insight. The WIP's goal, of course, is to promote scholarly activity, publications, and peer encouragement. Throughout my process of writing, I submitted three chapters to the WIP at different times, and members read and evaluated them. Those discussions made the three chapters stronger and more focused. They even caused me to change the title of one and the entire direction of another. I am so indebted to all my wonderful colleagues in that group, especially Yi Deng, Bill Balco, Victoria Hightower, Johanna Luthman, Geran Dodson, Ann Tucker, Robert Scott, Alex Wisnoski, Michael Proulx, Tamara Spike, Jennifer Smith, and Warren Rogers. To my fellow historians who took time out of their hectic semesters to read portions of my work, I thank you. It is an honor to serve in our department with all of you.

I would also like to thank some of my other history colleagues. First, Jeff Pardue is the most supportive and encouraging department chair I have ever worked with. Thank you, Jeff, for believing in me. I know I have talked about Elbert for years, but his time has now come, and all the research and travel funding you helped me get has finally produced fruit. I am so thankful for the assistance you provided along the way, especially your constant encouragement. Ben Wynne, you are a complete inspiration to me. Thank you, Ben, for the motivation you constantly provided and for listening to me babble on about Elbert for years and years. You are a true role model who challenged me to achieve big things. I wanted you to know that. Dee Gillespie is another encourager. Dee, you too heard about Elbert until you were sick of it. However, I want you to know that on some occasions when we spoke, I was struggling with writing. I remember the advice you gave me one day in my office when words were not flowing onto the paper. You said, "Write, Clay, write!" I followed your suggestion and I thank you for that nudging. I want to thank Warren Rogers Jr., too. Warren, we had hundreds of conversations through the years about Elbert and the direction I should take this study. I want to thank you for your advice because I followed it and this manuscript is much the better for it. You also read some of the chapters and offered criticism. I will always remember the day you and your family came to visit me at my bucolic cabin in the woods during the holidays. In the rustic comforts of my cabin kitchen, I thrust the introduction to the manuscript, which I had just finished cutting for a third time, on you to read and you patiently complied. Please forgive me for that intrusion on your visit. Thank you, too, Pam Sezgin. You were a valuable resource for me concerning Jewish history in Colonial and Revolutionary Georgia. I would like to thank George Justice for sharing with me his deep insight and knowledge about early Georgia history and for alerting me to valuable resources that I had not considered. I want to thank also Lee Cheek. Lee, we talk a good bit about everything under the sun, but you were always interested enough to ask me how the Elbert project was going in each conversation. You may not know it, but each time you inquired, you pushed me to complete this work. Thank you for having faith in me.

Another person who deserves special recognition is Mary Anne Abbe. Mary, I cannot recall how our paths crossed, but from the moment I met you I have been thoroughly impressed with your deep knowledge of archival research, courthouse records, and Georgia history. When this project was in its infancy, you took your valuable time to gather sources for me while you were engaged in your own archival research. I will never forget the days that you showed up at my Oconee office with all sorts of things you had discovered—wills, inventories, and many other items—and then explained them all to me. Thanks, too, for setting me straight on the difference between a land grant and a bounty. Much of what you gave me found a place in this study. I still think I owe you twenty-five dollars for copies.

I also thank Bob Holiday for reading the manuscript in its entirety and offering constructive criticisms. Thank you, Bob, for your insights and friendship and for allowing me to give my first historical talk on Elbert to the Tallahassee Historical Society in May 2021. Gina LaMedica Duck-Mincey offered much support in the early stages of this work, and I thank her for the encouragement. Thank you, Gina. After all of the revisions and editing, any remaining errors in this work, grammatical or otherwise, are mine alone and in no way reflect on all the wonderful people who devoted their time and expertise to this project.

My father was a big history enthusiast, especially when it came to the Revolution. He died in 2007, and I am sorry he is not around to see this work. He is the person who originally fired my passion for the American Revolution. In many ways, this work is the fruit of his love of history, which he passed on to me. I know he would be proud of this accomplishment. My mother has always stuck with me in my life through all its hills and valleys. She has pushed me to finish Elbert, and I am sure she is glad to see this work completed. As always, she is my rock. Thank you, Mama. I love you.

Finally, to my children Forbes, Addison, Graham, and MacKenzie, thank you for your patience. I know Elbert has intruded into many things you wanted us, and me, to do. I cannot fathom how boring I seemed as I sat wedded to a laptop in the cabin for all those days, even years, with books, notecards, and papers strewn on tables, chairs, and the cabin floor. I apologize for my messes and self-absorption. This work is a tribute to you for allowing me the space I needed to research, think, and write—and now you have it to cherish forever. I love each of you tremendously—more than you can comprehend. Now you can have your Daddy back, and I think we should celebrate by going camping, hitting the beach, and floating the mighty Broad.

Abbreviations

CGHS *Collections of the Georgia Historical Society*

CNYHS
"Proceedings of a Court Martial...for the Trial of Major General Howe, December 7, 1781." *Collections of the New York Historical Society for the Year 1879.* Vol. 12. New York: New York Historical Society, 1880.

CRG
Candler, Allen D., ed. *The Colonial Records of the State of Georgia.* 39 vols. Atlanta: Franklin-Turner Company, 1904.

GGCJ, 1772–1773
Warren, Mary Bondurant, and Jack Moreland Jones. *Georgia Governor and Council Journals, 1772–1773.* Athens: Heritage Press, 2004.

GGCJ, 1774–1777
Warren, Mary Bondurant, and Jack Moreland Jones. *Georgia Governor and Council Journals, 1774–1777.* Athens: Heritage Papers, 2006.

GHQ
Georgia Historical Quarterly

LBGSE
"Letter Book of Governor Samuel Elbert, from January, 1785, to November, 1785." *Collections of the Georgia Historical Society.* Vol. 5, pt. 2. Savannah: The Morning News Print, 1902.

LSJW
"Letters from Sir James Wright." *Collections of the Georgia Historical Society.* Vol. 3. Savannah: Morning News Office, 1873.

MMAR
Moultrie, William. *Memoirs of the American Revolution, so far as it Related to the States of North and South-Carolina, and Georgia.* 2 vols. New York: David Longworth, 1802.

OBSE
"Order Book of Samuel Elbert, Colonel and Brigadier General in the Continental Army, October 1776, to November, 1778." *Collections of the Georgia Historical Society*. Vol. 5, pt. 2. Savannah: The Morning News Print, 1902.

PCS
"Proceedings of the Georgia Council of Safety." *Collections of the Georgia Historical Society*. Vol. 5, pt. 1. Savannah: Braid & Hutton, Printers and Binders, 1901.

PLM, pt. 1
Hawes, Lilla M., ed. "Letter Book of Lachlan McIntosh, 1776–1777. Part I." *Georgia Historical Quarterly* 38/2 (1954): 148–69. http://www.jstor.org/stable/40577509.

PLM, pt. 2
Hawes, Lilla M., ed. "The Papers of Lachlan McIntosh, 1774–1799. Part II." *Georgia Historical Quarterly* 38/3 (1954): 253–67. http://www.jstor.org/stable/40577710.

PLM, pt. 3
Hawes, Lilla M., ed. "The Papers of Lachlan McIntosh, 1774–1799, Part III: Letter Book of Lachlan McIntosh, 1776–1777." *Georgia Historical Quarterly* 38/4 (1954): 356–68. http://www.jstor.org/stable/40577545.

RRG
Candler, Allen D., ed. *The Revolutionary Records of the State of Georgia*. 3 vols. Atlanta: Franklin-Turner Co., 1908.

Samuel Elbert (1740–1788). This portrait, which went into a locket, is the only original likeness of Elbert that exists. Elbert had it made when he visited London in 1773. He is wearing a red captain's uniform of the Grenadier Regiment, a Georgia militia unit which he commanded before the Revolution. The portrait and locket, passed down through direct decedents of Elbert, belonged to Richard Elbert Whitehead when he died in 2011.

Courtesy of Hargrett Rare Book and Manuscript Library/University of Georgia Libraries

Elizabeth Rae Elbert (1745–1792) was the daughter of fur trader and wealthy Savannah and Augusta merchant John Rae. She married Elbert on November 29, 1769. This locket and miniature painting of her was made when Elbert visited London in 1773 and was in the possession of direct descendent, Richard Elbert Whitehead when he died in 2011.

Courtesy of Hargrett Rare Book and Manuscript Library/University of Georgia Libraries

Royal Governor Sir James Wright (1716–1785) ruled Georgia from 1760 until he was driven out of the colony in March 1776. He returned after the fall of Savannah to resume leadership from July 1779 until the British evacuated the state on July 11, 1782. During Elbert's term in the Assembly in the early 1770s, he developed a dislike for Wright which never abated.

Courtesy of Hargrett Rare Book and Manuscript Library/University of Georgia Libraries

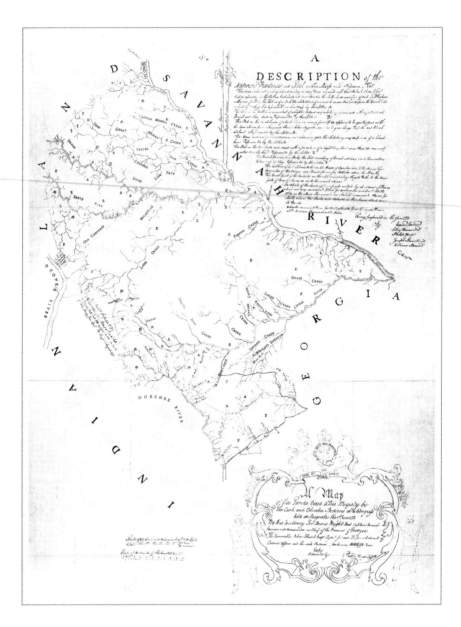

Map of the Ceded Lands, 1773. This map is based on a survey of the Ceded Lands after the New Purchase from the Creeks and Cherokee in Augusta during the summer of 1773. The area depicted in this map, which is north of Augusta, became Wilkes County in 1777.

Courtesy of Hargrett Rare Book and Manuscript Library/University of Georgia Libraries

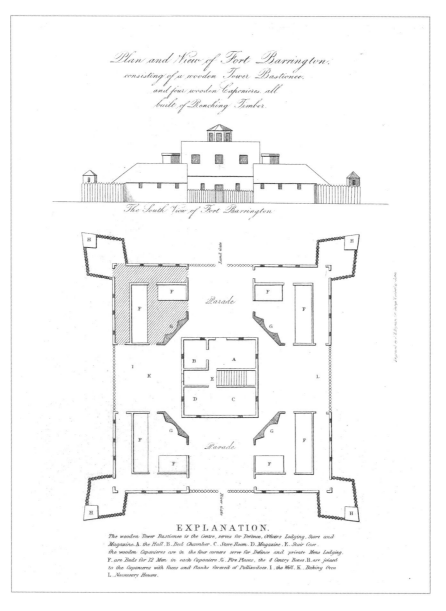

Fort Barrington (Fort Howe) on the Altamaha depicting the general layout of the outpost. Originally constructed in 1751, it was captured and burned by the British during the Revolution.

Courtesy of Hargrett Rare Book and Manuscript Library/University of Georgia Libraries

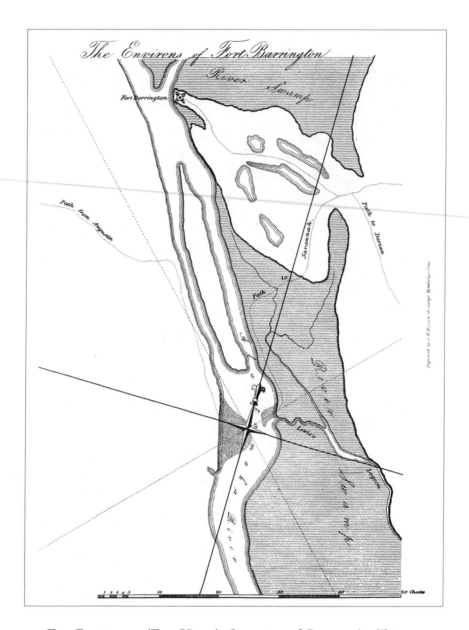

Fort Barrington (Fort Howe), Overview of Geography. This map shows the location of Fort Barrington on the Altamaha River. The fort was along a point at the river's bank and protected on three sides by water. Notice, too, the "Path to Savannah."

Courtesy of Hargrett Rare Book and Manuscript Library/University of Georgia Libraries

Joseph Habersham (1751–1815) was Elbert's closest friend. They fought together during the Revolution and when Elbert was governor, Habersham was the Speaker of the House. He was later appointed Postmaster General by President George Washington in 1795.

Courtesy of Hargrett Rare Book and Manuscript Library/University of Georgia Libraries

Lachlan McIntosh (1725–1806) assumed command of Georgia's Continental Battalions during the early years of the Revolution. As his subordinate, Elbert both admired and respected him as a commander. After McIntosh killed Button Gwinnett in a duel on May 16, 1777, his enemies chased him out of the state, putting Elbert in charge of the Georgia Line.

Courtesy of Hargrett Rare Book and Manuscript Library/University of Georgia Libraries

Archibald Bulloch (1730–1777) became Georgia's first "president" on April 15, 1776. He died under mysterious circumstances before finishing his term in office.

Courtesy of Hargrett Rare Book and Manuscript Library/University of Georgia Libraries

Button Gwinnett (1735–1777) was a signer of the Declaration of Independence from Georgia. He became temporary governor after the death of Archibald Bulloch. Gwinnett died in a duel with Lachlan McIntosh on May 16, 1777.

Courtesy of Hargrett Rare Book and Manuscript Library/University of Georgia Libraries

John Adam Treutlen (1734–1782) was elected governor in 1777 just before Button Gwinnett's death. During his term, Elbert undertook his western campaign into the Ceded Lands.

Courtesy of Hargrett Rare Book and Manuscript Library/University of Georgia Libraries

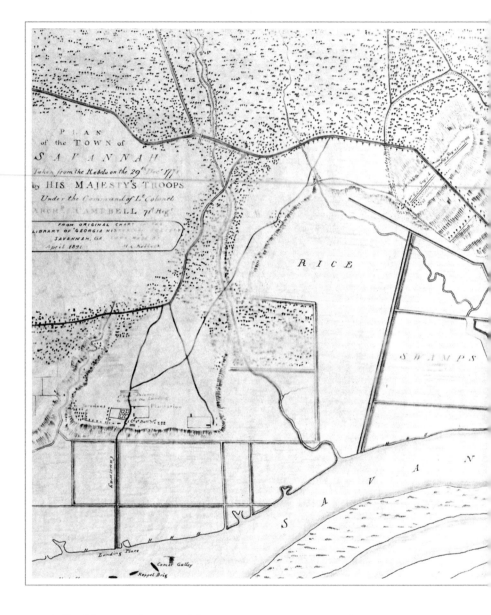

Fall of Savannah, 1778. This map clearly shows the American position on Fairlawn, the British advance from Girardeau's Plantation, the location of their flotilla in the Savannah River, and the retreat of Howe's forces through the city of Savannah, where most of the patriot forces were captured at Musgrove's Creek just on the city's northern outskirts, depicted in dotted circles.

Courtesy of Hargrett Rare Book and Manuscript Library/University of Georgia Libraries

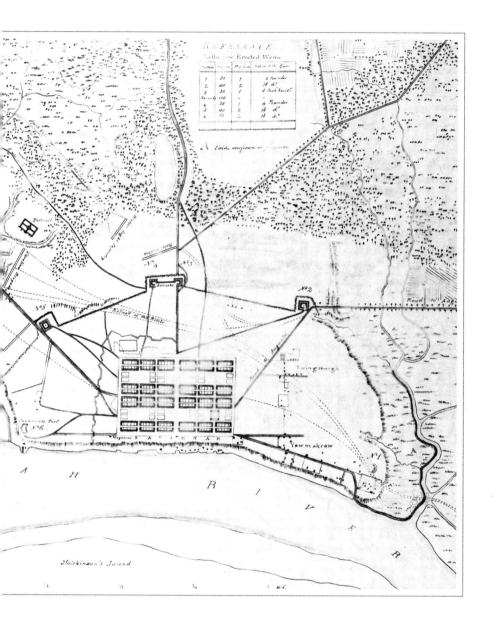

George Walton (1749–1804) was a signer of the Declaration of Independence from Georgia. In addition to being one of the state's Revolutionary politicians, he commanded the militia on December 29, 1779 when the British captured Savannah. During the battle, Walton was wounded and captured.

Courtesy of Hargrett Rare Book and Manuscript Library/University of Georgia Libraries

Mordecai Sheftall (1735–1797), a Jewish merchant in Savannah, was also a close friend to Elbert. During the war, he served as Commissary for the Georgia Line of Continentals before he was captured during the fall of Savannah on December 29, 1779.

Courtesy of Hargrett Rare Book and Manuscript Library/University of Georgia Libraries

Benjamin Lincoln (1733–1810) replaced Robert Howe as the commander of the Southern Continental Army after the failed third Florida campaign in 1779. He would later become the nation's first Secretary of War under President George Washington.

Courtesy of Hargrett Rare Book and Manuscript Library/University of Georgia Libraries

William Moultrie (1730–1805) from South Carolina commanded Continental troops from his state during the third Florida campaign in 1778. He also attempted to coordinate an attack on Archibald Campbell's British army after their evacuation of Augusta in early February 1779. The planned movement was canceled due to the crushing defeat of the American army at Brier Creek on March 3, 1779.

Courtesy of Hargrett Rare Book and Manuscript Library/University of Georgia Libraries

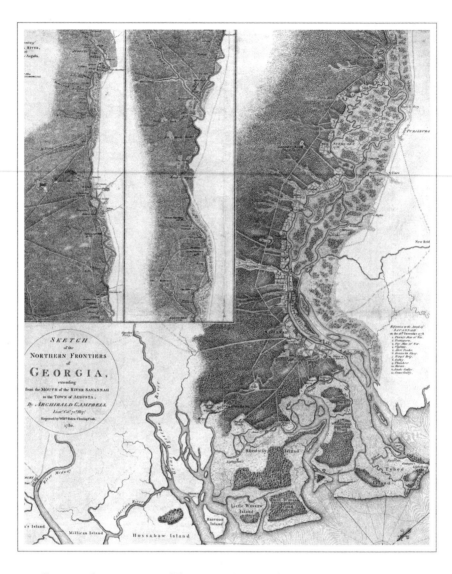

Savannah, circa 1780. This map depicts the fall of Savannah to the British on December 29, 1778. Notice the location of Girardeau's Plantation and the road that led to the American position at Fairlawn. The map also shows the disposition of Robert Howe's and Archibald Campbell's forces and the little path through the swamp that James Baird used to surprise the militia under George Walton on the American right. The inner smaller map shows the location of the Two Sister's Ferry.

Courtesy of Hargrett Rare Book and Manuscript Library/University of Georgia Libraries

Militia Colonel Elijah Clarke (1742–1799) participated in the third Florida campaign in 1778 where he was wounded at the Battle of Alligator Bridge. He also became one of Elbert's business partners after the Revolution.

Courtesy of Hargrett Rare Book and Manuscript Library/University of Georgia Libraries

William Few (1748–1828) and his militia joined others with Elbert in a vain attempt to stop Archibald Campbell's British forces from taking Augusta during late January 1779.

Courtesy of Hargrett Rare Book and Manuscript Library/University of Georgia Libraries

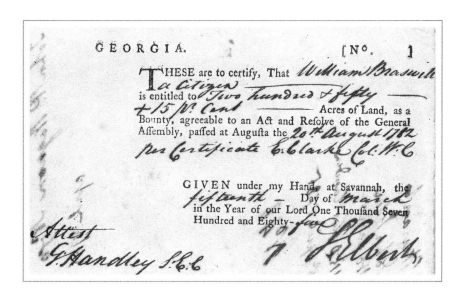

1785 Bounty Certificate. This bounty certificate for land displays Samuel Elbert's signature when he was governor.

Courtesy of Hargrett Rare Book and Manuscript Library/University of Georgia Libraries

Samuel Elbert Reburial, 1924. The Chapter of the Daughters of the American Revolution from Tennille, Georgia, placing a wreath on Elbert's tomb during his reburial ceremony in Savannah's Colonial Cemetery, March 10, 1924.

Atlanta Journal-Constitution via AP

Samuel Elbert Hotel. Sutton Square in Elberton facing west, showing the Elbert County Courthouse. The Samuel Elbert Hotel is the white building to the left of the courthouse, 2021.

Courtesy of Clay Ouzts

Samuel Elbert Monument, Elberton, Georgia, 2021. The image depicting Samuel Elbert is based on a locket painting from 1773.

Courtesy of Clay Ouzts

SAMUEL ELBERT

and the Age of

REVOLUTION IN GEORGIA,

1740–1788

Chapter 1

Parents, Patronage, and Professions: Samuel Elbert's Greening Years

SAMUEL ELBERT'S STORY in Georgia began on February 1, 1733, when his future mother, sixteen-year-old Sarah Greenfield, sailed up the Savannah River, stepped off the *Anne*, and ascended Yamacraw Bluff. There she stood for the first time, along with Georgia's founder, James Oglethorpe and the other original colonists, on the future site of Savannah. Accompanying Greenfield were her brothers, William (age nineteen), Charles (age sixteen), and a servant named Elizabeth Wallace (age nineteen). The uncle of the Greenfield children, forty-four-year-old William Calvert, led the group, along with his forty-two-year-old wife, Mary. When Calvert's family debarked from the *Anne*, it was the first time their feet touched the ground since leaving England on November 6, 1732.[1]

From the beginning, Georgia stood in stark contrast to the other twelve English colonies. For the first twenty years of its existence, twenty-one men called the Georgia Trustees ruled the colony. All resided in London, and during the trustee period, which ended in 1752, Oglethorpe was the only one who ever came to Georgia. The trustees created Georgia, in part, to serve as a buffer between the rest of the colonies and the Spanish and French to the south and west. The lands granted to Georgia through its charter caused immediate tensions with Spain, which claimed possession of the territory from Florida to the Savannah River. Defending against Indians also figured prominently into Georgia's buffer role. After South Carolina's successful but devastating war with the Yamasee Indians (1715–1717), that colony repeatedly petitioned Parliament for a protective zone with forts between themselves and the Indians beyond their borders

---

[1] Portions of this chapter appears in Ouzts, "Good Bargain for the Trust," 25–52. See also Coulter and Saye, eds., *List of the Early Settlers of Georgia*, 3, 20, 106; Temple and Coleman, *Georgia Journeys*, 9.

to the south and west.²

Georgia's uniqueness also included religious goals. Although the colony was officially Anglican, the Georgia Trustees envisioned it as a refuge for Europe's persecuted Protestants. The colony went far in providing religious freedom to a host of groups, such as Baptists and even Jews. For example, Calvert was a Baptist preacher, and for many years, he remained the only person in Georgia representing that faith, except perhaps for his family. By the time trustee rule ended, out of a total population of 5,200, just 0.13 percent (or only seven individuals) residing in the colony were Baptists.³

Philanthropy was a third goal of the trustees, and, like religion, it also impacted Calvert and his family. The trustees hoped that England's impoverished and destitute population could come to Georgia and start over. This, too, set Georgia apart from other colonies. The trustees funded passage across the Atlantic for those who could not afford it. Calvert and his family, like many on the *Anne*, came to the colony as charges of the trustees. As charges, they could expect a small plot of land, a year's worth of provisions from the trustee store, and agricultural tools to help them turn Georgia's forests into small farms and homesteads. According to the rules establishing the colony, each male adult was to receive a fifty-acre "trust grant" through a lottery system, which Calvert helped to coordinate and administer in Savannah. Calvert received lot number seven in Tything Decker Ward, which later became part of Ellis Square. Like all the other town lots, it measured sixty by ninety feet. He also received a five-acre garden plot on the edge of the new town of Savannah in addition to a forty-five-acre farm lot that he was expected to clear and cultivate.⁴

Within a month after the initial landing, the skeletal form of the planned town of Savannah, laid out on a grid of public squares surrounded

---

² Ramsey, *Yamasee War*, 2–3; Spalding, "Colonial Period," 13–15.

³ Gardner, "Baptists in Georgia, 1733–2010," 89, 100; Benedict, *General History of the Baptist Denomination in America*, 2:172; Spalding, "Colonial Period," 17. Trustee propaganda may have persuaded Calvert to come to Georgia. See Sweet, "The natural Advantages of this happy Climate," 6–15.

⁴ "The Minutes of the Common Council of the Trustees for Establishing the Colony of Georgia in America," in ed., *Colonial Records of the State of Georgia* (hereafter cited as *CRG*) 2:8–10, and 14 explains Calvert's role in administering land distribution in Savannah; C. C. Jones, *History of Georgia*, 1:114; Spalding, "Colonial Period," 19–20. For Calvert's lot, see Coulter and Saye, *Early Settlers of Georgia*, 3 and 295–99 for a list of passengers on the *Anne*. For the creation of Savannah's lots, see Cadle, *Georgia Land Surveying*, 12; Knight, *Standard History of Georgia and Georgians*, 1:81.

by trustee, business, and residential lots, took shape on Yamacraw Bluff. All the while, the colonists cleared the forest and lived in tents as they marked Savannah's boundaries. Work progressed along steadily, but with the arrival of summer's heat and humidity, calamity struck in the form of sickness. By the fall, forty of the original colonists were dead, including Calvert's wife, who died on July 4 during the outbreak's peak. While the exact cause of her death is unknown, she, like most of the other colonists who died, probably succumbed to either malaria or dysentery. The symptoms of those diseases were consistent with the colonists' experiences and included aches, pains, high fevers, convulsions, and the bloody flux. One survivor said that the illness, accompanied by a "great trembling," terrific "pain in my head," and "burning heat," laid her down for several days.[5] Sickness continued to plague the colony into the next year, bringing suffering and death to many more settlers.

As Savannah emerged out of the longleaf pine forest, Oglethorpe scoured the surrounding wilderness looking for places to establish forts. He placed one of his strongest outposts along the Ogeechee River, about twenty miles west of Savannah and called it Fort Argyle. Since Georgia was defenseless against an attack from any enemy, the governor of South Carolina, Robert Johnson, generously loaned Oglethorpe a handful of rangers to garrison the forts. One of the young rangers sent to Fort Argyle was William Elbert, the future father of Samuel Elbert. In 1742, nearly a decade after he came to Georgia, the elder Elbert wrote his only known surviving letter to the Georgia Trustees in London. In it, he said that he was born in England but came to South Carolina when he was young. For several years, he was a ranger in South Carolina patrolling between Port Royal and Savannah and served for two years as a lieutenant. During his time at Fort Argyle, Elbert carried out his duties as a soldier on Georgia's frontier, which often involved patrolling rudimentary roads looking for signs of danger.[6]

---

[5] For early descriptions of Savannah, see Oglethorpe to the trustees, March 12, 1733, in K. Coleman and Ready, eds., *Colonial Records of the State of Georgia*, 20:14. In the same source, see Thomas Causton to his wife, March 12, 1732, 16–17, and for disease, McIlvenna, *Short Life of Free Georgia*, 25–27.

[6] Governor Robert Johnson to James Oglethorpe, January 26, 1732, and South Carolina Resolution in White, *Historical Collections of Georgia*, 321–22; Martyn, *Impartial Enquiry*, 51 (description of Fort Argyle); Wesley, *Journal of the Rev. John Wesley*, 1:65; Tailfer, Anderson, and Douglas, *True and Historical Narrative*, 24; C. C. Jones Jr., *History of Georgia*, 1:147; Temple and Coleman, *Georgia Journeys*, 42–43; de Quesada, *History of Georgia Forts*, 13–14. Archaeology is discussed in Elliot, "Fort Argyle." A map illustrating early

Oglethorpe soon sent about ten families to Fort Argyle to settle, and among them was Calvert and his nephew, William Greenfield. Even so, Calvert retained his original lot in Savannah where Charles and Sarah Greenfield presumably lived. In 1762, when the magistrate probated Calvert's last will, the lot was still in his name. Calvert worked diligently on his new lot at Argyle. In 1736, Thomas Causton, who oversaw the trustee store and served as the colony's bailiff, observed that most of the settlers there "don't think of improving their Land (except Calvert)." It is hard to imagine that any land was cultivated since Oglethorpe pressed everyone there into service with the rangers. "The Setlers at Fort Argyle," wrote Causton to the trustees, "are *all of them* entered into Captain McPhersons Troop of Rangers." John Perceval, the Earl of Egmont and one of the trustees in England, penned in his journal that "the Settlers at Fort Arguile…had *all enter'd themselves* into the Rangers Troop." It was in the rangers where Elbert probably met Calvert and through him, his niece Sarah Greenfield. A courtship soon began, and Samuel Elbert's parents were married on June 22, 1734. As Elbert reminded the trustees in his 1742 letter, the marriage linked him into one of the first families in Georgia.[7]

Shortly after his marriage, Elbert left the rangers to seek other employment. For a short while, he served as a messenger running letters, packages, and other items from Savannah to Charleston, but that job barely allowed him to sustain his new household. Apparently, he fell upon hard economic times because in 1736, he became an indentured servant to Joseph Wardrope, a thirty-five-year-old carpenter from Scotland, who "let" Elbert lot 180 in Savannah.[8] The reasoning behind Elbert's decision to become a servant probably concerned the payment to Wardrope for leasing lot 180. For Elbert, the new situation was degrading. It surely made him rue the day that he left the rangers.

---

forts and roads in relation to Savannah is at the Hargrett Rare Book and Manuscript Library at the University of Georgia in Athens. See Lotter, Map of the County of Savannah. For the rangers in South Carolina, see Rowland, Moore, and Rogers Jr., *History of Beaufort County*, 1:141, and Ivers, "Rangers, Scouts, and Tythingmen," 158. Finally, see William Elbert to the trustees, April 20, 1742, in *CRG*, 23:281–82.

[7] Thomas Causton to the trustees, November 26, 1736, in *CRG*, 21:274; Earl of Egmont, *Journal of the Earl of Egmont*, 237; William Elbert to the trustees, April 20, 1742, in *CRG*, 23:282; Coulter and Saye, *Early Settlers of Georgia*, 20. I retain the spelling and punctuation of the originals throughout, adding clarification when necessary. Emphasis in these quotations has been added.

[8] Letter from William Elbert to the trustees, April 20, 1742, in *CRG*, 23:282; Coulter and Saye, *Early Settlers of Georgia*, 72.

No record exists describing the terms of Elbert's servitude or the tasks Wardrope expected him to perform. Elbert likely helped Wardrope with carpentry work in Savannah. He was only one of several indentured servants that Wardrope owned. According to the trustee rules, anyone transporting ten servants from England could qualify for a grant of 500 acres. Since Wardrope brought many servants with him, like George Bunkle from Scotland, he became a large landowner. Elbert and Bunkle probably helped clear Wardrope's land and plant his crops. They also likely became close friends, especially since Wardrope leased Bunkle lot number 179, adjacent to Elbert.[9]

Elbert was a disgruntled servant, and, like many others in his position, he ran away within weeks of beginning his indenture. In their notes, the trustees said that the day of Elbert's departure was February 24, 1736. Sarah probably went with him because the trustees noted at the same time that she "lives mostly in Carolina." Once in South Carolina, Elbert traveled in search of employment along the same roads he patrolled years earlier as a ranger. At the same time, Wardrope probably formed a low opinion of him just like the trustees, who frowned upon servants who ran away from their owners. Elbert's absenteeism caused William Stephens, the colony's secretary, to see the former ranger in a negative light. In his estimation, Elbert was just like all the other servants, which were generally "a Sad crew."[10]

Elbert did not stay away long. At some point in 1737, he and his wife returned to Savannah to take advantage of liberal trustee laws passed in August that allowed servants who finished their terms before Christmas of that year a grant of fifty-acres, along with a sow and cow. This plan proved that Elbert's service involved a debt he owed Wardrope and that he could work it off in a relatively short time. By the end of the year, Elbert satisfied his debt, became a freeholder, and obtained a lot from Oglethorpe. He built a house on his lot, but cultivating his forty-five acres was a challenge because most of it was swampland. He complained loudly

---

[9] Coulter and Saye, *Early Settlers of Georgia*, 72, 165; Temple and Coleman, *Georgia Journeys*, 185; Dobson, *Scottish Emigration to Colonial America*, 117; C. C. Jones Jr., *History of Georgia*, 1:196–97 (trustee rules on land distribution). Watson, "Consideration of European Indentured Servitude," 381–406, gives a good description of indentured servitude in a Southern colony.

[10] Melton, *Religion, Community, and Slavery*, 206; Coulter and Saye, *Early Settlers of Georgia*, 72, 100; Reese, *Colonial Georgia*, 46; Fraser, *Savannah in the Old South*, 26; Lockley, *Race and Class in Lowcountry Georgia*, 16.

about the worthless state of his land and, hoping that they would give him a more productive tract, even wrote the trustees. The land was useless, he informed them, and dominated by low pine barons and scrubby bushes. It would never be tamed, he claimed, because "My five Acres [are] a Deep swamp…so deep [yet] a man must be up to his armpits in clearing it." Georgia's first historian, Hugh McCall, explained early in the nineteenth century that Elbert's situation was related to the indiscriminate granting of land by the trustees regardless of quality. "Some of the lots were rich and valuable, others poor," he wrote. "The farmer who was obliged to cultivate pine land, was absolutely compelled to plant where he could not reap a valuable consideration for his labor." Furthermore, much of the land around the river or swamps required "twenty hands one year" just to cultivate forty acres.[11] Unfortunately, the trustees, who had the power to change Elbert's situation, ignored his complaints and did nothing.

Shortly after Elbert became a freeholder, he made an enemy of Causton, who was a powerful figure in Georgia but who was also petty, tyrannical, and loathed by most of the colonists. In 1734, Joseph Watson, a store clerk on Yamacraw Bluff, murdered an Indian servant named Skee. Watson claimed that it was an accident. He gave Skee alcohol, he said, but then Skee died of a head injury after he became drunk and fell. Causton had Watson arrested and confined under heavy guard. The bailiff claimed that Watson was lying, that he had poisoned the Indian instead. That was the story Causton passed along to the trustees, who also concluded that Watson was guilty of murder even before a trial. For three years, Watson remained in confinement. Finally, on October 20, 1737, his case went to trial. On that day, Elbert left his toil in the field and went to the courthouse to witness the proceedings. What he saw left him in shock. Causton, acting as chief judge, refused to let Watson call any witnesses. Instead, the bailiff became a witness against the accused, even as he berated the jury and used "very indecent Language." Because of Causton, the jury found Watson to be a lunatic and "guilty of unguarded expressions." The verdict was unpopular among many inhabitants, including Elbert. When the trial concluded, Elbert joined forty-six citizens who signed a petition stating that Causton violated Watson's rights to a fair trial according to English law. They also pointed out that Watson's treatment was unjust,

---

[11] William Elbert to the trustees, April 20, 1742, in *CRG*, 23:282–84. The trustees described Elbert's lot as "swamp overflow'd." See Coulter and Saye, *Early Settlers of Georgia*, 72; McCall, *History of Georgia*, 1:54; Reese, *Colonial Georgia*, 46.

particularly regarding his lengthy confinement. When Elbert put his name on the petition, he became an enemy of Causton. Since the petition was public, Causton was aware of everyone who signed it, and he nursed a grudge against them.[12]

The trustees' failure to award Elbert a different tract, coupled with Causton's violation of Watson's rights, caused the former ranger to question the limits of governmental power. What he witnessed, he believed, was a gross abuse of that power which resulted in the destruction of constitutional rights and liberties. It was enough to provoke Elbert to rise up against the trustees. In the wake of Watson's trial, Elbert became a protester and joined the ranks of an anti-trustee faction called the malcontents. On December 9, 1738, he and 116 other freeholders in Savannah signed a memorial protesting trustee rules that they believed ruined Georgia's economy. The memorial mentioned two laws. The malcontents felt the only way they—and Georgia—could prosper was to end the trustee ban against slavery and to abolish their land distribution system, which prevented many colonists from legally owning property.[13] This was certainly Elbert's viewpoint. If Elbert could obtain a vast acreage to be worked by slaves, he could escape his financial woes and eventually become a wealthy plantation owner. It would also free him from his valueless piece of swampland so that he could acquire a more profitable tract.

The 1738 memorial was the first of several formal complaints drawn up by the malcontents and sent to the trustees. According to Betty Wood, a colonial Georgia historian, the malcontents were "one of the most effective of all colonial pressure groups." She identified a malcontent as someone who actively opposed the trustees and their rules by signing one or more of the following documents: the three major petitions sent from Georgia between 1738 and 1740 and the Thomas Stephens's commission as "Agent of the Malcontents" sent to Parliament in 1741. Stephens was the son of the colony's pro-trustee secretary, William Stephens. The intent of the commission was to appoint Stephens as Georgia's first colonial agent who could deal with Parliament directly, thus completely bypassing

---

[12] "Benjamin Martyn, Secretary of the Trustees to the Bailiffs and Recorder of the Town of Savannah in the Province of Georgia in America, March 17, 1735," in *CRG*, 2:133–35, and, in the same source, "Petition from Savannah, October 20, 1737" and "Petition from the Petty Jury," September 12, 1737, 135–36; Coran, *Brief Account*, 52–53; B. Wood, *Slavery in Colonial Georgia*, 19–20.

[13] "Memorial to the Honorable Trustees for Establishing the Colony of Georgia in America, December 9, 1738," in *CRG*, 3:422–26.

the trustees. Elbert signed two of the four documents, making him a "hard-core" malcontent by Wood's definition. The petitions had little effect on the trustees or their policies, and they denounced the malcontents. Historian E. Merton Coulter noted that the malcontents were "entirely out of tune with the new order under which the Trustees were setting up in Georgia."[14] At any rate, the trustees, who never paid any attention to Elbert, were starting to notice him. The regular appearance of his signature on malcontent petitions, in addition to his absenteeism as a servant, caused them to believe he was a troublemaker and detrimental to the success of their colony.

In 1740, during the midst of malcontent protesting, William and Sarah Elbert became the proud parents of a second child, a son they named Samuel. A daughter, Elizabeth, was born a few years earlier. Historians cannot establish the month or day of Samuel Elbert's birth. For many years, there was considerable discussion about the place where he was born. Several have erroneously claimed that he was born in South Carolina, and one source has said he was born in Virginia. Surprisingly, even Elbert's first biographer, Charles C. Jones, got the location wrong. Samuel Elbert settled the debate long ago. In 1767, when he petitioned Georgia's governor Sir James Wright for a grant of 450 acres in St. David's Parish, he testified in a written statement that he was "born in the Province," most likely at his parents' home in Savannah.[15]

Around the time his son was born, William Elbert had an altercation with Causton. The tension had been building since the Watson trial, but the hopeless and inaccurate state of Causton's account books at the trustee store brought the conflict to a head. Although disorganization and accounting deficiencies partly explained the state of his books, Causton also had been quietly using trustee funds to reward friends and punish enemies. When the trustees discovered his unscrupulous behavior and the muddled state of their accounts, they removed the storekeeper from his duties, but first gave him an opportunity to correct his mistakes and balance the books as best he could. It was at this point that Causton struck back at his enemies. To save face and account for his own shortcomings, he labeled many

---

[14] B. Wood, "Note on the Georgia Malcontents," 264, 274; Stephens, *Journal*, xx; Reese, ed., *Clamorous Malcontents*, 248 (1738 petition), 341 (1742 petition). Elbert's name appears on the list of those signing the Stephens Commission in Coran, *Brief Account*, 93–97.

[15] C. C. Jones Jr., *Samuel Elbert*, 6; White, *Historical Collections of Georgia*, 215; Leiter, *Biographical Sketches*, 155; Purcell thought Elbert was born in Savannah but was not sure ("Public Career of Samuel Elbert," 1). See also *CRG*, 10:124–25.

that used the store as thieves who, through guile, lies, and underhanded methods, defrauded the trustees of money. He identified Elbert as one of those people and promptly reported him to the trustees. For example, Causton claimed to have found in his records a note showing that Elbert borrowed £400 on the trustee account when he was in South Carolina in 1734. Elbert was indeed in South Carolina during that year working as a messenger. Causton accused Elbert of swindling the trustees since he never paid the money back. Again, the storekeeper produced evidence to show that in 1738 Elbert purchased a horse and goods with £16, 15 shillings, and 6 pence (£16.15.6) loaned to him from the trustee account. Just as before, Elbert neglected to reimburse the trustees. According to Causton, he was a habitual thief who accepted the generosity of the trustees and then "fraudulently" took their money. Elbert's criminal activities went beyond theft; Causton also accused him of sexual misconduct. He promptly notified the trustees that Elbert, who was married, had made inappropriate advances toward his young niece.[16]

Elbert responded to Causton's charges with a letter to the trustees in 1742 in which he denied all the accusations. As for the money, Elbert insisted that he had settled his debts with the trustees. He blamed Causton, whom he believed had a record of the payment, but had either lost the papers or destroyed them intentionally. Elbert flatly denied the charge of "bringing Letters Contrary to [her] Entrust" against Causton's niece. His morals were such, he suggested, that he could never conceive of such behavior. Despite Elbert's profession of innocence, Causton had become his merciless "enemy" whose only goal was to ruin "Me and mine." He would go to great lengths to destroy his opponents, suggested Elbert. "How far he has or may write to [you] against me I don't know," he mused. Elbert wanted the trustees to know that he had never given them any trouble; to vie for their sympathy, the former ranger reminded them that he had been with the colony since its inception and wanted it to succeed, writing that he and his family "have ben Old setlers here." He appreciated all the trouble the trustees incurred in supporting himself and his family, even as he audaciously reminded them that he never received the farming implements

---

[16] "Thomas Stephens' Journal, 1737–1740," August 8, 1739, in *CRG*, 4:385, 2:363; William Elbert to the trustees, 23:281–85.

they promised new families.[17]

In his letter, Elbert also addressed one of the problems that weighed heavily upon his heart. He wanted more land. When he wrote the trustees, he (along with three other men) had already applied for a joint tract of 500 acres situated along the Ogeechee River near Savannah. That application, dated on March 7, 1741, was doomed from the beginning. All four men were malcontents and enemies of the trustees. Elbert even pressured William Stephens to have the tract surveyed, but the secretary refused without the trustees' specific instructions.[18] Almost a year later, on April 20, 1742, when Elbert wrote his letter, he still had heard nothing from the trustees concerning his land application.

Elbert believed that a face-to-face meeting with the trustees was necessary to clear his name and address his other concerns. He was planning a trip to London, he told them, until Causton interfered and arrested him, probably for theft and sexual misconduct, before he could leave. When Elbert wrote his letter, he was awaiting a court date that was not yet determined. He still intended to sail for England where he had many friends and contacts and was certain he could recruit them as servants for Georgia. Of course, Elbert knew that trustee laws allowed people who brought servants to Georgia could qualify for large grants. The only catch, he said, was that the trustees would have to pay for his passage and give him financial assistance in the beginning. Given that he was a prior escaped indentured servant and was at the time under arrest for theft and sexual misconduct, it's fascinating that Elbert thought the trustees would help him.[19] It was yet another ruse by Elbert to gain land from the trustees, but it failed, since they never replied to his letter.

As Elbert waited for a response, a Spanish flotilla invaded Georgia with the intention of capturing Savannah. Fearing for their lives, many inhabitants, including Elbert and his family, fled to South Carolina. According to trustee records, the day of Elbert's departure was August 23, 1742, almost a month after Oglethorpe's impressive victory over the Spanish at the Battle of the Bloody Marsh on St. Simons Island, which was the climax in England's conflict with Spain over Georgia known as the War of Jenkins' Ear. Fleeing with Elbert was his wife and daughter. There was also a younger, unnamed child with them that the trustees misidentified

---

[17] William Elbert to the trustees, in *CRG*, 23:281–85.
[18] "William Elbert Application for Land," March 4, 1741, in *CRG*, 6:23–24; 5:601.
[19] William Elbert to the trustees, April 20, 1742, in *CRG*, 23:283–85.

as a daughter. The unnamed child whom they identified as a female could only have been Samuel Elbert, who was about two years old at the time. The trustees concluded, correctly, that Elbert and his family had "run away."[20]

When Elbert abandoned Georgia, he had no intention of returning. The trustees believed that anyone who fled the colony during the Spanish invasion did so because they were cowards. That was not the case with Elbert, who showed his courage years earlier as a ranger patrolling the state's dangerous frontier. Elbert fled Georgia because of legal issues, economic hardships, and confrontations with the colony's leaders over their misuse of power. Causton's charges of theft, fraud, and sexual misconduct were serious enough by themselves to drive him away. Elbert decided to take his chances and escape while he could. Financial issues also contributed to Elbert's decision to abandon Georgia. After nearly a decade of toil in the fields surrounding Savannah as an indentured servant and then freeholder, he had nothing to show for his labor. He blamed the trustees and their bans on slavery and limits on property as the source of his problems and had no reason to believe his life would improve if he stayed in Georgia. Finally, Elbert's conflicts with the trustees and Causton caused him to distrust those in authority and gave him further incentive to leave. Those conflicts caused Elbert to protest abusive government. As time would tell, the willingness to rebel against an abusive government was Elbert's greatest legacy to his son.

When news of Elbert's departure reached Stephens, he was delighted. "'Twas now confirmed that Elbert also with his family were gone," he concluded in his journal. "It may look like a Paradox to say 4 families gone would not be missed. But from the appearance of any benefits the Colony were to expect from either of them, I think it may be maintained for a truth; as my Opinion…'twould have been a good Bargain for the Trust.'" Stephens's degrading remarks spoke much about Elbert's eroded status among the colony's leaders. Not only that, two weeks before Elbert left for South Carolina the trustees rejected his joint application for land. The Common Council, who made the ruling, said that the four applicants, judged on their past conduct, did not intend to cultivate the land and were therefore undeserving of the grant.[21] Elbert probably never knew of the

---

[20] *CRG*, 5:655; Coulter and Saye, *Early Settlers of Georgia*, 72.
[21] William Elbert to the trustees, April 20, 1742, in *CRG*, 23:283–85; and, in the same source, "Journal of the Trustees for Establishing America, Minutes of the Common Council, Queen's Square Westminster," August 7, 1742, 1:404; Stephens, *Journal*, 123.

trustees' decision. It was just as well; by that time, he had already made his decision to leave Georgia forever.

Elbert settled in Prince William Parish in the Carolina low country near a place called Euhaw. Early in the eighteenth century, South Carolina's legislature designated the area as "Indian Lands," but due to the devastating impacts of the Yamasee War, it was almost devoid of Native Americans when Elbert arrived. Euhaw was located between the Combahee and Savannah Rivers and west of Beaufort along the road leading from Savannah to Charleston.[22] It was here that Samuel Elbert spent his childhood, adolescence, and early adulthood. Elbert's early life in South Carolina is enshrouded in mystery. Although William Elbert was barely literate, his son was the opposite. As an adult, the younger Elbert emerged as an eloquent writer, but the source of his education is unknown. Nothing exists in historical documents to illuminate Elbert's early life. As he grew older, he was certainly required to serve in the militia, but there is no record of that either.

William Elbert arrived at Euhaw during a religious revival brought about by the Great Awakening. Caught up in the religious euphoria, Elbert and his family began worshiping with a group of nearby Baptists. Isaac Chanler, the group's minister, particular impressed Elbert. He became a devoted follower of the preacher and his Calvinistic viewpoints embracing the doctrines of limited atonement, unconditional election, irresistible grace, total depravity, and the perseverance of the saints. The whole Elbert family was probably present on May 5, 1746, when the group of worshipers formally drafted a constitution and organized themselves into the Euhaw Baptist Church. After that, Elbert became an active member, and his son grew up in the church. William Elbert fully embraced Chanler's teachings. There can be no doubt that he was eager to learn and serve in the church. Impressed with Elbert's enthusiasm, Chanler personally instructed him in the tenets of Baptist theology. On May 18, just two weeks after the church's formation, the minister granted Elbert and Francis Pelot, a Swiss Calvinist from Purrysburg, each a probationer's license to preach. As probationers, neither Elbert nor Pelot was ordained, so they could not preach beyond their home church.[23] Finally, after years of

---

[22] Helsley, *Beaufort*, 28; for the Euhaw Indians, see Bossy, "Spiritual Diplomacy," 369, 374.

[23] Little, "Origins of Southern Evangelicalism," 802–806, 803n108, 804n113; Townsend, *South Carolina Baptists*, 38–39; Totora, "From Purrysburg to Prosperity," 4, 4n7; Weis, *Colonial Clergy of Virginia*, 76. The original Euhaw Baptist Church, which is now gone, was

searching, Elbert had discovered his calling.

Elbert's midlife career change stood in sharp contrast to his earlier work experiences as a ranger, messenger, indentured servant, and freeholder. He had hardly embarked on his new life as a minister before tragedy struck his family: his wife, Sarah, died. The circumstances surrounding her death, as well as the date and the location of her grave, are lost to history. Since Elbert remarried on October 2, 1749, Sarah's death was before that date. She was probably buried in the church's original cemetery, which is now lost. Elbert's second wife was Hannah Sealy, a wealthy widow and church member. When her husband, John Sealy Jr., died, she inherited his chattel and plantation on the Euhaw River. As Sealy's second husband, Elbert suddenly had a stake in the Sealy plantation, and he entered the slaveholding ranks of the planter elite. After 1749, he experienced a significant rise in social status and wealth, all of which had eluded him in Georgia. He even acquired seven slaves and in 1752 was able to purchase three hundred acres more in Purrysburg.[24] Thus, it was in South Carolina, and not in Georgia, where Elbert finally attained his life-long dream of owning property and slaves and becoming a member of the planter class.

Shortly after his second marriage, Elbert, for unknown reasons, quit the ministry, but remained active in the community. In 1754, for example, he was on the petit jury and grand jury lists in the Saint Helena Port Royal Parish Ward. Even as Elbert climbed the social ladder, his health deteriorated and was probably a factor in his decision to resign from the pulpit. Evidence suggests that he suffered from "consumption," or tuberculosis. It was a losing battle; over time, the disease, with its constant coughing and spitting of blood, would be terminal. Finally, after a lengthy illness, Elbert died on November 16, 1754. His burial was alongside his wife, probably in the Euhaw Baptist cemetery.[25]

After William Elbert's death, Samuel and his sister became orphans. They probably continued to live at the Sealy homestead for many years,

---

near present-day Grahamville.

[24] Holcomb, *South Carolina Marriages, 1688–1799*, 74; Will of Hannah Elbert, November 10, 1766, Wills 11–13, 1767–1771, Charleston County, Charleston, SC, 447–48; Migliazzo, *To Make This Land Our Own*, 104, 366n83.

[25] Jury lists, 1751, Acts #783, 16, Family 115; for grand jury citation, see in same source family #867, 7, both in South Carolina Archives; Townsend, *South Carolina Baptists*, 39; St. Helena Parish Register, 61.

but when Hannah Sealy died in 1766, her will mentioned neither child.[26] The only document containing Elizabeth's name is the trustees' note about the Elbert family leaving Savannah in 1742, after which she vanished from the historical record. As for Samuel, he stayed in South Carolina through his teenage years and worked wherever he could find an opportunity. It is possible that he found employment as a clerk in a trading firm or business. If so, it was valuable experience when he established his own merchant business in Savannah a few years later.

Due to the lack of records, much about Samuel Elbert's early life is unknown, including the date he left South Carolina and came to Georgia. In 1971, Herbert Wilcox, an amateur historian and columnist for the *Atlanta Constitution*, suggested that Elbert arrived in Savannah during 1754 when he was fourteen years old. The catalyst that brought him to Georgia, claimed Wilcox, was the death of his father. Elbert was a minor in 1754 and much too young to venture out on his own to a city where he had no family or connections, except perhaps his great-uncle William Calvert, whose whereabouts at the time are uncertain. There is, however, one document after the 1730s providing a clue establishing Elbert's motive for returning to Georgia as well as pinpointing a date for his arrival. Calvert died in 1762, and his will, which was probated on December 7 of that year, states that "Samuel Elbert" was the sole heir to his farm and townhouse in Savannah, which was Calvert's original grant of lot 7 in Tything Decker Ward on Ellis Square.[27] This inheritance prompted Elbert to leave South Carolina and come to Georgia. Thus, Elbert arrived in Georgia shortly after the end of the Seven Years' War and claimed his Savannah inheritance. For almost the rest of his life, Calvert's lot served as Elbert's residence.

Additional evidence suggests that Elbert arrived in 1764. On January 12, 1764, Georgia's only newspaper, the *Georgia Gazette*, published a proclamation by Governor James Wright concerning recently granted lands and inheritances. What followed was an alphabetical list of people who had legal titles to those lands but had not claimed them. Elbert's name was on the list and next to it was Calvert's "Savannah Town Lot." According to Governor Wright's proclamation, if any land remained unclaimed after a set amount of time, it would go to others who applied for grants. For several months, Elbert's name appeared in the *Gazette* with the list of

---

[26] Will of Hannah Elbert, November 10, 1766.
[27] *CRG*, 8:744.

claimants. The list released on September 13 did not include Elbert's name.[28] Elbert arrived in Savannah during late summer 1764 to claim and occupy the lot he inherited from Calvert. At the time, he was twenty-four years old.

The Georgia that Elbert encountered was a growing colony and much different from the days when his father lived there. Barely three decades old, it had survived the difficult trustee years and, by the 1760s, contained a robust population of 10,000 inhabitants supported by a host of mercantile firms and businesses, mostly in Savannah and Augusta. There were an additional 3,500 slaves in the colony, mainly working on rice plantations scattered around Savannah and down the coast. Most merchants were involved in the shipping trade, where they imported goods from London and the West Indies and exported mostly raw products, like rice, skins, and lumber. They were the key to Georgia's phenomenal growth after the Seven Years' War because in addition to fostering trade and establishing financial connections across the Atlantic, they also provided credit to local shopkeepers, tradesmen, small businesses, entrepreneurs, and those who owned plantations and small farms. Rice and indigo were the predominant staple crops produced on Georgia's plantations. In the three months between October 1764 and January 1765, around the time Elbert arrived, the colony exported 7,686 barrels of rice (in addition to 376 half barrels) and 14,124 pounds of indigo. From the forests came 871,881 board feet of pine, 2,003,261 shingles, 352,451 stoves, 18,000 hoops, and 225 barrels of pitch and tar. Wildlife provided additional commodities through raw furs and skins, mostly from deer and beaver. Those products, in turn, became the basis of trade with the Indians, drawing them, through fur traders, into the Atlantic economy. The *Georgia Gazette* reported that during a three-month period in late 1764, the colony exported to manufacturers in England 130 hogsheads of raw deer skins and 1,115 bundles, 1 hogshead of raccoon skins and 18 bundles, 9 bundles of beaver pelts, and 1 bundle of otter pelts.[29]

For two years, Elbert worked at odd jobs, but in 1766, he entered a partnership with Samuel Douglass, an established Savannah merchant. It was Elbert's first documented entry into the world of business. Elbert,

---

[28] *Georgia Gazette*, January 12, 1764, 2, and September 13, 1764, 3; *CRG*, 9:356.

[29] K. Coleman, *American Revolution in Georgia*, 10; Spalding, "Colonial Period," 54; Pressly, "Scottish Merchants and the Shaping of Colonial Georgia," 150; *Georgia Gazette*, January 17, 1765, 3. A bundle was a stack of raw skins while a hogshead was a large, sealed wooden cask (or barrel) with skins packed inside.

Douglass & Company announced their grand opening with an advertisement in the *Gazette*. Their store was in a house lately occupied by Alexander Fyffe & Company. Fyffe, who had recently died, left behind an inventory of European and East Indian goods imported from London for Elbert and Douglass to sell. Their goods included Jamaican loaf sugar, West Indian rum, and large-grained salts, in addition to a stockpile of skins and indigo destined for London. Douglass, as the administrator of Fyffe's estate, was responsible for collecting debts and liquidating his personal property and real estate. Elbert, no doubt, helped Douglass with these matters. The inventory at Elbert's store expanded in 1767 when a vessel from Philadelphia brought them ship bread, flour, water, milk, butter in kegs, biscuits, beer, hams, turpentine in bottles, and other merchandise. Then, on June 10, 1767, after operating for almost a year, the partnership suddenly dissolved.[30] After that, Douglass and Elbert opened their own individual stores.

Charles C. Jones, an early Georgia historian, wrote that Elbert excelled at business and quickly emerged as a "leading and prosperous" Savannah merchant. He was correct, because in 1768, the young businessman sailed to Boston to purchase goods for his Savannah store. On February 1, 1769, Elbert returned to Savannah on the ship *Paoli* with a multitude of items for his new business. Three weeks later, on February 22, he announced his grand opening in the *Gazette* and then advertised his wares, such as hogsheads of New England rum, half barrels of cordials, and bohea tea, to the public. He also stocked cheese, onions, potatoes, and refined loaf sugar along with soap, tallow candles, bar iron, calamanco (a type of fabric), and shoes. Elbert was anxious to dispose of his goods quickly, and he offered them to customers at "very low" cash prices or on "credit."[31]

Elbert also emerged as a "formidable figure" in the fur trade with the Creeks and Cherokee. By the 1760s, the Carolinas and Georgia heavily regulated the fur trade, and Elbert's participation in it required a special license issued to him by Governor Wright. Elbert's role in the trade was not much different from Samuel Eveleigh's, one of Charleston's early merchants who acquired raw deerskins and beaver pelts from Georgia's Indians during the trustee period. Eveleigh sent the skins to London where

---

[30] *Georgia Gazette*, July 2, 1766, 3; August 27, 1766, 3; March 25, 1767, 3; June 10, 1767, 3.

[31] Ibid., February 8, 1769, 3; February 22, 1769, 2; C. C. Jones Jr., *Samuel Elbert*, 6.

manufacturers turned them into products such as hats and coats and then shipped them back to the colonies. Eveleigh sold those manufactured goods to customers who visited his store. Elbert engaged in the same mercantile activities. Like Eveleigh, he even provided fur traders with bartering items, like cloth and rum, used in their business negotiations with Native Americans on the frontier.[32]

Elbert also engaged in land speculation. On March 23, 1770, he advertised several tracts for sale in the *Gazette*. One, about thirty miles from Savannah along the May River in South Carolina (near his childhood home around Euhaw), was a four-hundred-acre rice plantation with a spacious home, numerous outbuildings, a new barn, and a large quantity of mulberry trees for raising silkworms. A dam on the property allowed the rice fields to be flooded at the proper time, and down by the river was a good landing where barrels of rice could easily be loaded onto boats. He advertised several other large tracts for sale, including seven hundred acres in Georgia on the Sapelo River and four hundred more along the Altamaha.[33]

By the late 1760s, Elbert could be proud of his business accomplishments. Midway through the decade, he had come to the colony with nothing to his name except a Savannah town lot, but in just five years, he was a successful young entrepreneur ascending the social ladder. While hard work contributed to his rise from obscurity, he could not take all the credit for himself. Government also contributed to his newfound prosperity. In 1767, he petitioned Wright to grant him 450 acres in St. David's Parish south of the Altamaha. As a testament to his rising fortunes, his request mentioned that he owned eight slaves at the time, but he had no land except for the Savannah town lot he inherited from Calvert. Wright approved Elbert's application, giving him enough property to qualify for a seat in the General Assembly.[34] By 1770, Samuel Elbert's achievements, with the aid of government, cast a long shadow over his father's experiences in Georgia two decades earlier. In addition to owning a substantial tract of property, he enjoyed a stable career as a merchant, a comfortable income, a rising social status, and a good reputation. William Elbert, in contrast, never attained any of those benchmarks during his tumultuous decade in Georgia. His misfortunes caused him to lash out at government,

---

[32] Pressly, *On the Rim of the Caribbean*, 178; Braund, *Deerskins & Duffels*, 113–18, 189–92; *Georgia Gazette*, June 3, 1767, 4; Sweet, "Encourager of Industry," 6–7.

[33] *Georgia Gazette*, March 23, 1770, 3.

[34] *CRG*, 10:124–25.

which he blamed for his hardships, and he ultimately abandoned the colony.

While Elbert may have been a Baptist during his youth, in Savannah he worshiped with the Anglican congregation at Christ Church. The church was the first established in the city and it counted among its earliest leaders John Wesley, the influential Anglican minister. Elbert joined Christ Church soon after he arrived in Savannah, and he remained a member for the rest of his life. During the 1760s when Elbert was establishing himself in the mercantile business, many of Savannah's most influential citizens and businessmen were part of the congregation. It was through the church and in the circles of business that Elbert established some of his earliest and most enduring personal relationships.

Elbert's closest friends were James, Joseph, and John Habersham, the three sons of James Habersham Sr., a merchant and political leader. The Habersham family was influential in Georgia from the earliest days of trustee rule. In 1738, the elder Habersham arrived in the colony and quickly launched the first successful mercantile establishment in Savannah. In time, his firm became the most dominant business in the city. As his business grew, so did his wealth and influence. In 1741, he assisted Great Awakening leader George Whitefield in establishing Savannah's Bethesda Orphanage. He also served on a commission to advance the cultivation of silk in Georgia. He entered politics during the administration of Georgia's first royal governor, John Reynolds, who appointed him as the colony's secretary. His political stature increased over the next two decades, especially during Governor Wright's administration. In 1767, when Elbert was opening his first business, Habersham served as the president of the Upper House in the General Assembly in addition to being a member of Wright's Council.[35] Wright had full confidence in Habersham's loyalty and leadership abilities. When he had to leave for London during the early 1770s, Wright made Habersham Georgia's temporary governor until his return about a year later.

Out of Habersham's sons, Elbert enjoyed his dearest friendship with Joseph (born in 1751), the middle sibling of the three brothers who became one of his most trusted and closest political allies in the future. Habersham's education was more formal and advanced than any Elbert received. During the 1760s, Joseph's father, determined that his son would

---

[35] White, *Historical Collections of Georgia*, 196–99; Mebane, "Joseph Habersham in the Revolutionary War," 78–79.

also be a merchant, sent him to Princeton. After earning a degree there, Joseph went to London to study under the guidance of one of Habersham's merchant friends. Upon returning to Georgia, he formed a partnership with his first cousin, Joseph Clay, and in 1773 established a successful Savannah firm.[36] Elbert and Joseph Habersham operated within the same spheres of Savannah's commercial circles and frequently saw each other. When Elbert attended Christ Church, the Habersham family were also there since all were members. No doubt, James Habersham Sr. developed a special fondness for Elbert particularly since Samuel was best friends with his sons.

Through the fur trade, Elbert made additional contacts, some of which profoundly shaped his life. Among his new acquaintances were Lachlan McGillivray, who owned a large plantation on the outskirts of Savannah. McGillivray operated a firm and spent much of his time living with the Creeks in the Chattahoochee River valley. Eventually, he fathered a son named Alexander with Sehoy Marchand, a member of the influential Wind Clan. When Alexander was older, McGillivray took him to Savannah to get an education and learn to be a merchant. At the age of seventeen, he got his first experience in a firm when Elbert hired him for a short time as a clerk.[37]

Elbert's most important relationship fostered through the skin trade was with John Rae, a wealthy and elite merchant. Rae (born around 1708 and alternately spelled Rea) arrived as a new immigrant to Georgia from Ireland on May 8, 1734, around the time that Samuel Elbert's parents married. By 1736, he was operating a scout boat along the Sea Islands and then, three years later, was the patroon, or captain, of a pirogue (a vessel carved out of large logs) ferrying deer skins, letters, packages, and passengers from Augusta to Charleston and Savannah. As a patroon, Rae gained his first exposure to the fur trade and Indians. In time, he became one of Georgia's most influential traders and many considered him an expert in Indian affairs. Though once a malcontent, Rae (unlike William Elbert) managed to stay within the good graces of those in positions of authority, including Stephens and Causton. His business ventures, leadership qualities, and connections with Indians also made him an asset to the government. When he moved to Augusta during the 1740s to become more involved in the fur trade, many viewed him, even then, as a prominent

---

[36] Lambert, "Father against Son, and Son against Father," 14–20.
[37] Cashin, *Lachlan McGillivray*, 75.

entrepreneur and one of the founding pioneers of that frontier community.[38]

Rae became a partner in the firm of Patrick Brown & Company, which was renamed Brown, Rae, & Company, or the Augusta Company, and obtained a license to trade with the Lower Creeks in Coweta and the Chickasaws in the Mississippi valley. When Brown died in 1755, the firm dominated the profession and handled 75 percent of the trade with the Creeks and Chickasaws. By then, Lachlan McGillivray and George Galphin were also partners. Other traders, like Thomas Bosomworth, complained that the company was destroying competition and that it looked upon their trade with the Creeks as their "undoubted Right." Outside traders who came to one of their Indian towns found themselves immediately "under their Influences and Authority." The General Assembly refused to curtail the monopoly because they recognized, as did those in Rae's firm, that the company was more acquainted with the Indians than anyone else in the colony. "It is us," one of the firm members proclaimed, "who by our Endeavours, have in a great Measure kept the Indians on good Terms with this Colony as well as Carolina."[39]

Recognizing Rae's importance, the trustees, on June 1, 1751, appointed him as conservator of the peace in Augusta. Rae held that position throughout the 1750s under Reynolds and Henry Ellis, Georgia's first two royal governors. Rae became the official voice of Royal government, and on November 1, 1754, he displayed notices in Augusta that Reynolds was Georgia's governor. He also advised Georgia's governors and the assembly concerning Native Americans and was widely heralded as "a Person well acquainted with Indian Affairs." During the Seven Years War (1754–1763), for example, he delivered many talks from the Royal governors to Creek headmen in their towns to keep them from aligning with the French. To the Creek *micos* (leaders), he always referred to himself as their "loving Friend and Brother."[40]

Rae's finances and landholdings increased proportionately to his rising status. His first large land grant occurred in 1743 when the trustees approved his request for five hundred acres. He accumulated even more land under Reynolds and Ellis. In 1759, Ellis granted his request for eight

---

[38] Memorial to the Honorable Trustees for Establishing the Colony of Georgia in America, December 9, 1738, in *CRG*, 3:422–26; Coran, *Brief Account*, 93–93; Cashin, *Lachlan McGillivray*, 49; G. F. Jones, "Portrait of an Irish Entrepreneur," 428–30.

[39] Braund, *Deerskins & Duffels*, 44–49; Juricek, *Colonial Georgia and the Creeks*, 182.

[40] *CRG*, 1:561; 7:16–18, 20–25; 8:425–26.

hundred acres on McBean's Swamp along the Savannah River. At the time, Rae owned thirty-six slaves, but more acreage was necessary, he said, to sustain his plantations and business interests. Rae's commercial interests went beyond trading firms to include pastures and cowpens for his many ranching operations. By the 1760s, he possessed thousands of acres containing cabins, gristmills, and at least one ferrying operation. Bodies of water on his land bore his name in their designation, such as Rae's Great Pond and Rae's Creek in Augusta. He even gained control of large islands in the Savannah River, including a three-hundred-acre tract on Argyle Island, just above Savannah where Pipemaker's Creek entered the river on the Georgia side. That grant gave Rae almost complete ownership of the whole island.[41]

By the 1760s, Rae was one of the wealthiest men in Georgia, and his acquisition of John Robinson's plantation and estate across from Argyle Island and bordering Pipemaker's Creek reflected his opulence. Purchased in 1760 for £305, the property contained fertile rice fields and a large residence on a high bluff along the river that he christened Rae's Hall. The spacious and eloquent building said much about Rae's political and social stature. Several visitors to Savannah, including English naturalist William Bartram, regarded the mansion as "one of the most public and best known places in Georgia." Also on the property was a flat-topped temple mound at the mouth of Pipemaker's Creek. Built by the Mississippian Indians hundreds of years before European contact, the mound and its history were a great mystery to everyone who saw it, including the Yamacraw Indians, who believed that spirits haunted it. Despite this belief, the Moravians, early in the colony's history, placed a school on top of the mound to Christianize the Yamacraw and named it "Irene," or "place of peace."[42] Rae, unaware of the mound's pre-Columbian and early colonial past or even that it contained human remains, marveled at its unique appearance and the panoramic view it gave to his estate and the river from its summit. Shortly after discovering it, he determined to turn the summit into a family cemetery. Over the next few decades, the mound became the resting place of Rae and many others in his family.

Rae's Hall served as Rae's primary home. In 1767, when one of his horses strayed, he placed an advertisement in the *Georgia Gazette* offering

---

[41] Ibid., 7:381, 922; G. F. Jones, "Portrait of an Irish Entrepreneur," 432–33.
[42] Savannah Unit, Georgia Writers' Project, "Rae's Hall Plantation, Part I," 225–37; Cashin, *William Bartram and the American Revolution*, 42.

20 shillings to anyone who brought it back to his address at Rae's Hall. A brand showing the letters "JR" within a circle on the horse's buttocks made it easily identifiable. In addition to being a residence, Rae's Hall also functioned as a trading firm. In 1767, he advertised in the newspaper a list of goods for sale at the residence, noting that he also accepted deerskins, rice, and indigo for shipment to London.

Around this time, Rae added John Somerville (or Sommerville), his son-in-law, as a business partner. Somerville married Rae's oldest daughter, Jane, in 1762. He was the son of Captain Edward Somerville, who pioneered sailing routes between Ireland and Georgia. In addition to their business in Rae's Hall, the two men opened a merchant house on Johnson Square in Savannah.[43]

Even after residing in the colony for nearly three decades, Rae's family and friends in Ireland were never far from his thoughts, and he led a colonization effort to help them migrate to Georgia. He continually wrote letters to his brother, Matthew, in Ireland, to entice newcomers to Georgia. "Now Brother," he penned on May 17, 1765, "if you think a number of good industrious families will come over here I will do everything in my power to assist them; for nothing will give me more satisfaction than to be the means of bringing my friends to this country of Freedom." Those who put too much emphasis on cultural things and the pleasures of social life would be better off staying in Ireland, he suggested, since Georgia was void of the comforts of civilization. Still, a good life was possible. "We have greater plenty of good eating and drinking," explained the fur trader, and the tables were always full with excellent food, punch, wine, and beer.[44]

In 1769, Elbert assisted Rae in his colonization effort; it was the first time the two men worked together on a project beyond their business interests. By the time of Elbert's involvement, many Irish immigrants were already settling at Queensborough, a new township established by Wright just south of Augusta along Lambert's Big Creek, a tributary of the Ogeechee and near present-day Louisville. Wright and his Council granted Rae and Elbert £200 to hire out wagons, purchase flax seeds, and settle the newcomers at Queensborough. Irish immigrants continued to filter into the township over the next few years, and Rae, as promised, gave them as much assistance as possible. That aid included applications for

---

[43] *Georgia Gazette*, November 25, 1767, 3; December 16, 1767, 2; December 14, 1768, 2; Pressly, *On the Rim of the Caribbean*, 178.

[44] Green, "Queensborough Township," 183–87.

large tracts of land, such as his 1772 request for 25,000 additional acres near Queensborough for distribution to more Irish arrivals. Although Queensborough's prospects promised much in the beginning, the Revolution devastated the community, and by the end of the war, the township no longer existed.[45]

For Elbert, 1769 was a watershed year. In February, he opened his first store. At some point in 1769, he met Rae's daughter, Elizabeth (or "Betsy"). Their initial friendship quickly blossomed into a romance, and they were married on November 29, 1769. Within a week of the marriage, Elbert was assisting his new father-in-law in Queensborough. Elbert's marriage represented the most fortunate development in his life up until that point. Through it, he obtained instant access to Rae's wealth, status, friends, and even Rae's Hall. According to Jones, the marriage "confirmed" Elbert's social status and influence in society.[46]

Almost immediately, Elbert found himself the beneficiary of blessings by association with Rae. The process of riding the coattails of others into positions of power or social distinction, known as patronage, was a legitimate pathway to success during the eighteenth century. As colonial historian Gordon Wood observed, people such as Elbert, who rose out of insignificance into positions of eminence due to patronage, were not unheard of during the colonial era. Patrons, like Rae, were often looking for promising individuals to assist. "Patronizing inferiors and creating obligations," wrote Wood, "were important marks of an aristocrat in that rank-conscious age." Patronage, therefore, was "the basic means of social mobility in the eighteenth century."[47] In 1769, that patronage opened the doors to elite circles in pre-Revolutionary Georgia for Elbert. For the rest of his life, Elbert's position in the upper class remained secure.

Beyond the benefits of social identity, Elbert's marriage provided business advantages. For one, Rae was heavily involved in financial schemes that went beyond his trading operation at Rae's Hall. He had, for example, investments in several additional firms around Augusta and Savannah that dealt in skins as well as vast cowpens and cattle operations. In addition to that, Rae, like Elbert, engaged in land speculation. Still, Elbert

---

[45] *Georgia Gazette*, December 7, 1768, 3, December 14, 1768, 2, December 27, 1769, 4; *CRG*, 19(1):182; Green, "Queensborough Township," 189–92; G. F. Jones, "Portrait of an Irish Entrepreneur," 440; Cashin, "Sowing the Wind," 237; Wright, *McGillivray and McIntosh Traders*, 93.

[46] *Marriages of Chatham County*, 1:13; C. C. Jones Jr., *Samuel Elbert*, 6.

[47] G. Wood, *Revolutionary Characters*, 75.

had much to learn from his father-in-law about these business pursuits. In a way, Rae became Elbert's mentor as the young merchant forged his own identity and reputation in Georgia's colonial society.

As was to be expected, Elbert soon immersed himself in Rae's business affairs. Elbert, Rae, and Somerville (Elbert's brother-in-law) created a joint account that they used to pool money to purchase goods on credit and increase their property and holdings. Over time, Rae and Somerville (more so than Elbert) faced insurmountable debt owed to many creditors and British firms. During the early 1790s, after the Revolution and the deaths of Rae, Elbert, and Somerville, a British creditor sued those still owning portions of their estates. In the case *Telfair et al. Executors of Rae & Sommerville, v. Stead's Executors* (1805), Benjamin Stead's English firm sued Rae's descendants and the owners of Rae's Hall for £3,864 that he owed the business as of January 1, 1775. That figure did not account for accrued interest and late penalties since the credit was first issued. According to the arguments presented in the case, the men mishandled their finances since a "considerable part of [Rae's] personal estate was purchased with monies, improperly drawn out of the joint funds." Rae and Somerville habitually withdrew "considerable portions of their partnership-funds, which they ought not to have done before payment of their debts." They then invested that money in "the purchase of lands and negroes as their own separate property." Since Rae and Somerville acted irresponsibly regarding their pre-Revolutionary War debts, the judges, despite the passage of three decades and the outcome of the American Revolution, ruled in favor of Stead.[48]

Since Elbert was now part of Rae's family, he, like Somerville, was in a position to benefit from the joint fund account. The money surely financed businesses he opened in partnership with John Rae's half-brother, Robert Rae, during the early 1770s. John Rae was a persuasive person and influenced many people from Ireland, such as Robert Rae, to build new lives in Georgia. Once in Georgia, the younger brother worked for a while in Rae's firms where he quickly learned the fur trade and cattle ranching businesses before striking out on his own. After that, Elbert and Robert Rae, drawing on the account for money and credit, established two new stores. One of the new firms was Rae's, Elbert & Company, which specialized in the fur trade. To conduct business, Elbert undoubtedly visited Indian towns and dealt personally with their leaders in negotiations over

---

[48] Cranch, *Reports of Cases Argued and Adjudged*, 2:407.

skins. Even before the new company was established, Elbert already had dealings with Indians on the frontier as evidenced by his purchase of a horse from the Creeks in 1769. Rae's, Elbert & Company became deeply involved in the trade and by 1775, the Creeks owed them £2,688.18.6 worth of deer hides. It was impossible for the Indians to produce enough skins to cover the debt. To maintain peace between the Indians and Georgia, Wright intervened and on November 7, 1775, offered Elbert's company land grants not exceeding five thousand acres to compensate for the debt.[49] The arrangement showed that the company also had thousands of acres in property assets, allowing them to engage in land speculation.

Elbert's partnership with Robert Rae and Thomas Graham became a second business. Like the former company, Rae's, Elbert & Graham also dealt in the fur trade. The firm offered additional incentives for Elbert to visit Indian towns in the Chattahoochee valley. In May 1775, Graham left Augusta and traveled along trading paths all the way to the Tallapoosa River to pick up a load of skins from the Ockfusky (or Okfuskee) Creeks. When he arrived, recent rains had flooded the river across from the *talwa* (or town) of Ockfusky almost out of the banks. It was perilous to cross the swollen river with his pack animals, so Graham borrowed canoes from the Indians instead. Robert Rae visited Ockfusky, too, and considered one of their leaders, Handsome Fellow (or Handsome Man) to be his friend.[50] Elbert knew Handsome Fellow as well, and, during the Revolution, he gave a talk to the Creek leader on behalf of Georgia. If Graham and Rae conducted the trade with the Indians in their towns, Elbert did as well. In the process, he gained valuable knowledge of major *micos* throughout the western frontier and personally knew many of them, like Handsome Fellow. He also became acquainted with the labyrinth of trading trails and rudimentary paths that wound through Georgia's western frontier beyond the colony's boundaries.

Rae's, Elbert & Graham also participated in cattle ranching. Elbert had little experience with cattle, and John Rae surely offered him much welcomed advice and guidance. Nevertheless, by the time of the Revolution, the firm's ranching enterprise included enormous tracts utilized for grazing cattle herds. Part of their empire of pastures was as a five-hundred-

---

[49] *Georgia Gazette*, January 10, 1770, 3; Warren and Jones, *Georgia Governor and Council Journals, 1774–1777* (hereafter cited as *GGCJ, 1774–1777*), 80, 85; G. F. Jones, "Portrait of an Irish Entrepreneur," 442; Cranch, *Reports of Cases Argued and Adjudged*, 2:409.

[50] Warren and Jones, *GGCJ, 1774–1777*, 44; *CRG*, 8:522–24; Braund, *Deerskins & Duffels*, 167.

acre tract on Brier Creek, which they acquired in 1772. According to the Minutes of the Proceedings of the Governor in Council on January 5, 1773, Rae's, Elbert & Graham petitioned for the land adjoining property already owned by John Rae. In an argument reminiscent of Elbert's reasoning for obtaining a land grant in 1767, they claimed ownership of 25 slaves, but the governor never granted them headright lands to account for them. Three years later, in 1776, British Loyalists informed Governor Patrick Tonyn in Florida that they had seen the large herds of cattle belonging to Rae's, Elbert & Graham ranging in several cowpens between Savannah and Augusta. They estimated some to contain at least six thousand head of cattle. The herds reported to Tonyn were exceptionally large and required several hands to maintain them. To oversee the cattle, the firm used cowboys (known as "cattle hunters"), who were likely slaves owned by Elbert and his partners.[51]

It is possible that Elbert's firms also sold slaves, since Rae, Whitefield & Company, one of John Rae's establishments in Augusta, advertised one for sale in the *Gazette* on December 20, 1769. According to the advertisement, they purchased the slave from the Creeks. They described him as a person standing "near six feet high, about 20 years of age, of the Bumbo Country." Apparently, he had been with the Creeks for some time since he could "speak no English, but can talk Indian." Elbert probably saw the slave since he visited the company at the time they placed the advertisement in the paper. While Elbert was there, the horse he recently purchased from the Creeks broke out of the stable and escaped. He put a notice in the *Gazette* on January 10, 1770, offering £20 sterling for anyone who caught and returned it. He described the horse as a large white gelding fifteen hands high, about seven years old, with a soft trot and a brand on its buttock. Elbert would pick up the horse and deliver the reward at Rae, Whitefield & Company.[52]

Samuel Elbert had two father figures during his greening years, and both, for their own reasons, had major influences on his life. William Elbert passed along to his son a rebellious spirit against authoritarian leaders who deprived people of natural rights and liberties enshrined in constitutional law. Since he was a former ranger, he may have even fostered his son's early fascination with the military. In contrast, his father-in-law,

---

[51] Searcy, *Georgia-Florida Contest*, 35; Wright, McGillivray and McIntosh Traders, 73; Warren and Jones, Georgia Governor and Council Journals, 1772–1773 (hereafter cited as GGCJ, 1772–1773), 107.

[52] *Georgia Gazette*, December 20, 1769, 3; January 10, 1770, 3.

John Rae, became a mentor to Elbert and taught him much about being a merchant in the fur trade. Through Rae, Elbert learned about Indians, cattle, and many other things necessary for his survival in business. Rae also opened avenues for social advancement to Elbert, and his marriage to Elizabeth linked him to one of the most prominent families in Georgia. Rae may have even persuaded Elbert to become involved in politics. On October 10, 1769, about a month before his marriage, the citizens of St. Matthew's Parish and the town of Ebenezer elected him as a representative to the General Assembly.[53] His election represented yet another milestone for 1769 and formally marked his entrance into the arena of government and politics. By the time he took his assembly seat in November, he had come far in establishing a reputation and identity for himself. There was more to come, but for the moment, Elbert basked in the light of a bright future that was full of promise and hope.

---

[53] Ibid., October 25, 1769, 2; *CRG*, 15:4–5, said the election was on October 31.

Chapter 2

"The Bulwark of Our Liberties": Samuel Elbert, the Assembly, and the Voice of the People, 1769–1771

On November 1, 1769, twenty-nine-year-old Samuel Elbert entered the Commons House of the General Assembly in Savannah as one of nineteen newly elected members. He, along with William Ewen and Samuel Farley, represented St. Matthew's Parish. The oddly shaped, rectangular district encompassing the Salzburger's historical town of Ebenezer was located between the Savannah and Ogeechee Rivers, just north of Savannah's Christ Church Parish. The assembly could not officially convene until everyone made public declarations of loyalty to England's King George III and Governor James Wright and then took an Oath of Abjuration as required by law. After those preliminaries, the assembly moved to elect its speaker. They unanimously chose Noble Wimberly Jones, a delegate from Savannah and the son of Noble Jones, a prominent Georgia politician and member of Wright's Council who built the immaculate Wormsloe Plantation outside of the city. In his first communication to the Commons House, Wright expressed his pleasure that Jones was the speaker and said that he "greatly approved" of the choice.[1] Thus began the first of Elbert's four sessions in the assembly, which continued through spring 1771. For Elbert, his service was a mark of civic duty and devotion and he saw it as a great honor to serve at His Majesty's pleasure in Georgia's royal government.

Elbert had come a long way since first arriving in Georgia. Looking back, he probably never envisioned that he would one day serve in the colony's government. Undoubtedly, John Rae prodded Elbert to enter politics. During his courtship of Elizabeth Rae, Elbert frequently visited Rae's

---

[1] *CRG*, 10:911–12, 15:4–5. See also "Journal of the Upper House of Assembly, January 17, 1763 to March 12, 1774," in *CRG*, 17:436; *Georgia Gazette*, October 25, 1769, 2.

Hall. There, he certainly engaged Rae, and even John Somerville, in hours of conversation about everything ranging from Indians and cattle ranching to business and politics. Those discussions revealed to Elbert that Rae, in addition to his many other talents and experiences, was himself a veteran of the assembly who first entered that body on March 7, 1755, to replace an expelled member from St. Paul's Parish and Augusta. In 1769, he still entertained political ambitions and once again ran for the Commons House as a representative from St. Paul's. Perhaps Elbert relished the opportunity to serve alongside his father-in-law in the assembly; his entry into politics may have been an effort to impress Rae since he would marry his daughter in less than a month. When writs for the elections were returned by the provost marshal in late October, they showed that Rae, in addition to Edward Barnard and John Walton, were the new representatives from St. Paul's Parish.[2]

In Georgia's royal government, there was an Upper House (or Council) selected and approved by the royal governor, the king, and other London superiors, and there was a Commons or Lower House selected by the people—it was their voice. The Commons House traditionally consisted of nineteen members, all elected by White, male freeholders over twenty-one who owned at least fifty acres in the parish where they lived and voted. When the governor summoned the assembly, writs were issued for elections in the different parishes; to determine winners, deputies took voice polls from voters at pre-determined times and places.[3] The *Gazette* published polling times and places to maximize voter participation and ran notices announcing the winners. Outlying towns also displayed broadsides showing election results. In that way, citizens always knew their assembly representatives.

To qualify as a member of the Commons, a candidate was required to own at least five hundred acres in the parish or district where they ran. That meant that Elbert owned a minimum five hundred acres in St. Matthew's, giving him a total of around 1,000 acres in 1769, although he lived in Savannah. The St. Matthew's property probably came from a government grant. His estate included the 450 acres he obtained from Wright's grant in St. David's Parish two years earlier, in addition to his residential and business lots in Savannah. Elbert's limited number of acres in the city

---

[2] *CRG*, 10:911–12, 13:79–80.
[3] Abbot, *Royal Governors of Georgia*, 9–11; Saye, *Constitutional History of Georgia*, 59–60; Reese, Colonial Georgia, 22; CRG, 10:911.

disqualified him from running as a delegate from the "Town of Savannah," which provided the House with four representatives, more than any other parish.

Elbert's membership in the Commons House was a testament to his character, rising social status, and comfortable financial situation. Only wealthy and prosperous colonists could afford to serve in the assembly. Once elected, representatives had to leave their work or business for several weeks at a time to attend legislative duties in Savannah. Since they served without monetary compensation or benefits, any expenses became their responsibility. Unlike many other representatives, Elbert was in a better position to simultaneously manage his business affairs and carry out his legislative duties since his home and stores were in Savannah. When the assembly adjourned, he could avoid onerous lodging expenses by simply returning to his residence or to Rae's Hall. Members of the assembly were required to attend all the proceedings. If, for whatever reason, they failed to appear, they faced fines and, occasionally, jail time. Such was Rae's experience when he was absent in spring 1771 because he was delivering necessities to new arrivals from Ireland destined for Queensborough. Even that valid excuse did not waive him from his fine.[4]

Elbert entered the assembly during a period of relative calm in Georgia after the turmoil caused by the Stamp Act in 1765 and the Townshend Duties in 1767. Both controversies negatively affected royal government in Georgia and strained the earlier harmonious relationship between Wright's Upper House (Council) and the Lower House. Constant bickering also damaged the relationship between the governor and the lower house. Although Wright still maintained control of his assembly, that body contributed to the friction since it was testing boundaries of its legal authority in the late 1760s and early 1770s. However, the assembly could also make the claim, as it did, that Wright, too, often stepped outside of constitutional limits. The repeated clashes between Wright and the Lower House intensified as the years flew by, but at least the ongoing conflict had an identifiable origin in the Stamp Act crisis.

Britain's troubles in the colonies, and Wright's problems in Georgia, began in 1764, when Parliament passed the Sugar Act as part of their New Imperial Policy to impose taxes to administer their American empire after the Seven Year's War. Parliament passed the Stamp Act in the following year. Both acts became law without American consent and signified a more

---

[4] *CRG*, 15:254–57, 282.

active British government in the lives and pocketbooks of the colonists. Neither were welcomed news in America. It was the Stamp Act, however, that generated violent protests and set the colonies on a course that eventually led to the American Revolution. Largely an internal tax levied on paper, the Stamp Act created pandemonium in the colonies, and many protests, like those in Boston, featured destructive mobs. Almost everywhere, stamp collectors were threatened and hunted down. There were protests in Georgia, too, where a Sons of Liberty organization quickly formed, as it had in other colonies. Although the Stamp Act caused some disorder in Georgia, Wright managed to maintain political control despite the liberty folks who orchestrated small mobs to prowl the streets and vent their frustrations. They also organized meetings of resistance in local taverns, threatened the stamp collector, plotted to steal the stamps, wrote political pieces in the *Georgia Gazette* questioning British authority, and once angrily confronted the governor at his home in Savannah.[5] There is no evidence to suggest that Elbert took part in Georgia's Stamp Act protests, and nothing exists to validate his affiliation with the Sons of Liberty in Savannah at this time. Elbert, in 1765, had only recently arrived in the colony and was still struggling to find employment, although he witnessed the impact that the crisis had in his city.

Despite the protests, Georgia, through Wright's steadfast leadership, became the only colony that sold the stamps. The chaos created by the Stamp Act finally dissipated when Parliament, after much debate, repealed the law in 1766 and then passed the Declaratory Act, claiming its authority over the colonies "in all cases whatsoever." By then, much damage had occurred in the hearts and minds of many colonists, including some in Georgia, who continued to seethe. Wright noticed that the Stamp Act produced a peculiar strain of Americanism in Georgia that he had never seen before. A few years later, he observed that the steady erosion of royal government in his colony began with the Stamp Act controversy. He was correct in his observation because after the Stamp Act, things were never quite the same in his colony.[6]

Although the Stamp Act's repeal eased tensions somewhat in America, Britain's financial problems remained, and in 1767 Parliament passed another law, the Townshend Duties, without American consent, to raise

---

[5] Alden, *American Revolution*, 4–5; Spalding, "Colonial Period," 58–60; Miller, "Stamp Act in Colonial Georgia," 322–23.
[6] Spalding, "Colonial Period," 58–60; Miller, "Stamp Act in Colonial Georgia," 329.

revenue by imposing an external tax on lead, paper, paint, glass, and tea. All these items were vital components of the colonies' material culture as well as important mercantile goods in the Atlantic trade. America's response was swift, dramatic, and more dignified since it lacked, for the most part, the rioting and destructive mobs characterized by the Stamp Act protests. In general, Americans viewed the Townshend Duties as an assault not only on liberty but also on property and constitutional rights. John Dickenson, who wrote a series of newspaper columns on the matter and published them in pamphlet form under the title *Letters from a Farmer in Pennsylvania*, argued that the duties were unconstitutional and that they would reduce the colonists to the level of slaves with no rights.[7] However, it was the 1768 Massachusetts Circular Letter, written by Samuel Adams and James Otis, which had the greatest impact in Georgia.

The Massachusetts Circular Letter called upon all colonies to unite against the Townshend Duties. Although the document was not radical, it did include a strong statement on the colonists' constitutional rights as British citizens. The Georgia General Assembly opened on November 7, 1768, and the House was already in session when Wright issued a stern warning about the circular, which had not yet arrived. Both he and King George disapproved of its contents, he said. When it reached the Commons, as it most surely would, Wright instructed the members not to consider it. If the House disobeyed these explicit instructions, the governor stated that he would dissolve the assembly, pursuant to instructions he had previously received from London. The House assured the governor that they were only concerned about carrying out the legislative affairs of the colony and professed the deepest affection and loyalty to Wright and the king. Shortly afterwards, the Massachusetts Circular arrived, along with another from Virginia. On Christmas Eve, the House, despite its promises to Wright, delved into a discussion concerning the constitutionality of the Townshend Duties and then brought both circulars to the floor for debate. After due consideration, the House determined that the letters, contrary to Wright's professions, were neither radical nor dangerous. Instead, they represented the sacred right of all British subjects to openly debate ideas and petition the Crown for redress of grievances. The House resolved to inform Massachusetts and Virginia that they approved of the arguments presented in the circulars and then ordered their proceedings published in the newspaper for all to see. Wright's earlier warning was no veiled threat.

---

[7] Dickinson, *Letters from a Farmer*, 74–76.

When he heard what the House was doing, he was infuriated. The governor did not waver in his response and promptly dissolved the assembly on Christmas Eve, the same day that it considered the circulars.[8]

There the matter rested until the next assembly met in fall 1769, with Elbert as a delegate. Though tensions remained, and some members still bristled over Wright's actions, the fall session was remarkably calm despite a few combative moments between the governor and the Commons House, as Elbert soon witnessed. As a legislator, Elbert surely contemplated the larger meaning of recent political events in his colony. Unfortunately, his feelings about the Stamp Act, the Townshend Duties, the circular letters, and Wright's dissolution of the assembly in 1768 are unknown. No doubt, he felt, as did others, that the governor abused his power by dissolving the assembly to stifle debate over a valid concern. Although Wright's actions were controversial, they were also fully within his legal parameters, since all governors, as the executive head of government within their respective colonies, possessed the right to dismiss assemblies. Wright's actions signified the beginnings of a protracted struggle between the executive and the assembly over constitutional rights and division of powers in royal government. At the core of these problems, the issue at stake was liberty. Surely, that idea lurked in Elbert's mind, and soon, in the name of liberty, he would take action to bring about the collapse of royal authority in his colony.

Elbert had other reasons to worry about the Townshend Duties. From a business perspective, they could adversely affect his trade. However, he remained silent, even while other merchants voiced dissent. When some of Savannah's merchants finally erupted in open protests over the duties in September 1769, one month before Elbert became a member of the House, he still avoided the controversy. There is no evidence to put him in the league of merchants who, following the lead of neighboring South Carolina, held a mass meeting headed by Jonathan Bryan, a member of Wright's Upper Council, on September 19. There, a handful of merchants adopted a watered-down nonimportation agreement. Elbert could surely understand the merchant's complaints, but a boycott held potentially negative ramifications for his firms. Joining with the protesters could also incur the wrath of Wright and others in prominent government positions, even in far-away London, further damaging his business. Nor was

---

[8] Middlekauff, *Glorious Cause*, 158, 160–61; K. Coleman, *American Revolution in Georgia*, 28–29.

nonimportation a popular, widespread policy. It hardly extended beyond a few Savannah merchants. The boycott was voluntary, entirely unenforceable, and without punitive reprisals for those who broke it. If anything, its existence was largely symbolic. Nevertheless, Elbert, like most of the other merchants in the city, did not endorse it. Even most planters questioned the measure and distanced themselves from it.[9] Additionally, Elbert may have purposely kept any criticisms of Parliament or Wright to himself because he was trying to impress his future father-in-law, who supported royal government.

Despite the aftermath of the Stamp Act crisis, the Townsend Duties controversy, and Wright's dismissal of the House, Elbert's first term in the assembly was mostly calm. One of the top items on the agenda concerned a law to regulate the fur trade and punish those who mistreated Indians on the frontier. The debate that followed certainly garnered much of Elbert's attention since the fur trade was integral to his businesses. James Habersham Sr., who addressed Wright from the Upper House in the opening meeting, set the tone for the upcoming Indian bill by acknowledging that it was "absolutely necessary" to do something about the encroachment by colonists on lands and hunting grounds controlled by the Creeks. The trade, he said, needed tighter regulation and stricter punishments of those who committed offenses and abuses toward the Indians. "[We must] remedy those evils," he told Wright, "and for the future prevent the…grounded and repeated complaints of the Indians." The overall intention of the bill, of course, had nothing to do with protecting the rights of Indians and guaranteeing their ownership of lands. The aim, instead, was to avoid a brutal frontier Indian war. The assembly formed a committee on November 3 to draft the legislation. It was no shock or surprise to anyone that John Rae was on the committee.[10] In Georgia, no one rivaled Rae's credentials or experience when it came to Native Americans.

On the same day that Rae was charged with drafting a law to regulate the Indian trade, Elbert was placed on a committee to come up with a bill to better order and govern slaves, particularly regarding trials. Additionally, Elbert's committee was instructed to incorporate provisions preventing the "inveigling and Carrying away [of] Slaves from their Masters, Owners, or Employers." By the end of the week, on November 10, he

---

[9] K. Coleman, *American Revolution in Georgia*, 30–31; C. C. Jones Jr., *History of Georgia*, 2:113–15; *Georgia Gazette*, September 20, 1769, 3.
[10] *Georgia Gazette*, November 8, 1769, 1; *CRG*, 15:20.

joined another committee to produce a port bill to ascertain the rates of wharfage, shipping, merchandizing, and storage of goods in harbors throughout the province. A second charge was to appoint a harbor master for Savannah's port. Serving on this committee with Elbert was William Ewen. A native of England, Ewen came to Georgia early in the trustee period as an indentured servant where he worked for two years in Thomas Causton's store. Eventually, he became involved, like William Elbert and John Rae, with the malcontents, who protested trustee rule. He signed the malcontents' 1738 memorial as well as the commission to appoint Thomas Stephens as Georgia's colonial agent. His activities drew the ire of William Stephens, the colony's secretary and later president.[11] In the assembly, Elbert worked closely with Ewen to draw up a satisfactory port bill. They served on additional committees together, forming political and personal bonds that would benefit Elbert in the days to come. The committees regulating slaves and the ports both affected Elbert personally since one concerned the governance of his chattel and the other involved his businesses.

During the fall, Elbert witnessed two incidents that brought into question the constitutional divisions of power between Wright and the assembly. One involved the freedoms of speech and protest, while the other highlighted the deepening conflict between Wright and the House. The first concerned the fate of Bryan, a member of Wright's Upper Council who led the merchant's protest back in September that resulted in the adaptation of a weak nonimportation agreement. The king, having learned of Bryan's actions, was incensed and expressed a determination to confront "every measure that tended to violate the Constitution and excite opposition to the laws." As a member of the Upper Council, the king, who earlier approved Bryan's appointment, expected him to not only support royal government but also the Crown's polices. He was certainly not supposed to align himself with an opposition. Accordingly, George III ordered Wright to "immediately suspend" Bryan not only from his council seat but also from any other "office he might hold in Georgia." Thus, observed early Georgia historian Charles C. Jones, Bryan, who was a "pure patriot, an influential citizen, and a brave man," became the colony's first political martyr.[12] The firing of Bryan for voicing his opinion against royal policies was an eye-opening moment for many colonists who cherished their

---

[11] *CRG*, 15:21, 39, 2:74; Tailfer, Anderson, and Douglas, *True and Historical Narrative*, 42; White, *Historical Collections of Georgia*, 199–200.

[12] C. C. Jones Jr., *History of Georgia*, 2:115.

liberties. Elbert, too, noticed this assault on the freedom of speech and protest. Perhaps a fear of the same sort of reprisal against his business explained why he followed his instincts and distanced himself from the merchant's protest over the Townshend Duties.

The second confrontation involved the ringing phrase "no taxation without representation" that had been heard repeatedly in the colonies since the time of the Stamp Act. In this instance, it featured a unique Georgia twist. The problem concerned the colony's four newest parishes to the south—St. David, St. Patrick, St. Thomas, and St. Mary—all of which lacked representatives in the assembly in 1769. Those parishes were below the Altamaha River on lands gained from Spain after the 1763 Treaty of Paris. Although grants and headrights had enticed several families to move there after the Seven Years' War, the whole area was still a sparsely populated expanse of longleaf pines, swamps, and tidewater marshes. One of the prerogatives of the House was that it controlled the colony's purse strings and any money bill or legislation aimed at raising taxes originated in that body. Anticipating that they would soon issue a general tax on the province and provide a budget and finances to fund the government's operation in the following year, the House, on November 15, asked Wright to issue writs for elections in Georgia's southern parishes to ensure they had representation and an assembly voice. Without proper representation, the House informed the governor that they would, out of fairness and justice, exempt all four parishes from any general taxes they issued. Why the House concerned itself with the rights of the parishes at this specific time is a matter for debate since they had never raised the issue before. During previous sessions, they had taxed those parishes without any representation in the assembly. Wright's reply on the following day seemed promising. He told the House that he agreed with them in principle and had even brought the matter before the King's Council in the previous year. However, he did not believe that a royal governor's powers gave him authority to accommodate their request. Issuing writs and increasing the size of the assembly was something that needed specific approval from London. He promised the House that he would seek the Crown's permission, await the answer, and promptly notify them when the king voiced his pleasure. That reply did not satisfy the House and they disagreed with the governor. The Proclamation of 1763, they explained, gave Wright full authority to act since it mandated that all sections affected by it must have assembly representation. The confrontation between the governor and the House over representation in the southern parishes was still unsolved when the assembly's fall session adjourned on December 20.[13]

On January 8, after a brief Christmas recess, the assembly reconvened. There was still much unfinished business from the previous session in addition to several new items for the House to consider. For Elbert, this term would be much busier than the fall session, and, by the end of April, he was on five committees. He took a more active role because on some he was their liaison and speaker, verbally delivering messages, bills, and resolutions to the whole House for deliberations. In the process, the young politician tested, for the first time, his leadership skills and speaking abilities in the setting of a legislative body.

Some of Elbert's committees had simple tasks. On January 25, he found himself on a committee to appoint hemp and flax inspectors for the ports of Savannah and Sunbury. A few weeks later, Elbert read their new bill to the House. The bill, with few amendments, passed a House vote and then became law. Elbert also joined a committee with John Rae to develop a fire prevention bill. In March, he, Rae, and Ewen were on another committee to regulate the town of Savannah. One of their tasks was to establish a burial ground for Jewish residents. Elbert read their bill to the House before delivering it to the table for consideration. On April 11, he became part of the committee to create a tobacco bill, which appointed inspectors in Augusta to curtail the selling and exportation of inferior or unmarketable tobacco in order to protect consumers.[14] Serving on so many committees was time-consuming, but it was also a great honor for Elbert. It was certainly a special pleasure to work on two of them with his new father-in-law.

Elbert's immersion into the disagreement between Wright and the House over representation during the assembly's spring term was unavoidable. The controversy, carried over from the fall, constantly simmered under the surface. Historian Harvey H. Jackson referred to the House members, including Elbert, who sought to extend representation into the parishes, as the "Liberty party-led assembly." Their agenda, claimed Jackson, was to "limit executive authority and enhance that of the assembly." They were part of a growing "Christ Church" coalition of conservative Whigs largely from Savannah and its environs, later identified as the

---

[13] K. Coleman, *American Revolution in Georgia*, 32–33.

[14] *CRG*, 15:98, 117–18, 169, 176; *Journal of the Upper House of Assembly, January 17, 1763 to March 12, 1774*, *CRG*, 17:590–91.

"Liberty party," who sought to establish "local control and legislative supremacy."[15] Elbert's dispute with Wright, through the assembly, over the parish controversy was the first indication of his association with the "Liberty party," or conservative Whigs, who helped usher in the Revolution in Georgia. Thus, it was while he served in the assembly, and not during the Stamp Act and Townsend Duties controversies, when Elbert first expressed his radical tendencies and aligned himself with the anti-Wright faction in his colony.

On February 20, the House sent Wright an address expressing their concerns. Their earlier request in November was "just and reasonable," they argued. Having thought about it further, the House believed that "partial Representation is a measure unknown in any part of his Majesty's wide extended Domains and entirely inconsistent with the Bulwark of our Liberties the glorious Bill of Rights the Pride of our Nation and the envy of the rest of Mankind." They asked him, once again, to issue writs for elections. Without representatives from the four parishes, they cautioned, "we dare not impose a General Tax," which would be unjust, unequal, unwise, and against the principles of liberty that all held dear. Forcing them to impose the tax would be nothing less than "virtual representation" and everyone knew the level of "abhorrence, and detestation…the Community" had for that concept.[16]

Irritated by their request and persistence, Wright fired off an angry letter. He reminded them that when they first inquired about the parishes back in the fall, he said he did not have the power to expand representation in the assembly and that he would seek permission from the Crown. That situation had not changed. The question was still before the King's Council and no specific instructions were forthcoming. Since the assembly refused to drop the matter, he added in frustration, "I find that was not satisfactory to you." The House suggested that the King's Council had not paid due attention to their request, but Wright assured them that it was getting appropriate consideration. Clearly annoyed, he advised that they take a closer look at the wording in the king's royal proclamation of October 3, 1763. Then, they too would admit that they were in error. Governors in the four new provinces created from the proclamation were the only executives who could grant or increase representation in the assembly. However, this was not the case for Georgia's four parishes, which were not

---

[15] Jackson, "Georgia Whiggery," 258–64.
[16] *CRG*, 15:124.

provinces but rather part of a royal colony. Enlarging the assembly's size went beyond Wright's powers to act. While he still supported their argument that all citizens should have representation in the government, the governor also believed that the House was testing its limits beyond legal boundaries and attempting to assume rights and prerogatives that were explicitly reserved for the king and his council. Thus, the governor concluded, "I cannot therefore agree with you in opinion on this point, but apprehend I am to conduct myself agreeable to my commission and instructions from his Majesty…which [I will] certainly do." He promised once again to "lay this matter before them [the King's Council], and whatever further determination or opinion they may come to thereupon I will communicate to you."[17]

Elbert became deeper involved in the conflict on April 5 when he was placed on two committees related to the complex issues of taxes and finances. One estimated the costs of running Georgia for one year, between September 29, 1769, and September 29, 1770. He joined Ewen on the other, which was a Ways and Means Committee charged with finding methods to defray government expenses for the same time frame. Elbert was the speaker for both committees and frequently carried their communications to the House. Dealing with finances was a complicated assignment, and Elbert often told the House during his updates that the committees had to have "leave to sit" for further discussion. The Ways and Means Committee was especially tricky since it had to raise more than £3,355.16 to fund the government for the fiscal year. Most of the money came from taxes, but the House, after wrangling with the problem of the parishes for two sessions, had already decided to exempt them from the requirements of any money bill.[18] At this point, there was nothing Wright could do except approve the measure since the government needed money to operate. Of course, this never solved the disagreement, which spilled over into the following year.

The assembly was still in session when sobering news arrived in Savannah from Boston. On March 5, British soldiers fired upon a large gathering of citizens, killing five and wounding many others who were protesting at the Custom House on King Street. The event was old news by the time it appeared in the *Gazette* on April 11, but it was the first time that Elbert and his peers in the assembly heard about the altercation that the

---

[17] *Georgia Gazette*, February 28, 1770, 1.
[18] Ibid., April 11, 1770, 1; *CRG*, 15:170–71.

paper labeled a "massacre."[19]

The *Gazette* portrayed the soldiers as the instigators of the trouble and painted them as brutes and savages. The newspaper claimed that, apart from a few unruly teenagers, Boston's citizens were innocent onlookers who did nothing to warrant being fired upon. According to the story, soldiers paraded the streets, harassing and abusing citizens, and even clubbing them before the massacre. As the soldiers gathered at the Custom House, one teenage lad asked them if they intended to murder people. The instant reply from one was, "yes, by G—d, root and branch." As the crowd increased, some hurled snowballs at the soldiers. The British commander of the troops, according to the *Gazette*, shouted, "Damn you, Fire, be the consequence what it will." With that, the soldiers discharged their weapons. The paper ended its story by saying the whole event showed "a degree of cruelty unknown to British troops." What transpired in Boston was a "general if not universal massacre" and a "barbarous outrage."[20]

Elbert did not record his thoughts on the Boston Massacre, nor is there any documentation that the House discussed it, but it was apparent that a pattern was emerging. The blatant assaults against liberty by Britain's Crown and royal governments, not only in Georgia, but in all the colonies, were occurring with more frequency. Just like it did in 1768 when Wright dissolved the assembly for considering the circular letters and the next year when the king removed Bryan from the Upper House for publicly protesting the Townshend Duties, the incident in Boston brought into focus the rights of citizens to assemble and protest against their government. It also highlighted the real threat that standing armies posed to ordinary citizens who lived in their midst. At its core, these incidents threatened constitutional liberties. That point was made clear in the *Gazette* on April 25, when an editorial appeared discussing the "inhuman tragedy lately exhibited in Boston." What transpired there encompassed "every species of evil." The paper reminded all the kings of the earth and the judges of humanity to beware, for the masses were committed to their care, and they would pay for shedding innocent blood. The piece ended with a melancholy sigh: "Oh liberty. Oh my country!"[21] Surely, editorials such as this caused Elbert, along with many of his legislative colleagues, to pause and think about what British power was doing *in* America and *to*

---

[19] *Georgia Gazette*, April 11, 1770, 4.
[20] Ibid.
[21] Ibid., April 25, 1770, 1.

Americans.

The spring session of the 1770 General Assembly closed on May 10, after achieving much beneficial legislation, and Elbert could feel pride in the meticulous and detailed work he put into his committee assignments. All the bills associated with him passed the House and with Wright's approval became law, even though the assembly failed to achieve some of its goals. Bogged down in the committee and plagued with resolutions and questions, Rae's Indian bill, one of the primary goals set forth by Habersham in November of the previous year, was still unfinished. Before he adjourned the assembly, Wright told them that it was of the upmost "Utility and Necessity" to quickly pass an Indian bill, since its significance increased "more and more every Day." He hoped that the members would think about the importance of completing their task over the long recess, so that they could create a law to relieve tensions with the Indians during the next session. Each member, he suggested, should "inform and prepare himself in such a Manner that at our next Meeting, something effectual may be agreed upon relative to this Point so essential to the Peace and Safety of the Province." With that, the governor dismissed the assembly, and everyone went home except Rae. On the day the assembly adjourned, the House voted him £80 to repair the fences, porch, and other parts of Wright's Savannah residence.[22]

Elbert relished his short break from demanding committee work. Over the next six months, he focused on his mercantile businesses and spent time with Elizabeth at home. He and his wife also sometimes rode out to Rae's Hall where he reminisced with Rae about their shared time in the assembly. Undoubtedly, they took short exploratory jaunts to survey the property surrounding Rae's Hall. Those trips sometimes wound up at the Indian mound in the forks of Pipemaker's Creek and the Savannah River. Upon seeing it for the first time, Elbert, like Rae, could not help but marvel at its commanding presence. The mound offered visitors a peaceful and beautiful setting with a panoramic view of the river and Rae's Hall plantation. Ascending the summit, as they surely did, Rae revealed to Elbert his grandiose plans to turn the whole "mount" into a family cemetery. The thought appealed to Elbert, and he decided that his burial would one day be in the mound. It was the perfect place to spend eternity, he later told someone, because there he could hear the Savannah singing in

---

[22] "Journal of the Upper House," *CRG*, 17:593, 19(1):194.

his dreams forever.[23]

On October 22, 1770, Elbert began his third session in the assembly. He became a member of six committees during the fall, but of them all, he must have relished his first appointment the most. On November 7, he and Ewen joined a committee to better order the province's militia.[24] For Elbert, the committee perfectly matched his military interests. His experience expanded his limited knowledge about the condition of Georgia's militia in the years before the Revolution. Although all able-bodied males, including Elbert, were required to serve in the militia, the committee assignment was the first documented example of his being associated with the military in any official capacity.

Beyond the militia assignment, committee work piled up in successive order. Some allowed Elbert to leave the city for a few days to carry out his mission. On November 9, he and seven other House members set out to determine the best place for a new fort at the mouth of the Savannah River. Again, the topic interested Elbert since it touched on military matters. Elbert and those with him also inspected the old lighthouse on Tybee Island, a few miles south of the city, to determine repair needs and estimate restoration costs.[25] While there, they explored the maze of tidal marshes, swamps, and coastal scrubs at the river's mouth to ascertain an appropriate fort location. It took a few days for the committee to complete its fact-finding task. Afterward, they came back to Savannah, put their observations and recommendations into writing, and then presented their findings to the House.

Elbert was on two additional committees before the end of November. On November 13, he and Ewen became members of one that studied the condition of ferries that crossed the Savannah into South Carolina. Their job was to help formulate a system to better establish, maintain, and regulate ferries to aid navigation. On November 14, Elbert learned that he was on yet another committee, this time one to craft a law to prevent people from hunting with fire in the night. Elbert certainly had much to contribute to the committee's discussions since he had helped to write an earlier fire prevention bill for the House. Perhaps this experience led the

---

[23] Purcell, "Public Career of Samuel Elbert," 102. According to Purcell, Elbert's quote was passed down through his family and recorded in a letter written by Stella Muse Whitehead, a descendant, to Mrs. J. E. Hays early in the twentieth century (102n11). See Wheeler, *Images of America*, 75.

[24] *CRG*, 15:224.

[25] Ibid., 15:225.

committee to choose him as their speaker. Just before the assembly adjourned, Elbert found himself on a committee to prepare a bill for the relief of parishes from the upkeep of orphans. Finally, he delivered an address in person to Wright informing him that the House had come up with a resolution providing £17.5 to the several officers and men comprising the watch in Savannah. It was likely the first time that Elbert and Wright ever spoke. After he delivered his short report to the governor on December 20, Wright responded that he was pleased with the resolution and immediately issued orders to that effect.[26] On the following day, the governor dismissed the assembly for a short Christmas break.

If any of the House members felt that the spring term of the assembly in 1771 was going to run as smoothly as the previous one, they were in for a surprise. Everything appeared to be in order when the assembly convened on January 8. Shortly afterwards, problems with the governor arose over the larger power struggle between Wright and the House. On January 30, just before the difficulties began, the House placed Elbert, Rae, Ewen, Archibald Bulloch, and a few others on a committee to examine the proceedings of the courts and public offices. On February 18, the committee summoned Wright's deputy secretary of the colony, Thomas Moodie, to give testimony. When he arrived, the committee instructed Moodie to take an oath before they took his testimony. The oath stated, "you shall true answer make to all such Questions as may be required of you by this Committee relative to Fees allowed to be taken by the several Officers respecting Lands laid out and reserved for the use of the Irish and other settlers So help you God." Moodie flatly refused to take the oath, saying that this request had never been required from anyone testifying before the House or one of its committees and he would not set a precedent for the future. The House immediately reprimanded Moodie and issued a statement saying that his refusal to comply with their request was a "presumptuous Breach of the Privilege of the House and a daring Contempt of the Authority of [the] Committee." Moodie's actions, they said, obstructed the "Course of Publick Justice" and exposed their constituents to the "rapacity and Insolence of [his] Office." The House arrested Moodie and hauled him away to the "Common Goal" where he remained "during the Pleasure of the House."[27]

The Moodie affair was yet another confrontation with Wright that

---

[26] Ibid., 15:227, 229–30, 254, 255–57.
[27] Ibid., 15:295–96.

involved Elbert, and it further jaded his opinion of the governor. Gradually and for many reasons, Elbert was losing respect for Georgia's executive, whom he believed to be a dictatorial leader who often exceeded his constitutional authority. Wright was livid, too. Clearly, the House, by requiring an oath and then having the witness arrested and jailed when he refused to obey, had gone far beyond its legal limits. Wright insisted that the House had no right to compel anyone to take an oath to a mere committee and that their demands were beyond the ordinary. Even the House of Commons in England, he explained, did not routinely compel witnesses to take oaths before they testified to committees. In the midst of this controversy, the House still refused to pass a tax bill because the four southern parishes continued to lack representation. At this stage, Wright's patience was exhausted. He informed the House, as he had stated many times before, that only the king could grant representation and that the House of Commons could not just assume any powers that it chose to have. Unless the House released Moodie from jail and passed a tax bill, Wright would have no other choice but to dissolve it. The House did neither and, consequently, Wright dissolved it on February 22, only to receive word a few days later that the king had agreed to allow assembly representation in the four parishes.[28]

Wright's dismissal of the House ended Elbert's brief term in the assembly. Although his tenure in colonial politics concluded on a low note, Elbert benefited from the experience in at least three ways. First, based on his observations of and participation in the struggles between Wright and the House, he was able to form opinions about the governor and the divisions of power in government. His conclusions aligned him with the conservative coalition of Savannah's Christ Church Whigs, which included such people as Jones, Ewen, Bulloch, and Joseph Habersham. Elbert came to believe, as did many of his fellow House members, that the authority given to royal governors was dangerous without proper checks. Those left to suffer were the citizens who often sacrificed their liberties in the process. This lesson was plainly evident when Elbert considered the unfortunate case of Bryan, Wright's refusal to allow representation in the southern parishes, and the governor's habit of dissolving assemblies. In short, Elbert's time in the Georgia General Assembly enabled him to gain a deeper appreciation for liberty, natural freedoms, representation in government, and constitutional rights. He believed that curtailing the governor's authority

---

[28] K. Coleman, *American Revolution in Georgia*, 33–34.

was the only way to uphold those ideals. At the same time, the young leader hoped to enlarge the powers of the House and the voice of the people.

Elbert benefited in a second way. As a first-time politician, he gained valuable legislative experience. He saw, for example, how the House delegated authority through committees to achieve legislation. He also learned about the importance of compromise and debate in the legislative process. Beyond that, he explored and improved upon his skills as a leader and a speaker. These lessons would all provide useful knowledge and experience in Elbert's future.

Finally, many of Elbert's new friends and acquaintances in the House became revolutionaries just a few years later. Of the nineteen members in the House when Elbert began his first term, the overwhelming majority expressed Liberty party sentiments and later became active participants in Georgia's Revolutionary movement. At least four of the members, Jones, Ewen, William Young, and John Morel, served with Elbert on the Council of Safety when it formed in 1775. Ewen became the council's first president. Bulloch, an assemblyman from the town of Savannah, later became Georgia's first president. Button Gwinnett, from St. John's Parish, signed the Declaration of Independence in 1776 and then went on to become one of Georgia's Revolutionary governors. The list of later Patriots in the House did not include John Rae, who died shortly before the Revolution. Overall, the assembly during Elbert's four terms was decidedly patriotic and highly sensitive to issues involving liberty and House prerogatives. As for Elbert, the friends he made then became important influences when the time came for him to choose between king and country.

In 1771, the time for making that choice had not yet arrived. Elbert was still a faithful British subject who, despite his problems with Wright and his association with the liberty crowd, was devoted to the Crown and its government. Along the way, the young leader discovered something about himself. He understood now that he had a servant's heart. He would still seek ways to serve and make positive contributions to the betterment of society, even as he deepened his involvement in prominent organizations within his community. He also wanted to be a father and raise a family with his wife. Perhaps, at some point, he traveled out to the "mount" alone one day, ascended its summit, and then sat to contemplate his accomplishments and ponder the future. There, in the presence of the serene Savannah and nature's splendor, he could have arrived at only one conclusion. His life was truly blessed.

Chapter 3

A Devotion to the Duties of Life: Fatherhood, Brotherhood, and Grenadiers, 1771–1773

With his assembly days over, Samuel Elbert discovered new ways to serve his fellow citizens. In 1771, he became a justice of the peace for St. George's Parish between St. Matthew's (Ebenezer) and St. Paul's (Augusta) parishes along the Savannah River. Queensborough was within the parish, and, when Elbert assumed his duties, he resided in Savannah and owned no land in St. George's until he received a grant there in early 1772. His primary responsibilities as a justice included enforcing laws, regulating the militia, overseeing the proper trial of slaves accused of crimes, repairing roads, and establishing watches and guards to protect the inhabitants.[1] He was familiar with at least some of these tasks. As a representative in the assembly, he served on committees and passed laws dealing with the militia and the regulation of slaves. He also helped ensure a salary for the watch in Savannah and personally delivered an address to Governor Wright about it a year earlier.

Again, as was the case with so many other things in his life since coming to Georgia, Elbert's new father-in-law, John Rae, may have influenced him to seek the position. Since Rae had years of experience as a justice of the peace in St. Paul's Parish, he was well acquainted with the major responsibilities associated with the office. There were perils and dangers, too, as Rae well knew, particularly regarding the Indians. In 1771, those same challenges existed in St. George's Parish.

Queensborough was dear to Rae's heart. When Elbert became a justice, Rae was still a member of the assembly. All the while, he funneled Irish immigrants to the settlement. By 1772, the original tract was full,

---

[1] *CRG*, 11:376.

and newcomers needed additional acreage. On February 4, 1772, at Wright's council meeting in Savannah, the governor read a memorial from Rae requesting 25,000 more acres for Queensborough. The new grant was to accommodate two hundred recent Irish arrivals on the ship *Britannia*, quarantined in their vessel at Tybee Island due to a smallpox outbreak. The council made no decision at the time but promised to consider the request.[2]

Unfortunately, Queensborough's location on the fringes of Georgia's frontier put it in a precarious position due to its proximity to Indians. Rae continually worried about its safety. In early December 1771, his fears were justified when John Carey, a Queensborough resident, was killed by a party of Creeks. Inhabitants retaliated by killing Indians.[3] Since Rae had enticed the Irish to settle at Queensborough, he felt obligated to ensure their protection. With Elbert as a justice, Rae was assured that someone trustworthy oversaw the militia there. Furthermore, through Elbert, Rae maintained a commanding influence in Queensborough over slaves, the militia, roads, and the community.

With a possible Indian war looming, Elbert and Rae were much relieved when they heard about a communication sent to the governor and his council from Salagee, Tallegee, Fullokey, and Catagee, four Lower Creek *micos*, about Carey's murder. The Indians expressed remorse for the incident, and, following previous treaty agreements reached with Georgia, they executed the killer in the presence of several traders serving as eyewitnesses. The Creek leaders hoped that the execution proved their "Love & Friendship for the English" and served as a warning to their errant warriors. They promised that they would strive to keep their "Mad people" from venturing into the settlements and to "prevent all bad doing." They only wanted "peace and Quietness between our Nation and the White People our Friends" so that the trading paths "will be white to Charleston…[and] Savannah." Acting governor at the time, James Habersham Sr., replied to the Indians, telling them that he was "perfectly satisfied with what you have done in this affair, and I receive[d] your talk with a Streight and good heart, and shall acquaint the great King over the Water with your good Behavior."[4] While this situation was resolved, it foreshadowed growing

---

[2] Ibid., 12:192, 212–13, 243–54; G. F. Jones, "Portrait of an Irish Entrepreneur," 444.

[3] Holmes, *Those Glorious Days*, 8–9.

[4] "Talk from the Cheehaws," March 17, 1772, *CRG*, 12:316–17, and, in the same source, "Reply to Cheehaws," April 20, 1772, 318.

tensions between the Creeks and Georgia during the early 1770s, and sparsely settled areas, such as St. George's Parish, became especially vulnerable.

Although his duties as a justice required frequent absences from home, Elbert still spent time in Savannah, running his businesses and enjoying Elizabeth's companionship. Elbert had a good marriage, and the love he felt for his wife was deep and genuine. Throughout his marriage, he never engaged in scandalous relationships or affairs. Those who knew him maintained that he was always a loyal and devoted husband.[5]

He was also a loyal and devoted father to six children, but due to the lack of records, it is impossible to pinpoint with certainty the precise year any were born.[6] At least two were alive before 1777. The first indication of Elbert's fatherhood appeared when he applied to Wright for land on June 5, 1771. In his petition, he said that he now had a wife and child and that he had not received a grant for them. His intention, he claimed, was to cultivate the land and use it for a cowpen. He knew the specific plot he wanted, which was one hundred acres in St. George's Parish on Boggy Branch. Wright granted the petition on January 7, 1772. Again, just a month later, on February 24, 1772, Elbert sent the governor a second request for land. In it, he said that he already had land granted to him "on Family Right," referencing his acquisition back in January. But now that he had a wife and child, "for whom he never had any land," he was requesting additional acreage. He identified the property, which was one hundred acres on Lambert's Creek, again in St. George's Parish. It was his desire, he told Wright, to place a cowpen on that property, too. It was a curious appeal, because he had just received one hundred acres the previous month in the same parish for his wife and child. Nevertheless, Wright agreed to Elbert's petition.[7] The land on Lambert's Creek was close to Rae's cowpen and not far from Queensborough. Both grants were probably associated with Rae's, Elbert, & Graham's vast cowpens below Augusta described by Loyalists to British superiors in 1776 during the

---

[5] In Elbert's obituary that appeared in the *Independent Gazetteer*, December 8, 1788, 2, he was described as "a most affectionate husband."

[6] *Georgia Gazette*, December 8, 1788, 2. Two important primary sources indicate six children. Elbert's last will lists all six children by name (see Elbert, will, July 2, 1788, 105–107). The *Independent Gazetteer*, December 8, 1788, also lists six children in Elbert's obituary. The earliest accounts of Elbert in the nineteenth century, following the information given in the obituary lists six children (see, for example, White, *Statistics of the State of Georgia*, 241).

[7] *CRG*, 11:392; 12:191; 12:224–25.

Revolution. Since he was a justice of the peace at the time, Elbert's grants were convenient in that they allowed him to keep watch over Queensborough and at the same time oversee his cowpens and those nearby belonging to Rae. The addition of the two grants in St. George Parish increased Elbert's land holdings to at least 1,200 acres in 1772 widely scattered across four Georgia parishes.

Elbert's child, listed in the applications for land in St. George's Parish, was a daughter born in 1770 or 1771. It could have been Catherine ("Caty" or "Kitty") or Elizabeth. In Elbert's will, signed on July 2, 1788, he listed the names of his children. That Catherine was the first mentioned may imply that she was the oldest. After Catherine appeared Elizabeth's name. Another will from John Rae Jr. (Elbert's brother-in-law and Elizabeth's brother) probated in 1777 mentions his two nieces, Catherine and Elizabeth. The will named Elbert as an executor, along with Rae's sister, Jane Somerville, and his uncle, Robert Rae. The document identified both children as daughters of Colonel Elbert, which was his military rank at the time. "To Miss Caty Elbert," read the will, "[I bequeath] the sum of one-hundred pounds sterling." To a second child, "Miss Elizabeth Elbert," Rae left the "sum of two-hundred pounds."[8] Both children carried family names. "Caty" came from Elizabeth Rae's mother, Catherine Rae. Elizabeth carried her mother's name. Elbert also had a sister named Elizabeth.

According to Elbert's will, he and his wife had four additional children. They were Sarah, Samuel Emmanuel de la Fayette, Matthew, and Hugh Rae, all born between 1777 and 1788. Sarah, probably born in 1777 or 1778, got her name from Elbert's mother. Samuel Emanuel de la Fayette was named not only for his father but also for the Marquis de Lafayette, a famous French commander in the American Revolution whom Elbert met during the 1781 siege of Yorktown in Virginia. This is important in establishing a timeframe since Elbert did not know Lafayette before Yorktown. Thus, Samuel Emmanuel de la Fayette could only have been born after 1781. Matthew, the fifth child, carried the name of John Rae's brother in Ireland, but he died before reaching adulthood. The youngest child, Hugh Rae, carried the last name of his mother's family.[9]

"In private life," wrote the *Independent Gazetteer*, after Elbert's death

---

[8] S. Elbert, Last will, July 2, 1788, 105–107; J. Rae Jr., Last will, 59.

[9] S. Elbert, Last will, July 2, 1788, 105–107. See McMullan, *Equity Cases*, 475, for *Thos. Holt et ux. and John Kerr et ux. vs. Benoni Robertson, 1831*, which was a land case in South Carolina involving a portion of Elbert's disputed estate several years after his death. The case lists all the children except Hugh Rae.

in 1788, "he was among the first to promote useful and benevolent societies." One of those societies that Elbert affiliated with prior to the Revolution was the fraternal order known as the Free and Accepted Masons (F&AM). The Masonic craft, with its secrets, rituals, and bonds of brotherhood, intrigued Elbert. It also expanded his business connections since many of Savannah's merchants and political leaders were Masons. Elbert probably joined the Lodge in Savannah sometime after 1771. His name was not on a list of members in Solomon's Lodge #1 in Savannah, Georgia's only Masonic organization, which incorporated a set of bylaws in 1771.[10]

Everyone in the lodge had to approve Elbert's application for membership when he first petitioned; it took only one dissenting vote to reject his request. Once admitted, Elbert entered a phase of training where he advanced through three Masonic degrees. It took several months of intense training and practice for a candidate to pass through Masonic ranks and attain the final level of Master Mason. Each degree had its own oral catechisms, rituals, and symbols to memorize, patiently taught to Elbert by one or several lodge members. Devotion, diligence, and discipline were necessary to advance through the degrees. Since none of the catechisms were written down, Elbert had to perfectly memorize them for each level of masonry. After that, he had to pass an oral exam in the presence of the entire lodge before advancing. A ritual ceremony full of Masonic symbols and rights followed the final test after which he became a Master Mason for the rest of his life.

Solomon's Lodge was the second oldest in the colonies, even predating the lodge that appeared later in Charleston with the same name. It was an offshoot of the Grand Lodge of England and subject to its bylaws, guidance, and authority; its history dated back to James Oglethorpe and Georgia's founding. In 1733, Oglethorpe and a few other colonists who had been Masons in England established the Savannah Lodge at Sunbury under a long-gone live oak tree, south of Savannah on the Midway River. Two years later, in 1735, Savannah Lodge received a formal charter from England and changed its name to Solomon's Lodge #1. During the trustee and royal periods in Georgia, Freemasonry rapidly grew as a social and community institution. In lieu of a formal gathering place in Savannah,

---

[10] Solomon's Lodge F&AM Papers, 1735, 1771, "The Rules or By Laws of Solomon's Lodge, 1771," MS 0940, Georgia Historical Society. See *Independent Gazetteer*, December 8, 1788, 2.

public buildings, people's homes, and other suitable locations served as meeting places. Freemasonry's influence in Savannah was evident when, in 1757, Solomon's Lodge had the honor of being one of the city's community organizations that received Henry Ellis when he arrived in Georgia as the colony's second royal governor.[11]

Many of Elbert's closest acquaintances were members of Solomon's Lodge. Foremost among them were James Habersham Sr. and all his sons. Noble W. Jones, who was speaker of the House when Elbert was in the assembly, was also a member, as was his father, Noble Jones Sr. Two additional friends, Oliver Bowen and Joseph Woodruff, were also Masons. The lodge also accepted Jewish residents, such as Mordeci Sheftall, one of Elbert's business friends. His Masonic bonds even extended to included Governor Wright, who was a past grand master (or leader) of South Carolina's lodge. Another friend was Grey Elliot, a member of Wright's Council when Elbert was in the assembly. In 1760, Elliot became the leader of Solomon's Lodge with the title "Provincial Grand Master of Georgia." He served in that position for many years and presided over the lodge when Elbert became a member. In 1773, Elliot joined Philadelphia's Benjamin Franklin as the colonial agent to solicit the affairs of Georgia in England. His primary task was to act as a substitute in case Franklin had to be absent from his duties. When Elliot left, Noble Jones Sr. probably filled his position and held it until around 1775 after which Elbert became provincial grand master through the authority of the Grand Lodge of England. Elbert remained in that position until after the end of the Revolution.[12]

Masonic duties made heavy demands on Elbert's time. According to the Seventeen Rules or Bylaws of Solomon's Lodge adopted in 1771, the organization scheduled two-hour meetings on the first and third Thursday of each month "at some convenient place in Savannah." They began at six in the evening between September 25 and March 25 and at seven during

---

[11] Solomon's Lodge, F&AM Papers, 1735, 1771, "William Young to a Worshipful Brother," June 11, 1771; Tabbert, *American Freemasons*, 33–34; *Freemason's Chronicle*, 242; Knight, *Georgia's Landmarks, Memorials and Legends*, 2:649; C. C. Jones Jr., *History of Savannah*, 555–56.

[12] "Journal of the Upper House," August 7, 1773, in *CRG*, 17:736; G. Smith, "Georgia Grenadiers," 406; *Leaves from Georgia Masonry*, Educational and Historical Commission of the Grand Lodge of Georgia, F&AM, 1946, 211, 234. C. C. Jones Jr., *Samuel Elbert*, 39, wrote that his character was based on "moral endowments of a high order." For grand master appointments from the Lodge of England, see Clarke, *Early and Historic Freemasonry of Georgia*, 25, 63.

the other half of the year. Fines ensured that members follow all lodge rules. Attendance at meetings, for example, was mandatory. If a member failed to attend a regular meeting or function, the fine was one shilling. If that person was an officer, the fine was two shillings. The lodge documented absences from regular meetings and other functions. "The Secretary shall take down minutes of what is transacted in the Lodge, and to deliver to the Treasurer a list of absent Members every Lodge night," specified one of the bylaws. Some rules governed behavior when the lodge met. "Any brother," read the seventh rule, "that shall so far forget himself as to swear or use any indecent expression shall be fined one shilling, and for the third offense shall be expelled [from] the Lodge." Any member who neglected his quarterly dues or lodge attendance for a period of one year, decreed another rule, "shall be erased and [looked] upon no longer as a Member."[13]

With the strict penalties and regulations, it is a wonder Elbert would subject himself to the rigors of lodge membership in the first place. However, the benefits of Masonry to Elbert were many. On one level, the lodge elevated his community status, winning for him the respect of not only his Masonic brothers, but also others outside of the organization. That respect was rooted in Elbert's virtuous character, which lodge membership outwardly displayed. Additionally, Solomon's Lodge afforded Elbert the opportunity to enhance his business and political networks since many members were associated with Savannah's mercantile firms, as well as with the assembly. It also gave him another opportunity to develop and display his talents as a leader, especially after he became provincial grand master. Finally, all Masonic brethren were obligated to help each other in times of distress or need. Elbert knew that if he suddenly died, his fraternal brothers would care for his wife and children. This thought was particularly comforting to him since he was once an orphan himself.

The duties in Elbert's life seemed to magnify with each passing year, and he was frequently away from home. He had to travel often on business errands, for example, and that meant trips to Augusta to purchase items for his stores or to Indian country to procure deerskins. On other occasions, he made visits to his cowpens to make sure that things were in order there. As justice of the peace, he spent considerable time in St. George's Parish, about a five- or six-day journey on horseback from Savannah.

---

[13] Solomon's Lodge F&AM Papers, 1735, 1771, "The Rules or By Laws of Solomon's Lodge, 1771."

Fraternal demands carved away even more of his time. In Savannah, he regularly attended Christ Church on Sunday and for special services. He also successfully managed the operation of his firms by keeping books, stocking merchandise, engaging in land transactions, and faithfully serving his many customers.

On June 20, 1772, Elbert's responsibilities expanded when he became captain of a new flank company of grenadiers in Savannah's First Regiment of militia. The First Regiment was one of three militia companies organized for the city's defense. Since Wright was in England from summer 1771 until spring 1773, acting governor James Habersham Sr. made the promotion.[14] Elbert's elevation to captain represented his first appointment to a position of military rank, and it occurred almost as rapidly as his rise in politics and masonry. It was a remarkable turn of events for him, particularly since he lacked formal military training, at least beyond required militia service.

There is little doubt that Elbert had a lifelong interest in the military. It was probably first kindled by his father, who spun the tales of his ranger experiences on the South Carolina and Georgia frontiers to Elbert when he was young. From the days of his youth, soldiers and armies captivated him with their uniforms, weapons, drills, and discipline, claims the first person who wrote about him in 1807. The author, in a moment of romanticized hero worship and without any evidence, states that Elbert was "born a soldier" and that his "fondness for tactics was evinced even in childhood." One of the most fascinating things about the military to Elbert, he believed, was the "forming [of] little companies and teaching them the exercise [drills]." Late in the nineteenth century, Jones echoed the same idea, saying Elbert had always shown a "decided taste for military affairs."[15]

As a member of Savannah's militia, Elbert learned the fundamentals of soldiering by participating in frequent musters, drills, and training exercises. He gained additional knowledge in the General Assembly. In fall 1770, he helped author a bill to better organize the colony's militia. Later, he served on a committee to determine the best place for a fort at the mouth of the Savannah River and another to better the pay for Savannah's watch. Finally, as a justice of the peace in St. George's Parish, one of his

---

[14] G. Smith, "Georgia Grenadiers," 406 and 412n6, which identifies the First, Fourth, and Fifth companies as the three units comprising the First Regiment.

[15] Charlton, "Sketch of the Life of General Elbert," 2; C. C. Jones Jr., *Samuel Elbert*, 6.

responsibilities was to order and regulate the militia. Collectively, these experiences formed Elbert's rudimentary understanding of military affairs and, along with his social status, political influence, and natural tendencies for leadership, helped pave the way for his promotion in 1772, but so did Georgia's political climate and the escalating Indian threats.

The formation of an elite branch of foot soldiers, or grenadiers, within Savannah's militia was Elbert's idea. It was also Elbert's intention to gain a commission as a captain so that he could command the unit. Elbert presented his proposal to Wright before the governor left for England in summer 1771. Wright showed no interest in Elbert's proposition and refused to sanction it. The reason for the governor's rejection, surmised Judge Thomas U. P. Charlton in 1807, was "on account of Mr. Elbert's principles."[16] Those principles were on visible display for Wright to see when Elbert was in the assembly. Although Elbert did not take a public role in the protests against Parliament's policies in the 1760s, he did confront Wright during the Thomas Moodie affair and the dispute over representation in the parishes. From Wright's perspective, Elbert was part of the opposition crowd who created trouble in the assembly and questioned the governor's authority. It was unwise, he thought, to give Elbert command of an elite unit of militia while he was away in London. In the hands of radicals, that unit could do great mischief in his absence. Simply, Wright did not trust Elbert or any of his radical friends in the assembly, like Noble W. Jones. For this reason, the governor followed his instincts and refused Elbert's request.

Elbert and Jones enjoyed close political and Masonic ties. When Elbert was in the assembly, Jones served as speaker of the House, and initially Wright applauded him for his leadership. Though Jones was an effective politician, he aligned himself with the Sons of Liberty elements in the colony. It was Jones's outstanding qualities as a leader that disturbed Wright the most because the young politician had the ability to sway many to his line of thinking, especially in the assembly. This situation set up another showdown between the governor and the House when the assembly met for a late spring session in 1771, just before Wright left for England.

Elbert was probably in St. George's Parish fulfilling his duties as justice when the next assembly convened on April 23, but Rae, having won another term from St. Paul's Parish, arrived in Savannah to assume his

---

[16] Charlton, "Sketch of the Life of General Elbert," 2; G. Smith, "Georgia Grenadiers," 406.

seat. As usual, the House moved to elect a speaker, and they unanimously again chose Jones—much to Wright's dismay. Wright, without citing reasons and acting within his parameters as governor, told the House that he disapproved of Jones and instructed them to elect someone else. Obeying the governor, the House chose Archibald Bulloch instead. That, however, was not the end of the matter. On April 24, the House formally thanked Jones for his service and then adopted a second resolution contesting Jones's dismissal. The resolution called Wright's interference a serious breach of the House's privilege to choose their speaker. That action, claimed the House, subverted the rights and liberties of all Georgians. When Wright heard about the resolution, he was incensed. So was his council, who called it a "most indecent and Insolent denial of His Majesty's Authority." The council suggested that Wright dissolve the assembly if it did not rescind the second resolution. The House refused to comply, and, on April 26, after much back and forth, Wright dismissed the assembly after being in session for only four days. Two months later, on July 10, he departed for England, making James Habersham Sr. the acting governor until he returned.[17] Unfortunately for Habersham, he had to deal with the fallout from Wright's actions.

Although Elbert was not directly involved in the assembly at the time Wright dismissed it, he disapproved of Wright's actions. To him, the governor displayed a growing disregard for constitutional law and violated House prerogatives. Such abuses of power cost him Elbert's respect. During the course of 1771, Elbert turned against Wright, aligned himself with the Conservative Whigs, and sought ways to undermine the governor's leadership and power as evidenced by his role in the creation of the grenadiers.

Nearly a year passed before Habersham summoned the next assembly. The temporary governor sensed a lingering resentment over the fate of the last assembly. On February 17, 1772, he predicted to Wright in London that trouble would soon "shew itself" although this "unnatural opposition to Government in England is daily losing Ground." It saddened him, he admitted, that "we are distroying our own Internal Peace, and like Vultures [are] tearing out our own Bowels."[18] Still, much business from the previous session needed attention, including the passage of revenue bills

---

[17] *CRG*, 15:644; see also K. Coleman, *American Revolution in Georgia*, 34–35.
[18] James Habersham to James Wright, February 17, 1772, in "Letters of Hon. James Habersham," 166.

so the government could function. Reluctantly, Habersham called the next assembly into session. It met on April 21, 1772, and representatives once again chose Jones as their speaker.

While the House did not know it, Habersham already had instructions to deny Jones the position. The reason, according to Habersham, was that the upstart radical led the House in its "unwarrantable and rash Resolution" in April 1771, "which not only called in Question but in fact denied the right of the King's Representative [Wright] to negative a Speaker." In addition, Habersham, like Wright, did not like Jones. In a letter to the absent governor just before he summoned the assembly, Habersham suggested that Jones and his followers misled many "Poor people," by their incendiary rhetoric, turning them into "Cats-Paws to carry on the sinister Views of a few designing men."[19]

When the assembly began its session, it sent two members to Habersham's chamber to inform him that they had selected Jones as speaker. Habersham negated their choice and directed them to choose another. A second vote later that day, which Habersham refuted, produced the same results. On the following day, Habersham went to the council chamber with the "intention to dissolve the Assembly, if they persisted in their Choice," only to be told that Bulloch was now the speaker, which Habersham approved. That satisfied Habersham, until later that evening when he asked to see the House journal. There, Habersham learned that Jones had been elected a third time. The only reason Bulloch was speaker was because Jones had stepped down and refused to serve. The next day, Habersham told the House that it would have to remove the minute referencing the third election from their journal and that he would not do business with them as long as it remained. He gave the House two days to reconsider their position and strike the minute. Finally, he sent the House a message saying that if they did not delete the minute in question, he would terminate the assembly. They did not, and, as he explained to the Earl of Hillsborough in a letter, "I dissolved them" on April 25 after "a fruitless Attempt on my Part to make the Commons House sensible of their Duty to the King." The assembly had been in session only five days.[20]

Twice within one year, Georgia's governors dissolved the assembly over the Jones controversy. Now, Habersham faced the consequences of

---

[19] James Habersham to James Wright, March 12, 1772, 168, and James Habersham to the Earl of Hillsborough, April 30, 1772, ibid., 6:176.

[20] James Habersham to the Earl of Hillsborough, April 30, 1772, ibid., 6:74–75.

his actions, and there were already signs that something was astir. Some of the militia officers in the First Regiment of foot (in which Elbert was a member), were refusing to muster their men to celebrate the king's birthday according to custom. The source of their complaint, Habersham told the Earl of Hillsborough a week after he sent the assembly home, was the "sultry heat of the Weather, which might prejudice the People's Health." The men were especially concerned about the "vexatious Suits" they were required to wear. They hoped that the celebration could "be postponed to a more temperate Season." Their excuses did not fool Habersham. "I am not mistaken in their Motives for this Hint," he said in reference to "Mr. Jones and his Party." Jones's conduct, said Habersham as he dipped "his pen in Gall," was "very ungrateful and unworthy of a good Man." The acting governor was determined to force the militia's hand. "I shall put it to the Test," he told the earl, "and order a general Muster as usual."[21]

In this atmosphere of uncertainty and potential rebellion, Elbert perfectly timed his approach to Habersham about his plan for the grenadiers. To be fair, Habersham was probably unaware of Wright's earlier refusal to form the unit with Elbert in charge. Believing that the government would need all the help it could summon if the need arose, Habersham granted Elbert's request on June 20 and formed the grenadiers containing fifty enlisted men and three officers. Habersham commissioned Elbert as a captain and made him the commanding officer of the new unit. The nervous governor evidently had more faith in Elbert than Wright did and believed the new captain could rein in the militia and keep them loyal if the situation got out of control. There were other reasons that factored into Habersham's decision. Unlike the potential threat posed by radicals, the Indians were an ever-present danger; a strong and reliable militia, undistracted by political squabbles, was critical for the colony's protection. Although Habersham could mask his feelings and smooth-talk the Indians when the occasion demanded it (as he did to the Lower Creek leaders who earlier apologized for the murder of Carey), he felt nothing but contempt for them. On March 16, he wrote to Wright, complaining about how the "Savages" had no respect for treaties and "with arms and violence [they] rob [the inhabitants] at Noon Day." In a letter to his sister, Mary Bagwith, he called the Creeks a "nation of Savages" who continuously inflicted "cruel and barbarous insults" on Georgia's citizens. Thus, the fear of Indian violence also factored into Habersham's decision to sanction

---

[21] Ibid., 6:178–79.

Elbert's grenadiers. In addition to that, Habersham made his son, Joseph, second in command behind Elbert. Both men received their commissions on the same day. This honor not only elevated his son but also put another check on any rebellion hatched within the militia. There was one final reason Habersham gave the grenadiers his blessings: he, like Elbert, was a member of Solomon's Lodge.[22] While Wright did not allow Masonry to override his intuitive feelings about Elbert, Habersham was more trusting of his fraternal brother. Conversely, Noble Jones Sr. was Georgia's provincial grand master at the time, and Habersham detested Noble's son, who was also a Mason. What likely warmed the temporary governor to Elbert more than anything else was his close relationship with Habersham's three sons.

In the midst of the assembly's chaos and Elbert's scheming to form a grenadier regiment, calamity struck the Rae family. In fall 1771, the new captain and his wife heard the shocking news that John Rae was under arrest for the murder of Ann Simpson in Savannah. The news was unbelievable, given Rae's character, reputation, and social standing. While the circumstances surrounding the crime are mysterious, Rae claimed that her death was accidental. That excuse did not insulate him from a conviction for manslaughter in the jury trial that followed. Rae appealed to Habersham to overturn the conviction. On December 18, in a meeting of the Upper Council in Savannah presided over by the acting governor, a memorial from Rae about the death was read. Rae claimed that he had acted out of "Indiscretion, [rather] than bad intention towards the unhappy deceased." For this reason, and because of his standing in the province where he had resided for decades, he was humbly appealing to the governor as a "fit and deserving Object of the Royal Mercy." He sought a "gracious pardon" that he hoped would free him from "any pains[,] punishments[,] and forfeitures Consequent to…his Conviction." Many petitions on Rae's behalf accompanied his memorial. They all attested to his "unblemished character" and noteworthy service as a public official in various capacities. After reading the petitions, the governor and his council took the "unhappy case" of Rae into consideration and unanimously agreed, based on the circumstances, that Rae was "a fit Object of Mercy." Much to the dismay of Simpson's family and friends, Habersham granted him a royal

---

[22] Joseph Habersham to James Wright, March 12, 1772, ibid., 6:170; James Habersham to Mary Bagwith, February 3, 1774, in James Habersham Papers, May 1772–May 1775, MS 337, folder 17, Georgia Historical Society. For the unit's size and Habersham's commission, see G. Smith, "Georgia Grenadiers," 406–407.

pardon.[23]

A year later, toward the end of 1772, the Rae family endured another tragedy. In early December, John Rae died unexpectedly from unknown causes. So widely known had he become that reports of his death reverberated outside of Georgia. The *South Carolina Gazette and Country Journal*, for example, notified its readers on December 15 that Rae was dead.[24] Rae's family reeled in mourning, and the loss deeply touched Elbert, who had not dealt with the death of someone so close since his father died in 1754. Indeed, since the late 1760s, Rae had become something like a second father to Elbert, who constantly sought his advice, guidance, and encouragement. He had been tremendously influential in Elbert's life, persuading him to seek political positions in the General Assembly and as a justice of the peace in St. George Parish. In business and other affairs, Rae and Elbert partnered in the fur and cattle trades and in the establishment of the Queensborough settlement. Although he had only known him for four years, Elbert greatly respected his father-in-law, and the two shared many experiences and memories from their time together in the assembly and at Rae's Hall. For these reasons, Rae's death was a personal blow to Elbert.

In accordance with Rae's wishes, the family gathered at the "mount" just north of Rae's Hall near the mouth of Pipemaker's Creek to bury their patriarch in an ancient Indian temple mound. If not the first, he was among the earliest members of the Rae family interred there. After Rae's death, his heirs divided his vast estate. The will specified that Rae's Hall, the adjoining plantation, and most of the other land assets went to his son, John Rae Jr. Thus began the long chain of inheritances that kept Rae's Hall out of Elbert's possession. Claire Purcell observed that Elbert assumed the "head of the clan" position in the family after Rae's death but neither he nor Elizabeth ever owned Rae's Hall. Nor did Elbert inherit Rae's business interests. Instead, those went to Rae's half-brother, Robert,

---

[23] *CRG*, 12:154–55.

[24] *South Carolina Gazette and Country Journal*, December 15, 1772, no. 368, in Warren and Jones, *GGCJ, 1772–1773*, 99.

including two large firms in Augusta known as Rae, Whitefield & Company and Rae & Whitefield.²⁵

Beyond real estate and Rae's businesses and firms, personal property passed to his heirs, including Elizabeth. An inventory and appraisal of Rae's Hall on July 12, 1773, showed that his personal belongings there were worth £6,090.4.7, excluding land. That was almost twice the amount voted to fund the government in spring 1770 by Elbert's assembly. The appraisal did not include Rae's other homes and cabins around Augusta, or even his cowpens scattered over many parishes. The inventory extended for six pages, front and back, on long sheets of parchment. Since it was the first item listed, Rae's large clock, which greeted guests to his residence, must have most impressed the appraisers. Expensive mahogany furniture adorned Rae's Hall and included such items as cupboards, coffee tables, stands, drawers, desks, chairs, and two large dining tables, on which sat a silver coffee and tea service. There were many silver items scattered around the house, including castors, tankards, waiters, spoons, forks, knives, strainers, punch ladles, skewers, and pepper boxes, in addition to sets of fine china. Clothing, bed sheets, and blankets for his family and slaves filled closets, drawers, and trunks. Many of the items were inventory for the store that he and John Somerville (Rae's son-in-law, married to Rae's daughter Jane) operated out of Rae's Hall. The appraisers recorded the tools at his plantation, as well as wagons, saddles, straps, and other property. Rae's cows, mules, and horses were also included. One large section listed Rae's slaves by name and their value. The list identified all married and unmarried slaves, as well as those with children. According to the appraisal, Rae had more than 120 slaves on his Savannah plantation, not counting those he owned at his cowpens and other places.²⁶ Based on the inventory alone, he was, by all accounts, one of the wealthiest men in Georgia despite his many debts.

Rae's passing bequeathed to his family internal strife and substantial financial liabilities. A clue to the discord appeared in the will of John

---

²⁵ Wheeler, *Images of America*, 75; Purcell, "Public Career of Samuel Elbert," 5. Both companies were partnerships owned by John Rae and designated to receive payments for deerskin debts owed to them by the Creeks and Cherokee through a major Indian land cession in 1773 coordinated by Wright (National Archives, formerly the Public Record Office, Kew, England, Audit Office A. O. 13/36 Part 2, folio pages 833–37, in Warren and Jones, *GGCJ, 1772–1773*, 139–41).

²⁶ Estate Papers of John Rae, July 25, 1773, oversized folder 23, box 19, Telamon Cuyler Collection, MS1170, series 1, Hargrett Rare Book and Manuscript Library.

Somerville, who died almost a year later, in 1773. As the will suggested, disputes over Rae's inherited chattel created problems in the family. The disharmony was such that he asked his executors not to "interrupt my wife Jane Somerville in the quiet and peaceable enjoyment of all such negroes that has already been or may hereafter be received from the administrators of her late father John Rae." Meanwhile, John Rae Jr. struggled to keep Rae's Hall plantation intact. As heir to the bulk of his father's estate, John Rae Jr. became an instant target of creditors who sought to recover debts. Some of Rae's financial liabilities were so excessive that the only way to satisfy them was to relinquish whole tracts of valuable property. Such was the fate of Rae's fertile fields and pastures on Argyle Island on the Savannah River. Shortly after Rae died, a crediting firm seized the entire section of the island that he owned.[27] That was only the beginning. Rae's debts haunted his posterity until, ultimately, there was nothing left of his once impressive estate for future generations to inherit.

Rae's death did not deter Elbert from his primary goal of training and disciplining his new grenadiers. The militia leader knew that Wright would return to Georgia in early spring 1773 and that became the target date for the grenadiers' first public appearance. He wanted his grenadiers to greet the governor and impress him, and everyone else watching, with flawlessly executed drills and performances. Intense training could only take the grenadiers so far; perfection required that they also look professional. For this reason, Elbert requested funding to purchase special uniforms, made in London, for his unit. For himself, he ordered a red captain's outfit, trimmed in white, with epaulettes that fit his rank. Elbert's plan to surprise and amaze the governor would be compromised without the uniforms, so time was of the essence.

By late January, it appeared that Elbert would have to parade his grenadiers without uniforms, which had not arrived. Then, on February 3, the House received a petition from the unit's officers and men asking for permission to incorporate. Historian Gordon Smith, an authority on Elbert's Grenadiers, observed that this was "an unusual move at the time for a military company." The reason for incorporation, read the petition, was that it would make the grenadiers a more effective force to protect the colony in case of emergencies. They were always willing, they pledged, "to

---

[27] John Somerville, will, October 8, 1773, Book AA, Chatham County, Court of Ordinary's Office, Savannah, Georgia, 62–64. The reference to Argyle Island is in Granger, ed., *Savannah River Plantations*, 355, and Savannah Unit, Georgia Writers' Project, "Rae's Hall Plantation, Part I," 240.

turn out upon duty whenever there was the least probability of danger in the Town." Incorporation would "better serve the Province upon any alarm of danger" since it would "exempt [them] from some particular duties." The chief exemption they had in mind was to be relieved from serving the office of the constable. Without that burden, they explained, they could better fulfill their purpose of serving and protecting Savannah's citizens. Incorporation would thus establish the grenadiers as an independent arm of the militia and increase Elbert's autonomy as its captain. The petition also mentioned that the grenadiers had ordered "Necessary Cloaths and Accoutrements" from a company in England, which they expected to arrive any day. The uniforms and gear were the highest quality and the best available and came "at a very great expense." No one recorded the fate of the grenadiers' petition, and Smith concluded that the assembly probably tabled it.[28]

Six days later, on February 9, the ship from England carrying Wright back to the colonies arrived in Charlestown. The governor stayed in that city for few days before he began the slow trek back to Georgia, finally reaching Savannah at the end of the month. While in England, King George III baronetized Wright for his excellence in leadership and loyalty to the Crown. That news preceded the governor's entry into Savannah, so his return took on added significance as a celebration of that honor. Apparently, the long-anticipated uniforms had finally arrived because Elbert had his grenadiers mustered and paraded to greet "Sir" James Wright when he entered the city. Wright's reaction is unknown, but his feelings probably vacillated between surprise and anger at Elbert's defiance of his wishes. At the same time, the grenadiers' appearance in their new, brightly colored and unblemished outfits certainly created a positive impression. With their perfectly timed salutes and coordinated responses to Elbert's commands, they surely met and exceeded the mark of excellence Wright expected from his militia, especially since none of them, including the officers, received any compensation for their services.[29]

---

[28] *CRG*, 15:374; G. Smith, "Georgia Grenadiers," 407.

[29] In a report on the "Condition of the Province of Georgia" made to the Earl of Dartmouth on September 20, 1773, Wright stated that "Officers of the Regiment of foot Militia…have neither pay nor perquisites." See Warren and Jones, *GGCJ, 1772–1773*, 162, and for Wright's entry into Savannah, G. Smith, "Georgia Grenadiers," 407.

The House received the governor with a warm address on March 2, but by then, Elbert was already finalizing his plans for a trip to London with his wife. His primary motive in going was to perfect himself in the art of military command. While there, he hoped to get a professional artist to paint a portrait of him in his new uniform, so he carefully packed it for the journey. Leaving Joseph Habersham and other trusted subordinates in charge of the Grenadiers, Elbert and Elizabeth boarded *The Planter* in Savannah's harbor, and, on March 31, in fair winds, the ship sailed over the horizon on its long voyage to England. For the next two months, Elbert sought the advice of professionals in London who instructed him in military matters respecting the command of an elite militia. He even found a composer to write a march for his regiment titled "The Georgia Grenadiers," which, according to Charlton, was "still extant in the the British Books of Musick, and…an excellent composition."[30]

The two miniatures that exist of Elbert and his wife were most likely created in London during this trip. Based on the artistic style and the rendering of facial features, backgrounds, color hues, and brush strokes, they were also created by one painter at the same time. Elbert looks confidant and brave in his miniature, ringed in an oval gold, beaded frame. It features a profile of his right side, set in a background of dark sienna and cream. Large gold buttons cascade down a white border on the front of his brick-red uniform. From the shoulder, two thin gold strips lead to an epaulet of the same color. A dark necktie underneath a short white collar complements the outfit. Elbert's physical features show a young, fit, handsome man with large blue eyes, perfectly formed eyebrows, robust red lips, and a prominent (but not overly large) nose. His wavy, long sandy-blond hair, neatly tied with a fine black ribbon, cascaded far below his shoulders. The painting exudes the pride that he must have felt as he sat for his portrait in his new officer's uniform. His distinguished presence reflects the physical appearance detailed by Jones one hundred years later, when he described Elbert as "gentlemanly in deportment, handsome in person, erect and graceful in carriage, and gallant in bearing." The image in the painting projects a person who was, as Jones said, "magnetic in his intercourse and commanding in his influence." As Charlton observed, Elbert was "easy [in] manners" and had a "majestic form."[31] Elbert's miniature reflects those

---

[30] Charlton, "Sketch of the Life of General Elbert," 2. For Elbert's departure, see, Warren and Jones, *GGCJ, 1772–1773*, 183.

[31] Charlton, "Sketch of the Life of General Elbert," 2; C. C. Jones Jr., *Samuel Elbert*, 39. The miniatures are the only known images of Elbert and his wife.

attributes.

Elizabeth's oval miniature is a frontal view cast in a background of cobalt blue, which takes on a darker hue below the shoulders. She appears to be in her late twenties or early thirties and wears a dark blue or black dress with a V-neck and a broad collar of crimped white lace. Short sleeves rest high upon her arms. She wears a two-stranded red necklace that drapes down to her bosom, closed by three small dress buttons. Physically, she is dainty with small shoulders, but not frail. She has a pale complexion, thin lips, and an oblong face framed by a mass of long, curly dark-brown hair pulled into a bun typical for the time. Small strands of curls drop across her forehead, setting off her large brown eyes, which stand out as one of her most striking features. Elizabeth's portrait depicts a woman who is content, graceful, and confident. She also appears happy. Together, both miniatures show a beautiful young couple in the blissful early days of their marriage.

The story of the grenadiers' formation opens up doors of understanding into Elbert's character that go beyond the persona of virtue conveyed by his Masonic image. In addition to being honest and trustworthy, he could also be defiant, strong-willed, calculating and manipulative, opportunistic, and self-promoting. When Wright refused to let him have his regiment and command, Elbert sought a different avenue to achieve his goal. It seemed that nothing could deter him from his plan of establishing the grenadiers under his leadership. In Wright's absence, Elbert quietly took advantage of Habersham's fears of an internal rebellion and an Indian war to push his agenda and get the acting governor's cooperation. Although Elbert's parading of the grenadiers when Wright returned appeared to be a show of honor and respect, from another perspective, it represented a willful, brazen, and public act of disobedience of the governor's wishes. In the spirit of the liberty faction, Elbert's command of the grenadiers was not only a visual defiance of Wright but also a challenge to his authority and an indication of the new commander's dwindling respect for the governor. For Wright, it could only have reaffirmed his earlier reservations about giving Elbert the command in the first place. Whatever the governor's feelings, he let it pass and never said a thing about it.

The creation of Elbert's grenadiers was visionary but not unique. South Carolina, for example, had a grenadier unit at the time Elbert initially approached Wright with the suggestion. In Georgia, it was certainly a novel idea and even a good one, given the unstable situation on the frontier. The episode with the grenadiers showed that Elbert had initiative, drive, and independent-mindedness. The constant drilling of his grenadiers exposed another side of Elbert, who delighted in "forming little companies, and teaching them the exercise," which Charlton believed was "his principal amusement." Not only that, but Elbert was a perfectionist and held both his men and himself to the highest standards of performance in both drill and, later, war. Elbert was proud of his accomplishments and the grenadiers, but he was not pompous or boastful. As a "soldier without arrogance," he always thought of those he commanded first and placed their well-being above his own.[32]

While in London, Wright was on the cusp of attaining one of his greatest achievements as governor. Before he left for England, he received word that the Cherokee were interested in trading land to eradicate their deerskin debt. Through the years of the fur trade, the Cherokee and Creek had both accumulated tremendous debt to the traders amounting to thousands of skins. Subjected to the laws of supply and demand, deer populations in the colony crashed due to increased hunting pressures, making it impossible for Indians to rectify their debts. Deerskins formed the basis of credit in the fur trade. Any interruption in their availability reverberated up the system and affected the ability of traders, such as Elbert, to meet their credit obligations to merchants and settle their accounts. By the early 1770s, the situation was untenable. The debt problem, coupled with the traders' insistence on Indians producing skins and the declining deer population, contributed significantly to frontier friction between colonists and Indians.

One of the primary reasons for Wright's trip to England was to hammer out specifics of a major land cession to eradicate the Indians' debt, and he spent much time working with his superiors in London to formulate a plan. The broad outline of the deal, according to the Earl of Dartmouth, the secretary of state for the colonies, was that the transfer should "acquit & forever discharge the Indians from all debts." In turn, the "traders [will] agree to take their chance of being paid by and out of the monies which may arise by the sale of the lands." In this way, everyone, including Elbert's firms, could be satisfied. Rae's, Elbert & Company; Rae, Whitefield & Company; and Rae & Whitefield had significant claims against the Creek and Cherokee. The Indians could be relieved of their debt, and the traders,

---

[32] Charlton, "Sketch of the Life of General Elbert," 2.

merchants, and manufacturers could get their payments. The settlers could also have access to newly opened and fertile lands where they could create homes and farms.[33] It was a win-win situation for everyone except the Indians, who liquidated their debts but also lost their land.

When Wright arrived in Charleston from his London trip, he met with John Stuart, the Indian superintendent of the Southern tribes in North America, and told him to schedule a conference with Cherokee and Creek headmen in Augusta, hopefully in May, to discuss a land-for-skins agreement. Wright was optimistic that the upcoming congress would be a success, and, as he informed the Earl of Dartmouth in a letter, "we shall be able to obtain a proper Cession." The General Assembly celebrated the news of the proposed cession and heaped praise upon the governor when he arrived in Savannah from South Carolina. Enlarging Georgia's boundaries was "of the utmost importance to us," they told Wright, and the "Province is indebted to you, on this Occasion…for your effectual endeavours exerted while in England."[34]

The land Wright sought began about twenty-two miles above Augusta between the Savannah and Oconee Rivers. The cession included two major river systems, the Little and the Broad, both tributaries of the Savannah and also the upper headwaters of Brier Creek. The major ridge between the Broad and Oconee Rivers marked the western boundary all the way down to the headwaters of the Ogeechee River. To the north, the line stretched to the highest springs of the Broad. Wright added an additional unconnected narrow strip to the cession owned by the Creeks between the Ogeechee and Altamaha Rivers southwest of Augusta.[35]

The Augusta Conference (thereafter referred to as the "New Purchase") began on June 1. Among those attending were three hundred Creeks and one hundred Cherokee along with twenty-one headmen, Wright, Stuart, and William Bartram, an English naturalist who intended to explore the lands after they were acquired and give a detailed description of the flora and fauna. The royal governors from Virginia, North Carolina, and South Carolina also attended, as did many traders and merchants,

---

[33] Earl of Dartmouth to James Wright, December 12, 1772, Sir James Wright Papers, folder 1: Loose Papers, 1772–1784, MS 0884, Georgia Historical Society.

[34] James Wright to the Earl of Dartmouth, March 24, 1773, in Warren and Jones, *GGCJ, 1772–1773*, 151. For Elbert's and Rae's firms, see ibid., 139–41. For the House address, see *CRG*, 15:394.

[35] At the time, the cession was known as the "ceded lands." In 1777, during the American Revolution, Georgia designated it as Wilkes County.

including Elbert, who barely made it back in time from England. Elbert had ample reason to be at the conference since the negotiations involved Rae's, Elbert & Company. As a representative of his business, Elbert and all the other traders were required to provide the governor with a detailed list of debts owed to them by the Indians. Furthermore, Wright arrived in Augusta accompanied by militia, which included Sir Patrick Houstoun's company of light infantry and "three discharges of small arms from Capt. Elbert's Grenadier Company." Without a doubt, Elbert proudly marched from Savannah to Augusta at the head of his grenadiers to ensure the governor's safe arrival. A military presence was necessary at the conference to keep the peace, should anything happen, especially since some of the Creeks were in a surly mood and did not want to cede any land.[36]

Disagreements went beyond those between the colonists and Indians. There were also heated disputes between Creek and Cherokee leaders over their own boundaries since both claimed some of the lands in question. Wright wanted to include the Oconee lands in the treaty, but the Creeks refused to budge on that suggestion. As he later reported to the Earl of Dartmouth, the Creeks were unwilling to let go of their Oconee claims because it was "their *beloved* hunting Grounds for Bear and Beaver." Instead, "the lands above the Line marked by the Cherokees two years ago were ceded in Lieu of going to [the] Oconee River." Stewart's bribery with liberal presents and alcohol convinced the Indians to give up a total of 2,100,000 acres to eradicate a debt of 200,000 skins. Of this amount, the largest portion, 1,616,298 acres, were north of the Little River. The majority of the Creeks left Augusta dissatisfied, but they had sworn during the conference that they would not "disturb any of his Majesty's subjects in their settlements or otherwise within the lines aforesaid." As surveying parties accompanied by Indians set out to mark the new boundaries, Wright returned to a hero's welcome in Savannah where the council and House lauded him.[37]

Land courts soon opened in Savannah, Augusta, and at the mouth of the Broad and Savannah Rivers where a small stockade called Fort James was erected. On the first day alone, Wright reported applications for about

---

[36] Sir James Wright to the Earl of Dartmouth, August 10, 1773, in Warren and Jones, *GGCJ, 1772–1773*, 154, 139–41, 184; Cashin, "Sowing the Wind," 240.

[37] Cashin and Robertson, *Augusta & the American Revolution*, 2; Braund and Porter, eds., *Fields of Vision*, 5; *CRG*, 17:707; C. C. Jones Jr., *History of Georgia*, 2:129.

300,000 acres. The flow of settlers into the ceded lands continued at a steady pace, swamping the governor with piles of warrants to sign. On November 2, 1773, for example, 71 people received 17,230 acres. Unfortunately, clashes between settlers and Indians in the ceded lands began almost immediately, particularly with the Creeks who, refusing to acknowledge their loss of territory, retaliated against frontier inhabitants. Rising tensions caused Wright to assess the state of his militia. Writing to the Earl of Dartmouth on August 16, he informed him that all he had were three regiments of foot militia comprising 2,828 men, ranging from the age of sixteen to sixty, to defend the province. Those numbers included Elbert's grenadiers. "This, my Lord," he agonized, "is our whole Strength, scattered about a great face of Country and not a Soldier in the Province in His Majesty's Pay."[38] Wright's apprehension was well founded. The new settlers were not safe, and reports of Creek depredations filtered into Savannah with increasing frequency. The region teetered on warfare, and, when it finally came in 1774, Elbert and his grenadiers played a role in the unfolding frontier drama.

As pressures mounted between the colonists and Indians in Georgia, another unrelated incident several hundred miles to the north dangerously escalated the conflict between Great Britain and her colonies. In 1770, Parliament repealed the Townshend Duties except the tax on tea in order to keep the government-backed East India Tea Company solvent. Financial problems continued to plague the company, and Parliament responded by passing the Tea Act of 1773, giving the East India Tea Company a monopoly in the American tea trade. Americans opposed the act. The three-pence duty placed on the tea served as another example of Parliament taxing the colonies without their consent. In late fall 1773, ships carrying tea were sent to the major port cities in the colonies except Savannah; Boston provided the most dramatic response. On the night of December 16, about fifty men, dressed like Indians, boarded the cargo ships in Boston's harbor and destroyed 342 wooden casks of tea, which they broke open with hatchets and then tossed overboard. The perpetrators then escaped into the night, but the results of their actions were obvious to anyone who gazed upon the tea-stained harbor on the following

---

[38] Sir James Wright to the Earl of Dartmouth, August 16, 1773, in Warren and Jones, *GGCJ, 1772–1773*, 155; *CRG*, 15:465; "Georgia Council Orders, 1772–1773," in box 15, folder 10, Telamon Cuyler Collection, MS1170, series 1, Hargrett Rare Books and Manuscripts Library; C. C. Jones Jr., *History of Georgia*, 2:131; Cashin, "Sowing the Wind," 241.

morning. What they saw was 90,000 pounds of floating and ruined East India tea valued at £10,000.[39] The destruction of the tea was dramatic and symbolic, and it demanded a firm response from Parliament, which came a few months later with the passage of the punitive Coercive Acts.

News of Boston's intrepid actions did not arrive in Georgia until a few weeks later. When it did, scattered columns supporting Boston's protest appeared in the *Georgia Gazette*, but at the time, the prospect of an Indian war in the ceded lands consumed the colony's attention. Elbert found himself caught between the pinchers of two intensifying but separate conflicts, one with the Creeks and the other with the Crown. He was destined to play a role in both.

For Elbert, 1773 was an eventful year. There were moments of grief as the family struggled to cope with the death of John Rae and settle his estate. There were also challenges, accomplishments, and even a trip to England. One of Elbert's biggest tasks during the year was to train and discipline his new grenadiers. He even tried, and failed, to get them incorporated in February. Then, in March, his grenadiers, in their first public appearance with new uniforms, greeted Wright when he arrived in Savannah from England. In June, he participated in the Augusta conference, which resulted in a major land cession by the Creeks and Cherokee and a promise by the government to compensate his firm for Indian debts. All the while, he maintained his business, home, and Masonic commitments. The year was so full of activity that he mistakenly let another grant of one hundred acres given to him by Wright in St. George's Parish, expire in the surveyor's office. Elbert asked the survey general to recertify it, and he allowed Elbert six more months to sign the necessary paperwork and get it registered.

Despite his busy schedule, Elbert found time to ask England's Grand Lodge for permission to constitute a second lodge in Savannah. Elbert called the new organization the Unity Lodge and he sought to be its grand master. Smith suggested that the primary motivation for Unity Lodge was Elbert's desire to bypass the House and pursue another avenue to incorporate the grenadiers. He also believed that Unity Lodge had a political purpose since it would serve as a secret venue for members to "discuss the growing controversy between England and the American colonies."[40] The attempt to constitute the new lodge was yet another example of Elbert's

---

[39] Middlekauff, *Glorious Cause*, 219–26.
[40] Warren and Jones, *GGCJ, 1772–1773*, 106; G. Smith, "Georgia Grenadiers," 407.

drive, vision, and ambition. He was still awaiting the Grand Lodge's response to his application for a new charter at the end of the year.

As a loving father and husband, son-in-law, businessman, justice of the peace, Masonic brother, and captain of the grenadiers, Elbert showed that he was a man deeply devoted to the duties of life. He was also loyal to the people and causes that he embraced. Still, as was shown when he defied Wright and created the grenadiers, his loyalty ran only so deep. His loyalty would soon be tested as dark and ominous clouds gathered on the horizon. They signified the approach of furious storms carrying frontier war and revolution in their howling and destructive winds. Those storms would soon consume Samuel Elbert.

Chapter 4

"That Love for My Country Which Prompted Me": The Americanization of Samuel Elbert

At some point in 1774, Samuel Elbert assessed his multitude of benefits as a loyal subject in His Majesty's British Empire. Under Crown rule, for example, he became a substantial landowner. In St. George's Parish alone, he accumulated two hundred acres in grants from Governor Wright with an additional one hundred acres pending when he completed administrative paperwork in the surveyor's office. There were more government grants in St. Matthew's and St. David's parishes. In total, well over one thousand acres of Elbert's growing estate was due to royal government. That same government afforded him the opportunity to gain political experience in the assembly. It also bolstered his businesses, particularly when Wright negotiated the New Purchase with the Indians in 1773 and secured debts owed to Elbert by the Creeks. Finally, royal government fulfilled Elbert's dream of attaining military rank and commanding an elite grenadier militia unit.

Despite these benefits, 1774 was the last year of Elbert's life as a loyal subject. As the year progressed, he faced a personal crisis regarding his own loyalty to the very government that nourished his advancements, opportunities, honors, and aspirations. His decision to become a Revolutionary came only after a period of deep soul-searching that autumn; the catalyst was Parliament's passage of the punitive Coercive Acts in 1774 in response to the Boston Tea Party. Those acts energized Georgia's Revolutionary movement like nothing else in the previous decade. They also galvanized Elbert.

Chronological categories charting the evolution of Elbert's slow transformation into a Revolutionary help to explain his Americanization. The first, a period of realization, represented a growing awareness in Elbert about threats posed to liberty by Parliament and Georgia's royal government. This period began with the Stamp Act in 1765 and continued until the Coercive Acts and the reaction they caused in Georgia during summer 1774. Elbert's time in the assembly was an important milestone in this phase because it caused him to develop a negative view of Wright, and he aligned himself with the Conservative Whigs. The second phase, a period of decision, began in late summer 1774 and lasted through the fall. It represented a time of deep reflection for Elbert in the aftermath of the Coercive Acts and a brief frontier war with the Creeks. This phase ended when Elbert, after carefully weighing his options, openly joined Georgia's Revolutionary movement on January 23, 1775. The last phase, a period of action, took place during the remaining months of 1775. It was during this time that Elbert actively engaged in bold acts of resistance to Georgia's royal government; by the summer, he was a major figure in the colony's Revolutionary movement.

Elbert was still loyal to the British government when 1774 began. The year opened with a predicted Indian war in the ceded lands, and, before it was over, both he and his grenadiers were involved. The struggle began on Christmas Day in 1773 when a Coweta Creek war party attacked William White's house on the headwaters of the Ogeechee River near the Quaker town of Wrightsborough and killed him, his wife, and four children. The murders initiated four brutal months of warfare and atrocities on both sides. On January 14, the Creeks struck again and killed seven settlers, this time at William Shirrell's home, about four miles from White's residence. In the wake of the "Shirrell Massacre," the militia pursued the Indians, only to be routed themselves on January 23 by a party of sixty Creeks led by a warrior named Big Elk. To add insult to injury, the Indians captured militia commander Lieutenant Daniel Grant, tied him to a tree, and tortured him to death. Though the assembly howled for war, a guarded Wright wisely advised restraint. Both he and Indian Superintendent John Stuart "disavowed those Outrages," and blamed the violence on the rashness of a few young men. The Lower Creeks did not want war, he counseled, but the crimes still demanded satisfaction.[1]

Wright's caution was justified. Lower Creek headmen did not sanction the murders. Seeking to restore peace, Mad Turkey (also called Head Turkey), an Upper Creek from Ockfusky where Elbert's firms carried on

---

[1] *Georgia Gazette*, February 2, 1774, 2; March 16, 1774, 1; March 23, 1774, 2; April 27, 1774, 1; J. M. Johnson, *Militiamen, Rangers, and Redcoats*, 97–98; Braund, *Deerskins & Duffels*, 159–60; Cashin, "Sowing the Wind," 241; C. C. Jones Jr., *History of Georgia*, 2:132–33.

trade, took it upon himself to end the fighting. He visited Coweta's leaders to gauge their intentions. They agreed that he should go to Wright, apologize, and tell him that the Cowetas were not at war and only wanted reconciliation.[2] Accordingly, Mad Turkey, a few other Indian leaders, and a fur trader set out for Savannah in late March on a diplomatic mission.

On their way to Savannah, the entourage stopped at Augusta, which became the scene of another grisly crime. The *Georgia Gazette* told the story as it unfolded. "Last Thursday," it informed readers on March 30, "the Mad Turkey, who, with two other Creek Indians, accompanied by one of the Traders from the Upper nation, and who had done his utmost in the Lower Towns to persuade his countrymen to endeavor to make peace with this province…was barbarously murdered in Augusta." The murderer was a local blacksmith named Thomas Fee. According to a slave eyewitness, Fee invited Mad Turkey to have a drink with him. When the Indian tipped the bottle to his mouth, Fee hit him in the back of the head with an iron bar purchased from Robert Rae's store. The slave tried to intervene, pleading with Fee to "not kill the Indian." Fee hit the slave in the head with the iron and then continued his "barbarous" beating of Mad Turkey, crushing the chief's head "in a terrible manner" and killing him. On April 6, the *Gazette* labeled the killing as a "most cruelly and inhumanly murder." The Indians would seek reprisal, it warned, destroying the "lives of his Majesty's subjects, and the peace and happiness of these provinces." Wright's response was to issue an immediate proclamation on March 30, saying that anyone who molested, assaulted, or insulted Indians "behaving themselves quietly and peaceably," could expect a swift and severe punishment. Meanwhile, Fee fled the province into South Carolina. Wright issued a £100 reward for anyone apprehending him. The *Gazette* described him as a "slim man, of about six foot high, ruddy complexion, sandy or reddish hair, and about 26 or 27 years-old" who was "supposedly from North Carolina."[3]

Authorities in South Carolina captured Fee a few days later and confined him in a jail at a town called Ninety-Six. A mob declaring Fee a hero then broke him out. South Carolina's governor responded, offering £200 for his capture. All the while, the situation in Georgia reached a critical state. The problem was not just with Indians. Wright's Council charged that "disorderly white people" in the backcountry without property fanned

---

[2] McCall, *History of Georgia*, 2:11; C. C. Jones Jr., *History of Georgia*, 2:134.
[3] *Georgia Gazette*, March 30, 1774; April 6, 1774, 1; April 13, 1774, 3.

the flames hoping to benefit from the confusion caused by an Indian war. "Our situation is precarious," the council informed the House. Expecting the worst, the House appealed to King George III to send British regulars for protection. "Far as such treachery must have been from our expectations [after the land cession], we have...lately experienced many very lamentable proofs of the baseness of these Barbarians," they explained to the king. "[We] have too much reason to fear the frequent repetitions of such unspeakable...acts of Cruelty," they predicted, "unless effectually prevented by the speedy interposition of your Majesty's arms in our favor."[4]

The requested troops never materialized, but Wright's invitation to Creek headmen to come to Savannah, establish peace, and witness Fee's execution bore fruit. On April 20, Emistisiguo, a *mico* of Little Tallassee; Captain Allick from Cusseta; St. Jago, another Creek leader; and a host of additional Indians met with Wright and his Council at the courthouse. The Creeks were certainly disheartened to learn that Fee escaped despite the governor's reassurances about his capture. Addressing the recent string of violence on the frontier, Wright informed the headmen that the only way to preserve peace was to execute those Indians responsible for murdering innocent people. This method of retribution went against Creek tradition, but it was already something they agreed to in prior treaties with Georgia. The colony did not want a war, but unless the Indians ceased robbing and terrorizing settlements, Wright promised that the king would send a great army against them. If the perpetrators of the murders were put to death, the governor assured his Creek audience that the "chain of friendship" would be made "strait and bright," and that the "blood which had been spilt might be washed away." The governor also wielded the deerskin trade as a weapon, which he promised to cut off until the Indians met his demands.[5]

Recalling Mad Turkey's fate, the Indians expressed concerns about their own safety, especially when returning to their villages and towns in the Chattahoochee valley. To ease their fears, Wright provided them Elbert's grenadiers and its sister flank company, the light infantry, under the command of Sir Patrick Houstoun, as an escort through the settlements

---

[4] Ibid., March 2, 1774, 1; *CRG*, 15:542–43; Cashin, "Sowing the Wind," 241–42; McCall, *History of Georgia*, 2:12.

[5] *Georgia Gazette*, April 20, 1774, 2; May 25, 1774, 2; June 22, 1774, 3; Juricek, *Colonial Georgia and the Creeks*, 7–9, 161, 169; McCall, *History of Georgia*, 2:12–13; Braund, *Deerskins & Duffels*, 161.

to the Ogeechee.[6] Elbert's appointment to lead the mission was a logical choice. His task was potentially dangerous given most Georgians' hatred of Indians. The appearance of the grenadiers in their impressive uniforms could simultaneously win the respect of civilians and curtail their insults to the Indians. The choice of Elbert also showed that Wright had confidence in his leadership and that the young captain could discipline and control his soldiers to accomplish the task. Elbert's familiarity with the Indians was another factor in Wright's decision. While he may not have known those he escorted personally, the Indians were acquainted with him through the trade. He also knew how to communicate with them by signs, gestures, and perhaps even a few phrases or words. Additionally, Elbert knew the labyrinth of trails and paths leading to Indian country, so he had at least some knowledge of the terrain. Finally, he had ample reason to ensure the Indian's safety. After all, his businesses depended upon the restoration of the trade. When he left Savannah in late April with the grenadiers and Indians, he was fully cognizant of something else. This was his first field command. As such, it was important to Elbert, not just to Wright and others, that the undertaking be professional and successful.

Elbert was away for several weeks escorting Indians. When he returned to Savannah, he once again publicly displayed his grenadiers. As usual, a big celebration took place on Saturday, June 4, to honor King George III's birthday, and the grenadiers were required to participate. On the morning of the observance, ships in the harbor hoisted colorful flags to commemorate the occasion. Later, Wright and other dignitaries reviewed the militia as it mustered on the commons. Prominently displayed in the formation were Elbert's grenadiers and the light infantry. The militia made a "fine appearance," wrote the *Gazette*, and they went through their exercises with "great dexterity and exactness." No doubt, Elbert amazed his audience with a drummer and fifer on hand to play the "Georgia Grenadiers." At 1:00, cannon added their rapport to the celebration, and the ensemble then moved to the courthouse, where the governor provided entertainment. Present were members of both Wright's Council and the General Assembly, clergy, and militia officers, which included Elbert. It was probably at the courthouse, where, in great ceremony, Elbert, Joseph Habersham, and other officers took a qualification oath of loyalty to the king. The oath was a prerequisite to their holding commissions in the military, and it weighed heavily on the mind of Elbert in the months to

---

[6] G. Smith, "Georgia Grenadiers," 407–408.

come. According to the *Gazette*, the celebrations finally concluded in the evening with a display of "great illuminations, &c. as usual."[7]

The gala atmosphere may have suggested that all was well in Georgia, but the façade of calm was already dissipating. Parliament was in no conciliatory mood when news of Boston's tea party reached England in mid-January, and it was nearly unanimous in its desire to punish the city for its disobedience. In spring and summer 1774, with few dissenting votes, it passed five separate bills collectively called the Coercive Acts. Together, they set the stage for the colonies' final descent into revolution.

The first measure, the Boston Port Act (or bill), was voted on by Parliament and approved by the king in March. It indefinitely closed that city's harbor to all trade as of June 1, with certain exceptions made for food and fuel. Compensation for the destroyed tea was required from Boston, but the king was the ultimate authority in lifting the ban. That was followed by the Massachusetts Government Act, passed by Parliament and then approved by the king in May, which called for the council in that colony to be nominated by the Crown. It also limited town meetings without permission, put the sheriff in charge of selecting juries, and allowed the governor more power to appoint and remove officials. An Impartial Administration of Justice Act (Jury Act), also signed by the king in May, called for any royal official or servant accused of a capital crime to be sent to England or some other colony away from his peers to stand trial. A Quartering Act was also approved, which forced the colonists to provide housing and provisions for soldiers in their midst. Finally, the Quebec Act, which became law at the same time, fanned the flames of religious controversy by encouraging French Catholics living in Canada to settle among the Puritans in Massachusetts's western frontier.[8]

The Coercive Acts unleashed a torrent of protests in the colonies that reverberated all the way from Massachusetts to the Carolinas and Georgia. In Georgia, the acts galvanized the liberty crowd who believed their chartered rights were being "literally annihilated" by a "completely tyrannical" government. On July 14, an invitation, signed by Noble W. Jones, Archibald Bulloch, John Houstoun, and George Walton, appeared in the *Gazette* calling for all concerned citizens to convene at Tondee's Tavern in Savannah on July 27 to discuss the dire state of affairs and determine a response. On the appointed day, there was a public reading of the letters

---

[7] *Georgia Gazette*, June 8, 1774, 3; Purcell, "Public Career of Samuel Elbert," 8.
[8] Middlekauff, *Glorious Cause*, 230–31.

and resolutions from committees of correspondence in the different colonies. They appointed a Committee of 31 to draft a set of resolutions from Georgia to share with other colonies. On the committee were some of Elbert's closest acquaintances, like Jones, Bulloch, and Habersham. Without representation from Georgia's distant parishes, the meeting adjourned until August 10. Then, the discussion would resume at Tondee's Tavern with representatives sent from each of Georgia's parishes.[9]

Wright denounced the July 27 meeting a week later in a published proclamation, claiming that a few "artful and designing men" with mostly "imaginary Grievances" masterminded the unlawful gathering. Such summonses, he warned, tended to "raise fears and jealousies in the minds of his majesty's good subjects." To keep them from being deceived, he declared future such meetings, like as the one planned for August 10, "unconstitutional, illegal and punishable by law." All involved in orchestrating future gatherings, he threatened, would "answer the contrary at their peril." The proclamation was criticized by the liberty folks, who, according to Wright, saw it as an "*arbitrary & oppressive…attempt to debar them of their natural and Lawful Rights*" of assembly, speech, and petitioning for the redress of grievances.[10]

The governor's threats did not deter concerned citizens from holding their meeting on August 10, when, with more delegates in attendance, they adopted eight resolutions drawn up by the July 27 committee. According to historian Kenneth Coleman, these resolutions were the "first real statement of revolutionary sentiment in Georgia." One attacked the Boston Port Bill as something "contrary to our idea of the British Constitution." Another assaulted the Massachusetts Government Act as a law that subverted American rights. Unlawful, too, was the Jury Act. The most Revolutionary statement of all proclaimed that Parliament "hath not, nor ever had, any right to tax his Majesty's American subjects." To coordinate Georgia's efforts with other colonies, they agreed to send their resolutions to like committees in the provinces. Additionally, a committee of nine was appointed to solicit supplies and aid for Boston's suffering citizens. The members of this committee were from Elbert's town and district of Savannah, except for two. Before adjourning, those at the meeting decided to

---

[9] K. Coleman, *American Revolution in Georgia*, 40. Coleman said it was a committee of thirty, but the member list produced in C. C. Jones Jr., *History of Georgia*, 2:149, contains thirty-one names. For the quote, see McCall, *History of Georgia*, 2:27.

[10] James Wright to Lord Dartmouth, August 24, 1774, in "Letters from Sir James Wright," 181 (cited hereafter as LSJW). See also McCall, *History of Georgia*, 2:22–24.

hold a provincial congress in January composed of delegates from all of Georgia's parishes.[11]

As before, Wright denounced the August 10 meeting as a "Junto of a very few [people]." Because of this, he told Lord Dartmouth in a letter, that their resolutions "were not the voice of the People, but unfairly and insolently made." The gathering, read one notice by opponents in the *Gazette* on September 7, was "held at a tavern, with the doors shut for a considerable time: and it is said 26 persons answered for the whole Province." Meanwhile, a "Tavern-keeper…stood in at the door with a list in his hand" barring entry to everyone but the "resolutioners." The whole world would judge, they predicted, whether a meeting "held by a few persons in a Tavern, with doors shut, can, with any appearance of truth or decency, be called a General Meeting of the Inhabitants of Georgia."[12]

The July 27 and August 10 meetings were significant steps on Georgia's road to revolution, but the glaring question during those momentous and historic occasions is, *where was Elbert*? McCall said that the July 27 meeting was composed of "a number of respectable free-holders and inhabitants" in addition to those placed on the committee to draw up resolutions against the Coercive Acts. Those unnamed participants could have included Elbert, but there is no record of how many people attended either meeting or even what parishes they represented. Opponents claimed that most were from Christ Church and St. John's parishes. McCall described the August 10 gathering as "a general meeting of the inhabitants," refuting the critics' claim that only those creating resolutions could enter.[13] Without a list of names to reference other than those selected to committees, it is impossible to know who was present at either meeting, including Elbert.

If Elbert did attend, why was he not on any of the committees? There are three possible answers to this question. For one, Elbert, unlike others who took leadership roles and committee assignments, held an officer's commission in the militia. Consequently, Wright and his council watched him closely; any move to support the dissenters could jeopardize his command. The loyalty oath Elbert recently took to the king also restrained him. Joining any of the committees or taking part in what was viewed by

---

[11] K. Coleman, *American Revolution in Georgia*, 40–41; C. C. Jones Jr., *History of Georgia*, 2:151–55; "Proceedings of the First Georgia Provincial Congress, 1775," 1.

[12] Sir James Wright to Lord Dartmouth, August 23, 1774, LSJW, 180; C. C. Jones Jr., *History of Georgia*, 2:154.

[13] McCall, *History of Georgia*, 2:18, 22; K. Coleman, *American Revolution in Georgia*, 40–41.

Wright as Revolutionary proceedings would violate that oath. The combination of his rank and oath perhaps left Elbert torn and prevented him from openly siding with his Whig friends. At the same time, those concerns did not stop Habersham from openly serving on Revolutionary committees. Elbert's loyalty may have been tested a few days after the August 10 meeting, when Wright petitioned his supporters to attend a courthouse rally. About one-third of Savannah's inhabitants showed up. McCall said that among them were Wright's Council and "other civil and military officers."[14] Those military officers could have included Elbert, who was probably compelled to appear.

The ongoing Indian conflict also tempered Elbert's actions. The situation on the frontier was still unsettled in summer 1774, and the fears among backcountry people caused many to denounce the July and August meetings. For them, royal government offered the best protection against the Indians through treaties, the militia, frontier forts, and outposts. Elbert understood these sentiments since he owned land in sparsely settled St. George's Parish on the fringes of Georgia's border and in proximity to the killings earlier in the year. Beyond the issue of safety, one of Elbert's top priorities as a merchant was to settle the colony's Indian affairs and restore the trade. This was especially important because the government had still not compensated him or any other merchant for Indian debts. Funds garnered from the sale of property in the ceded lands were to generate money to pay creditors, but frontier turmoil severely curtailed the area's flow of settlers. Thus, financial considerations became another reason for Elbert's hesitancy. There was a direct correlation between Indian peace and the payment of Indian debts. Elbert may have distanced himself from Revolutionary events in Savannah to allow Wright time to restore peace, lift the trade restrictions, and settle debts with merchants and traders. This was a plausible reason for Elbert's hesitation to confront royal government at this time. If this were true, he approached the July and August meetings with an abundance of caution.

Finally, Elbert may have backed away from supporting the liberty faction in summer 1774 simply because he was not ready. At the time of the August 10 meeting, Georgia's Revolutionary movement was in its infancy, and it divided large numbers of colonists. "Many people," wrote Coleman, "who later decided that American rights could not be secured by constitutional means within the British Empire had not yet made up their minds."

---

[14] McCall, *History of Georgia*, 2:24.

This group could have included Elbert. After all, observed Coleman, the "Revolution had not yet come to Georgia" in 1774.[15] For this reason, the six months after the August 10 meeting became Elbert's time of decision. He finally resolved his conflict in January 1775 and joined the Whig movement. What caused Elbert to embrace the American cause? What transformed him into a Revolutionary, and what were the sources of his Americanization?

The events Elbert experienced and witnessed during a decade of strife between England and the colonies laid the foundation for his Americanization. It was during his period of realization, between the Stamp Act in 1765 and the Coercive Acts in 1774, when he developed an increasing awareness that Britain's government, instead of American rights, had become liberty's greatest enemy. As Elbert and countless others came to recognize, each new parliamentary attempt to regulate the colonies, from the Stamp Act forward, increasingly fit into a pattern of repeated and progressive abuses. Yet, in the protests against Parliament's policies through the years, he was never an active participant. He was not involved in Georgia's Stamp Act protests or the Sons of Liberty in 1765. Nor did he engage in Georgia's remonstrations against the Townshend Duties in 1769. When the opportunity arose to join a boycott thrown together by a handful of angry colonists, he did not participate. When tempers boiled over during the Boston Massacre in 1770, Elbert remained silent. Nor did he publicly speak out against the Coercive Acts after the Boston Tea Party, although they caused him to reconsider Britain's intentions in the colonies and his response to it. While he may have attended the July 27 and August 10 meetings organized by Georgia's revolutionaries, he did not actively participate in them, their committees, or the drafting of resolutions.

Attacks on liberty from Georgia's royal government, however, struck a more responsive chord in Elbert. There, he witnessed the dissolving of assemblies at the whim of the governor, the erosion of House prerogatives and constitutional powers, and Wright's retribution against those who voiced the wrong opinion. The examples seemed almost endless. The most recent example was Wright's proclamation after July 27 stifling free speech and outlawing town gatherings. As the governor's authoritarian efforts increased by degrees over the people, their liberties decreased accordingly, in addition to their voice in the General Assembly. By late 1774 and early 1775, the situation had become almost intolerable for those who cherished

---

[15] K. Coleman, *American Revolution in Georgia*, 41, 44.

their constitutional rights as Englishmen.

Those opposing Wright's usurpation of power were a proliberty faction in the House that included Elbert, Jones, Ewen, Bulloch, and several others. This bloc formed the basis for Savannah's Christ Church coalition of Conservative Whigs during the early 1770s. Originally, their goal was to check the growing authority of the executive branch, and they confronted Wright when Elbert was a member of the assembly. At that time, they clashed with the governor over the issue of representation in the parishes and in the Thomas Moodie affair involving one of Elbert's committees. Those controversies, suggested historian Harvey Jackson, placed Elbert in league with the assembly's liberty-loving faction. The Christ Church coalition continued to oppose Wright beyond Elbert's time in the assembly. On the eve of the American Revolution in Georgia, they still sought to limit his authority, but instead of destroying royal government, they wanted to restructure it in their favor and preserve their status. Due in part to the later influence of more Radical Whigs (like Button Gwinnett and Lyman Hall) from St. John's Parish, that goal soon became the complete overthrow of royal government. Thus, in 1774, Georgia's Whigs found themselves divided. Elbert and the conservatives were more limited in their goals of decreasing Wright's power but increasing their own within the government. According to Jackson, they sought "reform, not revolution." This desire to check Wright's unbridled power helped to fuel Elbert's patriotism. The radicals, in contrast, wanted to join the other colonies and plunge Georgia headlong into the Revolution.[16]

A second source of Elbert's radicalization involved his relationships with others. Those relations revolved around the circles of family, political and business connections, and the Masonic lodge. Some people, like the Habersham brothers, transcended all three circles. In the area of family, Elbert's male relatives through marriage became outspoken opponents of British rule. They included John Rae's brothers James and Robert, and his son, John Rae Jr. Of these, Robert Rae stood out in particular importance since he and Elbert were also business partners. This circle included Joseph Habersham when he married Isabella Rae, Elizabeth's sister, on May 19, 1776, and became Elbert's brother-in-law.

---

[16] Jackson, "Georgia Whiggery," 258, 264; Jackson, *Lachlan McIntosh*, 22.

Many of Elbert's business and political connections became revolutionaries. In business, those included not only the Habersham brothers and Robert Rae but also merchants Joseph Clay and Mordecai Sheftall. Most of Elbert's friends from his days in the assembly also became revolutionaries. Foremost among them were Jones, Ewen, and Bulloch, all from Elbert's Christ Church Parish who were instrumental in orchestrating Georgia's embryonic Revolutionary movement in 1775. Additional friends and acquaintances during his assembly days who became revolutionaries included John Milledge and William Young (also from Savannah), John Morel, Philip Box, Henry Bourquin, Samuel Farley, Edward Barnard, John Walton, Button Gwinnett, Benjamin Andrew, John Stevens, and John Glen, who chaired the July 27 meeting and, later, the first Provincial Congress. The Committee of 31 appointed on July 27 included several of those same assembly members.[17] These men influenced Elbert's decision to oppose Wright and the Crown.

The Masonic lodge made up a third circle of relationships that contributed to Elbert's radicalization. After 1773, when Grey Elliot stepped down as grand master and permanently left for England, Elbert eventually became the provincial grand master, heading an organization whose membership included several Conservative Whigs, including Noble W. Jones and Habersham. They could not express their political sentiments openly in the lodge however, since many devotees of royal government were still members. For this reason, and to incorporate his grenadiers, Elbert sought permission from the Grand Lodge of England to charter Unity Lodge in Savannah with himself as grand master. The Grand Lodge authorized Elbert's request and chartered Unity Lodge No. 465 in fall 1774. By the end of the year, Unity Lodge, with Elbert as the grand master, was holding regular meetings at the home of Joseph Woodruff in Savannah. Woodruff was a fellow Mason, a captain in the militia, and a future Revolutionary. Smith believed that much of the lodge's activities at Woodruff's house involved discussions about the "growing controversy between England and the American colonies."[18]

In 1774, Elbert again petitioned the Grand Lodge of England for permission to charter a third lodge in Savannah, this time for his grenadiers. In 1775, the same year he probably became provincial grand master,

---

[17] See *CRG*, 10:911–12, for a list of members elected to Elbert's assembly in fall 1769. The list of the July 27 Committee of 31 is in C. C. Jones Jr., *History of Georgia*, 2:149.

[18] Harris, *Outstanding Georgia Freemasons*, 71–72; G. Smith, "Georgia Grenadiers," 407.

he received a warrant from England to constitute Grenadier Lodge No. 481 with himself as its leader. That warrant created an unprecedented situation in the world of Masonry by making Elbert grand master in three separate lodges simultaneously. Grenadier Lodge, unlike the others, had a decidedly military presence, and, according to Smith, it brought a "warlike" aspect to Savannah's Freemasonry. It was more than that. The Grenadier Lodge allowed Elbert to wield another level of control over his company of militia. Grenadier Lodge, explained Smith, was the "alter-ego" of Elbert's company. In 1775, it became a "sharpened instrument for cutting Georgia's ties with England" and the military expression of the early movement.[19]

Finally, the defiant mindset Elbert inherited from his father factored into his rebellion against British authority. During the time of trustee rule in Georgia, William Elbert became a malcontent and protested against their rules and regulations primarily because they presented insurmountable obstacles to his economic dream of ownership of land and slaves. Twice, he signed memorials contesting the trustees, but, for him, those protests only resulted in the cultivation of enemies in powerful political positions. Although Elbert's stance against the trustees was motivated by self-gain, he also exhibited a concern for the constitutional rights and liberties of others. For example, he complained loudly about the abuse of power and authority in the courts during the Joseph Watson trial in 1737. William Elbert's defiance of political authority and his concern about rights and liberties in the face of oppressive government were traits that he passed down to his son. When Samuel Elbert became a Revolutionary, he was only following the path that his father blazed three decades earlier. William Elbert expected government to be just and fair in its dealings with the citizens it ruled. Samuel Elbert expected the same thing, and, when government overstepped its bounds of authority, whether it was Parliament or Wright, he wanted it held accountable to the people.[20]

Elbert's Americanization emanated from the events he witnessed regarding Parliament's attempts to regulate the colonies and Wright's authoritarian approach to royal government at home, his personal relationships in family, business, political, and Masonic circles, and the spirit of rebellion he inherited from his father. These complex and interwoven

---

[19] G. Smith, "Georgia Grenadiers," 408. For the alter-ego comment, see G. Smith, *History of the Georgia Militia*, 1:284.
[20] Ouzts, "Good Bargain for the Trust," 48.

webs of causes and effects became the cradle of Elbert's Revolutionary sentiments, but the overriding reason was probably simpler. In a letter written to House speaker Noble Jones in 1777 while commanding scattered American forces around Augusta after an embarrassing failed invasion of British East Florida, Elbert laid bare his real motivation. The reason for his patriotism, he informed the speaker, stemmed from a deep "love for my Country." It was that love, he explained, "which prompted me to engage in its service."[21]

The excitement generated during Georgia's Revolutionary summer in 1774 temporarily subsided as fall approached, but the changing temperatures did not dampen the spirits or determination of the liberty faction. Wright was clearly distressed and complained to Lord Dartmouth that everything was becoming "unhinged and Running into—Confusion." Even voicing opposition to the revolutionaries was dangerous. "At such times as these," he lamented in late August, "if a man has resolution & integrity Enough to stand forth and attempt to do his Duty it [is] like being set up as a mark to be Shot at and [it raises] the Resentment of great numbers against him." He had come to believe, he confessed, that "neither Coercive or Lenient measures will settle matters and restore any tolerable Degree of Cordiality & Harmony with the Mother Country."[22]

As Wright pondered the deteriorating situation in his colony, a Continental Congress made up of delegates from all the colonies except Georgia met in Philadelphia on September 5. Georgians debated sending delegates during the August 10 meeting, but because of divisions, decided against it. On October 20, the Continental Congress approved a boycott, known as the Association, as a means of economic pressure to force Parliament into repealing the Coercive Acts and its unjust tax laws in the colonies. The Association called for a nonimportation policy against England, Ireland, and the West Indies that would go into effect on December 1. To enforce the Association, it authorized committees to inspect customhouses and other venues related to trade. If anyone broke the boycott, the committees published their names. Despite pressure from South Carolina and even some of Georgia's Radical Whig parishes (such as St. John's and St. Andrew's), Georgia did not formally adopt the Association until summer 1775.[23]

---

[21] Samuel Elbert to Noble Jones, September 11, 1777, in "Order Book of Samuel Elbert," 55 (hereafter cited as OBSE).

[22] Sir James Wright to Lord Dartmouth, August 24, 1774, LSJW, 180–82.

[23] K. Coleman, *American Revolution in Georgia*, 42; Middlekauff, *Glorious Cause*, 248.

While the Continental Congress convened in Philadelphia, Elbert and his grenadiers were in route to meet a delegation of Creeks at the Ohoopee River. The Creeks were anxious to have a talk with Wright and Stuart about restoring the trade and putting things "upon the old footing." Aware of their impending visit, Wright once again sent Elbert, his grenadiers, and part of the light infantry to escort the Creeks through the settlements to Savannah, which they reached on October 19. In his history of the grenadiers, Smith maintains that the "boldness and expertise of Elbert and his command" were evident during this march and that they regularly performed drills to maintain their proficiency and impress the Indians. The Indians who gathered in Savannah included Emistisiguo and about seventy Upper Creeks. Another group joined them headed by Pumpkin from the Cusseta, the Cherhaw king of the Lower Creeks, and Tallachea (or Talechee) of the Ockmulges. They all congregated, along with Elbert's grenadiers and the light infantry, around the courthouse where they met Wright, Stuart, and other officials. On October 20, the day the Continental Congress adopted the Association, the governor convened his conference with the Creeks. His foremost concern, as before, was the execution of those Indians responsible for murdering innocent people and the return of all the horses, cattle, and slaves stolen from the inhabitants. Only then would he restore the trade. The Creeks agreed to satisfy Wright's demands, and he followed through by reopening the trade.[24]

With lingering anger among some Indians, all was still not well on the frontier. A few months later, during spring 1775, one of Elbert's business associates had a dangerous encounter with the Creeks. Thomas Graham, a partner in Rae's, Elbert & Graham, went to Mad Turkey's former town of Ockfusky on the Tallapoosa River to obtain deerskins when he had an altercation with some intoxicated Indians. When the Ockfusky Creeks saw Graham, many gathered around him, and one ran up to give the trader a handshake. Graham suspected trouble. When he reached out, the Indian grabbed his hand firmly and would not let go. The Indian said that Mad Turkey was his murdered uncle and a beloved man in the town. Since Fee had escaped, Graham would have to die in his place to avenge Mad Turkey's death. Several nearby Indian warriors then ran off to gather their weapons. Fearing for his life and with no time to lose, Graham struck

---

[24] *Georgia Gazette*, May 25, 1774, 2; October 19, 1774, 3; G. Smith, "Georgia Grenadiers," 407–408; Braund, *Deerskins & Duffels*, 162–63.

the Indian holding him in the face with his fist. The Indian staggered and loosened his grip, giving Graham the chance to break free and seek the safety of three Chickasaw Indians who were accompanying him.[25] Fortunately, for Graham, the Chickasaws intervened and diffused the situation. Had the Chickasaw not been present, the Ockfusky would have murdered Graham on the spot.

In December, Elbert was on the grand jury in Savannah. It would be his last civic duty as a loyal citizen in the British Empire. Serving with him were Habersham, Ewen, and John Morel. After deliberating memorials and complaints on the docket, the jury made a presentment of grievances on December 28, which included the need to have a night watch in the city, better regulation of the taverns, and a revising of the balloting methods for those serving on the grand and petit juries. Surely, in secret, the group discussed political grievances that had nothing to do with the grand jury. No doubt, Georgia's Provincial Congress, which was to meet on January 18 in Savannah, loomed as a major conversation topic. Already, on December 8, Christ Church Parish had selected a slate of delegates to attend, which included Habersham and Morel, but not Elbert. In an atmosphere charged with excitement and uncertainty, the men shared their sentiments about the upcoming congress. It was probably during the grand jury assignment when Elbert finally decided to join the others in their challenge to royal authority. Wright, too, was alarmed. He considered the approaching congress an illegal body, but there was little he could do to prevent it without causing a riot. On December 13, he informed the Earl of Dartmouth that the Continental Congress and the influence of South Carolina radicals had "greatly encouraged the spirit of political enthusiasm which many were not possessed of before." The frenzy was such that "God knows what the consequences may be or what man or whose property may escape their resentment." One week later, he confessed to Dartmouth that the liberty folks were "really very active in tormenting a flame throughout the Province."[26]

On January 17, the assembly convened in Savannah, and the Provincial Congress met as planned on the following day. The congress contained forty-five members, six of whom were also in the assembly. Still, only five parishes out of twelve (Christ Church, St. Paul's, St. Matthew's,

---

[25] Warren and Jones, *GGCJ, 1774–1777*, 43–44.
[26] *Georgia Gazette*, December 28, 1774, 4; C. C. Jones Jr., *History of Georgia*, 2:157–60.

St. Andrew's, and St. George's) sent delegates, so a problem from the beginning was that it did not represent the people and had no mandate to act. St. John's Parish, which should have attended, refused to send delegates until the congress joined it in the adoption of the Association. Meanwhile, Wright gave his opening address to the assembly. It was one of the most beautiful and eloquent speeches of his tenure as governor and epitomized his conservative views about the crisis in America. He advised the assembly, in an obvious reference to Jones, Bulloch, Ewen, and others, to not be swayed "by the voices and opinions of men's over-heated ideas." The liberty group was composed of "inconsiderate People" who wanted to plunge Georgia "into a state of distress and ruin." The governor admitted that he was an advocate for liberty just like everyone else, "but in a constitutional and legal way." The rash actions of those in the Provincial Congress threatened to destroy law and order. "Where there is no law," he reminded the assemblymen, "there can be no liberty." He urged the assembly to take heed and not embrace the ideas of those who sought to "trample upon law and government." That path led to "dreadful calamities," he warned, and he trembled at the "apprehension of what may be the resolution and declaration of the new Parliament relative to the conduct of the People in some parts of America."[27]

As the assembly sat in session, the Provincial Congress, plagued by a lack of proper representation and without legislative authority, attempted to push forward its agenda. The members wanted to adopt resolutions similar to those decreed in other colonies, appoint delegates to the Second Continental Congress in Philadelphia scheduled to begin in May, and enact the Association. Since fewer than half of Georgia's parishes had delegates in the Provincial Congress, their goals required assembly approval. Despite their limitations, the congress agreed to a number of resolutions; selected Jones, Bulloch, and Houstoun to represent Georgia in the Second Continental Congress; and adopted a watered-down version of the Association set to go into effect on March 15.[28]

The Association sanctioned by the Provincial Congress was not an official policy of Georgia, and, without the Assembly's blessing, it was only binding on those who endorsed it. Nevertheless, many supported its provisions of nonimportation, nonexportation, and nonconsumption,

---

[27] Brooking, "Of Material Importance," 254; C. C. Jones Jr., *History of Georgia*, 2:162–63.

[28] K. Coleman, *American Revolution in Georgia*, 46–47; C. C. Jones Jr., *History of Georgia*, 2:165–66.

including people who were not members of the Provincial Congress. One of those signing the Association on January 23 was Elbert. He was in good company with Habersham and nearly forty others who signed the agreement and pledged to "associate under the sacred ties of virtue, honor, and love of our country." The group included sixteen active commanders in the militia, and five of them, such as Elbert and Habersham, had taken the oath of loyalty to the king the previous June. As an added inducement for Elbert, several Savannah merchants signed the document.[29] For a long time, Elbert contemplated such a move, but for a variety of reasons, he was not ready to commit. The process of Elbert's Americanization that began with the Stamp Act crisis in 1765 finally bore fruit on January 23. On that day, Samuel Elbert became a Revolutionary.

Two days later, on January 25, the Provincial Congress sent their recommendations to the assembly for endorsement and then adjourned. The House had previously told Wright that they would uphold their duty to the king, but they would also consider the "interest, liberty, and welfare of our Constituents." Toward that end, they deliberated the same resolutions, and papers that had been before the Provincial Congress. To prevent the House from acting upon the resolutions of the Provincial Congress, the Association, and its selection of delegates to the Second Continental Congress, Wright prorogued it on February 10 and sent the members home. Without the backing of the assembly and representation from all parishes, Jones, Bulloch, and Houstoun declined to serve, leaving Georgia unrepresented for a second time in the Continental Congress.[30]

For the moment, Wright could bask in a narrow victory over the "Liberty Boys" (Whigs who opposed him), but the year was young. The tide of liberty was already swelling in Georgia and soon it would overwhelm royal government. Americanized and radicalized in the name of liberty, Samuel Elbert became an active participant in the destruction of royal government in Georgia. Future generations would laud him as a hero for the decision he made on January 23, but his accolades came with a high personal price. Glory and honor lay ahead in the future, but so did tremendous suffering and hardship.

---

[29] Warren and Jones, *GGCJ, 1774–1777*, 126; J. M. Johnson, *Militiamen, Rangers, and Redcoats*, 105; White, *Historical Collections of Georgia*, 58–61; K. Coleman, *American Revolution in Georgia*, 47.

[30] K. Coleman, *American Revolution in Georgia*, 49.

Chapter 5

"Judged by the Law of Liberty": Samuel Elbert and the Making of a Revolution in Georgia, 1775

On June 17, 1775, the same day that the battle of Bunker Hill between American and British armies occurred outside of Boston, Governor James Wright sat down at his desk and wrote to Lord Dartmouth in England describing the royal government's deterioration of his colony. "It gives me much concern to acquaint Your Lordship," he informed his superior, "that…the Liberty Folks here assembled…and put up a Liberty Tree and a Flagg and in the Evening paraded about the Town[.] I am informed to the number of 300, some say 400." These actions, he believed, showed much "contempt and defiance…of all Law and Government…which here as well as elsewhere seems now nearly at an end." Clearly, it appeared that royal government was unraveling. Already, it had been a difficult spring. For one, the General Assembly refused to meet when the governor summoned it for a late spring session. Even with a royal proclamation demanding they convene, members ignored him.[1]

The problem with the assembly was the least of Wright's worries. Earlier, on May 10, news of the first battles of the Revolution at Lexington and Concord on April 19 in Massachusetts reached Savannah. Reports of the fighting unleashed a fountain of pent-up anger in Georgia and spurred the "Liberty Boys" into action. Their response was almost instantaneous. On the night of May 11, several Whigs, including Joseph Habersham, Edwin Telfair, and Noble W. Jones, broke into the king's powder magazine and stole six hundred pounds of gunpowder. Although Wright issued a reward for the capture of the culprits, which he referred to in the *Georgia*

---

[1] Sir James Wright to Lord Dartmouth, June 17, 1775, LSJW, 183; K. Coleman, *American Revolution in Georgia*, 51; Middlekauff, *Glorious Cause*, 281–92.

Gazette as "evil disposed persons unknown," he never discovered their identity. Nor did he learn who was responsible for spiking the cannons along the Bay Battery on the night of June 2 and throwing them to the bottom of the river bluff, just before the annual celebration of the king's birthday.[2] It is possible that Samuel Elbert was involved in these protests, especially given his close relationships to the ringleaders, but there is no evidence beyond circumstantial guilt by association.

Summer 1775 was a trying time for Wright, but for Elbert, it was full of excitement. Events proceeded rapidly, and, with the governor's power crumbling, the Whigs seized every opportunity to push their Revolutionary agenda forward. At this confusing time, there were two groups of Whigs steering the movement's course in Georgia. The first sought to create a Council of Safety and hold a second Provincial Congress. The other pursued a middle ground involving compromise.[3] Elbert was associated with the first group. In 1774, he was a cautious and reluctant Revolutionary. That was not the case in 1775, and by the end of the year, he stood out as one of Revolution's central figures in Georgia.

Given Elbert's proven leadership qualities and devotion to Whig principles, it was inevitable that he would eventually find himself on one of the committees that charted the movement's progress in Georgia. On June 21, a notice appeared calling for a gathering of concerned inhabitants near Tondee's Tavern "at the Pole" on the following day at ten o'clock to elect delegates to the Provincial Congress in July and create a committee to enforce the Association. At the meeting, a local Council (or Committee) of Safety was formed with William Ewen as president. As a testament to Elbert's Revolutionary verve, they selected him to be a member of the council along with Habersham. The council's instructions included maintaining frequent correspondence with the Continental Congress in Philadelphia and coordinating Savannah's Whig activities with other like-minded bodies in the colonies. Once this business concluded, they hoisted a patriotic flag on the liberty pole above two cannon. Elbert and his fellow Whigs then celebrated their accomplishments with a fine dinner at Tondee's. At the conclusion of their meal, they gave thirteen toasts in honor of the rebelling colonies, each followed by the discharging of cannon accompanied by martial music. By June 1775, Elbert's sympathies were

---

[2] K. Coleman, *American Revolution in Georgia*, 52; Mebane, "Joseph Habersham in the Revolutionary War," 77; C. C. Jones Jr., *History of Georgia*, 2:176; *Georgia Gazette*, May 17, 1775, 1.

[3] K. Coleman, *American Revolution in Georgia*, 56.

decidedly pro-Whig. Precisely one year earlier, on June 4, 1774, he, along with Habersham who was a first lieutenant in the grenadiers, publicly took an oath of loyalty to King George III and Wright.[4] Now, that loyalty was aligned with His Majesty's enemies in America.

During summer 1775, two places in Savannah became epicenters for Whig resistance. Elbert had connections to both. One was Tondee's Tavern, which proudly flew the liberty flag and hosted Whig gatherings such as the June 22 meeting that produced the Council of Safety and made Elbert a member. The tavern was fated to take on additional significance as the scene of Georgia's Second Provincial Congress, scheduled to convene on July 4, with Elbert as a delegate. A second locale was the residence of Mrs. Jane Cuyler, the widow of a ship captain named Telamon Cuyler. Savannah's Whigs often met to discuss their business at Culyer's bayside home. At one of their meetings on June 13, they created a list of five resolves to bring before the upcoming Provincial Congress for its consideration. Among the thirty-three men who gathered there were Jones, John Glen, and John Joachim Zubly, who was the local minister of the Independent Presbyterian Church in Savannah. They called for unity in protest and for the Provincial Congress to send an application to the king seeking redress. They also vied to uphold the freedoms fueling their own protests, proclaiming that no one behaving themselves "peaceably and inoffensively, shall be molested in his person and property, or even in his private sentiments, while he expresses them with decency and without any illiberal reflections upon others."[5]

Cuyler's home also became the scene for clandestine activities hatched up by Elbert under the guise of a Masonic lodge. In 1774, Elbert petitioned the Grand Lodge in England for permission to constitute a third lodge in Savannah. The Grand Lodge approved his request in 1775 and chartered Grenadier Lodge No. 481 with Elbert as the grand master. By 1775, Elbert was grand master in all three lodges in Georgia (Solomon's, Unity, and Grenadier) and two of them (Unity and Grenadier) were engaged in some level of Revolutionary activity. Grenadier Lodge stood out in importance during 1775 because Elbert used it to scheme against the government and gain Whig influence over the militia. One of Grenadier Lodge's most esteemed members was Oliver Bowen. A Rhode

---

[4] *Georgia Gazette*, June 21, 1775, 3; McCall, *History of Georgia*, 2:44–45. There is a list of all the officers who took the oath of loyalty on June 4, 1774, in Warren and Jones, *GGCJ, 1774–1777*, 26–27.

[5] "Proceedings of the First Georgia Provincial Congress, 1775," 4–5.

Island native, Bowen rented a room at Cuyler's home where the Grenadier Lodge met. In summer 1775, he gained a reputation as one of the most radical Whig leaders and, through Masonry, developed a friendship with Elbert. Bowen was also a second lieutenant in the grenadier company and, along with Habersham, provided additional Whig influences in the militia. According to historian Gordon Smith, there was a constant flow of armed men in and out of Cuyler's home. There, in the presence of Elbert, Habersham, and Bowen, they quietly plotted and formed committees to carry out their subterfuge.[6]

Through the Grenadier Lodge and the grenadier company, wrote Smith, the "Liberty Boys, Elbert, Habersham, and Bowen, were now firmly in control of a sharpened instrument for cutting Georgia's ties with England."[7] It is significant that Smith linked Elbert, Habersham, and Bowen together as "Liberty Boys" and then chose the word "cutting" to describe the impact of their activities in relation to Crown rule. The implication was, correctly, that all three had become Americanized by summer 1775 and no longer entertained possibilities of reconciliation. That position contradicted the informal list of resolves drawn up by the group who met at Cuyler's home on June 13, but neither Elbert, Habersham, nor Bowen was present.

As a Conservative Whig, one of Elbert's goals before 1775 was curtailing Wright's power. He felt the same way about Parliament's control over the colonies when he joined the Association in January 1775. Maybe, at that time, he hoped for reconciliation, but something changed in Elbert's heart during the summer. Most likely, the spilling of blood at Lexington, Concord, and later, Bunker Hill, first reported in the *Gazette* on July 12, transformed his thinking.[8] By the end of the summer, his actions left no doubt that he wanted to destroy Wright's government and force a separation from England. Thus, Elbert's political philosophy, like that of many other Conservative Whigs, temporarily found common ground with the goals of Radical Whigs, and, for a short while, their differences blurred—at least until early 1776 when the Provincial Congress moved to appoint officers to Georgia's 1st Continental Battalion.

Elbert's changed attitude was apparent in June before he even heard about the Battle of Bunker Hill. Georgia's stormy political climate made

---

[6] G. Smith, "Georgia Grenadiers," 408–409, 413n27; G, Smith, *Morningstars of Liberty*, 1:25.

[7] G. Smith, "Georgia Grenadiers," 408.

[8] *Georgia Gazette*, supplement, July 12, 1775.

Wright concerned for his safety, and he ordered Elbert's grenadiers to protect him. Elbert, Habersham, Bowen, and the other officers would have none of it. They "positively refused to pay any attention" to Wright's directive and then "threw down their commissions." They would only fight, they declared, "in defense of their liberties." Later that same month, a traveler dined with some grenadiers at a local Savannah tavern and was stunned when he saw them rebelliously lift their glasses in a toast to Lexington, Concord, and "Success to American Arms." These incidents collectively showed that by June 1775, even the elite grenadiers, under the influence of Elbert, Habersham, and Bowen, were radicalized and Wright's hold on government was slipping. The governor admitted as much in a letter to Lord Dartmouth on July 8, when he lamented that his powers "are wrested out of my Hands [and]…Law & Government are nearly if not quite annihilated." When the assembly had last met in January, Wright urged the members to avoid the impassioned rhetoric of misguided people who stirred up dissension and led Georgia's good citizens astray. "Don't catch at the shadow and lose the substance," he cautioned them.[9] Those comments became something like an omen for Wright six months later, but in reverse. In summer 1775, it was Wright's government, and not the Revolutionary movement he abhorred, that was becoming a shadow without substance.

The governor was powerless to prevent the meeting of a second Provincial Congress in Tondee's Long Hall on July 4 called for by Elbert's Council of Safety. Unlike the First Provisional Congress in January, ten of Georgia's twelve parishes attended. The exceptions were two small and isolated parishes (St. Patrick and St. James) just below the Altamaha River. Of the 103 delegates, 39 (or roughly one-third), were from Christ Church Parish and included Elbert, Habersham, Bowen, Jones, Zubly, Glen, Archibald Bulloch, and William Ewen. Elbert's business partner, Robert Rae, and his brother James were representatives from Augusta's St. Paul's Parish. Rae's loyalty was never in question, and the Revolutionary sentiment constantly expressed at Rae's, Elbert & Graham in Augusta showed that even Elbert's business ventures were entwined in Whig opposition. In

---

[9] *Virginia Gazette*, July 15, 1775, Dixon and Hunter, , 2; *CRG*, 38(1):454–55; Sir James Wright to Lord Dartmouth, July 8, 1775, LSJW, 192; C. C. Jones Jr., *History of Georgia*, 2:163.

July, as the Provincial Congress was in session, an eyewitness heard one customer, Robert Hamilton, openly suggest to an audience of White and Black people at the store that if the situation deteriorated much further, slaves should be armed for "Killing the King's troops." For their patriotism, he said, "Each Negro…should be entitled to…have his Freedom." Three justices of the peace later reported the remarks to Wright, who considered punishing Hamilton for treason but then did nothing. It was an ironic twist of fate that at the time of this incident, Wright awarded Rae's, Elbert & Company £2,688.18.7 for Indian debts stemming from the 1773 cession and Rae & Company £1,272.4.7 for the same purpose.[10]

Meanwhile in Savannah, the Provincial Congress elected Bulloch as president and George Walton as secretary. Afterwards, everyone adjourned to the Independent Presbyterian Church and heard Zubly preach a lively sermon titled "The Law of Liberty." The text came from the New Testament book of James 2:12, which called on others to "speak, and so do, as they that shall be judged by the law of liberty." Most in Zubly's audience, including Elbert, were familiar with the pastor and regarded him as a biblical scholar. Since 1760, he had lived in Savannah and ministered to one of the city's largest congregations. By the time of the Provincial Congress, Zubly's published tracts were widely read and many considered him "Georgia's revolutionary pamphleteer." One historian later referred to him as "the most influential minister in Georgia" prior to the American Revolution.[11]

Zubly's sermon emphasized reconciliation. While he opposed the oppressive acts of Parliament and George III's ministers, he still upheld the rule of law and felt that loyalty was a Christian's duty, even in the face of injustices. The interest of America, he said, "lies in a perpetual connection with our mother country" and that the king's greatest sin was that he surrounded himself with "evil counselors." He appealed for moderation on both sides of the Atlantic, observing that it was easy to extinguish a spark, but it was "folly to blow up discontent into a blaze: the beginning of strife

---

[10] "Proceedings of the First Georgia Provincial Congress, 1775," 1–3; *CRG*, 12:414–15; K. Coleman, *American Revolution in Georgia*, 56–57. In addition to Elbert, several other members of this congress were also Masons. See Clarke, *Leaves from Georgia Masonry*, 232; "Proceedings and Minutes of the Governor and Council of Georgia, October 4, 1774 through November 7, 1775," in *CGHS*, 10:27.

[11] Nichols, "Man True to His Principles," 297–99; Schmidt, "Reverend John Joachim Zubly's 'The Law of Liberty' Sermon," 351–57.

is like the letting out of waters, and no man may know where it will end." Thus, in all of their actions, God and posterity would judge the king, his ministers, and even the Provincial Congress by the law of liberty. Elbert's opinion of the sermon is unknown, but the Provincial Congress noted in their minutes that the minister's speech was "excellent," and they created a special committee to thank him for his words of wisdom.[12]

The Provincial Congress sat in session from July 4 until July 17. While Wright regarded them as an unconstitutional entity, they considered themselves lawful since the assembly was not functioning and they represented most of Georgia's parishes. On July 5, the day after Zubly's message, Bulloch had the resolutions drawn up at Culyer's home on June 13 read to the members. The Provincial Congress next petitioned Wright to appoint a day for fasting and prayer in the hopes that a "happy reconciliation may soon take place between America and the parent State." Wright replied to their appeal two days later after conferring with his council. "The request made by the gentlemen who have assembled together by the name of a Provincial Congress," he wrote, had come from an unlawful gathering. However, since their request was "expressed in such loyal and dutiful terms, and the end proposed being such as every good man must most ardently wish for, I will certainly appoint a Day of Fasting and Prayer, to be observed through this province." Accordingly, Wright selected July 19. Shortly afterward, word arrived that the Continental Congress in Philadelphia had coincidentally set aside July 20 as a day of fasting and prayer in the colonies. The Provincial Congress also wanted Wright to observe this day, but he refused. Their response was to ignore the governor and mark both days for observance.[13]

On July 6, the Congress adopted sixteen resolves to enact policies outlined by the Continental Congress. Among them was the formal adoption of the Association and a series of resolves to cause its enforcement. Of particular importance to Elbert was the Thirteenth Resolve, which expanded the presence and power of the Committee of Safety. Committees appeared in every town, district, and parish to "observe the conduct of all persons touching this Association." Anyone violating the agreement would have their name published in the *Gazette* so that "all…foes to the rights of British America may be publickly known and universally

---

[12] Zubly, *"The Law of Liberty,"* 21, 45–47, 50; "Proceedings of the First Georgia Provincial Congress, 1775," 2–3; Nichols, "Man True to His Principles," 298.

[13] "Proceedings of the First Georgia Provincial Congress, 1775," 3–5, 9.

contemned as the enemies of American liberty." As a member of the committee, Elbert collected signatures from supporters of the Association, even as he kept a separate list of those refusing to sign. Thus began, according to Coleman, an "all-out attempt" to force the Association on Georgians. "High-pressure methods were used to secure signatures wherever they were not forthcoming voluntarily," he observed. The usual methods were financial pressure and public humiliation, but they employed stronger inducements when necessary. The actions of Elbert's committee were not much different from its counterparts in other Southern colonies. In North Carolina, for example, committees ruthlessly pushed for the collection of signatures. Alan D. Watson, an authority on the Council of Safety in that colony, said that committee members and even militia units forced Association documents on the people at large. At New Bern, the committee demanded that everyone sign the Association within five days or face being disarmed and denounced as enemies to America. In one county, people could not even work as a public servant unless they signed the Association.[14]

The Association that Elbert signed in July denounced the king's ministers and vowed "never to become slaves" to Parliament's acts and measures that punished the colonies or taxed them without representation. To salvage their rights and liberties, they called on a "firm union of the inhabitants" and a vigorous effort to secure their safety. In light of Wright's decaying powers and the nonexistent Assembly, immediate precautions were necessary to prevent "the anarchy and confusion which attend the dissolution of the powers of government." Toward the end of the document, signees swore to "associate, under all the ties of religion, and honor, and love to our country, to adopt and endeavor to carry into execution whatever may be recommended by the Continental Congress, or resolved upon by our Provincial Convention." This statement represented an oath of allegiance not just to the Continental Congress but also to the Provincial Congress. Finally, the Association called for all signees to be responsible for its enforcement, even "at the risk and peril of [their] lives and fortunes."[15]

---

[14] Ibid., 5:5–8; C. C. Jones Jr., *History of Georgia*, 2:197; K. Coleman, *American Revolution in Georgia*, 61; Watson, "Committees of Safety," 143. Elbert was placed on the committee to enforce the Association on July 13, along with Bowen and Walton. See the supplement in the *Georgia Gazette*, July 18, 1775.

[15] *RRG*, 1:252–53.

There were other pressing matters on the Provincial Congress's agenda. On July 7, Zubly prepared a humble memorial to the king, which was sharp in tone and content. Then, the body chose five delegates to represent Georgia in the Continental Congress. Four of them, Bulloch, Jones, Zubly, and John Houstoun were from Elbert's Christ Church Parish. The only exception was Lyman Hall, a Radical Whig who was currently in Philadelphia attending the Continental Congress as an observer from St. John's Parish. The adoption of nineteen resolves on July 8 representing Georgia's Whig sentiments soon followed, putting the colony on the same Revolutionary footing as the others. Many of the resolves contained, or at least represented, the ideas expressed by the group who met at Culyer's house on June 13. They included the statement, "we were born free, have all the feelings of men, and are entitled to all the natural rights of mankind." Additionally, they said, Americans claimed all rights and privileges of English citizens as a birthright. As for the destructive acts of Parliament, the Congress admitted that it was at a loss for words to express "our abhorrence and detestation." The Provincial Congress assembled, it said, to seek some means of reunion with the Mother Country. To do nothing, in the absence of an Assembly, would suggest that "we must [be]…a people without all thought or council." In lieu of the Assembly, the Provincial Congress assumed its functions and began deliberating ways to raise £10,000 to defray the cost of government and on July 12, it issued a general tax on the colony's inhabitants.[16]

Elbert was involved in two important measures taken by the Provincial Congress near the close of its session. On July 15, he joined a committee to ascertain the state of Georgia's militia and to make suggestions for its improvement.[17] The existence of this committee suggests that the Provincial Congress sensed an armed conflict on the horizon. The task of assessing the military was an assignment normally given by the Assembly and indicated how far the Provincial Congress had usurped the powers of government. Elbert's selection was a foregone conclusion. No one else in the Congress had the level or quality of his military experience or even his rank, except perhaps Walton, who, like Elbert, was also a captain in the militia. Elbert surpassed even Walton's qualifications because he had been the captain of an elite unit for at least three years and had an additional

---

[16] "Proceedings of the First Georgia Provincial Congress, 1775," 9–13; C. C. Jones Jr., *History of Georgia*, 2:189. For Zubly's background and claims that he was a Loyalist in Georgia, see Nichols, "Man True to His Principles," 299, 301–302.

[17] C. C. Jones Jr., *History of Georgia*, 2:198.

advantage of proven service in the field. Elbert was intimately acquainted with the militia and its structure, abilities, organization, and needs. Compared to the knowledge and talents of others in the Provincial Congress, he loomed as an expert in military affairs.

Through the Council of Safety, Elbert was in a position to orchestrate the revolution. Just before the Provincial Congress adjourned on July 17, it legitimized the council, broadened its scope, and gave it "full power [to act] upon every emergency." The Provincial Congress appointed members to the council. When it was not in session, the council assumed all government powers. Initially, it enforced the Association, but its influence quickly expanded into other areas. Before long, it completely controlled the militia, including the commissioning of officers, the issuing of orders to units, and the securing of weapons. It even negotiated with the Indians. These activities, which traditionally and constitutionally rested with Wright, showed that the council functioned as an executive branch. Additionally, it acted like a treasury, borrowing and issuing money and providing funds to carry out its directives. For example, on January 20, 1776, it drew up a certificate, signed by Walton, paying the sum of £4.9 out of the public account to John Stirk. The council also censured the *Gazette* and turned it into a pro-Whig propaganda machine. "The Council of Safety was the most powerful force in the Whig movement," wrote historian Harvey Jackson, and "there was little check on its powers." Watson echoed the same conclusion: "Who or what was responsible for organizing and converting the whig movement, whether psychologically, politically, or militarily, into a demand for Independence?" The answer, he said, were the committees of safety that "proved indispensable in effecting the Revolution." It was not surprising that many members of Georgia's Council, like Elbert, Habersham, Walton, Houstoun, and John Morel, were also Masons, further solidifying fraternal ties to the Revolutionary movement.[18]

Finally, as a member of the Provincial Congress, Elbert approved of its memorials delivered to the king, Wright, and Georgia's inhabitants. Zubly's appeal to King George III notified the monarch that "Though we bring up the rear of American petitioners…we must take the liberty to speak before we die." Referencing the fighting in Massachusetts, he

---

[18] *Georgia Gazette*, supplement 616, July 18, 1775; "Council of Safety Certificate to John Stirk," January 20, 1776, George Walton Papers, 1749 or 1750–1804, Rubenstein Rare Book and Manuscript Library; K. Coleman, *American Revolution in Georgia*, 62–63; Jackson, *Lachlan McIntosh*, 27–28; Clarke, *Leaves from Georgia Masonry*, 232; Watson, "Committees of Safety," 132–33.

pointed out that His Majesty's arms "now everyday make mothers childless and children fatherless!" and that the "blood of your subjects has been shed with pleasure, rather than with pity." Zubly held to a forlorn hope that the king would intervene and restore peace. Lifting a page from his "Law of Liberty" speech, he implored George III to "hearken to the cries of your loyal and affectionate subjects" and to "let the goodness of your own heart, interpose between weak or wicked Ministers, and millions of loyal and affectionate subjects."[19]

The memorial to Wright, also sanctioned by Elbert, explained why the Provincial Congress was necessary. "In these very critical and alarming times," it read, "the good people of this Province found themselves under an absolute necessity to take some measures for the security and preservation of their liberties and every thing that is near and dear to them." The Provincial Congress had to be summoned to relieve the citizens from their "many and very heavy grievances." The cumulative impact of Wright's adjourning, proroguing, dismissing, and controlling the assembly through the years also surfaced in the petition. The Provincial Congress feared that Wright had "received very strong instructions not to suffer the Assembly to enter into any measures to secure the rights of America, or even to petition for relief, unless in terms which would have been giving up the rights of, and fixing lasting disgrace on, the petitioners." Georgia had been the defaulting link in the protesting thus far, they said, but no more. Wright found the memorial insulting, without "any just foundation" and a misrepresentation of facts.[20]

The address to Georgia's citizens stoked fears of a civil war in America. Referencing earlier clashes between British and American armies during the year, the petitioners acknowledged that the slaying of "their brethren" would forever be an "everlasting blot" on British "character for humanity and generosity." In spite of this, the Provincial Congress sought "reconciliation on honorable principles" and prayed that this "unnatural" quarrel with Britain cease and that "no more blood may be shed." Until that time, the Congress urged Georgia's inhabitants to "use all possible caution not to say or do anything unworthy of so glorious a cause," and to

---

[19] *Virginia Gazette*, October 28, 1775, Dixon and Hunter, , 2.
[20] C. C. Jones Jr., *History of Georgia*, 2:194–95; Sir James Wright to Lord Dartmouth, July 18, 1775, LSJW, 196–99; for his Council's response, Council Minutes, July 17, 1775, in "Proceedings and Minutes of the Governor and Council of Georgia, October 4, 1774 through November 7, 1775," *CGHS*, 10:32–33.

"promote frugality, peace, and good order."[21]

By the time it adjourned, the Provincial Congress had adopted the policies of the Continental Congress and elected five delegates to that body, endorsed the Association, legitimized the Council of Safety, established two days of fasting and prayer, aligned itself with resistance in the other colonies, begun the organizing of the militia, and sent memorials to the king, Wright, and the people. For all of these accomplishments, it represented, according to Claire Purcell, a "milestone in the history of revolutionary Georgia." Jones called it "perhaps the most important [Assembly] ever convened in Georgia" and "Georgia's first secession convention." Coleman observed that it was "Georgia's first revolutionary government."[22] Elbert could share in the credit for these accomplishments as he advanced the "glorious cause" in his colony during 1775.

Although attending the Provincial Congress and running the Council of Safety were time-consuming, Elbert never wasted an opportunity to engage in insurrectionary acts. While the Provincial Congress was in session, an incident took place at the mouth of the Savannah River with the *Phillipa*, a British ship carrying powder and arms to Savannah for the Indian trade. The Council of Safety in Charleston first learned of the ship's expected arrival, immediately laid plans for its capture, and then notified the Provincial Congress of the plot. Already, forty South Carolinians were waiting at Bloody Point near Tybee Island for the ship to appear. Smith claimed that some of the men got in touch with Elbert, who, along with Habersham and Bowen, secretly coordinated efforts to seize the ship and steal the gunpowder. Much of the scheming, no doubt, occurred at Culyer's home under cover of the Grenadier Lodge. Historian Leslie Hall believed that the grenadiers participated in the action. Meanwhile, the Provincial Congress commandeered a schooner from a Savannah merchant, armed it with carriage and swivel guns, and christened it the *Liberty*. Habersham and Bowen assumed command of the ship, rounded up a crew of about fifty (which probably included some grenadiers), and then sailed toward Tybee to wait on their target. On July 10, the *Phillipa* arrived at the river's mouth, dropped anchor, and waited for a pilot boat to take it up to Savannah. Suddenly, the *Liberty* hoisted sails and emerged from hiding to overtake the *Phillipa*. The slow and cumbersome British ship tried to

---

[21] C. C. Jones Jr., *History of Georgia*, 2:198–200.

[22] Purcell, "Public Career of Samuel Elbert," 15; C. C. Jones Jr., *History of Georgia*, 2:183, 202; K. Coleman, *American Revolution in Georgia*, 61.

escape, but after a short chase it surrendered without a fight. Victorious Whigs quickly boarded the vessel and confiscated nearly 13,000 pounds of powder, shot, and numerous weapons. Georgia and South Carolina shared the bulk of the prize, and the remainder, some say, went to American forces in the North. The capture of the ship and the loss of the powder almost broke Wright's will to govern. As soon as he learned about it, he wrote Dartmouth detailing all that happened. As he closed his letter, he confessed that he could no longer "submit to these daily Insults" and asked for leave to return to England. As for Elbert, he had once again participated in a milestone event resulting in the Patriots' first capture of an enemy vessel in Southern waters. The *Phillipa* Affair also gave birth to the Georgia navy, which soon expanded and fell under the command of Bowen.[23]

With the Provincial Congress in recess after July 17, Elbert's Council of Safety assumed control of government and quickly went after the opposition. His committee to induce people to sign the Association was relentless in its efforts. "Throughout the province," wrote Wright to Dartmouth on August 7, "every Method has been used to *Compell* the People to Sign the Association." If anyone refused, explained the governor, they opened themselves up to violent acts upon their person and the destruction of their property. "Great Numbers have been Intimidated to Sign," he said, "and I Suppose by far the greater Part of the Province have Signed it, indeed it is said there are few in the Country who have not."[24]

Refusing to sign the Association was only one way to draw the ire of the Council of Safety. Hadden Smith was the rector at Savannah's Christ Church and a pro-Wright sympathizer. As a member and former vestryman at the church, Elbert knew Smith. On July 19, Smith opened the doors to his church, preached a sermon, and had the bells toll in observation of the governor's day of fasting and prayer. On July 20, instead of recognizing the Continental Congress's day of fasting and prayer, the church remained closed and the bells were silent. The Council of Safety immediately sent a group of men to confront Smith for his defiance. According to Smith's later deposition to the governor, five men came to the front porch of his chambers on July 22, produced a piece of paper, and read

---

[23] G. Smith, *Morningstars of Liberty*, 25; G. Smith, "Georgia Grenadiers," 409–10; K. Coleman, *American Revolution in Georgia*, 53; C. C. Jones Jr., *History of Georgia*, 2:181–82; Sir James Wright to Lord Dartmouth, July 10, 1775, LSJW, 194–95; Hall, *Land and Allegiance*, 26.

[24] Sir James Wright to Lord Dartmouth, August 7, 1775, LSJW, 205.

its contents to him. Because he failed to do his duty on July 20, they notified him that he could no longer preach in Savannah and that he should immediately leave the colony. "You are deemed an Enemy to America," they decreed, and "by Order of the Committee [of Public Safety] We are to inform you that you are to be suffered no longer to officiate in this Town." Since the order to vacate came from the Council of Safety, Elbert surely knew about the document's contents beforehand. There is a good chance that he even helped write it, since three of the five men delivering the message to Smith were Habersham, Bowen, and Walton, all Masonic brothers and his close friends. The pressure on Smith to leave was enormous, and he feared for his life. The threats were so forceful and frequent that they produced the desired results in just three days. On July 25, Wright said that he fled the colony into South Carolina although he was not safe there, either. Apparently, Smith came to this conclusion as well and wisely chose to go back to England.[25]

Threats and intimidation reached new levels of intensity on July 24 when they turned into vicious personal attacks. Wright was at his Savannah residence when, around 9 o'clock in the evening, he "heard a very great Huzzaing in the streets." He sent someone to see what all the commotion was about and learned that a mob had "seized upon one [John] Hopkins...and were Tarring and Feathering him." Hopkins, a mariner by trade, was intoxicated at one of Savannah's taverns and unwisely ridiculed the Sons of Liberty and the Council of Safety. Eyewitnesses saw him raise a glass and give a toast, saying, "Damnation to America." Hopkins, in a later deposition, claimed that he went home after that and sat down with his family for supper. He had just started eating when a number of men, some in disguise, burst through the door and seized him. Without saying a word, they dragged him out of his house to one of Savannah's squares where they stripped off his jacket and shirt and tarred and feathered him. Humiliated, Hopkins was thrown into a cart and wheeled around town for three hours. The mob made sure to parade their spectacle in front of Wright's home. The governor peered out of his window and was shocked to see the cart with Hopkins in it. It was a "Horrid Spectacle," he informed Dartmouth, the worst "I really [ever] saw." They "made the Man Stand up in a Cart with a Candle in his Hand and a great many Candles were

---

[25] Ibid., July 29, 1775, 3:200–204; Council Minutes, July 25, 1775, in "Proceedings and Minutes of the Governor and Council of Georgia, October 4, 1774 through November 7, 1775," *CGHS*, 10:34–35; *Georgia Gazette*, May 17, 2.

Carried round the Cart and thus they went through most of the Streets in the town." One eyewitness thought it was a "terrible indignity, the poor creature being stripped naked, tarred all over, and then rolled in feathers." She refused to further gaze out of her window and watch the torture because the "idea was too dreadful." Wright did not observe the mob's threats to hang Hopkins. One of his attackers said that although the victim was "rather fat" he would personally "go up the tree & hang" him unless Hopkins drank to the "Damnation [of] all Tories & Success to American Liberty." Hopkins complied with their demands, but they persisted in their abuse. He heard one of the mob say that they would not stop until all "Tories" received the same treatment. When asked in his deposition to identify his attackers, Hopkins specifically named Habersham and Bowen. One historian noted that the mob included a number of merchants and militia officers. Hopkins stated there were "several others" who attacked him, beside those he named.[26] None of the documents place Elbert at the scene, but he could have been present, particularly since the episode involved the Council of Safety, Habersham and Bowen, and some militia officers and merchants. Having said that, inflicting personal harm on someone through tarring and feathering seemed beneath Elbert's dignity, and it is hard to believe that he participated in such brutality although he probably condoned it.

The incidents with Smith and Hopkins revealed the ugly side of revolution in Georgia, and it was only the beginning. Wright believed that Georgia's near plunge into anarchy was due to the "very illegal, Insolent and Dangerous Transactions of the Liberty People." Hopkins was not the only person tarred and feathered by those enforcing the dictates of the Council of Safety. Anthony Stokes, a member of Wright's Council, claimed that many underwent that "severe discipline" for refusing to sign the Association. Two comments from Georgia's legislative bodies in 1775, one from the assembly's last gathering in January and the other from the Provincial Congress which recently adjourned, warned that liberty could be a double-edged sword and that those who committed acts in its name were also subject to its consequences. One of those consequences was the absence of law and order. When Wright addressed the assembly on January 18, he told them, "You may be advocates for liberty: so am I, but in a

---

[26] Sir James Wright to Lord Dartmouth, July 29, 1775, in LSJW, 200–203; McCall, *History of Georgia*, 2:45–46; K. Coleman, *American Revolution in Georgia*, 65; J. M. Johnson, *Militiamen, Rangers, and Redcoats*, 109; E. Johnston, *Recollections of a Georgia Loyalist*, 44.

constitutional and legal way.... take heed how you give a sanction to trample upon law and government, and be assured...that where there is no law there can be no liberty."[27] Another consequence, exposed by Zubly when he addressed the Provincial Congress, was that those fighting for liberty would be judged by its laws. By late July, it seemed that all Whig assurances about protecting people and property, as expressed the June 13 resolves at Culyer's residence, the Provincial Congress's resolves adopted on July 8, and the memorials delivered to Wright and the inhabitants of Georgia on July 17, were forsaken. Simply uttering a dissenting opinion opposing Whig rule could expose a person to public humiliation, severe economic reprisals, and, as the case of Hopkins emphasized, bodily harm. The irony was that the Whigs, through their Congress, committees, councils, lodges, and mobs, mirrored the same threats to liberty that Wright posed through his proclamations, decrees, threats, and censoring to stifle opposition to the royal government. As Wright's power and authority ebbed, a new division between Whigs and Loyalists rapidly filled the void and ensured that the Revolution would become a merciless civil war. That was the long-range significance of Smith's and Hopkins's unfortunate experiences.

Even with a weakened government, Wright still maintained authority over the militia—or so he thought. In early August, the Whigs moved to sever that control as well. The Council of Safety sent Wright a letter, endorsed by Elbert and others, demanding that, instead of the governor appointing and commissioning militia commanders, the soldiers should instead pick their own leaders. In these perilous times, read the letter, the accustomed channels for getting things done were too slow. Georgia, surrounded by dangers, had to act quickly. Since the colony was a "frontier Province, bordering upon the Indian[s], and too near the Spanish settlements...both of which 'ere long, may be our declared Enemies," it was necessary to put Georgia in the best defensive footing possible to protect citizens from the "dreadful Enemy within its Bosom." It was therefore imperative to have the militia commanded by "Officers of their own Chusing." Either that, they warned, or the province would face the "Miserable alternative...of being Sacrificed." While dismissing commissioned officers was a delicate matter, they assured Wright that their only motive was the safety of the province. They were certainly not plotting the "idea

---

[27] *CRG*, 12:429–30; Sir James Wright to Lord Dartmouth, August 7, 1775, LSJW, 204–205; C. C. Jones Jr., *History of Georgia*, 2:163.

of an attack upon the Prerogatives of our Gracious Sovereign," nor did they mean to disparage "the Courage, Conduct or Integrity, of any Officer now in Commission." They were only listening to the voice of the people and thinking about what was best for Georgia's protection.[28]

The letter astonished Wright and pointed toward a "very extraordinary and dangerous Tendency." He understood the real purpose of the request, which was a thinly veiled ruse to "Wrest the Power and Command of the Militia from the Crown, and out of [my] Hands, and to vest it in the Congress and Committees" in a "most Arbitrary and Tyrannical manner." The petitioners, he correctly surmised, only wanted new officers because they were members of the Association. He admonished the petition's authors as the "cause" of the whole pandemonium. They were the ones who committed and encouraged the "Many Acts of Violence and Oppression." Since Elbert helped author the petition and then signed it, he was, in Wright's estimation, one of the guilty parties. Their claim about following the voice of the people was a mere pretense. The voice they followed, he said, came from the Provincial Congress, the Council of Safety, and the committees. If the Indians or the Spanish attacked the province and caused a calamity, it would arise from the misconduct of the rebels, who could only blame themselves for the disaster. According to Wright's Council, it was nothing more than an attempt to purge the militia of those not supporting the Association. Stokes said that the men they wanted to replace were all officers of "distinction" and that the Association was only a "test" to distinguish those who wanted to take up arms against His Majesty from those who did not. He labeled the application a "Clumsy Artiface," full of "misrepresentation," and an "Affront" to the governor.[29] Wright rejected the request; the Council of Safety responded by ignoring his rejection.

On August 9, the Council of Safety, in complete defiance of the governor, ordered Elbert to march his grenadiers and several other units to Augusta to quell a domestic insurrection that threatened to erupt over the tarring and feathering of Thomas Brown, a Loyalist who refused to sign the Association. It was to be another noteworthy accomplishment for Elbert since it represented the first time that he commanded an army in the field during the American Revolution. As a member of the council, Elbert surely had much input in the decision to send the militia northward with

---

[28] *CRG*, 12:421–23.
[29] Ibid., 12:421–23, 429–33.

himself in command. Normally, orders to summon, muster, and march the militia issued from Wright. When the council bypassed the governor and ordered Elbert and the militia to Augusta, it signified that Wright's control over the military had vanished. They left, complained Wright to Dartmouth, "without any Application or Authority from me, but I am well Informed were ordered to do so by the Council of Safety." The governor heard that along the way, they, "by Persuasions and threats, Prevail'd on a Great Number of People to Join them as they went through the Country." At this stage, he said, it was difficult to say "what Outrages or Acts of Violence they may Commit before they return."[30]

Elbert's mission was to protect the citizens of St. Paul's Parish from reprisal by Brown's followers. When the commander finally arrived in Augusta, other area units joined his force, giving him a combined strength of about 140 men. The Council of Safety funded the expedition with public money and paid the soldiers for their service. Captain John Conyers and his company, who marched to Augusta and joined Elbert, received four shillings per day. Ann Johnston hired out her horses for the march at forty shillings, also credited to the public's expense.[31]

Once in Augusta, Elbert gained information from the local Committee of Safety and other sources about Brown and the tense situation engulfing the town and countryside. He learned, for example, that Brown was a twenty-four-year-old recent arrival in Georgia and that Wright had made him a magistrate and granted him 5,600 acres above the Little River in the ceded lands. There, he built a plantation called Brownsborough in the forks of Kiokee Creek. In summer 1775, as Georgia's Revolutionary crisis heated up, Brown defended royal government. When Augusta Whigs tried to force the Association on the inhabitants, Brown helped organize a frontier counterassociation that included Loyalists in both Georgia and South Carolina. Because of this, wrote his biographer Edwin Cashin, he became a "marked man in the Georgia backcountry." On August 2, a party of nearly one hundred Liberty Boys accosted Brown at a residence near Augusta and demanded that he sign the Association. Brown informed the mob that he had only recently taken an oath of loyalty as a magistrate and that he (unlike Elbert and Habersham) could not simply profess allegiance to another group opposing the king. Brown

---

[30] Sir James Wright to Lord Dartmouth, August 17, 1775, LSJW, 208.
[31] "Proceedings of the Georgia Council of Safety," December 16, 1775, 18–19 (hereafter cited as PCS). See also J. M. Johnson, *Militiamen, Rangers, and Redcoats*, 120–21.

steadfastly defended his position and paid dearly for his recalcitrance. The crowd, having become impatient with his stalling, drew their swords and rushed him. Brown responded by producing two concealed pistols that he fired into the mob. Although one weapon misfired, the other put a lead ball into the foot of an assailant. In a final effort to defend himself, Brown pulled out his sword, but it was already too late. The crowd swarmed over him. In the scuffle, someone hit him in the head with a rifle butt and fractured his skull.[32]

The mob threw a barely conscious Brown into a cart and hauled him to Augusta where they tied him to a tree, scalped him in three or four places, tarred and feathered his legs and feet, and thrust tiny strips of kindling between his toes, which they then set on fire, burning off some of them. Somehow, Brown survived his ordeal. It took several days for him to regain his composure and begin to heal. With his head and feet covered in bandages, he was a pitiful sight and could barely even sit on a horse. In many respects, he never really recovered from his torture. His face permanently scarred, he suffered severe headaches from the fractured skull for the rest of his life. In his heart, he burned with fury toward the Whigs and nourished an insatiable spirit of revenge. He never forgot his humiliation in Augusta and, during the Revolution, "Burnfoot" Brown would have his day, spreading his wrath all along Georgia's exposed frontier with an army of Loyalists he commanded called the King's Rangers.[33]

In Augusta, the possibility of a frontier uprising placed everyone, including Elbert and his men, in potential danger. After the tarring and feathering, word spread that Brown fled into South Carolina to raise an army of Loyalists numbering in the hundreds to retake the city and punish the Whigs. Anticipating the worst, several militia units from South Carolina soon arrived and took up positions above and below the town along the river. Fortunately, for them, Brown's invasion never materialized. On August 18, Colonel Stephen Bull, a commander in one of the South Carolina units near Augusta, informed Henry Laurens, a delegate of that colony's Provincial Congress, that the danger appeared to have dissipated. For several days, he said, there were constant reports that Brown and his men were coming against the town, but they all turned out to be unfounded. It was a good thing, he added, since the militia around Augusta were in a sad shape. They "have not three pound[s] of Powder or lead

---

[32] Cashin, *King's Ranger*, 17–18, 25–28.
[33] Ibid., 28; *Georgia Gazette*, August 30, 1775, 2.

among them…[and] should a sudden Insurrection of our Domestics happen, they have not Powder to make the least defense."[34]

With the crisis over, Elbert directed his units back to Savannah and resumed his duties on the Council of Safety. He became a delegate to the Third Provincial Congress on September 15, set to convene on November 16, and was selected as its president. At the same time, the Council of Safety began recording minutes of its meetings. Elbert's first documented meeting with the council occurred on November 3. It met next on December 11 and again, Elbert was present. That meeting was significant for four reasons. First, they elected Walton as president to replace Ewen, who had served in that position since the summer. Second, it drew up a list of guidelines for members to follow during meetings. According to the rules, when the president took the chair, each member had to take his seat immediately or face a fine of two shillings and six pence. If a member anticipated an absence for more than a week, he had to obtain special permission from the president. If someone addressed the president directly during a meeting, he had to stand with his head uncovered. Only one person could speak at a time, and, if two simultaneously arose to give their opinion, the president determined who should have the floor first. For Elbert, the council's rules were not unlike those in the Masonic lodges over which he presided. For example, regular attendance was required from both bodies and fines enforced the rules. The formulation of rules was a common practice in the councils and committees throughout the colonies because they helped establish "proper decorum" for the "transaction of business." In North Carolina, one committee subjected members to a fine if they became drunk, swore, or engaged in disorderly behavior during meetings. Thirdly, the council delivered commissions to sixteen officers, all of whom endorsed the Association. Four of the new commanders were elevated to the rank of captain. This action provided further evidence of how thoroughly the Council of Safety had usurped Wright's military powers. Finally, it formalized a list of sixteen members, which varied as time went on. In addition to Elbert, Ewen, and Walton, membership on the council also included, not surprisingly, Habersham and Bowen.[35]

---

[34] Col. Stephen Bull to Henry Laurens, August 18, 1775, in Chesnutt, ed., *Papers of Henry Laurens*, 10:309.

[35] While the notice about the election appeared in the *Georgia Gazette* on September 20, 1775, 3, the article said delegates were chosen on the previous Friday, which would have been September 15. See also, Council of Safety Minutes, December 11, 1775, in PCS, 16–18; Watson, "Committees of Safety," 135. For the notice of Elbert's selection as

December was incredibly busy for Elbert, and demands on his time came from every direction. In addition to maintaining his home and family, he continued to operate several businesses, lead three Masonic lodges, drill his grenadiers, and meet military emergencies such as the Brown uprising in Augusta. At the same time, he fulfilled a multitude of political roles. He was still gathering names for the Association, even as he served as president of the Third Provincial Congress. He was a dedicated member of the Council of Safety and took an active role in its discussions and decisions. He rarely missed a meeting, even the special session that convened on Christmas Eve, which happened to be a Sunday, where the council considered ways to curtail the "wicked and daring attempts" by some merchants in the southern parishes who violated the Association by secretly supplying lumber to the West Indian market.[36]

Elbert soon found himself mired in the council's committee work. After reading a letter from the Council of Safety in Charleston to the members on December 18, he joined a committee to draw up instructions for a deputation to confer with them. On December 27, he formed a second committee with Bowen, Habersham, Edward Telfair, and Basil Cowper to propose some method for supplying the province with arms and ammunition.[37] His knowledge about the militia's needs and state of readiness made him a valuable member of this committee since Georgia lacked adequate supplies for defense other than stolen gunpowder and weapons.

On December 19, the Council of Safety read a resolution sent to Georgia from the Continental Congress in Philadelphia. The letter had significant ramifications for Elbert since it called for the raising of a Georgia battalion of the Continental Line (or 1st Battalion), containing 728 men divided into eight companies. Each company was to consist of seventy-six privates, two drummers or fifers, four corporals, four sergeants, one ensign, two lieutenants, and one captain. Pay scales for the men were included, ranging from twenty-six dollars per month for a captain to just over six dollars for a private. A colonel, receiving fifty dollars per month, was to lead the battalion and under him, a lieutenant colonel (forty dollars per month) and a major (just over thirty-three dollars per month). The council did not act immediately on the resolution and deferred its creation until the Fourth Provincial Congress, scheduled to meet in January 1776.

---

president of the Provincial Congress, see *Georgia Gazette*, November 22, 1775, 2.

[36] Council of Safety Minutes, December 24, 1775, in PCS, 23–24.

[37] Ibid., December 18, 1775, 20–21, and December 27, 1775, 24–25.

Wright fretted over the news when he heard about it. "Thus your Lordship Sees," he immediately informed Dartmouth, that "they are Preparing throughout, to Support their Usurped Powers, and to resist the King[']s troops." He readily admitted that a few Whigs in leadership positions were men of distinction, but the majority were of the "Inferior Class, and it is really Terrible my Lord that Such People Should be Suffered to Overturn the Civil Government and most arbitrarily determine upon, and Sport with Other Men[']s Lives[,] Liberties[,] and Propertys."[38]

Amazingly, after all that Elbert had done to destroy royal government in 1775, he had the audacity to ask Wright for another grant, this time in the ceded lands. On November 7, Wright shared with his council a memorial signed by Elbert and several others representing firms involved in the Indian trade. Speaking for Rae's, Elbert & Company and Rae, Whitefield & Company, Elbert informed the governor that many debts stemming from the 1773 New Purchase treaty were still outstanding due to Indian troubles that curtailed the sale of land and the flow of money. To compensate, he suggested grants not exceeding five thousand acres to all complainants, either individually or to companies, equaling the amount of debt.[39] Nothing happened with Elbert's request, and it was among the last things considered by Wright's Council before the collapse of Georgia's royal government.

In the beginning of 1775, Wright was the supreme authority in Georgia, and his government was intact. Due to the unremitting efforts of Elbert, Habersham, Bowen, and a host of others, Wright's government, by the end of the year, lay in shambles. Isolated, abandoned, and stripped of all power except granting property and signing paperwork related to wills and estates, he was governor in name only. His orders were no longer obeyed, the assembly no longer existed, the Council of Safety controlled the militia and the treasury, the courts were dysfunctional, and British regulars that he had requested since the summer to back his disintegrating government never materialized. All that he had left was his Upper Council, but even that was in a weakened state. James Habersham Sr., seeking to improve his failing health and escape Georgia's chaotic descent into revolution, had gone North during the summer to visit his sister. He never

---

[38] Ibid., December 19, 1775, 21–22. See also Sir James Wright to Lord Dartmouth, December 19, 1775, LSJW, 228. Many primary sources inconsistently varied their use of pounds and dollars when discussing financial matters.

[39] Council Minutes, November 7, 1775, in "Proceedings and Minutes of the Governor and Council of Georgia, October 4, 1774 through November 7, 1775," *CGHS*, 10:47–48.

made it to his destination. Old, infirm, and suffering from gout, he died en route off the coast of New Jersey on August 28. Another stalwart ally in the council, Noble Jones Sr., died in early November. Ironically, the sons of his two most spirited supporters, Joseph Habersham and Noble W. Jones, were among Wright's primary antagonists. Disheartened, Wright believed all was lost. He described Georgia's "Wretched State" to Dartmouth and admitted that he had nearly reached the limits of his toleration. Royal government was "totally Annihilated, and Assumed by Congresses, Councils and Committees." All he could do was to stand by and watch as the "greatest Acts of Tyranny, Oppression, Gross Insults &c. [are] committed, [without] the least means [given for] Protection, Support, or even Personal Safety, and these almost Daily Occurrences are *too much* my Lord."[40]

As Wright's government slipped into oblivion, Elbert had cause to celebrate. He was no longer just a rising star among the revolutionaries. He was one their brightest luminaries. Looking back over the year, he could take pride in the movement that he helped to spawn. As a member of the Provincial Congress, he helped launch Georgia's first republican government and link it with the Revolution in the other colonies. Through the Council of Safety, he gained control of the militia, enforced the Association, made efforts to acquire weapons and ammunition, and helped to consolidate Georgia's budding revolution. As commander of the grenadiers, he kept the peace in Augusta. As a grand master in Georgia's lodges, he infused Masonry with Whig ideology. In religion, he condoned measures to ensure that Christ Church had a pro-Whig parson.

In all of this, the fact remains that Elbert engaged in activities depriving his opponents of their liberties. If he was not personally involved, he looked the other way while the Whigs beat, tarred and feathered, tormented, harassed, intimidated, and publicly and economically ruined the supporters of royal government. Judged strictly by the laws of liberty, he and his cohorts fell short of the mark regarding their treatment of Loyalists, even as they professed the righteousness of their cause. It is likely that Elbert never thought about those contradictions. He justified his actions

---

[40] C. Smith, "Habershams," 209. On October 14, Wright told Dartmouth, "there is hardly a shadow of Government remaining.... I have scarce any Power left, but Proving Wills and Granting Letters of Administration." Based on Elbert's application for land, he was still awarding grants, as well. See Sir James Wright to Lord Dartmouth, October 14, 1775, LSJW, 217. For Wright's "Wretched State" quote, see Sir James Wright to Lord Dartmouth, September 23, 1775, LSJW, 213.

because he saw a bigger picture of a country free from the tyranny of a king, a Parliament, and even, in Georgia's case, a royal governor. Having instilled a new government in Georgia, the hard work of maintaining it against a mighty and powerful foe lay ahead. The task was not going to be easy since Georgia faced almost insurmountable disadvantages. Winning victories for liberty in the congresses, committees, and councils was one thing, but winning them on battlefields was an entirely different matter.

Chapter 6

"To Do Them Honor": Samuel Elbert and the "Spirit of '76" in Georgia

On January 2, 1776, Samuel Elbert entered the room in Savannah where the Council of Safety was holding its first meeting of the year. Other members soon arrived, and he exchanged greetings with his Whig friends, Joseph Habersham, George Walton, and Archibald Bulloch. All four significantly contributed to the destruction of royal government in 1775, and now they faced the daunting task of consolidating their revolution and moving forward in an atmosphere of uncertainty. Before long, six additional members joined, and Walton, the president of the council, called the meeting to order.[1] With the Provincial Congress in recess, the Council of Safety assumed total leadership of the revolution. There was much to discuss, particularly since Georgia, exposed and defenseless, was in a state of emergency. No one knew what lay ahead, but enemies perched at every corner and military preparedness sat at the top of their agenda.

In August 1775, when Elbert and the council requested that Governor James Wright allow the people to choose their own officers in the militia, the petitioners referenced the "dreadful Enemy within [Georgia's] Bosom," which they identified as the Spanish and the Indians. In 1776, the Spanish were the least of Georgia's worries. Now, other enemies loomed that did not exist earlier. First, the colony was wide-open to a British invasion from the sea with massive fleets and professional armies intent on capturing Savannah and crushing the rebellion. Georgia was not prepared to ward off a determined British attack, and Savannah, defended by unreliable militia and woefully inadequate fortifications, was vulnerable.

Loyalists were a second new threat. The incident with Thomas Brown in Augusta a few months earlier exposed the deep divisions that existed in Georgia, particularly among backcountry residents, and many of

---

[1] Council of Safety Minutes, January 2, 1776, in PCS, 26.

them refused to join the revolutionaries. Several, including Brown, fled to safety in British East Florida, where royal governor Patrick Tonyn provided them sanctuary at St. Augustine. Once in Florida, they flocked to Loyalist regiments, like Brown's King's Rangers, which organized in spring 1776. Others stayed home and waited to aid British forces when they finally appeared to crush the rebellion.

The Indians constituted a third problem for Georgia's Whigs, and their threat was the most dreaded. Some believed that the Creek, Cherokee, Choctaw, and Chickasaw could muster at least 14,000 men against the Whigs, and that number did not even include Seminole warriors. Memories from the 1773–1774 Creek war in the ceded lands were fresh on the minds of Georgians, and they feared another brutal Indian conflict. The Seminoles in Florida and several Creek *talwas* (or towns) like Coweta were under British influence, and they constantly raided into Georgia's wide-open southern and western borderlands, creating pandemonium as they stole livestock, burned buildings, and murdered settlers. Georgia historian Hugh McCall suggested that British Indian superintendent John Stuart encouraged their hostility. This certainly was the conclusion of Georgia's Whig leaders, who chased Stuart from Savannah in July 1775, accusing him of trying to instigate an Indian war. Those accusations, according to Stuart, were fallacious. His ardent wish, he said, was to keep the Indians peaceful through normal trade relations, which Georgians had disrupted with their protests. While Stuart professed Indian neutrality as his ardent goal, other British leaders had different ideas. Shortly after he arrived in St. Augustine, Brown convinced Tonyn to embrace the Indians as allies. Tonyn needed little persuasion. He promoted Brown to colonel and authorized his mission into Indian country to recruit Seminole, Creek, and Cherokee warriors. Utilizing the Indians, Tonyn believed, would be a "very great" service to the British, especially since the colonists "were a thousand times more in dread of the savages than of any European Troops." He told one British commander that the Creeks should be used to England's advantage. They could "lay waste" to the whole of Georgia "at a moment's notice…hovering on the back country perplexing and harassing the enemy, keeping…that province in a warm alarm." Failure to utilize the Indians, he warned Lord George Germain, the secretary of state for the American department who had recently replaced Lord Dartmouth, would be a mistake, especially since they were "ready to join the British troops." The involvement of the southern tribes was, according to historian Edwin Cashin, directly linked to the efforts of Stuart, Tonyn, Brown, and

Germain, and their policies were responsible for the Indian warfare that erupted in the Southeast during the Revolution.² Nevertheless, Native Americans had a stake in the fight. Most could not remain neutral in a war that was, to them, ultimately about control of their ancestral lands.

For Georgia's Whigs, the disrupted flow of customary trade goods exacerbated their Indian problems. Elbert was to blame for some of it. The military stores seized from the *Phillipa* in July was all destined for the Indian trade. The *Phillipa* was not an isolated incident. The Whigs captured other ships containing goods for the Indians and then confiscated the cargo. Wright knew that Indian peace depended on the trade. On November 1, 1775, he told Lord Dartmouth that if the Creeks and Cherokee were "not Immediately supplied with Ammunition, and the Trade opened as usual, it will be Impossible to restrain them." Toward that end, he sent a message to the Whigs who usurped his government imploring them to maintain the steady and expected flow of goods or else face the Indian's terrible wrath. To keep the Indians friendly and perhaps win their loyalty, the Council of Safety supplied them with some goods, but the quantity was far less than normal. To ward off any rise in tensions brought about by the paucity of goods, the council passed a resolution ordering the committees of safety in the backcountry to "apprehend any white person who shall molest or disturb any Indian…[within] this Province."³

To mollify the Indians, the Whigs made other efforts to keep them peaceful. On July 4, 1776, the day Americans declared their independence from England, Archibald Bulloch, Georgia's newly elected first president, sent the Lower Creeks a talk informing them that the colony did not have it within its power to supply them as usual. If the Creeks would be patient, he suggested, the trade would resume. For now, Georgians "intended to…leave off planting Indico [Indigo] and go to work at making cloath and Ammunition." This frugality, he promised, would soon supply the Creeks with "every necessary [item] as usual." He advised the Creeks not to listen to the superintendent's words and to "look upon every talk that

---

² McCall, *History of Georgia*, 2:77; J. M. Johnson, *Militiamen, Rangers, and Redcoats*, 109; K. Coleman, "Georgia in the American Revolution, 1775–1782," 72; Cashin, *King's Ranger*, 57. For Tonyn's quote, see Kokomoor, "Burning & Destroying All Before Them," 309. For Tonyn's remarks to Germain, see Piecuch, *Three Peoples, One King*, 75, and for the estimate of Indian warriors among the Southeastern tribes, see pg. 26.

³ Sir James Wright to Secretary Lord Dartmouth, November 1, 1775, in LSJW, 218–19; Council of Safety Minutes, January 8, 1776, in PCS, 29.

came from Captain Stuart as lyes as he was paid for what he did from the King." There is no doubt that Stuart, contrary to his earlier professions about keeping the Indians peaceful, engaged in double-talk, since he also enticed the Creeks and Seminoles to make war against the colonists. In summer 1776, during a conference in Augusta between Creek *micos* and American commissioners, the Cusseta king, Handsome Fellow, from the town of Okfuskee, and the Tallassee king alluded to Stuart's secretive efforts to persuade them to take up the hatchet. While he was having some success, an equal number of Creeks, including the Cusseta king, pledged themselves to neutrality. "It was a mistaken notion of Mr. Stuart," he informed the American commissioners, "to ask my people to take up Arms against them or any of the white-people.... As to the red flag [of war] that was sent up to me [from Stuart] I mean to carry it back...to [his headquarters in] Pensacola."[4] The Cusseta king's comment only verified what the colonists already knew. Stuart could not be trusted; he was surreptitiously waiting for the right moment to unleash the fury of Indians against Georgia's settlers.

The triple dangers emanating from British armies, Loyalists, and Indians were foremost in the minds of the Council of Safety when they met on January 2. On December 27, Elbert served on a committee with Habersham to explore ways to acquire weapons. Now, they issued their report, and the council responded with a number of resolutions. Any merchant ship bringing the province "gunpowder, saltpeter, Sulphur...brass field pieces or good muskets fitted with bayonets," would be permitted to forego the Association and reload their vessels with produce from the colonies to the value of the munitions they carried. Furthermore, the council agreed to set aside money to obtain munitions and placed Elbert, Habersham, and Edward Telfair on a committee to find a person to oversee this directive. The purchaser had the authority to draw funds from Elbert's committee for the acquisition of weapons, including "400 stand of arms, with bayonets, as nearly to the size recommended by the Continental Congress as possible, 20,000 lbs. of gunpowder [and] 60,000 lbs. of ball, bullets, bar lead, grape, swan and goose shot, properly proportioned." Finally, the stores of powder lodged at different places throughout the colony, like

---

[4] "Talk from the Committee in Savannah to the Lower Creeks," July 4, 1776, Archibald Bulloch Papers, MS103, folder 103, item 1, Georgia Historical Society. For the Cusseta King's quote, see Rindfleisch, "Our Lands Are Our Life and Breath," 588–89. See also K. Coleman, *American Revolution in Georgia*, 112–13.

at the forts at Frederica on St. Simon's Island and on Cockspur Island at the mouth of the Savannah, should immediately be secured and hidden.[5]

Elbert was present at a special meeting of the Council of Safety on Sunday, January 7, to address rumors that British warships were sailing from Charleston to Savannah. While their intentions were unknown, the council speculated that they were coming to plunder the colony for provisions. The news generated alarm and the council implemented immediate measures for defense. The initial response was to summon part of the militia to duty around Savannah. They were given only hours to gather their arms and assemble in town at noon on the following day. Elbert was promoted to "Colonel and chief in command" over them, making him the highest-ranking commander in Georgia. They also commissioned Habersham as major. To safeguard ships and goods in the lower part of the river, the council ordered all vessels at Cockspur to take their cargo up to Savannah. If British ships appeared sooner than expected, the commander at Cockspur was to scuttle all vessels to keep them from falling into enemy hands. Finally, the council gave Elbert the power to "restrain any Crown officer from going without the limits of Savannah, if he should deem it expedient."[6] These measures and Elbert's elevation to the position of supreme command both rested on the bedrock of speculation. In this case, the rumors proved true. British vessels were indeed headed to Savannah.

Scrambling to obtain weapons, organize the militia, and prepare for the worst, the Council of Safety held two separate meetings on Monday, January 8, and Elbert attended both. To deprive the British of rice or any other commodity, they reiterated their commitment to temporary nonimportation, set to expire on March 1. To supply the growing number of militia congregating in Savannah, they appointed Levi Sheftall, one of the city's Jewish residents and an acquaintance of Elbert, as commissary. A major concern was the lack of firearms, powder, and shot. The council, once again violating the laws of liberty, ignored the property rights of others and issued orders to confiscate weapons from the "houses of all overseers and negroes throughout the Province, together with those on the plantations in South Carolina, bordering upon [the] Savannah River." Search parties were to examine each house for "all guns and ammunition" and then confiscate any found. Always watchful for any opening that could increase the chance of a slave rebellion, overseers could retain one gun and

---

[5] Council of Safety Minutes, January 2, 1776, in PCS, 26–27.
[6] Ibid., January 7, 1776, 27–29.

thirteen cartridges to suppress an insurrection. The council authorized Elbert, the commanding officer in Savannah, to carry out these directives. In compliance, he sent parties of his militia to the respective plantations, where they seized weapons and ammunition and then stored them in Savannah.[7]

The Council of Safety received a letter from Henry Laurens, the president of the Council of Safety in South Carolina, on January 9. Its contents confirmed Georgian's deepest fears. Four British ships, the *Tamar* (sixteen guns), *Cherokee* (ten guns), the *Sandwich Packet*, and an unnamed armed schooner set sail from Charleston several days earlier and were headed toward Georgia. "They are intended for your river," warned Laurens, "in order to obtain provisions (of bread particularly) which…we have refused to supply them with." The grand design, it seemed, was "overawing the friends of liberty" in Georgia. He hoped that Georgians, when the time came, would respond in a way that would "do them honor." That was precisely what Savannah's Whigs intended to do. As Elbert drilled the militia, fortified positions, and procured weapons and gunpowder, he also gathered all of the town's cannon, cleaned them, made sure they were in working order, and placed them in the best positions to watch the river and defend the city. A few days later, the Council of Safety instructed him and the other commanding officers to patrol the town in an effort to conserve precious gunpowder. "It shall be considered as an offense in any person, who shall idly fire a gun in the Town or Common of Savannah," read the council's resolve, and anyone caught aimlessly discharging weapons would be detained and have their gun confiscated.[8]

The *Tamar* arrived off the coast from Tybee's lighthouse on January 13. In response, the council ordered Elbert to send an officer and some of his men to Causton's Bluff, one of the strategic points overlooking the river just below Savannah, to keep watch. The bluff was a slight elevation jutting out along a small peninsula and surrounded by swamps and rice fields, but from its summit, the river was visible across the flooded lowlands. If any British vessels made their way upriver, Causton Bluff lookouts were to send an alarm.[9] Elbert certainly accompanied his men to the position initially, but due to other military and political responsibilities, such

---

[7] Ibid., January 8, 1776, morning meeting, and January 8, 1776, afternoon meeting, 29–31.

[8] Ibid., January 9, 1776, 33; January 16, 1776, 27; Sir James Wright to Secretary Lord Dartmouth, March 10, 1776, in LSJW, 233.

[9] Council of Safety Minutes, January 16, 1776, in PCS, 38.

as attending the Fourth Provincial Congress as a delegate on January 17, he could not remain. While Causton's Bluff was a good observation point, its value was negligible since it was just two miles or so south of town; by the time word arrived from Elbert's lookouts, the British would already be at Savannah's doorstep. Since geography dictated the bluff's occupation, there was little else Elbert could do. As he left his men on Causton's Bluff and headed back to Savannah, it probably never occurred to him that the hill's name honored Thomas Causton, one of his father's most bitter enemies during the early trustee years.

More enemy ships, including the *Raven* (eighteen guns), *Scarborough* (twenty guns), and *Syren* (twenty-eight guns) accompanied by many supporting vessels, soon arrived off Tybee's bar. The *Scarborough* was the first of several ships sent from Boston by British major general William Howe to procure supplies for his troops facing the American Continental Army commanded by General George Washington. The flagship of the fleet was the *Scarborough*, captained by Andrew Barclay, who assumed command over the flotilla. Wright was thrilled when he heard about the presence of British ships. Only days before, he complained to Dartmouth that his situation was hopeless with "no Troops, no Money, no Orders, or Instructions…no Arms, no Ammunition, [and] not so much as a Ship of War of any kind." The British fleet breathed new life into Royal Georgia and Wright, for the first time in months, sensed an upper hand. Taking advantage of the moment, he fired off a notice to the Whigs on January 18, informing them of the British fleet's presence. He desired a personal conference with two of the town's representatives, Noble W. Jones and Joseph Clay, to discuss the new turn of events. Jones and Clay could then disseminate Wright's message to the council or anyone else that had unlawfully seized his government.[10]

During the evening of January 18, Jones and Clay arrived at Wright's residence fully aware of the British presence in the harbor. Wright told his visitors that he was confident the Royal Navy would treat Georgia as if it was in a state of rebellion and that it had both the authority and the power to "destroy their Towns & Property." He did not believe that was their intention, however. Their business was merely to secure provisions, and he

---

[10] Sir James Wright to Secretary Lord Dartmouth, January 3, 1776, in LSJW, 229–30; Hall, *Land and Allegiance*, 33–34; Warren and Jones, *GGCJ: 1774–1777*, 151–54; *Georgia Gazette*, January 24, 1776, 3. McCall stated that the *Syren*, *Raven*, *Tamer*, and *Cherokee* were already lying at anchor off Tybee on January 18 (*History of Georgia*, 2:61).

was certain that, once supplied, they would depart. Wright wanted assurances from the Whigs that they would not antagonize the British as they gathered supplies. If they would cooperate, he said, he would "settle every thing with the Officers in such a manner as to prevent their doing any Injury to this Town or the Inhabitants of the Province or their Property." If they resisted, though, the British would take what they needed by force and, if they wanted, "attack this Town & destroy it."[11]

Instead of causing the Whigs to back down, Wright's threats had the opposite effect. The Council of Safety responded by holding a late-night session at Tondee's Tavern to explore alternatives. Present were Elbert, Habersham, Bulloch, William Ewen, and four others, in addition to Walton, who chaired the meeting. There was only one way to interpret Wright's message, which was to surrender in dishonor. A few days earlier, the council entered a resolve into its minutes issued from the Continental Congress in Philadelphia, calling for the arrest of those "whose going at large may…endanger the safety of the Colony or the liberties of America." Not trusting Wright and in line with the dictates of that resolve, they issued an order for his arrest, as well as his council. All of them were to be captured, disarmed, and paroled in their homes under the solemn promise that they would not "aid, assist or comfort any of the persons on board his Majesty's ships of war, or take up arms against Americans in the present unhappy dispute." The council authorized the "commanding officer," or Elbert, to oversee Wright's arrest and then await further orders. Instructions followed to several commanders in the colony to march their men to Savannah as soon as possible. According to historian Gregg Brooking, the decision to secure Wright ensured "the ruination of nearly two decades of [the governor's] inexhaustible work and dreams."[12] The orders to arrest the governor highlighted the degree to which the council coordinated the revolution and showed the depth of Elbert's involvement in the movement's leadership.

As orders disseminated summoning more militia to Savannah, Habersham, with Elbert's blessing, selected a group of armed men and led them though the town's dark streets to Wright's residence. Habersham and his accomplices brushed aside the sentinel posted at Wright's home and strolled into the midst of a conference that the governor was having

---

[11] Warren and Jones, *GGCJ: 1774–1777*, 151.

[12] Council of Safety Minutes, January 18, 1776, in PCS, 38–39. For the resolution from the Continental Congress, see in the same source, January 9, 1776, 32. See also Brooking, "Of Material Importance," 256–60; Jackson, "Battle of the Riceboats," 231.

with his council. Placing his hand upon the governor's shoulder, Habersham proclaimed, "Sir James, you are my prisoner." Shocked and astonished, Wright's council members hastily bolted but were apprehended later. Wright remained in his home, closely watched by some of Habersham's men for the rest of the night. On January 19, the following day, the council held a morning session to discuss the conditions of Wright's arrest and parole. Present were Elbert, Jones, Habersham, Bulloch, Ewen, Walton, and seven others. Wright's confinement was indefinite. He was under heavy guard and forbidden to leave town or hold any correspondence with officers on the British ships without permission of the council. The council forced him to swear upon his honor that he would not break parole and flee. Later that day, Elbert attended a second meeting of the council that drew up parole conditions for the others who fled Wright's home the night before.[13] That was the last time Elbert attended a Council of Safety meeting.

Elbert was in good company when the Fourth Provincial Congress opened its session on January 20, and he took his seat alongside Habersham, Jones, Ewen, Oliver Bowen, John Houstoun, and other Revolutionary allies. It had been a year since Elbert initially signed the Association in January 1775. Since then, his rise to the pinnacle of Whig leadership was nothing short of meteoric. He not only was involved in almost all of the major events that helped topple royal government and bring the revolution to Georgia over the previous twelve months but also was an instrumental figure in both the Council of Safety and the Provincial Congress that orchestrated the rebellion. Additionally, he was now supreme military commander over the province's militia. Finally, he was involved in the arrest of Wright, which signified the complete erosion of royal authority.

Wright's arrest aside, Georgia's problems were only beginning. The gathering British armada at Tybee and Cockspur, which seemed to grow daily with the appearance of new schooners, sloops, transports, and auxiliary ships, loomed as an ominous and expanding danger. Despite Wright's suggestion that they only wanted provisions, none of the Whigs really knew the intentions of the British navy. The consensus was that they were formulating plans for an attack on Savannah. Such uncertainty created an atmosphere of urgency as the Provincial Congress began its deliberations.

---

[13] Council of Safety Minutes, January 19, 1776, in PCS, 39–41; C. C. Jones Jr., *History of Georgia*, 2:211–12.

Organizing Georgia's 1st Battalion with eight companies, authorized by the Continental Congress during late fall 1775, was a high priority for the delegates. One writer to the *Gazette* saw the battalion as "absolutely necessary," considering the "open and defenseless state of the province." Another declared that it was "expedient...[and] indispensably necessary" and a "matter of the highest concern." On paper, it was to have 728 men, including officers, but filling those ranks proved to be difficult. For one, Georgia's small population meant that there were only around three thousand men available for duty, and, given the choice, many of those preferred service in the militia rather than the Continental Army. In the militia, soldiers had more freedom to return home after completing their missions, as opposed to the Continental Army, which bound men to serve for specified amounts of time while increasing their chances of fighting in areas far beyond Georgia's borders. There were other problems, too. The money Congress promised Georgia to pay for recruits had not yet arrived, and the province's currency was practically worthless in other colonies. There was confusion on terms of enlistment, as well, which ranged from six to eighteen months. South Carolina, in contrast, offered many more incentives to its enlisted men, including larger bounties. This meant that many Georgians, rather than serving in their own Continental unit, opted for those in South Carolina. For these reasons, recruitment in Georgia's battalion lagged far behind expectations, and, by mid-March, it contained only about twenty-five or thirty inexperienced soldiers.[14] Undermanned, underfunded, and ill equipped, it was no match for the enemy host gathering below Savannah.

The old divisions between Conservative and Radical Whigs became evident when the Provincial Congress moved to appoint field officers to command the battalion. For the highest rank of colonel, Conservative Whigs threw their support behind Elbert. In the field of potential commanders, Elbert was by far the most qualified because, while his military experience was not extensive, it was more than anyone else could offer. Furthermore, he already commanded the militia in Savannah and, since he was in charge of preparing the city's defenses, he had first-hand

---

[14] *Georgia Gazette,* January 3, 1776, 4; January 10, 1776, 2; J. M. Johnson, *Militiamen, Rangers, and Redcoats,* 134–37; Searcy, *Georgia-Florida Contest,* 24–25; Sir James Wright to Secretary Lord Dartmouth, March 10, 1776, LSJW, 234; White, *Historical Collections of Georgia,* 93; Lachlan McIntosh to George Washington, April 28, 1776, in Hawes, ed., "Letter Book of Lachlan McIntosh, 1776–1777. Part I," 153 (hereafter cited as PLM, pt. 1).

knowledge of strategic key points, their conditions, and the number of men detailed to garrison each position. As a member of the Council of Safety and the Provincial Congress, he was a perfect liaison between the militia and Georgia's Revolutionary government and best poised to carry out directives issued from both bodies. Radical Whigs, however, objected to Elbert. Instead, they wanted their own candidate, Button Gwinnett, an opportunist from St. John's Parish without any military experience, to fill the position.

On the eve of the Revolution, political infighting over command of the battalion ripped apart Georgia's Whigs, and Elbert found himself in the middle of the chaos. Having come so far as to foster the revolution, it was a frustrating turn of events and the enemy within seemed just as dangerous to Whig aspirations as the British fleet stationed below Savannah. Habersham reflected on the sad situation in a letter to Henry Drayton, one of his Revolutionary contemporaries in South Carolina. "I am sorry to inform you," he wrote in February 1776, "that we are at present a little unhappy in our [Congress], owing to the ambitious views of some of our leading people. I think this province is remarkable for a number of parties and I am afraid we shall find it too true that a house divided against itself can never stand."[15]

To be sure, Elbert was a towering figure among the Conservative Whigs. Historian Harvey Jackson argued that their original goal during the late 1760s and early 1770s was to increase the power of the legislature over the executive branch, while at the same time protecting and enhancing their own political status. In short, they wanted to reform the system and to preserve self-interests, not overturn it.[16] However, judging from the brazen acts of rebellion by many in 1775, a large number had evolved their thinking to embrace the earlier Revolutionary stance of the Radical Whigs, which was to bring Georgia in line with protests in other colonies. For some Conservative Whigs, this was already further than they wanted to go.

Geography continued to divide the Whigs, but a new element, personalities, became more pronounced by the beginning of 1776. The base of radical support was in St. John's Parish, the home of Gwinnett and physician Lyman Hall. Gwinnett and Hall were prominent radicals and the most famous citizens in Sunbury, the parish's major town. In 1775, St.

---

[15] Jackson, "Georgia Whiggery," 251–73.
[16] Ibid.; Jackson, *Lachlan McIntosh*, 22–24.

John's Whigs were quick to embrace the Revolutionary movement and they adopted policies and positions that went far beyond the goals of conservatives. According to Jackson, they wanted to "go outside the system, creating new mechanisms of government which could threaten the old," and this included a desire to unleash popular democracy and unhinge Savannah's chokehold on government.[17] For example, when the Provincial Congress in summer 1775 failed to send delegates to the Continental Congress, the radicals sent Hall from St. John's Parish on their own accord as an observer. Since Hall had no mandate from Georgia, he could not vote, but he did offer opinions and contributed to discussions in Congress. On top of that, leaders in St. John's Parish still seethed over the continued dominance of Savannah's conservatives in government spanning the previous decades. The Revolution presented them an opportunity to recast government on their own terms and shift the balance of power toward Sunbury. In 1775, under the leadership of Gwinnett, Radical Whigs expanded their coalition, combining their efforts with the frontier parishes that were also at odds with Savannah's conservatives.

Like the radicals in St. Johns, many frontier leaders also fumed over the continued dominance of Savannah's leadership in government and while the tension had been building for years, Georgia's Revolutionary crisis allowed them to strike back. Their frustrations prior to 1776 were many, but in spite of their protests, they still felt ignored by Savannah's elite, who advanced legislation that only promoted themselves, their merchants, and their region. Many settlers wanted additional Indian cessions, for example, so they could obtain new and fertile lands. Instead, the focus of Wright and Savannah's leading class was on maintaining the trade and pursuing diplomatic approaches to gaining Indian territory. Backcountry settlers also made the same argument about the colony's land policies, particularly in the ceded lands, which favored the wealthier class, who could afford the required fees and initial payments for grants over less affluent settlers, who could not. Georgia's frontier protest against low country elites was not unique in the southern colonies and it mirrored the struggle in the Carolinas and Virginia at the same time. In Georgia, many backwoods protesters, such as fiery George Wells from Augusta, longed for the day when they could topple Savannah's political class and assert a strong frontier voice in government. Originally from St. John's Parish, Wells had long been an opponent of Savannah's Whigs, and he was rightly cast as one of

---

[17] Jackson, *Lachlan McIntosh*, 23–24.

the major leaders of the "country" faction of radicals. In 1775, he merged his protest with Gwinnett, and, according to Cashin, the combination was "more radical than the Savannah Whigs might have liked."[18] The radicals were in no mood for concessions when the Provincial Congress met in January 1776, and when conservatives put up Elbert's name for colonel, they balked. To them, it was just another conservative ruse, this time through the military, to gain even more control over Georgia's revolution.

While opposites in many ways, Elbert and Gwinnett had much in common. Both had roots in England. Elbert was born in Savannah, but his parents were from England. Gwinnett was born in Gloucestershire in 1735 and migrated to America in the early 1760s. The fathers of both men were ministers. William Elbert was a pastor at Euhaw Baptist Church in South Carolina for a few years, and the Reverend Samuel Gwinnett was a prominent member of the Welsh clergy. Both also came to Savannah around the same time. Elbert arrived in 1764, followed by Gwinnett, who moved there from Charleston in 1765. Once in Savannah, both became merchants although Elbert was the more successful of the two. Gwinnett soon left the merchant trade to try his hand as a planter. After liquidating his stock, he obtained a hefty loan and purchased St. Catherine's Island along Georgia's coast for £5,259. The purchase made Gwinnett a large plantation owner, and, like Elbert, he soon acquired slaves. Though both were mired in debt, Elbert found ways to manage his while Gwinnett lacked the discipline to keep his financial house in order.[19]

Drive and determination were important elements undergirding Elbert's rise in social stature, but he also benefited from the patronage of his father-in-law, John Rae. To propel himself socially upward, Gwinnett had to rely completely on himself. Although he possessed a domineering personality and evidenced much promise as a leader, his poor management abilities were an ever-present threat to his ambitions. One historian remarked that he was a "man of limited commercial skill, prone to questionable, almost desperate, financial dealings, who realized few of the goals he initially sought." His reckless finances finally caught up to him. Buried in debt and defaulting on loans, he was soon borrowing money from one creditor to pay another. His financial situation was untenable. His most crushing blow before the American Revolution occurred when creditors

---

[18] Cashin, *King's Ranger*, 15–16.
[19] Jackson, *Lachlan McIntosh*, 30–32. See also C. C. Jones Jr., *History of Georgia*, 2:271; W. Robertson, "Rare Button Gwinnett," 298.

seized his landholdings on St. Catherine's to liquidate his mound of debt. Desperate, Gwinnett tried to salvage himself and his honor through the avenue of politics, where he benefited from his close personal friendship with Hall.[20]

Gwinnett and Elbert also shared political experiences. In 1767, Gwinnett, like Elbert later, became a justice of the peace for St John's Parish. Both also worked together in the General Assembly during 1769–1770. Still, Gwinnett's accomplishments in politics, like his business ventures, were far from impressive. Overall, his achievements before the Revolution were mediocre, and, according to one historian, he was a "financial failure whose record of political activity since 1770 was nil." Blessed with an abundance of political ambition, he also had a talent for stirring controversy. He could be petty at times and was easily affronted. On the eve of the Revolution, he positioned himself as the leader of the Radical Whigs in St. John's Parish after Hall left for Philadelphia. Taking the opportunity to further his own ambitions, he came out as an enemy of the Conservative Whigs and vowed to terminate their dominance in Georgia's Revolutionary movement. Toward this goal, he joined forces with Wells and other backcountry leaders who shared his concerns. Thus, Gwinnett's revolution had dual objectives. One was to fight for independence against England. The other was to remove Conservative Whigs from power and redistribute it in favor of St. John's and the frontier parishes with himself as their leader.[21]

The Provincial Congress spent January 29 and 30 wrangling over the 1st Battalion's superior commander. The gridlock broke when Elbert and Gwinnett removed themselves from consideration, opening the way for a compromise candidate, Lachlan McIntosh, to be colonel. A planter and businessman from Darien and St. Andrew's Parish below Savannah, McIntosh was politically neutral, but he had strong business connections with Conservative Whigs such as the Habersham brothers and Joseph Clay. As was the case with Gwinnett, Elbert also surpassed McIntosh's military qualifications. McIntosh had almost no military experience to offer. However, he did have a distinguished name and reputation, in addition to being an astute businessman and politician. According to Jackson, a common belief was that if a person held a position of status and respect in society, it could easily translate into high levels of military leadership.

---

[20] Jackson, *Lachlan McIntosh*, 31.
[21] Ibid., 30–32.

Such was the case with the "cautious and conservative," McIntosh. In politics, wrote his biographer, he was wise, logical, and understanding. He was also "serious, conscious of status and procedure, and often [struck] contemporaries as cold and abrupt." Even though he was a loyal friend, loving father, and even honest, he had his share of negative traits. Foremost among them was a difficulty controlling his temper. McIntosh's anger was sometimes so intense that it caused him to lash out at others and make regrettable, costly decisions.[22] Although he was politically neutral in early 1776, he could hardly avoid getting involved in the ongoing controversy between Georgia's Whigs, especially given his commanding position in the battalion, and in the months to come, he became increasingly affiliated with the conservatives.

The next two positions in the 1st Battalion's chain of command went to conservatives when Elbert became lieutenant colonel and Habersham a major. Elbert's promotion became official on February 4. Many of the remaining field commands went to Radical Whigs, with some exceptions, like John Habersham (Joseph's brother) who became first lieutenant in the 1st Company, John Rae Jr. (Elbert's brother-in-law) who became its ensign, and Bowen, who was appointed captain of the 2nd Company. Part of the compromise that made McIntosh colonel and Elbert lieutenant colonel also made Gwinnett one of Georgia's delegates to the Second Continental Congress. Although Gwinnett did not know it at the time, this appointment would enshrine him in the annals of history as one of Georgia's signers of the Declaration of Independence later that year, along with Hall and Walton.[23]

Two incidents concerning oaths and honor swirled around Elbert in early February. The first, Wright and his parole of honor, involved Elbert indirectly since he was in charge of the governor's arrest and the drawing up of conditions of his confinement. Since January 18, Wright was a prisoner in his own home, but he was just biding his time, waiting for an opportunity to escape to the British ships off Tybee. The hostility of Georgia's Whigs toward those who supported royal government made him fear for his life and only strengthened his determination to flee. Furthermore, he believed that the colony's welfare depended on his ability to speak to British officers in the ships. His chance to escape occurred on the night of

---

[22] Ibid., 18, 24, 33–34.
[23] Ibid., 33–34. See also J. M. Johnson, *Militiamen, Rangers, and Redcoats*, 134–37; McCall, *History of Georgia*, 2:65; *Georgia Gazette*, February 7, 1776, 3; C. C. Jones Jr., *History of Georgia*, 2:217.

February 11, when he snuck past his house guards with his family and hid in the swamps where he waited for a pre-arranged small boat to pick him up and row him to the British fleet. Early in the morning of February 12, he arrived on board the *Scarborough* at Cockspur where Captain Barclay greeted him with a fifteen-gun salute.[24] To the Whigs, Wright's action was disgraceful since he broke parole and violated his oath of honor.

Safely on board the *Scarborough*, Wright wasted no time in formulating an address to Georgians, which he sent to the assembly, or if they were not sitting, to "those that are called the council of safety," on the following day. Although he meant to extend an olive branch, his letter had the opposite effect and reinforced the conviction that the enemy's design was to take the city. In a letter to George Washington about three weeks later, McIntosh claimed that Wright's escape underscored the British intentions to "land at or near the town, *destroy it* [italics mine], and carry off about twenty sail of shipping lying in the river." Wright's message promised, unconvincingly, that the king's fleet was interested only in gaining provisions and that Barclay would pay full price for them. He vowed that once supplied, the "forces now here, will not commit any hostilities against this province." The Whigs were not inclined to believe him since he violated his own solemn oath of parole. However, they could take stock in his observation that the British fleet was "fully sufficient to reduce and overcome every opposition that could be…made." If the Whigs resisted, Wright warned that it might "not be in my power to insure them the continuance of the peace and quietude they now have, if it may be called so." The result would be "total ruin and destruction, which…I most clearly see at the threshold of [your] doors." This was Wright's final warning, "in the most earnest and friendly manner," for the rebels "to desist from their present plans and resolutions." Only then, could the embattled governor "endeavor to obtain for them, full pardon and forgiveness" for their sin of rebellion.[25]

Wright's letter arrived at the same time that Elbert and the other officers of the 1st Battalion were taking oaths of loyalty to the Provincial Congress and the Council of Safety commensurate with their commissions. On February 16, Elbert stood before the Congress and swore to hold himself to the "supreme and civil powers of this Province…for the purpose of defending our rights and liberties." As a soldier and a man of honor, he

---

[24] Brooking, "Of Material Importance," 259–61.
[25] Lachlan McIntosh to George Washington, March 8, 1776, in PLM, pt. 1, 150; Sir James Wright to Honorable Gentlemen, February 13, 1776, in McCall, *History of Georgia*, 2:62–65.

bound himself to "obey and carry into effect…the orders and commands of the present or any future Congress or Council of Safety of this Province." The next section of the oath was fraught with confusion. He, and all other commissioned officers, promised to follow the dictates of Georgia's Whig government as long as it did "not contradict, or interfere with the orders or directions of the General Congress or a Committee…or any General or other officer by them appointed over us."[26] Although not immediately apparent, the oath created gray areas of uncertainty. It did not specify, for example, who commanded militia troops when they worked in conjunction with the Continental Army. Nor did it establish the authority, if any, that the Provincial Congress had over the 1st Battalion or any others that were later mustered in Georgia. The oath's ambiguities plagued Georgia's entire Revolutionary experience as McIntosh, Elbert, and other Continental Army commanders soon discovered in the midst of crucial military events.

These discrepancies did not surface during the escalating conflict churning around Savannah in February and March. Following the spirit of the oath, Elbert yielded his position of command over the militia to McIntosh, who now outranked him as the colonel of the Continental Line. McIntosh was not comfortable with the change. As he later informed Washington, "I ventured to take command of the Militia…though, I must acknowledge, with some reluctance." Instead of protesting the move, Elbert stepped aside. Twice, in the span of about two weeks, he removed himself from controversies surrounding command to maintain unity in Whig ranks. In the first instance, he relinquished his desire to be colonel of the 1st Battalion to McIntosh, the compromise candidate. Similarly, giving up his militia command was a selfless act. Maybe this is what Jones had in mind when he described Elbert as a leader possessing "moral endowments of a high order." Elbert's reputation, he wrote, "was above reproach," and he stood out as "one of those excellent and good men" who made the earth wholesome.[27]

Even as Elbert formalized his oath to the Provincial Congress and the Council of Safety, the high drama in Savannah moved toward a climax. On February 19, Barclay delivered a message to the council asking for provisions. Even though the British commander promised to pay market

---

[26] C. C. Jones Jr., *History of Georgia*, 2:216–17.
[27] Lachlan McIntosh to George Washington, March 8, 1776, in PLM, pt. 1, 150. See also, C. C. Jones Jr., *Samuel Elbert*, 39.

price, the council refused to consider his request. Barclay now had to come up with his own scheme to get the much-needed supplies. He soon became aware through informants that around twenty fully loaded rice boats were tied to their docks on the upper end of Hutchinson Island, a long, oddly shaped body of land in the Savannah River directly across from the city. The council confined the rice boats and all others to port because of the crisis and the nonimportation agreement. Barclay knew that in a matter of days, nonimportation would expire, and, if he would just wait, the rice boats would freely leave port and sail downriver directly into his hands. As he contemplated options, more British ships appeared off Savannah's coast. In late February, the *Hinchinbrook* (eight guns), commanded by Major James Grant, and two transports, the *Symmetry* and the *Whitby*, arrived from Boston carrying about two hundred light infantry and marines. Their addition increased the number of British warships to at least a dozen, all accompanied by a multitude of smaller supporting vessels. The British commander also had at his disposal nearly six hundred sailors and marines.[28]

In the face of seemingly hopeless odds, Elbert remained calm and focused. Without knowledge of Barclay's intentions, or even a navy to contest the British fleet, he busied himself shoring up defenses and waiting for the enemy to make a move. He probably also directed the work of slaves, who were forced to hastily construct earthworks and fortifications in and around the town. According to McIntosh, the whole scene was one of "anarchy and confusion." To protect Savannah, Georgia only had about three hundred militia. This small army, noted McIntosh, was all that he had to "defend an open, straggling, defenseless, and deserted town, with numberless avenues leading to it."[29] In these trying times, the abrupt appearance of nearly one hundred militia from South Carolina surely bolstered morale in the city. It is significant that McIntosh called Savannah "deserted." The implication was that Elbert's wife, Elizabeth, along with

---

[28] Jackson, "Battle of the Riceboats," 235–36; Sir James Wright to Lord Dartmouth, March 10, 1776, in LSJW, 233; J. M. Johnson, *Militiamen, Rangers, and Redcoats*, 141–42.

[29] Lachlan McIntosh to General George Washington, March 8, 1776, in PLM, pt. 1, 150. Wright's estimation of the militia forces in Savannah, gathered from Loyalists who escaped to the British navy and from other sources, were nearly three times what McIntosh claimed and included "about 800 men in arms [and] about 200 of their Regiment or Battalion already Inlisted and daily increasing." He estimated that South Carolina had sent "600 of their [militia] to reinforce and assist the People here." See Sir James Wright to Lord Dartmouth, March 10, 1776, in LSJW, 234.

his two children, had fled their home to a less dangerous location, probably Rae's Hall, just above the city. As it turned out, Rae's Hall was not a safe place to be either.

On board the *Scarborough*, Barclay waited for the termination of nonimportation. Aware of this possibility and determined to deprive the British of any provisions, the council, following South Carolina's lead, extended nonimportation at the last moment for two additional months. This development forced Barclay's hand, and he decided to seize the rice. Already, several British ships had inched their way toward Savannah, congregating in the river channel about two miles below the city where the Whigs partially obstructed passage with a sunken hulk. For several days, British ships lingered and drew sporadic fire from small arms and a little battery overlooking the river, but to little effect. Although the British did not return fire, on March 2, a portion of the fleet, including the *Hinchinbrook*, the *St. John*, and some other vessels, with Barclay and several hundred soldiers on board, finally sailed away from the sunken vessel toward Hutchinson Island. As darkness fell, they disappeared behind the island into a small channel called the North River.[30]

Although Elbert's precise location in Savannah between March 1 and March 3 is unknown, the escalating crisis showed just how much he would have to sacrifice for his decision to become a Revolutionary when the Council of Safety held another emergency meeting. Believing that Savannah was under imminent threat of an invasion, it passed a resolution stating that all of the homes and businesses in the city belonging to the "friends of America" be appraised. Should the British attack, the plan was to set the city and vessels ablaze in a "noble conflagration" and deprive the British of their prize. As a leading Whig, commander, and former member of the council, Elbert supported the resolution. "There was not one dissenting voice," claimed McCall.[31] Elbert's endorsement of the council's scorch-and-burn approach showed how deeply personal the conflict had become for him, and he laid everything he had on the altar of liberty. Not only was his city in jeopardy and his wife and children refugees, but there was now a real possibility that his home and businesses would be reduced to ash heaps.

The personal nature of the revolution to Elbert again became

---

[30] K. Coleman, *American Revolution in Georgia*, 69. See also Jackson, "Battle of the Riceboats," 237.

[31] C. C. Jones Jr., *History of Georgia*, 2:223–25; McCall, *History of Georgia*, 2:68.

apparent when the British ships disappeared behind Hutchinson Island. If their intention was to round the island and land troops across from it just north of the city, Rae's Hall would be in jeopardy. To ward off this threat and foil "their scheme upon the town," McIntosh had three four-pounder cannon carried up to the former village of Yamacraw accompanied by militia commanded by Habersham, who hastily threw up entrenchments.[32] Yamacraw was on land once owned by John Rae. This meant that the possible bridgehead for the British invasion was on family land associated with Elbert. Since Elizabeth was also probably at nearby Rae's Hall, Elbert must have rushed to Yamacraw in great haste to ensure the safety of his family. He was not the only person concerned about Rae's Hall. Habersham, too, had a personal stake in defending the mansion since he would soon wed Isabella Rae, Elizabeth's sister, who was likely at Rae's Hall, as well.

Unknown to McIntosh or any other Whigs, attacking the town was never Barclay's goal since he was only after the rice. Early on the morning of March 3, about two hundred British soldiers secretly landed on the back of Hutchinson Island with orders to march across the marshy ground and secure the rice boats. Barclay's plan was to come around on the upper side of the island with his ships and take control of the vessels. The North River, with its shallows, mud banks, sandbars, and other obstructions, was not part of the major river channel, and navigating it was a challenge. Twice, the *Hinchinbrook* ran aground, once on a sandbar across from Rae's Hall, where it remained until the tide shifted around 4:00 in the afternoon. During this time, wrote McIntosh, Habersham's "little battery of three guns began to play upon them, which they returned, and was continued very smartly with ball, langrage, and small-arms, from both sides for several hours."[33] Those at Rae's Hall surely heard the report of weapons and probably witnessed some of the action.

Having captured the rice boats, British soldiers on Hutchinson Island waited for the larger ships to come up, secure the vessels, and take them back around the North River behind the island and down to Tybee. As the British ships moved closer to the rice boats, they came under a hail of fire from American arms and Habersham's battery. At this moment, Captain Bowen and some militia burned the British out by setting two ships

---

[32] Lachlan McIntosh to George Washington, March 8, 1776, in PLM, pt. 1, 151; J. M. Johnson, *Militiamen, Rangers, and Redcoats*, 148.

[33] Lachlan McIntosh to George Washington, March 8, 1776, in PLM, pt. 1, 151; J. M. Johnson, *Militiamen, Rangers, and Redcoats*, 148.

on fire upriver and floating them down into the mass of rice vessels and warships. The first fireboat grounded and never made it to its target, but the second, a sloop, became entangled in the rice boats and two caught fire. While the British failed to take all of the rice boats, they did capture ten, after which they slipped back upriver out of danger. They soon rounded the island where the soldiers once again, out of sight of the Americans, boarded their ships. Apparently, McIntosh was shocked that the British were able to get their ships around Hutchinson Island in the first place. He was unfamiliar with Savannah, he later told Washington, and the British ships worked their way around the island through a "channel never known before."[34] Had McIntosh thought to ask Elbert, he would have learned that the channel not only existed, but that large ships could maneuver through it. Having explored Savannah and its environs for fort locations and defensive positions as a member of the General Assembly years earlier, Elbert was well aware that the North River was navigable by warships if the tide was right. He had an extensive knowledge of the North River and all of its channels, especially since they were directly across from Rae's Hall and the Indian mound where one day he hoped to be buried. Elbert fully expected Barclay's ships to come around Hutchinson Island directly across from Rae's Hall, which is exactly what they did.

The so-called "battle of the riceboats" was over. It was Georgia's first military engagement in the Revolution, and it was only appropriate that Elbert was a participant. Although it took Barclay five days to get his ships and captured prizes back to Tybee, there was little the Whigs could do to stop them without a navy. On March 6, Grant sent McIntosh a letter from the *Hinchinbrook* telling him that they would proceed to Cockspur without offense to the province "if we are not fired upon." Grant's warning had little effect since Elbert's shore batteries continued to harass the British fleet below Savannah, but their impact was minimal. Finally, on March 9, the British ships with their rice boats anchored next to the *Scarborough* and unloaded their captured provisions. As Grant had informed McIntosh three days earlier, the British were "determined to get up to our declarations on coming there [to Savannah]," and they did just that. Waiting on board the *Scarborough* for the expedition to return, a jubilant Wright glowed in the mission's accomplishment. Barclay brought in several merchant ships, he informed Lord Dartmouth, loaded with not only rice, but

---

[34] Lachlan McIntosh to George Washington, March 8, 1776, in PLM, pt. 1, 152; Jackson, "Battle of the Riceboats," 239.

also deerskins. In total, he reported capturing at least fifteen vessels and merchant ships, including 1,600 barrels of rice with little loss to the king's troops other than four wounded. Several Savannah merchants experienced severe economic setbacks due to the British confiscation of their vessels and goods. Thomas Tallemach and James Jones, two Savannah merchants, swore in an affidavit to President Bulloch two months later that they lost two schooners in addition to goods and wares valued at £3,251. Despite these losses, McIntosh, convinced that he had frustrated the British "scheme upon the town," claimed victory. While he was unclear what Barclay intended to do next, he took pride in informing Washington that the British "rather lost than gain'd any reputation, and have done us great Honour by being the Second Province on the Continent which they have attacked and were shamefully foiled." His units also suffered minimum casualties, and he reported to the commander-in-chief only three wounded men, including an Indian. As for the British, he believed they suffered much worse, since "several were seen to fall." Still, the British got away with the rice, he told Washington, "without paying a farthing for it."[35]

For the next few weeks, Barclay's fleet remained anchored at Tybee, even while additional militia arrived from South Carolina under Colonel Stephen Bull to bolster Whig defenses. Wright had reason to believe that General Sir Henry Clinton would send reinforcements from North Carolina, but he was grievously disappointed to learn that the British commander was engaged in military operations of his own and was unable to provide any assistance. Feeling that all was lost, Wright finally abandoned Georgia on March 31 and sailed away on the *Scarborough* with the rest of Barclay's fleet except the *Raven* and the *Cherokee*, which remained at Tybee. Wright's departure to London ended royal government in Georgia and placed the Whigs in absolute control of the colony.[36]

With the immediate crisis over, the Whigs could not relax their guard because of the continued presence of enemy ships, the general uncertainty

---

[35] Sir James Wright to Lord Dartmouth, March 10, 1776, in LSJW, 233–34; Lachlan McIntosh to George Washington, March 8, 1776, in PLM, pt. 1, 152; James Grant to Lachlan McIntosh, March 6, 1776, in Lachlan McIntosh Papers, Rubenstein Rare Book and Manuscript Library; "Affidavit of Thomas Tallemach and James Jones, May 11, 1776," in box 2, folder 1776–1779, Edward Telfair Papers, Rubenstein Rare Book and Manuscript Library; J. M. Johnson, *Militiamen, Rangers, and Redcoats*, 152–53.

[36] Sir James Wright to Secretary Lord Germain, April 26, 1776, in LSJW, 243; K. Coleman, "Georgia in the American Revolution, 1775–1782," 70. J. M. Johnson claimed that Bull's reinforcements numbered 289 militiamen (*Militiamen, Rangers, and Redcoats*, 153–54).

about British plans, and the state of open warfare on the southern border. While additional recruits in the Continental Battalion had increased its strength to 236 men, McIntosh claimed that barely one hundred were fit for duty. The remaining militia were dispersed throughout Georgia's western and southern frontier and along the seacoast, with others remaining in Savannah as a precaution. With the collapse of royal authority, it was essential for Georgians to establish a new government in its place with a temporary constitution, which they accomplished on April 15. Known as the Rules and Regulations of 1776, the document, in thirteen paragraphs, laid out a broad outline for government and the machinery to make it function. Under it, the General Assembly, on May 1, chose Bulloch for a one-year term as Georgia's first "president and commander-in-chief." Of particular interest to Elbert was the seventh regulation, forbidding anyone holding a civil or military place of profit to be eligible as a member of the Congress or of the Council of Safety. For Elbert, the point was moot since his military obligations made it impossible for him to attend the proceedings of either body. According to McIntosh, in the aftermath of the rice boats episode, Elbert busied himself drilling soldiers. "The officers who are not recruiting," he wrote, "employ all their time in Training themselves & the Battalion on which Spectators are pleased to pay high compliments for the proficiency they have already made, and appearance of the men." Since Elbert was not out recruiting and instead with parts of the battalion and the militia in Savannah, his primary occupation at the time was training men and acquiring weapons. On May 2, the council approved his application for "arms, bayonets and gun locks," which the battalion desperately needed. Additionally, Elbert constantly sought funding for the battalion from the council. He authorized Habersham's request for £900 sterling on May 23, which it granted. One month later, on June 25, he signed a receipt acknowledging the transaction of an additional £50 for the battalion drawn from the public trust.[37]

Earlier in February, while Savannah was embroiled in its struggle with Barclay, the Continental Congress created a Southern Military Department to coordinate the revolution in the Carolinas, Virginia, and Georgia. Congress sent General Charles Lee, a former British commander

---

[37] Lachlan McIntosh to George Washington, April 28, 1776, in PLM, pt. 1, 153. For Elbert's request for arms, see Council of Safety Minutes, May 2, 1776, in PCS, 48. For Habersham, see Council of Safety Minutes, May 29, 1776, 57, and June 25, 1776, 66; C. C. Jones Jr., *History of Georgia*, 2:220, 231; K. Coleman, *American Revolution in Georgia*, 76–78.

before the war and now one of Washington's best officers, to Charleston to head the new department. A distinguished veteran of the Seven Years' War, Lee was a man highly qualified to lead armies. In June 1775, while still holding rank in the British military, he confirmed his allegiance to the colonies and emerged as a potential commander of the Continental Army, until Congress finally settled on Washington. Lee believed he was more qualified and took the snub personally. Although his large and bruised ego often caused him to clash with Washington, the commander-in-chief recognized his value to the American cause. Later that year, Washington admitted that Lee was the "first Officer in Military knowledge and experience we have in the whole Army."[38]

Soon after coming to Charleston, Lee received a letter from Elbert, whom he had never met. "I congratulate your Excelly. on y[your] arrival in South Carolina," began the communication. Elbert was obviously acquainted with Lee's fine reputation and was "happy" to hear about the appointment of a "Gentleman of your Character [and] abilities to the Chief Military Command in the…Colony of Georgia." Since McIntosh was away mounting a defense on the southern frontier, Elbert felt duty-bound to brief Lee about Georgia's military situation. The colony had a Continental battalion, he told the new commander, and its soldiers were highly qualified. Highlighting his own obsession for drilling soldiers, Elbert proudly admitted that the few officers and men he had "take Disciplin very fast." What they really needed, he said, was proper arms and clothing "to make them appear formidable." The appearance of a military unit was of paramount importance to Elbert, just as it had been back in 1773 when he insisted on impressive uniforms for his grenadiers. Uniforms were important, but they mattered little without troops to wear them, even though recruiters were out scrambling to enlist soldiers. Elbert also relayed recent intelligence from an escaped officer in St. Augustine saying that at least 1,000 enemy troops were in Florida and poised to strike at Georgia with their Indian allies. A great fear in the colony, wrote Elbert, was that the "Savages…are inclin'd [to use] the Hatchet against us & should that [happen] this Province…would be reduced to the greatest [destruction] Imaginable."[39] Elbert's letter was one of Lee's earliest indications that Georgia's perilous situation required immediate attention.

---

[38] Papas, *Renegade Revolutionary*, 5; Mazzagetti, *Charles Lee*, 79–80.
[39] Samuel Elbert to Charles Lee, May 14, 1776, in PLM, pt. 1, 155.

A few days after writing his letter, Elbert attended the wedding of Habersham and Isabella Rae, the daughter of Elbert's deceased father-in-law, John Rae. It is inconceivable that he was not there since Habersham was his best friend and Isabella was Elizabeth's sister. The wedding took place on May 19 at Belmont plantation near Savannah, formerly owned by Habersham's father. The marriage further cemented the close ties between Elbert and the Habersham brothers.

Despite the wedding's festive atmosphere, Elbert and Habersham were soon back with their battalion. The sordid condition of Elbert's soldiers weighed heavily upon his mind. On May 28, he again wrote Lee, urging him to provide sufficient arms and supplies to his men. Even though his force was small, the officers and soldiers he commanded were exceptional and would cover "themselves with Honour, whenever put to Try[al]." It was an unfortunate "Pity…that they are badly arm'd" and lacked proper "camp equipage." Even so, Elbert assured Lee that his men were some of the finest he would ever have at his disposal in the South. The soldiers were so hearty "in the glorious [cause of] their Country," he explained, that they would "cheerfully" take the field when called upon, even though they had nothing covering their bodies except "the canopy of heaven." Elbert then relayed intelligence showing the dire situation on Georgia's southern border. The gathering enemy around St. Augustine was a constant source of danger to the colony's southern parishes, especially since they raided at will across the border, taking fresh provisions and cattle from the citizens. To counter the threat, Elbert suggested that Lee quickly send an additional force to protect the colony from the incursions of the British and "Savages" who accompanied them. Elbert's concerns were no exaggeration. Even Bulloch and the council were convinced that the British were planning an invasion from St. Augustine. On June 25, Georgia's president directed Elbert to order in "all the out detachments of the Battalion" and to "march [them] without loss of time to headquarters at Savannah." The militia, likewise, were ordered to be in a full state of readiness.[40] Despite widespread fears of impending disaster, the dreaded invasion never materialized, at least not in 1776, although the border situation remained in turmoil.

---

[40] Ibid., May 28, 1776, 156; Council of Safety Minutes, June 25, 1776, in PCS, 66.

On July 5, the council sent McIntosh, John Houstoun, and Jonathan Bryan as a delegation to confer with Lee in Charleston about Georgia's situation. Having just thwarted a major British naval effort to take Charleston, Lee was riding a crest wave of popularity. With the British threat to South Carolina temporarily checked, the general felt more at liberty to concentrate on Georgia's southern frontier. The meeting was cordial and much of the discussion concerned the Florida threat. One of the remedies suggested was the addition of more battalions to defend the province. "In our opinion," they informed Lee, "less than six battalions will not answer the purpose." Impressed by the delegation's arguments, Lee hastily agreed with the necessity of a southern campaign and authorized a late summer expedition to crush St. Augustine.[41] The complications and difficulties associated with an impromptu Florida campaign soon caused Lee to second-guess himself after the meeting, but by then, Georgia's Whigs were fully committed to the effort.

The meeting between Lee and Georgia's delegation directly affected Elbert. During the summer and at Lee's urging, Congress authorized two additional Georgia battalions at the cost of $60,000. It was much less than what Georgia's leaders desired. Since Georgia lacked a pool of available men to fill the ranks, Congress requested Virginia and North Carolina to allow recruitment in their states. It also ordered the construction of four row galleys to protect Georgia's coast in addition to two artillery companies of fifty men each to garrison the forts in Savannah and Sunbury further to the south. Although the new units existed only on paper, Elbert was selected to command the 2nd Battalion of Georgia's Continental Line. His new appointment came with a promotion to colonel on September 16.[42] By September, Elbert's leadership role in Georgia's military consisted of two separate ranks. As a colonel of the militia, he exercised first command over that force and as a colonel in the Continental Army, he stood second in command behind McIntosh over Georgia's Continentals.

Elbert, McIntosh, and many of the 1st Battalion were present in Savannah on August 10 when a messenger from Philadelphia arrived with a

---

[41] Council of Safety Minutes, July 5, 1776, in PCS, 70–74; C. C. Jones Jr., *History of Georgia*, 2:248.

[42] G. Smith, *History of the Georgia Militia*, 1:285; C. C. Jones Jr., *History of Georgia*, 2:251. White, *Historical Collections of Georgia*, 215, wrote that Elbert was promoted to colonel in September. At this same time, the 4th Georgia Battalion was authorized by the Continental Congress. McIntosh was also promoted to brigadier-general. For Lee's role, see Searcy, *Georgia-Florida Contest*, 52–53.

copy of the Declaration of Independence, signed about five weeks earlier. Bulloch had the document publicly read several times during the day at different locations. Elbert was probably present for at least two of the readings. His grenadiers and the light infantry companies in Savannah formed up and, despite a scarcity of powder, fired a salute during a reading on the public square. A subsequent reading occurred at Tondee's Tavern in the presence of the grenadiers and the 1st Battalion. When the reading was finished, McIntosh ordered a thirteen-gun salute from the field artillery, followed by another from the muskets. A final reading occurred at the Trustee Garden to a large crowd, after which a battery of siege guns nearby bellowed honorary volleys to salute American independence.[43]

While Georgians were celebrating their first independence day, Lee was pulling together an army for his Florida campaign. He left Charleston during the first week of August with a force estimated at 1,500 soldiers consisting of Virginia and North Carolina Continentals, parts of the 1st, 2nd, and 3rd South Carolina Battalions, and thirty men from a South Carolina artillery unit. With them was General Robert Howe from North Carolina, whom Congress had appointed brigadier general to assist Lee in the Southern Department. Convinced that invading Florida would solve all of their problems, Georgians were ecstatic when they heard that Lee's Continentals were on the way. The scene was somewhat comical since British ships still prowled at will off Tybee, even as Lee's makeshift army gathered a few miles upriver for an expedition in the opposite direction. The continued presence of British ships at Savannah only underscored Georgia's weak and exposed position. As late as July 26, McIntosh reported to Lee that three British ships, including the *Cherokee* and the *Raven*, remained anchored below Savannah. An informant told him that he saw another, estimated to be a fifty-gun warship, "sailing over our Barr into the River" while five others were "under Sail out side [Tybee] which fir'd several Gu[ns] and are probably in by this time." Seemingly besieged on all sides, Georgia's leaders, including Bulloch, were willing to believe—and act on—almost anything they heard. The rumors prompted Georgia's executive to fire off a letter to Lee, who had not yet left Charleston, warning him of another British attempt to reduce Savannah with their navy. Only after sending the letter did Bulloch learn the reports were false. Following with a second letter, the president apologized for misstating the facts. "I gave you…information respecting the Ships of War appearing off

---

[43] C. C. Jones Jr., *History of Georgia*, 2:243–44.

our Coast," he informed the general, but "from the Examination of sundry Persons since, I find we have nothing to apprehend from this invincible armada, & that they are not as yet at Cockspur."[44]

When Lee arrived in Savannah, he met with Bulloch and the council. During his meeting, he openly questioned the wisdom of a Florida campaign that he recently encouraged. Instead of invading Florida, Lee proposed a more tangible goal, the creation of a strong defensive perimeter along the Altamaha River. The council would not be deterred. It was convinced that "an irruption into the Province of East Florida will be attended with the most salutary consequences to this Province." Unfazed by Lee's arguments, the council blazed ahead with plans for an attack. Bulloch informed him that the invasion must happen to protect the citizens he swore to uphold. "We are happy in having your Excellency's Presence among us," he wrote, but the state's leaders were all "answerable for our Conduct to the People." As such, they were "obliged in all our proceedings to conduct ourselves in such [a] manner, as to justify our Conduct to them, as guardians of their rights and Privileges, for which our fellow Citizens...are daily bleeding." Frustrated, Lee later confided that the "people here are if possible more harum skarum than their sister colony. They will propose anything, and after they have propos'd it, discover that they are incapable of performing the least....I should not be surpris'd if they were to propose mounting a body of Mermaids on Alligators."[45]

Lee's heart was not in the Florida campaign he helped to instigate. He remained in Savannah for a few more days as Georgia's leaders scrambled to gather supplies, transports, and other items for the undertaking. Just before the army left Savannah for Florida, he held a grand review on August 19 of all the Continental troops in the city, including Georgia's 1st Battalion and the militia. Elbert was present with his men for the review. The battalion, going through its drills and performances, particularly impressed Lee, who remarked that it was equal, if not superior, to any other

---

[44] Archibald Bulloch to Charles Lee, July 26, 1776, Archibald Bulloch Papers, MS103, folder 103, item 1, Georgia Historical Society; Lachlan McIntosh to George Washington, July 25 and July 26, 1776, in PLM, pt. 1, 158–59; Searcy, *Georgia-Florida Contest*, 54–55.

[45] Council of Safety Minutes, August 19, 1776, in PCS, 92–94. For Bulloch's comments, see Archibald Bulloch to Charles Lee, August 23, 1776, MS 0103, folder 103, item 1, Archibald Bulloch Papers, Georgia Historical Society; Jackson, *Lachlan McIntosh*, 44–45.

Continental Line in the United States. The compliment was a great honor to Elbert and a reflection of his devotion to the battalion since he was the person most responsible for disciplining and training the soldiers.[46]

Although Elbert surely desired to participate in the campaign, threats from the British navy kept him confined to Savannah. It was just as well. Plagued by poor planning, technical difficulties, a lack of food and medicine, an inability to coordinate movements, dissension among the commanders, and the oppressive heat and humidity, Lee's Florida invasion fell apart as quickly as it materialized. It never even got close to St. Augustine. The main body only made it as far south as Sunbury before Lee terminated the invasion in mid-September. By then, Congress brought a merciful end to Lee's miseries in Georgia and recalled him back to the northern theater of war.[47] There was a lesson embedded in Lee's fiasco for Georgia's Whigs to learn, which was to fully prepare and plan for any future campaigns into the remote wilds of Florida. They never learned the lesson.

On September 16, as the Florida invasion fell apart, Elbert received word in Savannah of his promotion to colonel over the 2nd Battalion. At the same time, the Continental Congress made McIntosh a brigadier general over Georgia's Continental Line. Fresh from returning to Georgia after signing the Declaration, Gwinnett, who felt he should have gotten the appointment instead, was infuriated by the news of McIntosh's promotion.[48] This development represented the opening salvo of a bitter feud between McIntosh and Gwinnett, which only intensified in the coming months and, ultimately, produced unfortunate consequences.

When Elbert assumed his duties as a colonel in the Continental Army, he began keeping an order book where he meticulously recorded, for the next two years, written commands, letters, returns, movements, and other information pertinent to his troops. It was not surprising that on the first page, he listed all the drum signals used to maneuver soldiers. For example, striking the snare with a single stroke and a flam signaled a unit to face right. Two single strokes followed by a flam would cause the soldiers to face left. There were drum stroke commands for wheeling units, causing them to about face, charging bayonets, and even forming the battalion. Since his earlier days with the grenadiers, Elbert fascinated himself with military drummers and fifers. To him, they were indispensable, like

---

[46] Charlton, "Sketch of the Life of General Elbert," 2.
[47] Searcy, *Georgia-Florida Contest*, 56–61.
[48] Jackson, *Lachlan McIntosh*, 52.

the uniforms he always coveted for his men. Collectively, both made his fighting force appear professional and, as he indicated to Lee earlier, "formidable." He was not alone; drummers and fifers were vital elements in eighteenth-century armies. Elbert apparently knew what made a quality drum and wanted the best available for his men. In the order book's first letter on October 2, he instructed Lieutenant Colonel John Stirk and Major Seth John Cuthburt, his new field officers who were headed to Virginia to recruit men for the 2nd Battalion, to find excellent musicians and instruments. "Do what you can to get good drummers and fifers," he advised. "At any rate, buy some good drums and as none are to be had here [and] you may have [them] marked 1 to 8 with battalion upon them, but no more paint—it spoils the sound of a Drum."[49]

Elbert wanted Stirk and Cuthburt to recruit, as "soon as possible," many "brave fellows" who would be "the Salvation of their Country." He offered a bounty of seventy dollars to attract soldiers, as well as the promise of one hundred acres, although new recruits were required to pay for their own clothing. Elbert was also concerned about instilling discipline in his raw soldiers. "Once the men begin to assemble," he advised, "one of you must be constantly with them and introduce subordination as soon as possible but not with so much severity at first." One day after writing this letter, Elbert learned that his salary as a colonel was seventy-five dollars per month. He was also promised a new uniform annually, two linen hunting shirts, two pairs of overalls, a waistcoat, two pair of hose, a pair of breeches, a hat, two shirts, and two pair of shoes.[50]

Although was not the scene of major battles, such as those Washington fought in New York in the summer and fall and in Trenton, New Jersey, on Christmas Day, the "Spirit of '76" was alive and well in Georgia. The Whigs had much to celebrate despite Lee's fiasco. They had toppled royal government and installed a new one in its place with Bulloch as its first president under a temporary constitution called the Rules and Regulations of 1776. Additionally, the colony could boast four Continental battalions (the 4th Georgia Battalion was authorized in September) although three of them had no recruits at all. In December, McIntosh reported 538 men in the 1st Battalion, dispersed on guard duty across the state, including deserters, and two artillery companies. There was also a Continental

---

[49] Samuel Elbert to John Stirk and John Cuthbert, October 2, 1776, OBSE, 6. The order book's last entry was on November 11, 1778.

[50] Ibid., 7.

horse regiment consisting of three hundred undisciplined soldiers patrolling the frontier.[51] These were paltry numbers compared to the nearly three thousand combined soldiers that all of the units would have if they were full.

In the midst of all of this stood Samuel Elbert. In the beginning of 1776, he was still orchestrating the Revolution from his positions of authority in the Council of Safety and the Provincial Congress. In that capacity, he played a significant role in bringing down Wright's government while simultaneously rising in military rank to become the head commander of the militia in his state. Between January and March, he emerged as an instrumental military figure when the British navy threatened his city. Elbert courageously participated in the effort to protect Savannah and led the way in mounting an honorable defense against a powerful and superior foe. Further honors came when he was elevated to the rank of colonel and given command of Georgia's 2nd Battalion. Elbert's achievements did not come without a price. He risked life and limb as he stood up against his adversaries, even as his family became temporary refugees while his home and business faced a potential patriotic inferno. As the year ended, Elbert enjoyed the reputation of a man of honor firmly committed to the cause of liberty. He was a promising military commander who could effectively lead and discipline men. His bravery was never in question, but much was still unknown about Elbert, especially since he was untried in battle. All of that was about to change as events showed his true mettle as a commander.

---

[51] Searcy, *Georgia-Florida Contest*, 64.

Chapter 7

"For God's Sake Let Me Hear from You": Samuel Elbert and the Second Florida Campaign, 1777

During 1776, Samuel Elbert's military activities remained concentrated around Savannah. That situation changed in 1777 when threats along Georgia's borders called for him to mount a defense against enemies to the south and west. During the spring, he participated in a second Florida invasion, and, due to circumstances beyond his control, found himself leading a campaign for the first time. In the summer, he went to the western frontier to stabilize the region and ensure Indian neutrality. Both experiences placed Elbert in situations that demonstrated his decision-making abilities and skills as an independent commander even as they tested his resolve and determination in the face of countless obstacles.

Early in 1777, the ongoing crisis along Georgia's southern border drew Elbert's attention toward a defense of that sector. Frequent and unchallenged raids across the St. Marys River by Indians and Loyalists continued, and it was incumbent upon Georgians to formulate a strategy to fortify and protect the vulnerable southern parishes. The burden fell upon Lachlan McIntosh, whose proposed plan was defensive in nature and essentially the same that Charles Lee suggested to the Council of Safety earlier, which was to create a series of outposts along the southern border anchored on the Altamaha River and supplied by its ports. Patrolling scouts linked communications between the forts so if the enemy attacked one, reinforcements from another could come to its defense.[1]

The scheme was far from perfect. There were hardly any naval vessels available to guard the Altamaha, and, although Congress authorized the creation of four row galleys, they were not ready. The forts were isolated,

---

[1] Jackson, *Lachlan McIntosh*, 46.

separated by great distances, and barely garrisoned. Soldiers inside suffered from boredom, poor living conditions, sickness, a want of supplies, and a lack of payment for their service. These problems, in turn, contributed to a decline in morale, frequent insubordination, and desertion. There was also the problem of establishing communication between the outposts and McIntosh's headquarters in Savannah, where troops under Elbert's command continued to drill. Should any situation require reinforcements, McIntosh reasoned that he could send them from Savannah, but given the time it took to relay messages, organize troops, and shuffle them to the frontier, it would be days before their arrival.[2] These conditions made it highly probable that key points in the defensive perimeter would fall if attacked. In defense of McIntosh, there was little else he could do given his limited resources and the almost insurmountable task of defending an entire southern border while hoping for the best outcome. The whole situation harked back to Lee's earlier observation that Georgians were mounting "mermaids on alligators" by refusing to temper lofty expectations with reality.

During fall 1776, McIntosh funneled militia, companies of the 1st Georgia Battalion, and part of his mounted troops to the south with instructions to repair forts, build new ones, and coordinate opportunistic raids into Florida. Four major posts stood out in McIntosh's defensive line, and three were located along the Altamaha. Chief among them was Fort Barrington, renamed Fort Howe by the end of 1776 in honor of Brigadier General Robert Howe, who commanded the Southern Military Department after Lee's removal. Fort Howe was about ten miles from McIntosh's home of Darien at the river's mouth. Constructed just before the Seven Years' War, it occupied a low bluff overlooking a ferry crossing along the only road from Savannah, but in 1777, the structure was in a pitiful condition. At the mouth of the Altamaha a second fort protected Darien from the sea. McIntosh also constructed a third defensive post at Beard's Bluff, a high rise along the Altamaha's north bank about forty miles above Fort Howe. An Indian trail connected Beard's Bluff to Fort Howe. The colonel built a fourth outpost some thirty miles below Fort Howe on the north side of the Satilla River, again on the same road linking Fort Howe to Savannah. Christened Fort McIntosh, it contained a small stockade about

---

[2] The galleys were the *Congress*, *Lee*, *Washington*, and *Bulloch*. They were all more than likely lateen-rigged with twenty oars and armed with small guns. Georgia acquired eight row galleys and two sloops at the same time. See Fraser, *Savannah in the Old South*, 119.

one hundred feet square, with a bastion in each corner and a blockhouse in the middle serving as a barracks and magazine. Early in 1777, it was commanded by Captain Richard Winn from South Carolina and manned by forty men from the 3rd South Carolina Regiment and twenty troops from Georgia's 1st Battalion. Winn was no newcomer to warfare. By the time he came to Georgia, he had already distinguished himself during the failed British naval attack on Charleston in summer 1776.[3]

Georgia's limited forces were thinly scattered between these forts, smaller outposts, and other garrisons, in addition to those protecting the backcountry settlements, and were in no position to thwart a determined effort by the enemy from any direction. To make matters worse, as of December 17, not a single new recruit for Elbert's 2nd Battalion or even the 3rd Battalion had appeared in Savannah. The situation caused McIntosh to fire off a letter to George Walton, Lyman Hall, and Nathan Brunson, Georgia's delegates in the Continental Congress, informing them of the state's woeful predicament. The overall condition of Georgia's ordinances and military stores, he reported, was "very Scant" while most of the cannon were "not mounted & in bad order." Nor was there "a Single quire of Cartridge paper" for the soldiers to use with their weapons, much less lead balls. The fortifications were in sad shape, and, although two galleys had been constructed and launched, they were still unfitted. "Surely," he remarked in closing, "the Congress will See the necessity of making every Effort to Secure this frontier State, exposed to Danger & daily in Expectation of being attacked." Highlighting Georgia's empty coffers, on December 27 he lamented to Howe that "our Convention have voted but the trifling sum of £50 for Fort Howe…and nothing for the Lower Fort at the 1st Landing of the Altamaha, which I think the 2 most Important posts in this State."[4] Faced with a myriad of obstacles, Georgians confronted a hopeless situation.

---

[3] Lachlan McIntosh to Robert Howe, December 13, 1776, in Hawes, ed., "Papers of Lachlan McIntosh, 1774–1799. Part II," 255 (hereafter cited as PLM, pt. 2); Cashin, *William Bartram and the American Revolution*, 39; Lenz, *Longstreet Highroad Guide*, 201; McCall, *History of Georgia*, 2:97–98; C. C. Jones Jr., *History of Georgia*, 2:260.

[4] Lachlan McIntosh to George Walton, Lyman Hall, and Nathan Brunson, December 17, 1776, and Lachlan McIntosh to Robert Howe, December 27, 1776, both in PLM, pt. 2, 256–57; 259–60. A quire was a collection of leaves of paper for wadding, generally in four.

Without adequate men and horse troop on the frontier, McIntosh's defenses were weak and exposed. In late December 1776, Indians overtook Lieutenant Jerimiah Bugg and one of his companies of light horse with twenty-seven men at Beard's Bluff. Bugg's troops hardly put up a fight and, after it was over, fled the post. According to McIntosh, the men deserted not only out of fear but also because they were "seven Months Inlisted, & never received any pay." The skirmish at Beard's Bluff only underscored McIntosh's belief in a looming Indian uprising. Without paid soldiers to defend the state, Georgia was lost to the enemy. "I am afraid the Indians in General are determined upon a War, which we are unprepared for," he informed Howe. To make matters worse, as of January 7, 1777, Elbert's 2nd Battalion, as well as the 3rd, still had no men. McIntosh could not assure Howe that new recruits were even on the way.[5]

The affair at Beard's Bluff convinced McIntosh of something else. He needed a reliable commander to oversee border operations and instill confidence and discipline in the men. He had the perfect person in mind. As he informed Howe, he intended to send Elbert to take control on the Altamaha. Along with Elbert, he was also sending forty soldiers from the 1st Battalion under the command of Captain Chesley Bostwick to reoccupy Beard's Bluff. Elbert received notification of his orders on January 8. There could be little doubt that McIntosh had the utmost assurance in Elbert's qualifications for the assignment. "I flatter myself [that] your taking the Command [on the Altamaha] will bring things into some order there," he informed the colonel. "I am sure it [will] make me much easier & happier than I have been for some [time]." One of the concerns for McIntosh, among many, was that the men needed discipline, particularly the unruly and insubordinate horse regiment, and he believed Elbert had the abilities to instill it "on the Spot." Increased Indian raids also concerned McIntosh. If they crossed the Altamaha, he instructed Elbert to use his "utmost exertion to pursue them & prevent their entering or coming near the Settlements." The inhabitants were going to tax him with requests to protect their property, he warned, but the overall goal was "the security of the whole collection." Toward that end, Elbert should do his best to protect plantations and cattle and make regular visit to the forts on the Altamaha and Satilla. "I only mean upon the whole to give you a General Idea of my plan," suggested McIntosh, "& leave [the rest] to prosecute…as you think best." At any rate, McIntosh expected a continuous

---

[5] Lachlan McIntosh to Robert Howe, January 7, 1777, in PLM, pt. 2, 263–64.

stream of intelligence from Elbert "as fully & frequent[ly] as possible." He concluded by wishing him "every Success" on the mission.[6]

A new level of order became evident with Elbert's arrival at Fort Howe, yet even his presence could not eliminate the ever-present danger posed by lurking armies of Indians and Loyalists. Immersed in his duties, the colonel neglected to establish contact with McIntosh. About a week after his arrival, he received a letter from the general who was "very anxious to hear" a report from the Altamaha. McIntosh wanted to send more troops to Elbert, he said, but the lack of money to pay them was the greatest hindrance in recruiting good soldiers and keeping them from deserting. He instructed Elbert to continue strengthening Fort Howe's defenses and to build proper magazines in all of the other posts to store provisions. Desiring a full report, McIntosh also wanted Elbert to send "a person…with a full Acct. of your proceedings since you went from here." Elbert could determine the duration of his stay at Fort Howe. "Your future plans & how long you think your presence will be necessary to the So. Ward,…I leave…to you," wrote the general. Exactly how long Elbert remained at Fort Howe is uncertain. He was gone by February 17 when a combined army of British regulars, Thomas Brown's Loyalists, and Indians attacked Fort McIntosh on the Satilla.[7]

The forts that Elbert visited not only protected the settlements above the Altamaha. They also functioned as bases for raids into East Florida to gather cattle and rice. The raids, in turn, inflicted terror on St. Augustine's inhabitants and caused the city's population to swell with panicked residents fleeing their outlying farms and plantations to seek protection. The population surge put additional demands on an already limited food supply, and by early 1777 St. Augustine was facing famine. The British response was to send regulars, Brown's King's Rangers, and a host of Indian warriors on counterraids into Georgia. The free-roaming herds on Georgia's frontier were prime targets for many raids, which sometimes

---

[6] Ibid., 264, and Lachlan McIntosh to Samuel Elbert, January 8, 1777, 266–67. Concerning the lack of discipline in the horse regiment, see Lachlan McIntosh to Lyman Hall, Nathan Brownson, and George Walton, January 23, 1777, in Hawes, ed., "Papers of Lachlan McIntosh, 1774–1799. Part III," 357–58 (hereafter cited as PLM, pt. 3). Bostwick was one of the men who assaulted Thomas Brown in Augusta during August 1775. During the altercation, Brown shot him with a pistol. See Searcy, *Georgia-Florida Contest*, 14.

[7] Lachlan McIntosh to Samuel Elbert, January 17, 1777, in PLM, pt. 3, 356–57; McCall, *History of Georgia*, 2:94. According to K. Coleman, one of the greatest complaints of the Continental troops in Georgia at this time concerned pay (*American Revolution in Georgia*, 110).

penetrated deep into the state's interior. When Brown was traversing the Georgia frontier in 1776 recruiting Indians, for example, he noticed a herd of six thousand cattle owned by the firm of Rae's, Elbert & Graham ranging in an open cowpen. The Loyalist leader reported his sighting to East Florida's Governor, Patrick Tonyn, and suggested driving the cattle of these "violent partisans" below the St. Marys to feed a starving populace. It is significant that Brown specified Elbert's firm, especially since one of the partners, Thomas Graham, was a leader of the Augusta mob who assaulted him in 1775. As for Elbert, Brown called him "one of the most violent partisans of the Congress." Georgia's wandering herds were vulnerable targets, and in early 1777 Tonyn, largely because of St. Augustine's worsening food crisis, went on the offensive.[8]

Late in January, a foraging party of regulars under the command of Lieutenant Colonel Lewis Fuser consisting of 162 men, 120 rangers under Brown's command, and about 60 Indians, left St. Augustine and set out toward the Satilla. At the time, Elbert was at Fort Howe but, unaware of the British advance, set out on a return trip to Savannah. Near the Satilla, Brown and the Indians separated from Fuser and headed toward Fort McIntosh garrisoned by Winn and his Continentals. On February 17, Brown besieged the fort and a seven-hour battle ensued. Although Winn sent an express for help, none arrived in time to assist the defenders, underscoring the inherent weakness in McIntosh's defensive scheme. On the next day, Fuser arrived, and Winn, outnumbered and out of ammunition, surrendered. Fuser paroled Winn's men, sent them to Fort Howe, and made them promise not take up arms again until exchanged. Before the prisoners left for Fort Howe, Winn insisted that Fuser provide a British escort to protect them from the Indians and vengeful Loyalists, and Fuser agreed. On February 19, Fuser set fire to Fort McIntosh, and the American prisoners began their journey to Fort Howe under a British guard. Hardly had the group gotten underway before the escort violated their agreement and abandoned Winn and his men to their fate. Fearing a sudden ambush, Winn secretly led his unarmed troops through swamps and thickets and avoided surprise Indian attacks until he reached Fort Howe.[9]

---

[8] Thomas Brown to Governor Patrick Tonyn, [February?] 1776, in Davies, ed., *Documents of the American Revolution*, 12:72; Cashin, *King's Ranger*, 42–44; Searcy, *Georgia-Florida Contest*, 35, 83–84.

[9] Searcy, *Georgia-Florida Contest*, 86–88. For Elbert's intelligence, see McCall, *History of Georgia*, 2:97.

The British promise to protect American prisoners from Indians at Fort McIntosh was significant for Elbert. In just a few months, he invoked the terms of Fort McIntosh to a British commander when Indians under his authority captured and massacred many of his men.

The loss of Fort McIntosh was a turning point in Georgia's 1777 border war, and it set in motion a chain of events that placed Elbert in command of a second Florida campaign to capture St. Augustine three months later. News of the incident created pandemonium among Georgia's leaders. It took two days to get dispatches from the Altamaha to McIntosh in Savannah and, given the piecemeal knowledge of facts, they sometimes contained exaggerated and erroneous information. Informing Howe of the disaster, McIntosh proclaimed it was the beginning of a "General Attack upon the State." He then ordered Colonel James Screven, a former member of the Council of Safety and now the commander of Georgia's 3rd Battalion (that still had no recruits), to gather scattered militia and rush them to the Altamaha. In his message to Screven, McIntosh claimed, erroneously, that the fort was taken by "300 regulars & 500 [Indians]." The situation was desperate. "For God's Sake," he implored, "be expeditious to prevent their crossing of the Altamaha, if possible." The Altamaha was the line that the British and Indians could never cross, and he told Colonel Bostwick at Beard's Bluff that he must hold his position "to the last" man. He also ordered Joseph Habersham to march to Fort Howe immediately with parts of the 1st Battalion and, if possible, prevent the enemy from crossing the river and attacking the settlements. Leaving Elbert in charge of Savannah's defenses, McIntosh saddled his horse and hastily rode southward to take personal charge, but he did not remain gone for long. Wounded in a skirmish when he arrived, he was soon back in Savannah recovering from his injury.[10]

These last-minute efforts may have discouraged Fuser from taking Fort Howe. He was already marching in that direction, but after some encounters with militia and Continentals near the Altamaha, he suddenly turned south, followed by Brown's men and the Indians. There could be

---

[10] Lachlan McIntosh to Robert Howe, February 19, 1777, in PLM, pt. 3, 361. See in the same source, Lachlan McIntosh to Colonel Screven, February 19, 1777, 362; Lachlan McIntosh to Chesley Bostwick, February 20, 1777, 362; Lachlan McIntosh to Joseph Habersham, February 20, 1777, 362. For the mention of his wound, see Lachlan McIntosh to Button Gwinnett, April 13, 1777, 366–67. There is great discrepancy in the estimate of soldiers who attacked Fort Howe. C. C. Jones Jr., for example, estimated that Brown commanded seventy Florida Rangers and eighty Indians (*History of Georgia*, 2:261).

no doubt that Fuser's raid was a resounding success. In addition to taking Fort McIntosh and all of its men, weapons, and horses, they also exposed the vulnerability of Georgia's southernmost defenses, all while achieving their primary objective of getting provisions. When they finally arrived at St. Augustine, they had with them two thousand head of cattle and thirty tierces of rice (a cask containing roughly forty-two gallons) confiscated on the Satilla.[11]

The psychological impact of Fuser's raid was perhaps the greatest damage inflicted on the Whigs, and when the gloomy news reached Savannah, it threw them into a panic. Like McIntosh, they believed that the dreaded invasion of Georgia had commenced. They responded on February 22 by taking the extraordinary step of granting President Archibald Bulloch temporary dictatorship powers for one month. On the day Bulloch became dictator, he attended a Council of Safety meeting where Whig fears were evident in the minutes. The council agreed that Fuser's raid had produced a "present alarming situation" in Georgia and now it was "absolutely necessary, that every friend of American liberty should stand forth." The council then ordered most of the state's militia into the field. After that meeting, something else extraordinary happened. Bulloch, after being dictator for just two days, suddenly died. The news jolted Georgia's leaders, especially since he was just forty-seven and presumably in good health. It is possible that his enemies poisoned him, given the mysterious circumstances surrounding his death.[12]

Elbert was surely saddened to hear of Bulloch's demise. As a Conservative Whig, he likely was troubled by the political implications of his passing. Already, the Radical Whigs dominated the assembly, and on February 5, they created the Constitution of 1777 to replace the Rules and Regulations of 1776. Conservative Whigs bristled at the new constitution's democratic tendencies, but the radicals silenced their opposition. The key to the radicals' mandate to govern rested in the unleashing of popular democracy to break down Savannah's chokehold on political power. All males twenty-one years or older could vote for representatives in the assembly if they had at least £10 worth of taxable property. In lieu

---

[11] Searcy, *Georgia-Florida Contest*, 87–88.

[12] PCS, Council Minutes, February 22, 1777, 124–25; C. C. Jones, "Biographical Sketches of the Delegates from Georgia to the Continental Congress," 47, original unpublished manuscript, box 7, Addresses and Writings, Charles C. Jones Papers, Rubenstein Rare Book and Manuscript Library; W. Wilson and McKay, *James D. Bulloch*, 7, for a reference to Bulloch's possible poisoning.

of that, they could still vote if employed as mechanics or in some other skilled trade. Furthermore, if a man could prove he was a Georgia resident for at least six months, he could also vote. As in the Rules of 1776, the governor still served for a one-year term and was commander-in-chief of all military forces in the state. This power would shape the trajectory of Georgia's revolution in just a matter of weeks. Recalling Governor James Wright's earlier abuses of power, the framers made sure that the real authority rested with the General Assembly. Under the new constitution, the governor and his council (appointed by the assembly) were powerless to veto any actions of the legislature. The Radical Whigs also disestablished the Church of England and replaced all of the parishes with Georgia's first eight counties. Overall, much to the horror of conservatives, the Radical Whigs created a government with little check on their power.[13]

On March 4, the assembly appointed Button Gwinnett, already the leader of the council, as temporary president until May, when the Constitution of 1777 went into effect with the election of a new governor. Gwinnett, in his leadership positions, was one of the loudest advocates for another Florida campaign that he sought to lead. The new turn of events set the temporary governor on a collision course with some of his most conservative opponents, including those in the Continental Army, and foremost among them was McIntosh. Gwinnett still seethed over McIntosh's earlier appointment to command Georgia's battalions, and he continued to nurse his resentment as governor. Having taken control of government, he and the radicals sought to purge the army of its conservative leaders, and their first target was McIntosh. They initially went after his brothers, charging William McIntosh with desertion for failing to protect citizens in the southern parishes from enemy raids. Then they intercepted a letter from Governor Tonyn suggesting that a younger brother, George, was colluding with the British. Gwinnett, in his position of authority, charged George with treason and had him arrested and put in irons on March 14. George's supposed dealings with the enemy was particularly galling to Gwinnett, who believed that "Tory friends in this state" were supplying the garrison at St. Augustine with cattle, rice, and corn. McIntosh viewed both attacks as a personal affront to his honor, and, while the charges were all questionable, he knew the goal was to tarnish his reputation and remove

---

[13] K. Coleman, *American Revolution in Georgia*, 80–84; Jackson, *Lachlan McIntosh*, 52–53. The eight counties were Camden, Glynn, Liberty, Chatham (Savannah), Effingham, Burke, Richmond, and Wilkes, created out of the New Purchase ceded lands.

him from command.[14]

The quick succession of events in February—the fall of Fort McIntosh, the new democratic constitution, Bulloch's death and his replacement by Gwinnett, the growing feud between McIntosh and the new governor, and the renewed push to take St. Augustine—all had implications for Elbert. He surely sensed that another Florida campaign beckoned, and there was little time to train the raw recruits of the 2nd Battalion slowly drifting into Savannah. At least some were present on March 15 for a review by General Howe, who was newly arrived in Savannah from Charleston to confer with Georgia's leaders. Elbert's first command to the 2nd Battalion was to parade before Howe, but he could not have expected his recruits to give an impressive performance. He admitted at the time that the regiment was "greatly in need of being well disciplined." To remedy that, Elbert ordered his officers to exercise them "every morning from six to eight o'clock" and then again in the afternoon, placing the most awkward into "squads by themselves, with the most expert Officers to drill them." At four o'clock each afternoon, Elbert reviewed the men's progress during routine parades. The troops were hardly acclimated to the new regime before McIntosh ordered Colonel John Stirk to immediately take fifty soldiers from the 2nd Battalion (perhaps a half or a third of the total present) to Fort Howe to relieve part of the 1st Battalion whose times had expired. Their mission, which was to "guard every part of the Altamaha," was simple but a tall order for such a handful of untrained men. To make their stay more pleasant, Elbert purchased a hogshead of rum (about fifty-seven gallons) for £30.19.6 and sent it along with Stirk to Fort Howe for the men.[15]

On March 22, just before they left, Elbert gave Stirk some final orders highlighting one of his most enduring traits as a commander, which was the care and compassion he felt toward his soldiers. In this instance, he was concerned about the paltry state of their equipment and desired some "means fallen on to carry their Ammunition as the Pouches are not yet arrived." Health concerns related to food, medicine, and living conditions

---

[14] Jackson, *Lachlan McIntosh*, 54–55; E. Coleman, "Letter from Governor Patrick Tonyn of East Florida to Lord George Germain," 289–92; Hall, *Land and Allegiance*, 59.

[15] Samuel Elbert, "Regimental Orders, Second Georgia Battalion," March 15, 1777, in OBSE, 8; Lachlan McIntosh to Lt. Colonel Francis Harris, March 23, 1777, in PLM, pt. 3, 363; Button Gwinnett to John Hancock, president of the Continental Congress, March 28, 1777, in Drewien, *Button Gwinnett*, 300; Account Book, 1769–1788, 3, 27, Samuel Elbert Papers, Rubenstein Rare Book and Manuscript Library.

bothered him as well. Toward that end, two large wagon trains were stocked with "a few Necessary Medicines" in addition to "as much Indian Meal as possible…camp Equipage, [and] Nine tents." Having recently been at Fort Howe, the colonel knew that trying circumstances associated with camp life on Georgia's isolated frontier would test his men's willpower, especially since they were new to the army. He instructed Stirk to keep his men in high spirits. "By all means," advised the new commander, "make them incamp on a dry spot of Ground…and…let no time be lost in teaching the men discipline."[16]

As Elbert drilled the rest of his battalion, Howe conferred with Gwinnett and heard, for the first time, the plans for a second Florida expedition. The general was shocked. From the time he arrived in Savannah on March 8, he and Gwinnett were at odds. On March 4, the day he became temporary governor, Gwinnett and the council authorized a militia and naval force for the undertaking without consulting Howe. As Gwinnett informed John Hancock, president of the Continental Congress, three weeks later, the naval force was "superior (I think) to anything they may meet with on our Coast." Georgia's fleet comprised three sloops of fourteen, ten, and eight guns respectively and two completed galleys, both armed with cannon ranging from four to eighteen pounders.[17] Despite his bellicose boasting, it was no match for the fleet of galleys, schooners, and sloops at Tonyn's disposal for St. Augustine's defense.

Even though Gwinnett was adamant in commencing the campaign, Howe said it was destined to fail, just as Lee's did a few months earlier and for the same reasons. On a practical level, there was simply not enough men, naval ships, supplies, or even planning to ensure the mission's success. While he acknowledged Georgia's defenseless state, he predicted that the successful reduction of St. Augustine required at least seven to eight thousand troops. The proposed force was a utopian dream and more than double what General George Washington commanded in his Northern army at the same time. At any rate, Howe believed defense was the best offense, especially since no one knew exactly how many British troops were in East Florida. Almost a year earlier, passengers on a captured schooner leaving St. Augustine revealed that the city contained at least seven hundred regulars, but that news was outdated and unreliable in early 1777.

---

[16] Samuel Elbert, "After Regimental Orders," March 22, 1777, in OBSE, 11.

[17] Button Gwinnett to John Hancock, President of the Continental Congress, March 28, 1777, in Drewien, *Button Gwinnett*, 299–301.

The estimate also did not include Brown's rangers and other Loyalist units or even the host of Indians flocking to Tonyn and the British. At the time Howe came to Georgia, his best guess based on scattered intelligence was that East Florida contained an aggregate force of around 1,000 soldiers, 120 partisans, and perhaps about 300 Indians. Political infighting among Georgia's Whigs further tempered Howe's commitment to a southern campaign. At times, he seemed thrust into the middle of it, especially concerning the escalating conflict between Gwinnett and McIntosh. Much to Gwinnett's dismay, Howe had nothing but the highest praise for McIntosh, whom he described a few months earlier as an "active, vigilant, and spirited officer." Despite this, Gwinnett went to great lengths to disparage McIntosh and even implied that his loyalty might be in question due to the (trumped-up) charge of Toryism hurled at Mcintosh's younger brother. From Howe's perspective, Georgia's toxic political climate destroyed unity and spelled doom for any invasion. Unfortunately, Howe contributed to the animosity by socializing with Gwinnett's enemies and attending their dances.[18]

Gwinnett desperately badgered Howe to cooperate, but all the general was willing to concede was Colonel Thomas Sumter's 6th South Carolina Regiment, which he sent to occupy the fort at Sunbury, a small port town just below Savannah along Blackbeard Creek flowing into the Atlantic between Ossabaw and St. Catherine's islands. Gwinnett did not help his cause when he informed Howe that the Continentals would be under his authority during the campaign according to the powers delegated to him by the Rules and Regulations of 1776. Thus, the old debate concerning blurred lines of authority between civil and military leaders in Georgia, initially breached in early 1776 when Elbert and others took oaths for commissions in the 1st Battalion, again erupted in the heated arguments between Howe and Gwinnett about a second Florida campaign. While Gwinnett attempted to exercise what he felt was his legal right as president, Howe found the proposition absurd. The whole idea of a St. Augustine invasion perplexed him. He could not understand how "A State which but a few days before had thought itself in [great] Danger as to implore

---

[18] Naisawald, "Major General Robert Howe's Activities," 25–26; Searcy, *Georgia-Florida Contest*, 46; Bennett and Lennon, *Quest for Glory*, 61; Ranlet, "Loyalty in the Revolutionary War," 729; Button Gwinnett to John Hancock, president of the Continental Congress, March 28, 1777, in Drewien, *Button Gwinnett*, 300.

the assistance of this country to save them from instant destruction, could without any addition to their Strength think themselves able to carry on an offensive war against [a foe] so lately dreaded." The whole notion was nothing short of "romantic" in light of the "crude[,] indigested[,] unprepared manner in which it was to be undertaken." Gwinnett was openly frustrated as well. Writing to Hancock a few days later, he expressed his dismay: "Finding the Council had deputed the President of this State," he angrily wrote, "after they could obtain no Assistance to proceed on this Expedition, he [Howe] appeared [unwilling] to concur & assist & rather seemed to obstruct the Attempt." After that, the general abruptly left for Charleston with the rest of the Continental troops, who accompanied him to Georgia. As Gwinnett sarcastically concluded, "He came, he saw, and left us in our low estate."[19] Howe's refusal to endorse the campaign meant that Gwinnett had only the state's militia to carry out his plans unless he could somehow wrest control of Georgia's battalions from McIntosh.

Meanwhile, Elbert worked with his battalion. On March 19, he instructed his tailors to be "constantly at work making Coats" so that the men could have uniforms. Professional soldiers also needed to be well armed. On April 3, he ordered each officer to ensure that every soldier had powder horns. The commander also dealt with complaints by local inhabitants about the behavior of his men concerning their use of private wells and drunkenness. He responded by detailing a party to clean the well in the barrack yard containing "very good" water to use instead. As for alcohol, Elbert condemned the "vile practice of hard drinking" and instructed the confining of drunk soldiers in the guardhouse. Sounding much like James Oglethorpe when summer sickness gripped the young Georgia colony soon after settlement, he claimed that alcohol was "more the cause of Fevers in Savannah than the climate," even though he routinely provided rum to his men. A good deal of his time in March and early April was spent on court-martial trials, where he often showed mercy to his men, perhaps because they were new recruits. Although the offenses and sentences were unspecified, two men received punishment in the presence of the battalion on April 4. A third, John Sack, who also faced a sentence, endured the humiliating experience of a verbal reprimand by the colonel on the parade ground before he was pardoned the crime. Again, on April

---

[19] Robert Howe to (?), May 29, 1777, Robert Howe Papers 1777–1778, Rubenstein Rare Book and Manuscript Library; Button Gwinnett to John Hancock, president of the Continental Congress, March 28, 1777, in Drewien, *Button Gwinnett*, 301; Bennett and Lennon, *Quest for Glory*, 61–62.

9, two men scheduled for discipline before the battalion for unknown reasons were forgiven and released by Elbert.[20]

As Elbert drilled his men, Gwinnett proceeded with his plans to take St. Augustine. He established his headquarters at Sunbury, where he oversaw naval preparations and waited on the militia, but only those from St. John's Parish showed up. It soon became obvious that he would need more help. Although he intended to lead the campaign himself and did not want McIntosh involved, circumstances forced his hand. It must have been particularly galling for Gwinnett to send McIntosh a letter on March 27 asking for the cooperation of the Georgia Line. The request surprised McIntosh. While much talk floated around Savannah for several weeks about the possibility of an expedition, this was his first indication that it was happening. He probed several of his officers about the matter, but no one knew anything. Since Elbert was second-in-command and the highest militia commander in the state, he was surely among the first McIntosh asked, but he too was oblivious. The confusion proved that Gwinnett, in positioning himself to reap glory for the liberation of Florida, had taken great caution to isolate McIntosh. On the following day, McIntosh replied to Gwinnett's request. Although incensed by Gwinnett's marginalization, the general vowed that his soldiers were ready at the "Shortest notice" to aid the president in "any measure that appears to have probability of Success, or tends to promote [the betterment] of this or the United States."[21] It was Gwinnett's belief that he would command the combined army, but the cooperation that McIntosh offered never included a willingness to surrender control of his battalions to a civil authority, especially one led by Gwinnett.

On April 2, McIntosh relayed Gwinnett's request to Howe. "I promised to the utmost of [my power to help], whenever it was necessary," he explained, "but I dont hear that he has [recruited] any Militia yet, nor do I know the particular intention of [the expedition]." By the time McIntosh composed his letter, the nature of Gwinnett's request finally dawned upon him. Since the militia were not turning out as expected, Gwinnett wanted to shift the burden of the campaign to the Continental Army, with himself in charge. McIntosh sensed a trap. If he refused to participate, he would reap blame for the campaign's failure. If he did participate and the

---

[20] Samuel Elbert, "Regimental Orders," OBSE, March 19, 1777, 10, April 3, 1777, 13–14, April 4, 1777, 14, April 9, 1777, 15.

[21] Lachlan McIntosh to Button Gwinnett, March 28, 1777, Lachlan McIntosh Papers, folder 1, Letterbook (1776–1777), MS 526, Georgia Historical Society.

campaign failed, as it surely would, he would stand out as the scapegoat. As McIntosh put it, Gwinnett was looking for a "hole to creep out of [so he could] throw the blame upon the [Military] if nothing was done." Despite his suspicions, he still offered assistance. Most of Elbert's battalion were now in Savannah and ready to march, but the army remained idle. A week passed before he received another letter from Gwinnett wondering why the general was not in Sunbury with his battalions. Apparently, Gwinnett accused McIntosh of delaying with the intent to make the mission fail and discredit the president. "[I] can only inform you *once more* [emphasis added] that I am so far from *retarding* this [campaign], or any other service for the good of the State," shot back the general on April 11. The only reason for the delay was that he was waiting to "hear [from] you." After sending off that response, McIntosh immediately ordered Georgia's two battalions to Sunbury.[22]

The army assembling for the reduction of St. Augustine was half the strength of Lee's forces during the first aborted campaign. Even though the 1st Battalion contained seasoned veterans, they were mostly twelve-month recruits; their enlistments were expiring, and they were down to only two hundred men. On April 13, Elbert's untried 2nd Battalion, with four hundred recruits, arrived in Sunbury. Georgia's finances were so depleted that Elbert personally paid the bounty for some of the men to bolster the strength of the 2nd Battalion. For example, he paid £7.10 bounty money out of his personal account to John Strong and did the same for many other new recruits through 1778. McIntosh could also call on the Light Horse Troop with nearly four hundred mounted soldiers, which comprised independent companies recently attached to the Continental Army, although most were scattered in the backcountry. Their reliability was in question since they were, according to McIntosh, undisciplined and "very badly horsed." Finally, the massive army of militia that Gwinnett promised never materialized, and only about two hundred under the command of Colonel John Baker answered the call. In total, the American invasion force consisted of around eight hundred soldiers, but that number was just on paper. Sickness and other factors reduced the army's strength as it waited more than two weeks before setting out for Florida.[23]

---

[22] Lachlan McIntosh to Robert Howe, April 2, 1777, in PLM, pt. 3, 365, and, in the same source, Lachlan McIntosh to Button Gwinnett, April 11, 1777, 365; "General Orders, by General McIntosh," April 11, 1777, OBSE, 15.

[23] Lachlan McIntosh to George Washington, April 13, 1777, in PLM, pt. 3, 366–97; Account Book, 1769–1788, 3, Samuel Elbert Papers, Rubenstein Rare Book and

Oliver Bowen commanded the naval force assembling in Sunbury. When Congress commissioned the construction of Georgia's four row galleys in late 1776, it also promoted Bowen to commodore. According to Elbert's Order Book, three of the row galleys, the *Congress*, the *Washington*, and the *Lee*, were fit to sail, contrary to Howe's opinion. A schooner, the *Dolphin*, and a sloop, the *Hope*, also joined the small fleet. While the exact number of transports in the flotilla is unknown, Elbert identified at least one, the *Polly*, in his Order Book. Several of the transports had cannon loaded on their decks for use in the campaign. All of this was no secret to Tonyn, whose intelligence told him that the Whig navy at Sunbury contained at least sixteen transports.[24]

Elbert ordered his men to be ready to embark at any time, but meanwhile, he scrutinized their behavior. Realizing that he commanded a people's army, he advised them to govern their actions around Sunbury's inhabitants. On the day they arrived in Sunbury, the colonel told his officers and men to preserve their honor by acting "in such a manner as to gain the Esteem of the Inhabitants." Not everyone followed his advice. For example, Elbert soon learned about (and probably heard) the random firing of guns in camp. Since this "irregularity" created tensions with the citizens and wasted precious powder and cartridges, he condemned the practice and ordered a patrol sent about the camp to find the perpetrators and arrest them.[25]

Controversy erupted when McIntosh finally arrived and Gwinnett called a council of war. Believing Gwinnett was overstepping his bounds, the general refused to attend and instead summoned Elbert and the other officers to his own war council. Then, to deny Gwinnett control over the Continental Army, McIntosh, on April 16, ordered his officers, including Elbert, to take an Oath of Fidelity to the United States. The oath specified that the loyalty of the Continental officers was first to the country they served and implied that civil control did not supersede the authority of the national government over Continental troops in the state. This did not clarify matters for Gwinnett, who heaped abuse upon the general and insisted that he would lead the army into Florida despite McIntosh's

---

Manuscript Library.

[24] Robert Howe to (?), May 29, 1777, in Robert Howe Papers 1777–1778, Rubenstein Rare Book and Manuscript Library; Searcy, *Georgia-Florida Contest*, 90–93.

[25] Samuel Elbert, "Regimental Orders, 2d Battalion," April 13, 1777, in OBSE, 16, and, in the same source, "Regimental Orders, 2d Battalion," April 16, 1777, 16–17, and "Regimental Orders, Second Battalion," April 17, 1777, 17.

objections. The escalating quarrel threatened to undermine the whole campaign before it even commenced. To salvage the expedition, the council recalled McIntosh and Gwinnett to Savannah and placed Elbert in temporary charge of the battalions but without the general's orders to proceed on the mission.[26]

Eager to defend himself before the council and assembly, McIntosh left Sunbury before Gwinnett. He was gone by April 24 because, on that day, Elbert sent him an urgent express concerning a meeting he had just had with Gwinnett. According to Elbert, Gwinnett handed him a letter from the council (which he sent with his dispatch for McIntosh's perusal) ordering him to proceed "immediately on the Southern Expedition." If Gwinnett's purpose was to use Elbert's ambition as a way to seize control of the battalions, then he failed. Gwinnett did not realize that Elbert's sense of honor outweighed any desire he entertained to command the battalions. Gwinnett wanted Elbert to abide by the council's orders. This would have effectively removed McIntosh from command and placed Gwinnett in charge of the expedition through the council. Instead, Elbert adhered to his recent Oath of Fidelity and the chain of command. Much to Gwinnett's bewilderment, the young colonel informed him that any orders from the council putting him in charge of the undertaking would have to come directly through McIntosh. These concerning matters represented the heart of what "passed between the President and self Just before he left this place," Elbert explained to the general, and he desperately sought immediate clarification from McIntosh. "For God's Sake let me hear from you Immediately," he implored. He continued, "If you think proper that I should proceed On the Expedition, let me have your Orders of directions as full as possible. I am sure you wish well to the Undertaking and therefore will occasion no delay on your part."[27]

McIntosh did not tarry in providing Elbert an answer, which arrived in Sunbury on April 26. To McIntosh, the council's letter and order were further proof that—through Gwinnett's scheming— he had fallen out of favor with the state's leaders since the offer to make Elbert commander of the expedition was "kept a profound secret from [me]." As he informed the colonel, attacks upon his character and abilities to command had become so intense that he would rather step down than "sacrifice [my]

---

[26] Ibid., Lachlan McIntosh, "General Orders, by Gen'l McIntosh," April 16, 1777, 16; Jackson, *Lachlan McIntosh*, 62–63; Searcy, *Georgia-Florida Contest*, 90; C. C. Jones Jr., *History of Georgia*, 2:265; K. Coleman, *American Revolution in Georgia*, 104.

[27] Samuel Elbert to Lachlan McIntosh, April 24, 1777, in OBSE, 19.

Country." He did not know how the council intended to "forward this Expedition," but he was convinced that their effort to find "some flaw in my conduct" contributed to the long delays. At least Gwinnett achieved one of his goals. Exasperated, McIntosh "cheerfully" resigned command of the expedition and turned it over to Elbert, confident that he would do everything to "serve our Country & [the common] cause that can reasonably be [expected]." McIntosh ordered Elbert to proceed into Florida under "Great Caution" and with the "utmost of your power."[28] Elbert did not have much "power" to draw from. By the time the campaign commenced, only about five hundred soldiers were fit to make the journey, hardly enough to accomplish the task of subduing East Florida. Nor did he have the element of surprise, since Tonyn was aware of the invasion.

As Elbert formulated plans to move forward, Tonyn bolstered his defenses. He sent Brown and his rangers to the St. Marys River and requested aid from the Indians. He hoped, unrealistically, that the Cherokee would undertake a diversionary raid into South Carolina as the Upper Creeks did the same along Georgia's frontier. To harass the Patriot army's advance, the Lower Creeks and Seminoles were encouraged to coordinate with Brown while British regulars from the 14th and 60th regiments guarded the St. Johns. The governor told civilians to remain on their farms and plantations and serve as informants if the enemy appeared. Tonyn's naval defense was far less than expected since many of the larger ships normally at his disposal, such as the *Hinchinbrook*, were temporarily on other missions. Still, he had the sloop *Rebecca*, a ten-gun ship, in addition to three ten-gun service transports, two schooners, and a handful of smaller boats at his disposal.[29]

Elbert's Florida expedition was his first campaign as a commander and, unwilling to entertain further delay, he issued orders for its commencement. On April 27, he sent Baker a message requesting consultation to discuss the mission's strategy. He told Baker to send his mounted militia, now numbering about 109 men, to Fort Howe to link up with Sumter's 6th South Carolina Regiment sent there from Sunbury. Unbeknownst to Elbert, Sumter's regiment, since recalled to South Carolina, would not participate in the campaign. During their meeting on April 28, Elbert and Baker devised a two-pronged movement into Florida. Baker would take his men southward along the King's Road (the only thoroughfare linking

---

[28] Lachlan McIntosh to Samuel Elbert, April 26, 1777, in PLM, pt. 3, 368.
[29] Searcy, Georgia-Florida Contest, 57, 92–93.

Savannah to St. Augustine) to a place on the Nassau River called Sawpit Bluff, directly south of Amelia Island on the Florida side of the river. Meanwhile, Elbert and his Continentals would travel down the inland waterway in transports. The wings would unite on May 12 at the bluff.[30]

Before boarding his Continentals on transports, Elbert reviewed the 1st and 2nd Battalions and ordered his men to turn out "clean & neat" with their blankets and knapsacks. He planned to conduct live fire exercises along the way, but, to conserve precious wadding, he suggested using dry black moss instead. Everyone was to have an ample supply of powder in their horns, extra flints, and wadding in their pouches. There was to be no unauthorized discharging of guns, he mandated, because of the "great risque of killing one another, added to the useless expenditure of Ammunition." Some men still lacked necessities, such as shoes. Those men, Elbert suggested, should "make Mockasines for themselves…with raw Deer Skin." Elbert provided oil to prevent the rusting of muskets in the salty air and allocated each man a gill of rum per day.[31]

When Howe learned Elbert was taking the army into Florida, he wanted to countermand the order, but it was already too late. On the morning of May 1, the fleet finally sailed from Sunbury and after traveling just a few miles, anchored off St. Catherine's Island later that afternoon. Elbert's flagship was the *Polly*, from which he now referred to himself in written orders as the "Commanding Officer." As the "commanding officer," he was responsible for ensuring that his fleet arrived at Sawpit Bluff on the appointed day before the enemy detected Baker's militia. Given the strict time schedule, it was inexcusable that he allowed the fleet to tarry around St. Catherine's for five days, especially since they had to travel seventy-five miles through Georgia's Inland Passage to reach the rendezvous point. Believing that he had sufficient time to deal with unforeseen problems, he ambled along, said one historian, at a "leisurely pace." As expected, he encountered setbacks over which he had no control, such as strong headwinds and unfamiliarity of the passageway by some of the pilots. On May 4, while still offshore from St. Catherine's, the *Congress* ran aground, and much time was lost trying to free her. He also had to ensure the health of his battalions. There were frequent stops along the way, such

---

[30] Samuel Elbert to Colonel John Baker, April 27, 1777, in OBSE, 20, and, in the same source, Samuel Elbert to Colonel Thomas Sumter, April 27, 1777, 20; Siebert, "East Florida as a Refuge of Southern Loyalists," 232.

[31] Samuel Elbert, "Genl. Orders," April 27, 1777, in OBSE, 21, and, in the same source, "General Orders," May 3, May 4, and May 14, 1777, 23–25.

as the one at Frederica on May 14 (two days beyond the rendezvous date), where the men left the transports to "air" themselves. Some probably looked forward to a brief respite on land. They were sorely disappointed to learn that their commander would never squander an opportunity to drill and parade his battalions. Nor did he excuse them from parades without written explanations from doctors. Elbert's army also had to eat. During the voyage, time was lost as parties canvassed islands and inland plantations searching for fresh beef. Often, much to the detriment of Elbert's hungry soldiers, they returned empty-handed.[32]

By Friday, May 16, Elbert's fleet was skirting Jekyll Island. He was four days behind schedule and still miles from his destination. On the following day, as the ships rounded the southern end of Jekyll, they observed several "large fires in the Woods" between the Satilla and St. Marys Rivers. Elbert assumed, incorrectly, that they were from Baker's men.[33] While he could not have known it, on the day he spotted fires in the forest, Baker's militia were being routed by a combined force of British regulars, Brown's rangers, and Indians, and without a doubt, the "commanding officer's" tardiness was a deciding factor in their fate.

At the same time and unknown to Elbert, the bitter feud between McIntosh and Gwinnett reached its bloody climax. Once in Savannah, their bickering continued, and the quarrel boiled over into the General Assembly as it elected a new governor. Convinced the assembly would choose him, Gwinnett suffered a major reversal when they elected John Adam Treutlen, a moderate radical, instead. McIntosh gloated over Gwinnett's defeat. After Treutlen's election, the assembly discussed the Florida campaign. Conservatives sought to have Gwinnett censured for its mismanagement, and radicals pushed to remove McIntosh from command and send him out of the state. Neither happened, since the assembly approved Gwinnett's actions and McIntosh retained his position. At this point, McIntosh reached the limit of his tolerance and lashed out at Gwinnett in front of the assembly, calling him a "Scoundrell & lying Rascal." Gwinnett responded to the public insult by challenging McIntosh to a duel. At dawn on May 16, they met with their seconds in Wright's former pasture just outside the city. During the duel, both men shot each other in

---

[32] Ibid., Samuel Elbert, "Genl. Orders," April 30, 1777, 21, and, in the same source, "General Orders," May 4, May 14, and May 15, 1777, 23–25, Robert Howe to (?), May 29, 1777, Robert Howe Papers, Rubenstein Rare Book and Manuscript Library; Searcy, *Georgia-Florida Contest*, 93; McCall, *History of Georgia*, 2:123.

[33] Samuel Elbert, "Gencral Orders," May 15–16, 1777, in OBSE, 25.

the leg. McIntosh recovered. Gwinnett died from his wound three days later.[34]

There is no question whose side Elbert would have taken had he known about the duel. He greatly respected McIntosh, not only as his military superior, but also as a Conservative Whig. He did not feel the same toward Gwinnett. No surviving documents record Elbert's opinion of Gwinnett, but he surely held him in contempt because of his all-consuming, vainglorious drive for power and fame to promote his own self-interest. Elbert's Conservative Whig ally, George Walton, who signed the Declaration of Independence with Gwinnett, believed that he had "no criterion by which you might fix any character." In a letter to McIntosh just a few weeks before the duel, Walton called Gwinnett a "self elected [demagogue who] is dispised more or less every where...he must, sooner or later atone for these things."[35] Elbert would have interpreted Gwinnett's character flaws as unvirtuous. Perhaps the most compelling evidence of Elbert's attitude toward Gwinnett rested in the person McIntosh chose to be his second in the duel. That honor went to Elbert's brother-in-law, Joseph Habersham.

On May 17, the day after the duel, Elbert's fleet crossed the sound below Cumberland Island, and during the night of May 18, they arrived at Amelia Island at the mouth of the St. Marys. Already the invasion was in jeopardy. He was six days behind schedule and still not at Sawpit Bluff. The enemy also knew of his presence. A resident on the island informed him that Brown had seen the fleet and estimated that it carried at least two thousand Continentals. In addition to that, the British had fortified key defensive positions between the island and St. Augustine, and there were a number of Tonyn's ships prowling along the coast. Unwilling to imperil his mission any further, Elbert hurriedly sent Lieutenant Robert Ward and twenty of his best men on rowboats to the island to "make Prisoners," secure all of the inhabitants, and "prevent the Enemy getting intelligence of our Approach."[36] It was an interesting order, since Elbert was already aware that "the enemy" knew he was on Amelia Island.

---

[34] Jackson, *Lachlan McIntosh*, 64–65.
[35] George Walton to Lachlan McIntosh, May 1, 1777, in P. Smith, ed., *Letters of Delegates to Congress*, 7:11–12.
[36] Samuel Elbert, "General Orders," May 15–18, 1777, in OBSE, 25.

Elbert's predicament became glaringly evident on the morning of May 19, when fifteen of Baker's men abruptly appeared on the north end of Amelia Island and informed him that their entire command was routed at Thomas Creek, a tributary of the Nassau River several miles west of Sawpit Bluff. Pressing for information, Elbert learned that Indians and regulars ambushed them and, despite Baker's pleas, they refused to fight and instead fled in all directions. Elbert's gut response was to blame the militia, and he refused to yield from his position as more details about the encounter emerged in the days ahead. He informed McIntosh about a week later in a letter that he "lament[ed] the Behavior of Colonel Baker's men." The problem, as he understood it, was a lack of discipline; and such outcomes were expected "where Subordination is wanting."[37] Apparently, Elbert did not realize that he, because of his failure to link up with Baker on schedule, was partially responsible for the defeat.

Baker's journey to Sawpit Bluff was no easy matter. Recent spring rains flooded the Altamaha, and two days were lost at Fort Howe building rafts and ferrying men and horses across the river. Not long after that, Indians attacked their camp, wounding two men, but they escaped into the swamp before Baker could retaliate. When they reached the Satilla, they found it flooded as well and additional rafts had to be constructed. Despite all of this, Baker made it to Sawpit Bluff on time. He arrived on May 12, where he waited three days for Elbert's transports to appear. The delay was fatal. Brown's spies discovered Baker's camp and reported their findings. On May 14, about forty rangers and Indians inched toward Sawpit Bluff and spotted Baker's camp. That night, stealthy Indians stole nearly forty of Baker's horses. Baker dispatched a party to find them the next morning and discovered them tied up in a swamp several miles away. As the militia were retrieving their horses, Indians ambushed them and, after a brief fight, fled into the swamp, leaving a dead warrior behind. Upon discovering the dead Indian, the militia made the mistake of scalping him and mutilating his body.[38]

---

[37] "General Orders," May 19, 1777, ibid., 25–26, and Samuel Elbert to Lachlan McIntosh, May 26, 1777, ibid., 31.

[38] Searcy, Georgia-Florida Contest, 95.

Believing his position at Sawpit Bluff no longer tenable, on May 16, Baker moved further west and inland to Thomas Creek, a tributary of the Nassau River in the northeastern tip of Florida, not knowing that he was trailed by Indians and about two hundred of Major Mark Prevost's regulars and Brown's rangers. During the night, Prevost and Brown quietly moved toward Baker's position on Thomas Creek and planned their attack for the next morning. Brown's men were to ambush the militia from one direction, while Prevost swung his three columns around Baker's rear to cut off a retreat. At mid-morning on May 17, the British sprung their trap. Brown's men struck first, suddenly materializing out of the woods and catching the militia by surprise. At fifty feet, they leveled a volley at the stunned Americans, who turned and fled right into Prevost's advancing columns with fixed bayonets. Panic ensued as the militia realized they were surrounded, and the whole command was routed in less than five minutes. Half of Baker's militia at the Battle of Thomas Creek were casualties. Some, including Baker, escaped into the swamps, carrying nine of their wounded with them, most of whom later died. They left behind several dead patriots and about forty prisoners captured by the British.[39]

Then, one of the most atrocious episodes in Georgia's Revolution took place. Seeking vengeance for the Indian killed and mutilated two days earlier by the militia, the Creeks fell upon the prisoners and brutally executed them. One eyewitness recalled that they "were all put to death…except for 16 who were saved by Major Prevost and some regulars," and the British commander had great difficulty even sparing those. When Tonyn heard about the massacre, he blamed it on the militia for cutting all the "features" off the dead Indian during the swamp skirmish on May 15. Because of this, he said, the Indians were "greatly exasperated," and it was impossible to control their blood lust when they sought revenge.[40]

Back on Amelia Island's north end, Elbert's troubles only compounded. Shortly after learning the fate of Baker's militia, he received word on May 20 that Loyalists shot and killed Ward as he scoured the

---

[39] Ibid. See also Raab, *Spain, Britain, and the American Revolution*, 102. The Battle of Thomas Creek took place in what is today Duval County, Florida.

[40] Raab, *Spain, Britain, and the American Revolution*, 102. See also, Cashin, *King's Ranger*, 65. Accounts vary on the number of prisoners taken and those killed by the Indians. For example, McCall wrote that thirty-one men were taken prisoner, five of whom were murdered by the Indians (*History of Georgia*, 2:123). McCall's estimate of the five murdered prisoners corresponds with Elbert's report ("General Orders," May 22, 1777, in OBSE, 27).

island for beef. He also learned that some inhabitants were fleeing the island and informing the British of their advance. Incensed, Elbert made the rash decision to destroy each dwelling on the island. "I dispatched Lieut. Winfree with Twenty good men," he wrote, "with Orders to Burn every house on the Island & destroy all the Stock." The wisdom of this decision was questionable. Although there were many Loyalists living on the island, there were also friends of America residing there as well, such as the woman who warned of Brown's presence when he first arrived on May 17. His action surely created more Whig enemies at a time when he greatly needed their loyalty. Meanwhile, the angry commander sent another party to scour the island for "all the Beef and Hogs." All of them were to be "Jerked and cured with…Salt taken…on the island."[41]

Elbert's situation was far more perilous than even he realized. Out at sea, not far away from Amelia Island, a number of Tonyn's ships were gathering to cripple Elbert's fleet. On May 21, not long after Winfree left to burn the homes, Elbert heard, about three-o'clock in the afternoon "several Cannon fired towards the South End of the Island which we suppose to be at our People." While he could not pinpoint the exact origin of the shooting, he had a good indication as to its source because he saw two enemy vessels racing out of Nassau Sound. The ships that Elbert spotted were probably the ten-gun sloop *Rebecca*, commanded by Captain John Mowbray, and one of its escort ships, either the transport *Hawke* or the ten-gun *Meredith*. Strong winds forced them out of Nassau Sound and into open waters, where they happened upon one of Elbert's brigantines and gave chase. As the ships closed their distance, a hotly contested sea battle ensued. Mowbray tried to maneuver his ship to board the brig, but at that moment, a cannonball carried away the *Rebecca*'s topmast, giving the Americans an opportunity to escape. Mowbray and his men observed many dead rebels on the brig's deck as she pulled away; the damaged *Rebecca* was unable to pursue, and the American ship vanished on the horizon. When Tonyn heard about Mowbray's encounter, he praised the captain for his "zeal, activity, and unwearied industry."[42] Though unaware, the sea battle further weakened Elbert's invasion force and represented an additional setback for his campaign.

---

[41] Samuel Elbert, "General Orders," May 20 and May 21, 1777, in OBSE, 26–27, and, in the same source, Samuel Elbert to Joseph Habersham, May 30, 1777, 33.

[42] Buker and Martin, "Governor Tonyn's Brown-Water Navy," 66–67; Samuel Elbert, "General Orders," Amelia Narrows, May 21, 1777, in OBSE, 26–27. The name of the American brig is unknown.

Stranded and in grave danger, Elbert was running out of time. Provisions were nearly gone, and the men were becoming ill. The most direct route to St. Augustine was to continue down the Inland Passage with his fleet for nearly fifteen miles to the mouth of the St. Johns, but that option put his whole force at risk. He already knew about two enemy ships, and he had no intelligence about any others with them or even their location. The other option was to get his fleet into the Nassau River at the south end of Amelia Island and work his way through the narrows toward the St. Johns. To explore that possibility, Elbert and a company of men went to observe the narrows, but what he discovered was disappointing. In some places, the passageways were barely six feet wide, and, at others, it was either too shallow or the turnings were too tight for his row galleys. "I judge it Impossible to get the smallest Galley through them," he observed, "without first taking out her Guns & all the Stores which will be attended with the greatest difficulty, if Practicable at all." On May 22, he ordered Bowen to hold a council of war with the captains of the galleys and transports to decide if the fleet could navigate the narrows. Elbert wanted everyone's opinion recorded. The commander was "anxious to have this matter determined without loss of time as the Provissions in the Fleet are nearly Expended." If passage was deemed impracticable, then "some new mode of Operations should be adopted before 'tis too late." He had barely gotten off his order before three more of Baker's men appeared on the island with additional information about their defeat. They told Elbert that "all the Creek-nation were coming…against us" and that the British "were prepared" to resist the invasion.[43]

Bowen's council agreed that they should salvage the campaign. For four days, they desperately tried to overcome the narrows, but with no success. When Elbert wrote McIntosh on May 26, he was frustrated and ready to abort the mission. "I think from every Information we can get that the enemy are at present on their Guard," he observed. At this point, little could be done, "unless by a formidable Invasion, which I Judge to be rather too much for Georgia to undertake [until] her Forces are put on a more respectable footing." Elbert's strategic thinking was now aligned with McIntosh and Howe, and he recommended "confining our Operations intirely to the defencive till a more favorable opportunity [presented itself]." There could never be success in Florida, observed the colonel, until

---

[43] Samuel Elbert, "General Orders," Amelia Narrows, May 21 and May 22, 1777, in OBSE, 27.

the "Secret Enemies" who kept up a regular correspondence with the British were stopped. Even more than that, provisions were exhausted. "I find it will be prudent," he told McIntosh, "for want of Beef to leave this place in a Day or two—and retire to the St. Illa [Satilla]." Facing such bleak odds, he still boasted that "flying Parties of my Virginians" would soundly defeat the Florida scouts and Indians if they only had an opportunity. Elbert closed his letter asking McIntosh for directions on how to proceed, but he had already determined to abandon Florida. On May 27, he told Colonel Francis Harris that "we shall proceed with the fleet up [to the] St. Illa immediately and as soon as we come to a proper place on the North side for a post, shall make a Stand."[44]

On May 28, after ten torturous days on Amelia Island, Elbert's fleet sailed north. His departure marked the end of Georgia's 1777 Florida campaign. As the *Polly* came into the sound between Amelia and Cumberland Islands, he observed on shore a white flag atop a crude pole. Coming over to investigate, he discovered three more of Baker's men. They told him a fourth was in the woods, but he refused to come out. The renegade soldier highlighted another problem for Elbert, which was desertion. Writing to Joseph Habersham on May 30, Elbert claimed that desertions were the primary reason for his "retreating," since the "Enemy will from them be informed of our Strength and what is worse, our having had nothing but Rice to Eat for five days past." Despite everything, he told Habersham that his "brave fellows" were still in "high spirits." Two days later, as the fleet entered the Satilla, they were on the verge of mutiny for want of provisions.[45]

Before leaving, Elbert received a dispatch from Prevost criticizing his inhumane treatment of civilians on Amelia Island. Prevost was infuriated that "Harmless & Innocent Planters should find themselves the object" of Elbert's excursions and that "Sending…Parties to take or assassinate any Particular Individuals is…Contrary to the rules of war." In the future, he warned, whenever any of the rebels engaging in such activities were taken, they would be given "no quarter" and any found beyond the limits of Georgia would be regarded as "Robbers & Murderers." Elbert replied to Prevost in kind, calling into question the so-called "humanity" that the British

---

[44] Ibid., Samuel Elbert to Lachlan McIntosh, May 26, 1777, 31, and Samuel Elbert to Colonel Harris, May 27, 1777, 32.

[45] Samuel Elbert, "General Orders," May 28, 1777, 32–33, and, in the same source, Samuel Elbert to Joseph Habersham, Cumberland Island, May 30, 1777, 33–34; Samuel Elbert, "General Orders," Old Town, Satilla, June 1, 1777, 35.

professed. "Sir," he began, "it hurts me, as I am sure it must you, to be informed that some of the unfortunate men of Colo. Baker's Detachment who fell in your hands, were cruelly Butchered by the Savages, in cool Blood, and in the presence of some of your people." The murder of prisoners by Indians, he pointed out, was uncivil and contrary to the terms reached at Fort McIntosh back in February. "If Savages can't be restrained," he angrily inquired, "why are they Employed?"[46]

On that note, Elbert's first campaign in the American Revolution concluded. It was a disaster from its inception and none of its objectives were achieved. Even the cannon they took along with them to help conquer St. Augustine remained stored on the transports for the campaign's duration. Neither of his superiors fully endorsed the scheme—Howe refused to give it his blessings while McIntosh's support was only lukewarm. Howe reported afterward that he "foresaw that the matter would end just as it did and I took the liberty to express…to the Council my Sentiments upon the occasion," but they refused to listen. The general rushed to defend Elbert, whom he deemed a good commander and outstanding citizen, from any attacks for the disastrous adventure and instead put the blame on Georgia's political leaders. The only person in the state's military establishment entertaining a remote possibility of its success was Elbert himself. Young and deeply devoted to his cause, Elbert believed, naively, that a liberation of St. Augustine was just within his grasp, if only he could navigate the shallow narrows, instill more discipline in his soldiers, obtain reinforcements, prevent desertion, silence Loyalist spies and informants, find adequate provisions, gather better intelligence about British forces, and make his men suffer just a bit longer through the stifling heat and humidity. As he informed Habersham in retrospect on May 30, he only wished for "an opportunity of a Trial of Skill with the Floridians," and, had he gotten into the St. Johns, he boldly predicted that his limited force would have "made the whole Province of East Florida tumble."[47] The statement showed that Elbert, too, had fallen into the delusional trap of mounting "mermaids on alligators." Realistically, there was never a hope for success in Florida with such few men.

The campaign's failure was not all Elbert's fault, but some of it was.

---

[46] Ibid., Samuel Elbert to Mark Prevost, Cumberland Island, May 31, 1777, 35, and, in the same source, Mark Prevost to Samuel Elbert, May 27, 1777, 36–37.

[47] Ibid., Samuel Elbert to Joseph Habersham, Cumberland Island, May 30, 1777, 33–34; Robert Howe to (?), May 29, 1777, in Robert Howe Papers, Rubenstein Rare Book and Manuscript Library.

He set the place and date for the rendezvous with Baker's wing of the invasion at Sawpit Bluff but appeared a week behind schedule. The result was the obliteration of Baker's command at Thomas Creek. The torch-and-ash policy Elbert unleashed on Amelia Island made even more enemies for the Whigs and caused the British to declare that all rebels taken beyond the limits of Georgia would be given no quarter. The 1777 Florida campaign bruised Elbert's ego and even threatened to tarnish his image, but his reputation survived. There were other pressing dangers ahead, particularly on the state's western border, which required his immediate attention. Refusing to dwell on the past, Elbert looked forward to those future challenges and with them, a chance for redemption.

Chapter 8

"To Save Your Country from Ruin": Samuel Elbert's Western Campaign in the Ceded Lands, 1777

On Sunday, June 1, Colonel Samuel Elbert's fleet arrived at Old Town on the Satilla River after a fruitless excursion into Florida. His men were sickly, starving, and near revolt. For two long days, he waited in vain for supplies requested before leaving Florida. Anticipating trouble and having heard nothing from his superior, General Lachlan McIntosh, Elbert put his ragged army into motion and marched them inland to Fort Howe on the Altamaha. There was ample incentive to reach the fort since nearly one thousand head of cattle, rounded-up by Whig partisans between the Satilla and St. Marys, were headed there. To ensure the herd reached their destination, Elbert ordered Colonel James Screven and his freshly recruited 3rd Battalion at Darien to assist the drivers while he led his exhausted troops, with the promise of fresh beef, to the fort. He placed those unfit to make the journey on galleys and transports and sent them to Frederica.[1] Thus, one thousand cows were all Elbert had to show for a month-long campaign to reduce St. Augustine, but the food they represented went far in suppressing a potential mutiny caused by empty stomachs.

When he finally reached the fort on June 9, his troops received much-needed provisions, but not rest because he marched them down the Altamaha to the town of Darien at the river's mouth the next day. There he received orders to return to Savannah. The colonel departed Darien on Sunday, June 15, and was back in the city a few days later, followed by a trickling stream of exhausted Continentals. Once in Savannah, Elbert reestablished his routine of drilling the battalions, writing reports, filling out returns, and overseeing frequent court martial trials. He also made it

---

[1] Samuel Elbert to Lachlan McIntosh, July 18, 1777, in OBSE, 45–46.

his duty to instill patriotism and morality in his soldiers. He supported McIntosh's order respecting the Independence Day celebration in Savannah on July 4, featuring a grand review and parade of soldiers in front of the general and the city's citizens. The soldiers were to look their best to honor, as McIntosh said, "the most Extraordinary & glorious Revolution in the History of mankind." The celebration included a feast of barbequed beef and pork chased by rum. Hopefully, most of Elbert's soldiers drank responsibly because on the following morning, the colonel had his 2nd Battalion up early and marched them to church. He expected the men to be "clean Dressed with their Hair Combed & beard shaved." Once inside the church, they were to sit in the gallery and not disturb any of the members in their pews. Above all, in the presence of God, they were to "behave with decency."[2]

If the late Florida campaign taught Elbert anything, it was that his soldiers needed reliable muskets, which he requested McIntosh to furnish. "It would make me Happy," wrote the colonel, since the "Sorry trash I have at present [is] a medley of Rifles, old muskets & fowling pieces." He professed that he had "no faith" in such a ragged assortment of unreliable firearms. To remedy the situation, he even purchased weapons for some of his men with his own money, such as the £2 he spent for a musket he gave to William Dobbins a few months earlier. The Florida experience also made him aware of something else. The semitropical climate of the coast was playing havoc on the health of his battalion, and the effects were obvious after a grueling campaign. With many of the battalion sick, Elbert reasoned that a temporary move to the upcountry would bolster their health, especially since most were from Virginia and unaccustomed to Georgia's coastal climate. He expressed his concern to McIntosh. "Our new Troops begin already to be Sickly," he told the general. "I am well convinced [this] could be remedied by marching them about 140 miles back" into the state's interior. At first, McIntosh balked because it would weaken Savannah's defenses, but after some consideration, he agreed with Elbert. On July 24, he ordered the colonel to take his men to Wilkes County (formerly the ceded lands of 1773) north of Augusta and patrol the Savannah River and its branches, but to be ready to return immediately to headquarters in case of an emergency. "The lives and health of the

---

[2] Ibid. See also, in same source, Samuel Elbert, "Left St. Illa," 37, Lachlan McIntosh, "General Orders, by Genl. McIntosh," July 3, 1777, 42, and Samuel Elbert, "Regimental Orders, 2d Battalion," July 5, 1777, 42.

Troops shall ever be an essential consideration," declared McIntosh, who found the "sickness and disorders" in the returning regiments "alarming."³ The place where Elbert was heading stretched westward as far as the Ogeechee and Oconee Rivers, the boundary between Georgia and Indian country. As was the case with the southern border, Elbert's small force could not adequately cover such a vast area, but for him and his men, it was a welcomed change from the brutal heat and humidity. Unlike Florida just two months earlier, on this occasion he was at least familiar with the geography of the Augusta area.

Elbert's presence on the western outskirts of semi-civilization was not just for health reasons. His primary purpose was to secure the area from a wave of renewed Indian attacks. Ever since the New Purchase in 1773, the region was the scene of violent clashes between settlers and Creeks, who resented the loss of their territory. Frightened inhabitants responded to Indian threats by building forts in key defensive positions stretching from the Savannah all the way back into the Little and Broad River valleys deep in Wilkes County. Local militia defended the forts, if garrisoned at all, and so did elements of McIntosh's Continental horse troop when they were around. According to local resident Malaciah Culpepper, settlers spent much of their time in forts and blockhouses because "the Creek Indians particularly from the Coweta and Cusseta towns were extremely troublesome and daring." Thus, one of Elbert's goals was to visit and inspect as many forts as possible. Additional objectives included protecting settlers from Loyalist and Indian raids, bringing order to frontier troops, and coaxing Creek *micos* to keep their people neutral in America's war with Britain. While seeking neutrality, he was also ordered by Governor John Adam Treutlen to "punish those faithless and cruel savages and to protect our back inhabitants against the excursive and rambling enemy."⁴

Treutlen's directive represented a push for war against the Creeks called for by many in the General Assembly and backcountry. It put Elbert in a quandary since the Continental Congress and his military superiors emphasized maintaining peaceful relations with the Indians. The opposing viewpoints served as only another reminder of the blurred divisions between state and federal authority in relation to the Continental Army.

---

³ Samuel Elbert to Lachlan McIntosh, July 18, 1777, ibid., 45–46, and, in the same source, Lachlan McIntosh, "General Orders by Genl. McIntosh," July 24, 1777, 48–49. For the purchase of muskets, see Account Book, 1769–1788, 3, Samuel Elbert Papers, Rubenstein Rare Book and Manuscript Library.

⁴ Haynes, "Patrolling the Border," 103; Hall, *Land and Allegiance*, 61.

Elbert was to pursue war and peace against the Indians simultaneously while maintaining the appearance of following conflicting orders from both his governor and his military superiors.

From the outbreak of the Revolution in Georgia, Native Americans played an increasingly significant role. The British long recognized their importance, and devising a strategy to win them over as allies was a goal since the war's onset. Britain's pro-Indian policy had the blessings of Lord George Germain, the secretary of state for the American Department, and several top military commanders, such as William Howe, Sir Henry Clinton, and Thomas Gage. Even Sir James Wright, Georgia's deposed colonial governor now residing in London, believed that assistance could be "expected" from the Indians, and, with their help, the province "might be recovered from the Rebels." East Florida's governor, Patrick Tonyn, constantly sought assistance from the Lower Creeks and Seminoles to aid Loyalist units, such as Thomas Brown's King's Rangers, as they raided Georgia's interior. Brown himself was a proponent of Indian warfare as a weapon to terrorize the Whigs and restore British rule. John Stuart, British Southern superintendent of Indian affairs, also worked from his base in Pensacola to entice the Indians to support England through lucrative trade goods and presents. Records show that his Pensacola inventory of Indian goods nearly doubled from £19,000 in 1776 to £37,729 in 1777. The trend upward continued into the following year with a stockpile estimated to be worth nearly £55,000. What trading items the Whigs had to offer, in contrast, paled in comparison to Stuart's endless stream of guns, powder, shot, and rum. While Stuart wanted to prevent a general Indian uprising, he did hope to coordinate their efforts with the British military when the opportunity arose. Stuart's deputies, Alexander Cameron with the Cherokee, and David Taitt, David Holmes, and assistant deputy William McIntosh (not to be confused with Lachlan McIntosh's brother) among the Creek worked in concert with Stuart to win Indian loyalty. Georgians believed that Cameron and Stuart enticed the Cherokee to violate earlier treaties and attack the South Carolina backcountry in summer 1776 to coincide with the failed British naval effort to take Charleston. In response, militia units from both Carolinas, Virginia, and Georgia joined forces and devastated most of the lower, middle, and upper towns. Among the Creek, Taitt obtained an agreement from some Lower towns in 1777, including Coweta, to raid Georgia in September. Tait told Stuart that the Cowetas, "to a Man" were "firm friends...with us." Stuart passed the information to Germain in a letter acknowledging Coweta's promised attack.⁵

Although not all Creeks, Cherokee, and Seminoles sided with the British, the activities of those who did caused many of Georgia's military leaders, such as Elbert and McIntosh, to fret about an impending Indian war. Georgia's most experienced and respected Indian agent was George Galphin, a fur trader and former close friend and associate of Elbert's deceased father-in-law, John Rae. As a federal Indian commissioner for the Southern Department and the most influential agent among the Whigs, Galphin believed that peace with the Creeks depended on trade, and, unless it became competitive with the British, war with them was inevitable. Speaking of the Creeks in 1776, he predicted that if the trade was stopped, "they will all go to Florida, & then we may Expect an Indian War." Elbert's superiors, McIntosh and General Robert Howe, the leader of the Southern Military Department, wanted to avoid a disastrous war with the Creeks. Howe even sent letters to Georgia's General Assembly and the Continental Congress in August and September 1777 warning about the dangers of an Indian uprising provoked by "the wantonness and indiscretion of several persons" in the state. While Howe did not specify those "persons" he suspected, it undoubtedly included British agents as well as several frontier settlers, such as radical assemblyman George Wells and his followers, who sought an Indian war as a pretext to seize more land. Congress responded to Howe's concerns by ordering Georgia's authorities to "use their utmost exertions to cultivate peace and harmony with the Indian nations." Toward this end, Congress urged Georgia to pass laws "inflicting severe penalties on such of their inhabitants as may endeavor to provoke a war which may endanger the state...and entail great injury and expense on the United States."⁶

Based on a series of talks he gave the Creeks at the time, Elbert was also an advocate of peace. Despite saber rattling by radicals, keeping the Southeastern tribes neutral was critical in the state's war effort, especially given its limited number of men and resources. An Indian war would cripple Georgia and divert attention away from the objective of defeating British forces in Florida. To Elbert, the greatest instigators of Indian violence

---

⁵ Sir James Wright to Secretary Lord Germain, October 8, 1777, in LSJW, 247; Cashin, *King's Ranger*, 67–68, 71; K. Coleman, *American Revolution in Georgia*, 113; C. C. Jones Jr., *History of Georgia*, 2:245–46; Morris, "George Galphin and John Stuart's America," 39; Rindfleisch, "Our Lands Are Our Life and Breath," 592.

⁶ *Journals of the American Congress*, 2:297; Cashin, *King's Ranger*, 67; Cashin, "Trembling Land," 31. For Galphin, see Piecuch, *Three Peoples, One King*, 73–74.

were the British superintendent and his minions. Without their influence, in addition to the provocative actions of Indian haters on the frontier, the young commander naively believed there would be no conflict with Native Americans.

Elbert was unable to fathom that Native Americans had their own "Indian" reasons to take up their war clubs. Protecting their territory and hunting grounds against land-hungry European Americans offered ample incentive for Native Americans to resist the Whigs. Many Creeks, for example, still resented the 1773 New Purchase (a treaty that Elbert witnessed and supported; it benefited his businesses) and could never accept the loss of hunting grounds there. Their response was to send out border patrols and conduct raids to terrorize settlers and drive them away. One authority on the Creeks during the Revolution believed that their raids in Georgia were more about political agendas than a sign of British support. During the war, the Creek towns, or *talwas*, acted autonomously based on their self-interests, and there was no unified Muskogee policy. Some *talwas*, like the Lower town of Coweta, often participated in raids either by themselves or in conjunction with Loyalists. Cusseta, another lower town, preferred to keep the trading path with Georgia and the Carolinas "White" and remain neutral. The divisions between Coweta and Cusseta were indicative of the Revolution's impact on Creek society. Indian raids served several purposes for those engaging in them, such as revenge killings, reclaiming land lost in illegitimate treaties, and offering young warriors opportunities to test their bravery and combat skills. It is not surprising that most raids during the Revolution took place in the ceded lands. Throughout the war, 181 raids occurred in Georgia. Out of those, approximately 122, or 67 percent, took place in Wilkes County. In 1777, their frequency increased. In 1776, for example, there were 12 raids in Georgia. That number tripled in 1777 to about 30, and most of them occurred in the ceded lands.[7]

On June 17, 1777, just a few weeks before Elbert set out for Wilkes County, Galphin and the colonel's business partner, Robert Rae, held a conference with several Creeks at Old Town, the agent's cowpen on the Ogeechee River. Present were Handsome Fellow (also called Handsome Man) from Cusseta (some say Okfuskee), the Cusseta King, the Hallowing King from Coweta, and some four hundred warriors. Galphin warned the Creeks that if they waged war against the Whigs, their fate would be worse than what happened to the Cherokee in 1776. His talk intimidated

---

[7] Haynes, "Patrolling the Border," 6–7, 60, 90, 103, 110.

the Indians, and he later reported that only a few lower towns remained steadfast in their opposition. The agent underestimated the level of Creek resistance. Already, a Coweta war party thought to contain over one hundred warriors was heading toward the western settlements. Acting independently, the Upper Creek *talwas* of Kialiee, Hookchoie, and Alabama sent additional warriors into the area. Galphin showered his Creek delegation with presents and then accompanied ten of them to Charleston where they met Governor John Rutledge and his council. They also saw the might of America's friends overseas represented by the presence of French naval vessels anchored in the harbor. The timing of the trip was intentional and bolstered the hopes of impressing neutrality upon the Creeks. One of the first things Creek visitors did after arriving in the city on July 9 was to tour some of the vessels.[8]

As Galphin awed Creek headmen in Charleston, a series of events converged along Georgia's western frontier, flinging the region into chaos and thrusting Elbert, once again, into a violent border situation. By midsummer, Coweta war parties were already raiding backcountry settlements. Terrified survivors poured into nearby forts when the raids occurred. While they offered temporary protection, the forts did not guarantee safety since the Indians sometimes attacked and burned them, too. One party of Cowetas, for example, attacked and burned a fort on the Ogeechee during the 1777 raids.[9]

Creek war parties were not the only ones invading Georgia's frontier. Stuart fumed over Galphin's efforts to coax Creeks away from Pensacola. He admitted to Germain that Galphin's diplomacy significantly diminished the prospect of Creek assistance. The only way to ensure Creek loyalty, he reasoned, was to eliminate Galphin. Supposedly, Stuart offered £500 for Galphin's murder, and a party of Loyalists commanded by Sam Moore, in addition to some Indians, set out from Florida to assassinate the agent. On top of that, scouting parties of Brown's rangers spread across the state. One of them got within five miles of Savannah, another supposedly passed through Augusta, while a third overtook Frederica and St. Simons Island and captured some prisoners.[10]

---

[8] Cashin, *King's Ranger*, 68; Haynes, "Patrolling the Border," 105–106; Piecuch, *Three Peoples, One King*, 111–13; Davis Jr., "George Galphin and the Creek Congress of 1777," 15–16; Kokomoor, "Burning & Destroying All Before Them," 327–28.

[9] Kokomoor, "Burning & Destroying All Before Them," 331–32; Cashin, *King's Ranger*, 69.

[10] Piecuch, *Three Peoples, One King*, 112; Cashin, *King's Ranger*, 68. Davis claims that

On July 31, a party of Cowetas struck the home of Samuel Delk in Wilkes County near the Ogeechee border. Delk was not present, but they killed and scalped his wife and four children and captured an older daughter, about fourteen years old. A militia scouting party tracked the Indians some forty miles but then lost their trail. No one ever saw the girl again. They later discovered a lock of her hair near the river and assumed she was dead. Afterward, when Stuart heard about the massacre, he blamed it on Delk, whom he said caused the murders by being abusive to the Indians and trespassing on their lands.[11]

War parties also engaged the militia. One group skirmished with Captain Elijah Clarke's militia in Wilkes County along the Broad River, killing three of his men and wounding the commander. Another lured some militia out of a frontier stockade and then ambushed them, killing twenty. Additional raids occurred along the Altamaha. An ambush in August by 150 Florida Rangers near Fort Howe resulted in the deaths of fourteen patriots. The attacks were widespread. Captain Thomas Dooly, fresh from a recruiting trip in Virginia for the 3rd Battalion, marched his ninety-seven new men into Wilkes County and camped on the edge of Georgia's border, near Skull Shoals on the Oconee. During the night of July 21, a war party of Cowetas led by pro-British headman, Emistisiguo, stole some of their horses. On the following day, Dooly, Lieutenant John Cunningham, and twenty-one men set out to recover the mounts when Indians ambushed them in a cane swamp. David Haley, one of the survivors, remembered they were "waylaid by the Indians about 50 in number [who] killed six of our men and wounded two badly that got in and lived." In the skirmish, a musket ball shattered one of Dooly's legs just above the ankle. Haley recalled that Dooly "had his heelstring shot off the first fire and could not run." Another participant, Isham Ward, stated in an affidavit that when the shooting began, he heard one officer (probably Cunningham) say, "boys make your Escape." Ward believed the Indians shot Dooly in the initial exchange of gunfire, disabling him so he could not stand. He saw "Captain Dooly fire in a Sitting posture on the ground" and heard him cry out loudly for help, but that "Availed Nothing," since the militia "Continued Runing [*sic*]," abandoning many of their fallen comrades on the field. The last person who saw Dooly alive claimed that he was fighting off Indians with the butt of his gun. Unable to escape, the Indians captured

---

Stuart offered the reward money for Galphin's death ("George Galphin," 18).

[11] McCall, *History of Georgia*, 2:130–31; Searcy, *Georgia-Florida Contest*, 112–13.

Dooly and three others and then executed them.[12]

Thomas Dooly's brother, Captain John Dooly of the 12th Rangers in the Continental horse troop, was also in Wilkes County. Upon hearing of his brother's death, he decided to seek revenge. Dooly saw all Indians as the same and he made no distinctions between them. Outraged, he and his men rode into South Carolina and intercepted Galphin's party on their way back from Charleston. Dooly, surely knowing that Handsome Fellow and those with him had nothing to do with his brother's death, had the Indians arrested anyway and taken to Augusta, where they were badly mistreated. News of the event spread rapidly, and it galled leaders in South Carolina. John Lewis Gervais, a Charleston merchant, wrote to South Carolina Congressman Henry Laurens in Philadelphia, informing him of Dooly's actions. "It is a great Insult offered to this State, under whose protection & the Law of Nations, they were as Ambassadors from the Creeks," Gervais angrily noted. "It is also an Insult to the United States," he observed, "as they were taken by force of arms from the Continental Comiss. of Indian Affairs." Rutledge believed that Dooly's recklessness would lead to bloodshed. It was impossible to know what would happen if Handsome Fellow ever made it back to his people, he admitted, but war was a potential outcome. To prevent it, Rutledge ordered some South Carolina troops to free the Indians.[13] In taking matters into his own hands, Dooly undermined everything Galphin and Rutledge sought to achieve with the Indians. His behavior characterized the type of lawless frontier vigilante justice that eroded Indian relations, destroyed diplomatic gains, fueled Indian raids, drove Native Americans into the British camp, and intensified the probability of an Indian conflict.

In early August, Elbert left Savannah and headed toward Augusta with his 2nd Battalion. Georgia's western border, with its Indian raids, roaming Loyalists and assassins, frequent clashes between militia and Creeks, and provocative actions against Native Americans by backcountry settlers wanting Indian blood and Indian land, was in turmoil. He wrote his last orders from Savannah on July 31 to Captains Francis Moore and Charles Middleton, two officers from the 2nd Battalion headed to

---

[12] "Affidavit of Isham Ward, August 11, 1777, Wilkes County," Keith Read Collection, box 7, folder 13, document 1, Hargrett Rare Book and Manuscript Library; Davis, "Frontier for Pioneer Revolutionaries," 329; McCall, *History of Georgia*, 2:85–87; Searcy, *Georgia-Florida Contest*, 112–13; Cashin, *King's Ranger*, 69; Davis, "George Galphin," 19.

[13] Starr, "Letters from John Lewis Gervais," 22; Piecuch, *Three Peoples, One King*, 113; Davis, "George Galphin," 18–19; Cashin, *King's Ranger*, 69.

Philadelphia for private concerns and then to Virginia to find deserters and enlist more recruits. Elbert was reluctant to let them go, but while in Philadelphia, he hoped they could speak to Georgia's delegates in the Congress about getting wagons and teams for the battalion. He even entertained the remote possibility that his officers would encounter General George Washington while in Pennsylvania. If they did, Elbert told them to "give my most respectful compliments to that great man," and to bring to his attention the "true state of our regiment." Regardless, Elbert wanted Moore and Middleton to make all efforts to acquire ample clothes and weapons for the battalions. He also requested that the two officers find him a "neat, light pha[e]ton or post chaise" carriage suitable for the streets of Savannah and a pair of good bay horses while they were in Pennsylvania.[14] After that order, Elbert put his men on the road to Augusta.

The 140-mile march to Augusta from Savannah consumed nearly two weeks. The men probably averaged about ten miles per day at a steady pace. Riding his horse at the head of the column, Elbert had ample time for reflection. While it is impossible to know his thoughts, it surely occurred to him that the last time he marched up the same road at the head of an army was in summer 1775 during the unrest caused by backcountry Loyalists that resulted in the tarring and feathering of Brown. Given the uncertainty along the border, he undoubtedly also pondered the Indians. For most of the early 1770s, Elbert's contact with Native Americans occurred through the fur trade, and he often made trips to *talwas* in the Chattahoochee valley to conduct business. In the process, he cultivated personal relationships with some Creek leaders. Not all of Elbert's contact with Native Americans involved trade. Twice in 1774, during the Creek war spurred by the New Purchase, Elbert and his grenadiers escorted Indians back and forth through the settlements on their way to Savannah for peace talks with Wright. While he could never boast expertise as an experienced Indian diplomat, like Galphin or even his deceased father-in-law, Elbert could at least claim that he, along with Robert Rae, were the most versed military commanders in the state on Indian affairs.

Elbert's personal relationship with a few Creek leaders did not overshadow his general attitude about Indians, which mirrored those shared by almost all Whites in American society at the time. That view was best enshrined in the Declaration of Independence, which proclaimed American rights and liberties to the western world. According to the Declaration,

---

[14] Samuel Elbert to Captain Francis Moore, July 31, 1777, in OBSE, 51.

Britain's King George III "endeavored to bring on the inhabitants of our frontiers the merciless Indian savages, whose known rule of warfare is an undistinguished destruction of all ages, sexes, & conditions of existence." Thus, according to historian Colin Calloway, the Declaration put Native Americans on the wrong side of history as "savage allies of a tyrannical monarch" and "vicious enemies of liberty." This was precisely Elbert's view of Native Americans, whom he frequently referred to in his writings as "savages." In a letter written to Charles Lee on May 14, 1776, shortly after he assumed command of the Southern Department, Elbert advised the new general that the "Savages…are inclin'd [to use] the Hatchet against us." About two weeks later, he again warned Lee that the "savages" had joined forces with Loyalists to terrorize citizens and steal their provisions and cattle. Most recently, during his aborted Florida campaign, he complained to British Major Mark Prevost about the fate of some of his militia, who were "Butchered by the Savages in cool Blood." Once in the ceded lands, he told McIntosh on August 27 that it was "a little strange that we cant be victorious in one skirmish with the savages." Underscoring Elbert's notion of Indian savagery was a belief that he was fighting barbaric and ruthless murderers who, with hatchets and knives, scalped and mutilated their victims in "cool Blood," much like John Baker's men had ironically done to the warrior they killed in Florida a few months earlier. Elbert refused to acknowledge that Indian modes of warfare were effective methods in achieving their goals of terrorizing the enemy, reclaiming disputed territory, and exacting clan vengeance. To him, the Indians had no role to play in the Revolution outside of remaining neutral or becoming American allies. He could never comprehend that Native Americans, just like himself, were viable military combatants in the broader struggle for rights and liberties embedded in the Revolution.[15]

---

[15] *Declaration of Independence* (1776); Calloway, *American Revolution in Indian Country*, 293; Samuel Elbert to Charles Lee, May 14, 1776, and Samuel Elbert to Charles Lee, May 28, 1776, in PLM, pt. 1, 155–56; Samuel Elbert to Mark Prevost, Cumberland Island, May 31, 1777, in OBSE, 35, and, in the same source, Samuel Elbert to Lachlan McIntosh, August 27, 1777, 53. For the argument that Native Americans were not seen as viable Revolutionary combatants, see Kokomoor, "Burning & Destroying All Before Them," 336.

The Indians were definitely on Elbert's mind when he arrived in Augusta and learned about Dooly's treatment of friendly Creeks. It was incumbent on the colonel, clearly angered, to release the Indians and diffuse the crisis. In his first order from Augusta, on August 13, Elbert sent some of his men, with written instructions, to the local Sheriff and directed him to release Dooly's prisoners and bring them to him. The carefully worded orders never mentioned Indians or "savages" in case they fell into the wrong hands and exacerbated the situation. Elbert promised the sheriff a "sufficient force to enable him to effect the purpose he goes on." Once the Indians were in Elbert's presence, he planned to give them a talk and then have them safely escorted back to their respective towns.[16]

Elbert's talk occurred on August 14, the following day. Present were nine Creek leaders representing different upper and lower towns, including Handsome Fellow and his son and nephew, the Oakchee Warrior, the Cusseta Second Man, Hollowing King, Singee and his son, and the Palachacola Second Man. Many of them knew Elbert. The colonel began by reminding the Indians that the words he spoke in Savannah during an earlier talk were just as true as those he was now uttering. "The people of this State, hold the same Friendship for the good men of your Nation, which they then Professed," he announced, and the bonds of respect and amity were especially strong for Handsome Fellow, who was a "wise, Just, & good man, not fond of spilling the Blood of Innocent Women & Children." The friendship Elbert avowed was contingent on one thing—Indian neutrality. America's quarrel, he pointed out, was with the "King of Great Britain & his people [on] the other side [of the] Broad-Water" and the "Red-people [could not] interfere." The reward for Indian neutrality was trade. Although trade goods were scarce, Elbert assured his audience that "what we had we woud readily share with [you] our Friends." Each day, he assured them, trade articles destined for the Indians arrived in Charleston and Savannah on French and Spanish ships so that soon the Whigs could supply them with everything they needed.[17] This promise was an exaggeration since Elbert's own state could hardly supply its soldiers with the necessities of war.

---

[16] Samuel Elbert, "Orders to Lt. Bough of the 2d Battalion," August 13, 1777, in OBSE, 51.

[17] "Samuel Elbert's Talk to the Handsome Man," Augusta, August 14, 1777, Keith Read Collection, box 7, folder 42, document 1, Hargrett Rare Book and Manuscript Library.

Elbert moved to the heart of his talk, which was that British agents in the towns threatened continued friendship with the Creeks. "I dare say," explained the colonel, "that you have been told a great deal by the King's people, which since you have been with us, you are Convinced were Lies, and you may depend upon it that they will continue to tell many, in order to get you Innocent Men to fight Battles, which they dare not shew their faces in." In truth, their goal was "to bring you into a War with the people of this Vast United Continent, who are as numerous as the Trees and bound togather like a bunch of Twigs." Should the Creeks become deceived and make war on the Whigs, annihilation would follow, just as it had for the Cherokee. American armies, he assured them, were able to "crush you…and any body else who dare make war with them, to Atoms." These were not just idle words: "I don't speak like a madman. I tell you that I know what I say, and I know further, that the day will come when some of your young men will be convinced it is true." Elbert, like the "King's people," was not above misleading the Indians to get desired results. He informed them that America was already winning the contest and "our Great General Washington at the Head of our grand Army to the Northward, had drove all the King of Great Britains Soldiers out of our Land and…they are now on an Island, surrounded by their Men of War to save their Throats from being Cut." Furthermore, America's friends overseas were supplying the Whigs with "more Guns, powder & bullets than we want," and there were already many of France's "great Generals" with Washington's army.[18]

Elbert then brought up the "murder" of Captain Dooly and the others. The murders were intolerable, he said, and the colonel required full satisfaction for their deaths, but not "an Indian for a white-man" as usual. Instead, he wanted to turn them into assassins with instructions to "*Kill* those men, who the King sends amongst you." It was, he said, the only way "for you to save your Country from ruin." Otherwise, the British would drag them into a "War against your brothers, who are born on the same Land and suck the same milk with yourselves." To make amends and set matters right, Elbert demanded, in the name of the United States, "the Lives of those white-men in the Nation who set them on and who of course are the sole cause of what had been done." Should the Indians refuse, they would feel the wrath of angry frontier settlers, which Elbert could not control. The only reason he came to Augusta with his battalion

---

[18] Ibid.

was because "of the late mischief on the Ceded Lands" and he was determined to protect the inhabitants from both Indians and Loyalists. "I should be Sorry to spill the blood of an Indian," he warned his Creek audience, "but I fear the day is not far off when I shall be obliged to do it." After that, Elbert sent the Creeks back to their people. "[I] am in hopes," he told them in parting, "that you will be able…to save your Country from Ruin & may the Great-Master of the Breath assist you."[19]

After the meeting, Elbert summoned Captain Benjamin Porter to assemble some men to escort the Creeks back to Galphin's cowpen. "You are to march with the detachment under your Command, as soon as the Handsome Man is ready, and Guard [him] & protect him & his party from any Insults & Outrages, through our Settlements," commanded the colonel. Rae was to accompany Porter, while Galphin stayed at Silver Bluff to attend other business. Elbert was cognizant of the dangers Porter might encounter along the way. At all times, he was to keep his eyes open for trouble, especially from other Indians. "Be always [on] your Guard," cautioned the commander, "as the Savages come as a Thief in the night."[20]

Elbert next sought details about the Indian ambush on July 22 that resulted in the death of Dooly and several of his men. Preliminary reports told him that Lieutenant Cunningham, who was second in charge during the fight, ordered a retreat without offering any resistance. Based on that information, Elbert relieved Cunningham from command and then directed him "without loss of time" to report immediately. The lieutenant was to bring with him "two or three of the Men who were with him in the Action…in order that [the] matter may be inquired into" through sworn affidavits. Initially, Elbert believed that Cunningham acted in cowardice and put him under arrest. Later, much to the commander's delight, a court of inquiry exonerated Cunningham, who they said conducted himself "with the honor & valor becoming an officer" during the engagement.[21]

The problem with John Dooly still lingered. He reported to Elbert on August 16 to explain his behavior toward the Indians in Augusta. While Elbert was sympathetic to Dooly's plight, he had him arrested, but then made him a prisoner on parole because he needed the captain's leadership and influence with the unruly troop of horse troop in the ceded lands. Shortly before Elbert left Savannah, McIntosh ordered all of the

---

[19] Ibid. Emphasis original; "Kill" is underlined in the original text.
[20] Ibid., Samuel Elbert to Captain Benjamin Porter, August 14, 1777; Cashin, *King's Ranger*, 69.
[21] "After Orders," October 13, 1777, OBSE, 59; Davis, "George Galphin," 19–20.

Continental cavalry in the state to move southward toward Fort Howe and the city. Some of the regiments around Augusta defied McIntosh's order and refused to abandon their homes and families while parties of Indians and Loyalists prowled the region. On August 25, Elbert produced a letter from Governor Treutlen in Dooly's presence. The letter notified all officers and men that Elbert was "appointed commander of the Continental Troops stationed or sent to the westward," and that they must submit to his authority. Treutlen praised Elbert, calling him a "courageous, active and brave commander." In all circumstances, said the governor, the men must be "obedient to his orders."[22]

Elbert then told Dooly to "take a circuit with a sufficient number of your troops of horse to the different forts & stations in the western frontiers" to force all the remaining cavalry to comply with McIntosh's instructions. Elbert specifically mentioned Colonel John Baker's light horse militia, which defied orders from both he and McIntosh. Surely, Baker was in no mood to follow the dictates of Elbert, whom he blamed for his Florida defeat back in May at Thomas Creek. The feeling was mutual since Elbert also partially faulted Baker for his failed campaign. As he told McIntosh at the time, Baker's men were afraid to face the enemy. Nor did he have much respect for Baker, whose regiment was "in the greatest confusion for want of a proper leader." Unwell, unpaid, and plagued with low morale and still recovering from their Florida disaster, Baker's men, unsurprisingly, were reluctant to march southward again. Elbert was unmoved and insisted on the obedience. "All who refuse or are refractory must be made examples of," demanded the colonel, and he instructed Dooly to arrest any insubordinate officers and soldiers and confine them in Wrightsborough until further notice. The friction between Elbert and Baker was so great that, within two months, Baker resigned his commission. He was replaced by Lieutenant Colonel Leonard Marbury, Elbert's friend and a person "more entitled" and "better qualified" than Baker to "collect & bring [the Light Horse] into some order." The troop of light horse was an endless source of frustration for Elbert. "I don't know what to say about the behavior of the Light Horse," he complained to McIntosh on August 27. He continued: "[I] lament that the field officers of that regiment had not attended to see their men march [and] the Capts. and

---

[22] Lachlan McIntosh, "General Orders by Genl. McIntosh," July 24, 1777, in OBSE, 48–49, and, in the same source, John Adam Treutlen to the officers commanding the First and Second Minute Battalion, no date, 52–53.

subalterns have no more authority over them than if they had no commissions at all."[23]

As Elbert tried to gain control over the troop of light horse, Handsome Fellow's group, led by Porter's escort, neared the Ogeechee. It was there that Sam Moore and sixteen of his rangers ambushed the party. In the ensuing fight, the Loyalists killed Captain John Gerard, whom they assumed, because of his looks, to be Galphin, according to what Rutledge and several Georgia leaders later claimed. The rest of the escort and their Indians fled. When Elbert heard about the encounter, he immediately left with eighty men of the 2nd Battalion to find the Rangers and engage them in battle. He marched his men almost sixty miles over the next few days, twelve of which was through a canebrake swamp four miles wide. The men were jittery and expected an ambuscade at any time. At one point in the undergrowth, they saw what they believed was a tent holding some of the enemy. Slowly, they surrounded it, but as they got closer, they discovered that their "tent" was nothing more than a large white log. Later, when Elbert described his pursuit of the Loyalists in a letter to McIntosh, he mentioned the humorous incident and noted that the only damage done to himself and his men was a few mosquito bites.[24]

While Elbert chased elusive Loyalists, Galphin's Indian delegates approached their towns. Before they arrived, Handsome Fellow died of natural causes, but the others with him were able to relay the talks that Elbert and Galphin had given them. Elbert never knew it at the time, but his talk made an impression upon the Creeks who heard it, and they determined to kill all the British agents and confiscate their goods. During their absence, William McIntosh at Cusseta assembled a raiding party of Creek and Cherokee warriors and Loyalists refugees for a planned September 22 attack on Georgia's frontier. Joining them was another group of 200 traders and refugees and 150 Cherokee rounded up by Cameron. Elbert's friendly Indians frustrated the planned attack and instead hatched their own plots to murder McIntosh, Taitt, and Cameron. Alexander

---

[23] Ibid., Samuel Elbert to John Dooly, August 25, 1777, 52, and, in the same source, Samuel Elbert to Lachlan McIntosh, August 27, 1777, 53, Samuel Elbert to James Screven, October 13, 1777, 58–59, and, for Baker's resignation, Samuel Elbert to Robert Howe, October 15, 1777, 61–62; Searcy, *Georgia-Florida Contest*, 24–25; Cashin, *King's Ranger*, 71. For Elbert's relationship to Marbury, see Account Book, 1769–1788, 5, 49–50, Samuel Elbert Papers, Rubenstein Rare Book and Manuscript Library.

[24] Samuel Elbert to Lachlan McIntosh, August 27, 1777, in OBSE, 53; Cashin, *King's Ranger*, 69–70; Davis, "George Galphin," 22.

McGillivray, the half-Indian son of wealthy fur trader Lachlan McGillivray and a rising anti-American leader among the Creeks, heard about the planned murders and helped the agents escape to Pensacola. Stuart's immediate response was to suspend all trade with the Creeks until they expelled Whig agents in their midst and declared total allegiance to the British. Stuart's new policy further exacerbated the deep Revolutionary divide among Creeks and the complete loyalty he sought never materialized since several *talwas* continued trade negotiations with Galphin and Whig commissioners.[25]

Meanwhile, Elbert confronted the mountain of problems that came along with his western command. Given the state of anxiety in the region and the widely dispersed nature of the forts, he decided to leave small detachments in each. This activity took almost two weeks and left him in a much weaker position to oppose the enemy if confronted by an overwhelming force in any one location. On September 9, he told McIntosh that the bulk of his healthy soldiers were scattered over five forts. Nevertheless, their value was negligible since each fort was still undermanned. Elbert stationed twenty-five men at Folsom's Fort on the Ogeechee and nearby, at Wells' Fort, he left an additional forty-seven men. He posted twenty-eight more at Captain Phillips' Fort on the Little River. Joel Phillips' Fort, on Beaverdam Creek (a tributary of the Little River), received nineteen men. Carr's Fort, just below Phillips' Fort, only received eleven Continentals, hardly enough to make any difference. Having seen no Indians during his brief tour, he pronounced the frontier quiet. On September 11, a relieved Elbert wrote to fellow Conservative Whig and current Speaker of the House, Noble W. Jones, and suggested that the immediate danger in the ceded lands had ebbed. "The inhabitants are at present in peace," acknowledged the colonel. Still, the lull could be shattered at any time by another Indian attack. "How long the savages will permit them to remain [at peace]," he rhetorically pondered, "I am at a loss to guess." Only time would tell, but one thing was certain. If any of the forts fell, it would produce substantial civilian casualties since, as Elbert witnessed, they were "crowded with the inhabitants who have not yet returned to their habitations which they quit at the late alarm when Capt. Dooly and others were killed." Elbert spoke too soon. The peace he prematurely hoped for dissipated within months, and by 1780, Indians had attacked all the forts he visited and some of them more than once. Only Carr's Fort remained at

---

[25] Searcy, *Georgia-Florida Contest*, 114–15.

the end of the Revolution.[26]

Another issue facing Elbert were desertions from his army. It was not a new problem, but, as he learned in Florida, the secluded frontier offered irresistible opportunities for soldiers to flee. "Not less than twenty deserted since I came up here," he fumed in a letter to McIntosh in late August. Little wonder, he added, since they only risked one hundred lashes if caught and even that was often remitted. Elbert's own remedy was much more severe. "Pity it is, we can't have a court-martial who dare sentence a man to be shot for this crime," he told McIntosh. Desertion, claimed the colonel, was the most "scandalous & unmanly crime" that a soldier could ever commit. It also hampered the army's strength, especially since half of the battalion was already sick and confined at Wrightsborough.[27]

Although Elbert threatened to shoot deserters, he rarely followed through and instead showed compassion. He often reduced their sentences to some form of corporal punishment to keep them with the army. At times, he was even willing to remit punishment altogether if the deserters would return to their ranks. Such was the case for fifteen of his Virginians who deserted from the 2nd Battalion in the ceded lands. Believing that they had returned to their homes, Elbert sent Captain Shem Cook of the battalion to Virginia with orders to bring them all back to Georgia. He promised them a "free pardon" if they gave themselves up and rejoined the battalion. Otherwise, he offered a twenty-dollar reward for the return of each missing soldier.[28]

---

[26] Samuel Elbert to Noble Jones, September 11, 1777, in OBSE, 55, and, in the same source, Samuel Elbert to Lachlan McIntosh (?), September 9, 1777, 54–55. See also Hall, *Land and Allegiance*, 62. A period map from 1770 showing the close location between Phillip's Fort and "Cers [Carr's] Fort" can be seen in Elliot and Davis Jr., "Captain Robert Carr's Fort," 11.

[27] Chandler, "To become again our brethren," 371; Samuel Elbert to Lachlan McIntosh, August 27, 1777, in OBSE, 53, and, in the same source, Samuel Elbert to Lachlan McIntosh (?), September 9, 1777, 54; for the "unmanly" quote, "Parole—Arnold," Headquarters, Savannah, November 17, 1777, 72–73.

[28] *Virginia Gazette*, Purdie, November 28, 1777, 3, col. 1. Desertion continued to plague the army in Georgia for the duration of the Revolution. In 1782, General Anthony Wayne in Savannah complained that deserters were interested in preserving their "life and health, in a more hospitable and native climate." This observation was certainly applicable to Elbert's Virginians in the 2nd Battalion. See General Anthony Wayne to Governor John Martin, April 22, 1782, John Martin Papers, 1782, Rubenstein Rare Book and Manuscript Library.

A matter involving Elizabeth Elbert in Savannah arose in early September causing the colonel to shorten his presence on the western frontier and accompany her in the city toward the end of the month. While Elbert never specified the reason, he told his commander that Mrs. Elbert was in "a situation, which requires her being in Savannah." This suggests that Elbert's wife and their two daughters were probably staying outside of the city, perhaps at Rae's Hall or maybe even in Augusta. The circumstances bringing the Elberts to Savannah may have included the birth of their third child, a daughter named Sarah, who was born in 1777 or shortly thereafter. A second explanation may have to do with extensive renovations to his Savannah home. According to his account book, in 1777, Elbert hired out Henry Rolland, a local carpenter, to repair his residence, and perhaps both he and his wife needed to be there to oversee the work. It is possible that the anticipation of a new child prompted the remodeling.[29]

Back in Savannah, political infighting reached new levels of intensity stemming from the McIntosh-Gwinnett duel a few months earlier. For a while, it seemed that the fallout from the duel would slowly fade, especially after McIntosh apologized to Gwinnett's widow for killing her husband. Resentment among Gwinnett's friends festered, however, and they sought to avenge their fallen leader. A group calling itself the Liberty Society relentlessly assaulted McIntosh. Foremost among its leaders were Lyman Hall and Joseph Wood, who circulated petitions calling for McIntosh's dismissal. During the summer, they collected 574 signatures from several counties and then presented them to the assembly as evidence of McIntosh's inability to lead. Their efforts to crush the general bore fruit, and they convinced many that as long as he retained command in the state, Georgia could never be safe. "The radicals' victory was at hand," explained one historian, "but it was won at a terrible cost. Army discipline was shattered, morale was gone, and for a large segment of the population all faith in Georgia's Continental forces and their commander had disappeared."[30]

George Walton and Henry Laurens, two of McIntosh's friends in the Continental Congress, rushed to his defense at the last hour. In August

---

[29] Account Book, 1769–1788, 31, Samuel Elbert Papers, Rubenstein Rare Book and Manuscript Library; Samuel Elbert to Lachlan McIntosh (?), September 9, 1777, LBGSE, 55.

[30] Jackson, *Lachlan McIntosh*, 66–69.

and early September, as Elbert inspected forts in the ceded lands, the congressmen exerted their influence to have the tarnished general transferred to Washington's army. This arrangement, of course, would accomplish the objective of the radicals, which was to drum McIntosh out of the state. Rather than waiting on word from Congress, the General Assembly asserted their own civil authority and passed a resolution eliminating McIntosh from command. Arguing that only Congress could terminate his command, McIntosh refused to abide by the assembly's resolution. The assembly disagreed and drew up a petition denouncing the general for refusing to bow to its will. Simultaneously, it picked Elbert to replace McIntosh.[31]

Elbert learned of these developments on September 8 while still in Wilkes County, when an urgent letter arrived from Jones, the speaker of the House, offering him command over Georgia's Continental forces. After a stunned Elbert read the letter, he carefully formulated his response, and the result, claimed one historian, was "a masterpiece of composition." He began by acknowledging the receipt of Jones's communication "covering some resolves of your honorable assembly," but their request gave him much "pain." After due reflection, he rejected the promotion based on principle:

> I am obliged to decline accepting the Command they do me the honor to offer, nor can you judge how much I am embarrassed at being under the necessity of differing in opinion with so respectable a body. While General McIntosh contends for the command of the Continental Troops in the State, and I continue to hold my commission, I am bound to obey him, and were I presume to do otherwise, I should subject myself to be tried by a court-martial.[32]

Elbert's decision was a point of honor, and he vowed to leave the army if forced to violate his oath and commission. "That love for my Country which prompted me to engage in its service will have equal weights when I find myself a clog to its interests," eloquently explained the colonel, and he would never allow any error of judgment on his part to "prejudice" the country's success. Under the circumstances, he was willing to step aside and "leave an opening for those, who may have a different opinion, by

---

[31] Ibid., 69.
[32] Samuel Elbert to Noble Jones, September 11, 1777, in OBSE, 55; Searcy, *Georgia-Florida Contest*, 104.

resuming the character of a citizen."[33] Thus, twice in the span of just a few months, the radicals tried to usurp McIntosh through an appeal to Elbert's ambition by offering him a Continental command, and both times they failed due to his feelings of honor, duty, and loyalty.

Shortly afterward, Elbert left for Savannah, leaving his 2nd Battalion scattered in Wilkes County. He was back in the city by October 9 after only about a month on the frontier. On the following day, October 10, the Continental Congress transferred McIntosh to Washington's army in Pennsylvania. On that same day, McIntosh named Elbert as his replacement and ordered the army to "respect & obey him as their commanding officer." Thus, on October 10, 1777, Elbert became the leader of Georgia's Continental Line with a continuing rank of colonel even as he still held his state commission as a militia colonel.[34]

Elbert inherited the myriad problems plaguing McIntosh's command, such as the lack of pay and limited supplies for the soldiers, low morale, and the loss of faith by the people in the army. Friends and family members profited from his promotion. On October 13, for example, he named family member, James Rae Jr., to be the commissary general of purchase for the state and, on the same day, he promoted John Habersham (Joseph's younger brother) to major of the 1st Battalion.[35]

The difficulties facing Elbert were apparent from the beginning. On his first day, he learned that some soldiers in Savannah were on the verge of mutiny for want of pay. At the same time, the colonel discovered that the Light Horse Troop, without orders or permission, suddenly abandoned Fort Howe. Enraged, Elbert told Colonel Screven that their behavior was intolerable and while he commanded, he was "determined…that duty shall be attended to." The new leader was even unsure of the total number of men he commanded, or where they were stationed. Seeking information, Elbert asked McIntosh for a return of Georgia's troops before he left, but even the general was unsure. He then ordered his officers to prepare immediate returns on their units and to include an estimate of reliable weapons and supplies. As he tried to gain a comprehensive picture of his defensive and offensive capacities, word arrived about an imminent attack on Georgia from St. Augustine. His response was to order the 2nd Battalion to Savannah, but luckily for him and for Georgia, the attack

---

[33] Samuel Elbert to Noble Jones, September 11, 1777, in OBSE, 55.

[34] Ibid., Lachlan McIntosh, Orders, Headquarters, Savannah, October 10, 1777, 56.

[35] Ibid., Samuel Elbert, "Parole—McIntosh," Headquarters, Savannah, October 13, 1777, 57.

never materialized although bands of rangers and Indians continued to infiltrate the borders. After nearly two weeks, Elbert's understanding of his command was still incomplete. On October 25, he complained to Howe that his troops were "so scattered that I can't obtain accurate returns to send you."[36]

There was still the lingering issue with John Dooly, who remained on parole and continued to ride with his regiment. Finally caving to pressure from South Carolina's leaders, Howe sent Elbert instructions to arrest Dooly and the other three men involved in the abuse of Indians at Augusta. In compliance, Elbert reluctantly sent Colonel John Stirk with some men to find and apprehend Dooly. Elbert remained sympathetic to Dooly's plight. Back on September 9, when Elbert reported the incident to his superior, he admitted that he arrested Dooly's party and put them on parole. Beyond that, he did not know what to do with them. The colonel needed them in the army and wanted to overlook their transgressions, especially since the Indians were safely back in their towns. "The gentlemen [are] very sensible of their error," explained the commander. "Poor Dooley [Dooly] had lost a brother," while Major Joseph Pannell only went along to prevent mischief. The other two, Lieutenants Gideon Booker of the 3rd Battalion and John Bilbo of the Light Horse Troop, did not know any better and were just "giddy young men." Elbert believed that arresting all four served the purpose of showing them "that they are not always to do as they please."[37]

When Stirk finally located the men, they refused to submit and instead took refuge in a frontier fort. Stirk, apparently confused by the order to arrest Dooly a second time, sent Elbert a dispatch for clarification. Elbert exploded in anger for defiance of his specific instructions. "Dear Sir," he wrote back, "It astonishes me that you should send to know whether you are to take Dooley [Dooly] or not after my positive orders to do so." Stirk was to apprehend Dooly no matter what. "If he will not surrender himself to you lay the fort in ashes," and if that did not work, "collect all the troops to the westward for the purpose." Elbert's expectations were

---

[36] Ibid., Samuel Elbert to Colonel James Screven, October 10, 1777, 56–57, and, in the same source, Samuel Elbert to Lachlan McIntosh, October 10, 1777, 57; "Parole—McIntosh, Headquarters, Savannah," October 13, 1777, 57; Samuel Elbert to Colonel John Stirk, October 13, 1777, 58; Samuel Elbert to Robert Howe, October 25, 1777, 68.

[37] Ibid., Samuel Elbert to Lachlan McIntosh (?), September 6, 1777, 54, and, in the same source, Samuel Elbert to Colonel John Stirk, October 13, 1777, 58. See also Searcy, *Georgia-Florida Contest*, 114.

clear. The "business" was to be "executed" immediately and successfully. Elbert believed that Dooly's actions breached ethical standards governing soldiers, especially since he violated a verbal "parole of honor" personally given to the commander a few weeks earlier.[38]

Stirk's threats eventually coaxed Dooly's compatriots to give up, but the errant captain remained barricaded in the fort. When Major Pannell surrendered, Elbert interrogated him in Savannah. After listening to Pannell, Elbert pronounced him blameless. On October 25, he sent the major, under guard, to Howe in Charleston for further questioning, along with a supporting letter proclaiming Pannell's innocence. Even at that late date, Elbert could not assure Howe that Dooly was in custody, but soon afterwards, the defiant captain surrendered. A military court of inquiry was held on November 7 into the conduct of Dooly, Bilbo, and Booker. When it concluded, Elbert sent Howe a copy of the court's report. The men remained under arrest until released by Howe's order. "I will be obliged to you to release them as soon as possible," implored Elbert to the general, especially since "we are scarce of officers." Howe did release them, and Bilbo, Pannell, and Booker continued to serve in the military. Humiliated, Dooly resigned his commission. Despite the troubles he caused, his popularity remained high in Wilkes County, and within the year, he was again leading local militia as a colonel.[39]

By mid-October, those guilty of causing the Light Horse Troop to abandon their post at Fort Howe were also apprehended and punished. Three ringleaders received one hundred lashes on their bare backs and four others who accompanied them got sixty. Elbert believed their conduct was disgraceful and strictly commanded the officers administering the sentence to "see the lashes laid on with uncommon severity, as by articles of war the offence should be punished with death."[40]

---

[38] Samuel Elbert to Colonel John Stirk, October 13, 1777, in OBSE, 58, and, in the same source, Samuel Elbert to Robert Howe, October 17, 1777, 62–63.

[39] Ibid., Samuel Elbert to Robert Howe, October 25, 177, 68. See also, in the same source, "Parole—Washington," Headquarters, Savannah, November 7, 1777, 70, and Samuel Elbert to Robert Howe, November 17, 1777, 72; Davis, "George Galphin," 23. The court's findings were never specified, but the men apparently were reprimanded and then released.

[40] Samuel Elbert, "Parole—Harris," Headquarters, Savannah, October 18, 1777, in OBSE, 63.

The episode with the Light Horse Troop brought into focus a more widespread issue plaguing Elbert's command, which was the lack of money to pay soldiers for their enlistment. It was an old problem. A year earlier, McIntosh connected the desertion of Jerimiah Bugg and his men from Beard's Bluff to their seven months of service without pay. Elbert knew that the absence of pay increased desertion rates, and perhaps this is why he often showed mercy when soldiers were punished in spite of his talk about executions. After the punishment of the light horse deserters, Elbert went directly to the paymaster and scolded him. "You entirely neglect the duty of paymaster," he barked, and "I desire that you do immediately…let the matter be settled to my satisfaction & the men paid, or as my duty requires I shall be under the necessity of appointing one in your stead."[41]

From the onset of the Revolution, Georgia struggled financially, but by the time Elbert assumed command, the state's economy was much worse. The majority of Georgia's military funding came from state issued bills of credit, and, by 1777, the whole system was overextended and the treasury nearly empty. Additionally, Georgia's currency depreciated in value far below the rates in other states and even below Continental bills. During the summer, while Elbert was in Wilkes County, the commissary general appealed to the public for funds to pay the army. At Treutlen's urging, Congress finally voted the state $700,000 to redeem its credit and cover future expenses. In September, it gave Georgia an additional $1,000,000, but the money never seemed to arrive fast enough. On October 24, for example, Elbert was embarrassed to tell James Bradley that the twenty men he helped to recruit out of state for the Light Horse Troop could not be paid due to insufficient funds. "I would cheerfully send the money you want for the purpose of marching your men to this State," he lamented, "but at present we have it not."[42]

The state's money woes probably caused Elbert to consider his own finances. The war had all but ruined his merchant firms, even as Loyalists raided his cowpens and drove most of his cattle into Florida. As a man of means with large tracts of property, Elbert, unlike most Georgians, still had access to money. He had enough to spend on a phaeton earlier in the year, for example, and was able to finance expensive renovations at his Savannah home during the summer. His money may have been running out,

---

[41] Samuel Elbert to George Randal, Paymaster, October 17, 1777, ibid., 62; Lachlan McIntosh to Robert Howe, January 7, 1777, in PLM, pt. 2, 263–64.

[42] K. Coleman, *American Revolution in Georgia*, 92–93; Samuel Elbert to James Bradley, October 24, 1777, in OBSE, 67.

though. At some point in 1777, he sat down to figure out just how much the state owed him. According to his own reckoning, Georgia was in debt to Elbert for the sum of £5,479.6.5. The total included money due him by Georgia for his salary as a colonel, which was $50 per month, but also debts for other expenses he accrued on the state's behalf. He often used his money to buy items for the battalion, including flintlocks, powder, lead, and rum. Additionally, Elbert regularly paid bounties for new enlistments. In March, for example, he gave £7.10 to John Strong for bounty money, along with countless other new recruits. He even loaned money to Treutlen for state business. Elbert kept a tally in his account book to record the state's debts to him, listing the reason for the expenditures and the amount due. When news of the great American victory at Saratoga by Generals Horatio Gates and Benedict Arnold over John Burgoyne's British army in New York reached Georgia in early November, Elbert ordered his Continentals in Savannah to form up and fire a six round "feu de joye," which was a joyous musket salute. He then threw a lavish party for his officers, which he funded, to celebrate the "happy news."[43] Elbert, of course, charged the party to the state's account.

Elbert and Elizabeth were shocked to hear later in the year that John Rae Jr., his wife's brother and owner of Rae's Hall, had suddenly died. He was probably interred near his father in the family cemetery on top of the Indian mound at Pipemaker's Creek. The death was unexpected considering that back in the spring, Rae identified himself as a "planter" who was "sound in health and mind" in his last will. The will, signed on April 12, named Elbert as an executor, along with Rae's uncle Robert, and sister Jane Somerville, who inherited Rae's Hall. Elbert's two daughters received a small inheritance from Rae. Elizabeth, the oldest, was bequeathed £200 while her younger sister, Caty, received £100. The will never mentioned Elizabeth.[44] It also put the dream of owning Rae's Hall further from Elbert's grasp; neither he nor his heirs ever gained control of the property.

---

[43] Account Book, 1769–1788, 3–4, 9, Samuel Elbert Papers, Rubenstein Rare Book and Manuscript Library; PCS, February 22, 1777, 125; Samuel Elbert, "Parole—Gates," November 11, 1777, in OBSE, 71.

[44] Will of John Rae Jr., April 12, 1777, Will Book B, Court of Ordinary, Chatham County Court House, Savannah, 59; Savannah Unit, Georgia Writers' Project, "Rae's Hall Plantation, Part I," 240.

Samuel Elbert matured as a commander in 1777. Although he had not yet fought a major battle, or even exchanged gunfire with the enemy, he did lead two campaigns as an independent commander. Earlier, in the spring, he commanded a failed invasion of St. Augustine against all odds of success. During the late summer and fall, he assumed command on the state's western border where he toured and strengthened frontier defenses, negotiated with Indians, and tried to bring order to the troops under his leadership. Both campaigns highlighted elements of Elbert's leadership style and abilities. He showed himself to be decisive, determined, and optimistic even when faced with the worst possible situations. In most instances, his decisions were sound, but sometimes he acted rashly out of anger, such as when he ordered all of the homes and outbuildings burned on Amelia Island during the invasion of Florida in retaliation for the deaths of some of his soldiers. Overall, Charles C. Jones assessed him as an excellent commander who was a "brave, active, and intelligent" leader and a "dashing officer and hard fighter."[45] Elbert showed much respect for his superiors, especially McIntosh and Howe, and followed their orders, even when he disagreed with them. Twice in the span of the year, McIntosh's enemies in the state's government tried to replace the general with Elbert. It was Elbert's deep sense of duty and honor that caused him to turn down both offers, and he only assumed the position of supreme command in Georgia's Continental Line after Congress sent McIntosh to join Washington's army. While he enjoyed the support of Georgia's General Assembly and Treutlen, who deemed him a "courageous, active, and brave" leader, Elbert tried to rise above the political squabbles dividing his state and concentrated instead on disciplining and leading his army. Devoted to independence and duty, Elbert refused to acknowledge that civil authority superseded that of the federal government regarding Georgia's Continental forces.

Above all, Elbert showed concern and compassion for his men. His officers respected him. Colonel James Jackson, a militia commander in the state, once quipped that "every officer" ought to have "esteem" for Elbert.[46] It was not just the officers. Elbert's men thought much of him. He struck a healthy balance when it came to his soldiers; he drilled them incessantly but also recognized their need for rest and encouragement. Elbert always

---

[45] C. C. Jones Jr., *Samuel Elbert*, 39.
[46] Regimental Book, First Regiment, Chatham County Militia, James Jackson, June 1, 1780, in box 10, Charles C. Jones Papers, Rubenstein Rare Book and Manuscript Library.

did his best to ensure that his men were well supplied, often at his own expense. He was an advocate for them when it came to payment for their service and sometimes confronted authorities about the matter on behalf of his men. He expressed an ongoing concern for their health. After all, it was Elbert who initially suggested that his battalion be marched to the interior of the state during summer 1777 to recover their health. Finally, he showed mercy when soldiers were found guilty of crimes in court martial trials, including desertion.

The campaigns of 1777 also exposed many things that Elbert detested. He abhorred cowardice and desertion, but even then, Elbert could be forgiving. He complained loudly about the violence perpetrated on the frontier by both Loyalists and Indians. He particularly loathed British Indian agents, whom he blamed for much of the depredations and murders taking place there and even urged friendly Creeks to kill them. The colonel demanded respect due to the level of his rank. He also expected officers and soldiers to follow his orders to perfection. When they failed, Elbert often lashed out at them. Still, when his temper cooled, he was quick to forgive the offenders, like Dooly, and said nothing else about it. Sometimes, though, Elbert harbored resentment, such as that he felt toward John Baker after the defeat of his militia during the Florida campaign. Pressure from Elbert finally caused Baker to resign his commission.

At the end of 1777, Elbert could rest assured that he did everything possible within his limited abilities to keep his state safe, but Georgia was not out of danger. Although no British armies had landed on Georgia's shores, Florida, with its Loyalists and Indians, represented an imminent threat, and it seemed that nothing could stop them. While he confronted many problems as commander, like desertion, insufficient recruitment in the battalions, lack of pay for soldiers, an empty treasury, deficits in firearms and powder, raiding Indians, incomplete troop returns, and low morale, among others, they all seemed to be connected to the growing Florida menace and the state's ability (or inability) to defend itself. Georgians believed they could never live in safety until St. Augustine was subdued. While Elbert did not relish the thought of another Florida offensive, rumblings of a third campaign soon began in the General Assembly, and in early 1778, they turned into a clamorous roar calling for the final reduction of St. Augustine.

Chapter 9

"You Must Imagine What My Feelings Were": Action on the Frederica River and the Third Florida Campaign, 1778

"From many circumstances it appears that an invasion of the state is intended shortly from St. Augustine," wrote a frantic Colonel Samuel Elbert on October 13, 1777, to Colonel James Screven, commander of Georgia's 3rd Battalion. To meet the threat, Elbert ordered him to send one of his officers to the western frontier and promptly bring the Continentals stationed there to Savannah. Two days later, he informed his superior in Charleston, General Robert Howe, that an invasion was imminent. "[I] believe that our southern neighbors intend [on] paying us a visit very soon," he warned. He based his evidence, he said, on information obtained from prisoners and secret letters in possession of Governor John Adams Treutlen. "I have been busied in collecting & putting in order our scattered forces," he explained to Howe, "and as soon as I can possibly obtain it, [I] shall send you a return of the brigade."[1]

Elbert did not need Treutlen's letters or any other intelligence to remind him of Florida's menace since Loyalist raids from St. Augustine kept Georgia in perpetual crisis. There was little the state could do to prevent the raids and its response was largely reactionary. For example, Sam Moore and his band of Loyalists, who attempted to assassinate George Galphin a few weeks earlier, were still at large. In mid-October, Elbert learned that they were camped near the forks of the Canoochee River, a tributary of the Ogeechee just south of Savannah. On October 19, he told Screven to take a body of men to the area and either apprehend or annihilate them. Determined to catch Moore, Elbert sent fifty men from Savannah under

---

[1] Samuel Elbert to James Screven, October 13, 1777, in OBSE, 58, and, in the same source, Samuel Elbert to Robert Howe, October 15, 1777, 61.

Colonel Francis Harris to join Screven and snare the raiders. To avoid friendly fire, he suggested to both commanders that every man "put a white piece of paper or linen as a cockade in your hats." As an added precaution, the parole was "Washington." If both parties encountered each other, he told Screven, the sign of friendship would be a "loud *hem*," to be answered with two loud claps of the hand. Elbert cautioned Screven to keep his mission secret. "Don't let any person, even your brother, know the errand you are going upon, or the rout you intend to take," he warned. His orders to Harris were almost identical: "You are to use every means in your power to intercept and take those villians [*sic*]." Harris was to "March all night" and quietly "secrete yourself in the day, or they will get intelligence." Not a soul could be trusted and if anyone saw them, they were to be impressed so that "information cant be given about you; those you detain will act as guides." Since the mission's success depended on secrecy, severe punishment awaited anyone who so much as fired a gun. "Be vigilant," advised Elbert. Evidently, neither Screven nor Harris had any luck because a frustrated Elbert was still sending units up the Canoochee in early December. On December 9, he told Joseph Habersham to take twenty-five men and find Moore, whose "gang" numbered about forty Loyalists split up into small groups. "[I] am in hopes you will have the honor of making prisoners of that gang of thieves," he said. Habersham was to "leave no stone unturned" in his effort. Habersham had about as much success as the others and returned to Savannah a few days later empty-handed.[2]

Defending Georgia from Loyalists and Indians was challenging enough, but given the wretched state of the army and the treasury's depleted funds, an offensive strike southward made little sense. For one, Elbert could never be sure how many men he commanded, despite numerous requests for accurate returns. The best estimate during fall 1777 showed 1,526 troops in the first three battalions, the horse regiment, and scattered companies of artillery. However, due to sickness, desertions, the end of enlistments, and other factors, only six hundred (well under half of the army) were available. The precise number of militia was anyone's guess, but under any circumstance, not over two thousand could be collected in an emergency.[3]

---

[2] Ibid., Samuel Elbert to James Screven, October 19, 1777, 64–65, Samuel Elbert to Francis Harris, October 19, 1777, 66, and Samuel Elbert to Joseph Habersham, December 9, 1777, 79.

[3] K. Coleman, *American Revolution in Georgia*, 105. Recruits from Pennsylvania for the 4th Battalion were just arriving in Savannah during late October. See Samuel Elbert,

In addition to low numbers, a scarcity of weapons plagued Elbert's army. While the problem was not new, the inadequacies became glaringly obvious as the war entered its third year. The state's artillery units did not even have brass fieldpieces for their batteries. Elbert notified Howe on October 15 that "we have not one in the State" and he hoped that the general would furnish three or four that were "properly mounted" along with some shot and canister. There was not even a single ream of cartridge paper available, and an anxious Elbert urged Howe to "Please…order us some" in a large quantity. The situation with the soldiers' uniforms was just as bad. Considering the importance that Elbert placed on appearances, it must have galled him to write on November 3 that his men were "very bare of clothes."[4]

Elbert's reputation, by fall 1777, was that of a stern disciplinarian, but even he could not control everyone in the army. He was mortified to learn in mid-October that some of his officers were sneaking beds into their guard barracks and sleeping on duty. The angry colonel notified the whole army on October 19 that if he ever visited the guard during the day or night and found an officer asleep, he would "immediately have him relieved & put under arrest to be tried for [such an] unsoldierlike practice." If an officer could not perform guard duty for twenty-four hours without sleeping, quipped the colonel, then he was unqualified to bear a commission.[5]

Just before Christmas, Howe moved his headquarters from Charleston to Savannah and one of the first things he noticed, much to Elbert's embarrassment, was the colonel's undisciplined men. On Christmas Day, he rebuked Elbert's guards for their appearance and behavior. "The loose, disorderly manner, in which reliefs of guards march up; the awkwardness of the sentries, in the most common movements of their firelocks; the ignorance of sergeants & corporals in their duty, and the general want of discipline…are circumstances of anxiety and surprise to the General." He continued,

> It is painful to…add, but…he has, as yet, hardly met with one soldier, who has treated him with a proper [respect]. The relief of guard yesterday was performed in so loose and disorderly a manner as to impress

---

"Parole—Roberts," Headquarters, October 31, 1777, in OBSE, 68–69.

[4] Samuel Elbert to Robert Howe, October 15, 1777, in OBSE, 61, and, in the same source, Samuel Elbert, "Parole—Laurens," Headquarters, 69.

[5] Samuel Elbert, "Parole—Demere," Headquarters, October 19, 1777, ibid., 64.

him with inexpressible concern; and what enhanced his mortification was, that he did not observe one officer of the guard exerting himself to correct the mistakes of men. The motions of the feet, of all others so essential for a soldier to be instructed in, as every thing depends upon proper movements, seem entirely unknown to most of the soldiers he has met with; they walk indeed, but do not march.[6]

Compounding Elbert's humiliation, Howe, on December 31, again brought up the unprofessional demeanor of the battalions. "The soldiers appearing in the manner they do," complained the general, "with flapp'd hats, in any place…is slovenly and unsoldierly. Hats, however ordinary, may surely be cocked." The criticism did not end there. "Do officers of companies take no pride in the appearance of their men, or can they possibly conceive that their credit is not concerned in it?" he wondered. "Every want of attention to the men is displeasing to the General. A soldierly appearance in troops renders them respectable to their fellow citizens, and formidable to their enemies."[7] Elbert certainly concurred with this latter observation.

Insufficient men, deficits in weaponry, ill-clad soldiers, and an overall lack of discipline all suggested that Georgia's offensive capacity was severely limited. The only logical response to Florida's threat was defensive, yet Georgia's weakened state rendered it practically incapable of even that. Howe, despite his harsh criticisms, felt sympathy for Elbert's men. In early April 1778, after spending almost four months with Georgia's Continentals, he wrote to the president of the Continental Congress, Henry Laurens from South Carolina, explaining the sad conditions he witnessed. Georgia's treasury was nearly exhausted, he said, and payments due to the soldiers were in such arrears that mutiny lurked around the corner. "Most of the men [were] so naked that it was indecent to Parade them," and if there was a serious attack, there was not a stock of powder available to defend a garrison for five days. Nor were there enough provisions to feed the army for three days if forced to march.[8]

As Georgia's military strength dwindled, the power of East Florida's garrison increased. This was, paradoxically, due in part to the anti-Loyalist policies enacted by Georgia's General Assembly during fall 1777. On September 16, it passed "An Act for the Expulsion of the Internal Enemies of

---

[6] Robert Howe, "Parole—Georgia," December 25, 1777, ibid., 80–81.

[7] Robert Howe, "Parole—Houstoun," December 31, 1777, ibid., 85.

[8] Robert Howe to Henry Laurens, April 25, 1778, in Chesnutt, ed., *Papers of Henry Laurens*, 13:185; McCall, *History of Georgia*, 2:134.

this State," or simply, the Expulsion Act. Georgia was not alone in enacting legislation aimed at driving out Loyalists, although it was the last to do so. The measure was justified, claimed its authors, because Georgia's Loyalists colluded with their counterparts in Florida to destroy the state, even as they incited the Indians to conduct their brutal warfare on the frontier. "The savages," claimed the new law, made an "extremely dangerous and crucial situation" worse by "continually infesting our frontiers settlements, and sacrificing, in the most barbarous manner, numbers of our worthy citizens." Their war against civilians was "encouraged and supported by the Governor of Saint Augustine" along with the "internal enemies of this state." Exiling Loyalists seemed the only remedy to the problem. The law formed twelve member committees of inquiry in each county to judge people suspected of treason. If a person appeared before a committee, they had to bring two or more witnesses to vouch for their loyalty after which they were required to take an oath of allegiance to Georgia and another to renounce the king. It only took seven people on a committee to vote for banishment. In that case, those exiled had forty days to vacate, and, if they returned without permission, or were ever discovered bearing arms against Georgia or the United States, they faced execution for high treason. To provide an appearance of justice, the Expulsion Act allowed convicted Loyalists to retain half of their property even as they forfeited the rest to the state.[9]

Almost immediately, committees of inquiry charged inhabitants of Toryism, and the state seized their property. While it sounded patriotic, the Expulsion Act was flawed, and Elbert was among the first to criticize it. On October 16, he wrote Howe, who was still in Charleston, informing him that the law created new problems in his command. Since there were no large vessels in Savannah's port, the commander was flooded with requests for boat passes, and he sought the general's opinion on how to proceed. At least Elbert was certain of one thing. He assumed, correctly, that their immediate destination was St. Augustine. For this reason, he questioned the law's wisdom, which he pronounced as unsound since it strengthened "the hands of our east Florida neighbors." Even worse, those banished were "well acquainted with the situation and strength of the state, and at a time when we have every reason to think an invasion from them

---

[9] H. Robertson, "Georgia's Banishment and Expulsion Act," 274–82. Historians cannot agree on the number of people banished although the committees convicted 177 people of treason in March 1778 and drummed them out of the state (K. Coleman, *American Revolution in Georgia*, 87).

is intended."¹⁰ In other words, the Expulsion Act's intention of making the state secure was counterproductive because it transferred vital information to the enemy about the true condition of Georgia's weak defenses, even as it funneled more men into Loyalist armies and, once unleashed, those strengthened forces and their Indian allies could overrun the state.

Elbert was not alone in opposing the act. Others did too, but for different reasons. Although its supporters claimed that it upheld justice, it was an assault on individual rights since it made a mockery of the ideals encompassing the Revolution, such as the freedom of speech, the ownership of property, and the right to a fair trial by a jury of peers. John Wereat, the state's agent to the Continental Congress, believed that the Expulsion Act was unconstitutional. Writing to Lachlan McIntosh on March 13, 1778, he admitted that some of the Loyalists probably deserved their fate, but the assembly's actions were unreconciled to the law. "Our Constitution says Trial by jury shall remain sacred and inviolate forever," he protested, "but this Law condemns many without any trial at all to forfeit both their life and property. Thus Sir, you see the plighted fate of the state. [Whatever] ought to be sacred is set at nought [sic]."¹¹

Georgia's Expulsion Act, in addition to the one passed earlier in South Carolina, caused a mass exodus of Loyalists through and from the state to St. Augustine. They traveled by any means available, even by foot. Midway Loyalist William Lyford Jr. traveled by boat. On October 2, Midway's Council of Safety gave Lyford forty days to vacate for refusing to produce vouchers and take a loyalty oath. He filled his boats with family, slaves, and all the possessions they could hold. When he left, rebels burned his plantation on St. Catherine's Island and confiscated everything else. The sudden invasion of Loyalists appearing in Georgia concerned Elbert and represented yet another reason why he thought the act was harmful. "Some steps [must] be immediately taken in South Carolina to prevent an intercourse between their back settlements and the thieves of Florida," he warned Howe. "All in our power will be done in this state but the river Savannah has so many fording places, that to guard them all would require an army of ten thousand men."¹²

As Loyalist refugees poured through the state, Howe consolidated all

---

[10] Samuel Elbert to Robert Howe, October 17, 1777, in OBSE, 62–63.

[11] John Wereat to Lachlan McIntosh, March 13, 1778, Lachlan McIntosh Papers, Rubenstein Rare Book and Manuscript Library.

[12] Samuel Elbert to Robert Howe, December 5, 1777, in OBSE, 76–77; Braddock Sr., "Plight of a Georgia Loyalist," 255–56.

four battalions into one brigade of Georgia Continentals under Elbert's command. Despite the fusing of units, the battalions retained their unique identities. On January 21, 1778, he ordered flags for all the battalions, each with their own camp colors. Elbert's former 2nd Battalion received two flags with white backgrounds and blue insertions. The 1st Battalion's flag had a blue background with yellow insertions, the 3rd Battalion had a green background (the color for the insertion is not known), and the 4th Battalion had a red background with blue insertions. The insertions probably included some numerical designation of the battalion's identity.[13] Soon, those flags would flutter in the field as Georgia's political leaders trumped up calls for their annual campaign into Florida.

According to the state's constitution, Treutlen's term ended after one year and the General Assembly, on January 8, chose John Houstoun as his successor. Born in St. George's Parish in 1744, Houstoun emerged as a prominent leader during Georgia's Revolutionary movement. The Provincial Congress elected him as a delegate to the Continental Congress in 1775, but none of those chosen attended due to deep political divisions within the state. Selected again as a delegate to the Continental Congress in 1776, Houstoun chose instead to remain in Georgia and fight against those (like John Zubly) who sought reconciliation with the Crown.[14] The decision cost Houstoun fame. Had he gone to Philadelphia, he would have been one of Georgia's signers of the Declaration of Independence, along with Button Gwinnett, Lyman Hall, and George Walton.

Like his predecessors, Houstoun enthusiastically embraced the goal of invading Florida, despite the miserable condition of Georgia's battalions and the state's treasury. On January 29, he shared with his council and the General Assembly a report from Mordecai Sheftall, the commissary of the Continental troops. Appointed to that position in 1777 by Elbert, Sheftall intimately knew the needs of Georgia's battalions, and, according to him, provisions and almost all other necessities were nearly exhausted. Sheftall's dire picture forced the assembly to pass a bill providing nearly £1,000 in temporary funding. Clearly, Georgia was in no position to undertake an offensive against anyone, but unbelievably, on the same day, the assembly passed a resolution recommending that Howe immediately lead a third incursion into East Florida. Although he opposed the assembly's resolution, Howe called a council of war at his headquarters in Savannah on

---

[13] Robert Howe, "Parole—Moultrie," January 21, 1778, in OBSE, 93.
[14] White, *Historical Collections of Georgia*, 209.

February 7 to consider the proposal. Present were Elbert, Habersham, and several other officers. After some discussion, the general put the proposal to a vote. The unanimous sentiment of everyone was that any general "would be doomed culpable in marching the Continental Troops out of Georgia." Following the vote, Howe informed Houstoun that a Florida invasion was not feasible, that his officers unanimously opposed it, and that it would leave the state defenseless.[15]

Houstoun did not like Howe's response, and it was the beginning of a stormy relationship with the new governor. Few in Georgia's government held Howe in high esteem. The primary reason, of course, was that he stood as a deterrent to their own plans for conducting the war. From Howe's perspective, scheming up another Florida invasion, plagued with the same problems that doomed the others, while hoping for the best was sheer fantasy. No wonder, he remarked around the same time, that Georgia's defenseless state and bickering politicians made his command "embarrassing" and a "circumstance of anxiety and fatigue."[16]

A host of reasons for not marching the army into Florida mimicked the previous ones, but limited funding and inadequate forces were common threads tying all three invasions together. Howe would have willingly supplied the men with shoes, entrenching tools, firearms, and everything else they needed, but he had no stores to draw upon despite repeated requests to Congress. That left the state's government responsible for supplying the men, but there again Georgia's coffers were practically empty. The only logical response, argued Howe, was to strengthen the state's defenses along the Altamaha and Satilla and defend them with the battalions and militia. He also advocated for the construction of more forts, particularly around Savannah and Sunbury, as an additional layer of protection. The general's defensive plan had the full support of his officers, who believed that it was the most prudent option for protecting the state under the circumstances. In short, surmised the exasperated commander, Georgia was "destitute of almost every military requisite [yet] they were for

---

[15] C. C. Jones, "Biographical Sketches of the Delegates from Georgia to the Continental Congress," 124–25, original unpublished manuscript, box 7, Addresses and Writings, Charles C. Jones Papers, Rubenstein Rare Book and Manuscript Library; *RRG*, Minutes of the Executive Council, January 29, 1778, 2:18; Robert Howe to the Governor of Georgia (Houstoun), February 7, 1778, in Robert Howe Papers, MS 400, Georgia Historical Society; Ranlet, "Loyalty in the Revolutionary War," 730; K. Coleman, *American Revolution in Georgia*, 106.

[16] Ranlet, "Loyalty in the Revolutionary War," 728; Hühner, "Jews of Georgia," 94.

impelling the Army to undertake an Expedition into and against East Florida." He expressed his feelings to Laurens and told him that the state was "deplorably weak," everywhere assailable, and nowhere prepared to repel an attack.[17]

The radicals refused to listen to Howe, whose counterarguments offended them. At any rate, Congress took the matter out of the general's hands. On February 13, it passed a resolution ordering Howe or Elbert to proceed on the campaign. Acknowledging that Georgia's military was too weak to undertake the mission alone, Congress instructed Howe to augment it with troops borrowed from South Carolina. Bolstered by the blessings of Congress, a delighted Houstoun, on February 21, held his own "civil government" council of war. The governor invited Howe to attend, but the cautious general refused and stirred up even more animosity against himself from civil authorities. The constant bickering between the general and the governor soon trickled down to Elbert. In mid-March, John Wereat informed McIntosh in the northern Continental Army that the "Civil and Military departments are not upon a better footing with each other than when you presided at the head of the latter," and both Howe and Elbert were "dissatisfied and think themselves ill treated."[18]

Although Howe repeatedly assured Houstoun that he would cooperate as much as possible, he still hoped to dissuade the state's leaders from embarking on a campaign doomed to fail, but to no avail. To make matters worse, in February he became ill with a recurring "contagious sore throat and a very dangerous fever" that plagued him for the next two months, further sapping his drive. Despite the "distracted situation" in Georgia's civil government, which he described in detail to Laurens in a letter on April 25, the general, in accordance with Congress's directives, began the process of summoning his forces for the upcoming campaign. Georgia's 550 troops in the four battalions were insufficient for the task ahead, even with the addition of the state's militia under the command of Houstoun, whose numbers when they turned out was anyone's guess. Howe also ordered Major Roman DeLisle, commander of the state's Continental artillery with four field pieces, to accompany the army. To augment the invasion force, Howe told Colonel Charles Cotesworth Pinckney to bring his

---

[17] Robert Howe to Henry Laurens, April 25, 1778, in Chesnutt, ed., *Papers of Henry Laurens*, 13:184; Bennett and Lennon, *Quest for Glory*, 67–68.

[18] Congress's full resolution can be found in Crawford, et al., eds., *Naval Documents of the American Revolution*, 2:332–33; John Wereat to Lachlan McIntosh, March 13, 1778, Lachlan McIntosh Papers, Rubenstein Rare Book and Manuscript Library.

600 men in the 1st, 3rd, and 6th South Carolina Continental Battalions, with a small detachment of artillery, to Georgia. He also commanded Colonel Andrew Williams with nearly 800 South Carolina militia to join the invasion force. Howe ordered Commodore Oliver Bowen to participate as well with Georgia's galleys and other naval vessels. In total, the general could accumulate around 2,000 troops for the campaign, making it the most formidable army, at least in strength, to threaten Florida during the Revolution. Georgia's leaders were elated when they heard that South Carolinians were coming to assist their neighbors. In Congress, Walton told Laurens that the prospects for success looked much brighter. "The prompt assistance of Carolina…gives chearfullness and vigor to our present operations," he wrote, "and I really think well of our situation."[19]

As Howe waited for his army to materialize, other events set off a panic in the state. On March 13, Thomas Brown, with about one hundred rangers and a handful of Seminoles, secretly swam a quarter mile across the chilly Altamaha just below Fort Howe and captured the outpost after a brief fight. Brown took twenty-three prisoners and all of the fort's supplies and munitions, including its artillery. Exposed, unsupported by British troops, and far from his base, Brown had no alternative but to burn the fort and beat a hasty retreat southward, but he still sent small parties further into Georgia to harass settlements, gather recruits, and round-up cattle and other provisions.[20] The destruction of Fort Howe further highlighted the vulnerability of Georgia's southern flank, especially since there were no forts left on either the Altamaha or Satilla for the state's defense.

The loss of Fort Howe was bad enough, but the presence of thousands of plundering Loyalists roaming freely through the state on their way to St. Augustine further alarmed every friend of liberty in Georgia. One particularly large group formed around Ninety-Six in South Carolina in early April and headed toward the Savannah River below Augusta. Numbering between five hundred and eight hundred Loyalists and led by Colonel Joseph Scovel (or Scophol), the so-called Scopholites were joined

---

[19] Howe to Henry Laurens, April 25, 1778, in Chesnutt, ed., *Papers of Henry Laurens*, 13:184–85, and, in the same source, George Walton to Henry Laurens, April 26, 1778, 13:196; C. C. Jones, "Biographical Sketches of the Delegates from Georgia to the Continental Congress," 129, original unpublished manuscript, box 7, Addresses and Writings, Charles C. Jones Papers, Rubenstein Rare Book and Manuscript Library; Samuel Elbert, "Brigade Orders," April 6, 1778, in OBSE, 122; Searcy, *Georgia-Florida Contest*, 139; K. Coleman, *American Revolution in Georgia*, 106–107.

[20] Searcy, Georgia-Florida Contest, 130.

by several others once they arrived in Georgia. According to Houstoun, they "committed several outrages and many Robberies," as they passed through the state, stealing mostly horses and provisions, but also arms and ammunition.[21]

The wave of Scopholites spurred Howe into action, and he ordered Elbert to march Georgia's battalions southward to the ruins of Fort Howe. The principle aim of Elbert's mission, wrote the general, was to "prevent, if possible the Junction of the Insurgents with the Enemy." He also directed him to "dislodge & annoy" them wherever he could. There can be no doubt that Howe, like McIntosh earlier, had the utmost confidence in Elbert's abilities as a commander. For some time, he urged Congress to promote him to brigadier over Georgia's Continentals, but no word of their decision was forthcoming at the time Elbert set out for the fort. Even Walton thought a promotion for Elbert was proper. "I hope Congress in their promotions will not overlook Colonel Elbert," he confided to Laurens. "He is a good Officer, & will be much wounded if neglected. His leaving the service would be fatal to our Army."[22]

After much delay, Elbert issued marching orders for the 3rd and 4th battalions on April 6 and the long-awaited third Florida campaign finally sputtered to life. Their first destination was Midway, where the army arrived on April 9 followed by Howe one day later. While there, Elbert ordered twenty-four men from the battalions to board two of Georgia's galleys at Sunbury—the *Washington*, commanded by Captain John Hardy with two twelve-pounder cannons and the *Lee*, commanded by Captain John Braddock with one eighteen-pounder and one twelve-pounder. They were to accompany a large flat and a boat loaded with provisions and necessities up the Altamaha to Fort Howe and wait for the colonel's arrival there. Elbert also sent along two patroons familiar with the waterway to act as guides. One of the patroons hired out twenty of his slaves to help work the vessels through the Inland Passage and up the river. It was crucial that the galleys and flats get to the burned-out fort, Elbert noted, since the army could not cross the river or even cover a retreat without their presence.[23]

---

[21] Cashin and Robertson, *Augusta & the American Revolution*, 22; Olson, "Loyalist Partisan," 8–9.

[22] Robert Howe to Henry Laurens, April 25, 1778, in Chesnutt, ed., *Papers of Henry Laurens*, 13:186, and, in the same source, Robert Howe to Henry Laurens, April 26, 2778, 193, and George Walton to Henry Laurens, April 26, 1778, 186.

[23] Samuel Elbert, "Brigade Orders," April 6, 1778, in OBSE, 122, and, in same source,

Early on the morning of April 11, Elbert had his Continentals on the road to Fort Howe. Meanwhile, the General Assembly declared Georgia's situation "critical and alarming" and determined that a vigorous action was necessary to defeat the enemy and save the state. The evidence for impending ruin seemed everywhere. In addition to the uncontested raids, lost forts, Indian depredations on all borders, and roaming Scopholites, Georgians believed that East Florida's governor, Patrick Tonyn, was preparing to attack the state. Based on accounts Howe received from spies, prisoners, and deserters, there were almost 1,400 British regulars in the St. Augustine area scattered along outposts on the St. Johns and St. Marys Rivers. Added to that were perhaps three hundred Seminole and Creek Indians and close to four hundred rangers. He estimated that the Scopholites increased the enemy's strength by at least four hundred additional men. Georgians also knew that a number of British vessels lurked along the coast and could lend valuable support to any offensive strike unleashed from St. Augustine. The dire outlook prompted the Executive Council, on April 16, to give Houstoun temporary dictatorship powers "appertaining to the militia or the defense of the state against the present danger which threatens it."[24]

Elbert and the battalions arrived at Fort Howe on April 14 after two days of heavy rains foiled his attempts to pursue the Scopholites. While almost all of the Loyalists made it safely to East Florida, he did manage to gather intelligence from two of their own deserters and immediately relayed the information to Howe. Most were armed, on horseback, and short on provisions, he said. The colonel did discover that at least 1,500 more were gathering in South Carolina's backcountry intending to pass through Georgia and join their counterparts in St. Augustine. "As soon as we are refreshed," he informed the general, "and a convoy of provisions arrives, which I sent round with boats and a flat, I shall try a partisan party or two, and perhaps when they little expect it give them a brush at [the] St. Marys."[25]

Fate, however, had something else in store for Elbert. The same rainy

---

Samuel Elbert to Captain George Melvin, April 9, 1778, 123; V. Wood, "Georgia Navy's Dramatic Victory," 179, 195.

[24] Robert Howe to Henry Laurens, April 26, 1778, in Chesnutt, ed., *Papers of Henry Laurens*, 13:191; *RRG*, Minutes of the Executive Council, 2:73; C. C. Jones, "Biographical Sketches of the Delegates from Georgia to the Continental Congress," 124–26, original unpublished manuscript, box 7, Addresses and Writings, Charles C. Jones Papers, Rubenstein Rare Book and Manuscript Library; Searcy, *Georgia-Florida Contest*, 134.

[25] Samuel Elbert to Robert Howe, April 14, 1778, in OBSE, 125–26.

weather that plagued his efforts to intercept Scopholites also menaced a British fleet stationed in St. Simons Sound, between St. Simons and Jekyll islands. Howe's planned invasion was no secret to his East Florida enemies. Tonyn and British military and naval commanders also knew that Georgia's galleys would assume a central role in the rebel attack. Controlling the inner coastal passageway between Georgia and Florida became crucial for the defense of St. Augustine. In mid-March, three British ships tasked with the destruction of Georgia's galleys arrived in St. Simons Sound to carry out their mission. The commander of the triad of ships was Captain Thomas Jordan, a veteran officer on board his flagship, the HMS *Galatea*, with twenty nine-pounder cannon. The brigantine *Hinchinbrook* commanded by Lt. Alexander Ellis with sixteen four-pounder cannon and John Mowbray's sloop *Rebecca*, armed with fourteen four-pounders accompanied Jordan. On March 12, an unnamed watering brig joined Jordan's fleet.[26]

Navigating the sounds was risky for any larger vessel, especially with the prevalence of underwater bars and tricky, shifting river channels. The uncertainty associated with the sounds and back rivers behind the islands presented Jordan and his fleet with a formidable challenge. Nevertheless, since Georgia's galleys could not sail in open water, any plan to trap and annihilate them required the British to place their ships in narrow tidal rivers behind the Sea Islands. Two islands straddled St. Simons Sound. To the south was Jekyll Island and just across the sound to the north was St. Simons, which contained Fort Frederica, one of James Oglethorpe's defensive outposts constructed during the trustee years. Behind St. Simons and separating it from the mainland was the narrow Frederica River, which branched off the Altamaha and flowed through the river's marshy delta at the island's northern end.

For about a month, Jordan's ships lingered around St. Simons, taking fathoms and marking channels with buoys. He sent some of his men to occupy Fort Frederica and turn it into an observation post. In early April, another hazard presented itself to Jordan's fleet with the arrival of squally weather and strong gales. On April 9, the winds became so gusty that high swells threatened the safety of the ships. Unfortunately, Ellis, Mowbray, and some seamen were away in two small boats at the time gathering

---

[26] V. Wood, "Georgia Navy's Dramatic Victory," 171–72. According to note 11, the *Hinchinbrook* in Jordan's fleet was not the same HMS *Hinchinbrook* that participated in Savannah's Battle of the Rice Boats in spring 1776.

intelligence from inhabitants on the islands. During the storm, Ellis's boat sank, and the commander drowned. Mowbray survived in the other vessel. On April 13, Jordan received word that the galleys formerly stationed in Sunbury were heading in his direction. He dispatched the *Hinchinbrook* and *Rebecca* up the Frederica River above the fort to anchor and wait while he kept the *Galatea*, which had a deeper draft, further out in the sound. Between Jordan and the other two British ships was the watering brig.[27]

Elbert must have learned through informants about the location of Jordan's fleet as soon as he reached Fort Howe, and he wasted no time developing an impromptu plan to engage the enemy and capture their ships. He already knew that the *Washington* and the *Lee* were at Darien near the mouth of the Altamaha and that a third galley, the *Bulloch*, commanded by Archibald Hatcher and armed with two 9-pounders, had joined them. On April 15, a day after reaching the fort, the colonel gathered about 360 men from his four battalions (nearly two-thirds of his total force) and a detachment of artillery with orders to march to Darien at first light on the following morning. There, they would rendezvous with the galleys and head into the Frederica River. Elbert expected a fight and ordered each soldier to have fifty rounds of ammunition with him and enough provisions to last six days. Timing was crucial if he hoped to catch the British fleet by surprise, so to expedite his movement he ordered his men to "carry no baggage, except blankets."[28]

The trek to Darien took two days. Once there, Elbert hastily loaded his men onto the galleys. He boarded the *Washington* with a division under the command of his former business partner, Lieutenant Colonel Robert Rae. He would accompany them into the Frederica River and oversee their landing at Pike's Bluff on the island, about a mile and a half north of the fort. Rae's men, including a division of riflemen, were to take positions in the woods and cover the landing of a second division under Major Daniel Roberts and Captain George Young's artillery on board the *Bullock*. All boats were then to rendezvous with the *Lee*, where Elbert would debark with the rest just downriver at West Point Bluff, about a mile from the fort. The colonel kept some units on the galleys to assist in fighting and navigating those vessels. He promised his men that if they attended to their duty, they would achieve success "against the plunderers of their

---

[27] Ibid., 172, 175–79.
[28] Ibid., 180; Samuel Elbert, "After Orders," April 15, 1778, in OBSE, 127.

country and the common enemies of the rights of mankind."[29]

Elbert's scheme was a bold undertaking highlighting his aggressive abilities as a commander. It also displayed his talent for creative and spontaneous planning. Furthermore, the colonel showed that he was willing to take chances if an advantageous military situation with modest hopes for success presented itself. He was surely aware that any number of things could go wrong and turn his secret attack into a disaster. Surprise was of the essence, but so were favorable tides and winds, which factored into Elbert's timing for the attack.

Late in the afternoon on April 18, men on the *Hinchinbrook* spotted Elbert's galleys in the Frederica River. As they approached, the galleys fired upon the *Hinchinbrook*, but the sun was already low on the horizon and it was too late for Elbert to bring on a general engagement. Meanwhile, nearly one hundred of his men overran Fort Frederica and captured five British prisoners. At twilight, the Continentals found concealed positions in the woods flanking the eastern shore of the river. Soon after that, the *Hinchinbrook* and *Rebecca* hoisted anchors and drifted downriver in the dark to a place that seemed more suited to engage the galleys at dawn.[30]

At first light on Sunday, April 19, Elbert's galleys rounded a curve in the river and opened a barrage on the *Hinchinbrook* and *Rebecca* with their guns. Both ships tried to maneuver into a better position to meet the attack, but calm winds and unfavorable tidal currents put them at a serious disadvantage. The absence of a stiff breeze negated any hopes to sail toward the galleys and forced the ships into a defensive posture. At a half-mile away, the galleys anchored their vessels and, according to Jordan's after report, began a "galling fire" on the British ships that lasted for almost two hours. All the while, Elbert's men, sheltered in the thickets along the island's shoreline, mercilessly poured their lead and artillery balls into the walls and rigging of the ships.[31]

Since the guns on the galleys had a greater range than those on the enemy ships, the Americans were able to pummel the *Hinchinbrook* and *Rebecca* with hardly any damage in return. Nearly two hours of incessant pounding took their toll. With their rigging shot up and disabled,

---

[29] V. Wood, "Georgia Navy's Dramatic Victory," 181–82; Samuel Elbert, "Brigade Orders," on the *Washington*, April 18, 1778, in OBSE, 127–28.

[30] V. Wood, "Georgia Navy's Dramatic Victory," 182–83.

[31] Journal of H. M. Frigate *Galatea*, Captain Thomas Jordan, April 19, 1778, in Crawford, et al., eds., *Naval Documents of the American Revolution*, 12:139; V. Wood, "Georgia Navy's Dramatic Victory," 184–85.

ineffective artillery, and a rowboat sunk, both ships again weighed anchor and drifted further downstream toward the water brig in more open water, closely pursued by the galleys, who kept up a hot fire out of range from British guns. After floating with the tide for about a mile, all three vessels accidentally drifted out of the channel and simultaneously ran aground in the sound's mucky bottom. The *Hinchinbrook* and *Rebecca* became stuck with their head and stern to the stream, while the brig heeled over so much that the angle negated any impact from her guns. Perceiving the hopeless situation of the ships, the galleys quickly advanced to take possession of them. "In this Critical Moment," wrote Jordan, the captains had "no Alternative but to Abandon their Vessels & retreat in their Boats which with Great Difficulty they Effected & Returned to the *Galatea*."[32]

Shortly after 10:00 in the morning, an ecstatic Elbert boarded the *Rebecca* and prepared a detailed report for Howe about his action on the Frederica River. "I have the happiness to inform you," he began, "that…the Brigantine *Hinchinbrook*, the Sloop *Rebecca* & a prize Brig [watering brig] of theirs all struck the British Tyrants Colours & Surrendered to the American Arms." The colonel could hardly contain his excitement. "You must Imagine what my feelings were," he wrote, "to see our three little men of War going on to the attack of those three Vessels, who have spread Terror on our Coast & who were drawn up in order of Battle." Elbert attributed his victory to the "weight of our metal [which] soon damped the courage of those Heroes, who took to their Boats & as many as could abandon'd their Vessels & every thing on board, of which we immediately took possession." As Elbert and his men rummaged through their prizes for everything of value, they took some British seamen left behind as prisoners. In one of the ships, they discovered clothing destined for Continental troops seized by a British privateer near Charleston Harbor some time earlier.[33]

Elbert achieved his remarkable feat without losing a single soldier. Caught up in the euphoria of the moment, the colonel informed his superior that he would immediately consult with his field officers and the captains of the galleys about pressing an attack on the *Galatea*, now lying off Jekyll. That attack, however, never materialized, partially because the galleys were vulnerable in the sound's open waters. Furthermore, the captured

---

[32] Journal of H. M. Frigate *Galatea*, Captain Thomas Jordan, April 19, 1778, in Crawford, et al., eds., *Naval Documents of the American Revolution*, 12:139.

[33] Ibid., Samuel Elbert to Robert Howe, April 19, 1778, 12:138; C. C. Jones, *History of Georgia*, 2:291.

vessels were stuck fast in the mud and in no condition for a fight. For the next four days, the *Galatea* lingered around Jekyll, seemingly inviting an attack from Elbert, but the victorious colonel declined to press the contest further. He was running out of rations and the need to free and repair the ships and send them with Colonel John White and the 4th Battalion to Sunbury for safety took precedence over finishing off the *Galatea*. Elbert's window of opportunity closed on April 23 when Jordan hoisted sail and took his remaining ship back to St. Augustine.[34]

Thus, on April 19, in the span of about two hours on the Frederica River, Elbert scored Georgia's greatest victory in the American Revolution, at least up until that point in the war. His action was brilliant in its inception and flawlessly executed. The battle also represented the first coordinated combat activity between the state's navy and battalions, even as it significantly boosted confidence on the eve of another Florida excursion. Howe pronounced Elbert's exploits as "gallant." He told Laurens that the colonel deserved "great Applause" and that his achievement did him "high honor" and gave "sanguine hopes of further Success in future Service." Walton admitted that the capture of the British ships was bound to have "a good effect upon our affairs," even though it was "a lucky hit." When James Whitefield, an Augusta citizen, learned of Elbert's triumph, he attributed it to Divine intervention. "Had not the Almighty so signally interposed in our behalf," he surmised, "the State must have probably fallen before now; as it would have been entirely surrounded by its Foes."[35]

Elbert was back at Fort Howe by April 23 with a portion of his battalions. In his first orders since the action on the Frederica, he told Colonel White to secure the prizes in Sunbury and hurry with his men "by forced marches" to Fort Howe. "I know your anxiety for the safety of the State is such that no time will be lost," he reminded White. Before White left, he was to get the galleys and any other boats he could find loaded with barrels of rice and salt. They were to "proceed with all speed" up the Altamaha to Elbert's position. Some galleys escorted the captured ships from Sunbury to Savannah. According to Thomas Baker, a marine on one of the galleys, the captains of the American ships sold the prizes to the United States on

---

[34] Samuel Elbert to Robert Howe, April 19, 1778, in Crawford, et al., eds., *Naval Documents of the American Revolution*, 12:138; V. Wood, "Georgia Navy's Dramatic Victory," 189–91.

[35] Robert Howe to Henry Laurens, April 28, 1778, in Chesnutt, ed., *Papers of Henry Laurens*, 13:193, and, in the same source, George Walton to Henry Laurens, April 26, 1778, 195, and James Whitefield to Henry Laurens, May 6, 1778, 262.

the public wharf when they arrived. "We were promised the prize money—& after we had captured the vessels, the same promise was renewed to us by Captain Braddock," recalled Baker. Houstoun was present when the galleys and captured ships docked in Savannah, and he told Baker and the others that it would be worth a "fortune" to them, but no one knows if any of the men ever received a portion of the prize money.[36]

As Elbert basked in the glory of his recent exploits, the army that Howe threw together to invade Florida slowly coalesced at Fort Howe. A large body of perhaps four hundred militia, raised in Burke County by Houstoun, arrived on April 26, although the governor was not with them. Joining them about a week later were Pinckney's six hundred South Carolina Continentals and an artillery unit. One of the soldiers with Pinckney, Major John F. Grimké, commented on the scene that confronted the Carolinians. The men under Elbert's command, he noted, were "in general very ragged in their appearance." The fort was equally unimpressive, despite efforts at repair since Brown destroyed the structure a few months earlier. "Neither the lines nor the Stockade are finished," he observed, and both were inadequate. The lines were "too Extensive to be defended by the small number of men we have here, & the Stockade too small for those who defend the lines to Retire into." The "exceedingly Sultry" weather made matters worse since they contributed to the "Disorders prevailing in camp."[37]

After spending about two weeks at Fort Howe, even Pinckney was beginning to have his doubts. He admitted to General William Moultrie in South Carolina that Elbert's capture of the *Hinchinbrook* and the other vessels in addition to the proposed expedition "proved the salvation" of Georgia. Still, he was already concerned about the mission's success. Part of the problem, as he discovered after just two weeks at the fort, was the "candid gentry of this state" who were disparaging Howe and the army for not immediately marching off to attack the enemy. Houstoun, who finally arrived on the field from Savannah, tried to assume command of the galleys even as he issued orders that provisions destined for South Carolina troops be shared with his militia. "I am this moment informed," Pinckney complained to Moultrie, "that the governor of this state, has ordered from

---

[36] Samuel Elbert to John White, April 23, 1778, in OBSE, 128; Pension Application of Thomas Baker, March 22, 1826, S15299, fn39Ga, Revolutionary War Pension and Bounty-Land Warrant Applications.

[37] Searcy, *Georgia-Florida Contest*, 139; Grimké, "Journal of the Campaign to the Southward," May 9–10, 1778, 61.

us, to the militia, two-hundred barrels of rice: he likewise ordered the gallies 30 miles higher up the river than this place; when, on account of the shallowness of the water, they cannot come within 10 miles as high up as we are now: excellent generalship!" Apparently, Houstoun left after this to recruit more militia. Meanwhile, Pinckney confronted additional problems, like the lack of supplies for his own men that had not yet arrived aboard a South Carolina galley and schooner. How, he wondered, could eight men share just one canteen in such a hostile climate? Overcrowded tents were a problem, too, and the lack of camp kettles forced fifteen men to share each one. As for Fort Howe, Pinckney was as unimpressed as Grimké. The fort and surrounding encampment were "badly planned, and wretchedly constructed."[38]

Howe arrived on May 9, where he conferred with Elbert and the other commanders and reorganized his army. For the next few days after that, Elbert and Pinckney explored the other side of the river to discern a good location for the army's camp when it crossed the Altamaha to commence the march southward. They finally settled on Reid's Bluff about three miles south of Fort Howe. Beyond that, the army remained idle for the rest of the month as Howe waited on Williamson's South Carolina militia and Houstoun's recruits to arrive. With each passing day, the oppressive heat sapped the army's strength and morale. "I wish this matter had been determined upon two or three months ago," Moultrie warned Howe in a letter on May 31. "I fear the season is too far advanced…[the men] will sicken very fast, so as to prevent you from carrying on your operations and succeeding in your attempt." If the mission failed, he predicted, "it will be attended with bad consequences to these two southern states." He advised Pinckney on June 5 to move his men around "moderately" to help combat sickness and to keep "the devil out of their head."[39]

---

[38] Col. Charles C. Pinckney to William Moultrie, May 24, 1778, in Moultrie, *Memoirs of the American Revolution*, 1:212–14 (hereafter cited as *MMAR*); McCall, *History of Georgia*, 2:142.

[39] Grimké, "Journal of the Campaign to the Southward," May 12–13, 1778, 61–62; Searcy, *Georgia-Florida Contest*, 139–41; William Moultrie to Robert Howe, May 31, 1778, in *MMAR*, 1:215–16, and, in the same source, William Moultrie to Charles C. Pinckney, June 5, 1778, 220–21; Robert Howe, "Parole—Stirk," May 16, 1778, in OBSE, 143–44, and, in the same source, Robert Howe, "General Orders," May 21, 1778, 149–50.

The devil's temptation Moultrie may have been referencing was reflected through increased desertions from the army in May. On May 16, for example, a court-martial sentenced four men from the Georgia battalions to run the gauntlet for desertion. Days later, a subsequent court-martial sentenced Sergeant John Tyrrel of the 4th Battalion to death for the same crime. On the morning of May 21, Howe informed his whole command that he was "resolved never to pardon any future desertions." The punishment of death fit the crime of desertion, he said, because it was the "greatest a soldier can be guilty of" since it violated "every moral sanction." After that, Tyrrel was shot to death in the presence of the whole army. Grimké witnessed the event. The prisoner, he said, "met his fate with a Spirit & Resolution that would have done Credit to & was more worthy of a better Man & a proper behaviour. The Execution Guard & the Reserve failed in putting him to immediate Death: A Single Man therefore marched up & blew his brains out."[40]

At last, on May 25, Howe began ferrying the army across the Altamaha to their new bivouac on Reid's Bluff, where they remained until June 7. In those few days, sickness took a terrible toll on the American army. One officer reported on June 6 that three hundred soldiers required hospitalization at a makeshift facility in Darien. When the army left the bluff and headed toward the Satilla River on June 7, he estimated that only seven hundred Continentals were fit to march. Even as the Americans were breaking camp, a frustrated Howe informed Moultrie that he was "Puzzled, perplexed, disappointed, and the devil and all," especially since he had sacrificed the strength of his army waiting impatiently for the militia's arrival. All the while, the enemy were strengthening their garrisons and diminishing his chances of success. Unfortunately, Howe learned from Moultrie in a letter on June 22 that Williamson and Houstoun were still far to the rear. "I was told yesterday that Williamson with his militia, was not above 9 miles from Savannah," explained the South Carolinian, and the "governor with his Georgians, were about [at] Sunberry [sic]." The report was particularly deflating to Howe. "For God's sake!" asked Moultrie, "when will you all join[?]"[41]

---

[40] Grimké, "Journal of the Campaign to the Southward," May 21, 1778, 64; Robert Howe, "Parole—Stirk," May 16, 1778, in OBSE, 143–44, and, in the same source, Robert Howe, "General Orders," May 21, 1778, 149–50.

[41] Searcy, *Georgia-Florida Contest*, 141; Robert Howe to William Moultrie, June 7, 1778, in *MMAR*, 1:222, and, in the same source, William Moultrie to Robert Howe, June 22, 1778, 225–26.

From Reid's Bluff, the army advanced in good order. The target, according to Pinckney, was a British garrison hastily thrown together by Brown's rangers about twenty-five miles up the St. Marys on the Florida side called Fort Tonyn. Since early April, Brown knew that reducing Fort Tonyn was a major part of Howe's plans for overrunning Florida. On April 10, he wrote Brigadier General Augustine Prevost, who was in charge of British regulars in the province, and informed him that the rebel army, seven field pieces of artillery, and two-thirds of the militia in the state were marching with Elbert to the Altamaha with the intention of destroying the fort.[42]

For the next three weeks, the Americans pressed forward without incident. At times progress became so treacherous because of thickets and swamps that slave labor was necessary to construct roads, pathways, and bridges wide enough to let the baggage wagons and artillery pass through. On June 17 near the Satilla, Elbert's brother-in-law Joseph Habersham wrote his wife, Isabella, and informed her that they were only about fifteen miles from the fort. He hoped that soon the army could "give a good Account of Col. Brown and his Scouts unless he shoud prudently make his Escape to his good Friends the red Coats, who I fancy will hardly risk a Battle on this side of [the] St. Johns." Colonel Elbert, he noted, was "hearty" even though he "frets a little [on ac]cot. of Howe and the Govr's Tardi[ness]."[43]

On June 20, the army crossed the Satilla and rested for five days. Some men were already barefoot; they were given moccasins hastily constructed from cow hides. While at the Satilla, Bowen and the naval force arrived at Wright's Landing on the St. Marys with some of Elbert's Continentals. On June 25, Howe's main body was again in motion. At the same time, on June 26, the General Assembly empowered Houstoun to get two hundred slaves from confiscated estates to help cut roads and build bridges for Howe's army. By then, they were of little use. On June 28, the Americans began crossing the St. Marys on flats into Florida, landing about ten miles above Fort Tonyn.[44]

---

[42] Charles C. Pinckney to William Moultrie, May 24, 1778, in *MMAR*, 1:212; Thomas Brown to Brig.-Gen. Augustine Prevost, April 10, 1778, in *Report on American Manuscripts in the Royal Institution of Great Britain*, 1:227–28; Bullen, "Fort Tonyn and the Campaign of 1778," 253–54.

[43] Phillips, "Some Letters of Joseph Habersham," 148–49.

[44] Robert Howe, "General Orders," Camp, Sattilia [*sic*] River, June 21, 1778, in OBSE, 167–68; *RRG*, 2:77; Searcy, *Georgia-Florida Contest*, 142.

Houstoun finally appeared near the St. Marys with some of his militia as the last of Pinckney's Continentals crossed the river. Howe held an immediate conference with the governor to coordinate an attack on Fort Tonyn, but the meeting degenerated into an argument over supreme command. Nor could they agree on the object of an attack. The governor, having learned that Prevost's regulars were encamped nearby, wanted to concentrate the combined army on them and then make a push toward St. Augustine. Howe remained fixated on Fort Tonyn and was adamant that Brown's rangers should be the primary focus. Ultimately, both men retained their individual commands and in the absence of compromise, parted ways. Houstoun and his militia remained north of the St. Marys while Howe, Elbert, Pinckney, and the rest of the Continental Army completed their crossing to the Florida side and turned south toward the fort.[45]

Brown knew that the Americans were on his side of the river; three horsemen secretly observed the Continentals crossing the St. Marys. When discovered, some of Howe's men fired upon them and chased them into a swamp. They nearly caught one who dropped his baggage and coat as he fled. An examination of the baggage revealed that they had almost captured Brown. After his escape, the Loyalist commander made his way back to the fort and burned it. The rangers took what supplies they could with them and fled into nearby Cabbage Swamp where they hid and subsisted on Palmetto roots for a few days. Brown was not finished, though, and he planned to annoy and harass the Americans at every opportunity.[46]

Howe was sorely disappointed when his army entered the shell of Fort Tonyn on June 29. He expected to capture Brown, his men, and stockpiles of provisions and munitions. What he got instead was a pyrrhic victory. The feelings of discontent were widespread among the soldiers. One from South Carolina could hardly conceal his frustrations: "We have now with great toil and difficulty, thro' parching lands and uncultivated wilds, frequently in the Meridian Heat, Marched near 300 Miles to this place, and the Reward of our trouble has been to find in a half demolished stockade Fort, a few devil Cloaths [*sic*], [and] Blankets and trifling Necessaries buried under ground or thrown into the River."[47]

---

[45] Searcy, *Georgia-Florida Contest*, 143.
[46] Ibid. See also Cashin, *King's Ranger*, 77–78.
[47] Searcy, *Georgia-Florida Contest*, 143.

For the next two weeks, the Continentals occupied the charred remnants of Fort Tonyn. Meanwhile, on June 30, a party of about one hundred rebel mounted militia under Screven penetrated Cabbage Swamp in search of the elusive Loyalists. Already alerted, Brown led his men out of the swamp and toward Alligator Creek Bridge where British regulars under Major Mark Prevost camped behind a patchwork defense of logs and trenches. As Screven trailed Brown toward Prevost's position, the Loyalist leader ordered some of his rangers to backtrack around and behind the militia and to come up in their rear while the rest tried to reach the safety of British lines. About noon, as Brown's men approached Prevost's line, Screven's men smashed into their rear while his drummers played Elbert's "Grenadier March."[48]

Caught off-guard, the rangers panicked and ran into the British camp where unsuspecting regulars were cleaning weapons and bathing in the creek. Prevost's men hesitated in the confusion, then frantically formed ranks behind their works and fired into the militia. Meanwhile, Brown's rangers hanging on the rear of the militia attacked its flanks, blunting the forward momentum in Screven's assault. With his flanks collapsing, Screven broke off the attack and called a retreat. Instead of pressing his advantage, Prevost chose not to pursue the militia, which hastily made their way back to the American position. The Battle of Alligator Creek Bridge, representing the climax of the third Florida campaign, was over. It resulted in thirteen American deaths, including one African American patriot, while the British lost only one man. The engagement left scores of others on both sides wounded, including the emboldened Georgia militia commander, Colonel Elijah Clarke.[49]

Back in Fort Tonyn, the suffering of men and beasts intensified. On July 1, Howe informed the army that it was out of rice although a shipment was shortly expected. In the meantime, he admonished his men to "bear it like good soldiers." Hunger, heat, and disease took a daily toll. "Our little army now too fully experience the sickliness of this confounded climate," wrote Pinckney to Moultrie after a week in the fort. "The Carolinians have not been hitherto so sickly as the Georgians but, taking the sick of both brigades into the account, our numbers are now one half less than what

---

[48] Cashin, *King's Ranger*, 78; McCall, *History of Georgia*, 2:145–46.
[49] Cashin, *King's Ranger*, 78; Searcy, *Georgia-Florida Contest*, 144–45.

they were when we first joined at Fort Howe." On July 10, he informed Moultrie that the "continental troops have been so violently attacked by sickness, and the desolation made by it, is so rapidly increasing, that if we do not retreat soon, we shall not be able to retreat at all." Too weak to press forward or retreat, the expedition, once brimming with hope, seemed fatally stuck at Fort Tonyn. Even the pack animals suffered. "Our horses," Pinckney told Moultrie, "having no grain to support them, die daily." Already, thirty-five were dead from starvation and there were hardly enough left to drag along the artillery and wagons. "If we do not retreat soon by water," he predicted, "we shall be in a situation of not being able to retire or proceed by land."[50]

On July 4, Independence Day, Howe tried to boost morale and issued a gill of rum per man. At the same time, Houstoun, after a fruitless effort to find British regulars, arrived at the St. Marys. His presence temporarily aroused hope that a decision to move in some direction was eminent. "My dear Bella," wrote Habersham to his wife in Savannah, "The Governor and the Militia are to join us today, and I hope the Captain and Major General will lay their Heads together so that we may go on or return, for I am tired of staying here."[51]

Houstoun, after his arrival, dashed any hope of cooperation by informing Howe that he was not taking orders from the general. Howe's anger boiled over in a letter to Moultrie on July 5. "If I am ever again to depend upon operations I have no right to guide, and men I have no right to command, I shall deem it then, as now I do, one of the most unfortunate accidents of my life." He continued,

> Had we been able to move on at once…a blow might have been given [to] our enemies, which would have put it out of their power to have disturbed us…but delayed beyond all possible supposition, and embarrassed, disappointed, perplexed, and distressed beyond all expression; the utmost we can now achieve, will be but a poor compensation for the trouble and fatigue we have undergone.[52]

---

[50] William Howe, "G. O. [General Orders]," July 1, 1778, in OBSE, 173; Pinckney to Moultrie, July 6, 1778, in *MMAR*, 1:229, and, in the same source, Pinckney to Moultrie, July 10, 1778, 1:231.

[51] Robert Howe, "After Orders," July 4, 1778, in OBSE, 175; Robert Howe to William Moultrie, July 5, 1778, in *MMAR*, 1:228; Joseph Habersham to Isabella Habersham, July 5, 1778, in Phillips, "Some Letters of Joseph Habersham," 149; McCall, *History of Georgia*, 2:147.

[52] Howe to William Moultrie, July 5, 1778, in *MMAR*, 1:228.

It was unfortunate that the campaign's fate, assailed from every side by seemingly insurmountable obstacles, sustained its fatal blow from a lack of cooperation between those who led their brave men into the wilds of Florida. The cause of the confusion was the continued blurred lines of civil and military authority over the issue of supreme command. In the debate over military control, Elbert sided with Howe, as he had done when McIntosh was in charge. While he was the highest-ranking commander of the militia in the state, Houstoun's presence as a governor with dictatorial powers superseded Elbert's rank over those men.

Howe was exasperated. At one point, he hoped in vain to draw the militia into Florida where Houstoun's influence did not reach. On July 5, the general informed Moultrie that he and the militia were on opposite sides of the St. Marys about eight miles apart. "Ask me not how this happened," he angrily admitted, "but rest assured that it has not been my fault." On July 8, Williamson finally arrived with one thousand South Carolina militia and crossed the St. Marys two days later. By then, hospital returns contained nearly half of the army, and Howe was leaning toward a retreat from Florida. He told the quartermaster general to report on the number of wagons and horses fit for duty and to complete the teams as much as possible. He then ordered that a road be cut from the landing opposite Fort Tonyn to link up with the earlier one that led to the Satilla and had been constructed by militia pioneers and slaves.[53]

By July 10, disputes over command and powerful egos rent the whole invading force into quarreling factions. Pinckney was shocked. "After we have waited so long for the junction of the militia," he told Moultrie, "we now find that we are to have as many independent commanders as corps. Governor Houston [Houstoun] declaring that he would not be commanded; Col. Williamson hinting that his men would not be satisfied to be under continental command[,] or indeed any other commander but his own; and Commodore Bowlan [Bowen] insisting that in the naval department he is supreme." With this "divided [and] heterogeneous command," he wondered, "what can be done?" Indeed, he concluded, the only alternative was to quickly "retreat from this place, by water."[54]

Howe held a council of war on July 11 to discuss the campaign's fate. Present were Elbert, Pinckney, Rae, Habersham, DeLisle, and all of the

---

[53] McCall, *History of Georgia*, 2:145, 147; Howe to Moultrie, July 5, 1778, in *MMAR*, 1:228–29; Searcy, *Georgia-Florida Contest*, 146; Robert Howe, "G. O. [General Orders]," July 8, 1778, in OBSE, 175–76.

[54] Charles Pinckney to William Moultrie, July 10, 1778, in *MMAR*, 1:230–31.

other major field officers in the Continental Army. Neither Williamson, Bowen, nor Houstoun attended. The general gave his commanders a gloomy assessment of the army's condition and ended his remarks by suggesting that if they remained at Fort Tonyn, or if they pressed forward to St. Augustine, their force would "most probably be destroyed." Howe then posed a series of questions to his officers. Had not the mission accomplished its goal of driving the enemy out of Georgia and demolishing Fort Tonyn? All of the officers agreed. Since the enemy did not seem willing to attack the Americans so close to St. Augustine, were there any other objectives important enough to warrant a continued presence in the province? All agreed that there were not. Was the army in a condition to cross the St. Johns and attack the enemy? The officers unanimously agreed that the army was not capable of carrying out an advance. Does the sickness inflicting the army at an alarming rate render an immediate retreat necessary? All agreed in the affirmative. Could the general, with honor to himself and to his men, relinquish his command to the governor? All uniformly agreed that he could not. Could the army, with such a divided command, act with vigor to benefit the common cause? Without a dissenting voice, the officers said that it could not.[55]

That settled the matter. The third Florida campaign, so full of hope and promise, had come to its inglorious end. Howe sent Houstoun a copy of the council's minutes, and, on July 14, the evacuation of Fort Tonyn, to the relief of almost every soldier present, commenced. Howe detained 120 men to escort the wagons safely back by land. Elbert and Pinckney took their men to Wright's Landing at the mouth of the St. Marys where they boarded Bowen's galleys and flats and sailed to Savannah. Howe traveled by land to Charleston. Alone and abandoned in enemy territory, Houstoun's only option was to retreat as well. The experience left him bitter toward Howe and even Bowen. Before the year was over, he took command of the galleys from the commodore. The move was an assault on Bowen's honor, and he was still trying to seek redress in 1783. "I am injured by being suspended not for a military offense but by party resentment for a pretended offense against the civil authority," he explained to Jared Irwin, a former Revolutionary commander and member of the state's assembly after the war. "Houstoun and no other governor had no more right to command the gallies than they had the army[,] if he [even] had a

---

[55] Ibid., "At a council of war held in the camp, at Fort Tonyn, July 11th, 1778," 1:232–36.

right to one [or] the other."[56]

Despite the destruction of Fort Tonyn (which was accomplished by Brown and not Howe), the third invasion of Florida, predictably like all of the others, was an unmitigated disaster. It exacted a great toll in lives and treasure and all for little gain. Within months, British regulars and Loyalist raiding parties were once again probing Georgia's southern border. The number of Howe's men who died during the 1778 campaign is unknown, but the death rates were exceptionally high. One contemporary believed that "they had died by the hundreds." An early Georgia historian used the word "feeble" to describe the remnants of Elbert's battalions when they limped back into Savannah in late July. Two months later, in September, Elbert told Laurens that, based on the returns of his battalions, there were only a "few Men" remaining and their enlistments were expiring. "So great is their dislike to this service, that there is scarce an instance of one Man, who has been entitled to his Discharge, that could be prevailed on to engage anew," he added.[57] At least for some, the miserable experience in the Florida campaign was probably enough to dampen any desire to continue service one day longer than required.

Howe, under enormous pressure from Georgia's governor and Assembly, had led his army into Florida at the worst possible time of year, and many of his men paid the ultimate price for that unwise decision. However, the blame for initiating an invasion of Florida at the beginning of the sickly season rests not with Howe but with Houstoun and the General Assembly, who all but forced the general to undertake an ill-fated campaign into East Florida against his instincts. The elaborate plan failed, too, because of disunity in command. A stronger leader would have asserted his will over the disparate parts of the army to coordinate the whole. Howe was not that person.[58] Neither was Houstoun. Until the Florida campaign, the governor had never commanded a body of soldiers.

The leader so desperately needed to command the expedition was Elbert. The only ray of success during the entire two-month saga of suffering, setbacks, and embarrassments was his stunning defeat of the British

---

[56] Oliver Bowen to Jared Irwin, June 21, 1783, Jared Irwin Papers, 1783–1855, section A, box 71, Rubenstein Rare Book and Manuscript Library; Bennett and Lennon, *Quest for Glory*, 83.

[57] Hawes, ed., "Papers of James Jackson," 26; McCall, *History of Georgia*, 2:154; K. Coleman, *American Revolution in Georgia*, 108; Samuel Elbert to Henry Laurens, September 5, 1778, in Chesnutt, ed., *Papers of Henry Laurens*, 14:268.

[58] McCall, *History of Georgia*, 2:145.

navy in the Frederica River. There, he was able to do what Howe could not, which was to coordinate and lead a successful assault by land and naval units against the enemy. The colonel possessed the attributes of a great leader, including clarity of thinking and decision-making, creativity and initiative to execute bold maneuvers, and the confidence of his men to achieve success. He was a rock of stability in an otherwise chaotic command structure. It was a promising start, but the colonel's first real test lay just ahead. Within months, he would face, for the first time, the British army as it overran his city and home. Then, Elbert and his fellow revolutionaries would enter the darkest days of their rebellion.

Chapter 10

"We Have Lost the Day": The Fall of Savannah

By summer 1778, the outcome of the Revolution in Georgia was still in doubt. The state's only real military success was Colonel Elbert's victory over East Florida's brown-water fleet in the Frederica River back in April. Beyond that, there was little else upon which to hang laurels. Three failed Florida campaigns in just as many years were humiliating enough, but the loss of crucial forts on the Satilla and the Altamaha was devastating to the state's security against raiding Loyalists and Indians who continued to penetrate the borders. Stuck on the fringes of the United States, Georgia was vulnerable and in no position to withstand a concerted enemy invasion. Yet, such an invasion was precisely what the British intended in 1778 as they embarked on a new southern strategy to win the war.

Back in London, Georgia's exiled royal governor, Sir James Wright, constantly urged his political superiors to focus their attention on reconquering his colony and the Carolinas. Ever since arriving in London from Georgia two years earlier, the deposed leader insisted that the rebels' hold in his former colony was tenuous and that a small British army, bolstered with help from the king's Loyalist and Indian friends in the backcountry, could quickly reclaim the province and restore royal rule. Wright discussed his ideas with many people, most importantly Lord George Germain, secretary of state for the colonies, who favored a southern campaign. "There seems to be a Probability," he informed Germain on October 8, 1777, "that the People in general may be disposed to a return to their Allegiance, especially if they had any Assistance and a proper person to apply to." If the British army would just appear, Wright believed that both White Georgians and Native Americans would flock to them for their assistance. The aid of Loyalists and Indians gave Wright confidence to conclude that Georgia "might be recovered from the Rebels—and reduced to His

Majesty's obedience." His ideas were not far-fetched. Even Patrick Tonyn, East Florida's governor, sent messages to London calling for a strike in the South. "I am certain the four southern provinces are incapable of making any very formidable resistance," he advised, especially since "they are not prepared for a Scene of war." A concentrated push there would "operate to effect a quick surrender."[1] Persuaded that the new focus would work, Germain embraced the idea. Coordinating the resistance of Loyalists, Indians, and even slaves with an invading army in the South would overwhelm the revolutionaries and ultimately collapse their illegal governments.

In 1778, circumstances favored a new British approach to waging the war. The surrender of General John Burgoyne's army at Saratoga in New York during fall 1777 was a serious setback for England. Since then, the war seemed stalemated in the north. Furthermore, the entry of France into the conflict after Saratoga as an ally of the United States significantly complicated Britain's task of subduing the colonies. There was also the potential that America's rebellion could spill over into Europe and that Spain would enter as another adversary. Finally, the failure of a peace commission to the colonies led by Lord Frederick Howard, the Earl of Carlisle, earlier in the year left England little choice but to finish the fight. It seemed only logical to shift the focus to areas, such as the Southern colonies, that offered the most promise of success.

Stationed in New York with the bulk of His Majesty's forces, Sir Henry Clinton, who recently replaced William Howe as commander of the British army in America, shared the vision of Germain, Wright, and Tonyn. On November 8, 1778, Clinton informed Lieutenant Colonel Archibald Campbell of the 71st Regiment of Foot, also in New York, that he would command an effort to take Savannah in a joint operation with the British navy, under the leadership of Captain Hyde Parker, and Brigadier General Augustine Prevost's British troops in East Florida. Parker's fleet was to convey to Georgia three thousand soldiers consisting of the 1st and 2nd battalions of the 71st Highlander Regiment, the 1st and 2nd battalions of Delancy's Royalist Provincials, Sir James Baird's Corps of Light Infantry, the 3rd Battalion of Skinner's Provincials, two regiments of Hessian troops, and the 1st Division of the New York Volunteers made up of Loyalists. Once in Georgia, Campbell expected to receive a "Re-inforcement of 6000 Loyalists from the back Countries, in Conjunction with the

---

[1] Sir James Wright to Lord Germain, October 8, 1777, in LSJW, 247; Piecuch, *Three Peoples, One King*, 126.

Indian Tribes who were attached to the Government." The strictest secrecy surrounded the plans, and Campbell hoped to catch the Rebels off-guard to ensure a swift victory. After much preparation, Campbell's force, on November 26 in favorable weather, set sail from Sandy Hook in the Lower New York Bay and proceeded down the Atlantic coast toward Georgia. Before Parker's departure, Clinton notified Prevost to take a post along the St. Marys River with all the troops he could spare and to cooperate with Campbell as much as possible.[2] Clinton's letter neither specified Prevost's exact role nor established any timelines involving his troops. It did at least show that Prevost had some knowledge, however vague, about Campbell's mission to Georgia. Back in Savannah, however, Georgia's leaders were oblivious to the dangers encircling them.

Since returning from the recent costly and bitterly disappointing excursion into Florida, Elbert spent the rest of summer and fall 1778 trying to nurse his battered Continentals back to health. The colonel faced the same problems as always, which included grappling with desertions; replenishing his diminished command; supplying his men with uniforms, shoes, reliable weapons, provisions, and pay; and establishing efficient hospitals stocked with medicine and skilled doctors for the sick and wounded. As expected after a lengthy campaign, Elbert wanted to know how many soldiers remained in his units. "The Commandant is anxious for returns of the 1st, 3rd, and 4th Battalions," he informed his officers on August 6, "specifying the number of men lost since the commencement of the late expedition by deaths [and] desertions." As for the militia, their numbers were always in question, their dependability uncertain, and their availability a constant mystery. Elbert also dealt with desertions through a steady stream of court-martial trials. Luckily, those found guilty during the summer and fall escaped execution, but the punishment for some was severe. On August 19, a trial found William Wood, a "notorious offender," guilty of deserting his battalion, going to the enemy, and taking up arms against

---

[2] Sir Henry Clinton to Lieutenant Colonel Archibald Campbell, November 8, 1778, in C. Campbell, ed., *Journal of an Expedition*, 4. In same source, see also Archibald Campbell, General Orders, December 24, 1778, 19, and journal entries for November 8 and 26, 1778, 6–7, 11. For the reference to the letter from Clinton to Prevost, see in the same source, Sir Henry Clinton to Archibald Campbell, November 8, 1778, 4. Governor John Houstoun estimated that the British flotilla contained "A fleet of 37 Sail [that] arrived at Cockspur [Island] on the 24th of this month [December]" although the ships appeared on December 23 (John Houstoun to the President of Congress, John Jay, January 2, 1779, John Houstoun Papers, 1775–1784, MS 397, Georgia Historical Society).

the state. Those crimes resulted in a sentence of four hundred lashes to Wood's bare back. Elbert, who viewed desertion as the worst crime a soldier could ever commit, wanted each lash harshly delivered "with more than usual severity."[3] As before, Elbert was hesitant to put his soldiers to death for these types of offenses, largely because he needed them to bolster the strength of his already depleted battalions. He hoped the threat of severe punishment would curtail desertions.

Keeping the army supplied with food, clothes, weapons, and ammunition was another ongoing challenge. To better facilitate the provisioning of his soldiers, Elbert appointed Mordecai Sheftall as Georgia's deputy commissary general of issues. As one of Savannah's prominent Jewish leaders and merchants, Sheftall was well acquainted with Elbert in both business and Masonic circles. They enjoyed a close friendship, and Sheftall had the colonel's full confidence, evidenced by Elbert's appointment of him as the commissary of Continental troops in 1777. Thus, Sheftall was commissary and deputy commissary simultaneously; his job was not only to supply the soldiers with necessities but also to keep up with the stores, maintain accurate records for the dispersal of sundry goods to the army, and accurately document all financial transactions. Given the state's scarcity of resources and money, he was under tremendous pressure to keep the battalions and militia supplied, even as Elbert routinely issued him orders to that effect. On October 24, the commander directed Sheftall to "have magazines of every species of provisions stored at Savannah, Sunbury and Augusta." To carry out his task, the commissary was empowered to "employ as many hands as are necessary at those respective places." Elbert added that a "large quantity of barreled pork, and wheat flower, will be particularly wanted, which cant be done without." Sheftall was to collect certified copies of receipts for all purchases. As he had in the past, the colonel continued to rely on his own resources to help provide things for the army, such as brandy, rum, and sugar, which he charged to the state as debts owed to him.[4]

---

[3] Samuel Elbert, "B. O. [Brigade Orders]," August 6, 1778, in OBSE, 179, and, in the same source, Samuel Elbert, "B. O. [Brigade Orders]," August 19, 1778, 182; K. Coleman, *American Revolution in Georgia*, 111.

[4] Samuel Elbert, "B. O. [Brigade Orders]," July 28, 1778, 178, in OBSE, and, in the same source, Samuel Elbert Orders, "Parole—Lincoln," October 24, 1778, 188; Account Book, 1769–1788, 37–38, Samuel Elbert Papers, Rubenstein Rare Book and Manuscript Library.

Elbert also struggled with soldiers' pay. Part of the problem was that the state's currency was worthless outside of Georgia, so the men refused to accept it. Elbert notified his superior in Charleston, General Robert Howe, of the problem on August 11. The insistence by the General Assembly of paying the troops with state money was causing "great confusion" in the army, he reported. The colonel fully understood the sentiment and frustration of his men and urged Howe to take the matter to Congress and prevail upon them to pay the soldiers in Continentals instead. He was still lobbying for Continental pay one month later. "I hope Congress will find it convenient to send a sufficient sum of Continental Money for the purpose of paying the Troops," he wrote Henry Laurens, the president of the Continental Congress, on September 5. If something was not done soon, he predicted a "Mutiny will take place among them." A temporary response would not satisfy the men, he said, so a more permanent solution was necessary. Furthermore, since Continental money was more valuable, Elbert believed the state would save "nearly equal to one half, in the purchase of every thing necessary for the Army." The one area where the commander had direct control of soldiers' compensation concerned the paymasters who distributed their money. Always an advocate for his soldiers, Elbert admonished paymasters who failed in their primary responsibilities. "Pay-Masters may expect the most rigorous treatment," he warned on October 17, if they neglected their duty and caused the men to complain for want of pay. Evidently, Elbert's complaints and warnings bore fruit. Savannah merchant and first cousin of the Habersham brothers, Joseph Clay, who served as Georgia's deputy paymaster, worked diligently over the summer to get the soldiers back pay owed to them by the state. Around the same time, Congress voted an additional one million dollars in September to cover Georgia's expenses including soldiers' pay.[5]

Elbert also wanted to establish a professional hospital for his men, and he was not alone on this issue. Back in February, Howe addressed Governor John Houstoun and the General Assembly about many issues, including the poor health of the troops. He urged the governor to quickly appropriate money to build barracks in Savannah as well as a hospital containing proper medicines and staff. At the time, nearly one-

---

[5] Samuel Elbert to Robert Howe, August 11, 1778, Robert Howe Letters, MS 0400, 474, Georgia Historical Society; Samuel Elbert to Henry Laurens, September 5, 1778, in Chesnutt, ed., *Papers of Henry Laurens*, 14:269; Samuel Elbert, "Parole—Unanimity," October 17, 1778, in OBSE, 187; K. Coleman, *American Revolution in Georgia*, 105.

fourth of the soldiers were ill, and the sickly season had not even yet arrived. The assembly responded by constructing brick barracks in Savannah, but by the end of the Florida campaign, hospitals were still unregulated, and makeshift facilities were scattered across the state. "Every Regimental Surgeon has his own [hospital]," complained Elbert to Laurens on September 5, "which occasions some abuse that it is impossible to prevent." Those abuses infuriated Elbert, and there were many. On July 28, he suggested that the commissaries of hospitals were inaccurately recording financial transactions. The unethical practice hinted that some were probably lining their own pockets with stolen money. Surgeons, too, were neglecting their duty. "The sick," he reminded them, "are to be taken care of in the best manner, and to be accommodated with every thing necessary for their recovery." Some surgeons were even abusing the distribution of medicines. Elbert rebuked them, saying, the "greatest pains will be taken to detect and punish those who may presume to misapply any stores or other necessaries given out for the sick."[6] Still, by the end of 1778, the type of hospital that Elbert envisioned had not materialized although doctors, surgeons, and medical staff improved their efficiency and behavior.

Amid all these problems, Indian raids once again ticked up along the borders. Reports of Indian activity reached Elbert on August 13, and he responded by ending furloughs so that his army could deal with the threat. Six days later he scattered his battalions across the state's frontiers for the purpose, he said, "of securing helpless & innocent women and children from the scalping knife of the bloody allies of the British King."[7]

The reports reaching Elbert's ears were correct. Nearly five hundred Seminoles were prowling the area north of the St. Johns, while parties of Upper and Lower Creeks, including Okfuskees and Cowetas, were menacing the western settlements. One band of Upper Creeks attacked a fort on the Ogeechee, killing eight men. Afterwards, they went on a rampage destroying homes and plantations, causing locals to flee to nearby forts and blockhouses. Another party of 132 warriors from various Lower Creek towns raided homes and settlements along

---

[6] Hall, *Land and Allegiance*, 68; Samuel Elbert to Henry Laurens, September 5, 1778, Chesnutt, ed., *Papers of Henry Laurens*, 14:269; Samuel Elbert, "B. O. [Brigade Orders]," July 28, 1778, in OBSE, 178–79.

[7] Samuel Elbert, "Gen'l Orders," August 13, 1778, in OBSE, 181, and, in the same source, Samuel Elbert, "B. O. [Brigade Orders]," August 19, 1778, 182–83.

the Altamaha while a smaller group plundered farms on the Satilla. The raids extended to the Broad River valley in the ceded lands where Indians massacred almost thirty whites on August 9, killed their livestock, plundered their property, and burned their homes. Just a few weeks later, they attacked Nail's Fort on the same river and killed many more settlers. Houstoun was so concerned that he wrote Laurens and told him that eight Native American towns had "declared for War against us.…So that in addition to other Misfortunes we may consider ourselves as fairly in for an Indian War." Elbert kept Laurens apprised as well. "The Savages have, in the course of the last month, murdered upwards of twenty People on our Western Frontiers," he wrote, vowing to respond in kind. "Considering their former trespasses of the like Nature," fumed the colonel, "[it] is an insult that I hope will not be overlook'd with impunity."[8]

One of the state's goals in undertaking the Florida campaign earlier in the year was to end Indian depredations on the frontier. Measured against that objective, the events along Georgia's borders in summer and fall 1778 showed that the campaign only produced a brief lull in the violence.[9] John Stuart, British superintendent of Indian affairs in Pensacola, and his agents in Indian country played a role in instigating the raids, but Creek warriors also engaged in them as they continued to dispute lost territory in the ceded lands.

As Georgia dealt with a myriad of wartime problems, Congress, on September 5, removed Howe from command and replaced him with Massachusetts native Major General Benjamin Lincoln from Washington's army. A resolution from Congress on September 25 specified Lincoln's task in the South, which was to remain on the defensive. If the British did not attack, Lincoln was to go on the offensive and capture St. Augustine in yet a fourth Florida campaign. Howe did not learn of his removal until October 9, when the official papers reached his headquarters in Charleston informing him to turn his command over to Lincoln and immediately repair to Washington's headquarters. The removal was an affront to the general's honor. "Have I not sacrificed my Fortune & Peace to the service to

---

[8] Samuel Elbert to Henry Laurens, September 5, 1778, in Chesnutt, ed., *Papers of Henry Laurens*, 14:269; Searcy, *Georgia-Florida Contest*, 154–55; Hall, *Land and Allegiance*, 72.

[9] Samuel Elbert to Henry Laurens, September 5, 1778, in Chesnutt, ed., *Papers of Henry Laurens*, 14:269; Searcy, *Georgia-Florida Contest*, 154–55; Hall, *Land and Allegiance*, 72.

my Country!," he wrote Laurens on the same day. "Have I not by the most unwearied diligence & with a Zeal which at least has some merit attended to the duties of my station & by my every effort endeavored to do my Duty!... How Sir have I deserved this disgrace?"[10]

Despite Howe's excuses and professions of innocence, he must have known at least some of the causes for the transfer. His relationship with Georgia's authorities, particularly Houstoun, was terrible, and his reputation was even worse in South Carolina. There, a controversial relationship with a female had become a public and embarrassing affair. In addition, a duel he fought in August with South Carolina General Christopher Gadsden over a disagreement concerning command of the Southern Department further diminished Howe's popularity, even though he only grazed his opponent's ear in the contest. Finally, the failed Florida campaign also played into Howe's removal, especially since Houstoun and others loudly complained to Congress about the general's inability to command. Houstoun criticized every decision made by Howe in Florida, particularly the order to abandon the mission after the destruction of Fort Tonyn and the withdrawal of the British army. That decision especially was a "great surprise" to Houstoun since his militia, which the governor claimed numbered nearly two thousand men, were ready to march on St. Augustine. "I am happy in being able to say," he informed Congress, "that a more unpopular manuaver never was attempted than this," and all ranks of the militia who were present saw Howe's shameful decision for themselves.[11]

Howe remained in Charleston as he waited for Lincoln's arrival. Meanwhile, on November 11, a congressional committee that included Edward Telfair from Georgia and Henry Drayton from South Carolina formally authorized a fourth Florida campaign led by Lincoln. The new commander had full power to enlist men in the Georgia and South Carolina battalions as well as 1,500 militia from both states to subdue the province. Another campaign was necessary, they said, because ending the Florida threat was of "high importance to the welfare of the United States." Accordingly, "every exertion should be made during the course of the winter to reduce the Province of St. Augustine." As a final inducement for Lincoln, they offered him a bounty of three thousand

---

[10] Mattern, *Benjamin Lincoln*, 60; Bennett and Lennon, *Quest for Glory*, 86–87.

[11] Bennett and Lennon, *Quest for Glory*, 86–87; Godbold and Woody, *Christopher Gadsden*, 179–87.

acres just for leading the effort.[12] This report represented the height of the fourth Florida campaign, which never materialized due to the catastrophic magnitude of events that soon overshadowed it.

Around the third week in October, Howe sent Elbert a communication alluding to a new unspecified British threat in South Carolina and Georgia. The details of the communication are lost to history, but the reaction it caused in Elbert underscored the serious nature of the letter's contents. On October 24, the day Elbert received the message, he had all the troops in Savannah paraded so that he could access their readiness and issued orders to have the magazines in Savannah, Sunbury, and Augusta filled. He also admitted in his orders that a "very considerable army will be employed in this State in a little time." That army Elbert was referencing was certainly not Campbell's invasion force in New York. At that time, the British commander had not yet received his orders from Clinton to sail to Georgia. The only other possibility was that Howe had intelligence relating to renewed British activity stemming out of St. Augustine. Georgia's General Assembly also learned of the threat, probably from Elbert or Howe. They were so concerned that they sent Elbert to South Carolina on November 11 to discuss with Howe and Lincoln, if he arrived, what the colonel regarded as "matters of great importance to these States." Before he left, Elbert put Colonel John White from the 4th Battalion in charge of the state's Continental troops.[13]

The renewed British threat from East Florida was real. The increased population in St. Augustine due to fleeing Loyalists and the addition of more British troops compelled Prevost to scour Georgia once again for provisions. He sent his brother, Major Mark Prevost, with one hundred regulars and Lieutenant Colonel Thomas Brown with 300 rangers and Indians toward Midway to round up cattle and other necessities. At the same time, he directed Lieutenant Colonel Lewis Fuser to take five hundred soldiers from the 60th Regiment and some artillery up the Inland Passage in ships to the port of Sunbury, where they would act as a diversion. By November 19, Prevost's group had already crossed the Altamaha and were heading in the general direction of Midway. On that same day, Laurens sent some distressing news to Georgia's General Assembly. Apparently, after interrogating a

---

[12] Report from Committee to the House, Mr. Duer [?], Henry Drayton, Edward Telfair, November 10, 1778, in box 2, folder 1776–1779, Edward Telfair Papers, Rubenstein Rare Book and Manuscript Library.

[13] Samuel Elbert, "Parole—Lincoln," October 24, 1778, in OBSE, 188.

South Carolina Loyalist who had been in New York, Laurens learned that the British were about to unleash a mighty force on either Georgia or South Carolina. Although Laurens conveyed the message to Georgia's leaders, he admitted that he did not trust the source and doubted its accuracy.[14] It was the first evidence that the British were about to invade Georgia, but with Elbert gone and the Continentals and militia thinly scattered over a vast patchwork of outposts and forts, there was little else to do.

When White, who was at Sunbury, heard that Prevost and Brown were approaching Midway, he gathered some 120 Continentals and militia under the command of Colonel James Screven and Major James Jackson and rushed them to the community. Once in Midway, the Americans threw up a hasty breastwork across the major road near the Congregational Meeting House and decided to make a stand there, but, believing he was outnumbered, White abandoned that idea and opted for a surprise ambush along the road about a mile to the south instead. Brown's Loyalists were slightly ahead of Prevost as they neared Midway. Also believing he was outnumbered, Brown selected thirty-two rangers to set up an ambush precisely at the same location the Americans had chosen. On November 24, both parties bumbled into each other as they arrived at the same location around the same time. Heavy fighting ensued. Wounded in the opening salvo, Screven fell off his horse and was captured. Shot again as a prisoner by some of Brown's men, he died in enemy hands later that day. Prevost's regulars soon came up and closed in with Brown's rangers. The combined British forces, numbering some 400 men, drove the outnumbered American army back upon the church and beyond, forcing White to order a withdrawal toward the Ogeechee. During the retreat, White forged a letter from Elbert advising him to lure the British to the river where a large body of cavalry were approaching to encircle Prevost in the rear. White dropped his letter in a conspicuous place where someone discovered it and took it to the British major. The ruse worked because, shortly after occupying Midway, Prevost broke off his advance.[15]

Hugh McCall wrote early in the nineteenth century that Elbert "sent a flag to colonel [Major] Provost [Prevost] by Major John Habersham, requesting permission to furnish general Scriven [Screven] with such medical aid as his situation might require." Jones, in his

---

[14] Searcy, *Georgia-Florida Contest*, 161–63.
[15] Ibid.

history of Georgia later in the century, repeated the comment in a note. McCall erroneously believed that Elbert was in Savannah when he received White's dispatch dated November 24 informing him of the fighting at Midway; however, according to Elbert, he was in Charleston with Howe when Brown and Prevost attacked, and it was there where he received White's express. "I immediately received the General's [Howe] orders to return," remembered Elbert, "where, I think the second day after my arrival, I was joined by him."[16] It would have taken more than a day for White's express to get to Charleston and at least that long again for Elbert to arrive in Savannah. It was impossible, due to the constraints of distance and time, for the colonel to send Habersham under a flag of truce requesting medical aid for Screven, especially since he died on November 24, the day of the battle when White sent Elbert the express.

Elbert and Howe traveled to Georgia separately. Howe arrived at Zubley's Ferry on November 27, some twenty-three miles above Savannah, and Georgia's dreadful condition was the first thing he noticed. An express sent from Elbert, who entered Savannah probably on November 26, reached Howe on the day he arrived at the ferry. As Elbert later recalled, both commanders met up two days later in Savannah, which would have been November 28. Howe's alarm was such that he dispatched General William Moultrie in South Carolina a letter asking for reinforcements. Without assistance from South Carolina, claimed Howe, Georgia will "absolutely be lost." There was no time to spare. The general continued,

> Exert yourselves to the utmost to hasten up the troops under the command of Col. [Isaac] Huger; let them march with all possible expedition; baggage at this time is not to be considered, and provisions may be had at every house, let the men force on, and if some

---

[16] McCall, *History of Georgia*, 2:159; C. C. Jones Jr., *History of Georgia*, 2:306n2; Samuel Elbert testimony, January 12, 1782, in "Proceedings of a Court Martial for the Trial of Major General Howe," *Collections of the New York Historical Society for the Year 1879* (hereafter cited as *CNYHS*), 265. This source contains the transcripts of Howe's trial and several key eyewitness accounts about the fall of Savannah. George Walton also said at Howe's court martial trial that when "the troops from East-Florida first came into the State, neither the General [Howe] nor General [colonel at the time] Elbert was in the State" (*CNYHS*, George Walton testimony, January 9, 1782, 250). Emphasis added.

cannot march with the rest, let them proceed without the least delay; as this attempt upon Georgia is indeed a serious one.[17]

The abrupt appearance of the British in Georgia caused many leaders in South Carolina, including Moultrie, to see a different threat. Several believed the rumors that a large army was gathering in New York and about to head south. To them, the target was not Savannah but Charleston. On the following day, Moultrie informed Howe that people in his state were frightened. "The cloud from New-York, has not disappeared, but still hangs over our heads," he warned. The attack on Georgia confirmed the suspicions of many that the enemy was "causing a diversion there, while we are to be invaded here."[18]

In Savannah, Elbert hurriedly collected two hundred soldiers and rushed to the Ogeechee where he linked up with White and his Continentals. The colonel then sent a message to Prevost urging him to promise that he would protect the citizens and their property from the ravages of his army. In his reply, the British general refused to comply with Elbert's request since the people had voluntarily brought on their fate by rebelling against the king. While still lingering at Midway, Prevost learned from a scouting party that Fuser had not yet arrived at Sunbury. Without Fuser's support and unwilling to put his exposed army at further risk, Prevost abandoned Midway and headed back toward St. Augustine. Before he left, he burned the Meeting House and almost every dwelling and barn in his path.[19]

Had Prevost waited just a few more days, he would have established contact with Fuser at Sunbury, whose ships and transports, delayed by headwinds, arrived at the end of November. Fuser's immediate goal was Fort Morris along the Medway River at Sunbury, commanded by Lieutenant Colonel John McIntosh with around 127 Continentals. Fuser and his army of almost five hundred men, aided by his ships in the river, quickly laid siege to the fort and then sent McIntosh a demand to surrender the garrison. "Your answer," he mandated, "which I expect in an hour's time, will determine the fate of this country, whether it is to be laid in ashes, or remain [unscathed]." McIntosh's reply was memorable: "COME AND TAKE IT." Instead of moving against Fort Morris, Fuser sent out

---

[17] Robert Howe to William Moultrie, November 27, 1778, in *MMAR*, 1:243; Searcy, *Georgia-Florida Contest*, 162–63.
[18] William Moultrie to Robert Howe, November 28, 1778, in *MMAR*, 1:245.
[19] McCall, *History of Georgia*, 2:159–60.

scouts to locate Prevost. They soon brought back disheartening news. Prevost, believing he was outnumbered and without the support of Fuser, had turned his army back toward St. Augustine. Unable to form a junction with Prevost, Fuser lifted the siege, loaded his men back on the ships, and sailed to St. Simons Island where he put his army to work repairing Fort Frederica and gathering provisions.[20]

Georgians and South Carolinians were confused about the meaning of the incursions from Florida, but they gained a little clarity on December 3, when the *Neptune*, a British transport from Campbell's fleet, appeared at Tybee Island and anchored off the light house. The ship, separated from the fleet at Sandy Hook a few weeks earlier due to a storm, proceeded to Savannah, where it waited for the rest of the navy. While there, a sailor named William Haslam deserted and presented himself to Savannah's authorities. On December 6, Houstoun interrogated him and learned for the first time about Campbell's expedition. The deserter estimated that Campbell's force contained five thousand regulars and Loyalists. Haslam was just a sailor without accurate knowledge of details, which explains his exaggeration of numbers. Regardless, the implication to Houstoun was that the enemy's army was considerably larger than anything he had to oppose it. When questioned about where the fleet was going, Haslam said that Savannah, and not Charleston, was the target. He claimed that while he was at Tybee, he heard guns firing out at sea, which he understood to be some of the ships trying to establish contact with each other. Once the British army landed, Haslam admitted that the common order was "to burn and destroy all who would not submit." After a couple of days, the *Neptune* sailed away, but not before giving Georgians their first tangible evidence that Savannah was in peril.[21]

Georgians were not the only ones learning about Campbell's approaching fleet. On December 5, while off Cape Hatteras in North Carolina, the British commander dispatched letters to Tonyn and General Prevost by the sloop *Granby*, announcing his imminent arrival off Georgia's coast. In the communication to Tonyn, Campbell revealed that he was going to take Savannah with three thousand troops and then march into the backcountry where he believed "a considerable Body of Loyalists are happily disposed to join the Royal Standard." Once in Georgia, he

---

[20] Ibid., 2:160–61; C. C. Jones Jr., *History of Georgia*, 2:308–11.
[21] John Houstoun, "The Examination of William Haslam," in *MMAR*, 1:249–51; Searcy, *Georgia-Florida Contest*, 163; McCall, *History of Georgia*, 2:165.

hoped the governor could cooperate with the king's army. One of the first things Tonyn could do, he suggested, was urge Stuart to rouse the Indians and send them to the backcountry toward the settlements as a diversion while he moved up the Savannah River with his army toward Augusta. In the letter to Prevost, Campbell detailed the units he was bringing with him from New York. Parker's fleet, he said, had made it to their intended destination almost intact with the exception of one transport (perhaps the *Neptune*), which was missing. He suggested that Prevost move with his army across the Altamaha toward Sunbury and quickly take that port because of its naval significance. These letters did not reach Tonyn or Prevost until December 19, which gave them little time to coordinate efforts with Campbell. According to Searcy, neither leader in East Florida knew until December 19 that the invasion was a reality until they received Campbell's letters. Therefore, the earlier attacks on Midway and Sunbury by Mark Prevost and Fuser were independent actions and not directly connected to Campbell's invasion of Savannah.[22]

Border fighting caused Georgia's citizens south of Savannah and Chatham County to experience ruin and plunder from the war's beginning. By late 1778, as British armies increased their presence nearer to Savannah, Chatham's residents also felt the pangs of war on their farms and plantations. William Gibbons, a Whig planter in the county, could not prevent British soldiers from robbing his plantation in their endless search for provisions. They first arrived on December 6. "The Light Dragoons came to the quarters at Mrs. Sarah Gibbons['s] plantation…[and] killed seven hogs," he complained. After that, they turned their horses into his field without permission. Perhaps that is when they noticed that Gibbons had a quantity of food stored in his buildings. On the following day, a "Captain Cambel [*sic*]" took 783 sheaves of rice for his army along with some potatoes and corn. This was not Archibald Campbell, who was off the coast of Cape Hatteras with Parker's fleet at the time, nor was it Prevost's army or Brown's rangers, who were heading back to St. Augustine after fighting Americans at Midway. The only possibility was that these were some of Fuser's men from Fort Frederica. That area, stripped clean from the war, could not provide enough food and fodder for his army or horses, forcing the commander to send foraging parties further inland

---

[22] Archibald Campbell to Patrick Tonyn, December 5, 1778, in Campbell, ed., *Journal of an Expedition*, 11–12, and, in the same source, Archibald Campbell to Patrick Tonyn and Augustine Prevost, December 5, 1778; Searcy, *Georgia-Florida Contest*, 179–80.

toward Savannah. On December 11, Gibbons complained that the light dragoons came and confiscated an additional 1,553 sheaves of rice and more potatoes and corn. They took 200 more sheaves on December 12. He did not see them on the following day, but beginning on December 15 and continuing for the next five days, they pillaged his plantation for rice, corn, and potatoes. On December 19, they also robbed him of 234 sheaves of straw. Gibbons was not alone. On that same day, Houstoun informed Lincoln, who arrived in Charleston on December 4, that the British were confiscating pilot boats and taking slaves who were well acquainted with the rivers and that on one island, they robbed one or two plantations.[23]

As the sinews of war tightened around Savannah, Howe rode to Sunbury to check on the defenses at Fort Morris. While there, he wrote Moultrie on December 8, describing Georgia's desperate plight. "It is impossible for me to give an account of the confused, perplexed way in which I found matters in this state upon my arrival," he began. Savannah was so ill prepared that he predicted that it was not "defensible for half an hour, should it be attacked." He noted that several had heard the thundering of cannon at sea from different quarters, all of which "appear like signals given, and answered [and] confirm the accounts brought us by the man [Haslam]." If the enemy made any appearance with a large body of troops, he warned, they will "shake this state, in its weak unprepared situation, to its very foundation." His gut feeling was that Georgia "will probably be lost." Howe also referenced his ongoing struggle with Houstoun over control of the state's military forces. If the governor would only cooperate, the general promised to make the "purchase of this country dearer perhaps than our enemies expect."[24]

Houstoun and the executive council also felt premonitions of impending doom. Still fixated on invading Florida, the governor implored Lincoln to put the army in motion southward immediately. "I can assure you," he anxiously wrote, "with the greatest Truth, that the situation of this State is truly perilous, & unless some vigorous Impression is made, in the Course of the Winter, on our Southern Neighbors, I do not know whether the Existence of Georgia as a free & independent State is not endanger'd." The letter suggested that Houstoun was still uncertain about

---

[23] "List of Provisions Obtained by Campbell from Gibbons' Plantation, December 7, 1778," in William Gibbons Jr. Papers, 1772–1802, box 2, folder 1774–1784, Rubenstein Rare Book and Manuscript Library; John Houstoun to Benjamin Lincoln, December 19, 1778, John Houstoun Papers, 1775–1784, MS 397, Georgia Historical Society.

[24] Robert Howe to William Moultrie, December 6, 1778, in *MMAR*, 1:247–49.

British designs on Savannah, despite the overwhelming evidence like Haslam's interrogation, supporting an attack on the city. Determined to inform Lincoln about the true nature of affairs, the executive council met on December 17 and decided to send Walton and Lyman Hall to confer with the general. Walton and Hall were to impress upon Lincoln the absolute necessity of a "vigorous and decisive" defense against "the incursions of our Southern neighbors." Thus, just like Houstoun, the executive council focused its attention to the south and was impervious to the real threat hanging over Georgia's head from the north. Although Hall did go to meet Lincoln, the later appearance of the British fleet off Savannah caused Walton to remain behind since he deemed it improper to leave his militia regiment.[25]

Still off the coast of North Carolina, Campbell, on December 17, dispatched the *Alert* to the Savannah River to gather intelligence about the enemy's forces. The *Alert* went upriver as far as Cockspur but reported on December 24 that they had seen nothing. Parker's fleet arrived off the coast of Charleston on December 22. There, Campbell issued general orders to his army as they neared their destination. He was particularly concerned with the behavior of his men toward the city's inhabitants. His instructions contradicted the burn-and-destroy orders announced by Haslam earlier when interviewed by Houstoun. The troops were not to commit "a single Act of Depredation or Plunder," since they would "ruin a Country which was meant to be preserved [and] injure their Reputation in point of Discipline." Those who commit such acts were the "Bane and Disgrace of an Army, the stubborn Weeds of Riot and Licentiousness, and will be exterminated without mercy." Nor were they to enter any dwellings. "In a Country so much covered with Woods," he warned, and "possessed by an Enemy whose Practice it is, by every Species of Allurement to tempt and ensnare the unguarded; the Troops who straggle in Quest of Plunder, may expect to find in every Plantation, some lurking Villian ready to profit by their irregular Conduct." On December 24, Christmas Eve, Parker's fleet, almost all now at Tybee, hoisted signals to head into the mouth of the Savannah River. By the end of the day, the whole fleet was in the river except ten transports and a man-of-war.[26]

---

[25] John Houstoun to Benjamin Lincoln, December 19, 1778, in Mattern, *Benjamin Lincoln*, 61; Minutes of the Executive Council, December 17, 1778, in *RRG*, 2:124; *CNYHS*, George Walton testimony, January 9, 1782, 250.

[26] Campbell, ed., *Journal of an Expedition*, December 17, 1778, 13; December 22, 15; December 24, 1778, 18.

By this point, there could be no doubt about British intentions, and Savannah was hardly prepared to deal with the threat. "The cannon of this state are few indeed, and one-third at least are incapable of being made useful, and those that are capable of being made so are not in order," complained an exasperated Howe. There were, he admitted, some fine artillery pieces about the town, including a Howitzer, but they were all worthless since none had the proper shells. The general ordered all Continental troops in the state to Savannah, except the garrisons at Fort Morris and Augusta. "The Metropolis of Georgia was in the most defenseless condition imaginable," explained McCall. A battery on the eastern end of the city offered little protection from a determined enemy approaching by land, since it only guarded the river and the whole city was exposed.[27]

Despite Howe's efforts, there were hardly enough soldiers to mount a respectable defense. Those efforts included a call for militia from South Carolina and North Carolina to come and assist Georgia. Hundreds were on the way but had not reached Savannah by the time the crisis reached its climax. The arrival of Huger from South Carolina, around December 25, was welcomed news although it brought the total number of Continentals only to about six hundred. According to Elbert, the whole militia in the state at the time amounted to nearly three thousand men, and even they failed to turn out as expected except for nearly 120 with Walton. He believed that the prospect of losing the town and surrounding country prevented many from showing up. Instead, most spent their time relocating families and personal effects to more secure areas. Walton also felt that the ongoing feud between the general and the governor caused many to stay home. Thus, all Howe had to face a professionally trained enemy of three thousand soldiers was a paltry force of some seven or eight hundred men with four or five pieces of field artillery.[28]

In the face of such overwhelming odds, Howe tried to maintain a sense of calm although some of the general's detractors, such as militia commander James Jackson, who was in Savannah, interpreted it as overconfidence. Walton heard the general quip to a group of people around Christmas Day that the "enemy's army was composed of raw boys from the Highlands and of Delancey's green-coats, who would not fight" and "he did not care if they were double the number." On that same day,

---

[27] Robert Howe to [Moultrie?], December 25, 1778, Robert Howe Papers, 1777–1778, Rubenstein Rare Book and Manuscript Library; McCall, *History of Georgia*, 2:164.

[28] *CNYHS*, Samuel Elbert testimony, January 12, 1782, 266–67, 271, and George Walton testimony, January 8, 1782, 246.

Sheftall asked permission from the general to remove all the stores and provisions in Savannah to a more secure location. "He said," recalled Sheftall, "he thought there was no danger. I told him, I thought there was." John Wereat recalled that Howe hinted to the inhabitants of Savannah to remove their effects out of caution, and many did. Wereat claimed that more would have, but they could not find boats and carriages for that purpose. Howe later defended his actions, saying his intentions were not to lull citizens into a sense of false security, but to inspire them for Savannah's defense. His suggestion to remove personal effects was only precautionary, "for fear of accident."[29]

Elizabeth Elbert was certainly not going to take her chances, especially with children. As the wife of a high-ranking American officer, she could become a special target of abuse if Savannah fell and the enemy occupied the city. More than likely, she and her children evacuated at this time. The most logical place for them to go was Rae's Hall, just upriver from Savannah. However, that plantation's landing was a potential debarking site for the British army and not a safe option. She probably chose to move further away, perhaps to Augusta where she had family.

The enemy at Savannah's threshold did not stop the endless bickering between Howe and the state's politicians. Lieutenant Colonel Jean Baptiste de Ternant, Howe's French engineer and inspector general to the Army, recalled that the general complained many times in his presence about the governor's refusal to comply with simple requests for horses, entrenchment tools, laborers, and other things to help prepare defenses. "The chief command was even disputed with him, which occasioned confusion and delay in every measure," observed Ternant. "[I made] repeated applications to Houstoun for tools, hands, and many other matters," recollected Howe under sworn testimony in 1782, "and…no assistance was yielded me." Elbert concurred with the general. He saw letters that Howe laid before the legislative and executive bodies of Georgia to fortify certain places and prepare for a general defense of the state. There was one, in particular, that he remembered seeing on this subject laid before the General Assembly, but they were offended because they thought Howe was trying to "dictate to them."[30]

---

[29] Hawes, ed., "Papers of James Jackson," 8; *CNYHS*, Mordecai Sheftall testimony, January 11, 1782, 261, John Wereat testimony, December 15, 1781, 229, and Robert Howe testimony, January 21, 1782, 300–301.

[30] *CNYHS*, Jean Baptiste de Ternant testimony, January 12, 1782, 280, Robert Howe testimony, January 21, 1782, 289, and Samuel Elbert testimony, January 12, 1782, 273.

Finally, on the eve of a looming disaster, Houstoun caved. On Christmas Day, with a host of British ships congregating off Tybee and in the river, he reluctantly gave Howe authority over the militia. Even so, Walton recalled that he never received any orders from the general in the days prior to the invasion, including a plan of retreat if that were necessary. Not that it mattered since there were hardly enough militia in Savannah to make a difference. "Very few of the militia have as yet embodied," Howe lamented as he took command of all the troops in his midst. Apparently, due to Christmas celebrations or just unruliness, the militia now under his authority were difficult to control. After sunset on Christmas Day and in spite of the crisis, they strolled in and out of camp so much and created such disorder "that our guards were every moment in danger of firing upon one another."[31]

As mass confusion and uncertainty reigned among Georgia's military and political leaders, a confident Campbell readied his men to undertake their mission. While disruptive militia kept guards on edge in American lines, Campbell sent Sir James Baird and some of his Highland Light Infantry in two flat boats up the tidal creeks behind Tybee Island to gather intelligence. After searching all night through swamps and marsh, Baird returned at eight o'clock the following morning with a White overseer and a Black man named Peter. Upon interrogation, the British commander discovered (erroneously) that he faced two brigades consisting of 1,800 Continentals. Elbert commanded one while a "Colonel Eugee [Huger]" led the other. Over six hundred militia and ten brass field pieces augmented the American army, so Campbell's force nearly matched in number (he thought) the one he opposed. He also learned that the nearest place to debark was Girardeau's Landing, about twelve miles upriver from Tybee. A causeway, about a mile and a half long, linked the river to Brewton Plantation, which sat on top of Brewton's Hill, a forty- to fifty-foot bluff and the highest ground around Savannah. From there, a road led northward to Savannah through rice fields, gradual rises, and across a tidal creek made passable by a bridge. Beyond that, the ground gently rose again to a plateau at Fair-Lawn Plantation, just below the city. The rice fields were not flooded and were passable by Campbell's men. In all, the total distance from Brewton's Hill to Savannah was just over a mile.

---

[31] Ibid., George Walton testimony, January 4, 1782, 236, and George Walton testimony, January 8, 1782, 246; Robert Howe to [Moultrie?], December 25, 1778, Robert Howe Papers, 1777–1778, Rubenstein Rare Book and Manuscript Library.

Campbell immediately recognized the strategic importance of Girardeau's Landing and Brewton's Hill and determined to disembark his army there and march his force straight up the road and directly into the city.[32]

Campbell initially planned his attack for December 27, but blustery winds and choppy waves kept his army aboard the ships. The bad weather also grounded many of the transports downriver below the main fleet. There could be no attack on Savannah without them to funnel men and supplies from the ships to the shore. Campbell spent most of December 28 freeing transports and getting them into position at the landing. That night, both he and Parker lay in their uniforms on board the *Vigilant* anchored just below Girardeau's. From the ship's deck, Campbell could see the American campfires in the distance, along the general direction on the road he planned to follow into Savannah shortly after dawn.[33]

Although aware of the British fleet at Girardeau's, Howe spent December 28 trying to decipher the enemy's next move. Some officers, including Elbert, viewed Girardeau's as a likely landing place, but there were four additional sites below Savannah and two more above the city that offered possibilities, including Rae's Hall. Without better information, Howe could not commit his forces to any one site. The only thing he could do was detach small units at all the landings and keep watch.[34]

Tense hours passed, and still an overwrought Howe had no answers. Later in the day, he, Elbert, and some other officers rode down to Brewton's Hill to reconnoiter the enemy. From the bluff's summit, the entire British navy was in view. Still, Howe was unconvinced that Girardeau's was the chosen landing point. He decided to post a small picket there to observe developments and then returned to camp, leaving Elbert behind to situate the men and show them where to erect earthworks when they arrived. During this time, as Elbert quietly watched the enemy's activity in the river, he became convinced that Girardeau's was the location selected for debarkation. He believed they would form on Brewton's Hill for a march into Savannah along the road going through Fair-Lawn. To Elbert, the hill was a key strategic position to mount a stiff resistance. Soon, Captain John Smith and about thirty men from the South Carolina brigade met Elbert. The colonel informed Smith that he was going back

---

[32] C. Campbell, ed., *Journal of an Expedition*, December 25 and 26, 1778, 20–21; *CNYHS*, John Wereat testimony, December 15, 1781, 230–31.

[33] C. Campbell, ed., *Journal of an Expedition*, December 26 and 28, 1778, 20–22.

[34] *CNYHS*, John Wereat testimony, December 15, 1781, 230–31, and Samuel Elbert testimony, January 12, 1782, 266.

to General Howe and ask for reinforcements and some entrenching tools to strengthen the picket.[35]

When Elbert returned, he found Howe and gave the general his personal opinion. "I have every reason to believe," he predicted, "that the enemy intended to land at Girardeau's." To oppose them, Elbert suggested considerable reinforcements sent to Smith's picket, along with a large quantity of entrenching tools and some artillery. Elbert even offered his battalions as reinforcements. Still, Howe demurred. The congregating ships at Girardeau's could be a ruse masking their actual landing at another place. Furthermore, the hill lay open to shelling from British ships that could decimate any troops concentrated there. For these reasons, Howe relented and did not give Elbert a definitive answer, except for a promise that he would "consider it."[36]

Around ten or eleven o'clock that night, Elbert again met with Howe. From their conversation, Elbert understood that the entrenching tools were on their way. As for the reinforcements the colonel desired, Howe said that he could provide no more than twenty, giving Smith fifty men in all. The general could spare no field pieces, either. Howe told Elbert to accompany those troops to Smith's picket. When Elbert arrived at Brewton's Hill, he was stunned to discover that the tools he requested were not there. By then, it was too late to obtain them. As Elbert was leaving, he warned Smith that before daylight, he would surely see the enemy landed and marching up the hill to his position. He told Smith to reserve his fire until they were fifty or sixty yards away. Only then should his muskets spring to life with "cool" and "deliberate" fire. When the fighting began, Elbert directed Smith to retreat slowly up the hill until support arrived or his position became untenable. The colonel then returned to his battalions where he spent a restless night.[37]

At daybreak, British soldiers descended into transports and headed toward the landing. Arriving onshore in a whaleboat, Campbell arranged five hundred men for a rapid assault on Brewton's Hill where he learned "a small Body of the Rebels appeared in Readiness for our

---

[35] Ibid., Samuel Elbert testimony, January 12, 1782, 266.

[36] Ibid.; Bennett and Lennon, *Quest for Glory*, 94; McCall, *History of Georgia*, 2:171. According to militia commander James Jackson, who was present in Savannah, Howe was "begged…to permit two field pieces be sent to Brewtons." Had they arrived, "the British would have been severely handled & in all probability prevented [a] landing at that time" (see Hawes, ed., "Papers of James Jackson," 8–9).

[37] *CNYHS*, Samuel Elbert testimony, January 12, 1782, 266–67.

Reception." This, of course, was Smith's picket. In the absence of entrenchment tools, Smith's resourceful men found other ways to create defenses. During the night, they occupied the houses and barns on the plantation and knocked out planks to aim their firelocks through. As the British approached the summit and got within one hundred yards of the buildings, Smith's men fired. Campbell's soldiers responded by rushing the structures to flush out the Americans. It only took three minutes to gain possession of the hill and buildings as the "Rebels retreated with precipitation by the Back Doors and Windows," recalled Campbell. Although the skirmish cost no patriot lives, Campbell lost one officer and three Highlanders killed, with an additional five others wounded. It could have been worse. "Had the Rebels stationed four Pieces of Cannon on this Bluff with 500 Men for its Defense," the British commander admitted, "it is more than probable, they would have destroyed the greatest part of this Division of our little Army in their progress to the Bluff."[38] In other words, Elbert was right about Girardeau's Landing and Brewton's Hill. Had Howe listened to him a few hours earlier and sent Smith entrenching tools, artillery, and considerable reinforcements, the Americans would have possibly stood an outside chance of stemming the British advance, at least until Lincoln's reinforcements arrived.

After the affair on Brewton's Hill, Smith retreated and eventually linked up with the rest of the army encamped at Fair-Lawn. He reported the brief skirmish to Howe, but it was no surprise since the general and others heard the musketry from American lines. With the veil of uncertainty finally lifting, Howe summoned his officers to a council of war at ten o'clock to discuss their options. There were two choices. One was to abandon the city and wait on the arrival of reinforcements. A problem with that option was that Howe was unsure of the enemy's size although scouts and others who saw them guessed that it was between two thousand and three thousand men. Nor did he know when 1,200 troops from North and South Carolina, who left Charleston on December 27 with Lincoln, would arrive. While the promise of reinforcements gave hope, it did not help the Americans in their present predicament. The other option was to fight. The rise at Fair-Lawn offered the best place to establish a defensive line. Natural barriers, the Savannah River to the left and a wide and thick swamp on the right,

---

[38] C. Campbell, ed., *Journal of an Expedition*, December 29, 1778, 22–25.

protected the American flanks. Before them lay a broad swath of unflooded rice fields, affording a clear view of an approaching enemy with the exception of a few rises in the land. When Howe asked his officers their preference, a majority agreed to remain and "defend it to the last."[39]

The general then placed his troops for battle. He stationed Elbert's four battalions to the left of the road with a field piece in front of their brigade. In the road's center, he put two or three cannon and to their right, Huger's brigade with another field piece in front of them. Initially, Walton's militia was on Elbert's left, but frequent cannon balls fired from British ships fell onto their position, forcing them to relocate to Huger's right, where they guarded the extreme flank at the swamp. In his general orders concerning troop disposition, Howe admonished his officers and men to "distinguish themselves by their firmness and perseverance, and by an exact observance of orders." In case of a retreat, the troops, in an orderly fashion, would vacate the line in columns. Huger's South Carolinians would form the first column where they were to advance to Spring Hill at the northwestern outskirts of the city. The artillery came next and were to link up with Huger at Spring Hill. Once there, the artillery was to cover the Georgia brigade as they filed out last. Should a rout occur, advised the general, the troops were to assemble beyond Spring Hill on McGillivray's road.[40]

Out on the far right, Walton, unaware of Howe's retreat orders, was exploring the swamp near the militia. He became concerned about a number of passes traversing the boggy morass, some of which emerged from the thicket in the American rear. He rode to find the general and, upon encountering him, asked if the passes on the right were secure. Howe replied that there was no danger since he fortified the only one he knew of with a picket and some works. Walton then told him of another lesser-known unguarded pass beyond it. It was that pass, he insisted, and not the one with the picket, that posed the greatest danger to the American lines. Walton implored Howe to go and

---

[39] Bennett and Lennon, *Quest for Glory*, 93–94; Searcy, *Georgia-Florida Contest*, 164; *CNYHS*, Jean Baptiste de Ternant testimony, January 12, 1782, 280, and George Walton testimony, January 5, 1782, 241. For the order to fight to the last, see "General Howe's Order of Battle at Savannah," December 29, 1778, in *MMAR*, 1:252–53.

[40] *CNYHS*, "General Orders and Disposition of the Troops," in Jean-Baptiste de Ternant testimony, January 12, 1782, 282–83, and, in the same source, George Walton testimony, January 4, 1782, 238.

look for himself. "General," he explained, "in order that you may be convinced that what I say to you is true, I assert to you, upon my honor, that before the war I have frequently crossed the pass I mean in a chair, with young ladies, picking jessamines." Howe told Walton to reconnoiter it and then report his findings. Evidently, Walton's warning concerned Howe enough to send horse patrols to discover the hidden path, but they failed to find it. On another occasion, he sent Ternant and some aides. "I immediately went to visit it," recalled Ternant. "We attempted three times to go through the swamp at that place, and upon my guides pronouncing it impracticable we returned to the troops on Fair-Lawn." Howe did not take Walton's warnings lightly. The hidden paths on the right through the swamp "were sources of constant anxiety to me," he remembered, calling them "the disease of my position."[41]

It was midday before the whole of Campbell's army reached the top of Brewton's Hill, but shortly afterwards he formed his columns and advanced them up the road toward Savannah. Around two o'clock, Baird's Light Infantry maneuvered to within eight hundred yards of Elbert's line. Howe's artillery threw shot toward them, and Campbell directed Baird not to expose his men until he could ascertain the enemy's positions. The British commander climbed a nearby tree where he could see almost all of Howe's defenses. He also noticed that the bridge over the marshy creek that he would have to cross was in flames. Around this time, Quamino Dolly, a local slave, appeared and delivered Campbell a precious gift. He revealed the existence of a secret path through the swamp on the extreme right of the Americans leading to their rear and then agreed to guide some of the troops along it. With this information, Campbell determined to feint an attack on Howe's left and draw his attention there, while the slave led Baird's three hundred light infantry through the hidden pass on the American right. "A happy fall of Ground…concealed this movement," wrote Campbell, and behind it, Baird snuck his men from the front to the rear and, following the slave, entered the swamp unseen and came to the pass. Campbell instructed the officers with him to move forward briskly with

---

[41] Ibid., George Walton testimony, January 4, 1782, 239, Jean-Baptiste de Ternant testimony, January 12, 1782, 283, and Robert Howe testimony, January 21, 1782, 294–95.

their troops when they heard Baird's guns.[42] Baird and the light infantry slogged along the little-known trail through thickets and mud for nearly an hour before they emerged on Walton's flank around three o'clock.

Following Howe's suggestion, Walton was surveying the hidden pass when Baird's men burst upon the scene. They came on, he remembered, hopping over all obstacles with great agility. Although the light infantry saw Walton, he escaped before they could shoot at him. "Foreseeing that the enemy would soon [be] round, I rode full speed with the intelligence to the ground where the militia horse were posted," he recalled. He then scurried away and found Howe, to whom he announced that the "enemy [are] in force on our right." Howe ordered Walton back to the militia's position, and, when he arrived, Baird's men were already formed for an attack. A single field piece with the militia fired at them once or twice, but with no effect. The light infantry aimed their weapons and commenced a heavy fire into the militia. Almost instantly, Walton's men broke to the rear without even returning a shot. "I went up, and about three o'clock…the enemy appeared," remarked one eyewitness. "The militia appeared in confusion, and could not be reduced to order. A field-piece was fired once or twice in front of the militia, and though the Colonel [Walton] prevailed on them to advance and gave them three cheers, they were still in confusion." In the action, Walton was shot in the thigh and fell from his horse. Although his thigh was broken, he managed to get away for the time being.[43]

According to the prearranged signal, when Campbell heard Baird's guns, he ordered the rest of his army to rush the American line. He then wheeled out his battery, concealed behind a slight elevation, to pummel Howe's men. Howe's field pieces in the center of the road fired a couple of times with round shot at the close distance of 150 paces, but at this point, the right was folding and Baird was already in the American rear. Out of options, Howe gave the order to retreat.

---

[42] C. Campbell, ed., *Journal of an Expedition*, December 29, 1778, 24–27; McCall, *History of Georgia*, 2:174; Bennett and Lennon, *Quest for Glory*, 96. Several of Walton's militia later reported that Baird's force contained nearly three hundred men. See also *CNYHS*, John Gibbons testimony, December 15, 1781, 234.

[43] *CNYHS*, George Walton testimony, January 4, 1782, 240, and William Marbury testimony, January 12, 1782, 277. One eyewitness with the militia reported that they fled before Baird's Light Infantry even fired a shot. See in the same source, John Gibbons testimony, December 15, 1781, 235.

Benjamin Porter, a major in the Georgia line, recalled that the Continentals made little resistance before they started pulling out.[44] With the right engulfed in chaos, Howe's soldiers formed their columns and in good order vacated the line. Huger left first, followed by the artillery in the center, and both units headed toward the rendezvous point at Spring Hill.

For Elbert's battalions, waiting their turn in columns must have seemed like an eternity. Finally, he gave the order to march toward Spring Hill. It was during the retreat when the Georgia line sustained heavy casualties. As they gained Fair-Lawn's summit, Baird's light infantry emerged on Elbert's left flank and delivered a destructive volley into his men. Still, the battalions maintained their cohesiveness, but their organization dissolved when enemy artillery from the rear threw shot into the retreating brigade. One ball fell into the center, killing and maiming several men. It was probably at this time that John Newman, a member of the 2nd Battalion, had his arm shot off at the shoulder by a cannonball. Unable to go any further, the British captured him and put him on a prison ship near Savannah. To protect his men and reduce the size of the enemy's target, Elbert gave the command to turn the columns into a single file. This maneuver, executed under great difficulty, caused disorder. The appearance of additional British troops under Baird in the front of the file about one hundred yards from the city near the burial ground created utter chaos. That development cut off the escape route to Spring Hill. Flanked in the front, side, and rear, Elbert's center collapsed, causing the entire file to crumble, and the whole body fled into Savannah's streets. From the distance, a gleeful Campbell watched Howe's army scatter. Even he was amazed at its quick disintegration, which he called, "rapid beyond Conception."[45]

"Observing the few that followed me," Elbert recollected, "I led them through where a square of buildings had but late been burnt down, and halted before the Court-house door." There he consulted with his second-in-command, Lieutenant-Colonel Francis Harris of the 1st Battalion, about a place where he could lead the men to safety. Harris answered that

---

[44] Ibid., John Roberts testimony, January 12, 1782, 263, and Major Benjamin Porter testimony, January 10, 1782, 253.

[45] Ibid., Lieutenant William Glascock testimony, January 10, 1782, 258–59, and Samuel Elbert testimony, January 12, 1782, 269; Revolutionary War Pension and Bounty-Land Warrant Applications, Pension Application of John Newman, S1299, October 21, 1837.

Musgrove Creek, a tidal inlet on the Savannah River about twenty yards wide just north of the city, was the best option. He knew where a log spanned the creek, and the men could get across it. "Lead me to it," the colonel replied. "It is a happy circumstance, we will save our men." Elbert called out to those near him, "Follow me, soldiers, and I will conduct you to a safe retreat." Waiving his sword high over his head, he bounded toward the creek. "I sent Colonel Harris back to the rear with orders to push [my soldiers] on, and desired that he would join me in time before I got to the creek," explained Elbert. When Harris returned with more men, they found the creek, but no log. Apparently, the high tide covered it up or washed it away. As a last resort, Elbert ordered the men to jump into the frigid water and swim across. With the enemy close behind, many followed his command and some, like Harris, got to the other side. Elbert, who was a good swimmer, also made it to the opposite bank, but not with his horse and papers, which he abandoned.[46]

Faint from the loss of blood and excruciating pain in his hip, Walton arrived in town with the remnants of the fleeing army, barely able to stay on his horse. As someone helped him dismount, he noticed a scene of pandemonium: "I perceived scattered troops and citizens out of the town running and hiding in great disorder….The musket-bullets then began to reach the place where I lay." It was only then, with "Georgia troops running along the streets…in confusion," that he realized the day was wholly unfortunate. Someone helped Walton back on his horse, and he galloped away toward the northern part of town to escape. British soldiers captured him not long afterward.[47]

Back at Musgrove's Creek, more of Elbert's men threw down their weapons and plunged into the cold water. Many drowned. Faced with the prospect of drowning, surrendering seemed a better option for most. Mordecai Sheftall arrived at Musgrove Creek with his son, Sheftall Sheftall, a young Continental soldier in the Georgia line. Since his son could not swim, the elder Sheftall sat with him until the British arrived and they both surrendered. According to Sheftall Sheftall, on January 2, the British placed them on a prison ship. Elbert's longtime friend, Major John Habersham, also could not swim. His only choice was to give himself up to the British and become a prisoner of war, which he did.[48]

---

[46] *CNYHS*, Samuel Elbert testimony, January 12, 1782, 269–70; Charlton, "Sketch of the Life of General Elbert," 2.

[47] Ibid., George Walton testimony, January 5, 1782, 242–43.

[48] Robert Howe to Benjamin Lincoln, December 30, 1778, Robert Howe Letters,

As Howe gathered the shattered remnants of his command at Cherokee Hill, eight miles north of Savannah, Campbell rode up to Musgrove's Creek and oversaw the collection of prisoners. There he discovered Elbert's horse, stranded in the mud. The British victory could not have been more complete. In his post-battle return, Campbell tallied 453 prisoners, mostly taken at the creek, in addition to 83 Americans found dead on the field. The highest-ranking American officer now in British hands was Walton. The numbers revealed the depth of Howe's disaster, which was, shockingly, over half of his military strength. In the Georgia battalions alone, 244 soldiers surrendered. The one most severely affected was Elbert's beloved 2nd Battalion, who lost 137 men, including one major (Habersham). No longer would Elbert hear his old battalion play the "Grenadier March," either, since Campbell listed five drummers and five fifers as prisoners. The damage done to the 2nd Battalion was so catastrophic that it practically ceased to exist as a unit. Huger's troops also suffered. He compiled a return after the battle showing that fifty-five men in the 3rd Regiment, forty-five in the 5th, and nine in the Carolina corps of artillery were missing after the action, representing close to a third of his total strength. In comparison, the capture of Savannah cost Campbell only twenty-six men, further illuminating the lopsided nature of the British victory. Campbell netted more than just prisoners. He took almost all of Howe's cannon, ordinance, arms, and gunpowder, as well as the stores and supplies. A lack of ships and vessels prevented Howe from whisking them away to a place of safety. He admitted to Lincoln a day after the battle that one reason he chose to make a stand at Savannah was to prevent the British from taking the army's supplies. It was a fruitless endeavor because in addition to losing his army, he lost all of his stores as well. As British soldiers rounded-up prisoners and seized provisions, Parker's ships sailed up to Savannah's wharves and confiscated all the shipping. Toward the end of the day, as Campbell considered the totality of his victory, he could only remark that the "Capital of Georgia fell into my hands before it was dark."[49]

MS 400, Georgia Historical Society; Revolutionary War Pension and Bounty-Land Warrant Applications, Pension Application of Sheftall Sheftall, S31959, October 15, 1832; White, *Historical Collections of Georgia*, 340; Charlton, "Sketch of the Life of General Elbert," 2.

[49] "Archibald Campbell's Return of American Prisoners Taken in Action on December 29, 1778," in Archibald Campbell Papers, MS 0119, Georgia Historical Society, and, in the same source, "Archibald Campbell's Return of British Killed," December 29, 1778. See also C. Campbell, ed., *Journal of an Expedition*, December 29, 1778, 28; Robert Howe

At eight o'clock that night, seven miles from Savannah, a dejected Houstoun, surrounded by a handful of militia, jotted a quick note to Lincoln describing the horrifying events that had transpired. "Sir," began the message, "We have lost the day and the enemy are now in possession of Savannah." The attack began four hours earlier, he said, and because of the superior number of the enemy, "the matter was settled in a few minutes." He implored Lincoln to quickly march to Savannah: "Every thing will depend on your being [here] with us. A small party of militia are here and near to entrench…waiting for you coming up."[50]

Before he left Cherokee Hill, Howe issued orders for the Continental soldiers at Sunbury and Augusta to evacuate the state, although the commander at Fort Morris refused to comply. A few hours later, the defeated general arrived at Zubley's Ferry at the same place he entered Georgia a month earlier. There, he penned a quick note to Lincoln about his defeat. The army had suffered "considerable loss," he said. "I do not yet know exactly what numbers are lost, but this I shall have an opportunity of ascertaining [soon]." Most of his force would still be intact, he noted, "had not a part of the troops been attempting to cross the swamp [Musgrove's Creek], which though usually passable was…high…at that time and therefore those who could not swim were liable to be made prisoners." It was Elbert, explained Howe, who "put himself at the head of those troops who left the line" and went through the town to the swamp. The general hoped the bulk of them evaded capture. "They know the country so well," he told Lincoln, and this gave him "hopes that many of them will escape." In spite of everything, he had nothing but praises of "high merit" for Elbert and his men due to "their conduct thro the whole day."[51]

Howe remained at Zubley's Ferry for a few days, waiting on the remnants of his army to arrive. Not all of the soldiers linked up with Howe. Some went to Two Sisters Ferry, about ten miles above Zubley's and crossed the river there into South Carolina. George Gresham, a member

---

to Benjamin Lincoln, December 30, 1778, Robert Howe Letters, MS 400, Georgia Historical Society; Isaac Huger, "A Return of the Officers and Men Missing after the Action of the 29th December, 1778," in the Preston Davie Collection, #3406, Southern Historical Collection, Wilson Library, University of North Carolina at Chapel Hill.

[50] John Houstoun to Benjamin Lincoln, December 29, 1778, Benjamin Lincoln Papers, Rubenstein Rare Book and Manuscript Library.

[51] Robert Howe to Benjamin Lincoln, December 30, 1778, Robert Howe Letters, MS 400, Georgia Historical Society; *CNYHS*, Robert Howe testimony, January 21, 1782, 298.

of the Georgia line, said that many men "formed an encampment near Sisters ferry," where they remained throughout February. More than likely, Elbert arrived at Zubley's not long after Howe and began to ascertain what was left of his battalions, which was not much. The lack of papers and records forced him to perform his assessment from memory.[52]

On December 31, Lincoln arrived with his reinforcements at Pocotaligo in South Carolina, only a few miles from Purrysburg near Zubley's. Once there, he informed Laurens about Savannah's fall. At that point, details about the disaster were sketchy. He did not know, for example, the name of the British commander who took the city. Nor was he sure about the total number of troops Howe commanded when the British attacked. He knew that Howe lost several field pieces and "considering his weak state," had retreated to the north side of the Savannah River. Neither Howe nor Houstoun, Lincoln's chief sources of information, said anything about the number of prisoners taken, but at that time, they themselves did not know. Although the situation in Georgia was "distressed," Lincoln assured Laurens that not all was lost. "Though they are in possession of a town," he defiantly proclaimed, "they have not conquered a state."[53]

On January 3, Lincoln finally arrived at Purrysburg. Howe crossed the river and joined him in the evening. Their long-awaited meeting was probably a relief for the unfortunate general. Unceremoniously, he surrendered his position to Lincoln as the new commander of the Southern Department. Howe then reiterated his version of events at Savannah, but many unanswered questions remained, such as the fate of more than half of the Continental Army. He gathered some remnants at Zubley's, he told Lincoln, and there were others with Huger, recently arrived at the Two Sisters. Lincoln then dispatched an order for Huger to bring everyone with him to Purrysburg on the following day. After debriefing Lincoln, Howe headed to Charleston, forever leaving Georgia behind. He lingered in Charleston for two months before finally heading north to give Congress his account of the battle

---

[52] Revolutionary War Pension and Bounty-Land Warrant Applications, Pension Application of George Gresham, W2933, October 20, 1832. The last entry in Elbert's meticulously maintained Order Book was November 7, 1778. The reasonable assumption was that whatever records he had after that date were lost at Musgrove's Creek.

[53] Benjamin Lincoln to Henry Laurens, December 31, 1778, Benjamin Lincoln Papers, 1778, MS495, Georgia Historical Society.

and then join Washington's army.[54]

The loss of Savannah demanded a scapegoat, and, almost immediately, Howe became that person. His critics were relentless. Had he abandoned the city and waited on reinforcements, Moultrie believed the outcome would have been different. With militia converging on Savannah from Augusta, Ninety-Six, and many other parts of Carolina and Georgia, they could have united with Howe and formed an army of four or five thousand men. While Moultrie's claims were likely exaggerated, he still thought, "we could have marched down to Savannah, before the British could have had time to fortify, and before they were reinforced by the troops under Gen. Provost [Prevost] from Florida." Jackson blamed Howe for the disaster that overtook Elbert's men. "Indeed the manner in which the Georgia line was destroyed," he later commented, was due to "the disgraceful conduct of Genl. Howe." Like Moultrie, the Georgia Assembly was "greatly disappointed" at Howe for not trying to link up with Lincoln's reinforcements. The result was that Savannah was lost and the inhabitants around the city were "embarrassed." The backcountry suffered, too, since it was now "entirely open to the ravages of the enemy."[55]

Howe's most bitter enemy to arise out of the defeat was Walton, for whom the dispute was personal. After warning Howe several times about the unguarded pass through the swamp at Fair-Lawn, he continued to believe that Howe did not take adequate measures to secure the flank. From Walton's perspective, his subsequent wounding, capture, and imprisonment all stemmed from Howe's negligence. Walton's anger never abated, and, in January 1780, he led the state in an effort to get the general court-martialed for his lackluster performance at Savannah. Walton also charged that Howe's order to evacuate Continental troops in Augusta and Sunbury left the state defenseless in the face of the enemy. The trial began on December 6, 1781, and lasted for two months. During it, Walton was the state's star witness, but despite his efforts, the court, on January 21, 1782, acquitted Howe of all charges

---

[54] Moultrie, "General Howe's Order of Battle at Savannah," in *MMAR*, 1:254, and, in the same source, "General Orders by Gen. Lincoln, at Headquarters, at Purisburgh [sic]," 256; Bennett and Lennon, *Quest for Glory*, 100–101.

[55] Moultrie, "General Orders by Gen. Lincoln, at Headquarters, at Purisburgh [sic]," January 3, 1779, in *MMAR*, 1:256–57; Hawes, ed., "Papers of James Jackson," 26; "Minutes of the Executive Council," August 18, 1779, *RRG*, 2:162–63.

with the "highest honor."⁵⁶

Chided by many of his contemporaries, Howe has also been criticized by historians, particularly those who wrote in the nineteenth century. McCall called him a man of "moderate talents" with "questionable" military abilities who lacked "circumspection." McCall claimed without evidence that Howe's officers and soldiers lost confidence in him even before Savannah. Following the advice of his officers during the council of war on Fair-Lawn was his greatest failure, said McCall. Many of those officers, like Elbert, had personal interests and emotional attachments to the city that clouded their ability to make sound military judgments. Howe should have overruled their opinions and evacuated, saving both his army and his stores. C. C. Jones Jr. labeled many of the general's decisions as "fatal." Howe's refusal to follow Elbert's advice and make a stand on Brewton's Hill was a decision of "surprising stupidity" and a "fatal blunder," he wrote. One could only "marvel at the lack of observation and generalship which permitted such an opportunity to pass" since it was "the key to Savannah." His neglect to guard the pass Walton so emphatically warned about was another "fatal error," according to Jones.⁵⁷

To be sure, there was plenty of blame to go around. Houstoun's ongoing disagreement with Howe about civil versus military authority in relation to the militia contributed to the confusion that preceded Savannah's fall. That argument, as Walton explained during Howe's trial, caused many not to come and defend the city. Not until the last possible moment, in an act of desperation, did Houstoun finally relinquish control of his cherished militia. Houstoun regularly refused to cooperate with Howe, but so did the General Assembly. Howe made many requests to the governor, for example, to get Smith's picket entrenchment tools on Brewton's Hill, but they were all in vain. The governor and assembly ignored nearly all of Howe's recommendations concerning Savannah's defense. "From start to finish," observed Kenneth Coleman, "the defense of Savannah was handled poorly." Clashing personalities did not help, either. The chief players in Savannah's ill-fated drama, most notably Howe, Houstoun, and Walton, all despised each other, and their quarrels were an impediment to cooperation.⁵⁸

---

⁵⁶ *CNYHS*, Major General Baron von Steuben ruling, January 21, 1782, 310.

⁵⁷ McCall, *History of Georgia*, 2:180–81; C. C. Jones Jr., *History of Georgia*, 2:318–19.

⁵⁸ *CNYHS*, Robert Howe testimony, January 21, 1782, 292; K. Coleman, *American Revolution in Georgia*, 120.

Savannah was the first and only battle ever fought by Howe, and it permanently stained his reputation.[59] Regrettably for him, Savannah's fate was the same, no matter what he chose to do. Defending the city, and then losing it, inflamed his critics. However, had he evacuated Savannah and attempted to unite with Lincoln's reinforcements, the city would have fallen anyway. Again, his enemies would have ruthlessly pounced on him. If, following Elbert's advice, he had fortified Brewton's Hill, the outcome would have been the same. Since the American army was severely outnumbered, a determined defense there would have stalled but not stopped Campbell. As for Walton's pass, Howe did try to find it on several occasions, but the swamp was dense and impenetrable, and none of his scouts or horse patrols could locate it. The only avenue open to Howe was to defy all odds and defeat the British at Savannah's doorstep. That outcome was never possible.

One person who had ample cause to criticize Howe, but did not, was Elbert. When the general rejected his suggestion to defend Brewton's Hill, the colonel went along with his decision. When entrenchment tools did not reach Smith's picket there, Elbert did not criticize his superior. Nor did he blame Howe for the near annihilation of the Georgia battalions as they tried to escape the city. As was the case with Lachlan McIntosh earlier, Elbert respected his military superiors. While it diminished Howe's, the fall of Savannah enlarged Elbert's reputation. In a short piece written about Elbert in 1868, the author had nothing but praise for his performance at Savannah. While Howe was "outgeneraled" on that fateful day, Elbert, in contrast, shined as the "one bright point," especially as he led his battalions in a "brave but ineffectual stand against the victorious British regulars, and retreated fighting them." Elbert's calmness and courage in the face of disaster was even more remarkable since it was the first time he had faced a professional British army in a battlefield situation. Perhaps the biggest accolade Elbert received in the wake of Savannah's fall was his promotion to brigadier general over the militia early in January 1779, just weeks after the event.[60] That, more than anything, spoke loudly about the General Assembly's opinion of his conduct on December 29, 1778.

---

[59] Naisawald, "Major General Robert Howe's Activities," 29.

[60] J. Johnson, "Biographical Sketch of General Elbert," 35; C. Campbell, ed., *Journal of an Expedition*, 108n45.

Chapter 11

"Nothing Less Than a Total Rout": The Fall of Augusta and the Battle of Brier Creek

After the loss of Savannah, Georgia's patriots entered their darkest period during the Revolution. With few exceptions, those bleak days continued with little interruption for nearly three long years. One indication of the uncertain times was that many citizens loyal to the state fled into the Carolinas for refuge during the early months of 1779. That group certainly included Samuel Elbert's wife, Elizabeth, and their children, who probably crossed the Savannah River into South Carolina from Augusta.

Writing from Ebenezer a few miles north of Savannah on January 9, Archibald Campbell, the commander of all British forces in Georgia and the new governor for a restored royal colony, noted that the city he just conquered was almost devoid of women. In their haste to leave, he observed, they "abandoned their houses" and many of their possessions. He attributed their absence to the "wild conceptions" they formed about British officers, and, because of these "intolerable delusions," they suffered widespread damage to their property. In his opinion, the only ones who believed they had something to fear were rebel spouses. "When houses are abandoned," he opined, "it is natural to form unfavorable conclusions with respect to the principles of their owners." Abandoned homes with valuables left in them attracted "the Bandetty [*sic*]…who…do ten thousand times more mischief than the whole army put together." He hoped that in a few days, those women would return "and if they can possibly point out and make good their property either among the Publick Stores or [in] possession of any person of Savannah or the environs, it will afford me much pleasure in ordering them to be immediately restored to their proper owners."[1]

---

[1] Archibald Campbell to ?, January 9, 1779, MS1581, Archibald Campbell Papers, Georgia Historical Society.

Despite Campbell's professed concerns, citizens suffered privations at the hands of their conquerors. "To the families of those who maintained their devotion to the American cause...no mercy was shown," explained one historian. They were "stripped of property, their homes rendered desolate, often left without food and clothing, [and] were thrown upon the charity of an impoverished community." Governor John Houstoun knew the conditions of Savannah's conquered inhabitants and informed Congress about them on January 2. Although Campbell disavowed the actions of his troops, Houstoun heard from those who left town that "the spirit of Rapine Insolence and Brutality indulged in the soldiery exceeds description." General William Moultrie, on his way to Purrysburg to join General Benjamin Lincoln and his army, saw Georgia's wretched refugees pouring through South Carolina and felt compassion for them. "I have had before my eyes; the poor women and children, and negroes of Georgia, many thousands of whom I saw on my journey to this place...travelling to they knew not where," he wrote. To him and his men, it was a pitiful scene that "moved the hearts of soldiers."[2]

Georgia's citizens were not the only ones fleeing. The General Assembly in Savannah scattered when the British stormed the city. Houstoun, whose term expired due to limits set by the Constitution of 1777, joined the refugees in South Carolina. The executive council also abruptly dissolved, noting in its hurried minutes that all "public business of a civil nature" was finished. Those who could escaped to Augusta to reconvene the government. Once there, representatives from three of Georgia's upper counties not yet overrun by the British (Richmond, Burke, and Wilkes) were the only elected members of the assembly to appear. Unable to form a quorum and make their body constitutionally legitimate with representation from all the counties, they changed the General Assembly's name to "Convention," and on January 8, created a committee that called itself an executive council to continue state government.[3]

"There are no minutes of this convention and little is known of its actions," observed Kenneth Coleman. While they did not elect a governor to replace Houstoun, one thing they did before dissolving when the British

---

[2] McCall, *History of Georgia*, 2:185; William Moultrie to Col. C. C. Pinckney, January 10, 1779, *MMAR*, 2:259. For Houstoun's observation, see C. Campbell, ed., *Journal of an Expedition*, 110n64.

[3] Houstoun's escape is mentioned in "Memoir of William Few, Jr.," 19, William Few Collection, ac. 1955-0101M, Georgia Archives. See also Hall, *Land and Allegiance*, 75; K. Coleman, *American Revolution in Georgia*, 155.

captured Augusta on January 31 was to promote Elbert to the rank of brigadier general over the state's militia. Thus, Elbert's promotion, by an ad-hoc convention, took place between January 8 and January 31, 1779. The promotion came with a high salary. On February 3, 1780, one year later, the state sent Elbert a notice that it owed him $6,600 to cover his service for the past eleven months, which put the new general's salary at $600 per month. That commitment was a heavy burden for a financially distraught state whose government soon vanished into exile.[4]

There were hardly any Continental troops left in the state, either. The lone exception were 220 Continentals and militia at Fort Morris in Sunbury, now commanded by Major Joseph Lane. On December 29, as Howe tried to regroup his army at Cherokee Hill outside of Savannah, he ordered the evacuation of all Continental forces in Augusta and Sunbury. In an unwise decision, Lane refused to comply. By early January, General Augustine Prevost's British forces from East Florida, consisting of a detachment from the 16th Regiment, most of the 60th Regiment, and some Royal Artillery, were approaching Sunbury by land and sea. Loyalist units, the South Carolina Royalists, the East Florida Volunteers, and Thomas Brown's King's Rangers, accompanied them, bringing Prevost's strength to almost two thousand men. At the end of the first week in January, the British were already on the outskirts of Sunbury. On January 7, Lieutenant Colonel Mark Prevost, the general's younger brother by sixteen years, began a siege of the town with nine hundred men, but taking the fort was his chief objective. After a three-day siege, complete with a relentless pounding of the garrison by British artillery, Lane capitulated on January 10. News of the fort's surrender arrived at Purrysburg shortly thereafter. Moultrie was angered—but not because the fort was taken. The loss of men was irreplaceable, and that responsibility fell squarely on Lane's shoulders because he did not follow orders. "He, Don Quixote-like, thought he was strong enough to withstand the whole force the British had in Georgia," quipped the South Carolinian, and, for that, "I think he deserved to be hanged."[5]

---

[4] Samuel Elbert Receipt for Brigadier General's Subsistence, February 3, 1780, in the Preston Davie Collection, #3406, Southern Historical Collection, Wilson Library, University of North Carolina at Chapel Hill; K. Coleman, *American Revolution in Georgia*, 155–56. Georgia would not have a governor until August 6, 1779, when an illegal and unconstitutional Supreme Executive Council consisting of nine men unanimously elected John Wereat. See Cook, *Governors of Georgia*, 29.

[5] Searcy, *Georgia-Florida Contest*, 166–67; C. C. Jones Jr., *History of Georgia*, 2:332–

What remained of Georgia's battalions were scattered, but some were still with Elbert. Even so, there was little left of the state's once proud Continental Line. Muster rolls during summer 1779 showed only 158 soldiers left in the 1st, 3rd, and 4th battalions combined, but just 42 men were fit for duty. Elbert's 2nd Battalion was not even listed on the rolls. Georgia's militia dwindled, too. Before the fall of Savannah, Elbert predicted there were 3,000 in the state. In 1779, he was a brigadier general of no more than 750.[6]

The little army Lincoln collected at Purrysburg consisted of various Continental brigades, including remnants from Huger's battalions. Others arrived from the Carolinas. Militia units, some rather large, were either nearby or heading toward Lincoln's headquarters. Among them were 1,200 South Carolinians command by General Andrew Williamson around Augusta and 700 North Carolina militia led by General Griffith Rutherford. Political General John Ashe and 1,100 North Carolina militia and nearly 250 Continentals filtered into Lincoln's camp during January. Collectively, they gave him, at least on paper, some 3,600 troops, although most were untrained militia.[7] Still, the numbers bolstered Lincoln's prospects of successfully confronting the British on a near-equal footing when the opportunity arose.

The militia assembling at Purrysburg was difficult to control, and many of their officers suffered from deficits in character. Ashe's militia created trouble from the day of their arrival. Making matters worse, the enlistment terms for most were up on April 10, and they insisted on returning home. Not willing to tarry one day beyond their enlistment, they demanded to leave no later than March 10 so they could be back in North Carolina when their terms expired. Many junior officers in North Carolina's Halifax Regiment tendered their resignations during the march to Purrysburg, even as their own men mutinied. Philip Alston, the commander of the Wilmington Regiment from the same state, was a known swindler, unfit for the company of gentlemen. Finally, Lincoln lost patience and protested to South Carolina's governor, John Rutledge, and Washington about their insubordinate behavior. "I have no hold of them," he wrote Washington, "they leave the Camp

---

33; Cashin, *King's Ranger*, 84; *MMAR*, 1:259.

[6] Knight, *Georgia's Roster of the Revolution*, 7; Jackson, *Lachlan McIntosh*, 94.

[7] William Moultrie to Col. Charles C. Pinckney, January 26, 1779, *MMAR*, 1:269–70; McCall, *History of Georgia*, 2:206; Carrington, *Battles of the American Revolution*, 464.

and even their posts when they please with impunity."[8] Neither Rutledge nor Washington, who was hundreds of miles away from South Carolina with his northern army, could remedy the problem. Lincoln was on his own.

As Lincoln consolidated his army, Campbell prepared for a quick strike up the Savannah River to take Augusta and mobilize thousands of Loyalists expected to flock to the royal standard. However, logistical problems complicated his hopes for an early march. His intention was to pursue Howe's fleeing army on the day he took Savannah, but a lack of supply wagons and horses to drag along the artillery made that plan impossible. Another matter of great concern was the absence of maps containing information about an unfamiliar territory. Finally, the army could not venture into the dangerous backcountry without a secure base of operations in Savannah. That task was Campbell's first priority.[9]

Ebenezer became Campbell's initial defensive outpost. He first arrived there with part of his army on January 2. On the following day, he nailed a proclamation to the church door and on trees at every crossroad between Savannah and Ebenezer; it offered protection and the blessings of peace to His Majesty's loyal inhabitants. That same proclamation contained grim omens for Georgia's "deluded Subjects" who were in rebellion. "We lament the Necessity of exhibiting the Rigours of War," it read, "and call God and the World to witness, that they only shall be answerable for all the Miseries which may ensue." The proclamation was accompanied by loyalty oaths, and those who took them had to "disclaim and renounce that unlawful and iniquitous Confederacy called the General Continental Congress" and the "Claims set up by them to Independency." Protection of persons and property rested on future loyalty to the Crown since those who swore the oath pledged to "stand forth" and support King George III and his government "at all risks." At the same time, the proclamation pardoned all past sins of disloyalty, but taking the oath was the only gateway to forgiveness.[10]

On January 4, Campbell proceeded to Treutlen's plantation, across

---

[8] Heidler, "American Defeat at Briar Creek," 319–20; Howard, "Things Here Wear a Melancholy Appearance," 482; "To George Washington from Major General Benjamin Lincoln, 7 February 1779," Founders Online. Moultrie said that the North Carolina troops were "undisciplined" (William Moultrie to Col. Charles C. Pinckney, January 26, 1779, *MMAR*, 1:270).

[9] C. Campbell, ed., *Journal of an Expedition*, December 31, 1778, 31.

[10] Ibid., January 2–3, 1779, 34–36.

from the Two Sisters Ferry on the Savannah. British occupation of the former governor's plantation was another humiliation for Georgia's revolutionaries. After fortifying Treutlen's abandoned estate, Campbell went to the ferry, seized some vessels Howe used to transport his army across the river, and then burned them. For the next several days, he secured strategic locations, placing soldiers to guard each. Augustine Prevost arrived in Savannah on January 15 with part of his army from Sunbury and, because of his superiority in rank, assumed the governorship and command of all British forces in Georgia. By then, many Loyalists from Augusta were in Savannah offering Campbell their assistance. Their help bolstered Campbell's hope of Loyalist support once his army headed north. By January 20, the commander had all of the major outposts (Cherokee Hill, Ebenezer, Abercorn, Zubley's Ferry, Two Sisters Ferry, Treutlen's Plantation, and Fort Morris), secured and fortified.[11]

Finally, Campbell was ready to move. For that task, he picked 1,044 soldiers from his command, leaving the rest in Savannah and at the outposts. Campbell's detachment represented nearly one-fourth of the 4,330 troops in Georgia. Among those selected were 365 men from the 1st Battalion of the 71st Regiment, 299 from Sir James Baird's light infantry, 175 of the New York Volunteers, one troop of Georgia Light Dragoons consisting of 42 men, 75 Carolina Loyalists, 72 of Brown's King's Rangers, and 25 soldiers from the Royal Artillery. The field artillery included two six-pounders, two three-pounders (also known as "grasshoppers"), and one 5.5-inch howitzer. At daybreak on January 24, Campbell left Ebenezer and began his trek northward along the River Road with the rangers and the Carolina Loyalists in the vanguard.[12]

To mask the movement from Lincoln, Prevost created a diversion and sent two companies from the 60th Regiment and one from the 16th Regiment to threaten Port Royal and Beaufort on the South Carolina coast just south of Charleston. Lincoln responded by sending Moultrie with some Continentals, militia, and a fieldpiece to blunt the attack. Both armies clashed near Beaufort on February 4, and, after an hour-

---

[11] Ibid., January 4, 1779, 37, January 9, 1779, 39, January 15, 1779, 40, and January 20, 1779, 41–42.

[12] Ibid., Archibald Campbell to Augustine Prevost and Hyde Parker, January 21, 1779, 46; journal entry, January 24, 1779, 47–48; Carrington, *Battles of the American Revolution*, 467.

long fight, the British were severely repulsed. Although Moultrie defeated his opponent, the diversionary movement deprived Lincoln of extra troops at the time Campbell took Augusta.[13]

Also helping Campbell subdue upper Georgia was Colonel James Boyd, a North Carolina Loyalist with the British army in New York who received a commission and orders from Sir Henry Clinton to participate in the invasion. Once Savannah fell, he was to go into the Carolina backcountry and rally Loyalists to aid Campbell's army. After the capture of Savannah, Boyd snuck into Anson County, North Carolina, and began to gather disaffected inhabitants. In a short time, his followers created an army of nearly eight hundred men. As they traversed the Carolina Piedmont on their way to Augusta, Boyd's Loyalists struck fear into everyone in their path. Passing through the Ninety-Six district in South Carolina, they left a trail of death and destruction marked by looted and burned homes and murdered inhabitants. Word quickly spread about Boyd's presence. Scouts and others informed Lincoln of the danger, even as South Carolina militia units in the upstate under Lieutenant Colonel Andrew Pickens mobilized to stop them. While Campbell was aware of Boyd's activities, he did not know when to expect him in Augusta. At any rate, the thought of his impending arrival cheered the British commander's heart.[14]

There was hardly any opposition north of Purrysburg to counteract Loyalist threats in the region although Moultrie over-optimistically expected a "brilliant stroke" coming from that quarter. Elbert and a small force were already at Silver Bluff in South Carolina, a landing on George Galphin's Savannah River plantation below Augusta. Directly opposite the river from Augusta at Fort Moore's bluff were Williamson's militia. In Georgia, the only thing left to oppose Campbell was the militia in the upper counties. Half of them, from Richmond and Burke counties and commanded by the brothers William and Benjamin Few, were patrolling below Augusta. Around fifty or sixty more from Wilkes County led by John Twiggs soon joined them. In Wilkes County, Colonel John Dooly and Colonel Elijah Clarke were rallying their own units for Augusta's

---

[13] C. Campbell, ed., *Journal of an Expedition*, January 21, 1779, 45; Carrington, *Battles of the American Revolution*, 464. For Moultrie's account of the skirmish, see William Moultrie to Benjamin Lincoln, February 4, 1779, in *MMAR*, 1:291–95, and, in the same source, "Orders by Gen. Moultrie," February 4, 1779, 296–97, and William Moultrie to Charles Pinckney, February 1, 1779, 290.

[14] D. Wilson, *Southern Strategy*, 86–87; Elliot, "Stirring Up a Hornet's Nest," 67–68; C. Campbell, ed., *Journal of an Expedition*, January 10, 1779, 39.

defense. As always, it was impossible to know exactly how many militia were available, but William Few estimated that their numbers did not exceed five hundred.[15]

On January 25, Campbell reached Hudson's Ferry on the Savannah north of Ebenezer, where he posted a guard. The rest of the army marched fourteen more miles on the following day and finally arrived at Brier Creek, a slow black-water tributary of the Savannah thirty-six miles from Augusta. At Brier Creek, near its junction with the Savannah, Miller's long bridge (also called the Freeman-Miller Bridge) spanned the waterway along the major road leading to Augusta. Campbell observed that the creek there was about one hundred feet wide and eight or ten feet deep. He instantly recognized it as a key strategic feature since it controlled the only road through the area. Without the bridge, the creek's depth and width impeded all other means of crossing except for swimming. As Campbell pondered his surroundings, an express from Prevost in Savannah arrived ordering him to send Brown's rangers to the Burke County jail and free a number of Loyalists held captive there by rebels. Following his instructions, Campbell dispatched Brown to the jail and then departed Brier Creek, leaving behind a small detachment to guard the bridge.[16]

Reinforced with some Loyalists from South Carolina under Daniel McGirth, Brown arrived with several hundred men at the Burke County jail later that day and immediately engaged Patriot militia commanded by the Few brothers and Twiggs. Anticipating a confrontation with the British, the Patriots had turned the small town into a fortress, occupying the courthouse and most of the buildings as defensive works, including a log home that served as their fort. Though Brown outnumbered the Patriots, he could not break through their lines, and the Loyalists were initially repulsed. Near dark, additional reinforcements arrived, giving Brown confidence to renew his attack. This one, like the earlier attempt, failed. It also left Brown with a shattered arm caused by a musket ball. Compelled to retire, the Loyalist commander pulled his men back and returned to the main British army. The Americans also withdrew toward McBean's

---

[15] C. Campbell, ed., *Journal of an Expedition*, 115n95; Charles Pinckney to William Moultrie, January 25, 1779, in *MMAR*, 1:281, and, in the same source, William Moultrie to John Dart, January 20, 1779, 277; "Memoir of William Few, Jr.," 19–20, Georgia Archives; K. Coleman, *American Revolution in Georgia*, 122.

[16] C. Campbell, ed., *Journal of an Expedition*, January 25–27, 1779, 48–49. "Briar" appears to be the most consistent spelling in eighteenth-century sources although "Brier" is also correct.

Creek, several miles away to the north. The fighting at the Burke County courthouse was severe. William Few recalled that it was the first time he ever heard the whistling of bullets in a battle. "I found that those terrific messengers of death [lost] all their terror in a few minutes after the action began," he later wrote. "The exertion of the faculties—the action of the mind and ardent desire to destroy the enemy soon extinguished every sensation of fear."[17]

As Patriot and Loyalist militia engaged each other in Burke County, Elbert crossed the Savannah and briefly skirmished the British rear guard at Brier Creek. He then, through secondary roads, bypassed Campbell's army and linked his small band with those at McBean's Creek. There they entertained confident hopes that Williamson, Clarke, and Dooly would soon appear with reinforcements. They never did.[18]

Desperately in need of intelligence, Elbert got a lieutenant named Hawkins to pose as a Loyalist commander and sent him off to scout the area for the enemy. Elbert provided him with an old British uniform coat before he left. It was an extremely risky mission. If captured, the lieutenant would have suffered execution as a spy for passing himself off as a British officer. After traveling a short way, Hawkins fell in with three Loyalists heading toward the British lines and demanded to know their identity. They replied that they were on the way to join Daniel McGirth's army. Hawkins then told them that he was McGirth and accused them of being rebel spies worthy of death. All three Loyalists begged for mercy and swore they were fighting for the king. Hawkins still acted unconvinced. If what they said was true, he told them, they should hold up their hands in the manner of the Presbyterians and swear upon it. The three men, still believing they were talking to McGirth, put down their weapons and raised their hands to take the oath. At this point, Hawkins pulled out two pistols concealed underneath his officer's coat, cocked them, and marched his three prisoners to Elbert's camp.[19]

---

[17] C. C. Jones Jr., *History of Georgia*, 2:335; Cashin, *King's Ranger*, 87–88; Davis, "Civil War in the Midst of Revolution," 141; "Memoir of William Few, Jr.," 21, Georgia Archives.

[18] Cashin and Robertson, Augusta & the American Revolution, 26; McCall, History of Georgia, 2:191.

[19] Joseph Vallence Bevan Papers, MS 0071, Collection #71, box 1, folder 4, "History of Georgia, Revolutionary War," n.d., n.p., Georgia Historical Society.

Campbell had his spies too, and they informed him that Elbert's army at McBean's Creek numbered nearly nine hundred men. Those overblown estimates were well off the mark since Elbert's forces were under half that number. Campbell's false intelligence caused him to be extremely cautious as he passed through the densely wooded country south of Augusta. Having learned the rebels' location on the north side of the swamp, he determined to finish their resistance. During the night of January 29, he sent Baird's light infantry and Colonel John Maitland's 71st Regiment on a seventeen-mile circuitous route leading behind Elbert's position. Around four o'clock on the following morning, they reached their destination and waited until daylight to spring their attack. Elbert and the others knew about the movement because during the night, they captured two deserters from the King's Rangers who told them of Campbell's trap. Just when Baird and Maitland were ready to engage the enemy, the first rays of dawn revealed the whole rebel militia retreating quietly northward through the swamp. The British had little time to adjust to this new development, and Elbert's men got away. "It was more than probable that General Elbert's Party must have fallen into our hands," wrote a disappointed Campbell. Their retreat was so abrupt that "their pots with Beef and Pork were left standing on Fires just lighted up, and the water scarcely heated." In their haste to leave, they also abandoned blankets, weapons, and a large quantity of provisions, all of which the British confiscated.[20]

Pushing forward during the day, Campbell again encountered Elbert's "Party" at Spirit Creek, about ten miles above McBean's Swamp. There, observed Campbell, two hundred of their men occupied Fort Henderson, a wooden stockade on the opposite side of the creek. "I found a Piece of Ground on our Side of the Ravine," remembered Campbell, "which had a complete Command over the Fort at the Distance of 300 Yards. To this Rising the Howitzer and Two Six Pounders were brought up to play upon the Enemy, which in less than Ten Minutes made them abandon the Fort in a very precipitate manner." As the Patriot militia fled toward Augusta, a company of the 71st Regiment took possession of the fort.[21]

Elbert tried one last time to dispute Campbell's entrance into Augusta. He set up an ambush along the road at Cupboard Swamp about ten miles below the city, but scouts warned Campbell about it before the army

---

[20] C. Campbell, ed., *Journal of an Expedition*, January 28–30, 1779, 49–52.
[21] Ibid., January 30, 1779, 53.

passed through. Elbert apparently had second thoughts because he abandoned Cupboard Swamp before the British arrived, fled into Augusta, and from there crossed the Savannah where he joined Williamson's militia in South Carolina. William Few may have crossed the river before Elbert. In his memoirs, he claimed that he went to South Carolina and joined Williamson. If Elbert, who commanded all the militia in the state, had been there, Few surely would have mentioned his name.[22]

Campbell finally entered Augusta on the evening of January 31. Elbert's retreat at Cupboard Swamp ended Augusta's last hope, but the city was doomed regardless of his decision. Writing about Augusta's fall during the late nineteenth century, historian Charles C. Jones remarked that the "American forces retreated across the river and yielded Augusta without a struggle."[23] That harsh criticism did not consider Patriot efforts to dispute the British advance from Brier Creek all the way to the outskirts of the city. The repeated references by Campbell in his journal to Elbert (there were only two for "Feiu") showed that he believed his chief antagonist was the newly promoted commander. Despite their inferior numbers, Elbert and those with him made a noble effort to protect Augusta with their limited abilities. Just like Savannah's experience a month earlier, however, the odds they faced were insurmountable.

The loss of Augusta was a severe setback for Lincoln. "Genl Elbert who collected a small force of 300 in the upper part of Georgia is driven out…by Colo. Campbell who marched up to Augusta with about 1700 men," he informed Washington on February 7. He fully understood the cause behind Augusta's demise, which was the "want of a sufficient force" to check and harass the enemy. While Lincoln approved of Elbert's decision to evacuate Georgia, he also worried that Campbell, bolstered by thousands of Loyalists, would follow him into South Carolina. If that happened, he warned, "it is easy to see that many ill consequences will result…our supplies will be affected, the Indians uncontrouled [sic], and the Tories have an opportunity to triumph over & distress the good inhabitants of these States."[24]

Lincoln was correct to be concerned about a Loyalist uprising, and the problem went well beyond Boyd's roving army. Augusta exhibited in microcosm the guttural hatred existing in Georgia between Loyalists and

---

[22] Ibid., January 31, 1779, 54; "Memoir of William Few, Jr.," 21–22, Georgia Archives.
[23] C. C. Jones Jr., *History of Georgia*, 2:335–36.
[24] "To George Washington from Major General Benjamin Lincoln, 7 February 1779," Founders Online; Piecuch, *Three Peoples, One King*, 137.

Patriots. Those divisions were apparent from the moment Campbell stepped into the city and began administering loyalty oaths. Hundreds who kept a low profile when the Whigs were ascendant now came out of hiding, publicly denounced the rebels, and professed allegiance to the king. By February 10, Campbell's rolls contained the names of 1,100 inhabitants, which he formed into companies and placed into districts to collect intelligence and keep watch. While the British presence dampened the activity of Patriot sympathizers, it did not extinguish their zeal, and community divisions between the supporters of the king and devotees to the state often led to violence. That fear caused a captured rebel major to ask Campbell to give his wife and daughter protection in their home from vengeful Loyalists. Campbell, wanting to safeguard innocent citizens, placed a soldier from Baird's light infantry named MacAlister as a sentry to protect the major's family. According to Campbell, a small party of "Marauders" from Williamson's camp crossed the river, came to the major's house in the night, and killed MacAlister with a firearm. His death alone, however, was not good enough, so they hacked up his body with a hatchet and then escaped into the darkness. When Campbell learned of the murder, he called it a "shameful Act of Injustice" and "disgraceful in the extreme." The men in the light infantry were not happy, either. They vowed to avenge the gruesome killing at the first opportunity, which they would soon get.[25]

On February 3, Campbell received word that settlers in Wilkes County sought military protection from the Indians. Their request did not surprise him. On the eve of his Georgia campaign, the British commander requested Indian superintendent John Stuart to send the Indians on raids into the western settlements to create a diversion as he took Savannah and Augusta. While a few Indians answered the call, their numbers were well below what was expected. Although Campbell did not know it, by the time his letter arrived at Stuart's headquarters in Pensacola, there was no time left to coordinate help from England's Indian allies. Believing he could control the Indians, Campbell prepared an address to the inhabitants of Wilkes County offering protection to those who accepted the "benevolent Offers of the King" for pardons through loyalty oaths. His message for the "designing Men" who in their "Folly and Madness" waged war against His Majesty's army exhibited the same consistent theme of defeat and

---

[25] "To George Washington from Major General Benjamin Lincoln, 7 February 1779," Founders Online; C. Campbell, ed., *Journal of an Expedition*, February 3 and 10, 1779, 57–58, 60.

destruction broadcast all the way from Savannah to Augusta. Loyalist Captain John Hamilton from North Carolina, commanding around three hundred mounted troops, delivered the message to Wilkes County. While there, he administered oaths, demanded the prompt surrender of all frontier forts, and waited for Boyd's Loyalists to arrive. Enough of the frontier inhabitants cooperated with Hamilton to give the appearance that even Wilkes County was now under British control and the state was completely lost.[26]

Back in Purrysburg, Lincoln tried to decipher Campbell's next move, which he believed was to strike into South Carolina from Augusta. To prevent this, he developed a two-pronged strategy, unleashing Williamson and Elbert, reinforced with Ashe's militia, on Augusta while Moultrie's Continentals forded the river below the city. That would place Campbell between two pincers. The desired effect was to draw the British out of Augusta and make them fight their way back to Savannah between two American armies. Lincoln canceled the plan when Prevost's diversionary movement caused him to send Moultrie to Beaufort. His second option was to concentrate his army at Moore's Bluff to "check the plans of the enemy," but it entailed some risks. By strengthening the army at Augusta, Lincoln weakened the one in Purrysburg and made lower South Carolina vulnerable to another invasion from Savannah. Still, the general viewed Campbell as the major threat. According to Ashe, if the British moved out of Augusta into Carolina's frontiers, the disaffected and lukewarm inhabitants would be like a "snowball," growing in size to such large proportions that nothing could stop them from taking Charleston. That was also Lincoln's fear. On February 8, he informed Moultrie that the bulk of the army should link up with Williamson and Elbert. He proposed leaving behind the North Carolina Continentals and some militia (around one thousand men) to guard the Two Sisters and Purrysburg. Already, he believed there were around two thousand militia at Augusta and the addition of Ashe would make three thousand. Once united, the whole force could cross the river and reclaim the state. Moultrie wrote Lincoln back the same day agreeing with the general's proposal.[27]

Even though Elbert's state was lost, he had not given up. Believing

---

[26] C. Campbell, ed., *Journal of an Expedition*, February 3, 1779, 58; K. Coleman, *American Revolution in Georgia*, 123; D. Wilson, *Southern Strategy*, 87.

[27] Mattern, *Benjamin Lincoln*, 65–66; Benjamin Lincoln to William Moultrie, February 8, 1779, in *MMAR*, 1:301, and, in the same source, William Moultrie to Benjamin Lincoln, February 8, 1779, 302.

that he could rouse the Whigs' sagging hopes and scrape up more recruits, he made covert and dangerous forays across the river, but his Loyalist enemies soon found out about them. One angry Augusta Loyalist, on February 6, sent a letter to the *Royal Georgia Gazette*, the newly established pro-British newspaper in Savannah, detailing the general's secret activities. "The Leaders of sedition having at last fairly worn out the spirit and patience of the populace, by their infernal system of anarchy," it began, "have now the insolence to coax them by liberal offers of pardon, through the medium of Mr. Elbert authorized by an EXTERMINATED ASSEMBLY." Georgia's citizens should have enough "sense" to recognize that the blessings of peace, freedom, and happiness were more beneficial than war, poverty, and distress offered by Elbert's faction. In other words, claimed the author, "a good King is better than a bench of tyrants."[28] If the "Exterminated Assembly" authorized Elbert to grant pardons in the name of the state, it could only mean that the remnants of Georgia's government were in exile in South Carolina with the brigadier general when he was at Moore's Bluff.

During the evening of February 9, probably fresh from a clandestine visit to Georgia, an exhausted Elbert entered Lincoln's Purrysburg camp. There he delivered somber news to the American commanders. Instead of having two thousand men at Augusta, as everyone assumed, their total force was only around eight hundred, and Williamson was in grave danger should Campbell cross the river.[29] Alarmed, Lincoln hastily sent Ashe to Williamson's support, but before he got there, Campbell, on February 14, abruptly evacuated the city and began a march back to Savannah.

Campbell's sudden departure took everyone by surprise—especially Augusta's Loyalist community. The Reverend James Seymour, parson of the city's Anglican St. Paul's Church, was stunned. "These two weeks of sunshine at last expired," he said, expressing the feelings of almost all the other abandoned friends of the king left to fend for themselves against retaliating Whigs. When he heard about it, Williamson immediately embarked his militia across the river to reoccupy the city. On February 16, he wrote Henry Laurens in the Continental Congress, informing him with the "utmost pleasure" that the enemy "precipitously left Augusta about one o'clock Sunday Morning, after having destroyed the Flats which they had

---

[28] *Royal Georgia Gazette*, February 11, 1779, 4.
[29] William Moultrie to Col. Charles C. Pinckney, February 10, 1779, in *MMAR*, 1:309.

constructed in order to cross the River." That sentence contained a glaring clue about the next scene to transpire at Augusta if the British remained. The hasty exodus in the middle of the night underscored Campbell's urgency to get out of the city unseen by both Loyalists and Whigs. So did a letter left by the British commander addressed to Williamson and discovered in a conspicuous place when the Whigs came into Augusta. In it, Campbell politely asked the militia leader to take care of his wounded soldiers, all of which he left behind. With the backcountry temporarily spared from ruin and devastation, Williamson told Laurens that he would pursue the enemy with three hundred horsemen and "hang upon their skirts" keeping them in constant alarm.[30]

Many reasons existed for Campbell's hasty withdrawal from Augusta after a short two-week occupation. On February 11, he received word that Ashe was approaching Moore's Bluff with, according to his estimates, 1,600 militia to join with Williamson, Elbert, and other units also on the way. Additionally, he had not heard a word from Boyd and did not know if he was even in Georgia. The six thousand Loyalists he expected to rally in the upstate barely reached a third of that number. Many of those were unreliable since their allegiance shifted according to which side had control. The lack of Indian allies was another disappointment. In short, Campbell found himself abandoned and exposed in an inhospitable environment with no support as a powerful enemy gathered on the other side of the river to attack him. The great distance between himself and Savannah negated any hope of reinforcements coming from Prevost. Finally, the army was running out of provisions, especially rum. All of these problems factored into Campbell's decision to abandon Augusta. He reached that conclusion on February 12 and on the following day notified Hamilton to leave Wilkes County and join the rest of the army south of the city. He also sent an express to Prevost telling him of his plans. The army was not all that left. Georgia's exiled "council" claimed that many who received Campbell's protection while in Augusta, "imagining that they would be deemed traitors, and treated as such, went down with them."[31]

As Campbell contemplated leaving Augusta, high drama unfolded in Wilkes County. Hamilton was still commandeering frontier stockades when, on February 11, he came to Fort Carr, which held several families

---

[30] H. Robertson, "Reverend James Seymour, Frontier Parson," 150; Toulmin, "Backcountry Warrior," 27.

[31] C. Campbell, ed., *Journal of an Expedition*, February 11–13, 1779, 62–64; "Minutes of the Executive Council," February 1779, *RRG*, 2:163.

seeking protection from the Indians. He did not know that nearly 250 South Carolina militia under Pickens and around 140 more commanded by Dooly were close behind. Hamilton and his men entered the fort about the same time that the American militia appeared. After a brisk skirmish, the British retreated inside the fort and refused repeated demands to release the civilians and surrender. Pickens and Dooly then placed the fort under siege, which nearly succeeded. However, during the siege, Pickens received word that Boyd's Loyalists had crossed the river and were in the area. Given the option of continuing the siege or going after Boyd, the militia commanders chose the latter. As soon as the Americans left, Hamilton and his men evacuated Fort Carr and hurried to Augusta, but when they got there, Campbell was already gone. On February 15, he finally rendezvoused with the British army below the city.[32]

On the same day of the siege at Fort Carr, Boyd crossed the Savannah at Vann's Creek, several miles above the forks of the Broad River. He encountered stiff resistance from area militia in his attempt to ford the river and suffered nearly one hundred casualties, but he still managed to get his remaining men on Georgia soil. Determined to link up with Campbell in Augusta, he pushed across the Broad, deeper into Wilkes County. Close on his trail were over four hundred militia commanded by Pickens, Dooly, and Clarke. On the night of February 13, seven hundred Loyalists camped along the banks of Kettle Creek, a tributary of the Little River. Oblivious to the American presence, Boyd's men awoke the next morning and began preparing a breakfast of roasted corn. It was then that the militia burst out of the woods and into their thinly posted picket, catching the Loyalists by surprise. Unable to stop the onslaught, the picket fell back in confusion while Pickens drove hard into Boyd's center and Clarke and Dooly hit the flanks. Boyd tried to form his men, but in the confusion, all order evaporated. The fierce contest lasted for nearly two hours, and nothing was left of Boyd's routed force when it was over. Those who could bolted through the woods and nearby swamps to get away, but they left their mortally wounded commander behind. In addition to Boyd, nearly seventy of his men died in the battle and 150 became prisoners. In contrast, the Americans recorded nine killed and twenty-three wounded. Campbell received his first accounts of the battle on February 15, so the defeat of Boyd's Loyalists was not a factor in the decision to leave Augusta. He reported on

---

[32] McCall, *History of Georgia*, 2:192–96; C. Campbell, ed., *Journal of an Expedition*, February 15, 1779, 65.

February 18 that 270 lucky survivors of the battle arrived in his camp at Odom's Ferry along Brier Creek.[33] The astounding American victory at Kettle Creek was the highlight of Georgia's revolution in 1779, even as it was the state's greatest battlefield achievement since the beginning of the conflict. Unfortunately, the momentum it generated only lasted about three weeks due to events about to unfold at Brier Creek.

On February 16, before Ashe could reach Williamson at Moore's Bluff, Lincoln ordered him across the Savannah to follow Campbell's retreating army "with all the force you can muster and as quickly as you can." Elbert probably joined the North Carolinians at this time. With him were sixty or seventy Continentals and perhaps 150 militia and dragoons he recruited, led by Leonard Marbury. Altogether, Ashe had around 1,500 soldiers pursuing Campbell. Lincoln urged Ashe to keep strong pressure on the British rear to prevent them from crossing the river at the lightly guarded fords downstream where they could outflank his army.[34]

Campbell's column crossed Brier Creek at Odom's Ferry on February 17–18. Two days later, on February 20, his units arrived at Hudson's Ferry below Brier Creek. While there, Mark Prevost, sent up from Savannah by his brother, joined him. Prevost informed Campbell that his instructions were to assume command of the troops and that Campbell was to return to Savannah. Before Campbell left, Prevost sought his advice concerning the army's present situation. Campbell knew that a large American force was only a short distance behind, and he told Prevost that they would advance to Brier Creek. At this time, Prevost

---

[33] McCall, *History of Georgia*, 2:196–203; C. Campbell, ed., *Journal of an Expedition*, February 15, 1779, 65, and February 18, 1779, 66; Ashmore and Olmstead, "Battles of Kettle Creek and Brier Creek," 93–100. Elliot provides a detailed summary of historical and archaeological information about the battle and casualty estimates ("Stirring up a Hornet's Nest," 75).

[34] Mattern, *Benjamin Lincoln*, 66; Cox, "Brigadier-General John Ashe's Defeat," 297. There is much debate as to when Ashe crossed the Savannah and arrived at Brier Creek. McCall says he got to the other side on February 28 (*History of Georgia*, 2:207); Howard says it was on February 26 ("Things Here Wear a Melancholy Appearance," 486). Heidler fixes the date as February 27 ("American Defeat at Briar Creek," 321). Davis is probably closest to the correct date, which he established as February 22 ("Civil War in the Midst of Revolution," 147). Nor is there agreement on the number of men with Ashe. Moultrie places Ashe's strength at 2,300 (*MMAR*, 1:322). Ashmore and Olmstead estimate between 1,700 to 2,300 men ("Battles of Kettle Creek and Brier Creek," 101). Heidler estimates that it was somewhat lower at around 1,500 troops, which better aligns with Ashe's strength when he first appeared at Lincoln's headquarters in Purrysburg ("American Defeat at Briar Creek," 319).

may have ordered Miller's Bridge spanning Brier Creek destroyed to protect the British rear and check Ashe's advance, but historians cannot determine who destroyed the bridge or even when it occurred. Some have suggested that American militia burned it to prevent the British from wheeling around and advancing to engage Ashe before he got to Brier Creek. Leonard Marbury, who had recently joined Elbert, was scouting the area with his dragoons on February 22 and reported that the bridge was intact.[35]

It was at Hudson's Ferry where Campbell offered Prevost a grand strategy for defeating Ashe's army. He anticipated that when the Americans arrived, they would camp in the forks of the creek near the bridge commanding the road. He then produced a map showing a backroad that went up and around the creek. They could be easily surprised, he suggested, if some of the troops went forward "to amuse them in front," below the bridge, while the bulk of the army maneuvered through the backroad up the creek to Paris Mill. Once there, the troops should cross Brier Creek and take another road southward along the upper side of the stream. According to the map, that road would place Prevost in the American rear.[36] It was a classic encirclement maneuver, already successfully employed twice by Campbell, once at Savannah and again at McBean's Creek.

Before Campbell left for Savannah, he received a troubling report on February 23 from General Prevost in Savannah. New intelligence showed that Lincoln was preparing to enter Georgia at the Two Sisters ferry with 2,000 troops. If that were true, then the British at Hudson's Ferry risked entrapment between the pincers of Ashe and Lincoln. Campbell immediately set off for the Two Sisters and arrived there on the following day in "Readiness to meet General Lincoln." The American commander, however, was not there. Instead, he was still at Purrysburg waiting to hear from Ashe. Although Prevost's intelligence was faulty, it did affect Mark Prevost's command decisions at Hudson's Ferry. From his perspective, it was better to face one wing of Lincoln's army rather than both. It was then that the lieutenant colonel seriously entertained Campbell's encirclement movement. The only thing missing was Ashe.[37]

---

[35] C. Campbell, ed., *Journal of an Expedition*, February 20, 1779, 67–68; Davis, "Civil War in the Midst of Revolution," 147–48.

[36] C. Campbell, ed., *Journal of an Expedition*, February 20, 1779, 68.

[37] Ibid., Augustine Prevost to Archibald Campbell, February 23, 1779, 68, and, in

True to Campbell's prediction, Ashe arrived at Brier Creek on February 26 and spread his North Carolinians and Elbert's Continentals out in an open field near the bridge. According to Ashe's testimony at a court of inquiry on March 14, Elbert and North Carolina general William Bryan established the boundaries of their camp, which faced up from the creek's fork. The left almost touched Brier Creek, and the right terminated about a half-mile from an expansive swamp along the Savannah. They placed a picket about a mile in front of the main body to give an advanced warning of any approaching threat. Situated between natural features protecting both flanks, Ashe's camp appeared to be in a strong defensive position. Still, the security offered by natural barriers could be misleading, as Elbert discovered two months earlier when American lines buckled at Savannah. At Brier Creek, the wide stream and the sprawling swamp protected Ashe's flanks, but at the same time, they hedged his army into a small area and cut off escape routes with large bodies of water. Such water barriers could be fatal to panicking soldiers trying to cross them as Elbert learned earlier at Savannah when his retreating battalions encountered Musgrove Creek. In short, Brier Creek was a potential trap and the only way out in the event of an emergency was over Miller's Bridge that no longer existed. Recognizing the hazard, Ashe detached a work party to immediately repair the bridge.[38]

Lincoln ordered Ashe to remain at Brier Creek until a plan of action could be determined. He then called a council of war at Black Swamp with Ashe, Moultrie, and Rutherford. On February 28, Ashe departed his camp to attend Lincoln's meeting, leaving Bryan in charge. The mood must have been exhilarating at the council. Suddenly, after many setbacks, the tides of war were shifting in the Americans' favor. The victory at Kettle Creek and Campbell's retreat from Augusta bolstered Lincoln's confidence to the point where he was ready to undertake a bold offensive. The generals agreed to combine the whole army at Brier Creek, including Williamson's militia from Augusta, and create a grand force of seven thousand men. Since Brier Creek would be the new base, everyone sought assurances from Ashe that his position was secure. He guaranteed that it was. After the council, Ashe left

---

the same source, journal entry, February 24, 1779, 69.

[38] William Bryan testimony, John Ashe Court of Inquiry, March 14, 1779, in *MMAR*, 1:343–44, and, in the same source, John Ashe testimony, March 13, 1779, 338. Bryan is also referred to as "Bryant" in the sources.

Black Swamp with two artillery pieces for his militia, and on March 2 around noon he arrived back in camp.[39]

In Ashe's absence, Bryan and Elbert became apprehensive about their position, especially on the left. After discussing the problem with several officers, they advanced the lines nearly a mile upstream from the bridge. The new position buttressed a fork in the creek on the left and the swamp to the right. Though the move better strengthened the left, it also took the army further away from Miller's Bridge, which was still under repairs.[40]

On March 1, the day before Ashe returned from his meeting, Prevost sent his nine hundred troops toward Brier Creek after dusk. They included men from the 1st and 2nd Battalions of the 71st Foot, two companies of Baird's light infantry, and Loyalist units, including some previously with Boyd, Hamilton's Royal North Carolina Regiment, and two hundred cavalry from the King's Rangers. His reserve consisted of soldiers from the 60th Foot and a company of dragoons. He also carried along all five pieces of Campbell's artillery.[41]

As Prevost neared Brier Creek, he sent the 1st Battalion of the 71st Foot and some other detachments with two field pieces down the road toward Miller's Bridge to attract the attention of the Americans and mask the flanking maneuver. Prevost then led his main attacking column up the southwestern side of Brier Creek along the backroad to Pine Log Crossing, which he reached at ten o'clock in the morning on March 2. There he discovered that rebels burned the bridge across the creek. He spent the rest of the day getting his men over to Paris Mill on the opposite side on a makeshift pontoon bridge. At nightfall, with his men still crossing the creek, Prevost bivouacked at Paris Mill. Before daylight on March 3, the British army was again in motion down

---

[39] Mattern, *Benjamin Lincoln*, 66–67; Ashmore and Olmstead, "Battles of Kettle Creek and Brier Creek," 102; Davis, "Civil War in the Midst of Revolution," 148; William Bryan testimony, John Ashe Court of Inquiry, March 14, 1779, in *MMAR*, 1:345.

[40] William Bryan testimony, John Ashe Court of Inquiry, March 14, 1779, in *MMAR*, 1:345. Ashe maintained that he gave Bryan orders to move the camp further north before he left to meet Lincoln. See in the same source, testimony of John Ashe, March 14, 1779, 351; Howard, "Things Here Wear a Melancholy Appearance," 486.

[41] Howard, "Things Here Wear a Melancholy Appearance," 486–87; C. C. Jones Jr., *History of Georgia*, 2:347. This is also the number reported by General Prevost to Lord Germain on March 5, 1779 (Augustine Prevost to Lord George Germain, March 5, 1779, in Joseph Vallence Bevan Papers, MS 0071, Collection #71, box 1, folder 4, "History of Georgia, Revolutionary War," n.d., Georgia Historical Society).

the road on the northern side of the creek leading directly into the American position, some fifteen miles away. The entire circuitous route around Ashe's army, when completed, was fifty miles.[42] More remarkable, though, was that Prevost, even with the delay at Paris Mill, covered those fifty miles almost unnoticed in roughly two days.

The first indication of trouble occurred just before Ashe got back to camp. A colonel reported to Bryan that during the night of March 1, his men heard the sounds of the enemy near their lines around Miller's Bridge. The warning caused Bryan to send Major Francis Ross and sixty South Carolina cavalry, newly arrived from Williamson's approaching militia, out to reconnoiter the lines. Ross covered many miles between the road to Hudson's Ferry and Paris Mill and discovered compelling signs of an advancing British army. James Fergus, who was with Ross, remembered his experience. Recent rains made the river full and backed up Brier Creek for twelve miles before it became fordable. Miller's Bridge was still out, so they swam their horses over and then headed upstream toward Paris Mill. "About midnight," he said, "we came to a house where [there] was a woman & children. We pretended to be a party of Loyalists from North Carolina coming to join the British & wished to know…where they lay & how we could get to them." The woman, whose husband was with Prevost at Paris Mill, was "delighted." They were about a half-mile away along the creek, she said, and would soon "drive the Rebels out of the Forks." She suggested that her visitors remain at the house and wait for her husband's return. That way, she could confirm that they were friends. "From her we got all the intelligence we wanted," remarked Fergus, and "after giving our horses plenty of oats we returned to Camp." Fergus said that they found Ashe when they arrived during the afternoon of March 2 and told him about their discoveries. "We might expect them on us the next day at farthest," he warned. That was Ashe's first sound evidence that an attack was imminent. During that same afternoon, Bryan told him about the colonel who heard the enemy below Miller's Bridge. Unconcerned, Ashe replied that it was nothing more than roaming "horse thieves."[43]

---

[42] Howard, "Things Here Wear a Melancholy Appearance," 487; Davis, "Civil War in the Midst of Revolution," 150; Ashmore and Olmstead, "Battles of Kettle Creek and Brier Creek," 105; Carrington, *Battles of the American Revolution*, 464–65.

[43] William Bryan testimony, John Ashe Court of Inquiry, March 14, 1779, in *MMAR*, 1:344, and, in the same source, John Ashe testimony, March 14, 1779, 351; Ashmore and Olmstead, "Battles of Kettle Creek and Brier Creek," 105; Heidler, "American

Meanwhile, a jittery Elbert sent Marbury and his dragoons up Brier Creek to reconnector. Like Ross, Marbury also found signs of the enemy; he exchanged musket fire with them at Paris Mill. Ashe later complained at his court of inquiry that Marbury "did not send any information of their approach." Indeed, Marbury did report it, but the British captured his courier and the message never made it to the American camp. When Marbury finally returned, he informed Elbert of the encounter, who then told Ashe, so the North Carolina commander knew about the skirmish, contrary to what he stated at the court of inquiry. By nightfall, enough evidence existed even without Marbury's report to suggest that a substantial British force was near Ashe's camp. A concerned Bryan went to Ashe's tent to suggest more horse patrols. What he learned was shocking. None were patrolling, Ashe explained, because the horses in camp were fatigued and most of the riders were unarmed. When Bryan urged Ashe to consider the dangers that might arise from the lack of a vigilant watch, he replied that if the enemy did not surprise them during the evening, he "would take great care to have the country well patrolled for the future."[44]

Ashe's confidence stemmed from his belief that the American camp was, as he told his fellow generals earlier, defensively sound. He also believed that the size of his army intimidated the British and precluded any attack on his position. He was so self-assured that he parked most of his army's baggage and supplies eight miles upriver, making them inaccessible if quickly needed. In short, convinced of the superiority of his numbers and the strength of his position, Ashe became careless. Elbert did not share the same sentiments. He was still concerned about the vulnerable position of the American camp. To the front was an expansive open field with nothing to impede an advancing army, nor were there entrenchments or trenching tools. The supply wagons were miles away, and Ashe's undisciplined militia was wretchedly equipped with cartridges, powder, and weapons. Furthermore, the bridge was still out, eliminating that escape route. In addition to that, Elbert knew from firsthand experience that Campbell liked to take his army in wide circular marches that ended in the American rear. Such

---

Defeat at Briar Creek," 322; Revolutionary War Pension and Bounty-Land Warrant Applications, Pension Application of James Fergus, W25573, June 13, 1832.

[44] John Ashe testimony, John Ashe Court of Inquiry, March 13, 1779, in *MMAR*, 1:339, and, in the same source, William Bryan testimony, March 14, 1779, 345; McCall, *History of Georgia*, 2:209; Heidler, "American Defeat at Briar Creek," 325.

scenarios probably kept his eyes constantly peeled toward the front where the British could instantly appear along the little road leading down Brier Creek. All through the day of March 2, Bryan kept him informed about reports from scouts and patrols, so, along with Marbury's warning, he knew the British were nearby. To Elbert, Ashe's command decisions were unfathomable. The young Georgian, who highly valued order, discipline, and preparation, viewed the confused and disordered state of the American camp as an invitation to tragedy, and he held Ashe, the senior commander, solely responsible.

On the morning of Wednesday, March 3, as Prevost approached the American position from the north, Ashe sent out Ross's horse troop in the opposite direction toward Hudson's Ferry to determine the feasibility of an attack on the British army, which he believed were there. What Ross discovered instead was the unmistakable trail of a British advance toward Brier Creek. For reasons unknown, he never reported his findings to Ashe and never returned to camp.[45] Thus, throughout the morning of March 3 and into the early afternoon, Ashe was blind to the dangers enveloping his army, despite the mounting evidence. Some in Ashe's camp, like Elbert, Bryan, and even some of the common soldiers, understood their peril.

During these tense hours, the tale of three dispatches foretold the fate of Ashe's army. Ashe instructed Lieutenant Pleasant Henderson and John Taylor to deliver a written message to Lincoln at Purrysburg. Just as they were about to leave, Henderson suggested that Taylor take his saddlebags with him. Taylor followed Henderson's advice, but as they were leaving, he wanted to know the reason for getting his saddlebags. Henderson replied, "You nor I will ever see this place again. There will be a battle here before we return." A second dispatch came from Williamson, who was nearing Brier Creek with his militia. One of his scouting parties discovered Prevost's army almost on top of the Americans, and he sent an urgent express to Ashe giving the warning. About the same time it arrived, another came from the party guarding the supply wagons confirming Williamson's report. Ashe immediately conferred with Elbert and Bryan and advised them to "march out and meet the enemy," who were not yet present on the field. Hardly fifteen

---

[45] John Ashe testimony, John Ashe Court of Inquiry, March 13, 1779, in *MMAR*, 1:339; Ashmore and Olmstead, "Battles of Kettle Creek and Brier Creek," 105–106; Heidler, "American Defeat at Briar Creek," 324–25.

minutes passed from the time of the last dispatch until the moment when Prevost burst onto the scene.[46]

Pandemonium reigned in Ashe's camp as they readied themselves for battle. The drums beat to arms as men rushed to get cartridges, but as they did, Prevost's advance fired into the pickets and drove them back through the forming American lines. The surprise was complete. James Collins in the North Carolina militia remembered that when the battle opened "we were washing our clothes and amusing ourselves, some fishing and some at one thing and some at another, we were completely surprised, and routed." As the pickets rushed in, Prevost hastily formed his lines. Baird's light infantry filed into the right, the 2nd Battalion of the 71st and some of the rangers took the center, and about 150 cavalry formed on the left. Prevost ordered all of his artillery posted in front of the light infantry and the 71st Battalion. A reserve, nearly four hundred yards to the rear, consisted of three companies from the East Florida Volunteers and a troop of dragoons. About forty or fifty riflemen rushed out beyond the left to protect Prevost's rear.[47]

The Americans were completely disordered and were still gathering cartridges (most of which were incompatible with their muskets) when the British filed into attacking formation. Several had no cartridge boxes at all, so they carried their ammunition in hats, shirts, and anything else they could find. Many did not even have a musket. "The Americans troops were scattered and in the worst kind of order for battle," recalled North Carolina militiaman John Hancock. He attributed the mayhem to "the bad management of General Ashe." Hancock's observation was insightful since some of the militia later claimed they did not know how to deploy in case of a surprise attack. Their lack of training directly connected to a failure in Ashe's responsibility as a commander.[48]

Elbert advanced his Continentals and militia some half-mile above

---

[46] Heidler, "American Defeat at Briar Creek," 324; John Ashe testimony, John Ashe Court of Inquiry, March 13, 1779, in *MMAR*, 1:339, and, in the same source, William Bryan testimony, March 14, 1779, 345–46, 348.

[47] William Bryan testimony, March 14, 1779, in *MMAR*, 1:346; Revolutionary War Pension and Bounty-Land Warrant Applications, Pension Application of James Collins, S1653, August 8, 1832; Moore, *Diary of the American Revolution*, 2:140.

[48] D. Wilson, *Southern Strategy*, 93; Heidler, "American Defeat at Briar Creek," 325; Davis, "Civil War in the Midst of Revolution," 151; Revolutionary War Pension and Bounty-Land Warrant Applications, Pension Application of John Hancock, R4551, July 24, 1834.

the camp and formed the center of the first line along a small crest. With him was a two-pounder swivel field piece that was quickly loaded and aimed in the direction of the enemy. One of the earliest accounts of Elbert, a short article written in 1807, claimed that before the British fired into the American lines, he addressed his Georgians, and they swore to die with him rather than retreat. As Elbert readied his men, the remainder of the army, which was all North Carolina militia, took their places around him. The rest of the first line contained the New Bern Regiment on the left and the Edenton Regiment on the right. About seventy to eighty yards behind them was the second line with the Halifax Regiment on the left and the Wilmington Regiment on the right. Ashe posted Colonel Archibald Lytle's light infantry down near Miller's Bridge as a reserve.[49]

Around four o'clock, Prevost opened his attack with the firing of cannon, which generated fear and inflicted considerable damage to the rebels' front line. British columns then stepped forward to within 150 yards of Elbert's advanced position and changed into a charging formation. Elbert's soldiers steadied their muskets and fired one or two volleys. Then they advanced forward to within about thirty yards of the British line to improve the accuracy of their weapons. As they pushed ahead in good order, they drifted to the left in front of the New Bern Regiment, preventing them from discharging their muskets. At the same time, the Edenton Regiment shifted to the right, opening a huge gap between themselves and Elbert in the front line. Prevost immediately recognized the opening and, seeing the confusion in the American ranks, sent his soldiers charging into it at a quick step. As the 71st Regiment exploited the gap, Baird led a spirited charge into the American left. When the Halifax Regiment, on the left along the second line, saw the British charging, they immediately broke and fled without firing a shot. That set off a chain reaction fueled by panic. The New Bern Regiment shortly followed their comrades in a fast dash to the rear. Lytle advanced his light infantry from Miller's Bridge in an effort to stabilize the lines along the right, but he arrived just in time to see the Edenton Regiment melt away, followed by the Wilmington Regiment. When the enemy appeared, remembered Bryan, after a few volleys, the

---

[49] Ashmore and Olmstead, "Battles of Kettle Creek and Brier Creek," 108; Howard, "Things Here Wear a Melancholy Appearance," 490; Heidler, "American Defeat at Briar Creek," 328; John Ashe testimony, John Ashe Court of Inquiry, March 14, 1779, in *MMAR*, 1:352; Charlton, "Sketch of the Life of General Elbert," 2.

whole, including Ashe, gave away in great confusion and headed toward the creek and swamp. One North Carolina soldier recalled that their flight was "not from the fire of the Enemy…but it was from an apprehension [that they were] extending their lines and that [we] would be surrounded."[50]

Suddenly, all that remained were the Georgians standing alone against charging soldiers of the light infantry and the 71st Battalion. Baird unleashed his full fury against Elbert's wavering line. All around him, soldiers fell, either killed or wounded. As Baird's Highlanders swarmed the Georgians, the British commander yelled, "Every man of you that takes a prisoner shall lose his ration of rum." With that order, the light infantry lurched forward with fixed bayonets, plunging them into wounded and fleeing Americans. Over the sounds of battle, one Highlander called out, "Now my Boys, remember poor MacAlister!" Still, Elbert held on, not realizing that the army's right flank was gone until the British gained his rear. He fought so tenaciously that Prevost called up his reserves to help Baird overtake him. Assailed on all sides, the valiant Georgian continued to fight until a wound finally forced him to the ground.[51]

Much confusion among historians has centered on what happened next. Legend says that as Elbert was about to be pierced by a bayonet, he gave a Masonic sign of distress, and a British officer recognized it and spared his life. Some historians have questioned the accuracy of this story, and one, in particular, flatly stated that it never happened. None of the British accounts ever mentioned Elbert's Masonic sign. Most claimed that, when he surrendered, he "delivered his sword to a British officer and received quarter." The story seems "unrealistic," wrote the historian, since the "British were not in the habit of killing high-ranking Continental officers who were attempting to surrender, both for reasons of tradition and for the practical reason that such

---

[50] *Royal Georgia Gazette*, March 11, 1779, 4; Cox, "Brigadier-General John Ashe's Defeat," 300–301; Howard, "Things Here Wear a Melancholy Appearance," 490; Heidler, "American Defeat at Briar Creek," 329; William Bryan testimony, March 14, 1779, in *MMAR*, 1:346; Revolutionary War Pension and Bounty-Land Warrant Applications, Pension Application of Nathan Green, S3412, October 12, 1832; D. Wilson, *Southern Strategy*, 95.

[51] C. C. Jones Jr., *Samuel Elbert*, 32–33; Cashin and Robertson, *Augusta & the American Revolution*, 29.

captives were valuable commodities in prisoner exchanges."[52]

There can be no doubt that the British used bayonets at Brier Creek. An article in the *Royal Georgia Gazette* days after the event mentioned that rebel forces fled the field, their "panic occasioned by the terror of the bayonet." One contemporary included in his description of the battle that the British "rushed on with the bayonet." British soldiers "boasted of sheathing their bayonets in the bosoms of these poor supplicants." An eyewitness on the field the day after the battle saw "many clusters of Americans who had been massacred on their knees praying for quarter, most of their bodies disfigured with…gashes and stabs." Baird himself bragged that he personally put a dozen of those begging for quarter to death with his own hands.[53]

Hugh McCall, in his early history of Georgia written in 1816, did not mention Elbert's Masonic sign in his detailed description of the battle. "Elbert supported the conflict, until every avenue of a retreat was cut off," he wrote. When all appeared lost and hoping to save the lives of his men from useless slaughter, "he ordered his gallant little band to ground their arms and surrender." According to Nathan Green, a soldier from North Carolina on the battlefield, Elbert did not surrender "until most of his men were cut to pieces." The next Georgia historian to write about Elbert was Charles C. Jones. In 1887, he said that Elbert "gave the Masonic sign of distress" as he was about to be dispatched by a British soldier with an upraised bayonet. A nearby officer perceived the sign and intervened in time to save his life. Jones never cited his source for the story, and, according to some historians, he was only giving credence to an undocumented legend.[54]

It seems that the first time the Masonic story ever appeared in writing was in 1868, when Joseph Johnson published a sketch of Elbert in *The Historical Magazine*. In it, he said that Elbert was "on the point of being dispatched by a soldier with [an] uplifted bayonet, when he made the Masonic sign of distress. An officer saw it and instantly responded; he stayed the sturdy arm of the soldier, and Elbert's life was saved by the benevolent principles of brotherly love, even among

---

[52] Heidler, "American Defeat at Briar Creek," 329.

[53] *Royal Georgia Gazette*, March 11, 1779; Cox, "Brigadier-General John Ashe's Defeat," 299.

[54] McCall, *History of Georgia*, 2:212; C. C. Jones Jr., *Samuel Elbert*, 34, Heidler, "American Defeat at Briar Creek," 329; Revolutionary War Pension and Bounty-Land Warrant Applications, Pension Application of Nathan Green, S3412, October 12, 1832.

enemies."⁵⁵ It was likely that Jones got his story from Johnson. Johnson's source, however, is a mystery.

About fifteen years before Johnson published his sketch of Elbert, ninety-six-year-old Francis Weeks appeared at the Inferior Court in Gilmer County, Georgia, to give sworn testimony about his Revolutionary service to get a pension. Weeks was a Continental soldier with Elbert at Brier Creek, and he saw his commander fall with a wound. "He was about to be bayoneted by some of the British soldiers," recalled Weeks, "when he made a Freemason's sign which caused an officer of the British Army to rush in and [throw] the soldier's bayonet up and thereby saved the life of…Elbert."⁵⁶ Admittedly, Weeks was elderly, and his memory was probably fading. Still, witnessing Elbert's deliverance from death by a Masonic sign of distress was an event so remarkable that he could never forget it. The legend surrounding the Masonic sign of distress stemmed from a real occurrence. The Freemason's craft spared Elbert's life from the point of a bayonet at Brier Creek.

As Elbert and those with him lowered their weapons, British soldiers pursued Ashe's militia fleeing in all directions. With Miller's Bridge still out, the only option was to jump into Brier Creek or the Savannah River. Many drowned. Somehow, some of Elbert's men got away. Thomas Baker, a Georgia Continental, fled before Elbert surrendered. He jumped into a "Lagoon," which was probably his reference to the swamp. While locating the Savannah River was difficult, he finally found it, then "swam" across and joined Lincoln's army at Purrysburg some days later. George Gresham, a militiaman in Elbert's line, said that their "Regiment suffered very severely" before he bolted into a cane swamp. He soon crossed the river and ended up at the Two Sisters. "In the utmost disorder & confusion," recalled Thomas Hester from North Carolina, "[we] fled…[and] swam the River, leaving [our] clothes and baggage behind."⁵⁷

Swimming across large bodies of frigid water swollen by heavy rains offered the only chance of survival for those attempting to get away. Many jumped into the wide and rapid Savannah, observed

---

⁵⁵ J. Johnson, "Biographical Sketch of General Elbert," 34.
⁵⁶ Revolutionary War Pension and Bounty-Land Warrant Applications, Pension Application of Francis Weeks, W25934, September 22, 1853.
⁵⁷ Ibid., Pension Application of Thomas Baker, S15299, and, in the same source, Pension Application of Thomas Hester, S16299; Pension Application of George Gresham, October 20, 1832, W2933.

Moultrie, "to escape from the bayonet." Large numbers never made it to the opposite shore, and they were "sunk down, and…buried in a watery grave." Skilled swimmers made the other side, but "were so terrified, that they straggled through the woods in every direction." The cold weather only added to their miseries. "Many of our men were half naked having stripped to swim the river," explained James Fergus, and, making matters worse, there was a light frost that night. "Many suffered," he said, "with the cold [and] having nothing on but a shirt or breeches." Others secluded themselves in the swamps and canebrakes near the battlefield. The British captured and bayoneted almost all of them. To be sure, they set the cane on fire. British soldiers found "their half consumed [and] parched and blackening bodies" the next morning. One contemporary observed that it was a sickening sight of cruelty, seldom witnessed among civilized nations.[58]

The battle of Brier Creek lasted just five minutes. It was, angrily proclaimed Moultrie, "nothing less than a total rout." Never, he said, "was an army more compleatly surprized [*sic*], and never were men more panic struck." Ashe tried to rally his men in the swamp, but to no avail. He managed to find a way to the river, which he crossed around dark, and finally ended up at Mathew's Bluff in South Carolina late in the evening at Rutherford's camp. There, he wrote Lincoln, informing him of the disaster: "I am sorry to inform you…[that] the enemy came down upon us in force; what number I know not: the troops in my division, did not stand fire, five minutes; many fled without discharging their pieces; I went with the fugitives half a mile, and finding it impossible to rally the troops, I made my escape into the river swamp, and made [it] up in the evening to this place."[59]

The aggregate number of American casualties at Brier Creek is unknown. One historian estimated that between 150 and 200 Americans died in the battle while an additional 28 officers, including Elbert, Lieutenant Colonel John McIntosh, and 200 privates became prisoners. The loss of arms was nearly total and included all of the field artillery, most of the ammunition, and one thousand muskets. Provisions and baggage were also gone. British casualty figures displayed the

---

[58] William Moultrie to Benjamin Lincoln, March 3, 1779, in *MMAR*, 1:324–25; Cox, "Brigadier-General John Ashe's Defeat," 299; Revolutionary War Pension and Bounty-Land Warrant Applications, Pension Application of James Fergus, W25573.

[59] William Moultrie to Benjamin Lincoln, March 3, 1779, in *MMAR*, 1:324, and, in the same source, John Ashe to Benjamin Lincoln, March 3, 1779, 323–24.

totality of their victory. They reported five privates killed and one officer and ten privates wounded. "This unlucky affair at Brier-Creek, disconcerted all our plans," a disgusted Moultrie told Lincoln, "and through the misfortunes of Gen. Howe [at Savannah] and Ash[e], the war was protracted at least one year longer." Ashe received so much criticism for his lackluster generalship that Lincoln held a court of inquiry on March 13 in Purrysburg and another on the following day twelve miles upriver near Rutherford's camp to determine the necessity of a court-martial trial. The Inquiry found Ashe negligent in taking precautions and securing the camp but acquitted him of cowardice. Despite his ruined reputation, Ashe retained his command and remained in the field.[60]

As for Elbert, his brave stand was the only positive thing the American army experienced at Brier Creek. Now he was a prisoner. British soldiers probably led him to an open area near the battlefield with the other prisoners where they kept a close guard on them. Augustine Balthrop, a member of North Carolina's militia, was also in that field and remembered that at night, they forced the prisoners into a large barn to prevent their escape. For several days, they remained at Brier Creek and took verbal paroles in the absence of paper. As Elbert looked around at the mass of wounded and dejected soldiers in his midst, he felt sorry for them. As he considered the enormous, shameful disaster that brought them to this place, great resentment welled up in his heart. Only one person was responsible for the embarrassing nightmare: John Ashe. As he later told James Fergus, he believed Ashe betrayed the whole army to the British at Brier Creek. Elbert swore that if they ever met again, one of them should die before they parted.[61] For now, he was going to back to his home in Savannah, not as the triumphant savior of his city, but to begin his ordeal as a prisoner of war.

---

[60] Ibid., 326; Davis, "Civil War in the Midst of Revolution," 151; C. C. Jones Jr., *Samuel Elbert*, 8; Augustine Prevost to Lord George Germain, March 5, 1779, in Joseph Vallence Bevan Papers, MS 0071, Collection #71, box1, folder 4, "History of Georgia, Revolutionary War," n.d., n.p., Georgia Historical Society; Moultrie, "Opinion of the Court," March 16, 1779, *MMAR*, 1:353.

[61] Revolutionary War Pension and Bounty-Land Warrant Applications, Pension Application of Augustine Balthrop, August 29, 1832, W8113 and, in the same source, Pension Application of James Fergus.

Chapter 12

"A Day of Reckoning Is Hastening On": The Ordeal of Samuel Elbert, 1779–1781

Shortly after the American disaster at Brier Creek, the British marched Samuel Elbert and more than two hundred of his fellow soldiers to Savannah under heavy guard as prisoners of war. Word of his capture traveled fast and preceded his arrival in the city. Pro-British newspapers announcing the engagement, like the *Royal Georgia Gazette* on March 11, went out of their way to mention that Elbert was a prisoner, but so did Whig papers, such as the *Virginia Gazette*, that also told of his capture. General Augustine Prevost, the commander of British troops in Georgia, spread the news all the way to London. On March 5, two days after the battle, he informed the secretary of state for the American colonies, Lord George Germain, that among those captured was "Brigadier Gen. Elbert[,] one of their best officers."[1]

It took several days for the prisoners to reach Savannah, and, once there, most ended up on prison ships. Augustine Balthrop from North Carolina said that when they arrived, they stayed in town for a while, after which British soldiers escorted them down river and put them on a ship anchored at Cockspur Island, where he remained for three months. James McElwee recalled his eight-month incarceration in the "memorable and celebrated" prison ship *Munificence* lying in the harbor, where he remained "deprived of common necessaries of life" until he was exchanged. Those common necessities included things like food. During William Poplin's imprisonment below Savannah, he was allowed only a pint of rice per day and three-fourths of a pound of fresh beef each week. "The starvation and

---

[1] *Royal Georgia Gazette*, March 11, 1779, 4; *Virginia Gazette*, Dixon and Nicolson, April 9, 1779, 1; Letter from Augustine Prevost to Lord George Germain, March 5, 1779, in Joseph Vallence Bevan Papers, MS 0071, Collection #71, box 1, folder 4, "History of Georgia, Revolutionary War," n.d., n.p., Georgia Historical Society.

the intolerable filthiness and exposure" were terrible, claimed John Smith from North Carolina, who wound up on a ship off Cockspur with eighty other prisoners. When soldiers led Simon Whithurst from North Carolina onto the *Munificence*, he noticed a number of officers on board, including Elbert and Lieutenant Colonel John McIntosh, also captured at Brier Creek. Along with the *Munificence*, two additional prison ships, the *Nancy* and the *Whitley*, were at Cockspur. All three were crowded and filled to capacity.[2]

Life on the prisons ships was a living horror; while officers fared better than the rank and file, it was not by much. The stifling heat, lack of fresh air, cramped conditions, spoiled and rotten meat, putrid water, rank odors, rat infestations, sickness, and dark confinement below decks were an almost unbearable experience shared by all. As the highest-ranking officer in the state, Elbert had special privileges, including access to a servant. Still, the British abused some of the officers. Mordecai Sheftall, the commissary general for Georgia battalions captured at the fall of Savannah on December 29, 1778, was a prisoner on the *Nancy*. Because he refused to divulge sensitive information relating to the American army, the British ignored his rank and confined him with common prisoners. Knowing that he was an Orthodox Jew, they engaged in anti-Semitic abuses and offered him contaminated pork to eat for weeks, which he never consumed.[3]

American prisoners died on the ships in Savannah's harbor nearly every day, and those who survived verified the unspeakable cruelties of their ordeal. John Hancock was healthy when the British captured him at Brier Creek. When they put him on a ship below Savannah, his health deteriorated rapidly. In just nine months, he became so sick that he lost use of his limbs. His condition worsened when they sent him to a prison hospital in Savannah. There he stayed for one year, during which time he came down with many illnesses, including smallpox. Augustine Balthrop said that during his confinement, he suffered "very bad" for three months and only enlisted in the British army to end the torment. "Prison ships at Savannah were particularly crowded and unhealthy," explained one historian. "On one, six men slept in a space only five feet wide." During an

---

[2] Revolutionary War Pension and Bounty-Land Warrant Applications, Pension Application of Augustine Balthrop, W8113, and, in the same source, Pension Application of James McElwee, W9553, September 26, 1832; Pension Application of William Poplin, W10231, October 1, 1832; Pension Application of John Smith, November 17, 1832, S7540; Pension Application of Simon Whitehurst, W11795, October 7, 1834.

[3] C. C. Jones Jr., *History of Georgia*, 2:357.

exchange of prisoners sent up from Georgia to Charleston in April, South Carolina General William Moultrie noticed that most were "quite emaciated." Several could not walk without assistance. "They complain highly of their ill treatment," he wrote South Carolina governor John Rutledge, and "they say they were fed upon condemned pork and oatmeal, which the hogs would not eat." Often they received a week's worth of pork at one time so that it spoiled after just two days in the ship's putrid environment. "Our men die fast on board the prison-ships," reported an angry Moultrie, and they "are carried a-shore on the marsh, and buried so slightly as to be a horrid sight for those left alive, who see the buzzards picking the bones of their fellow soldiers." As Moultrie complained to Rutledge, Lincoln wrote Congress, detailing the wretched state of the men. "We have lately exchanged some prisoners," he said,

> those who have come out are in a most miserable condition—few fit for service. Their treatment on board the prison-ships...and the measures adopted to oblige them to renounce their allegiance to the United States, and engage them in the British service, have been cruel and unjustifiable; many inlisted with them, many are dead, and others [are] in a weak, dying state.[4]

Sometimes, even British doctors, whose job it was to help sick and wounded prisoners, ignored professional oaths and instead tried to kill them. One particular case concerned Donald McLeod, a British physician, accused by ship prisoners of committing many crimes against them. In 1783 after the war, McLeod applied to Georgia's Assembly for state citizenship. The assembly responded by gathering memorials and eyewitness accounts of the doctor's wartime actions from former prisoners. Some of the statements were fatally injurious to McLeod's case. While accused of sundry crimes, the most horrendous charge, and the one most often brought up in the sworn accounts, was that he "mixed fine, broken, or pulverized glass, in a parcel of medicines sent by him...for the use of said prisoners" on the ships. In one instance, American doctors who were also prisoners on the ships examined some of the medicines McLeod sent over and extracted fine splinters of glass

---

[4] Revolutionary War Pension and Bounty-Land Warrant Applications, Pension Application of Augustine Balthrop, W8113, and, in the same source, Pension Application of John Smith, S7540; Borick, *Relieve Us of This Burthen*, 6; William Moultrie to John Rutledge, April 16, 1779, in *MMAR*, 1:369. For Lincoln's quote, see C. Campbell, ed., *Journal of an Expedition*, 117n115.

from them. One former prisoner said that the doctor gave officers much better care than the rest of the men and did not taint their medicines only because he worried about his own fate should the Americans retake Savannah, in which case, he expected a return of his kindness. Little wonder, then, that Elbert's written testimony spoke well of McLeod. He praised the doctor's treatment of himself and his servant when they were sick in Savannah. He even credited McLeod with saving his servant's life. He never once witnessed the doctor mistreat any of the prisoners, he said, and always thought his intentions were well meaning. The contradictory testimony resulted in a close ballot by the assembly on July 31, 1783. They denied McLeod citizenship by only two votes.[5]

The unbearable conditions caused some to reach a breaking point, and several responded by jumping ship. Major John Habersham, himself a prisoner, wrote Lincoln and told him about the Reverend W. [Moses] Allen, the pastor at Midway Presbyterian and a chaplain for Georgia's Continentals, held captive on a ship. Wretched conditions pushed Allen to jump overboard, said Habersham, and he "drowned in attempting to make his escape from the prison ship at Coxspur [sic]." There were other ways to escape besides jumping ship. One night, John Love, a surgeon's mate in Georgia's 1st Battalion, snuck onto a barge belonging to his prison ship and quietly hid there until he could sneak away and rejoin the American army.[6]

The British used suffering and privation to coax prisoners to enlist in their army. To alleviate their agony, many did, at least until they could desert and return to American lines. To end his misery, Augustine Balthrop enlisted in the British army and stayed with them for a few months in Savannah until he could slip away. John Smith recalled that a British recruiting officer frequently came to prisoners on his ship. Sometimes they got one or two, and occasionally three, to join, but Smith always refused their offers. After six months on one of the ships,

---

[5] *The Gazette of the State of Georgia*, July 1, 1784, 2, and, in the same source, June 17, 1784, 1; May 13, 1784, 1; *Journal of the House of Assembly, August 17, 1781, to February 26, 1784*, July 31, 1783, *RRG*, 3:400–403.

[6] John Habersham to Benjamin Lincoln, February 21, 1779, Historic Augusta, Incorporated Collection of Revolutionary and Early Republic Era Manuscripts, MS 1701, folder 3, Georgia Historical Society; Revolutionary War Pension and Bounty-Land Warrant Applications, Pension Application of John Love, September 24, 1855, R21467. Allen drowned on February 8. See Judson, *Sages and Heroes*, 2:416.

William Poplin feared that he would starve to death unless he enlisted. Finally, one day, hunger drove him to abandon his friends and join the enemy. He remained in Savannah until the siege of the city in September and October and then fled to American lines. Sickness drove John Hancock into British ranks. Sent to Augusta to defend the city, he found his opportunity to flee in May 1781 and eventually linked up with the American army in South Carolina commanded by General Nathanael Greene.[7]

Recruiting agents also tried to persuade American officers, including Elbert, to turn against their country. The British treated him with great respect and kindness, wrote Jones in the late 1800s. On numerous occasions, they offered him promotions, honors, and rewards to sway him away from the Americans and become one of their officers. "His patriotism was proof against them all," claimed the historian, and out of duty to his country, he repeatedly declined their bargains. He was "subjected to many degrading insults," read a little piece on Elbert in 1807, but still the principle British officers respected him "as one of their most formidable opponents."[8]

From the day of his capture, Elbert became a prisoner on parole. In the absence of paper at the battlefield, his initial parole was verbal. In paroles, individuals promised to remain with their captors until exchanged for British prisoners. During that time, they pledged not to escape or take up arms against His Majesty's forces in America. Stipulations attached to paroles varied slightly from place to place. In Savannah, prisoners, at least on land, had freedom of mobility within reasonable limits. When Archibald Campbell first took the city, he ordered that prisoners, including officers, "shall not be permitted to go out of our Lines, even on Parole, before a general Change of Prisoners shall be settled between the Enemy and Us." This suggests that *within* British lines, they had limited abilities to mingle around or work in the city, as they did in Charleston after it fell on May 12, 1780.[9] It may even mean that Elbert, once he got off the *Munificence* after a few months,

---

[7] Revolutionary War Pension and Bounty-Land Warrant Applications, Pension Application of Augustine Balthrop, W8113; Pension Application of John Smith, S7540; Pension Application of William Poplin, W10231; Pension Application of John Hancock, R4551.

[8] C. C. Jones Jr., *Samuel Elbert*, 3; J. Johnson, "Biographical Sketch of General Elbert," 35; Charlton, "Sketch of the Life of General Elbert," 2.

[9] Archibald Campbell to Augustine Prevost and Hyde Parker, January 21, 1779, in C. Campbell, ed., *Journal of an Expedition*, 45; Borick, *Relieve Us of This Burthen*, 7.

could stay in his Savannah home, accompanied by his servant, while still on parole.

Civilians could pass through the lines and bring prisoners things necessary for their health and accommodation. Campbell even allowed limited interaction between civilians and prisoners. When civilians brought in items, they became the responsibility of the commissary of prisoners of war, who delivered them to their proper owners. Campbell's lenient policy was evident when he addressed the situation of a local resident who wanted to bring sundry items behind the lines for her captured husband. The prisoners, he told her, would get "whatever you may wish to send in for their relief." An officer will receive them, explained the commander, and then give a receipt. "Mrs. Bryan may be assured that every attention shall be paid to her aged husband," promised Campbell, and "whatever clothes or other articles she may wish to send for his use & comfort shall be punctually delivered."[10]

After three months in captivity, Elbert, his servant and his officers received formal, written paroles. On June 19, he and some forty additional officers, including Sheftall and Habersham, signed a parole adhering to the following terms:

> We, the subscribers being prisoners of War, taken by his Majesty's Troops, hereby engage and promise upon our words of honor, that we shall remain wherever the Commanding Officer of his Majesty's Army in Georgia shall think proper to have us quarter'd and remain within the bounds to us prescribed. And also that We shall not directly or indirectly act and serve against his Majesty and Government until we are properly exchanged either for Officers of the same Rank or on such terms as may be agreed upon whenever a Cartel is fixed.[11]

The terms in Savannah closely aligned to those signed by officers in Sunbury, where the British set up another prison camp, probably in Fort Morris. There the officers "solemnly and religiously" promised upon their honor that they would not leave the town or take up arms

---

[10] Archibald Campbell to Augustine Prevost and Hyde Parker, January 21, 1779, in C. Campbell, ed., *Journal of an Expedition*, 45; Archibald Campbell to ?, January 9, 1779, Archibald Campbell Papers, MS 1581, Georgia Historical Society.

[11] Hühner, "Jews of Georgia," 97.

until exchanged. They swore to abide by the parole conditions, pledging "our sacred words and honor as gentlemen officers."[12]

While Elbert was a prisoner, a strange and unverified incident involving an attempt on his life possibly occurred. The first written account of it appeared in 1868, when Joseph Johnson claimed that Loyalists sent two Indians to murder him, and, as they were about to carry out the act, Elbert gave them hand signals from his days in the fur trade. The Indians instantly recognized him, and according to Johnson, lowered their weapons and in friendship "came forward to shake hands." Johnson said that his story came from family tradition, but the tale was so extraordinary that Jones, later in the century, could not resist putting it into his short biography on Elbert as a factual event.[13] If the account was indeed true, that meant that Elbert saved his life twice, within the span of only a few months, by hand signs.

Before casting aside the incident as an unsubstantiated, hero-worshiping myth, is it possible such an event could have happened? In other words, did Loyalists despise Elbert enough to want him dead? Were there Indians around Savannah when Elbert was a prisoner? Are there any accounts at this time of Loyalists or Indians killing paroled prisoners, or even civilians, around Savannah?

From the start of the Revolution, Georgia experienced a civil war as Loyalists and Whigs routinely committed horrible crimes against each other, including murder. After British occupation of Georgia began, Loyalists, seeking retribution for Whig abuses, returned the favor in kind. Many Loyalists, such as the one who expressed an opinion in the *Royal Georgia Gazette* about the cruel and "barbarous Rebels" did seek justice. "Rebel governors," he complained, hung so many Loyalists who, after suffering the grossest calamities, received unjust death sentences in mock trials conducted by the "most abandoned juries and infamous Judges that ever disgraced human nature." Hanging, he mockingly said, had become second nature to *"those virtuous Sons of Liberty"* and putting a "Tory" to death was something "highly meritorious" among them. However, he warned, "a day of reckoning is hastening on, when all those Murderers, and the Tar and Feathering Gentry, must answer for their crimes." During British reoccupation of Georgia, many

---

[12] "Sunbury Prisoner of War Oath," n.d., MS 1340, Georgia Historical Society.

[13] J. Johnson, "Biographical Sketch of General Elbert," 35; C. C. Jones Jr., *Samuel Elbert*, 35.

did answer, including Colonel John Dooly, an officer on parole near Augusta, murdered by a party of Loyalists as he sat in his home enjoying a meal with his family. Loyalists burned Colonel Elijah Clarke's home north of Augusta and forced his wife and daughters into the wilderness with only a pony, which another party later confiscated. They also drove rebel leader Lieutenant Colonel Stephen Heard's wife and infant from their plantation residence in Wilkes County, into a raging snowstorm, where they perished. Sheftall Sheftall, confined at Sunbury, recalled that Loyalists prowled the countryside, and one killed an officer on parole near his prison.[14] In such a volatile environment, Loyalists were not above murdering American officers on parole, like Elbert, or even their families.

There were also Creek Indians in and around Savannah during 1779. Nearly five hundred assembled on the Altamaha waiting for instructions from John Stuart and his Indian agents. In April, a number of Creeks, led by Indian agent David Taitt and mestizo headman Alexander McGillivray, arrived in Savannah and lingered through the summer after many became sick. Later, still more came carrying with them about two hundred slaves plundered from area plantations. Prevost told them the slaves were theirs since whatever they plundered belonged to them.[15]

Finally, did Native Americans around Savannah at the time Elbert was a prisoner commit acts of violence against residents? Concerning the Indians in Savannah, McCall wrote that they had instructions, presumably from Stuart or Taitt, not to kill women and children. That, however, did not stop them from murdering others, such as the party who arrived at Ebenezer with five scalps as trophies and three female prisoners, all taken around Savannah. Thomas Brown, who was there at the time, rewarded them for their services.[16] Native Americans were not only in Savannah, but Loyalists enticed them to commit murder. Though the story's authenticity is unproven, it remains possible that hand signals saved Elbert's life from Indians sent to kill him when he was a prisoner. Loyalists nurtured a deep-seated hatred against Whigs, and, as the example with Brown attests, they employed Indians around Savannah to carry out their vengeance.

---

[14] *Royal Georgia Gazette*, January 13, 1780, 2; McCall, *History of Georgia*, 2:285–86, 306; Cook, *Governors of Georgia*, 40; Marcus, ed., "Sheftall Sheftall Describes His Career as a Revolutionary Solder," 140.

[15] McCall, *History of Georgia*, 2:217; Cashin, *Lachlan McGillivray*, 292–93; Brooking, "Of Material Importance," 277.

[16] McCall, *History of Georgia*, 2:238–39.

In late July, Sir James Wright returned to Georgia from London to resume his position as royal governor. At the same time, Georgia's Revolutionary government, barely surviving British occupation of the state, limped along in a limited capacity. As Wright reestablished his authority in Savannah, the General Assembly's remnants in Augusta created a Supreme Executive Council to keep state government alive. It was a desperate measure. The council was unconstitutional since it established a temporary dictatorship run by nine men. Elbert knew most of them, including his friend Joseph Habersham, William Few, Joseph Clay, John Dooly (later murdered by Loyalists), Seth Cuthbert, and John Wereat. After John Houstoun's term as governor expired at the beginning of 1779, the state had no chief executive. To create a figurehead for the state's government, the council, on August 6, unanimously elected Wereat as "president." The council's ascension and Wereat's election temporarily returned Georgia's leadership to the Savannah-dominated faction of Conservative Whigs, but not without a price. Congress refused to allocate $500,000 to the state's illegitimate government even with council member Clay's influence as Continental paymaster.[17]

As fall approached, Wright and Prevost in Savannah faced an impending crisis. On September 1, twenty-two French ships of the line appeared off Georgia's coast. The fleet, a product of France's military alliance with the United States in 1778, carried along nearly four thousand soldiers commanded by Comte d'Estaing whose goal was to retake the city. Lincoln, with almost one thousand troops in South Carolina, soon crossed the river at the Two Sisters and joined him. Over the next few days, militia from Georgia and South Carolina and around 370 Virginia Continentals augmented Lincoln's army, as did Polish count Casimir Pulaski's 300 American cavalry dragoons. General Lachlan McIntosh, Georgia's former embattled Continental Line commander, returned to the state from Washington's army during the summer and assumed command of three Continental regiments from South Carolina that joined Lincoln. By the middle of September, Lincoln had 3,155 soldiers under his command. When combined with d'Estaing's troops, the Allied force totaled 7,722 men.[18]

---

[17] Cook, *Governors of Georgia*, 29; Lamplugh, "To Check and Discourage the Wicked and Designing," 300.

[18] D. Wilson, *Southern Strategy*, 134–39, 177–80.

Believing that he now possessed an upper hand to extract concessions from Wright and Prevost, Wereat sent him a message from the Supreme Executive Council demanding Elbert's release. Wereat proposed an exchange of Elbert for Wright, himself a prisoner of the Council of Safety who broke his parole in March 1776 and fled the state in a British warship. "Your Excellency was never exchanged," read the note, and therefore "the Council of this State do claim you as their Prisoner, and expect that you will repair to this place [Augusta], and surrender yourself in consequence of your parole." Major John Habersham was an acceptable exchange if they could not have Elbert, "or any other of our friends who are now prisoners to the British Army, as may be equal to a person of your Excellency's Rank."[19] Wright, of course, ignored the ridiculous demand.

Meanwhile, Prevost bolstered his defenses and refused d'Estaing's request for surrender. The allied forces responded by placing Savannah under siege. The construction of siege trenches began on September 23, and heavy artillery soon appeared in the lines. Prevost called in all outlying troops from scattered garrisons in Georgia and South Carolina for Savannah's defense, including those in Sunbury and Lieutenant Colonel John Maitland's eight hundred men in Beaufort. When the British evacuated Sunbury, many of the American prisoners, including Mordecai Sheftall, who recently arrived there from Savannah, wound up in Antigua in the West Indies where the Jewish commander recalled that they "suffered…greatly." By the time Prevost got all of his reinforcements together, he had 4,813 men behind several defensive fortifications ringing the city, which included a thick line of sharp posts stuck in the ground and pointing toward the attacking force (called *abatis*) in front of hastily dug trenches, earthen redoubts, and breastworks.[20]

When the French fleet appeared, the British withdrew all of their ships at Cockspur, including the prison ships, upriver toward the city. To keep the French navy at bay, they sunk transports below the city to block the river. Remembering their experience during the battle of the rice boats in March 1776, British crews submerged smaller ships upriver and laid a boom across the waterway to prevent fire rafts from floating down and

---

[19] John Wereat to Sir James Wright, September 6, 1779, in *RRG*, 2:181; George Walton to George Washington, November 11, 1780, in P. Smith, *Letters of Delegates to Congress*, 16:324.
[20] D. Wilson, *Southern Strategy*, 157–58; 180–81; Mordecai Sheftall Papers, 1780–1796, "Mordecai Sheftall Memorial," 1779, MS 725, Georgia Historical Society; K. Coleman, *American Revolution in Georgia*, 128.

burning their fleet. Elbert was present during the siege of Savannah as a captive behind the lines, but his exact location is a matter of conjecture. Civilians and some prisoners remained in the city. Jonathan Curtis, a prisoner from the North Carolina militia, recalled that when the Americans besieged Savannah, "we were taken and placed in a strong house in the Town." It may be that Elbert was in the "strong house" as well, or perhaps he remained in his home. In any case, he witnessed a bombardment of his city, which began on October 4 and continued for the next four days. The bombs destroyed homes and buildings and set many on fire. They also killed civilians and slaves, even as they hunkered in cellars for protection. Some escaped to Hutchinson's Island for refuge. Wright and Prevost sought protection at the base of Yamacraw Bluff on the river.[21] Those options, of course, were not open to Elbert, who waited hopefully, and nervously, for the bombardment's end and the timely arrival of his liberators.

The shelling ceased on October 8, and d'Estaing prepared to storm British lines at the Spring Hill Redoubt on the following morning. The result was an allied catastrophe, much like the battles of Savannah and Brier Creek a few months earlier. The French lost 22.6 percent of their attacking force of 2,585 men, or roughly 585 soldiers. American casualties were high, too. According to Moultrie, out of 1,500 that participated in the engagement, close to 460 perished in the attempt, which amounted to nearly 30 percent of Lincoln's attacking force. Among those dead was Pulaski, killed by canister shot that pierced his thigh and chest while he lead a cavalry charge through the abatis. In contrast, Prevost reported 39 casualties, including 16 killed and the rest wounded. Crestfallen, the remaining Americans departed for South Carolina on October 19, followed by the French, who sailed away with their fleet on the following day.[22] The embarrassing episode was a supreme disappointment to Elbert. For himself and his men, the failure to retake Savannah extended indefinitely their ordeal as prisoners.

Still, Elbert had hope that an exchange with a prisoner of equal rank would happen soon. It did for Walton in October. Habersham was delighted to fill out a certificate of exchange on October 16. "I flatter myself," he said, if Lieutenant Colonel Munro [?], a British prisoner, "was offered

---

[21] "History of Georgia, Revolutionary War," Collection #71, box 1, folder 4, MS 0071, Joseph Vallence Bevan Papers, n.d., n.p.; C. C. Jones Jr., *Samuel Elbert*, 35; Revolutionary War Pension and Bounty-Land Warrant Applications, Pension Application of Jonathan Curtis, October 23, 1832, S8269; D. Wilson, *Southern Strategy*, 153–55.

[22] D. Wilson, *Southern Strategy*, 165, 770–74.

for me." He had no doubt that Prevost would agree to the proposal, despite Habersham's lower rank. Nevertheless, he did not want to injure the army by causing someone of a higher rank among his peers to remain prisoner. If the exchange did not happen, it was his "earnest desire" to remain a prisoner and "share the fate of my bleeding countrymen." Negotiations over Habersham's exchange broke down, probably due to rank issues. He was still a prisoner in 1780.[23]

Petitions from the state for Elbert's release continued, but not from the Supreme Council. The failed siege of Savannah discredited Wereat and his government. Already, Wereat called for constitutional elections to the General Assembly on December 1, but Radical Whigs, led by George Wells and Richard Howley, did not want to wait that long and they laid plans for a new body called the "House of Assembly" to assume control of state government. Like the Supreme Council, the House of Assembly was also extralegal, despite the name. To legitimize it, they needed a well-known figurehead to lead their movement. That person, of all people, was George Walton.[24]

It is hard to fathom how Walton, a longtime Conservative Whig, could align himself with the Radical Whigs, whom he considered bitter political enemies. He despised their champion, Button Gwinnett, and defended McIntosh, the person who killed him in a duel. Although an opponent of the "popular party," he reversed his attitude after his exchange. A letter Walton received from Lincoln shortly after the failed siege at Savannah may hold the secret to his political transformation. In it, Lincoln suggested that the state should convene the assembly soon and send delegates to Congress. Somehow, Walton understood Lincoln to suggest that he should go to Augusta and set up a government—and he did just that. Once in Augusta, Walton showed Wells and Howley his letter, and that was all they needed to usurp the council. Though unconstitutional, the radical-led House of Assembly promptly elected Walton as governor.[25] Thus, by late fall 1779, Georgia had three governors all serving at the same time. Two of them in Augusta were illegal, and the other in Savannah was propped into power by British bayonets.

---

[23] John Habersham to John Wereat [?], October 16, 1779, John Habersham Papers, 1779–1787, MS 0338, Georgia Historical Society; Borick, *Relieve Us of This Burthen*, 56–57.

[24] Lamplugh, "To Check and Discourage the Wicked and Designing," 301.

[25] Jackson, *Lachlan McIntosh*, 115.

Walton's elevation to governor and association with the Radical Whigs put him on a collision course with his old friend McIntosh. Time had not healed the wounds of Gwinnett's supporters, especially Wells, who was his second in that fatal duel. Nor had they forgotten the charges of Toryism leveled at McIntosh and his family, whom they still believed to be traitors. Now he was back in the state and, as the highest-ranking Continental officer in Georgia, in a position to once again command a new battalion and horse regiment authorized by Congress. Just like before, the radicals wanted him removed and, ironically, it was Walton, once McIntosh's most staunch defender, who shouted the loudest for his transfer. Walton's real motive for turning on McIntosh is still a mystery, although it probably had much to do with political ambition. While he continued to profess his friendship for McIntosh, he also worked behind the scenes to ruin him. On November 28, Walton and some of the radicals wrote a sham letter to Congress from their unconstitutional assembly demanding the general's employment in some other department because of the state's "common dissatisfaction" with his performance. The assembly never saw the letter. Neither did William Glascock, the speaker, although it contained his signature. Some months later, Glascock denied knowledge of the letter and declared his signature a forgery. Walton's forged letter had the desired result. On February 14, 1780, Congress, for a second time, removed McIntosh from command without a hearing or consultation with Lincoln or Washington.[26]

Oddly, the political backbiting had something to do with Elbert, languishing as a prisoner far from the epicenter of governmental chaos in Augusta, since the Radical Whigs wanted him to command any new Continental unit. Their plans, however, were compromised because Elbert was a prisoner. In their letter to Congress, the assembly recognized that Elbert "rendered much personal service in the course of the War" and that the people at large deemed him "a gallant and good Soldier." They urged Congress to facilitate a trade for James Inglis Hamilton, a brigadier general captured at Saratoga. Hamilton was a part of the Convention Army of British prisoners, mostly officers, waiting on cartels for exchange. Upon Elbert's release, the assembly suggested his promotion to the rank of brigadier general in the Continental Army.[27]

As the assembly worked with Congress to get Elbert released, they

---

[26] Ibid., 116–18; Hall, *Land and Allegiance*, 95.
[27] Minutes of the Executive Council, November 28, 1779, in *RRG*, 2:189.

also communicated with him about military matters in the state. This correspondence brings up several questions about the nature of Elbert's parole. For example, they requested a meeting to "confer" with him about the proper mode of officering the new Continental battalion and horse regiment. The reorganization was necessary since there were only forty men left in Georgia's Continental Line by 1780. Did Prevost allow Elbert the freedom to "confer" about ways to strengthen the army that opposed him? He certainly had to know about the correspondence. In an order relating to written communications sent to American prisoners in Savannah, guards and officers were to "stop and examine all letters going to them and if they contain anything improper [they] are to send them directly to the chief justice for his inspection." No doubt, authorities screened Elbert's replies, like the one he sent to the assembly's request on December 6. It contained a list of commanders in Georgia's four battalions, many of whom, like Habersham, were prisoners in Savannah. He sent another letter to the assembly on December 10, telling them that the "bad weather and my indisposition" would not permit a meeting "to day as you desired." What did Elbert mean by his "indisposition?" Was he referencing a sickness, perhaps the same one that nearly killed his servant? Did it mean the British prohibited him from meeting with assembly representatives? When Elbert mentioned "today" as the time for the meeting, did that mean assembly members traveled to Savannah for a conference with Elbert? If so, were they not putting themselves in jeopardy as leaders of the rebellion? In his December 10 letter, Elbert enclosed a paper signed by the officers with him agreeing to commanders for the new Continental regiments according to seniority. The assembly followed Elbert's suggestions and sent a copy of their proceedings to him. They requested that he make out a return for the units "if in his power."[28] All of this transpired under watchful British eyes, yet they unbelievably still let him make military decisions as a prisoner on parole.

Lincoln also tried to facilitate an exchange for Elbert. On December 23, he wrote Washington about the matter, hoping that his influence would expedite negotiations. Although Washington had never met Elbert, he was familiar with his name through reports from

---

[28] Ibid., 186–87; Knight, *Georgia's Roster of the Revolution*, 6; "Orders Concerning Letters Sent to American Prisoners," March 21, 1782, MS 0156, Walter Cliffe Papers, Georgia Historical Society.

McIntosh, Howe, Lincoln, and others. Lincoln told Washington about an exchange of prisoners taking place at Charleston. While most of the officers and privates were free, some, he said, remained in the enemy's hands and among them was Colonel Elbert. His case was further complicated because he held two ranks. "The enemy claim a Brigadier for him," explained Lincoln, since "he was appointed Brigadier of Militia by a number of the members of the Georgia Assembly, but not by a constitutional house." Lincoln, like Howe, was impressed with Elbert's abilities as a commander. "He is a valuable officer," explained Lincoln to Washington, "and his exchange is in every view to be desired."[29]

Elbert remained a prisoner despite attempts from state leaders and Continental commanders to free him. How he passed time during his confinement is unknown. Prisoners on parole sometimes engaged in the benevolent work of community organizations they affiliated with prior to the war. Before the Revolution, Sheftall was a member of Savannah's charitable Union Society. In Sunbury's prison, he tried to keep the Union Society alive by holding meetings and fulfilling in a limited capacity the philanthropic mission of the organization. Sheftall probably participated in small Masonic meetings there as well, since many of his fellow prisoners, such as Samuel Stirk and John Martin, were members with him in Savannah's Solomon's Lodge.[30] It is hard to imagine that Elbert did not practice Freemasonry while he was a prisoner, especially since it was such a large part of his life prior to the outbreak of hostilities. As the state's only provincial grand master, he had the legal authority and obligation to keep Masonry alive and the lodge functioning in some limited capacity during the conflict.

Being on parole did not preclude Elbert's involvement in civil litigations, and he had the right to sue. In August 1779, he hired attorney William Jones to collect prewar debts owed to him by Isaac Young. The defendant died shortly after 1775, but Young's debt did not insulate his wife from Elbert's lawsuit. Public notice of the case, listing Elbert as the plaintiff, appeared in the *Royal Georgia Gazette*, but since so many Savannah records were destroyed during the Revolution, the exact amount of the debt was "lost or mislaid." The only way to determine a base figure was to examine the provost marshal's book for 1775, before

---

[29] "To George Washington from Major General Benjamin Lincoln, 23 December 1779," Founders Online.

[30] *Minutes of the Union Society*, 126; Clarke, *Leaves from Georgia Masonry*, 180.

the commencement of hostilities, which showed Young owed Elbert £633.9. That figure included the principal and interest up through December 31, 1778. Jones asked for a total judgment of £1000 to cover Elbert's attorney fees and court costs.[31] Although Elbert won his suit, nothing exists to acknowledge if he ever recovered the money.

Just as he could initiate civil litigation, Elbert also found himself on the other side of the equation. In December, Storr and Reid, a Savannah firm on Johnson's Square, sued Elbert for defaulting on loans prior to the Revolution. Notice of the action appeared on December 16 in the *Royal Georgia Gazette*. The firm specifically sought to obtain the town lot containing Rae's, Elbert & Graham to satisfy the debt. Furthermore, his first business partner in the 1760s, Samuel Douglass, was now a partner in Storr and Reid. It could be that some of the debt was what Elbert previously owed Douglass. Political motivation may have also played a role since Douglass soon represented St. David's Parish as a member of Wright's Assembly. Regardless, several of Savannah's businesses took the opportunity of a restored royal government to collect money from defaulting individuals and firms, especially those formally owned by rebels. Little wonder, then, that Storr and Reid also filed suit in a separate case against James Habersham Jr. and his firm.[32] In a broader sense, the Storr and Reid case showed that pre-Revolution debts did not just vaporize because of the conflict. As Elbert discovered, they continued through the war and remained valid beyond it, with accrued interest.

While on parole, most officers had little access to their wealth if they had any left at all. John Habersham struggled to find money for daily necessities as he waited for an exchange. Frustrated, the major wrote Lincoln to complain about the problem. He desired, he said, "a weekly allowance to be paid the officers in lieu of rations." If that happened, he hoped the officers could better "pay for their washing and other trifling but unavoidable contingencies." Elbert, like Habersham, worried about money. While he no longer kept an order book, he did keep an account book. In it, he calculated that Congress owed him, between August 18, 1779, and April 18, 1780, $4,000 for his service as a colonel commanding a nonexistent Continental Line.[33]

---

[31] *Royal Georgia Gazette*, August 19, 1779, 4.

[32] Ibid., December 16, 1779, 2. For Douglass, see C. C. Jones Jr., *History of Georgia*, 2:419.

[33] John Habersham to Benjamin Lincoln, February 21, 1779, Historic Augusta,

The state was also financially obligated to Elbert. On December 1, elections for a new constitutional General Assembly authorized by Wereat and the Supreme Council took place. The new assembly promptly elected Howley as governor on January 4, 1780, thus continuing the same Walton coalition in government dominated by upstate radicals. As governor, Howley faced insurmountable challenges, including a worthless currency, a depleted military, and renewed British threats to reoccupy Augusta. In early February, for safety precautions, the assembly relocated the seat of government to Heard's Fort in the Wilkes County backwoods. It was during this chaotic time that Howley sent Elbert a receipt on February 3 for an eleven-month salary of $6,600 as brigadier general of the state's militia. The receipt was nothing more than a promissory note since the state had no means to fulfill the obligation. In May, when the British retook Augusta and Charleston fell, the assembly went into exile and Howley fled to Philadelphia. By then, the state's currency was in such a state of depreciation that it cost the governor $500,000 just to make the trip to Pennsylvania. After May 1780, explained Coleman, "the whereabouts or existence of the Georgia state government is unknown," at least until June 1781. "State government was in default and it was every man for himself," he wrote.[34] For Elbert, that meant that his salary, like the government who promised it, was in a state of limbo.

As a prisoner, Elbert still possessed chattel, mostly through Rae's, Elbert & Graham, and he had enough financial resources to hire an overseer. Those slaves, along with others belonging to Robert Rae, were likely at Rae's Hall. Desperate for hard money to maintain his chattel and pay the overseer, an advertisement in the *Royal Georgia Gazette* on January 13, from someone desiring between ten and five hundred cords of firewood, probably caught his attention. Not long afterwards, Elbert began providing firewood to customers. The backbreaking work of felling trees and chopping them into logs was enough to exert any fit person. Elbert, however, was not healthy. As a prisoner, he suffered through bouts of sickness that represented the beginning of a general

---

Incorporated Collection of Revolutionary and Early Republic Era Manuscripts, MS 1701, folder 3, pg. 17, Georgia Historical Society; Account Book, 1769–1788, 17–18, Samuel Elbert Papers, Rubenstein Rare Book and Manuscript Library.

[34] Samuel Elbert Receipt for Brigadier General's Subsistence Allowance, February 3, 1780, in the Preston Davie Collection, #3406, Southern Historical Collection; Cook, *Governors of Georgia*, 37–39; K. Coleman, *American Revolution in Georgia*, 161.

decline in his health. Due to his newfound health issues, and because of his gentleman status, Elbert performed little of the manual labor associated with his new venture. Instead, he used his slaves and probably his servant, under supervision from the overseer, to cut and haul the wood. Elbert's records indicated that he purchased his overseer a jacket for $150 and paid him a monthly wage during the first months of 1780. At the same time, his account book was full of references about the firewood he sold around Savannah. On March 18, he sent his close friend Joseph Habersham two cords for $50. Three weeks later, on April 1, he supplied him another cord, followed by a third load a week later. On March 21, he sold Joseph Kershaw four cords for $50, and, on April 7, he took another cord to Doctor Charlton at the hospital in Savannah. To further increase his earnings, he hired out slaves and wagons for full and half days to community locals.[35]

Some of the chattel Elbert used to cut wood were possibly eight inherited by his minor daughters in Robert Rae's will. Rae suddenly died in October 1779, around the time of the ill-fated siege of Savannah. His death shocked Elbert. Through the years, the men enjoyed a special relationship. In addition to being his wife's uncle, Rae was also a longtime business partner. Before the war, they carried on the fur trade with the Indians and operated joint cowpens as part of their firm. During the Revolution, Rae worked with Whig Indian commissioner George Galphin to build alliances with the Creeks. He also served as a colonel in the 3rd Battalion of Elbert's Continentals. Rae held the brigadier general in high esteem. In his will, he referred to Elbert twice as "my good friend" and bequeathed to him his "best Riding Horse." Leonard Marbury, Rae's other "good friend" received his "next best Riding Horse." Rae also named Elbert and Marbury as two of his executors.[36]

While Rae identified himself as an Augusta planter, he was also the owner of Rae's Hall plantation. After John Rae Jr.'s death in 1777, Jane Somerville, his sister, inherited it. She barely had the plantation a year before she died, and ownership passed to her uncle, Robert, who held it for about the same amount of time before his death. According to his will, Rae's Hall passed to his wife, Rebecca, for the rest of her

---

[35] *Royal Georgia Gazette*, January 13, 1780, 2; Account Book, 1769–1788, 41–47, Samuel Elbert Papers, Rubenstein Rare Book and Manuscript Library.

[36] Will of Robert Rae, October 13, 1779, Chatham Wills, Volumes A–B, 1775–1787, 31–35; G. F. Jones, "Portrait of an Irish Entrepreneur," 447.

life. After she died, he willed the plantation to his nephew, James Rae, and to his sister, Deborah Armstrong, both of whom still lived in Ireland.[37] By this point, Elbert and his wife could no longer entertain hopes of ever owning Rae's Hall.

As Elbert sold firewood, Congress debated the complications surrounding his release. In January, Lincoln wrote Samuel Huntington, president of the Continental Congress, informing him about the state of exchanges in the Southern Department. There was a recent general exchange of noncommissioned officers and privates, he said, leaving the British indebted with 106 men to the United States. For commissioned officers, however, there was only a partial exchange. That left many, like Elbert and Sheftall, still prisoners. On February 7, Huntington wrote Washington at his winter headquarters in Morristown, New Jersey, enclosing Lincoln's letter and apprising him of Elbert's predicament. He then brought the matter up before Congress, hoping that body could facilitate his release. The problem was that the British demanded a brigadier general in return for Elbert. While Elbert was a brigadier general in the state militia, that position was not considered equal to the same rank in either the Continental or British armies. In other words, the Americans would give up a high-ranking British officer in return for a militia brigadier general of lesser rank. Such an exchange favored the British and set a bad precedent for future cartels. The logical answer was for Congress to make Elbert a brigadier general in the Continental Army, but that move created its own problems. Promoting someone to facilitate an exchange ignored the established criteria of seniority and merit. For these reasons, Congress, on February 11, refused to promote Elbert and instead encouraged Washington to negotiate terms for his release with British authorities.[38]

Things did not get any better for Elbert as 1780 continued. He surely noticed Savannah's deteriorated condition due to the effects of war, and what he saw disheartened him. Destroyed by bombs and fires during the siege, many homes and buildings he once knew were now only piles of rubble. British soldiers did their share of the damage, too, dismantling structures for construction material to create defensive

---

[37] Will of Robert Rae, October 13, 1779, Chatham Wills, Volumes A–B, 1775–1787, 31–35.

[38] "To George Washington from Samuel Huntington, 7 February 1780," Founders Online, and To George Washington from Samuel Huntington, 12 February 1780," Founders Online.

works. A grand jury in June presented a list of grievances showing the city's pitiful condition. The odors must have been putrefying due to the "filth of the streets and the many slaughter houses in the town." Burials were no longer confined to cemeteries set aside for that purpose. Instead, gravesites were scattered everywhere "in various parts of the town, & its environs." The town's wells were in a "ruinous condition" and the roads and bridges in disarray. Even the soldier barracks no longer existed after the damage caused during the siege, forcing British troops to turn the homes of rebels into their quarters. Looters stole or destroyed much of the private property in residences so that hardly anything of value remained, including important papers and documents, destroyed by fires and scavengers.[39]

On July 1, Wright and his assembly passed a Disqualifying Act, punishing 151 of the province's most notorious "rebels" for their "audacious, wicked and unprovoked rebellion." It was the toughest piece of legislation passed during the restoration period. The list of names in the document read like an honor roll of Georgia's Revolutionary heroes and included Elbert, a "Rebel General," as the fourteenth person mentioned. He was in good company. The act also listed, among others, Lachlan McIntosh, George Walton, Joseph Clay, Leonard Marbury, Mordecai Sheftall, Seth Cuthbert, George Galphin, Joseph Habersham, James Habersham, John Stirk, Edward Telfair, Noble Wimberly Jones, Andrew Williamson, John White, Benjamin Few, and Oliver Bowen. All were disqualified from holding public office or a place of honor, trust, or profit in Georgia. Nor could they vote, sit in the assembly, or possess weapons without permission. Their former privileges would be restored only when they submitted themselves to British authority and took an oath to the king and his government, promising to "Maintain and defend" it. Elbert could only interpret the act as another blatant example of Wright's tyranny. The oath was particularly mortifying, and he refused to take it. Nothing in his constitution would ever allow him to join the enemy and betray the ideals of the noble revolution that he helped to ignite in Georgia. He despised Wright and the British government he represented. Like many captured officers, Elbert longed for the day he could return to the action and continue

---

[39] "Presentments of the Grand Jury," June 27, 1780, MS 2564, Stanford Brown Collection of Eighteenth Century Papers, Georgia Historical Society; K. Coleman, *American Revolution in Georgia*, 152.

his war against the king's forces.⁴⁰ For the time being, he humbly bore his burdens in captivity, waiting for an exchange and his own day of reckoning.

Sometimes later in the summer, after the passage of the Disqualifying Act, Elbert vanished from the province. Evidence of his absence first appeared in the *Royal Georgia Gazette* on September 7. On that day, a notification announced another lawsuit against him and several others by Samuel Douglass. Attached to the suit were the lands, tenements, goods, chattels, debts, and account books of the defendants, who were "absent from and without the limits of the said province." If they did not return to Georgia within a specified time, declared the notice, a judgment would pass against them by default.⁴¹

Where was Elbert during late summer 1780? Evidence suggests that the British placed some American prisoners from Savannah and Sunbury in Charleston. The siege in Savannah led to the relocation of Sunbury's prisoners. A vessel carrying Mordecai Sheftall and his son, Sheftall, left Sunbury for Charleston in October, but a vicious storm blew them off course and caused the pilot to change his destination. Instead of reaching Charleston, it docked at Antigua in the West Indies and dropped the prisoners off there. According to Mordecai Sheftall, all of the prisoners experienced squalid and inhumane conditions on the island. Another prisoner with them sent a letter to Huntington, presiding over the Continental Congress, begging lawmakers to "endeavor to facilitate our exchange." The situation of the "unfortunate men" housed there was deplorable and "twenty of our [fellow prisoners are] in goals [*sic*]," he said.⁴² Their number did not include Elbert, who, fortunately for him, never went to Antigua.

When Lincoln surrendered his army in Charleston to Sir Henry Clinton on May 12, the British took 5,611 American prisoners. They placed the officers at Haddrell's Point outside of the city and housed them in barracks. The rest of the Continental Army ended up on prison ships anchored in the harbor. To gather American officers into one place, those in Savannah most likely went to Haddrell's Point, across

---

⁴⁰ British Disqualifying Act, July 1, 1780, in *RRG*, 1:348–63; Hall, *Land and Allegiance*, 102; Borick, *Relieve Us of This Burthen*, 54.

⁴¹ *Royal Georgia Gazette*, September 7, 1780, 3.

⁴² Mordecai Sheftall Memorial, Mordecai Sheftall Papers, 1780–1796, MS 725, Georgia Historical Society; John Huntington to Samuel Huntington [?], December 16, 1779, MS 0410, Samuel Huntington Papers, Georgia Historical Society.

from Charleston on Sullivan's Island, where they joined other commanders captured with Lincoln's army. John Habersham, a prisoner with Elbert in Savannah, was at Haddrell's Point in August, where he got into trouble for violating his parole by corresponding with patriots in the interior. No doubt Elbert and his servant were there, too, along with 320 other paroled officers, according to a British report on August 7.[43]

Life at Haddrell's Point was much more restrictive than it was in Savannah. While officers still had servants, stricter rules limited their freedom. To travel into Charleston, for example, they now needed a pass. They could never go beyond six miles from the point, which they traveled by foot since the British confiscated their horses. Roll calls occurred every morning and evening, and any officer caught attempting to escape could expect long confinement on a prison ship. Even writing letters to the interior, as did Habersham, breached the terms of parole. Sickness plagued both officers and men, and many died during their incarceration. Many of the sick who went to the hospital to recover never returned alive; Moultrie, himself a prisoner at Haddrell's Point, informed Congress that the facility was "truly distressing."[44]

Months went by as Elbert waited for some positive word about his release, but no good news came forth. At times, he must have felt abandoned and maybe even forgotten. That was not the case, however. The same assembly that made Howley governor also selected Walton as a delegate to the Continental Congress. While in Congress, Walton wrote Washington on November 11 hoping to accelerate Elbert's exchange. The congressman reminded the general that the captured Georgian was a "Colonel and principal Officer in the line of the State, and Brigadier-general of the militia." He wanted to know if Washington, through his communication with British authorities, was close to negotiating terms for Elbert's release. If so, Walton wanted to inform Congress of any new developments regarding his confinement.[45] Washington's sway with Clinton to broker a deal for Elbert only went so far, and the British general seemed unwavering in his insistence that only a

---

[43] D. Wilson, *Southern Strategy*, 234; Borick, *Relieve Us of This Burthen*, 56–57.

[44] J. Money, town major, to William Moultrie, June 30, 1780, in *MMAR*, 2:122–23, and, in the same source, "Orders Received from the Commandant," August 6, 1780, 137, and William Moultrie to the President of Congress [Huntington], June 30, 1780, 129.

[45] George Walton to George Washington, November 11, 1780, in P. Smith, *Letters of Delegates to Congress*, 16:324.

brigadier general would be acceptable as an equal exchange.

Elbert was still a prisoner at Haddrell's Point at the beginning of 1781. As he waited for some breakthrough in negotiations, his personal estate left behind in Savannah was shattered under the heels of royal government. Without any access to Savannah's newspaper, he probably never knew about the numerous legal proceedings against him. In a way, his experience was similar to that of his father, William, who fled trustee Georgia to South Carolina in 1742 and lost, unknowingly, his town lot in a public auction. The difference was that Elbert's father left Savannah voluntarily. Samuel Elbert was in a forced exile, and his father's losses paled in comparison to his own. Even if he knew about the lawsuits stacked against him, he was unable to return to Savannah and defend his financial interests.

On March 8, the *Royal Georgia Gazette* published a notice that two hundred acres at Ácton in Christ Church Parish, formally belonging to Elbert, was subject to a marshal's sale at St. James's Square on March 21 at precisely ten o'clock. That same notice listed five hundred acres, more or less, known as Rae's Hall and containing a "dwelling house" as well as an additional two hundred acres on the upper end of Hutchinson Island, formerly belonging to James Rae, also for sale. This was certainly land John Rae, Elbert's deceased father-in-law, owned prior to his death. The "dwelling house" reference, however, seemed inadequate for a description of the plantation mansion now occupied by Rebecca Rae, Robert Rae's widow. Two new lawsuits appeared in the same issue of the newspaper. One was from a man named Robertson against the survivors of Rae's, Elbert & Graham, probably related to pre-war debts accumulated by the firm. The other was by Sarah Odingfell against Elbert personally, but the nature of that suit is unknown. On May 24, the marshal seized an additional Savannah town lot owned by Elbert and put it up for auction.[46]

As Elbert's former world in Savannah unraveled, his exchange drew nigh. While negotiations released some American prisoners in Charleston, a general exchange never occurred until nearly a year after the city's fall. Finally, on May 3, 1781, British commander Lieutenant-General Lord Charles Cornwallis and American Major General Nathanael Greene came to an agreement for a sweeping prisoner exchange. Elbert's special circumstance required the American

---

[46] *Royal Georgia Gazette*, March 8, 1781, 3, 6, and May 24, 1781, 3.

commissioners to yield on their position and Clinton got what he always wanted, which was a brigadier general in the British army in return for a brigadier general in the militia. In June, the Americans traded brigadier general James Inglis Hamilton for Elbert.[47]

Thus, after two years and three months as a prisoner of war, Elbert was finally a free man. During his confinement, he experienced tremendous emotional stress watching his own men suffer, but he was powerless to ease their burdens or even his own. The long period of separation from his wife and children must have been unbearable. On top of that, the revolution that he nurtured and led appeared lost, at least in Georgia and South Carolina. Lost too, were his once lucrative businesses and vast tracts of property. Almost everything he owned or cherished, except his home, was gone. This was the price of Elbert's revolution.

Elbert could restore many of his financial losses if America won the war. There was another loss, however, that bore lasting effects. While a prisoner, Elbert sacrificed his health. Contagious diseases like smallpox, measles, and tuberculosis ran rampant through cramped prison ships and overcrowded and unclean hospitals. Once, while in Savannah, both he and his servant became sick, probably from a contagious illness. The servant nearly lost his life. Evidently, something disastrous happened to Elbert's health during his imprisonment. When first taken prisoner after Brier Creek, he was healthy except for occasional bouts with minor maladies mentioned in his Order Book. It is possible that he had contracted tuberculosis in the closely confined environment of prison ships and hospitals because, after his release, Elbert frequently struggled with health problems that incapacitated him for long periods and that intensified over time. In short, Elbert sacrificed almost everything to free his country from the tyranny of a governor and of a king. As it turned out, his life also became part of that price of freedom.

The Cartel Articles stated that the delivery of prisoners in Charleston should occur on or before June 15 and that they would sail immediately under a flag of truce to Jamestown in Virginia for the exchanges. Some of the freed officers went to Pennsylvania, recalled Moultrie, while others stayed in Virginia. Instead of returning to

---

[47] "Articles of a Cartel," May 3, 1781, in *MMAR*, 2:198–200; C. C. Jones Jr., *Samuel Elbert*, 35.

Georgia, Elbert struck out for Annapolis, Maryland, but for good reason. He knew that just before his release, on April 9, Wright's Assembly passed an Act of Attainder, accusing several prominent Whig leaders of high treason for carrying out a "detestable and unnatural Insurrection" against the king's government. The list of those who were "Wickedly and Traiterously engaged" in rebellion included twenty-four people, and the ninth person mentioned was "Samuel Elbert, Rebel General." Additional esteemed revolutionaries accused of treason included McIntosh, Howley, Walton, Jones, Bowen, Clay, Wereat, Few, Telfair, and Hall. Apparently, every person named was out of the province. The act required that they return by October 9, stand trial for treason, and forfeit their estates to a marshal's sale. The money gained from the sale went to settle lawsuits against the person who formerly owned the estate and toward the financial relief of his wife and children if they remained in Georgia and took a loyalty oath to the king. The rest went into the Treasury to finance royal government.[48] Returning to Georgia had fatal consequences for Elbert. Everyone knew that the penalty for treason was death.

Some of Elbert's Revolutionary friends from Georgia, such as Leonard Marbury and Edward Telfair, one of Georgia's delegates to the Continental Congress, were also in Maryland. Accused of treason under the Act of Attainder, Telfair dared not show his face in Wright's colony. Wright had a particular disdain for Telfair, just as he did for Elbert. Associated with the "liberty crowd" that the royal governor despised, Telfair was among those with Joseph Habersham who broke into the king's magazine in Savannah during 1775 and stole all of the powder. He was also a member of the Council of Safety, along with Elbert, who directed the course of the Revolution during its early phase. He became a delegate to the Continental Congress in 1778 and then again from 1780 to 1782. The lone piece of evidence linking the two in 1781 exists in Elbert's account book. There Elbert listed several dealings with the congressman between March and November 1781. In March, for example, while still a prisoner in Charleston, he hired out a wagon to Telfair, perhaps to help carry his belongings from Georgia to Maryland. In June 1781, shortly after his release, Elbert sold him a black horse. That Elbert was in Maryland suggests Telfair was there, too.

---

[48] "Articles of a Cartel," May 3, 1781, in *MMAR*, 2:199–200; Charlton, "Sketch of the Life of General Elbert," 2; British Act of Attainder, April 9, 1781, in *RRG*, 1:364–70.

After Yorktown, when Elbert was in Annapolis, he hired out another wagon to Telfair on November 10 to draw bricks, maybe to build a house or barn. Just nine days later, he again hired out a wagon to him so he could "draw furniture to the country."[49] Elbert and Telfair would soon become business partners, but it was during those uncertain Maryland days in 1781 where they rekindled a friendship dating back to 1774 and 1775.

Meanwhile, Elbert's ordeal in Georgia was not over. The same Robertson who sued him earlier in the year went after the survivors of Rae's, Elbert & Graham again in August. He also sued Telfair at the same time. The notice appeared on August 16 in the *Royal Georgia Gazette*. To settle debts with the plaintiff, Robertson's lawyer sought another town lot belonging to Elbert, sixty feet wide in the front and ninety feet deep, known as Number 7. This was Elbert's home lot in Tything Decker Ward on Ellis Square that he inherited from William Calvert. Robertson also sued for an additional parcel of land at Yamacraw, possibly tied to Elbert's firm, which was a loading dock three hundred feet wide in front and extending to the tidal low water mark along the Savannah.[50]

Elbert probably did not know about this latest blow to the last vestiges of his property. Free to take up arms again, he sought the first opportunity to vindicate his honor and save his country. During spring 1781, Greene lured Cornwallis with the bulk of his British force into North Carolina where both armies clashed at Guilford Courthouse on March 15. After a two-hour battle, Greene ordered a retreat. The battle was far from a glorious victory for Cornwallis since his army suffered significant casualties. After the battle, the Americans fell back into South Carolina while Cornwallis's army, numbering over eight thousand men, limped into the North Carolina port of Wilmington where they stayed briefly before striking out toward Virginia. The vanguard of Cornwallis's army entered Williamsburg around the time of Elbert's exchange. There, the British commander received instructions from Clinton to set up base in Yorktown on the peninsula between the York and James Rivers and await the arrival of a British supply fleet. By the end of July, Cornwallis's whole army was bottled up in Yorktown.[51]

---

[49] White, *Historical Collections of Georgia*, 217; Account Book, 1769–1788, 63, Samuel Elbert Papers, Rubenstein Rare Book and Manuscript Library.

[50] *Royal Georgia Gazette*, August 16, 1781, 5.

[51] Middlekauff, *Glorious Cause*, 560–61.

Washington, facing Clinton in New York, was aware of Cornwallis's presence at Yorktown. He also learned that a large French fleet under Admiral de Grasse was sailing from the West Indies toward the Chesapeake. The American commander reacted immediately, slipped his army away from Clinton, and headed quickly toward Virginia, hoping to catch Cornwallis on the peninsula and cut off his escape routes by land and sea. When Washington's army arrived at Williamsburg on September 28, it numbered almost 19,000 men, nearly half of which were French troops commanded by Comte de Rochambeau. By the end of the day, most of the Allied army was within two or three miles of Yorktown.[52]

Sometimes after September 28, Elbert appeared at Washington's headquarters in Yorktown and offered his services. Aware of Elbert's bravery, abilities as a commander, and sacrifices for his country, Washington named him the "Superintendent of Materials in the Trenches," a position of great trust and honor since it gave the Georgian authority over the "grand deposit of arms and military stores." Meeting Washington in person was truly one of the highlights of Elbert's life. After all, he once referred to him as "that great and good man."[53] The appointment immediately put Elbert in Washington's inner circle where he fraternized with some of the most important commanders in the American army. Among them was Lincoln, whom Elbert already knew. For the first time, he met Henry Knox, Washington's chief of artillery. He must have loved conversations about military discipline and the art of training soldiers with Baron von Steuben, a Prussian officer in the army of Frederick the Great who came to America and became the drillmaster of the Continental Army. The inner circle also included Anthony Wayne, who soon helped retake Georgia from the British, and Lieutenant Colonel Alexander Hamilton, Washington's former secretary in command of units from New York and Connecticut. Elbert became acquainted with Rochambeau and several other French officers, too. However, the person who most impressed him, beyond Washington, was the Marquis de Lafayette and the men struck up a friendship. Lafayette so captivated Elbert that he later named one of his children after him.

---

[52] Ibid., 563–66.
[53] C. C. Jones Jr., *Samuel Elbert*, 35; H. Johnston, *Yorktown Campaign*, 112; Samuel Elbert to Captain Francis Moore, July 31, 1777, in OBSE, 51.

From the moment he arrived at Yorktown, Washington placed the city under siege, and Cornwallis's trapped army had no way to escape. De Grasse's fleet commanded the vast York River behind the city, cutting it off from British naval vessels sent by Clinton. The vessels carried reinforcements but didn't arrive in time to make a difference. The American lines formed a semicircle in front of Yorktown. Rochambeau commanded the French troops on the left side of the allied position while the Americans occupied the right. On October 6, sappers opened up the first parallel, or trench, six hundred yards southwest of the town in the American lines. During the night, 1,500 men dug the trench and threw the dirt toward the town, forming an embankment to protect them from enemy fire. Nearly 2,800 soldiers stood close by to guard them from any attack by the British. Under heavy enemy fire, workers constructed earthen redoubts protected with palisades along the first parallel and erected five batteries for Knox's artillery. When completed, the first parallel was two thousand yards long.[54] This was the first time that Elbert observed the creation of elaborate earthworks during the Revolution. He surely marveled as engineers laid out the trenches and workers formed the redoubts and batteries. Throughout the war, Elbert practically begged for entrenchment tools that always seemed in short supply. At Yorktown, they were in abundance.

Elbert's responsibilities in the trenches expanded on October 11 when the second parallel opened some three hundred yards from British lines. Workers rapidly dug all night to form a ditch three feet deep and seven feet wide. Two British redoubts on the southeastern section of their lines prevented an extension of the second parallel to the York River. On the night of October 14, American and French units stormed both strongholds and took them. Engineers incorporated the works into the second parallel and then pushed the trench to the river's edge. Two days later, Allied batteries began a destructive bombardment of the town. Faced with the helplessness of his situation, Cornwallis sent out a white flag of surrender on October 17.[55]

The formal capitulation took place on October 18 as 7,247 British soldiers and 840 seamen marched out of Yorktown's defenses and surrendered to French and American commanders, including Elbert.[56]

---

[54] Ward, *War of the Revolution*, 2:889–90.
[55] Ibid., 2:890–94.
[56] Ibid., 2:894–95.

Yorktown was Washington's greatest moment; it signaled the end of the Revolution although the war continued until 1783. To Elbert, Yorktown was highly symbolic. Just as it was for Washington, it was Elbert's greatest moment, too, and he shared it in the presence of the person he most admired. It also represented the dawning of his own day of reckoning. The road ahead was full of honors, but before he traveled down it, royal government in his state had to collapse for a second and final time. Only then, could he return to Georgia and rebuild his life from the ashes of victory.

Chapter 13

Land and Laurels: Samuel Elbert and the Consolidation of the Revolution in Georgia, 1781–1784

After Yorktown, Elbert headed to Annapolis, Maryland, joining other Georgians already there, such as Leonard Marbury and Congressman Edward Telfair. Returning home was not an option since Governor Wright and his Loyalists controlled the province. Wright's Royal Assembly also accused the men of treason and demanded their immediate presence to stand trial for rebellious acts against the king. Faced with that grim prospect, Elbert remained away from Georgia until conditions improved.

It was a wise decision. Gradually stripped of his property, almost all that remained of Elbert's pre-war estate were a number of chattel tied to Rae's, Elbert's & Graham likely located at Rae's Hall. On October 4, 1781, while Elbert was at Yorktown, Lewis Johnston, the junior provost marshal, announced in the *Royal Georgia Gazette* that he seized a plantation with 650 acres called Rae's Hall. That land, he publicized, was subject to a sheriff's sale on October 15, as were 31 slaves there belonging to Elbert, Robert Rae, James Rae, and Joseph Habersham, to be auctioned just over two weeks later. Charles C. Jones, writing in the late nineteenth century, observed that the Revolution in Georgia swept away at least half of the property owned by the inhabitants.[1] In Elbert's case, his loss was nearly total.

In December 1781, while in Maryland, Elbert received a summons to appear as a witness in the court-martial of his former commander, General Robert Howe, for his lackluster performance when Savannah fell on December 29, 1778. The trial, held in Philadelphia, was presided over by General Baron von Steuben, one of Washington's commanders Elbert met at Yorktown. George Walton spearheaded the movement to prosecute

---

[1] *Royal Georgia Gazette*, October 4, 1781, 4, and, in the same source, November 3, 1781, 3; C. C. Jones Jr., *History of Georgia*, 2:522.

Howe on behalf of the state back in January 1780. Then, the Georgia Assembly requested an investigation into Howe's conduct because his actions sacrificed the state to the enemy and led to the "distresses and consequences which ensued." By ordering the evacuation of Augusta and Sunbury, they accused Howe of leaving Georgia defenseless and without the benefit of any Continental troops.[2] Walton's motive to punish Howe was largely personal. After all, he held him responsible for a broken hip he sustained in the battle that still caused him to walk with a limp, in addition to his subsequent capture and imprisonment. Walton felt the same sort of animosity toward Howe as Elbert did toward John Ashe, whose mismanagement at the battle of Brier Creek resulted in the Georgian's injury and long ordeal in a British prison camp.

When the trial began on December 7, 1781, neither Elbert nor Marbury, who was also summoned, was present. Despite Elbert's absence, the hearings went ahead, and the court took testimony from several witnesses, including Walton, Mordecai Sheftall, and John Wereat. Walton's testimony, spread over a couple of days, was an effort to discredit Howe and portray his leadership in the worst possible light. On January 4, 1782, nearly a month after the trial began, von Steuben received a letter from Telfair and Noble Wimberly Jones, another Georgia delegate in the Continental Congress, informing him that Elbert's "indisposition" would likely prevent his attendance as evidence in the case against Howe. In their letter, they enclosed a certificate from doctors attending Elbert saying that he was too sick to travel, but they did not specify his illness. Despite his weakened state, Elbert defied doctors' orders and hired out two wagons from Thomas Wilson for £15.15. In those wagons, the unhealthy commander traveled to Philadelphia, and on January 12 he appeared before the court.[3]

If Walton hoped to use Elbert to vilify Howe, he was sorely disappointed. The opposite happened, and the Georgian's testimony vindicated the general. Elbert found no fault in Howe's command decisions. However, he suggested on a couple of occasions that Governor John Houstoun's and the General Assembly's refusal to cooperate with his superior's repeated requests to strengthen Savannah's defenses, give him control over the militia, and provide Georgia's battalions with entrenching

---

[2] *CNYHS*, Evidence, State of Georgia in Assembly, January 17, 1780, 217–18.

[3] Ibid., December 8, 1781, 221, and, in the same source, Edward Telfair and Noble Wimberly Jones to Baron von Steuben, January 4, 1782, 243; Baron von Steuben to Edward Telfair and Noble Wimberly Jones, 244; Account Book, 1769–1788, 65, Samuel Elbert Papers, Rubenstein Rare Book and Manuscript Library.

tools all figured prominently in the city's capture. After a detailed recounting of the events on that fateful day, including the retreat of his battalions through the city and their capture at Musgrove Creek, Elbert concluded his testimony and headed back to Maryland. After his departure, the trial continued for another week. Finally, on January 21, the last day of the hearing, an angry Howe spoke in his own defense. For most of his rebuttal, the general ripped holes in Walton's sworn statements and at times even mocked him. For Elbert, though, he had only kind and uplifting words and referred to him as "my friend." He approved of Elbert's account of the battle and felt his statements "justified" him against Walton's charges. Howe heaped praise upon his junior commander, calling him a "deserving officer" whose "spirit and abilities have served his country." He and Elbert enjoyed a close friendship for a length of time, he said, and in military matters, they were like-minded and seldom differed in opinion. He regarded Elbert's advice and assistance invaluable and felt indebted to the Georgia officer. After Howe finished his defense, those presiding over the trial deliberated for a short time and then, to Walton's embarrassment, exonerated the general of all charges.[4]

As Elbert recuperated in Annapolis, Wright's situation in Georgia deteriorated. When Cornwallis evacuated South Carolina early in 1781, he took many of the British regulars in Savannah with him except about five hundred Hessians commanded by Colonel von Porbeck. Augmenting the Hessian garrison were an additional 350 Loyalist militia scattered throughout the backcountry and an unknown number of Indian allies. The occupation army in Charleston also shuffled British regulars back and forth to Savannah, but their numbers were never large. Collectively, the whole force was inadequate to protect the entire province, and, by spring 1781, Rebel militia again controlled Wilkes County and most of the area around Augusta. On June 5, after a siege of nearly two weeks, Thomas Brown's Augusta garrison surrendered to American forces commanded by Henry "Lighthorse" Lee and Andrew Pickens. About forty miles away, on the Ogeechee River, some 1,500 Creek warriors were heading to assist Brown. Had he known of their presence, he probably would have held out a little longer before surrendering. The loss of Augusta, coupled with rebel dominance in the backcountry, spelled doom for Wright's government, even though he bolstered his defense by raising three new troop of horse

---

[4] *CNYHS*, Robert Howe testimony, January 21, 1782, 297–98.

and reorganizing the King's Rangers.[5]

After the fall of Augusta, the commander of the Southern Department, Nathanael Greene, sent Joseph Clay to Augusta to reestablish a constitutional government. Those efforts produced a legally elected assembly on August 16 that in turn named Nathan Brownson governor on the following day. Brownson's short tenure ended on January 2, 1782, when the assembly selected John Martin to succeed him for a one-year term, according to the Constitution of 1777. By then, most of Georgia was in Whig hands, but the British still tenaciously clung to the area around Savannah. In early January, Green dispatched General "Mad Anthony" Wayne with a few Continentals, Virginia militia, a small number of dragoons, and an artillery unit to coordinate with Georgia and South Carolina militia to drive the British out of the state. When he crossed the Savannah River at the Two Sisters ferry on January 12, Wayne had between five and six hundred men, hardly enough to oppose the nearly one thousand British and Hessian regulars plus Loyalist militia and Indians now arrayed against him. Outnumbered nearly three to one, Wayne went on the offensive, keeping steady pressure on the enemy for the next six months as he took outposts and turned back Indians coming to aid the Savannah garrison.[6]

Despite Wayne's efforts, Savannah remained in British control. Meanwhile, the assembly, now meeting at Ebenezer on the outskirts of the city, sat in session from April 20 until May 4. On the last day of the session, it revived the earlier Confiscation and Banishment Act, naming Wright and 279 other Loyalists as enemies of the state. The assembly ordered all of their property, both real and personal, confiscated and then banished the offenders from Georgia with the warning that if they ever returned, they would suffer death without the benefit of clergy. At the urging of Greene and Wayne, the assembly softened its harsh punishment to reclaim some Loyalists as state citizens. To take advantage of the state's leniency, Loyalists had to renounce their allegiance to the king, swear an oath to the Whig government, forfeit twelve percent of their property to the state, and serve in the Georgia Continental battalion. Ultimately, most named in the act left the state

---

[5] Cashin, *King's Ranger*, 130–33, 141–44.

[6] Ibid., 138–54, *passim*; Sears, *Anthony Wayne*, 187; K. Coleman, *American Revolution in Georgia*, 136, 141–42. Coleman estimates that, based on returns at the end of 1781, there were 970 British troops in Savannah (*American Revolution in Georgia*, 163). Among them, two-thirds were Loyalists, and the rest were Hessian and British regulars.

and lost all of their property.⁷ Many others, however, renounced the British, swore allegiance to the Whigs, and performed some type of Continental service.

With Wright's government reeling, Elbert headed back to Georgia hoping to recoup at least some of his losses under the Confiscation Act. Earlier in the Revolution when the act first passed, Elbert opposed it because it unleashed multitudes of roaming Loyalists through the state. In 1782, the situation was different, and he viewed the act as a path toward rebuilding wealth in land. He probably returned, in poor health, sometime around late May or early June. The first mention of his presence in Georgia was on June 13, when he purchased 140 acres of confiscated land on the Ogeechee River for £2,947. The property, known as Point Plantation, formerly belonged to Wright and comprised part of his extensive landholdings seized by the state.⁸ The fact that it was Wright's land gave Elbert an added sense of satisfaction. He felt nothing but contempt for the besieged governor, and it was only fitting that his resurgence as a landowner should begin at Wright's expense.

Around the time that Elbert purchased Wright's Ogeechee plantation, the royal governor received instructions to abandon Savannah and surrender the province to the Whigs. Reluctantly, he obeyed the orders of his superiors. Militia colonel James Jackson received the formal surrender of the city, and on July 10 and 11, British regulars evacuated to Tybee Island. From there, several, along with Wright, went to Charleston, while others sailed to New York to rejoin the British army there. Wright returned to London. The evacuation of Loyalists and their slaves continued into summer 1785. It is impossible to determine precisely how many Loyalists left Georgia with the British, but the number may be as high as 1,500, and with them went between three and six thousand slaves.⁹

An important step in Elbert's economic recovery was the reestablishment of his businesses. In his account book, he recorded that he sold sundry items to various people, including bacon and a ham to Noble Jones for £4.6.8. He still hired out wagon teams and, due to the scarcity of hard money, sometimes accepted payments in "Maryland

---

⁷ Candler, ed., *Revolutionary Records of the State of Georgia*, 1:413; K. Coleman, *American Revolution in Georgia*, 164, 183–85.

⁸ "Sales of Confiscated Estates," in *RRG*, 1:416; Cook, *Governors of Georgia*, 56.

⁹ K. Coleman, *American Revolution in Georgia*, 183–84; Hall, *Land and Allegiance*, 162.

currency," which was tobacco. He also rented out some of his newly acquired land. For example, he let thirty acres in February 1784 to Captain Bannister Winn for £7.10. At the same time, Elbert estimated that the state still owed him £2,947 for his war services. The money generated from business and other sources enabled him to purchase more confiscated land, such as the eight acres he bought at Tybee on January 3, 1783, formerly belonging to Wright's lieutenant governor, John Graham, for £40. He also reinvested in slaves. During 1783, he employed John Thomas as his overseer. That he hired an overseer suggests that Elbert had a considerable number of slaves, probably at Point Plantation. Elbert's account book shows that he purchased many necessities for them in 1783 and 1784, including beef, pork, sugar, coffee, duff blankets, blue plain shirts, checkered shirts, thread, linen, and flannel.[10]

Finally freed of British oppression, Elbert emerged as one of the state's greatest Patriot heroes, and the honors associated with his glory flowed accordingly. In a show of respect for the commander, the General Assembly, on January 21, appointed him as a commissioner in treaty negotiations with the Cherokee over a large swath of land adjacent to and north of Wilkes County. Having ended the war with Britain, Georgians were anxious to negotiate peace with the Cherokee and Creek, but at a cost, because what they desired more than anything else was an atonement of Indian land. That was just compensation, they reckoned, for waging a brutal war along the state's frontiers as allies of the British. The horrible memories from that experience, explained one historian, "warped Georgians by the close of the war into profound and inveterate anti-Indian people" despite their words of peace and friendship.[11]

Georgians initiated efforts to get Indian land even before the war's formal conclusion, which occurred with the signing of the Treaty of Paris on September 3, 1783. Earlier in the year, the state created two delegations to negotiate with the Cherokee and Creek separately at Augusta. The Georgia Assembly gave the commissioners "full power and

---

[10] Account Book, 1769–1788, 57, 63, 70, 79, Samuel Elbert Papers, Rubenstein Rare Book and Manuscript Library; "Sales of Confiscated Estates," in *RRG*, 1:416, and, from the same source, "Journal House of Assembly," February 23, 1784, 3:546.

[11] Kokomoor, "Burning & Destroying All Before Them," 302. For Elbert's selection to the Cherokee Commission, see "Treaty of Augusta with the Cherokee," 0001-01-025, Indian Claims (Treaties and Spoilations), Governor, Record ID Ahoo888, May 25, 1783, Georgia State Archives.

authority on the part of this State, to treat, confer, and agree with the aforesaid Indian Nations, on all matters relative to a cession of a claim of land." The delegation to the Cherokee included, in addition to Elbert, newly elected governor Lyman Hall and militia commanders General John Twiggs, Colonel William Few, and Colonel Elijah Clarke. Elbert's friend, Telfair, was also a commissioner. Due to his extensive knowledge of Indians, Elbert's selection was an obvious choice. He was also close to the state's superintendent of Indian affairs, James Rae, the nephew of his late business partner, Robert Rae.[12] The delegation to the Creek included some of the same members as the Cherokee commission, like Clarke, Twiggs, and Telfair, but not Elbert. All of the delegates sought to get their hands on Indian land. Some of them, like Clarke, recently returned from a vicious campaign against the Cherokee while pursuing Loyalists, were notable Indian haters.

Andrew McLean, an Augusta merchant selected to be secretary and to keep a detailed journal of the Cherokee deliberations, was an odd choice as commissioner given his questionable loyalties during the Revolution. In 1780, when Wright came back to rule as governor, the assembly listed him on the Disqualifying Act because of his support for the Whigs. Shortly after learning that he was on the list, McLean filed a petition asking for leniency and the removal of his name. He had never carried arms or fought for the Whigs, he said; they considered him inimical to their cause. As proof, he explained that they once imprisoned him for being a friend to the king's government. He was also present with the rebel army during the siege of Savannah in 1779, but he did not participate in any of the fighting. He was only there, he claimed, to help civilians if the city fell to the Americans and French. Convinced McLean was telling the truth, Wright and his council removed his restrictions on July 24 and restored his rights. Nearly two years later, on February 2, 1782, Governor Martin issued a proclamation offering full pardon and protection for those who saw the error of their past ways. What followed was a list of exceptions that included McLean. If McLean and the others named in the proclamation surrendered to General Wayne by March 15 and served in one of his units until the enemy departed, Martin promised that the state would forgive

---

[12] "Minutes of the Executive Council," in *RRG*, 2:422–23; Journal House of Assembly, January 13, 1783, 3:213 (Rae's appointment); Journal House of Assembly, January 12, 1782, 3:75 (Daniel McMurphy).

their disloyalty.¹³ Apparently, McLean turned himself in as directed, took up arms against the British for a few months before Wright's government collapsed, and resumed his life as a citizen. Although McLean's activities during the war made him highly suspect in the eyes of many Whigs, Elbert, like Martin, forgave him too, and they soon became business partners in the Indian trade.

Noticeably absent from both state delegations was any representative from the national government. According to Article VI of the Articles of Confederation governing the new nation, which Georgia ratified in 1778, states could not make war, peace, and treaties with any foreign prince or state. Though vague in its definition of prince or state, the implication was that it also included Indian *micos* and tribes. Article IX further stated that Congress had the sole right to enter into treaties and alliances.[14] Thus, federal commissioners needed to be present during Georgia's treaty negotiations with the Indians. Georgia would have none of it although it recognized the Indian tribes as "Nations" according to the assembly's instructions to the commissioners on January 21. During the war, the assembly constantly asserted states' rights over the federal government on military matters. After the war, it followed the same pattern negotiating land treaties with Indians.

In preparation for the upcoming negotiations, Hall sent out talks to the Indians. The assembly authorized £2,840.2.9 on goods to appease them when they arrived at Augusta. The state hired interpreters, too. In total, the treaties cost the state £3,235.16.6. Word traveled fast to the *talwas* because by the end of January, some Creeks were already gathering at the Big Shoals on the Oconee. According to Rae, they were "numerous," and more were coming. He expected Lower Creek headman Hoboithle Mico, or the Tallassee King, to arrive daily. "Considerable supplies of provisions will be wanted to support them," he advised the governor, at least until the conclusion of negotiations.[15]

---

[13] *RRG*, 2:422–23, and for the Disqualifying Act, July 1, 1780, 1:355; "Council Held at His Excellency's House in Savannah," July 11, 1780, in Hawes, ed., "Proceedings and Minutes," 204–205, and, in the same source, "Council Held at His Excellency's House in Savannah," July 24, 1780, 206–207; "Proclamation of Governor John Martin," February 2, 1782, in box 38F, folder 15, Telamon Cuyler Collection, MS1170, series 1, Hargrett Rare Book and Manuscript Library. The group working with the Cherokee also included Lachlan McIntosh and John Martin, but they did not attend.

[14] *Articles of Confederation*, Article VI, Article IX.

[15] "Journal of the House of Assembly," July 31, 1783, in *RRG*, 3:398–99, and, in the same source, "Minutes of the Executive Council," January 30, 1783, 2:431.

Meanwhile, Hall's talk reached the Cherokee. He told their headmen that Georgians only sought peace. He hoped to "sit down" with them and "smoak together as friends and talk about what has happened for a great while back." The friendship Hall spoke of, however, was conditional. "We are glad that you are so well Inclined to be at Peace with us," he explained, "and that Sensible of the wrongs, which we sustained," justice required that they "mark off a piece of Land which you can very well spare."[16]

Finally, on May 1, seventeen Cherokee headmen and warriors arrived at Augusta where the Georgia delegation greeted them. There they agreed to six stipulations laid out in negotiations by Elbert and the other commissioners. An informal agreement dictated by Clarke and General Andrew Pickens after their recent Cherokee campaign, formed the basis of the treaty. The only article benefiting the Indians was the promise of renewed trade, but even that instilled a form of dependence on Whites. As Elbert and the others knew, the trade was also a weapon for gaining future Cherokee cessions. Much to Elbert's delight, the Cherokee were still liable for all debts to merchants, probably including himself, incurred through the fur trade before the war. Additionally, the Indians agreed to restore all property taken from civilians during the conflict. By far, the greatest concession made by the Cherokee involved their loss of some hunting land, partially claimed by the Creeks, to the north and west of Wilkes County. The commissioners insisted on drawing a new line up the Savannah River from the present settlements to the northernmost branch of the Keowee River. From there, it angled westward to the top of Currahee Mountain and then turned south to the sources of the southernmost branch of the Oconee, which it followed to the Creek boundary. Just over a month later, in an effort to keep peace, Hall issued a proclamation forbidding anyone from marking trees or trespassing on Indian hunting lands across the new border.[17]

---

[16] Lyman Hall to the Headmen of the Cherokee, n.d., in Journal of the Georgia Commissioners Negotiating with the Cherokee Indians at Augusta, Including the Treaty of Augusta, 001-01-025, Indian Claims (Treaties and Spoilations), Governor, RG 1-1-25, Georgia State Archives.

[17] Ibid., The Treaty of Augusta, May 1, 1783; Lyman Hall Proclamation, *Gazette of the State of Georgia*, June 26, 1783, 1. Federal commissioners confirmed the Cherokee cession in the Treaty of Hopewell, signed on November 28, 1785. See Peters, *Case of the Cherokee Nation*, 249–50.

Elbert was not present when state commissioners negotiated a separate Treaty of Augusta with a handful of representatives from the Creeks on November 1, but the agreement's terms became an issue confronting him a few years later as governor. When Neha Mico (the Fat King), Tallassee King, and a few other minor chiefs and warriors from the lower towns headed up the old "beloved path" and finally met the commissioners at Augusta, they too received presents and heard the governor's peace talk. He hoped, as did the other commissioners, that now both parties could "sit down and smoke together in friendship [and] Eat out of the same dish and drink out of the same cup." The "Hatchet shall be buried deep," he promised, "and we will take fast hold of each other by the arm." The terms of the Creek treaty were nearly identical to the agreement forced upon the Cherokee. Again, the major consideration was a Creek cession of hunting ground, in this case, the much-coveted Oconee lands. Since the Creeks also claimed some of the land the Cherokee gave up in May, the treaty confirmed that agreement as well, but then added everything between the Oconee and Apalachee River to the west. The new line continued southward to where the Oconee met the Altamaha. The whole tract was between forty and sixty miles wide and nearly two hundred miles long—some 800,000 square miles of prime hunting land. Almost all Creeks who signed the treaty were friendly toward Georgians during the war and desperate to give up land in return for promises of renewed trade and a guarantee of hunting rights in the Oconee lands. Nearly a year later, Fat King and some of his warriors went to the home of James Rae in Augusta and, in the presence of John Habersham, Walton, and Clarke, admitted as much. The Indians were glad the trade was flowing once again, he said, and since they were poor, the need for goods "was the occasion for giving up our land."[18]

The Treaty of Augusta caused problems between Georgia and the Creeks, and war talk soon followed. As pointed out by Creek leader Alexander McGillivray, neither the Fat King, the Tallassee King, nor any others with them had the authority to give up land belonging to the Indians. Because of that, McGillivray denounced the treaty as

---

[18] Articles of a Convention held at Augusta, in the County of Richmond, November 1, 1783, in Keith M. Read Collection, MS 921, Hargrett Rare Book and Manuscript Library; K. Coleman, *American Revolution in Georgia*, 239; Braund, *Deerskins & Duffels*, 171–72; "Talk Delivered by the Fat King," John Houstoun Papers, 1775–1784, MS 397, Georgia Historical Society.

invalid. Unfortunately for Georgia, McGillivray, a gifted orator who claimed a leadership position among the Creeks, held much sway over the upper towns and villages. During the Revolution, he became a bitter enemy of Georgia and cast his lot with the British. His father, Lachlan McGillivray, also had pro-British leanings and had become a notorious Loyalist. The Whigs named him on their Confiscation Act, and, as a result, the state seized his property and plantations and permanently banished him. When state commissioners in Augusta coerced a handful of Creek headmen to give up the Oconee lands for trifling presents, it only magnified McGillivray's hatred of Georgians.[19]

Both treaties delighted Georgians, who insisted they were valid, despite McGillivray's protests, and settlers poured across the Oconee to take first possession of the most fertile tracts. Clarke predicted to Hall that by spring 1784, inhabitants from other states, upon hearing of the cession, would fill the Oconee lands. "With pleasure," crowed the *Gazette of the State of Georgia* on November 13, "we inform our readers, that the Indians, at the Treaty held at Augusta, have freely, fully, and absolutely relinquished all claims or pretention to lands, late in their possession, this side of and as far as the Oconees." McGillivray vehemently disagreed. For the time, he held his warriors back, but soon they would give Georgians the Indian war they dreaded in an attempt to "repel those Invaders [from] our Lands."[20]

On February 12, 1782, Congress promoted all colonels in the Continental Army holding their rank prior to May 1777 to brigadier general. That group included Elbert, who obtained his rank on September 16, 1776. The promotion put him on par with Lachlan McIntosh, the only brigadier general of Continental forces from the state during the Revolution. However, Elbert did not receive his commission until November 4, 1783, one day after Congress disbanded the Continental Army. At the same time, the state also made him a major general over the militia. It was the highest honor Georgia could bestow upon one of its military commanders.[21] Thus, at the end of 1783, when the

---

[19] Braund, *Deerskins & Duffels*, 168–73; K. Coleman, *American Revolution in Georgia*, 239; C. C. Jones Jr., *Samuel Elbert*, 38.

[20] Elijah Clarke to Lyman Hall, November 6, 1783, in box 39, folder 13, Telamon Cuyler Collection, MS1170, series 1, Hargrett Rare Book and Manuscript Library; *Gazette of the State of Georgia*, November 13, 1783, 2; Braund, *Deerskins & Duffels*, 172.

[21] "To George Washington from Ezekiel Cornell, 12 February 1782," Founders Online. The date of Elbert's Continental commission is in the "Minutes of the Executive

Revolution was over, Elbert became a brigadier general in the nonexistent Continental Army and a major general over Georgia's militia.

On February 17, 1783, the Georgia Assembly elected Elbert to the prestigious office of surveyor of Chatham County (Savannah), a position that further cemented his already honored status within the community. As surveyor, Elbert oversaw the creation of new land tracts. He also produced maps showing property lines that gave compass directions, numerical chain readings, and corner markings on trees and rocks. He then recorded those maps and other legal documents associated with them and stored them in their appropriate locations. Since he had no surveying experience, Elbert's role was largely administrative, and he appointed deputies to operate the equipment and draw up scaled maps. A second example of Elbert's advancement in civic life occurred a year later, on April 15, when Christ Episcopal Church (formerly Anglican) in Savannah elected him to be one of its vestrymen, along with James and Joseph Habersham and Joseph Clay. That appointment reflected Elbert's character as much as it did his community standing.[22]

Elbert also became a member of the Order of the Cincinnatus. In spring 1783, General Henry Knox, one of Washington's officers, founded the order as a fraternal organization dedicated to commemorating the memories and friendships of the Revolution among Continental Army officers. Named after a hero of the Roman Republic, Lucius Quinctius Cincinnatus, who victoriously served his country during war and returned to his farm as a civilian, the order quickly grew and established branches in all thirteen states. Elbert was honored to be part of the organization, especially since Washington was president of the order. To ensure the survival of the Cincinnati beyond the war generation, it bestowed membership to the oldest male heirs. It also created a charitable fund to help financially struggling members. There were no oaths or rituals associated with the Cincinnati and no formal meeting halls. Rather, members embraced their common bond of brotherhood and shared war experiences. To display publicly their affiliation with the organization, they received a prestigious badge for their apparel, which Elbert received. They also gained access to the charitable

---

Council," March 26, 1784, in *RRG*, 2:625. *Journals of the American Congress* places the date of Elbert's commission on November 3 (4:314). Cook wrote that the state breveted Elbert as major general at the same time of his Continental commission (*Governors of Georgia*, 56).

[22] "Journal of the House of Assembly," February 17, 1783, in *RRG*, 3:302; Hitz, "Georgia Bounty Land Grants," 342; *Gazette of the State of Georgia*, April 15, 1784, 2.

fund.²³

On August 13, 1783, Georgia Continental officers gathered at Captain John Lucas's headquarters in Savannah to establish a state branch of the Cincinnati, and on the following day they elected McIntosh president and Elbert vice-president. Joseph Habersham was also a member, along with his brother, John, who became the order's assistant treasurer. During their meetings held in 1784, the Cincinnati gathered at different locations in Savannah as members sat down to reminisce, enjoy meals, and give toasts. On January 29, 1784, they gathered at Murray's Long Room in Savannah for a festive meeting full of decorum, reflecting, claimed the *Gazette of the State of Georgia*, the "honour on its members, and the community to which they particularly belong." On October 14, they met at the house of Alexander Allison. The meeting lasted from ten o'clock in the morning until three in the afternoon, after which they sat down at a large table for a fine dinner.²⁴

After the Revolution, as it did before it, social, business, and family duties made tremendous demands on Elbert's time. Even as he maintained his various obligations, his family grew in size. The precise location of his residence in Savannah after the Revolution is unknown, but wherever he and Elizabeth lived, his dwelling had to be spacious. They did not reside at his former home or Rae's Hall plantation since both were lost in sheriff's sales during Georgia's reoccupation. Rae's Hall entered a period of transition after the Revolution when the plantation and the land around it depreciated. One study suggested that it no longer functioned as a plantation, but instead as a cattle range. That conclusion rested on a property tax return in 1791, which mentioned fifty-six slaves connected to the estate, but they all resided in different counties.²⁵ The Elberts had three daughters by the end of the war; Catherine "Caty" and Elizabeth were born before the Revolution. Sarah was probably born during the late 1770s and was likely the reason Elbert renovated his Savannah home in 1777. The other three children, all sons, were born after Elbert returned to Savannah during summer 1782. The first of those, Samuel Emanuel de la Fayette, was probably born between 1782 and 1784, and the other two, Matthew and Hugh

---

²³ Hünemörder, *Society of the Cincinnati*, 16–21.

²⁴ "Georgia in the American Revolution," 27–28; Peel, ed., *Historical Collections of the Joseph Habersham Chapter*, 1:39; *Gazette of the State of Georgia*, January 29, 1784, and October 14, 1784, 3.

²⁵ Savannah Unit, Georgia Writers' Project, "Rae's Hall Plantation, Part I," 241.

Rae, during the next four years.

Elbert's first opportunity after the Revolution to engage in state politics occurred when the assembly entered its new session on January 8, 1784. After electing John Houstoun to replace Hall for a second term as governor, the assembly moved to appoint members to Congress. On the following day, the House cast ballots and chose Elbert as one of the state's congressional delegation, along with Telfair, Joseph Habersham, and William Houstoun. Elbert's choice once again showed the respect House leaders had for him. Although honored by the appointment, Elbert, on January 21, after some consideration, declined to serve. At least two historians believed that his refusal was health-related.[26]

Despite health issues, Elbert remained focused on his business affairs and in particular, the Indian trade. As Georgia's political leaders knew, the trade was a vital component in maintaining peace with the Indians, especially after the 1783 Augusta treaties with the Cherokee and Creek, in which they promised a steady flow of goods in exchange for land. Unlike the trading arrangements before the Revolution that rested on deerskins and beaver pelts, the postwar trade was different. Frankly, Georgians were not interested in the decades-old deerskin trade after the Revolution. What motivated them more than anything else was keeping the Indians peaceful through presents as they sought additional avenues to acquire more of their land. As Georgia historian Edward Cashin observed, the "century-old British policy of trading with the Indians ended [after the Revolution] and a century-long policy of Indian removal began."[27]

While the Cherokee accepted the terms of Georgia's Treaty of Augusta with them, the majority of the Creeks, under McGillivray's influence, balked. Timothy Barnard, an old fur trader from Augusta with earlier ties to Brown, (John) Rae, & Company before the Revolution and one of the state's Indian agents and interpreters in 1784, sounded a warning of potential trouble coming from Creek country. "I believe they [the Creeks] are set on by the Spaniards and others not to let the Ockonie Lands be settled by the Americans," he informed Major Patrick Carr, one of the state's militia commanders. Already, some war

---

[26] "Journal House of Assembly," January 9, 1784, in *RRG*, 3:426; "Journal House of Assembly," January 21, 1784, in *RRG*, 3:455. Those historians were Cook, *Governors of Georgia*, 56, and Purcell, "Public Career of Samuel Elbert," 74.

[27] Braund, *Deerskins & Duffels*, 170; Ethridge described the new world of the Creek Indian trade after the war (*Creek Country*, 175).

parties were organizing for raids. "Two gangs set [off] from the upper towns to doe mischief," he wrote, "but were turned back by some of the head men." He also noted that the Spaniards were calling for Creek leaders from upper and lower towns to attend a great meeting in May at Pensacola.[28]

The Spanish connection mentioned by Barnard had much to do with McGillivray. According to the Treaty of Paris, Britain gave up East and West Florida to Spain, who now sought to assert their influence over the southeastern tribes, and they courted McGillivray as part of their effort. Southern tribes threatened Georgia's border security. The Creeks imperiled the Oconee frontier while the Choctaw and Chickasaw posed their own threats in the Yazoo lands to the west along the Mississippi River, which the state also claimed. McGillivray had his own reasons for cooperating with Spain, including access to weapons and the bolstering of leadership claims among his own people, even as he fought to preserve Creek territory from land-hungry Georgians. In summer 1784, he offered his services to Spain and negotiated a treaty to reestablish a relationship between them and the Creeks. At the same time, he signed a document outlining his duties as a Spanish commissioner that included a pledge to keep the Creeks subordinated to Spain. All the while, he routinely denied the validity of the Treaty of Augusta and called the Tallassee King who negotiated it a "roving beggar, going wherever he thinks he can get presents."[29]

Frontier vagrants further stoked tensions between Georgia and the Creeks through unlawful acts such as murder. In April 1784, the Fat King and some of his attendants met in Augusta with John Habersham, Hall, Walton, and Clarke at the home of James Rae, who also attended. The headman was upset and demanded satisfaction for the murder of one of his people by rogue settlers, or, as Hall earlier described them, "ignorant and ill designing men." On April 5, he gave a talk at Rae's residence detailing his complaints against Georgia since the Treaty of Augusta. Beyond violent acts perpetrated by lawless Whites upon the Creeks, the Fat King expressed disappointment at the quantity of goods flowing to the lower towns. Just two months earlier, Georgia's commissioners promised his people many presents for their "attachment to

---

[28] Braund, *Deerskins & Duffels*, 45; Timothy Barnard to Patrick Carr, April 13, 1784, John Habersham Letters, 1779–1787, MS 338, Georgia Historical Society.

[29] Saunt, *New Order of Things*, 75, 80.

their white brethren during the late war, and for their acquiescence and support in the late acquired Cession." The Fat King hoped that those promises were not just idle words. "I expected to have seen Goods come amongst us," protested the Creek *mico*. He continued, "For some time past I have talked often, and now talk again, and hope that Goods will be sent to every Town, even the smallest. When I gave up the Land, I expected to have plenty of Goods. At the Talk I was promised a pair of Colours to go through your Town, and to be stuck up there, and then to be brought to my Town."[30]

A paucity of trade, McGillivray's threats, Spanish influence, frontier violence, and ongoing disputes over the Oconee lands severely strained Georgia's relations with the Creeks, increasing the odds of an Indian war. As Hall recognized a year earlier when he was governor, such a conflict would "greatly distress" the state and "ruin the present settlers." To circumvent such a disaster, the General Assembly renewed efforts to reinvigorate the trade and called upon Elbert to help soothe the boiling tensions. In April, Georgia contracted with the commander to supply the Indians with goods through his new trade partnership, McLean, Elbert & Company. Thus, Elbert's businesses became part of Georgia's Indian diplomacy. Soon afterwards, he delivered £42.1.8 in goods to the Tallassee Creeks, including gun powder, gunflints, lead, and twelve gallons of India rum. The distribution of merchandise to the Creeks continued throughout June and July. At least some of Elbert's goods came from Telfair, one of his suppliers in the Indian trade. On June 24, John Habersham went to Telfair's store and obtained twenty-three shillings worth of trade goods on James Rae's credit, and then distributed it to McLean, Elbert, & Company for the Creeks. According to Telfair's accounts, he provided the Creeks with four and a half yards of Stroud cloth, three saddles, three large blankets, three white shirts, one trading gun, six papers of the best cut tobacco, four kegs of rum, a dozen gunflints, gunpowder, and lead for bullets. Elbert provided goods, too. On July 23, the state reimbursed him for presents given to the Tallassee King and the Fat King amounting to £52.16.11. Two days later, it paid £20.6.8 to McLean, Elbert & Company for

---

[30] Lyman Hall to John Houstoun, April 10, 1784, in John Houstoun Papers, 1775–1784, MS 397, Georgia Historical Society, and, in the same source, "Talk Delivered by the Fat King," April 5, 1784; "Journal of the House of Assembly," February 23, 1784, in *RRG*, 3:540, and, in the same source, "Minutes of the Executive Council," July 8, 1783, 3:2:510–11.

additional items distributed to the lower towns.[31]

The Creeks were not the only Indians getting presents from Elbert, McLean, and Telfair. It was imperative that Georgia keep the Choctaw in the Yazoo lands peaceful, too, and counter any Spanish influence among their leaders. In June and July, Mingohoope and another Choctaw headman came to Augusta and delivered a talk to Houstoun and the executive council. After the talk, the council gave the chiefs and each of their eight male attendants a blanket, shirt, and kettle. Each of the seven females with them received a blanket and two handkerchiefs. In addition to these items, Mingohoope's two wives received three yards of calico. Telfair's account book showed that at the same time, McLean, Elbert & Company delivered twenty-four gallons of rum and eight additional kegs to the Choctaw, a bushel of alum, and brass kettles, all valued at £10.17.4. A subsequent shipment later that month included ten white ruffled shirts, ten handkerchiefs, four cotton rumals (a type of handkerchief), eight shawls, eight tin kettles, two large yellow shawls, two quart tin pots, and red Stroud cloth, all valued at £94.2.½. Elbert and Telfair worked so closely together in the Indian trade that by the end of the year, they formed a partnership. In Telfair's accounts, he recorded that the state and others owed Telfair, Elbert & Company £6,400, some of which was for presents to the Indians. In addition to McLean, Elbert & Company and Telfair, Elbert & Company, there was also an Elbert & Company. The executive council recorded that it reimbursed Elbert & Company for £20 worth of presents that it furnished the Choctaw in July.[32]

Though Elbert's trading companies were part of Georgia's efforts to keep the beloved path "white" with the lower towns, taking possession of the Oconee lands without Indian interference was the ulterior motive for supplying the Tallassee King, Fat King, and other Creeks with presents. The state moved quickly to get new settlers across the Oconee, ignoring the complaints of some Lower Creeks who disputed the new boundaries. Despite Creek protests and before running the

---

[31] "Minutes of the Executive Council," July 8, 1783, in *RRG*, 2:510–11, 675–76; McLean, Elbert & Co. Account to State of Georgia for Indian Treaties, 1784, box 3, folder 1, Edward Telfair Papers, Rubenstein Rare Book and Manuscript Library.

[32] McLean, Elbert & Co. Account to State of Georgia for Indian Treaties, 1784, box 3, folder 1, Edward Telfair Papers, Rubenstein Rare Book and Manuscript Library; "Minutes of the Executive Council," July 17, 1784, in *RRG*, 2:670; "Minutes of the Executive Council," July 26, 1784, in *RRG*, 2:676–77.

boundary surveys, the assembly, on February 25, 1784, created Franklin County in the Cherokee cession and Washington County in the Oconee lands. Much like the earlier land distribution system, individuals could apply for headright grants of two hundred acres, plus fifty additional acres per family member and slave. After paying office and surveying fees, the individual had to live on the land for six months and make efforts to improve it before the grant was finalized.[33]

As vacant land in the new counties quickly became property, the state set aside thousands of acres for its own purposes. It preserved 20,000 acres in each county to establish an endowment for a state college destined to become the University of Georgia. It also granted Comte d'Estaing, the French commander who tried to liberate Savannah from the British in 1779, four grants totaling 20,000 acres of good land in Franklin County. Finally, the assembly established a military reserve, consisting of a twenty-mile square between the north and south forks of the Oconee, for granting war bounties to the state's Continental veterans. This fulfilled a promise by Congress to pay former soldiers for their service with a land bounty. Unlike headrights, there were no costs beyond office fees for the bounties, and grantees were not required to settle or cultivate the land in order to possess it. The state also rewarded militia veterans with land bounties.[34]

The Georgia Assembly followed a formula for land distribution that divided veterans (and others) into separate classes based on their military rank and type of service to the state. A private in the Georgia Line, for example, was entitled to 230 acres, while a private in the militia received 287½ acres. Bounties increased in size according to the rank of those getting warrants. A colonel in the Continental Line, which was Elbert's rank for most of the war, qualified for 1,150 acres. That was the amount the state was going to award Elbert until he informed the assembly that his bounty should be that of a brigadier general in the Continental Army. The assembly agreed and increased his bounty seven hundred more acres. A brigadier general of the militia, a category that only included Elbert, received a state bounty of 1,955 acres. To verify that soldiers getting bounties were veterans, their

---

[33] K. Coleman, *American Revolution in Georgia*, 217, 228.

[34] Ibid., 218–19, 228; "Minutes of the Executive Council," September 28, 1784, in *RRG*, 2:717, and, in the same source, "Minutes of the Executive Council," April 23, 1784, 2:639–40, and "Journal of the House Assembly," February 9, 1783, 3:267; Hitz, "Georgia Bounty Land Grants," 340.

commanding officer had to certify the validity of their applications. While the state granted most bounties to living veterans, the heirs of soldiers who died during the conflict could also claim them. On July 15, 1784, Elbert certified that David Crawford and three other veterans who died during the conflict had enlisted for three years in the 2nd Battalion. Although deceased, the men's heirs were entitled to the benefit of Continental and state bounties. The assembly hoped that certifications would prevent fraud, but it enhanced it. There is no evidence to suggest that Elbert manipulated the system to get additional acreage, but others did. A host of Georgia's state and militia officers signed certificates for soldiers who fought under them, only to receive the bounties themselves when the state issued their warrants. Among the worst offenders, observed one historian, were Marbury, Telfair, and Clarke.[35]

Elbert's workload increased when the state began issuing bounties. For one, he had to sign countless certificates for soldiers coming to him so they could get their warrants. Furthermore, as surveyor of his county, he had to direct and correctly lay out the increased number of applications for bounties and headrights under his jurisdiction, survey the land, and make plats to be signed by the secretary of state and issued in the name of the governor.[36]

There can be no doubt that Elbert benefited from the two Indian treaties signed in Augusta. For one, his various businesses prospered from the trade in presents to the Indians. However, his greatest personal gain came in the form of land, particularly in Washington County. Beginning in 1784 and continuing through 1786, the state issued Elbert five bounty and land warrants for an enormous total of 5,205 acres, some of which was in the military reserve. In a warrant dated November 30, 1784, and recorded the next year, Elbert received 402½ acres in the reserve bounded by the South Oconee River and lands claimed by McIntosh. His other two grants in 1784, one for 977½ acres along the Oconee and the other for 575 acres, were also in Washington County. In 1785, he obtained another grant, this time in Burke County, for 200 acres. The greatest bulk of his land was a tract consisting of 3,050 acres along Spirit Creek below Augusta, awarded in Richmond County in 1786. Altogether, because of his high military ranks

---

[35] Hitz, "Georgia Bounty Land Grants," 338–39; "Minutes of the Executive Council," March 26, 1784, in *RRG*, 2:625; Knight, *Georgia's Roster of the Revolution*, 154; K. Coleman, *American Revolution in Georgia*, 219.

[36] Hitz, "Georgia Bounty Land Grants," 342–43.

in the Continental Army and the militia, Elbert received more bounty land in Georgia than any veteran from the state including McIntosh who, by his own estimates, got 3,450 acres.[37]

As 1784 ended, Elbert was well along on his road to economic recovery. If measured in acres, his wealth was substantial, far surpassing the amount of land he owned prior to 1775. Though his pre-war trading firms were gone, he replaced them with at least three others in the war's aftermath. All the while, the state's political leaders smothered him in laurels. There were several examples of their adulation, such as naming Elbert a commissioner in the 1783 treaty talks with the Cherokee, promoting him to major general over the militia, using his firms to carry out Indian diplomacy, and even electing him to be a member of the state's delegation to the Continental Congress early in 1784. Despite failing health, he immersed himself in civic duties, as the surveyor for his county, a vestryman of his church, and as an officer in the Order of the Cincinnati. All the while, he enjoyed the blessings of a new home and growing family. As Georgia consolidated its Revolution, Savannah's inhabitants lauded him as one of their best-loved and praise-worthy citizens. Even with all of that, at the end of 1784 the commander stood on the cusp of attaining his greatest political laurel. Maybe he sensed what was in store, but when Georgia again required his services, he defied his illness, answered the call of his state, and again followed the voice of his servant's heart.

---

[37] Knight, *Georgia's Roster of the Revolution*, 216. For the 402½-acre bounty, see vol. A, 1784, record ID 19704, 323, in Georgia Colonial and Headright Plat Index, 1735–1866, Georgia State Archives. In the same source, for the 977½-acre bounty, see vol. A, 1784, record ID 19703, 323, and for the 575-acre bounty, see vol. A, 1784, record ID 19702, 323. For the 200 acres in Burke County, see vol. 1, 1785, record ID 19804, 1:469. For the 3,050 acres along Spirit Creek, see vol. L, 1786, record ID 19820, 213. For McIntosh, see Jackson, *Lachlan McIntosh*, 133.

Chapter 14

"Many Irregularities Have Taken Place": Governor Elbert's Trials, Triumphs, and Border Wars, 1785

On January 6, 1785, the Georgia Assembly opened a new session and cast ballots to elect another executive for a one-year term replacing outgoing governor, John Houstoun. In a near unanimous vote, Samuel Elbert became the new governor—although he did not seek the position.[1] It represented his first venture into politics since serving in the assembly some fifteen years earlier. Elbert probably never dreamed of someday becoming governor, but his experience highlighted the possibilities for upward mobility that existed in Georgia's frontier society for those with talent, charisma, drive, leadership skills, and the blessings of fortunate life circumstances. His Revolutionary legacy only magnified those attributes. He first came to Savannah from South Carolina in the mid-1760s as an unemployed orphan with little money or work experience, no immediate family in the province, and with small hopes for a bright future. From that humble beginning, he rose to the height of social, military, and political prominence in his state. His experience epitomized the classic example of a "rags to riches" story.

On the day Elbert became governor, the Georgia Assembly named his brother-in-law, Joseph Habersham, speaker of the House. Years earlier, both men worked together to foster the Revolution in Georgia. Now, they shared in the governance of the independent state spawned by that rebellion. Their deep and lasting attachment ensured a harmonious relationship between Georgia's executive and legislative branches, unlike the days when Wright constantly battled his assemblies.

---

[1] Cook, *Governors of Georgia*, 54. Purcell claims he did not seek the position due to declining health ("Public Career of Samuel Elbert," 75).

"It is with Pleasure I inform you," Habersham told Elbert as he presented the new governor to the assembly, "that the representatives of the People have this Day made Choice of you as Governor for the present year." According to Habersham, the primary reason for Elbert's selection was his "unwearied Exertions" in the war, which terminated in "Glory and Tranquility to our Country." Habersham and the assembly were confident that, as an executive, the former commander would preserve the liberties established by his military appointments. According to the speaker, Elbert, in sheathing his sword and becoming governor, provided clear evidence to the world that he was, like Washington, a true Cincinnatus who displayed "how readily the Distinction between Citizen and Soldier can be done away with."[2]

The new governor then addressed the assembly in a humble acceptance speech. "I shall ever be sensible of the Honour you have conferred on me," he began. Echoing Habersham's statements, Elbert promised that as a citizen, he would "merit the Confidence you are reposed in me." The former commander pledged to uphold the rights of citizens in every measure and to promote and protect the state.[3] While his acceptance rhetoric was uplifting, great challenges lay ahead to fulfill those inauguration promises.

Elbert's close relationship with Habersham and many in the assembly bode well for a successful term. The same was true for his assembly-appointed administration, many of whom were war acquaintances, such as Samuel Stirk, a former colonel in the 2nd Battalion, who became Elbert's attorney general. Walton, another wartime friend, became the state's chief justice. Elbert also knew former governor John Wereat, who served as his auditor, and Seth Cuthbert, the state's new treasurer. Other members in the administration included John Milton, secretary; Richard Call, surveyor general; and John Wilkinson, clerk for the assembly. James Rae continued to serve as the superintendent of Indian affairs though his role was limited and the state began to rely on others, like James Deveaux and Timothy Barnard, in its Indian diplomacy.[4]

---

[2] *Maryland Journal*, March 22, 1785, 3.
[3] Ibid.
[4] *Gazette of the State of Georgia*, February 10, 1785, 1, contains a list of those in Elbert's administration. The reference to Rae is in the same source, April 7, 1785, 1. See also, K. Coleman, *American Revolution in Georgia*, 193. "Deveaux" is alternatively spelled as "Durouzeaux" in the sources.

Elbert executed the duties of governor without scandal, but there existed a conflict of interest related to his firms in the Indian trade since they benefited from his position as executive. In April and June for example, Georgia contracted with Clarke, Elbert & Company, who in turn provided £31.6.4 worth of goods to the Creeks. Telfair, Elbert & Company also continued their trade with the Indians when he was governor. In April, Elbert sent him several items from Savannah, some of which were probably used as trade goods, like a cask of rum, a barrel of flour, and several iron cooking utensils, including two pots, a frying pan, and a dripping pan. During the year, his partnership with Telfair remained lucrative, and account books showed that customers owed them £7,393.15.8 by the end of 1785. Beyond this, little else in Elbert's administration hinted at corruption. The governor executed his office with "fidelity," read one commentary in Savannah's *Independent Gazetteer* a few years after his term. That same author observed that he discharged his duties with "attention and dignity." Another writer, some twenty years after Elbert's death, suggested that his "easy manners and…majestic form" further dignified his short term.[5]

Haunted by memories of Wright's abuses, the assembly limited the power of governors during the Confederation period. In the 1780s, Georgia's governors often followed the lead of their assemblies in passing legislation, and they rarely challenged any of it. As in the past, the governor worked closely with his executive council to carry out business, which included granting land, licenses, and passports, making civil and military appointments, discussing petitions from civilians to redress grievances, issuing bonds and warrants, and making proclamations to address emergences. Elbert participated in all of these activities, making his administration much like others during the decade. Beginning in 1783, the seat of government shifted between Savannah and Augusta to accommodate the growing frontier population and to help the land office distribute grants. That also meant that when the assembly was in Augusta, the governor also resided there. When Elbert was governor, the executive council decided to meet in the city on June 28 annually for three-month sessions, but after

---

[5] "Receipt for Express," Clark, Elbert & Company, September 16, 1785, in box 1, folder 11, Telamon Cuyler Collection, MS1170, series 1, Hargrett Rare Book and Manuscript Library; Elbert Receipt to Edward Telfair, April 21, 1785, in box 3, folder 2, Edward Telfair Papers, Rubenstein Rare Book and Manuscript Library, and, in the same source, "Accounts Due to Telfair & Elbert," December 1785; *Independent Gazetteer*, December 8, 1788, 2; *Public Intelligencer*, October 16, 1807, 2.

his term, Augusta became Georgia's acting capitol. The shift necessitated the removal of offices and documents from Savannah to the upcountry. On June 10, the secretary and the surveyor petitioned Elbert for one wagon with a good team to move their offices and boxes of papers to Augusta, which the governor granted. Still, many of the state's officers protested the move and remained in Savannah, including the attorney general and the auditor, who did not relocate until 1789.[6]

Petitions from citizens seeking redress, appointments, and other requests flooded Elbert's desk. The appeals from the state's inhabitants varied greatly and some concerned questions about slaves. On March 22, Edward Lloyd, possibly the jailer for Chatham County, wrote to the governor and the executive council about a female slave in his custody belonging to Jacob Hale, a prisoner sentenced to death but who was no longer in the United States. The slave's upkeep was expensive, and Lloyd hoped that the governor would facilitate her sale to release the state from the charges. Just a few days earlier, William Pierce informed Elbert about another incarcerated slave named James, who was jailed by the commissioners of confiscated estates for being a vagrant. "If you will please to order him released and delivered to me," explained Pierce; "I will take charge of him." Since "the Fellow was confined for no crime," Pierce hoped that the state would not "insist on the expenses of his imprisonment." In yet another incident involving a slave, South Carolinian William Harden complained to Elbert that one of his chattel stood trial in Georgia for an unspecified crime and that the judge sentenced him to death even though the attorney general forbade the execution. The constable hung the slave anyway. The attorney general informed the assembly about the hanging, but, to Harden's dissatisfaction, the report idly sat on the table and "was no more thought of during the session." Writing to Elbert, Harden hoped the governor would "grant such relief as you shall in your wisdom see fit," as he sought financial compensation for the loss of his slave.[7]

---

[6] K. Coleman, *American Revolution in Georgia*, 193, 199; *Gazette of the State of Georgia*, May 11, 1785, 4; John Milton and Thomas McCall to Samuel Elbert, June 10, 1785, in box 40, folder 39, Telamon Cuyler Collection, MS1170, series 1, Hargrett Rare Book and Manuscript Library.

[7] Edward Lloyd to Samuel Elbert, March 22, 1785, in box 40, folder 11, Telamon Cuyler Collection, MS1170, series 1, Hargrett Rare Book and Manuscript Library, and, in the same source, William Pierce to Samuel Elbert, March 15, 1785, box 40, folder 1; William Harden to Governor Elbert, April 5, 1785, box 40, folder 16.

Complaints of a domestic nature also came to Elbert's attention. On June 7, the governor and executive council received a petition from Michael Germain and Justice Hartmann, two brothers from different fathers, concerning bigamy accusations against James Story, a silversmith from Scotland living in Savannah who had been married to their deceased sister. Since her death, the men learned that Story had not been divorced from his prior wife in Scotland. When the brothers confronted Story about the allegations, he failed to "clear his Character to our joint Satisfaction." To discover the truth, they applied to the provost or chief magistrate in Edinburgh for sworn evidence concerning the legality of Story's marriage. They also requested a list of all marriages in the parish to prove that Story was still bound to his first wife when he unlawfully wed their sister. Having heard nothing from Edinburgh's authorities, the men asked Elbert to deliver a requisition to Scotland marked with Georgia's official seal to compel an official reply, but what happened after that remains unknown.[8]

Sometimes, people sought Elbert's influence to help them find employment. It was Peter Tarling's wish to become a public notary, as he informed the governor in a letter on May 19. Seeking Elbert's sympathy, Tarling explained that during the war, he lost his fortune and that everything was gone except his education. That, he said, was something that the enemy could never steal from him. Believing himself to be "equal to the task," he requested that Elbert "appoint and nominate" him as a notary public for the state. If he got the job, he promised to be "forever thankful."[9]

Petitions sometimes came from counties. On May 5, citizens from Burke County, including future governor Jared Irwin, sent a grievance to Elbert and the executive council seeking protection for some poor families in their community. Wright, during his administration, set aside two land surveys between Rocky Comfort Creek and the Ogeechee where destitute families could settle. Through the years, many unfortunate but "honest families" moved to the tracts, which the community acknowledged was theirs. Those people, claimed the petitioners, included some of the county's first settlers who often risked their lives as they "Stood as a wall against the Insults that might be

---

[8] Ibid., Petition of Michael Germain and Justice Hartmann, June 7, 1785, box 40, folder 37.

[9] Ibid., Petition of Peter Tarling to Samuel Elbert, May 19, 1785, box 40, folder 30.

Expected from the Savages." Additionally, most had improved their modest dwellings. Unfortunately, the residents heard that the land was about to be sold by the state to other people. "It would be very Cruel to Brake up those poor Families with their Helpless Children Being Good Citizens," explained the tenderhearted petitioners. Anyway, most of the land consisted of barren sand hills. They hoped that Elbert and his council would cancel or postpone the sale or at the very least allow them to continue in their homes, like some of the evicted Loyalists who still remained on their confiscated estates.[10]

A bizarre request to the governor came in a letter from Richard Burton, a former soldier in Elbert's 3rd Battalion. He participated, he said, in the commander's capture of three British vessels on the Frederica River in 1778. He understood that the ships were valuable at the time and that they later brought considerable prize money. Having played a role in the action, Burton concluded that he had a right to a fraction of the prize. Unfortunately, complained the veteran, he had "received not a Copper for his share of the same." He therefore hoped that the governor would consider his case and grant him relief.[11] Elbert must have been astonished by Burton's letter. Though he probably did not recall the soldier, staking out claims on war prizes seven years after the fact was audacious. In any event, the money was gone by 1785.

There were a number of state emergencies while Elbert was governor, including a smallpox scare. On July 19, Chesley Bostwick at Spirit Creek below Augusta sent the governor an express warning of a boat coming up from Savannah carrying smallpox. As word spread, inhabitants panicked. Bostwick hoped that Elbert would make a public proclamation and take other steps to stop the spread of the disease. The governor received the letter in Augusta on the same day and wasted no time in replying. "I am sorry to be informed by the [reception] of your letter on this date that a boat is now on the river intended for this place, with the small pox on board," he observed, and every precaution should be made to prevent it from spreading. Elbert told Bostwick to get a justice of the peace and to have the boat stopped before it came further upriver. He was to hire one or two people who survived the disease in the past to attend those infected. Elbert promised to pay all expenses

---

[10] Ibid., Petition of the Inhabitants of Burke County to Samuel Elbert and the Executive Council, May 5, 1785, box 23, folder 28.

[11] Ibid., Petition of Richard Burton to the Honorable Samuel Elbert, August 5, 1785, box 40, folder 55.

until everyone was well.¹²

Elbert also had to deal with criminals in his state. In mid-October, Elbert learned about three separate fugitives who refused to surrender. Theophilus Hill of Camden County killed Joseph Whitney on July 21 and then fled into East Florida. James McKay from Burke County shot and injured Richard Nichols, who died of his wounds on September 1. McKay's whereabouts were unknown. In Augusta, Christopher Teasdale "beat and cruelly ill-treat[ed]" John O'Neill, who died soon afterwards. Once in custody, Teasdale escaped and eluded authorities, who believed he was hiding in South Carolina. Elbert issued a proclamation urging citizens to be watchful and offered a £50 reward to any person who would apprehend any of them. When some rogue set the jail in Augusta on fire and burned it down, the governor issued another proclamation offering £40 specie for anyone giving information concerning the identity and whereabouts of the culprit.¹³

Florida continued to be a problem, too, even though Spain now controlled the province. During the Revolution, Indians and Loyalists constantly raided across the border, but the war's conclusion presented new threats in the form of vagabonds who committed robbery and violence against Georgia's frontier inhabitants. Their presence constituted an ongoing emergency. Both Lyman Hall in 1783 and John Houstoun in the following year tried to confront the issue when they were governors, but they had little success in curbing the rash of crimes committed by, according to the executive council, the roaming "idle and disorderly persons [who were]…notoriously bad characters."¹⁴

Elbert inherited the problem, and, on February 16, he ordered Colonel John Baker commanding the Liberty County militia to take a large force and "secure the villains" who were assembled somewhere between the Satilla and St. Marys Rivers. Though the governor had little confidence in Baker from his experience with him during the Revolution, he nonetheless ordered the militia commander to apprehend the gang and retrieve all stolen property. He estimated that their group contained around twenty-five men but predicted that others would join them. "It will

---

¹² Ibid., Chelsey Bostwick to Samuel Elbert, June 19, 1785, box 40, folder 49. See also Samuel Elbert to Chelsey Bostwick, July 19, 1785, in "Letter Book of Governor Samuel Elbert," 213 (hereafter cited as LBGSE).

¹³ *Pennsylvania Packet, and Daily Advertiser*, October 18, 1785; *Gazette of the State of Georgia*, October 13, 1785, 4, and November 10, 1785, 3.

¹⁴ *Gazette of the State of Georgia*, May 6, 1784, 3.

be a happy circumstance if you can fall in with them," he hoped, "as it will nearly put a stop to any further trouble to this State from that quarter." Though he tried, Baker did not accomplish his mission. On May 16, the governor again sent him to the Southern border with orders to capture the lawless marauders and *"make short work with them."*[15]

Like other governors after the Revolution, granting land consumed much of Elbert's time. Those grants, which required the governor's signature, included headrights and war bounties. The largest grant given out by the state when Elbert was governor was a 20,000-acre bounty in Franklin County awarded to Comte d'Estaing by the Assembly a year earlier for his Revolutionary service to Georgia. Despite requests from French Consulate Monsieur de la Forest in Charleston, d'Estaing still did not have legal papers formalizing his grant. Pressed for an answer, an embarrassed Elbert informed the consulate on May 16 that the documents would soon arrive. If it were up to him, he said, the papers would already be in d'Estaing's possession, along with a copy of the act naturalizing him as a free citizen of the state. "The delay in our public officers is the sole cause of their not being now sent," he apologetically replied, "but you may rest assured that as soon as I can have them properly authenticated they shall be forwarded to you." Finally, after much delay, state Commissioner John McQueen communicated to the Frenchman on June 28 that the titles were on the way. Elated, de la Forest told the governor about d'Estaing's pleasure in receiving the gift. "Nothing could exceed the flattering manner with which the gift is made to the Count," he wrote. Even more gratifying was to receive them from a fellow citizen of Georgia. That, said the consulate, would "please [him] highly."[16]

Land warrants, bounties, and certificates for service continually came to the governor's attention. On January 17, he received a request for a warrant from Jesse Winfrey, a Georgia citizen who fled the state during British occupation. He returned after the enemy evacuated and now desired land. He never had any granted to him, he claimed, so, taking advantage of the "common rights of his fellow citizens," he hoped to be awarded a

---

[15] Samuel Elbert to John Baker, February 16, 1785, in LBGSE, 195, and, in the same source, Samuel Elbert to John Baker, May 16, 1785, 204.

[16] Journal of the Land Court," May 13, 1784, in *RRG*, 2:795; Samuel Elbert to Monsieur de la Forest, May 16, 1785, in LBGSE, 203; Monsieur de la Forest to Samuel Elbert, June 28, 1785, in box 40, folder 43, Telamon Cuyler Collection, MS 1170, series 1, Hargrett Rare Book and Manuscript Library. The Assembly's Act granting the French commander land is found in *CRG*, 19(2):449.

warrant for 200 acres in Washington County. As an exile during the war, he also qualified for an additional 250 acres and 200 more as a headright, for a total of 650 acres. Elbert also continued to sign certificates verifying the service of Revolutionary soldiers under his command. On February 2, he signed a small, rectangular sheet of blue paper certifying that Christopher Hillary, a lieutenant, was entitled to bounty Number 200 containing 460 acres. Six months later, on August 18, he certified that Lewis Holloway, John Jordan, Littleton Williamson, Joshua Moss, John Rivers, Hardy Bass, and Thomas Bass served as privates in the 2nd Battalion, and all were "good and faithful soldiers" and due a bounty. He certified other 2nd Battalion privates, like Brittain Brantley, Timothy Simpson, William Vaughn, Lott Boyce, and Charles Clifton, all of whom died in service and whose bounties were due to their heirs.[17]

The widespread dishonesty in distributing land continued, and it galled Elbert. Determined to put a stop to the unsavory practice, on July 15, he wrote Charles Crawford, Garratt Irvine, and Arthur Fort on the assembly's Committee to Examine Land Certificates and complained about the abuses. Their purpose, he said, was to investigate the conduct of those issuing certificates for bounties in Washington and Franklin counties. Their probe was not just limited to former commanders since some surveyors were also involved in the illicit activity. "It appears to me that many irregularities have taken place in this business," he angrily observed. The dishonesty troubled the governor all year. He exposed his feelings in correspondence with his former commander Lachlan McIntosh in mid-September. Many of the grants were "surreptitiously obtained," he told McIntosh, and he wanted the assembly to declare the invalid grants "null and void."[18]

In 1785, Georgia was still dealing with former Loyalists. On June 22, the governor received a request from John Mulryne, a wartime Loyalist, for permission to abandon the state for the British-controlled Bahamas. Although Mulryne's name appeared in the 1782 Act of

---

[17] Petition of Jesse Winfrey for Land Warrant, January 17, 1785, in box 40, folder 1, Telamon Cuyler Collection, MS1170, series 1, Hargrett Rare Book and Manuscript Library. For Hillary's certificate, see Christopher Hillary Land Bounty, February 2, 1785, in box 10, folder: Legal Papers, 1757–1883, Charles C. Jones Papers, Rubenstein Rare Book and Manuscript Library, and for the rest, see Knight, *Georgia's Roster of the Revolution*, 20.

[18] Samuel Elbert to the Committee to Examine Land Certificates, July 15, 1785, in LBGSE, 211–12, and, in the same source, Samuel Elbert to Lachlan McIntosh, September 19, 1785, 218.

Confiscation and Banishment, the assembly allowed him to remain for seven years, but he barely made it through three. Probably because he refused to pledge an allegiance to Georgia or renounce his activities during the war, Mulryne felt pressure to leave. Spurned and rejected by his fellow Georgians, the former Loyalist told Elbert that he "relinquished" his right to stay and pleaded for an order sending him to the Bahamas. Never a friend to unrepentant Loyalists, the governor quickly obliged. Elbert ordered Edward Lloyd, the sheriff in Chatham County where Mulryne lived, to procure a vessel for his passage. On July 13, just a few weeks after the initial request, Mulryne boarded a ship commanded by Captain William Pinder, who promised the governor that he would land him safely at the Bahamas, "the dangers of the sea and death excepted."[19]

Georgia's finances remained in turmoil during Elbert's term, continuing a pattern stretching back into the war years. By 1783, the state's total accumulated debt was close to $1.5 million. Included in that sum were war debts owed to the federal government, estimated to be about £912,071 in 1787. With little hard currency to cover expenses, the state issued paper money in the form of funded and audited certificates. The certificates, which were worthless outside of Georgia, accrued interest and were valid as currency in the purchase of confiscated estates or other commodities.[20]

On May 30, William Ward and George Handley, both from Chatham County, pledged £880 in specie and certificates to Elbert or his successors for the purchase of a confiscated estate. They had little time to settle their debt since it was due in full precisely one year later, on May 30, 1786. Because of this, and for other reasons, people often defaulted on their payments, making the state's hoped-for income from confiscated estates far below initial estimates. Confusion reigned around Georgia's tangled web of debt and muddled finances. Attorney General Stirk pored over piles of confiscated account books in his office as he tried to figure out how to deal with them. One of them belonged to Belcher and Ingram, a Savannah firm operating during the British

---

[19] Petition of John Mulryne to Samuel Elbert, June 22, 1785, in box 40, folder 41, Telamon Cuyler Collection, MS1170, series 1, Hargrett Rare Book and Manuscript Library, and, in the same source, Receipt of William Pender to Edward Lloyd, July 13, 1785, box 40, folder 42.

[20] Hall, *Land and Allegiance*, 173; K. Coleman, *American Revolution in Georgia*, 256–57.

occupation that now owed the treasury money. The owners told Stirk that they would provide sufficient security if he turned the books over to them so they could undertake efforts at collection. They promised to pay the treasury half of what they recovered. Figuring out interest owed by the state to the holders of certificates was also daunting and almost overwhelmed the state's treasurer. "The Demand now begin[s] daily to be made upon the Treasury for Interest money arising from the Funded Certificates," Cuthbert warned the governor, and his office was "without capacity to answer there demands." He wanted Elbert and the council to suggest ways to generate more money, either through additional duties, taxes, or something else.[21]

The confiscation of estates to garner money for the state and the issuance of certificates due to the lack of hard specie contributed to Georgia's financial woes in 1785. By the time Elbert came to office, the auditor general reported that he had issued £261,317 in certificates. At the same time, Georgia only raised £1,234 in taxes to cover interest owed on certificates and other financial obligations. To be sure, additional revenue came from other sources, like the sale of land, fines, and import duties. The last large sale of confiscated estates in September 1785, for example, netted the state an additional £8,963. Still, Georgia struggled to raise enough money to meet pressing fiscal needs.[22]

In 1785, two years after the official end of the war, Georgia still owed many individuals for services and commodities given to the state during the conflict, and Elbert's assembly worked hard to clear past debts. In 1782, John Habersham signed a state promissory note to purchase four hundred bushels of lime from Frederick Treutlen for chimney construction in the barracks of a Savannah fort, but the state never paid the debt of £20. Still holding onto the note, Treutlen pressured

---

[21] Petition of William Ward and George Handley to Purchase a Confiscated Estate, May 30, 1785, in box 35, folder 30, Telamon Cuyler Collection, MS1170, series 1, Hargrett Rare Book and Manuscript Library, and, in the same source, Seth Cuthbert to Samuel Elbert, April 8, 1785, box 40, folder 17; K. Coleman, *American Revolution in Georgia*, 186; Samuel Stirk to Samuel Elbert, February 26, 1785, item 3, MS 232, Samuel Elbert Papers, Georgia Historical Society. According to Coleman, the attorney general issued audited and funded certificates used to pay half of the purchase price of a confiscated estate (*American Revolution in Georgia*, 201–202). The interest that Cuthbert complained of came from the state's use of certificates to pay off its indebtedness, which yielded a yearly interest of 7 percent. This, in turn, substantially increased interest payments owed by the state.

[22] *Georgia State Gazette or Independent Register*, March 3, 1787, 1; Hall, *Land and Allegiance*, 173.

Habersham for full payment in 1785. To satisfy Treutlen, Habersham wrote Elbert asking him and the council to rectify the situation, which, presumably, they did.[23] Though small, the debt owed Truetlen and others like him collectively put added stresses on an already strained state budget.

Desperate for money, the state went after defaulters. On October 3, Elbert petitioned Chief Justice Walton, on behalf of Georgia, to subpoena Thomas White and William West of Liberty County to appear before the Superior Court and answer for default on a confiscated estate. As Elbert informed Walton, they obligated themselves to the state for £372 in 1783, and, since that time, they had paid nothing. Now, complained the governor, they owed back payments in addition to £186 in interest despite repeated requests to make good on their obligation. To Elbert, defaulting on debts was as dishonorable as stealing land on fraudulent certificates. His recommendation to the commissioners of confiscated estates was that those who did not make full payments in audited or funded certificates a year from the date of the initial sale should be required to pay in "nothing else but gold or silver coin."[24]

Georgia's money problems stretched far beyond its borders and all the way to the halls of Congress in New York where it could hardly pay the salaries of its three delegates, Abraham Baldwin, John Habersham, and William Houstoun, the brother of John Houstoun. Although all were men of wealth who could rely on their own resources to cover at least some expenses, money from the state was necessary to maintain their living arrangements for extended periods while Congress was in session. Throughout the 1780s, delegates routinely complained about their poor salaries, and sometimes even the lack of them. Out of all the delegates in 1785, the one most mired in financial difficulties was Houstoun, and at times he felt abandoned by his state. He did not learn, for example, that Elbert was even governor until early April, after which he wrote the former commander and congratulated him on the appointment. That same letter detailed Houstoun's financial distress and a desire to return to Georgia unless the state remitted his expenses.

---

[23] K. Coleman, *American Revolution in Georgia*, 191–92; John Habersham to Samuel Elbert, May 3, 1785, box 40, folder 22, Telamon Cuyler Collection, MS1170, series 1, Hargrett Rare Book and Manuscript Library.

[24] Samuel Elbert Petition to George Walton, October 3, 1785, George Walton Papers, 1749 or 1750–1804, Rubenstein Rare Book and Manuscript Library; Samuel Elbert to the Commissioners of Confiscated Estates, July 20, 1785, in LBGSE, 212–13.

"I from time to time have been borrowing money in this Country for which I am now exceedingly pressed & so much involved that it is impossible for me to think of moving till I receive a pecuniary Relief sufficient to extricate me," protested the delegate. He continued, "I hope sir every principle of Justice as well as the Respect due to the Character and office I bear, will induce you to transmit to me, as soon as can be, the necessary supplies for my immediate assistance—as much as will enable me to return home, which is my earnest desire." Since becoming a delegate, the only pay he received from the state was a pittance of £100, hardly enough to sustain anyone for more than a few days in New York City. "My Case is singularly hard," he told the governor, "as Every other State…has made ample provision for their Delegates thinking it is a Matter of the first Consequence." The whole experience was degrading since he, unlike other delegates, had to work hard for "my daily support without any visible means." His immediate situation, he said, was "more distressing than I ever expected from my Circumstances in life."[25]

A sympathetic Elbert replied to Houstoun a month later. "I flatter myself the situation of a Georgia Delegate at Congress will be more agreeable than yours at present appears to be," he said. In the meantime, the governor prevailed upon Habersham and Baldwin to help, and he was happy to report that they "have generously undertaken to ease you of part of your present burthen." In another communication on the same day, he told Houstoun that all the money apportioned for the delegates was in the hands of Habersham and Baldwin, and he instructed them to divide it equally between all three. "I am hopeful the sum tho' small will answer your immediate demands," but in the meantime, Houstoun could "rest assured that I shall be attentive in collecting and forwarding to you a further sum as soon as it can possibly be collected." On June 9, Elbert gladly sent the delegates additional funds, including £43 sterling for a bill at Cox and Frazier of Philadelphia and an additional £150 for Hugh Newbigging & Co., another firm in the same city. "I will use every means I can to keep you fully supplied with cash," advised the governor, and he promised more money within a few days. Houstoun's situation still troubled him, and he followed up with a personal note, writing that it was never his wish to "make your

---

[25] K. Coleman, *American Revolution in Georgia*, 253; William Houstoun to Samuel Elbert, April 2, 1785, in P. Smith, *Letters of Delegates to Congress*, 22:301–302.

situation either in Congress or any where else disagreeable." Elbert acknowledged Houstoun's sacrifices and hardships, promising him that Georgia stood "bound in gratitude to make you full and ample compensation." The governor implored the destitute delegate to remain in Congress. Placing "you on a respectable footing" in that body was a top priority, he assured Houstoun.[26]

During winter 1785, Elbert's assembly produced legislation dealing with non-citizens residing illegally, taxes, Savannah's municipal laws, fees for public officials, and the gnawing problems associated with confiscated estates and funded certificates. It also passed an act regulating the marketing of tobacco, a cash crop that was just appearing in the upstate. The assembly foresaw tobacco as an important staple crop that could spur economic development on the frontier, and they encouraged its cultivation by authorizing the construction of inspection warehouses around Augusta and along the Savannah River. To enhance the establishment of morals in Georgia's frontier society, the assembly also passed an act protecting the freedom of religion among all Christian denominations and sects within the state.[27]

Waging war against immorality, civil disorder, and "Evils more horrid than the Wild uncultivated State of Nature" led, in part, to the most important and lasting achievement of Elbert's administration, which was the creation of an institution of higher learning that became the first state-chartered university in the United States. On January 27, the assembly passed an act creating Franklin College (later known as the University of Georgia), funded from an endowment of 40,000 acres set aside in Franklin and Washington counties in 1784. The charter established a Senatus Academicus as the governing apparatus of the college. Two separate bodies made up the Senatus Academicus—a board of trustees and a board of visitors. The governor appointed members to both boards and was himself on the board of visitors, along with his executive council, the speaker of the House, and the chief justice. The first board of trustees appointed by Elbert included James and John Habersham, Joseph Clay, former governors John Houstoun and

---

[26] Samuel Elbert to William Houstoun, May 5, 1785, in LBGSE, 202–203, and, in the same source, Samuel Elbert to William Houstoun, June 9, 1785, 209, and Samuel Elbert to William Houstoun, John Habersham, and Abraham Baldwin, June 9, 1785, 207–208.

[27] *CRG*, 19(2):397, for the act establishing freedom of religion. This volume contains all 1785 acts passed by the Assembly.

Nathan Brownson, and former speaker William Glascock. All of Georgia's delegates to Congress in 1785 became trustees, as did Adiel Holmes, Jenkins Davis, Hugh Lawson, and former war veteran Benjamin Taliaferro.[28]

Although Elbert had little, if any, formal education, he understood the value of an institution of higher learning to the future success and prosperity of his state and according to one historian, his influence was "considerable" in getting the bill passed. Without a doubt, chartering the college was the highlight of his administration. According to an article in the *Savannah Morning News* in 1920, it was Elbert's most "enduring and far-reaching" achievement spanning his entire "notable career." Beyond the initial flurry of activity after the college's charter, little else happened for the next sixteen years. Establishing the college on paper was one thing, but turning it into a reality was quite a different matter. For a variety of reasons—including finances, disagreements on choosing a site for the institution, a failure to get quorums for trustee meetings as specified in the charter, and a litany of additional problems—the college never advanced beyond the planning stages for the rest of the eighteenth century. Nevertheless, Elbert helped establish a foundation for higher learning in the state that would soon flourish; the University of Georgia became his enduring legacy.[29]

The assembly's most far-fetched idea in 1785 concerned the creation of Bourbon County in the Yazoo lands along the Mississippi River, the state's furthermost western frontier according to Georgia's original charter and the Proclamation of 1763. The scheme's genesis apparently came from Thomas Green, a resident of Spanish-held Natchez, who petitioned the assembly to establish a county on the Mississippi Delta. That body, needing little persuasion, enthusiastically embraced Green's vision and naïvely plowed forward with an unbelievable plan to plant Georgians on the banks of the Mississippi. Wholly ignorant of the land in question, the few people who lived there, and even the extent of Spain's dominion over the area, the assembly pored over primitive maps and drew out the new county's boundaries. It began where the Yazoo River met the Mississippi. From there, it traveled down the center of

---

[28] "An Act for the more full and Complete Establishment of a public School of Learning in this State," January 27, 1785, in *CRG*, 19(2):363–71; Coulter, "Birth of a University," 114.

[29] Coulter, "Birth of a University," 142–43; Purcell, "Public Career of Samuel Elbert," 79–80; Wilcox, "Early Governor's 'Lost' Portrait," 40.

the Mississippi to the 31st Parallel and then due east toward the land earlier relinquished by the Indians to the British. From that vague reference point, the line struck north back to the Yazoo River and then followed it down to the starting point. The county was massive (larger than any existing in Georgia at the time), and Spanish-held Natchez fell within its borders. The assembly's intention was to open a land office there, distribute grants according to Georgia's laws, and require everyone purchasing property to *occupy and cultivate it*. They went further, appointing several justices of the peace, all of whom took oaths of office administered by Elbert. Their instructions were to proceed immediately westward after qualification, lay out preliminary boundaries, and administer oaths of allegiance to Georgia among the area's inhabitants.[30] The state's leaders remarkably believed that when the justices appeared with their charters and official documents, the Spanish would simply relinquish the land without much protest.

The mission into unknown and remote lands was fraught with dangers and legal questions. The assembly instructed the justices not to infuriate the Spanish and to ignore areas they occupied or contested, but this directive conflicted with their task because of the Spanish garrison and fort at Natchez. Nor were they to enter into any discussion about navigation rights on the Mississippi with the Spaniards or their territorial disputes with the Chickasaw and Choctaw tribes. As for the Indians, the assembly only wanted to focus on cultivating trade and friendship. They authorized four justices, Green, William Davenport, Nathaniel Christmas, and Nicholas Long, to act as initial commissioners to set up Bourbon County's government modeled on Georgia's other counties. The presence of at least two of the commissioners was required to legalize any of their actions.[31] Soon, all commissioners set out toward Natchez along separate routes, and they arrived at their destination at different times.

Spanish officials already knew about the approaching Georgians long before they appeared because Alexander McGillivray, the Creek headman who was acting as a spy and already on the verge of war with Georgia over the Oconee lands, told them so. "I can inform Your Lordship," he wrote Estevan Miró, the Spanish governor of Louisiana on

---

[30] "An Act for laying out a District of land situate on the river Mississippi," February 7, 1785, in *CRG*, 19(2): 371–75; K. Coleman, *American Revolution in Georgia*, 261–62.

[31] K. Coleman, *American Revolution in Georgia*, 262–63.

May 16, "through authentic reports, that the Americans have sent commissioners especially to survey and fix the boundary of thirty-one degrees north latitude on the Mississippi." This could only mean, he hinted, that Spain, like the Creeks, would soon confront these "restless and turbulent American states, which keeps us in a constant state of alarm."[32]

Great confusion accompanied the Georgians upon their arrival. Green appeared first, about two weeks before some of the others, and announced his intentions to the Spanish commander in Natchez. Shocked at the demand, the commander said he had no authority to act without permission from his superiors. He instructed the commissioner to wait while he sent letters to them and received a reply. That answer, of course, did not sit well with Green, who in the interim named himself a colonel, began to organize a militia, and set up an illegal county government, without Spanish approval or the presence of two or more commissioners. His unauthorized actions astounded other justices when they arrived. Three of them, Richard Ellis, Tacitus Gaillard, and Sutton Banks, immediately formed an opposition against Green, whose behavior they deemed "alarming to the good people of this country." Far from Elbert and the assembly, the opposition violated their earlier oaths to the governor and predicted "ruin and destruction of this country if it should fall under the government of Georgia." What they demanded instead was a separate state. Former Loyalists in the area disagreed. Fearing retribution from the United States, they preferred to take their chances with Spain. Within a matter of weeks, Natchez's population found themselves divided into factions, with some wishing to be part of Georgia, others desiring to form a new state, and a third group determined to remain under Spanish rule. In the middle of the chaos stood Green. Facing scrutiny from almost all quarters, he soon abandoned Natchez and sought refuge with the Chickasaw, the only group in the region he had not offended.[33]

Marveling at the ridiculous demands of such a tiny, insignificant, barely developed frontier state to hand over without question lands possessed by His Most Catholic Majesty, Spanish leaders cast a wary eye toward Georgia and its intentions. Bits and pieces of information about

---

[32] Alexander McGillivray to Estevan Miró, May 16, 1785, in Burnett, "Papers Relating to Bourbon County," part 1, 73.

[33] Ibid., Richard Ellis, Tacitus Gaillard, and Sutton Banks to the Citizens of Natchez, June 1785; K. Coleman, *American Revolution in Georgia*, 262–63.

chaos in the Yazoo territory dribbled into Elbert's hands around mid-May. Having received an express from Creek country during the night of May 17, the governor promptly wrote Georgia's delegates in Congress on the following day apprising them of the situation based on the dispatch. "I have information that the Americans and Spaniards on the Mississippi have had two skirmishes," he began. In consequence of that, the Spaniards sent 1,200 soldiers upriver to reinforce their posts. The Americans were also gathering their forces, and Elbert "expected something serious would take place." The prospect of bloodshed deeply troubled him. There was at least a chance that the reports were either exaggerated or unsubstantiated, he said, especially since they came from the Indians. Nevertheless, he promised to keep the delegates apprised of any new developments.[34]

Desperate for information, Elbert fired off a letter to William Clark, one of the state's Indian agents at Beard's Bluff on the Altamaha, trying to substantiate rumors of the suspected skirmish, but no additional facts were forthcoming. While his fears of a potential war were justified, he made no effort to abort the Bourbon County scheme. Four months later, Green, still in a Chickasaw village, wrote to one of his contacts and told him that the Spanish refused to give up their Natchez garrison despite his repeated demands and instead had reinforced it. "Please…inform [the] government [that] thare is all the appearince of ware this way," he cautioned, and that spies were everywhere trying to ascertain American strength in preparation for an attack.[35]

On June 24, commissioner Davenport arrived at Natchez and witnessed a scene of confusion and disorder. After repeated attempts to speak to the Spanish commander, he received a reply that there would be no discussion until instructions arrived from Miró. Guards meanwhile arrested Ellis, Gaillard, and Banks and confined them in their fort. There, complained Davenport in a letter to Elbert, they were "obliged to sleep in the Calaboose, much inferior to our Dungeons."

---

[34] Samuel Elbert to the Delegates from the State of Georgia in Congress, May 18, 1785, in LBGSE, 205.

[35] Ibid., Samuel Elbert to William Clark, May 20, 1785, 205; Thomas Green to Anthony Bledsoe, September 10, 1785, in Burnett, "Papers Relating to Bourbon County," part 2, 333–34. In June, Elbert reported to Georgia's delegates in Congress that Timothy Barnard, another Indian agent, confirmed the rumors of a clash between the Americans and Spanish (Samuel Elbert to the Honorable Delegates in Congress from the State of Georgia, June 21, 1785, in LBGSE, 211).

He could not explain the cause of their ill treatment, but he suspected it was because of the "imprudent conduct or measures taken by Mr. Green."[36]

Christmas and Long joined Davenport around the end of August, but by then, Congress had learned of the Bourbon County fiasco through complaints from Spain's minister to the United States. On September 26, New York congressman and secretary of foreign affairs John Jay brought the matter before Congress, and on October 13 they passed a resolution condemning Georgia. Even though Congress acknowledged American rights to the territory, it did not approve of individuals or states disturbing good relations with Spain, Indians, or settlers already there. Embarrassed and under pressure, Georgia's delegates reluctantly joined their colleagues and voiced a modest dissent.[37]

As Congress debated Georgia's feeble and provocative attempts to establish Bourbon County, an express to Elbert arrived from Natchez from Davenport, Christmas, and Long. After causing much trouble, the commissioners explained the fate of Ellis, Gaillard, and Banks. One still sat in irons in the fort. Another faced a fifty-dollar fine, and they banished the third from the country. There was at least some positive news. Even though McGillivray's people were unfriendly to Georgians and he had openly sided with Spain, the commissioners reported that the Chickasaw and Choctaw "were in much favor of the Americans as the Creeks are averse to them." When they met the headmen of the Chickasaw, they displayed "a great deal of friendship" and expressed how happy they were before the war when the trade provided them ample ammunition and goods. Now, they explained, the Chickasaw claimed they were a forgotten people. Their heartfelt desire was to meet the beloved men of Georgia and establish "a firm and permanent peace with them." They wanted a talk from Elbert, who they said had "never deceived nor told them lies, and that they can beleave what he tells them." The Choctaw were likewise friendly. Mingo French Man Stubby, a Choctaw headman, wanted goods for forty of his chiefs and warriors. He longed for the day when he could receive the presents and take hold of the American people by the hand "without fear of letting go." The headman also sought a talk from Elbert.[38]

---

[36] William Davenport to Samuel Elbert, July 17, 1785, in Burnett, "Papers Relating to Bourbon County," part 1, 105.

[37] Burnett, "Papers Relating to Bourbon County, Georgia," part 2, 298; K. Coleman, *American Revolution in Georgia*, 263.

[38] William Davenport to Samuel Elbert, July 26, 1785, in Burnett, "Papers Relating to

The long-awaited answer from Miró finally came on November 10 when the commissioners received orders to leave Natchez within fifteen days and to be completely out of Spanish territory after a month. It was just as well. Given the circumstances, Georgia's chances for creating a county in the Mississippi delta was hopeless. Even if it did, remoteness from the seat of power that governed it doomed Bourbon County to failure. Nor could the state financially sustain the county. In early November, Elbert received dispatches from Green, still with the Chickasaw, asking for money. "I am sorry to find that your situation has been made unhappy," replied the governor on November 9. "It is not in my power of the Exe. to afford you any relief," he wrote. He promised to lay Green's letter before the next assembly when they met, but that was not until January. In the meantime, Elbert wanted him to impress the Indians with the goal of creating favorable sentiments toward Georgia and the United States.[39]

Elbert found the whole Bourbon business increasingly frustrating. Shackled by limited finances, rebuked in Congress, and facing the possible outbreak of hostilities with Spain, the governor was surely ready to abandon the project. Unruly, traitorous justices and self-serving commissioners, like Green, only compounded the problem, which dogged Elbert until the end of his term. Writing from a faraway Chickasaw village on December 16, Long, Christmas, and Davenport told him that Spain would not relinquish any land and that, as commissioners, they were powerless to act. They were certain of at least one thing. "If we were to judge from the appearances in this quarter," they predicted, "the conclusion would be that a war must be the inevitable consequence," especially since Spanish reinforcements were on the way to repair fortifications. In that case, they advised that Georgia should stand up for its claims, since the land "was worth contending for."[40]

Though the commissioners waited impatiently for an answer to their letter, it never came before Elbert's term ended, and the unresolved Bourbon mess passed to Edward Telfair, his successor in office. Despite the

---

Bourbon County," 305–306, and, in the same source, Nicholas Long, William Davenport, and Nathanial Christmas to Governor Elbert, September 13, 1785, 335–37.

[39] Samuel Elbert to Thomas Green, November 9, 1785, in LBGSE, 223; Burnett, "Papers Relating to Bourbon County," part 2, 299; K. Coleman, *American Revolution in Georgia*, 263–64.

[40] Nicholas Long, Nathanial Christmas, and William Davenport to Samuel Elbert, December 16, 1785, in box 1, folder 2, Samuel Elbert Papers, MS 232, Georgia Historical Society.

headaches it caused, nothing ever became of Bourbon County. In 1788, after much discomfiture, the assembly wisely repealed the act that created it and then ceded some of its western claims to the United States.[41] By then, the Bourbon troubles had both strained relations between Spain and the United States and embarrassed the state.

Georgia's border problems did not end in Mississippi. After the Revolution, it got into a border dispute with South Carolina over the Savannah River, and the issue was still unresolved when Elbert came to office. During the Confederation period, many states quarreled over their boundaries. Massachusetts argued with New York over its western boundary, and New York had disputes with New Hampshire about Vermont. Virginia and Pennsylvania disagreed over the area that now touches West Virginia. Virginia and North Carolina were also at odds over their border.[42] The disagreement between Georgia and South Carolina, which began in 1783 when Lyman Hall was governor, was no different.

According to the 1732 charter, Georgia sat between the northernmost stream of the Savannah and the southernmost stream of the Altamaha. From those two points, it extended due west to the South Seas, laying the basis for the state's claim in the Mississippi Delta. The problem, however, was determining not only the Savannah's most northern stream but also where the river began. It was generally believed that the Savannah River started where the Tugaloo and Keowee Rivers merged. Since the upper stretches of the Tugaloo was unchartered territory and in Indian lands, Georgia claimed the Keowee as the most northern branch and thus fixed its border on that river. In contrast, South Carolina's claim rested with its 1665 charter, which defined the land between the Tugaloo and Keowee as part of their state. The 1665 charter also extended South Carolina's southern border into Florida, providing the basis for later claims between the Altamaha and the headwaters of the St. Marys River all the way to the South Seas, even though the 1763 Proclamation after the Seven Years War awarded that strip to Georgia.[43]

Matters became more muddled in 1784 when governors from both states issued grants to their citizens in the disputed territory between the Tugaloo and Keowee. In January 1785, the assemblies in Georgia and South Carolina resolved to lay the issue before Congress. In lieu of a

---

[41] K. Coleman, *American Revolution in Georgia*, 264.
[42] Jameson, *American Revolution Considered as a Social Movement*, 42–43.
[43] K. Coleman, *American Revolution in Georgia*, 257–58.

satisfactory agreement, the matter would go to a federal court, according to the Articles of Confederation. Elbert, always wary of giving the federal government too much control over the states, desired to keep Congress and the courts out of the discussions and instead let commissioners appointed by Georgia and South Carolina come to a settlement. Georgia's commissioners were Walton and William Few. William Houstoun was also a commissioner, but he was in Congress at the time and unable to join the other two. Their instructions were to "defend and vindicate the Rights and jurisdiction" of Georgia using all of the legal means within their power. Meanwhile, on February 12, Elbert took the initiative and wrote South Carolina's governor and friend from the Revolution, William Moultrie, to propose a meeting of commissioners from both states at either Ebenezer or Purrysburg on March 10. He was optimistic about a successful outcome. "I flatter myself," he informed Moultrie, "that the difference between the two States will shortly terminate to their mutual satisfaction."[44]

Elbert's hoped-for conference produced no results because, from former governor John Houstoun's perspective, "there was not the least prospect of the Commissioners being able to adjust this matter." Houstoun continued,

> I conceive from the words of the Charter of Georgia all the lands which lie south and south west of the northern part of the stream of the river Savannah up to it's [sic] head or source. From thence within a direct line running due west to the River Mississippi, and extending southwards as far as the boundaries of East and West Florida, are the right of Georgia. This stream here described I take to be that branch of the River Savannah known by the name of Keowee—if so, all the lands which lie in the fork of the two branches of [the] Savannah River called Tugaloo & Keowee ought to fall into Georgia.[45]

Despite Elbert's efforts, federal intervention seemed a real possibility because on March 24, South Carolina's Assembly petitioned Congress to send the dispute to court. William Houstoun learned about this development from South Carolina's delegates, who were awaiting a letter from Moultrie formally requesting Congress to form a committee, hear

---

[44] Ibid., 257–58; *CRG*, 19(2):530–31; Samuel Elbert to His Excellency, the Governor of South Carolina, February 12, 1785, in LBGSE, 200.

[45] "The Dissent of John Houstoun to the Treaty of Beaufort," April 28, 1787, in John Houstoun Papers, Rubenstein Rare Book and Manuscript Library; William Houstoun to Samuel Elbert, April 2, 1785, in P. Smith, *Letters of Delegates to Congress*, 22:302–303.

arguments, and authorize the court. If the committee formed, Houstoun believed that the outcome would not be favorable to Georgia. "I shall only Mention," he told Elbert, "that the rooted prejudices in Congress agst. our State may subject us to [a] disadvantage [over the border question]. And from the great number of Members in Congress…Spirited Measures will certainly upon every occasion be adopted, and carried into Execution with force."[46]

Houstoun's warning alarmed Elbert as did a letter sent to him from Pennsylvanian Charles Thompson, the secretary of Congress, who substantiated Houstoun's report. "I have the honor to inform your Excellency," wrote Thompson on June 2, "that in consequence of a petition of the legislature of the State of South Carolina…a federal court may be appointed conformably to the Articles of Confederation…to decide a dispute Concerning boundaries between the said state and the state of Georgia." That letter prompted Elbert to dispatch an urgent message to Georgia's delegates telling them to defend the state's honor at all costs. "Georgia never at any one period stood more in need of a spirited and firm representation in Congress than at present" and he was certain they would "guard her honor and…vindicate her wrongs" against the "conduct of a neighboring State." The stakes were so high that not one of the delegates—including Houstoun, who desired to return to Georgia—could possibly withdraw while Congress was in session.[47]

With time running out, Elbert, on August 5, contacted a merchant he knew in London, seeking information to clarify Georgia's claims on the upper Savannah. The governor wanted him to obtain authenticated copies of charters, deeds, proclamations, and other documents relative to state's borders. The merchant, James Jackson (not the militia commander and future Georgia governor), had access to those papers, Elbert believed, because he knew both Georgia's founder, James Oglethorpe and Wright. "General Oglethorpe may yet be living," suggested the anxious governor and "I am certain he would readily explain on oath what he understood to be the boundary between Georgia & South Carolina." Elbert was certain that Wright would overlook his disdain toward him and give assistance if asked. The former commander pressed Jackson to "use every means in your

---

[46] William Houstoun to Samuel Elbert, April 2, 1785, in P. Smith, *Letters of Delegates to Congress*, 22:302–303.

[47] Ibid., Samuel Elbert to the Honorable William Houstoun, John Habersham, and Abraham Baldwin, June 9, 1785, 207–208, and Charles Thompson to Samuel Elbert, June 2, 1785, 426.

power to furnish me with the fullest information possible."[48] The effort to involve Oglethorpe and Wright went nowhere. Georgia's founder died on July 1, and Wright followed him to the grave four months later.

Georgia's border dispute, still unresolved when Elbert left office, passed to Telfair, the next governor, who also failed to settle it. Finally, in 1787, commissioners from both states agreed in the Convention of Beaufort to mark the boundary at the Tugaloo. Although Georgia's delegates gave up claims to the Keowee, they could take solace that the decision was a victory for states' rights since the commissioners ultimately resolved their differences without having to involve congressional committees and federal courts.

There was yet another crisis swirling around Georgia's borders, which, unlike the rest, posed an imminent threat to the state. The Oconee lands, west and south of Wilkes County, were a tinderbox that, due to McGillivray, was close to igniting. The Creek leader still denied the validity of the 1783 Treaty of Augusta, but in spite of this, Georgia's leaders wasted no time in distributing headrights and bounties there, even before surveyors could run the lines. Frontier vagrants complicated matters by trespassing well-beyond supposed Indian borders, where they committed all sorts of crimes against Native Americans, including murder.

Reports of frontier "irregularities" committed by rogue settlers reached Elbert early in his term. While he was sympathetic to the Indian's plight, he was more concerned about their retaliation against the state's citizens. On March 10, he wrote Walton at his home in Wilkes County and expressed his worries. "It is a pity that the people on our Frontiers will behave so cruelly towards those poor Savages," he lamented. The outlanders were not just content in having their lands, he observed. In addition to that, they "rob, beat and abuse them" and their disreputable behavior was "enough to bring down divine vengeance on their heads." More importantly, they invited Indian retaliation. "Did they but reflect," he predicted, "that the blood of some poor women & children, who might suffer in consequence of such conduct, will undoubtedly lay at their doors, it would surly deter them." He wished that someone could arrest the wrongdoers in the act of committing their crimes against the Creek and Cherokee. Only then could examples be made of such "notorious offenders."[49] That task, however, was nearly impossible in such a vast and untamed

---

[48] Samuel Elbert to James Jackson, August 5, 1785, in LBGSE, 214.
[49] Ibid., Samuel Elbert to George Walton, March 10, 1785, 196.

wilderness where there was little semblance of law and order, unrestrained Indian hatred, and no witnesses to crimes.

To ward off Indian revenge killings, Elbert quickly sent talks to the Cherokee and Creek. John Crutchfield, Georgia's agent to the Cherokee, delivered the governor's message to the headmen and warriors from their twelve towns as soon as he received it. Addressing them as his "friends & Brothers," the governor recalled their initial meeting in 1783 during negotiations in Augusta. There, he reminded them, "you gave us some land for our Warriors and People to sit down upon after they had beat the English King and his Soldiers." Everyone, he felt, left that meeting on good terms and the state's leader was sorry to hear reports of bad men now causing trouble. "Their numbers must be very small," he thought, since "all the great men and Warriors in Georgia love their friends & Brothers, the Cherokees, and wont suffer them to be hurt." That statement, as Elbert well knew, was not truthful, since persistent Indian hatred was prevalent in his state, even among its "great men and Warriors." If the Cherokee could catch or identify the culprits that "steal your horses & skins, & beat and abuse you in the Woods," he promised to punish them. The governor advised that they seek out "some of our white men, who you know, as witnesses, who understand how to read in our books, to come and tell me the names of any of the bad people who oppress you, and I will…make examples of them." Soon, he explained, the state would run a survey line and create a formal boundary between Georgia and the Cherokee. Once it was marked, Elbert promised that none "of our people will be suffered to go over it."[50] While it was a good gesture, Georgia's frontier borders, despite Elbert's assurances, were virtually impossible to monitor and control, just as they were during the Revolution.

It was the Creeks, however, and not the Cherokee, who required the governor's immediate diplomacy. The talk he sent the "Kings, Head Men & Warriors of the Creek Nation" in March nearly mirrored the one delivered to the Cherokee. Noticeably absent from those receiving his message was McGillivray. It was not an oversight since neither Elbert nor any other state leader recognized his claim as spokesman for the Creeks. The "Head Men" in his state, declared Elbert, desired to "hold you by the hand and keep the path open and straight between our two Countries" ensuring a bright "chain of friendship" so strong that "it might never again be

---

[50] Ibid., "Samuel Elbert's Talk to the Cherokee," March [10?], 1785, 197.

tarnished."[51]

Just as he did with the Cherokee, Elbert referenced the Treaty of Augusta. "The War is now over," he said, and "we have sheathed our swords and are at peace with all of the World." Ignoring McGillivray's protests, the governor upheld the validity of the treaty and the cession of 1783. "You gave us land for our Warriors to rest upon," he reminded them, "and we are satisfied." Acknowledging that the Creeks turned over their land in return for trade, the governor assured them that soon a great quantity of items were on the way, and they were sufficient to meet all of their needs.[52]

It was now time to survey the Oconee lands and mark the boundaries. Paper was not sufficient, since the Indians did not understand the written word. What was required instead was "beloved Men" from the state and the towns to walk the boundary together and "set up posts and mark trees and stones and drink out of the waters that lay on the line you shall agree upon." When this was done, Elbert promised that no "Land on your side of that Line shall be touched by our people on any pretense whatever." If anyone disturbed the lines or changed the markings on blazed trees and encroached on Indian land, they would surely pay for the transgression. Elbert wanted the lines marked quickly and prayed for the "great Master of Breath" to bless the endeavor, which would "cement our friendship and prevent the spilling of blood."[53]

The governor's professed sympathy and friendship for the Creeks was contingent on their cession of the Oconee lands. His determination to resolve the issue stemmed partly from a personal motive. After all, the bulk of his war bounties lay within the disputed territory, and it was therefore necessary to establish immediate boundaries. Regardless, time was running out for the governor to acquire the land on the state's terms. Even as he sent talks to the Indians, Congress appointed three commissioners, Benjamin Hawkins from North Carolina, Daniel Carroll from Maryland, and William Perry from Delaware, to form a committee on Indian affairs in the Southern Department. Their priority was to negotiate with the Creek and Cherokee about both 1783 Augusta cessions. When he learned of the committee, Houstoun quickly notified Elbert. Georgia's dealings with the Indians was not sitting well with Congress, he suggested in an April 2 communication. "I shall hasten to announce to you that the whole

---

[51] Ibid., 198.
[52] Ibid.
[53] Ibid.

body…are become so clamorous against our State, that I Shudder for the consequences." The alarmed delegate predicted that Congress would take "coercive measures" against the state and might even adopt plans for "Voting Georgia out of the Union." The state's predicament was serious. "In truth," he advised the governor, "I do not think at any one time since the Existence of Georgia [has] she been in a worse situation than at present." With twelve states railing against her on the floor, Georgia stood alone and half-represented. When Houstoun argued to place someone from Georgia on the commission, he was "severely replied [to]" for suggesting such a thing. Houstoun hoped that Elbert could use his influence to salvage Georgia's honor.[54]

This was a dreadful development for Elbert, who wanted no federal involvement to challenge states' rights and to end up muddling Georgia's Indian affairs. It thus became expedient to fix the boundary before the arrival of any federal commissioners. In May, he contacted William Clark at Beard's Bluff to arrange a meeting between the Creeks and state commissioners. The governor instructed him to pay James Deveaux £35 as an interpreter. "We have fixed the most proper place for the meeting [at] Scull Shoals on the Oconie River," he advised. Though he hated to admit it, any such meeting had to involve McGillivray. In lieu of the Creek leader's dissent, which would surely be vocalized, Elbert saw nothing else preventing the termination of the business at hand. He did not expect many Indians to attend, especially since he was sending only a few gifts for the talks. "Our Commissioners won't go to the Nation," he explained, "and as…running the Line is more to the advantage to the Indians than to ourselves, they need not expect great presents."[55] This decision virtually ensured that few would appear and perhaps that is what the governor wanted. Establishing the line quickly was the primary objective and fewer Indians meant less opportunity for disagreement and delay. The suggestion that the Indians would gain an advantage by running the line was absurd; the opposite was true. Elbert and others forced them to give away, under a dubious treaty unauthorized by a majority of Creeks, all of their prime hunting

---

[54] William Houstoun to Samuel Elbert, April 2, 1785, in P. Smith, *Letters of Delegates to Congress*, 22:301–302; Jackson, *Lachlan McIntosh*, 137.

[55] Samuel Elbert to William Clark, May 20, 1785, LBGSE, 205. On April 19, for example, Clark paid £20.10 to Colwele Eastus for taking one of Elbert's dispatches to the Creeks. See "Receipt for Carrying Gov. Elbert's Message to Creeks," April 19, 1785, in box 77, folder 32, Telamon Cuyler Collection, MS1170, series 1, Hargrett Rare Book and Manuscript Library.

ground in the Oconee lands.

As Elbert tried to arrange a meeting with the Creeks, Elijah Clarke and Lachlan McIntosh prepared to set out and mark the lines. The assembly also asked Hawkins to join them, but he declined because he was on the federal commission, which was in a state of flux. When Carroll became sick, Congress wisely placed a Georgian, McIntosh, on the federal commission and at the same time, they added two more Southerners, Andrew Pickens from South Carolina and Joseph Martin from North Carolina. Hawkins informed Elbert of these developments on May 27, but by then, Clarke was already marking boundaries.[56]

Meanwhile, a dispatcher handed Elbert a message from Deveaux with the Lower Creeks, which the governor laid out before the executive council. "The Fat King and the good Child King of the halfway House desired me to acquaint you of their coming down to meet the Governor or the beloved men at our place Beard's Bluff," explained the interpreter. Once there, the Creeks were prepared to "settle every point of the line and boundary of land and all other matters relative to their nation." According to Deveaux, both *micos* claimed that they had authority to "act in part of the nation." That statement, however, was not true since the Fat King and Good Child King never consulted McGillivray and the Upper Creeks about their intentions. There were only a few Indians coming, said Deveaux, and after gathering at Beard's Bluff, they preferred to continue their journey to Savannah and meet with the governor and commissioners. He predicted their arrival around June 11 and noted that they expected provisions. Because there were not many of them, "they will not be much trouble," and, since they chose Timothy Barnard to be their interpreter, Deveaux told Elbert he would not accompany them.[57]

On June 9, Elbert sent Hawkins a copy of Deveaux's letter. The Creeks, he said, were coming to Savannah to discuss the boundary with the state's commissioners and they would be there in five or six days. Having performed his duty of informing Hawkins, he then, on the same day, sent a quick note to Clarke in Wilkes County. It was urgent that the state's commissioners repair to the city immediately and treat with the Indians before any federal commissioners arrive. "If we get

---

[56] Jackson, *Lachlan McIntosh*, 137–38; Samuel Elbert to Benjamin Hawkins, June 3, 1785, in LBGSE, 206.

[57] Council Minutes, June 9, 1785, in George Handley Papers, 1783–1788, Rubenstein Rare Book and Manuscript Library.

thro' with this before they commence," he told Clarke, "it may be a capital point gained." On the same day, he sent a message to Georgia's delegates in Congress. The Fat King and a few others, including the Tallassee King, were on their way to Savannah to meet with the state's commissioners and fix upon a boundary. The governor left no room for misinterpretations about his thinking. This was a matter solely within Georgia's authority to settle and he hoped to get a boundary established long before those appointed by Congress "can enter upon their business." One of Elbert's concerns was that the federal commissioners would undo everything gained in the 1783 Augusta treaties. Apparently, he was not yet aware that McIntosh had joined the federal commission because he complained that no one from Georgia was in Hawkins' group. That, he protested, was an "insult" to the state and he directed the delegates to "enter a general protest against [Congress's] proceedings in a business in which we were refused a representation."[58]

The much-anticipated meeting with the Indians in Savannah never happened. The reason, as Elbert subsequently discovered, was that the federal commissioners sent the Creeks their own talk in which they sought a fall conference at Galphintown, a few miles above Old Town on the Great Ogeechee. Not only did Congress thwart Georgia's plans, but the commission also demanded money from the state to help defray costs for the meeting. "They have made a requisition of two thousand dollars from the State," bitterly complained Elbert to Georgia's congressmen on June 21. Georgia's woeful financial condition could hardly sustain that added burden, and, as he told the state's delegates, "we have not the ability to comply [with their request]." That was precisely the answer he delivered to the federal commissioners one month later. Writing from Augusta, the defiant leader told them that it was "entirely out of [our] power to comply even in part with the requisition you make of two thousand dollars to be paid by the second Monday in October next." The legislature would not meet until January, and since they allocated funds, it would be impossible to provide any money for Galphintown until then. He was willing, however, to send along a militia guard for the commissioners. Furthermore, since the talks concerned matters of great interest and consequence to the

---

[58] Samuel Elbert to Benjamin Hawkins, June 9, 1785, in LBGSE, 206, and, in the same source, Samuel Elbert to Colonel Elijah Clarke, June 9, 1785, 207, and Samuel Elbert to William Houstoun, James Habersham & Abraham Baldwin, June 9, 1785, 207–208.

state, the federal envoy could expect the presence of at least some representatives from Georgia at the negotiations.[59] The unspoken reason for this, of course, was to defend Georgia's sacred Treaty of Augusta from any attempts by outsiders to alter or nullify it.

With his plans frustrated, Elbert suspended talks and surveys until Galphintown, but the unabated flow of settlers into the Oconee lands continued, regardless of uncertainties about borders and even the cession itself. Thus far, the attempt to solidify control west of the Oconee proved to be an expensive endeavor. The constant changing of meeting locations with the Indians, for example, did not happen free of charge. On September 16, the state's government received a receipt from the governor himself for £31.6.4 owed to Clarke, Elbert & Company for their Indian expenses. Part of those charges included a payment to William Kerby, who delivered an express to the Lower Creeks stopping them from making their planned excursion to Savannah. It was also important that Elbert's firm keep the Lower Creeks satisfied with rum and provisions until the great meeting, perhaps to make them more inclined to cooperate.[60] In that way, Elbert—just like Wright when he was governor before the Revolution—used the trade as a weapon against the Indians to attain desired results. This "carrot and stick" approach to Indian diplomacy represented a strain of continuity that connected royal Georgia to the governors of the Confederation period, like Elbert.

On the same day that Elbert delivered his receipt to the state, the governor received a letter from Pickens informing him about the upcoming convention at Galphintown. The date was now set for October 24, after which Hawkins and his entourage would travel northward to Hopewell near Seneca and meet with the Cherokee on November 15 and with the Choctaw and Chickasaw soon afterward. Elbert promptly notified the officer commanding the Burke County militia to gather twenty mounted men under the guidance of a "careful Officer" and have them "ready on the spot" when the commissioners arrived at Galphintown. He expected their conduct to be professional at all times and to

---

[59] Samuel Elbert to the Delegates in Congress from the State of Georgia, June 21, 1785, in LBGSE, 211, and, in the same source, Samuel Elbert to Benjamin Hawkins, Andrew Pickens, and Joseph Martin, July 20, 1785, 212.

[60] "Receipt for expresses and provisions delivered to the Creeks," September 16, 1785, in box 1, folder 11, Telamon Cuyler Collection, MS1170, series 1, Hargrett Rare Book and Manuscript Library.

only carry out actions "agreeable to my formal order."[61]

The assembly selected Telfair, William Few, and James Jackson as the state's representatives at the talk. Their instructions from the governor could not have been clearer. They were to "aid and assist the Commissioners in forwarding this business as far as they are authorized by the Confederation to go." However, if they acted beyond their authority or in a manner contrary to the Confederation and laws of the state, the representatives were to "protest" their measures. Elbert informed the delegates in Congress of these developments and expressed to them his desire for a successful conclusion to the Oconee question. "I have not the least doubt but matters will be conducted in such a manner as will be pleasing," he wrote, and that "our State Commissioners will be able at the same time to have the temporary boundary line agreed on [and] marked between us and the Savages."[62]

The small number of Creeks in attendance at Galphintown on October 24 was expected, and only seventeen from the Lower Towns, led by Tallassee King and Fat King, appeared. Elbert extended an invitation to the Upper Creeks to attend through Deveaux, but McGillivray protested and refused to go. His actions had a cascading effect since many other Upper Creek headmen followed his lead. Since Few and Jackson declined to serve on the commission, Georgia's delegation, now consisting of Telfair, John King, Thomas Glascock, Elijah Clarke, and John Twiggs, anxiously desired to press ahead and conclude the business. This was not the position of the federal commission, who questioned the appropriateness of negotiating such a large land cession with only seventeen Indians present.[63]

McGillivray's absence further cast a dark shadow over the whole gathering, especially given his close connections with Spanish officials in the Gulf and lower Mississippi valley. Without him, any treaty with the Creeks could spark an Indian war that drew Spain into the conflict as his allies. The risks were too great, and the federal commissioners called off the negotiations. Before they left for Hopewell, they showed the Georgia delegation a draft of the treaty they were prepared to sign.

---

[61] Samuel Elbert to Colonel Lewis, Burke County Militia, September 16, 1785, in LBGSE, 216.

[62] Ibid., Samuel Elbert to the Honorable William Houstoun, John Habersham, and Abraham Baldwin, September 14, 1785, 220.

[63] Ibid., Samuel Elbert to James Deveaux, August 18, 1785, 215; Jackson, *Lachlan McIntosh*, 139; Saunt, *New Order of Things*, 79–80.

Upon reading it, the Georgians unanimously voiced their displeasure because, they claimed, it violated the rights of the state. Little did it matter because when the federal commissioners left, the state's delegation drew up their own treaty with the Creeks. That document, signed on November 12 and known as the Treaty of Galphintown, confirmed the earlier Treaty of Augusta in addition to ceding another strip of land east from the fork of the Ocmulgee and Oconee Rivers to the headwaters of the St. Marys.[64] By placing their marks on the document, Tallassee King, Fat King, and the others handed Georgia a *fait accompli*. Not only did the Indians confirm their earlier cession, but the state also got additional land, all without federal interference. It was a huge victory for states' rights in Georgia.

While Georgia's leaders crowed about their success at Galphintown, McGillivray pronounced the treaty as invalid and vowed to oppose it. Within months, he unleashed his warriors into the Oconee lands to settle the dispute with blood. That marked the beginning of a Creek war that stretched into the early 1790s, beyond the deaths of both Elbert and McGillivray. McIntosh's role in all of this remains unclear. According to his biographer, he was a minor player in the proceedings, but he also had a stake in the outcome at Galphintown since many of his bounty lands were in the disputed territory. He may have known beforehand that if his commission failed to get a treaty with the Creeks satisfactory to Georgia, the state's delegation would produce their own reconfirming the earlier agreement at Augusta that protected his economic interests.[65]

On January 9, 1786, Elbert's term as governor ended when the assembly chose Telfair as his successor. As the former governor stepped down, he had much to celebrate. In 1785, the state was at a critical juncture as it consolidated the Revolution, and it needed a steady and decisive executive. Elbert provided that leadership. He tackled emergencies, such as the smallpox scare below Augusta in the previous summer, with a calm and levelheaded approach and offered practical solutions to address them. Despite the conflict of interest in using his trading firms to carry out the state's business, his administration was free of corruption and scandal. He made it a point to go after corruption in the distribution of bounties and headrights. While he was quick to praise and reward honest and faithful

---

[64] Jackson, Lachlan McIntosh, 139; Saunt, *New Order of Things*, 80. Clarke and Twiggs signed the treaty on behalf of the state. See K. Coleman, *American Revolution in Georgia*, 243.

[65] Jackson, *Lachlan McIntosh*, 139.

citizens, he reprimanded wrongdoers, like frontier vagrants who caused problems with Native Americans and defaulters who refused to pay their debts to the state. Humble in nature and sympathetic to those he governed, Elbert also displayed a defiant and outspoken side when it came to matters concerning the defense of his state. The economic instability that the governor inherited was not his fault, but he and his administration deserved much credit for keeping Georgia from drifting off into a financial abyss. The relationship between the governor, his executive council, and the General Assembly was so harmonious that it served as a model for future administrations. Elbert's greatest success, however, was the creation of the nation's first state university, which stood out as the most far-reaching and consequential positive achievement of his administration.

The governor also had his share of disappointments, and they almost all involved his failed border wars. He tried, but did not curtail, the lawless bands prowling along the southern border with Florida. Far out west in the Yazoo lands, the fate of Bourbon County hung in limbo. Practically all Elbert and the assembly accomplished there was to stir animosity toward the state from both Spain and Congress. The border with South Carolina was also still in question when he left office. The Treaty of Galphintown failed to resolve the Oconee crisis since McGillivray and the Upper Creeks rejected it, and it did more harm to the state than good since its legacy was a war with the Creeks. Another legacy that Elbert did much to advance concerned the issue of states' rights. Throughout his administration, the governor constantly battled Congress over matters he believed fell solely within the state's power to address. His defiant stand for states' rights were most evident in Bourbon County, the Oconee Lands, and in the fight to clarify Georgia's border with South Carolina. Out of all Georgia's Confederation governors between 1783 and the state's signing of the United States Constitution in 1788, including Lyman Hall, John Martin, John Houstoun, Edward Telfair, and George Mathews, Elbert stood out as the greatest champion of the rights of his state in relation to the federal government. It was a strange reversal from his defense of federal authority over state government during the Revolution. Though he never knew it, the states' rights philosophy he so emphatically advanced as governor placed his country in future peril since it undermined the national government and nation that he fought so hard to establish during America's war for independence.

Chapter 15

Rest in Pieces

After an exhausting term as governor, Samuel Elbert found little time to rest and restore his health, since other matters intruded, such as finding a larger residence in Savannah to accommodate his family of eight by 1788. As he sought opportunities to expand his living arrangements, in 1785 he put his most recent former home up for lease, which he described in Savannah's newspaper as a "roomy and very convenient dwelling house" perfectly located in the heart of the city. The lot's selling features included several outbuildings and a large garden area, which he hoped would attract a buyer or tenant.[1]

The former governor may have already been considering a move to the Great Ogeechee, where a new town called Elberton, the first place in the state named for him, had just formed at Indian Hill in Effingham County north of Chatham. Located on the northeastern side of the Ogeechee, Elberton was approximately forty-eight miles from Savannah. Being on the Ogeechee also placed him closer to Point Plantation, which he purchased as Governor James Wright's confiscated estate in 1782. It is likely that he entertained ideas about running the plantation as another business. At the beginning of the year, he purchased ten horses, perhaps for use at the plantation, and described each in his account book. One was a cream mare "trot horse," thirteen-hands high with a heart and a "T" branded on the buttock. If any of the horses had distinctive brands, he drew them besides their descriptions in his records. Elbert also took careful notes about the husbandry of horses. On one page in his book, he jotted down a recipe to get rid of botflies. "Take a large handful of rue for herb-de-grace," it read, and then bound it with "half a pint of sharp vinegar." After straining the mixture, the next step was to add "allum grounded fine and give it to the Horse." This concoction worked, he pronounced, and if

---

[1] *Gazette of the State of Georgia*, February 10, 1785, 4.

the horse "hath the botts [*sic*], it will kill them."²

The possibility of relocating to the Ogeechee came with added risks. Most notably, Georgia was starting to feel the impacts of its ill-advised 1785 Treaty of Galphintown with the Creeks, who responded by raiding across the state's unprotected borders into the Oconee lands and beyond it into settled areas. The raids, initiated by Upper Creek leader Alexander McGillivray, ticked up in frequency through 1786 and became even more severe in the following year. In May 1786, one raiding party caught Elijah Clarke and his militia off-guard in the disputed area, and a brief skirmish ensued. The clash forced Clarke to retreat over the Oconee along with many inhabitants who fled for their lives. The frightened settlers were now concerned about saving their crops. Jared Irwin told Burke County militia commander General John Twiggs that the settlers would be "much obliged for every Incouragement [*sic*].... the Melitia [*sic*]" could give and he hoped he would use his influence to help restore them to their property and offer them protection.³ Such raids rekindled dreaded memories of Indian warfare along the border during the Revolution and further solidified a pervasive hatred toward all Native Americans. The violence surely caused Elbert to reconsider ideas about relocating to the Ogeechee with his family.

All the while, Elbert plied his trade as a merchant and kept his diverse customers satisfied with goods for their homes and plantations. For example, he listed in his account book after his term as governor a transaction with Dr. Samuel Russell, a local physician, where he sold him on credit coffee, sugar, salt, rum, corn, and several barrels of rice and hogsheads of bacon. Even as governor, Elbert continued to dabble in selling real estate. In March 1785, he placed an advertisement in the *Gazette* offering up a corner lot in Savannah near Major Fishbourne's property and opposite from Mr. Platt's residence. Another notice advertised a fifty-acre lot three miles from Savannah on the Thunderbolt Road. The land was well timbered with oak, hickory, and pine and

---

² Account Book, 1769–1788, 1–2, Samuel Elbert Papers, Rubenstein Rare Book and Manuscript Library; Worchester, *Gazetteer of the United States*, EGG–ELI, 1818.

³ Jared Irwin to John Twigs, May 19, 1786, John Twiggs Papers, 1781–1799, Rubenstein Rare Book and Manuscript Library. Between 1787 to 1790, every Georgia county reported Muskogee raids with newly created Greene County having the most (161), followed by Wilkes County (90) and Washington County (67). Even Chatham County during the same time reported eight raids. See the map in Haynes, "Patrolling the Border," 200.

formerly belonged to Jane Somerville, his wife's deceased sister.[4]

Many hailed Elbert as an excellent merchant, and they often came to him for advice in the trade. Though politics kept George Walton busy, he still hoped to open a store in Wilkes County. As he contemplated his decision, the first person who came to his mind was Elbert. On October 2, 1785, the upstate politician wrote then-Governor Elbert a letter seeking his opinion about entering the Indian trade, and he wanted the former commander to help stock his business. "I shall want some Indian goods this fall to the amount of five-hundred to a thousand pounds sterling," he requested, "if it is in your power to supply me with such articles as will suite the Indian trade on terms agreeable." Walton also asked for forty to fifty hogsheads of tobacco. He promised not to apply elsewhere for assistance until he received word from Elbert.[5]

If Elbert's intention was to distance himself from public service, the opposite happened. It was nearly impossible since he was the major general over Georgia's militia in the face of an intensifying Oconee crisis. Hardly had he finished his governorship when Chatham's citizens sent him to the assembly for the 1786 term under newly elected executive Edward Telfair. Elbert accepted the appointment in spite of his health and began his only post-Revolutionary experience in the assembly, which now met in Augusta. The sessions required an ailing Elbert to travel and be away from his family and businesses for several weeks at a time.

The 1786 General Assembly acted on several pieces of legislation, but among the highlights was an Act for the Encouragement of Literature and Genius, which established copyright laws and promoted research, writing, publication, and learning. The act was quite similar to those passed in other states, and, for Elbert, it meshed perfectly with the importance he placed on education. This assembly, more than any others prior to 1786, promoted the development of the frontier beyond Augusta. Recognizing the need to shift the capitol closer to a westward expanding populace, it established a new town called Louisville (in honor of the king of France who helped American during the Revolution), about twenty miles away from Galphin's Old Town, for that purpose. Louisville was little more than a name in 1786, and the town's

---

[4] Account Book, 1769–1788, 29, Samuel Elbert Papers, Rubenstein Rare Book and Manuscript Library; *Gazette of the State of Georgia*, March 10, 1785, 4.

[5] George Walton to Samuel Elbert, October 2, 1785, in box 3, folder 2, 1785, Edward Telfair Papers, Rubenstein Rare Book and Manuscript Library.

development, the selling of lots, and construction of government buildings required much time. It did not help matters that it was within the disputed Oconee lands and subject to Indian raids. Nevertheless, the state forged ahead and began surveys. In the interim, Augusta remained the capitol until Louisville was ready, which was not until 1795.[6]

Still focusing on the frontier, the assembly created Greene County out of the western portion of Wilkes. Named for deceased war hero Nathanael Greene (who died the year the assembly met), both the county and its seat of government, Greensboro, were the target of frequent Indian raids. On February 8, the assembly created two towns in the Broad River valley to promote the cultivation of tobacco. On the south side of the Broad at its juncture with the Savannah, it granted Zachariah Lamar land to lay out the town of Lincoln (named for Revolutionary War general Benjamin Lincoln) and to construct a tobacco inspection warehouse. In no time, Lamar's frontier town took shape, but instead of calling it Lincoln, he named it Lisbon. Across from Lisbon, on the northern side of the Broad, the assembly, on the same day, authorized Dionysius Oliver to construct another town, again with a tobacco warehouse. Oliver named his town Petersburg, and it quickly overshadowed Lisbon. To improve navigation to the two new towns, an act passed authorizing the clearing of the Savannah from Rae's Creek in Augusta all the way up to the forks of the Tugaloo and Keowee Rivers at the still-contested border with South Carolina.[7] Elbert was surely interested in the development of Wilkes County's northern section because it fell within the 1773 New Purchase from the Indians with which he was involved.

When compared to his time in the assembly before the Revolution, in 1786 Elbert was a passive member. He only found a position on one committee whose purpose was to oversee ship traffic and commercial activity in Savannah's harbor. On February 13, he, along with Joseph Clay, Seth Cuthbert, John Habersham, and a handful of others, were given "full power and authority" to appoint ship pilots, establish rules and regulations, and do everything else necessary to properly regulate the city's port.[8]

---

[6] K. Coleman, *American Revolution in Georgia*, 199.

[7] "An Act to authorize Zachariah Lamar, Esquire, to lay out a town at the mouth of Broad river, and to establish inspections in the county of Wilkes," February 8, 1786, *CRG*, 19(2):490–91; Ouzts, "Petersburg."

[8] *CRG*, 19(2):511–12.

By the time the assembly's term ended, Elbert was already busy trying to revive masonry in Georgia. During the Revolution, organized masonry in the state disappeared. In January 1785, Solomon's Lodge held its first formal meeting in a decade. Elbert was still grand master due to his pre-Revolutionary appointment to that position by England's Grand Lodge. By 1785, there were three other independent lodges in Georgia, including Hiram in Savannah, one in Augusta, and the last in Washington (Wilkes County).[9] Constituted without the permission of England's Grand Lodge, all three were illegitimate. It became Elbert's vision, along with fellow member James Jackson and other prominent Savannah Masons, to dissolve all ties to the English lodge and bring the state's separate masonic groups under one authority.

According to the *Georgia State Gazette*, on December 21, 1786, representatives from the state's lodges gathered at Solomon Lodge's meeting room in a Savannah coffee house and moved forward declaring their independence from England. Toward that goal, they abolished all bylaws, regulations, and appointments from England's lodge. In his last defiant swipe at a former enemy, Elbert resigned as grand master. By resigning, Elbert gave birth to free and independent masonry in the state. The members hailed him as the "Father of Independent Masonry" and appointed a committee to offer him thanks for his "generous and masonic behavior." They then presented him with an emblematic jewel as a token of their respect and brotherly affection. After Elbert stepped down, the craft installed new officers and made Solomon's Lodge #1 Georgia's premier lodge, with all present and subsequent masonic organizations falling under its jurisdiction.[10] Thus, Elbert began independent masonry in Georgia. It was, like the disestablished Anglican Church, one of the social results of the Revolution in the state.

Elbert invested much time and energy into providing leadership in the community. That extended beyond the lodge and included such organizations as the Order of the Cincinnatus, which continued to hold regular functions. On July 4, 1787, the Cincinnati held a special meeting to commemorate Independence Day. Before the celebration, members elected new officers and chose Elbert as their vice president. They spent the rest of the day and most of the evening in mirth, entertainment, and

---

[9] C. C. Jones Jr., *History of Savannah*, 556. Elbert's Unity Lodge and Grenadier Lodge ceased to exist when the Revolution began.

[10] *Georgia State Gazette or Independent Register*, January 13, 1787, 2.

"perfect harmony," giving countless patriotic toasts, including one to honor the memory of Nathanael Greene, who only a few weeks earlier died at his Savannah plantation called Mulberry Grove.[11]

Elbert's community activities were not constrained to Savannah. On April 5, 1787, he was at Elberton on the Great Ogeechee during Easter week helping settlers determine where to place a church and elect officers and constables. His motive, perhaps, was that he still contemplated leaving Savannah and moving to the town that bore his name. Purcell believed that health concerns largely lay behind the desire to relocate and suggested that he was already thinking about abandoning his businesses. Still, he maintained his residence in Savannah, likely due to the uptick of frontier violence in 1787.[12]

In 1786, when Elbert was in the assembly, the state negotiated yet a third treaty with the Lower Creeks, this time at Shoulderbone Creek on the Oconee River. Georgia invited McGillivray to attend, but he predictably refused unless the Whites withdrew from the Oconee lands. Such a withdrawal was never a possibility, so the Treaty of Shoulderbone, agreed to on October 21, was signed without McGillivray's presence or blessing. In it, the same Lower Creeks who negotiated earlier treaties with Georgia promised to give satisfaction for murders committed since the Treaty of Galphintown and to pursue peace. They also agreed, for a third time, to the cessions and boundaries established in the Treaties of Augusta and Galphintown. McGillivray balked at the new treaty and labeled it fraudulent, just like the other two. His response was to send out patrols and contest the treaty through scattered raids. In April 1787, when Elbert was down on the Great Ogeechee, McGillivray's warriors began random attacks on frontier homes and settlements all along the state's borders. The raids intensified through the summer. Georgia responded by revising the militia law and authorizing 1,500 to 3,000 troops to defend the state.[13] At that time, despite three treaties, an Indian war seemed no longer a possibility, but rather an inevitability.

The intensifying frontier conflict distressed Elbert, not only because he was thinking about moving to the Great Ogeechee. He knew that an Indian war would devastate his state and cause many fatalities. Despite this, neither he, nor any of Georgia's leaders, were willing to entertain

---

[11] *Gazette of the State of Georgia*, July 6, 1787, 2.

[12] Ibid., April 5, 1787, 4; Purcell, "Public Career of Samuel Elbert," 99.

[13] K. Coleman, *American Revolution in Georgia*, 244–49.

McGillivray's perspective. Instead, they considered their position on the Oconee lands, backed by three questionable treaties, legal and binding. On November 2, 1787, the former governor wrote revered and aged Pennsylvania sage Ben Franklin to seek insight on how to deal with Georgia's nagging Indian problems. Franklin, always willing to give wise advice, replied to the letter on December 16. "During the Course of a long Life in which I have made Observations on public affairs," he began, it seemed that "almost every War between Indians and Whites has been occasion'd by some Injustice of the latter towards the former." The elder statesman believed that wars with the Indians over land were not only unsettling to the frontier, but they also reduced settlers to poverty and distress, in addition to being financially disastrous. It was obvious, he thought, that obtaining cessions from Indians was was "much cheaper as well as honester, to buy their Lands than to take them by Force." He suggested that Georgia adopt a New England township model for the settlement of the frontier. By constructing a square with a fort, school, and church placed in it, surrounded by civilian homes on all sides facing inward, everyone could see each other. Thus situated, he believed that "one House could not be attacked without being seen & giving alarm to the rest, who were ready to run to its Succor." Georgia's mode of sparse and remote settlements did not offer these advantages, and, if frontier inhabitants managed to ward off Indian attacks, they were still, due to a lack of schools and other civilizing forces, in "danger of bringing up a Sett of Savages of our own Colour."[14]

As Elbert corresponded with Franklin, Chatham County was preparing to hold elections to the assembly and other civic positions. On December 4, 1787, citizens unexpectedly elected him, with a plurality of 271 votes, to be their new sheriff. This position of high esteem showed the level of great respect Chatham residents had for Elbert. It also showed something else: according to Purcell, Chatham County's citizens did not want Elbert to leave their city and move to Elberton. Their vote was, in part, an attempt to keep him in Savannah.[15] Because of health concerns, Elbert was in no condition to accept the position, but once again, he bowed to the people's wishes.

---

[14] Benjamin Franklin to Samuel Elbert, December 16, 1787, *Journal of the Society of Architectural Historians*, 11/3 (October 1952) 26–27.

[15] *Georgia State Gazette or Independent Register*, December 15, 1787, 3; C. C. Jones Jr., *Samuel Elbert*, 39; Purcell, "Public Career of Samuel Elbert," 99.

Being sheriff of Chatham County was no easy task. Within days of beginning his term, fourteen slaves escaped from a workhouse in Charleston, and authorities believed they were hiding around Savannah. Elbert's job involved their capture, and he placed a notice the *Gazette* to that effect. "All persons are therefore forbid[den] to buy or harbor" any of the slaves, it read, and he offered a reward of thirty shillings sterling for each one apprehended. On that same day, he also appeared at the Vendue House in Savannah to orchestrate a sheriff's sale. For years, the Vendue House served as the location for such auctions. Ironically, it was also where Elbert lost some of his property when he was absent from the state during Wright's restoration. The seizure and selling of land entailed another aspect of Elbert's role as sheriff. On this particular occasion, he placed a town lot, measuring thirty-four by ninety feet, with a fine dwelling house and attached buildings, up for sale to the highest bidder. The home's deceased owner faced substantial debt at the time he died. Those seeking payment of those debts sought an execution against the estate's administrator, resulting in the home's liquidation.[16]

The seizure of property to satisfy debts consumed most of Elbert's time as sheriff. Sometimes this included large tracts of land. In April, he listed 197 acres on Black Creek, 300 acres of tideland along the Savannah, and a 100-acre river swamp plantation on Hutchinson Island with a barn and several outbuildings seized for a sheriff's sale. He took the properties through a writ of *fieri facias*, which was a court order commanding the sheriff to sell the land to satisfy a judgment against the owner. During May, he seized Cherokee Hill, a 383-acre plantation, for the same reason. He even confiscated ships in the harbor. During the spring, the *John* lay at anchor as it awaited its fate in a sheriff's sale. Elbert boarded the ship and made an inventory of all of its furniture, tackle, and apparel, which he offered to the public, along with the ship.[17]

The disease that ravaged Elbert's frail body became worse in 1788, but he never slowed down. Being sheriff was exhausting, but he maintained a presence in the lodge, the Cincinnati, and at Christ Church. He kept up with Elberton, too, and had a stake in its success, despite setbacks there. He was disheartened to learn, for instance, that on February 13 an

---

[16] *Gazette of the State of Georgia*, January 10, 1788, 2, 4.

[17] Ibid., March 13, 1788, 2, April 3, 1788, 2, and May 5, 1788. Elbert also lost land due to debt. In 1787, he turned over his bounty land of 3,000 acres on Spirit Creek to Andrew Atkinson to liquidate a debt owed to him (Purell, "the Public Career of Samuel Elbert," 99).

Indian raiding party killed and scalped a young man who lived in Elberton. Given his status and support for educational efforts, his appointment to the Chatham Academy Board of Trustees by the assembly in that same month was no shock or surprise. He shared his position with many old friends and acquaintances, including Joseph Clay, Seth Cuthbert, John Habersham, former governor John Houstoun, and former speaker William Gibbons.[18]

Elbert generously continued to loan others money. In May, he loaned William Gordon £21.9. He also tried to provide his children with the best available educational and cultural opportunities. In April, he paid £3.5.3 to a teacher to help his daughter learn how to play the harpsichord. That music teacher was probably Edward Krutman, an immigrant to Savannah from Westphalia. In June, Krutman died, and he listed Elbert as one of the executors of his will. He also left him with all of his musical pieces and scores for use by "my scholars, the daus. of Gen. Elbert."[19]

Throughout summer 1788, Elbert continued to follow his servant's heart, giving to the community and others, but his time was running short. By then, the effects of his prolonged illness were noticeable to those around him. Though it cannot be proven, tuberculosis (or consumption), probably contracted when he was a British prisoner of war, was likely the disease that finally brought him down. His failing health prompted him to finalize a last will and testament, which he signed on July 2. In it, he admitted that he was "now sick," but still possessed a "sound mind and understanding." The first priority, he said, was to pay off his many debts by liquidating property. The rest of the estate, including his personal effects, he bequeathed to his wife and six children, Catherine ("Caty" or "Kitty") Rae, Elizabeth ("Betsy"), Sarah, Samuel Emanuel de la Fayette, Matthew, and Hugh Rae, to be divided equally among them. Since all of his children were minors, the ailing commander specified that they were entitled to their inheritance when they turned twenty-one years old, except for his daughters if they married before then. He then listed his executors, who were his wife, Elizabeth, and his friend William Stephens. He later added Joseph Habersham as another executor. Among those who witnessed Elbert sign the will was Clay.[20]

---

[18] *Georgia State Gazette or Independent Register*, March 1, 1788, 3; Watkins and Watkins, *Digest of the Laws*, 374.

[19] Account Book, 1769–1788, 22, 25, Samuel Elbert Papers, Rubenstein Rare Book and Manuscript Library; Purcell, "Public Career of Samuel Elbert," 100–101.

[20] Samuel Elbert, Last Will, July 2, 1788, Wills Record Book C, 1780–1791,

In September and October, Elbert continued his role as sheriff, but he hardly had the strength to fulfill his duties. The last notice announcing one of his sheriff sales appeared in the *Gazette* on October 9. Through the authority given him by his position, he seized the "good Sloop *Savannah*" against the owner, Edward White, and announced that the vessel was subject to a public auction in the following week. As the ship lay at anchor in the river, Elbert boarded it and took an inventory of its contents, including net tackle, furniture, apparel, and cargo. Those items were also up for public bidding, and he displayed them in his office for potential buyers. After that auction, he ceased his official, business, and community activities altogether. Though near death, he summoned enough strength to make one final trip to Elberton. He never saw the city of Savannah again. On Saturday, November 1, Elbert died in Elberton, surrounded by his family and friends. He only was forty-eight years old.[21] Had he lived just a few months more, he would have learned that George Washington, the person he most admired, was elected as the first president of the United States.

Elbert's death shocked the state. However, his burial came quicker than the solemn news could spread. He wished for interment in the Rae cemetery on top of the Indian temple mound (called the "Mount") between the forks of Pipemaker's Creek and the Savannah River. That resting place lay nearly fifty miles away, so, due to the effects of decomposition, his body had to be taken to Savannah in great haste. On November 2, the day after his death, Elbert's body arrived in Savannah on a wagon. Once there, a short, quickly organized funeral officiated by the Reverend Lindsay occurred in Christ Church. After Lindsay's oration, the militia and artillery bestowed upon Elbert full military honors, including the firing of minute guns. Soldiers at nearby Fort Wayne lowered their colors in mourning, as did all the ships in the harbor. A large and sorrowful funeral procession then formed to escort their fallen leader to the Mount, about three miles north of the city. Near the head of the procession were members of Elbert's family, several militia units, and artillery companies. The Masons and the Cincinnati followed along behind them while throngs of sad citizens formed the column's rear. The whole ensemble slowly snaked its way to the Mount, where they lay Elbert to rest in a wooden coffin near his father-in-law, John Rae, and other members of the Rae family. The

---

Chatham County, Georgia, Court of the Ordinary, 105–107.

[21] *Gazette of the State of Georgia*, October 9, 1788. McCall claims that Elbert died at the Great Ogeechee (*Roster of Revolutionary Soldiers in Georgia*, 3:74).

entire scene was "Solemn indeed," proclaimed the *Georgia State Gazette*, "for ELBERT is no more" and the state that he defended and led bid his "Immortal Spirit, farewell."[22] After his last rites, workers carefully lowered the coffin into the ground and covered it with earth. Soon, a marble tombstone appeared, marking his resting place for future generations.

Elbert's obituaries were full of adulation. "Stimulated *by love of country*," read one a week after his passing, he cheerfully participated in the controversies and struggles of his state and "undertook to encounter her enemies in the field." His bravery was unquestioned, and he disdained anything "that looked like shrinking back from danger." The statement was not hyperbolic. Elbert had proven himself as a courageous soldier during the Revolution as he faced insurmountable odds in campaigns and battles.[23]

The cause of death, according to newspapers, was a "painful illness." However, Elbert accepted his fate and faced the debilitating, "lingering" disease with "patience and firmness." Realizing his situation was terminal, he relied on his Christian faith as he bore the effects and "looked forward to his great *change* with an awful and fixed hope of future happiness." What people remembered most about him, in addition to his courage, was the "fidelity," "dignity," and "cool deliberation" he brought to his various civil and military appointments. He was a man with just principles, proclaimed one write-up, and possessed "an honest heart." In all things, it read, Elbert "showed himself to be a *man of honor*." That honor applied to his family, too. To Elizabeth and his children, he was a "most affectionate" husband and parent. "But alas! he's dead," the *Georgia State Gazette* proclaimed, "and all Georgia felt the stroke which deprived them of their *gallant friend*." Even the Masonic order felt death's sting. One of the first civic organizations to pay tribute to Elbert's memory was Solomon's Lodge. On December 29, they gave a toast in remembrance to their "late Right Worshipful Past Grand Master Elbert" during an elegant dinner.[24]

Elbert bequeathed his family both land and enormous debt. As one of the executors of his will, Elizabeth had the authority to liquidate

---

[22] Elbert's lengthy obituary appeared in the *Georgia State Gazette or Independent Register*, November 8, 1788, 3. There was a second obituary notice referenced by Jones that appeared in the *Georgia Gazette*, November 6, 1788, 302. See C. C. Jones Jr., *Samuel Elbert*, 40–41.

[23] *Georgia State Gazette or Independent Register*, November 8, 1788, 3.

[24] *Georgia Gazette*, November 6, 1778, 302, in C. C. Jones Jr., *Samuel Elbert*, 41; *Georgia State Gazette or Independent Register*, November 8, 1788, 3; January 10, 1789, 2.

property to cover her husband's liabilities. Over the next four years, she sold much of Elbert's lands to satisfy creditors. All the while, outstanding debts incurred compounding interest. Edward Telfair recorded in his books that his former friend still owed him money from the trading firm of McLean, Elbert & Company back in 1784. The debt then was £17.15.10, but, due to interest, it was now £29.17.8¾. Telfair was only one of many demanding money; an Augusta newspaper on April 30, 1791, told the sad state of affairs with a large headline reading, "To be Sold, Lands belonging to the late Concern of Rae, Elbert & Co." Altogether, 1,800 acres consisting of several tracts along the Savannah and Little Rivers were auctioned. On June 27, 1791, Chief Justice George Walton, presiding over the Superior Court in Richmond County (Augusta), issued an injunction momentarily suspending all lawsuits against the survivors of Rae's, Elbert & Graham and Rae's, Elbert & Company. Walton may have felt sympathy for Elizabeth and her family. At any rate, the injunction was only temporary. The debts remained outstanding and had to be paid.[25]

As legal obligations mounted and slowly drained Elbert's possessions, his wife managed to cling onto a semblance of their former wealth. She continued to own many of her husband's slaves, one of whom was a sawmill worker acquired from Andrew Atkinson's labor force on Spirit Creek shortly before Elbert died. When that slave ran away in 1790, she put an advertisement in the *Augusta Chronicle and Gazette of the State* offering a thirty-dollar reward for his capture and return. Nevertheless, the erosion of her finances was embarrassing, particularly given the social status of her father and husband when they were alive. In 1791, as creditors pressed her to satisfy debts, she appealed to the General Assembly on behalf of herself and her children for permission to purchase an estate called White Oak with a state bond. She offered hard specie for security against the bond, which she promised to repay over an agreed-upon term of limited years. The assembly considered her request, but despite her late husband's former stature with that body, they believed her finances were so unstable that the bond "ought not to be granted."[26]

---

[25] Account McLean, Elbert & Co. to Edward Telfair (1791–1793) in box 3, folder 1, 1784, Edward Telfair Papers, Rubenstein Rare Book and Manuscript Library; *Augusta Chronicle and Gazette of the State*, April 30, 1791, 3, and July 23, 1791, 3.

[26] *Augusta Chronicle and Gazette of the State*, October 23, 1790, 2; Mrs. Elbert Petition for Bond for White Oak Estate, December 10, 1791, in Georgia House of Representatives Papers, 1791, Georgia General Assembly, House of Representatives Certification and Resolutions, MS 285, Georgia Historical Society.

The fate of Rae's Hall paralleled Elizabeth Elbert's financial decline though she had no claim to the estate, which was sold in 1781 by the provost marshal during Wright's restoration. Once the center of opulence and her father's prized possession, the plantation home quickly deteriorated. The subsequent owners of Rae's Hall let the plantation fall into disrepair; they also neglected to pay their property taxes, so it was auctioned again in 1792 to Daniel Course for £128.19.4 (the amount due in outstanding taxes owed to Chatham County). Around the same time, the heirs of Benjamin Stead, an English merchant, sued the descendants of John Rae for outstanding debts incurred by the firm of Rae & Somerville before the Revolution. The stress from the suit was perhaps more than Elizabeth Elbert could bear. Georgia's former first lady died in 1792 on the Great Ogeechee, presumably at Elberton, and the family buried her in the Mount, next to her husband.[27]

Elizabeth's death created the worst of situations for Elbert's children who, like their father, became orphans. The oldest, Catherine, married John Burke in September 1791 at the Great Ogeechee shortly before her mother died. Elizabeth, the next oldest, married Dr. Michael Burke in 1799. The living arrangements for the rest of the children, who were minors, is unknown. Some probably lived with their older sisters and other members of the family, like Isabella Rae and Joseph Habersham.[28]

When Catherine and Elizabeth married, they received their portion of the remaining estate, but by then, much of Elberts' former landholdings were gone. The 1790s were particularly damaging to his legacy in property. In February 1793, the commissioners of Augusta sued Elbert's heirs for failure to pay off a bond on town lot No. 25, which ironically fronted Elbert Street on the west side. The court gave the late governor's children twelve months to pay off the principal, interest, and legal costs associated with the bond or face foreclosure. The responsibility for assuming the debt probably fell upon Catherine and her new husband since her siblings were minors and she was the only one married at the time. It is likely that she was unable to cover her father's debt, and the lot was probably lost in a

---

[27] Savannah Unit, Georgia Writers' Project, "Rae's Hall Plantation, Part I," 241–42; Elizabeth Elbert's death notice is in the *Georgia Gazette*, January 26, 1792.

[28] *Thomas Holt et u.x. and John Kerr et u.x. vs. Benoni Robertson*, 1831, McMullan, *Equity Cases*, 475–76; Samuel Elbert, Revolutionary War Bounty Land Applications, Bounty Land Warrant BLWt 1230–500, February 21, 1827; *Georgia Gazette*, September 22, 1791, for the marriage announcement between Catherine and John Burke.

sheriff's sale.²⁹

The erosion of property continued. On March 16, 1798, Elbert's Lot No. 5 and part of Lot No. 4 in the village of Yamacraw just north of Savannah and near his grave in the Indian mound, went up for public bidding in a sheriff's sale due to foreclosure. Three months later, on June 22, the *Georgia Gazette* listed a notice that 1,350 acres of "Cotton Land" at Mobley's Ponds in Burke County, formerly belonging to Elbert, was up for sale. The large tract, divided into smaller parcels, was foreclosed upon because "the former purchaser [had not] complied with the terms of the sale." Not surprisingly, Rae's Hall again reached the auction block about the same time. In 1797, the courts finally awarded the heirs of Benjamin Stead £13,634.14.7 to satisfy their claims against Rae & Somerville. By then, Daniel Course was dead, and his wife, Elizabeth, who inherited Rae's Hall but had nothing to do with the debt, lost the estate to satisfy Rae's creditors. Thomas Young purchased it off the auction block for $2,575, a fraction of the property's actual value.³⁰

Were Elbert alive during the 1790s, he would have been mortified to see his children's suffering, the demise of his landholdings, and the fate of Rae's Hall. Adding insult to injury, his beloved city of Savannah almost burned to the ground in 1796 due to a fire on November 26. Aided by favorable winds and inadequate preparations for such a disaster, the accidental fire consumed most of the city, including many homes and public buildings. Out of 358 residences in Savannah, only 129 remained when the fire finally burned itself out. Among the public buildings lost was Christ Church, in addition to many others Elbert once frequented or knew.³¹ Indeed, so much change had already occurred within a decade to the world that Elbert left in 1788 that he hardly would have recognized Savannah at the dawn of the nineteenth century.

The state's efforts to venerate Elbert offered a more positive legacy to his memory. On December 10, 1790, the assembly cut out a fertile section of upper Wilkes County between the Savannah and Broad Rivers and named it Elbert County.³² Within its limits was Oliver's new town of Petersburg, established in 1786 when Elbert was in the General Assembly.

---

²⁹ *Augusta Chronicle and Gazette of the State*, February 16, 1793, 4.

³⁰ *Georgia Gazette*, March 16, 1798, 4; June 22, 1798, 4; Savannah Unit, Georgia Writers' Project, "Rae's Hall Plantation, Part I," 242.

³¹ Fraser, *Savannah in the Old South*, 158.

³² *Augusta Chronicle and Gazette of the State*, February 26, 1791, 1; Ouzts, "Elbert County."

When the assembly created Elbert County, many inhabitants already lived in the Broad River valley where most cultivated tobacco. Warehouse inspectors at Petersburg and Lisbon graded their crops and then shipped them downriver to markets in Augusta and Savannah. During his life, Elbert never stepped foot in what became Elbert County.

The first few decades after Elbert's death represented a period of commemoration by the assembly and various localities. The initial commemoration, of course, was the little hamlet called Elberton in Effingham County that emerged shortly before his death. The original Elberton failed to prosper, and by 1800 it was already a dead town. The creation of Elbert County was a more lasting legacy, and it flourished during the early years primarily due to tobacco and the river trade. A small village called Elbertville soon formed around a spring in the county some fifteen miles or so north of Petersburg. In 1803, the inhabitants incorporated it into the town of Elberton, and it became the county's seat of government, complete with a courthouse and jail. The second town of Elberton had a much more promising future than the previous one, and by the early twentieth century, because of the county's expansive underground granite deposits, it became known as the "Granite City" and the "Granite Capital of the South." A final commemoration took place in Savannah when, in 1801, the city laid out Elbert Square to honor the general's services to the state. The city even created a neighborhood called Elbert Ward.[33] These were fitting memorials by Chatham's citizens and the residents of Savannah to one of their most illustrious sons. The square sat on the northwestern edge of the city limits, near the ward, in the vicinity of the Spring Hill Redoubt where American and French forces failed to break through British lines on October 17, 1779.

Meanwhile, Elbert's surviving children matured, but only one, Sarah, reached middle age. Catherine and John Burke had a daughter, Elizabeth, who later married Louis (alternatively spelled Lewis) Smith Muse. John Burke died on December 2, 1795, and Catherine died not long afterwards. Elizabeth and Dr. Michael Burke had two daughters, Catherine, who married John Kerr, and Elizabeth, who married Thomas Holt. Elizabeth, their mother, died at the age of twenty-seven in 1804. Samuel de la Fayette joined the United States Navy and received his commission on December 11, 1798, and a promotion to lieutenant on March 3, 1803. Elbert was still in the navy when he married Harriet Ann Jackson at St. Marys on June

---

[33] Ouzts, "Elberton"; Spracher, *Images of America*, 42.

30, 1809. When the War of 1812 broke out against England, he commanded Gunboat No. 2 along the Georgia coast. He died during that conflict, on December 20, 1812, although his wife survived him for many years. They had no children. Hardly anything exists to document what happened to Hugh Rae Elbert, and Matthew died before reaching a majority. In 1827, "Miss" Sarah Elbert, a "maiden lady" filed a petition with the state for a 500-acre Revolutionary land warrant in the name of her father. The petition showed that Sarah was the only issue of Elbert still alive. Other survivors included in the petition were Elbert's three granddaughters, Elizabeth Muse, Catherine Kerr, and Elizabeth Holt. Harriet Ann Elbert, Samuel de la Fayette's widow, also attached her name to the petition as an heir through her deceased husband. Sarah and Elbert's grandchildren received the warrant, but Harriet Ann Elbert's dubious claim created legal controversies that continued through the 1850s. She died in 1865.[34]

Soon, nature slowly enveloped the Indian burial mound known as Irene, according to an eyewitness account around the time of the War of 1812. The visitor described it as "a large Mount" right at the mouth of Pipemaker's Creek, which was a small, unnavigable, and shallow tributary of the Savannah. The mound, clearly visible from the river, towered many feet into the air. He compared its height to the steep bank at Yamacraw Bluff, where James Oglethorpe first laid out his city of Savannah in 1733. To him, the earthen structure's most profound feature, beyond its size and steep incline, were the large and impressive live oaks growing upon its sides and summit.[35] The onlooker may have ascended the mound. If he did, he probably found the Rae cemetery and stumbled upon the graves of Elbert and his wife marked with marble headstones.

The nineteenth century was a time of neglect for Rae's Hall and Rae's cemetery. Rae's former plantation home finally collapsed, and the cemetery, which was never maintained and rarely visited, passed out of memory, especially as later family members died or moved away. The surrounding property passed through the hands of many people, none

---

[34] Coltrane, *Lineage Book*, 58:302; McMullan, *Equity Cases*, 475–76; G. Smith, *History of the Georgia Militia* 1:285–86; Samuel Elbert, Revolutionary War Bounty Land Applications, Bounty Land Warrant BLWt 1230–500, February 21, 1827, and also the attached affidavit of Anne Cummings, May 2, 1836; McCall, *Roster of Revolutionary Soldiers in Georgia*, 1:214.

[35] Savannah Unit, Georgia Writers' Project, "Rae's Hall Plantation, Part I," 245.

of whom had a connection to the Rae family or knowledge of the land's past. Time took a toll on the Rae cemetery. Often, winds from fierce coastal storms and hurricanes battered and uprooted the exposed oaks covering the mound. As the large trees fell, they shattered and displaced grave markers. Briars and thickets overtook open areas. During the 1880s, Georgia historian Charles C. Jones ascended the mound and, with some difficulty, located Elbert's forgotten grave in a wilderness of "soulless brambles and envious forests" that "obliterated all traces of the inhumation" on the mount. Even Elbert's memorial stone had fallen, bringing into question the exact spot where his bones "mingled with the ashes of the ancestors of the venerable Tomo-chi-chi."[36]

In the nineteenth century, most of the land around Rae's Hall was devoted to rice and cotton production, but that changed in the early twentieth century as Savannah's industrial development expanded upriver toward Pipemaker's Creek. This growth, in turn, heralded a new age that destroyed many things associated with Elbert's memory. In other words, just as the late eighteenth and early nineteenth centuries represented a time of commemorating Elbert, the early twentieth century, fueled by Savannah's growth and expansion, assaulted his memory and the first place desecrated was the Indian mound containing his remains.

When Elbert chose an Indian mound as his burial place, he also, unknowingly, wedded his fate to Native Americans interred there. Georgians had little regard for the prehistory of Native Americans who once lived in their state, and this lack of respect became evident in the destruction of temple and burial mounds during the nineteenth and twentieth centuries. Such disregard for Georgia's ancient history placed the Irene Mound at Pipemaker's Creek in peril, as it did many others in the state. In 1916, the Savannah Warehouse & Compress Company purchased Rae's Hall and nearby adjacent tracts from Joseph Hull and Company, including the mound containing Elbert's remains. By then, several industrial and commercial enterprises, complete with modern wharves and up-scaled warehouses, dotted the banks of the Savannah at Rae's Hall. These companies, in cooperation with Savannah's city leaders, also decided to construct ditches along Pipemaker's Creek and enlarge existing drainage canals to channel water from low-lying areas

---

[36] C. C. Jones Jr., *Samuel Elbert*, 42.

for sanitation and expansion purposes.[37]

During spring 1916, convict laborers toiled in the soggy marshes around Pipemaker's Creek as ditch construction and expansion began. One of the drainage canals required a large quantity of soil for a sluice gate along the creek, and Irene Mound was a convenient source for backfill. Shovels and picks soon tore into the side of the mound and, before long, up into Rae's cemetery. The mound's destruction concerned some local historians, who became more alarmed when they recalled that it was the site of Elbert's lost grave. The Savannah chapters of the Sons of the American Revolution and the Daughters of the American Revolution sent R. J. Travis to investigate damage to the mound and to locate Elbert's burial spot. It took some close searching on top of Irene before Travis finally discovered the Rae cemetery and, ultimately, Elbert's (and his wife's) resting place. His most shocking observation were the widely scattered human bones lying on the ground across the whole area.[38]

When Clarice Purcell was researching her master's thesis on Elbert at the University of Georgia in the early 1950s, she wrote Travis to inquire about his experience. In a reply, Travis said that when he got to the top of the mound, he looked around and finally found the commander's grave. Unfortunately, convicts had already dug into one corner of it and exposed some bones. Lying on the ground was Elbert's skull, which he picked up and took back to Savannah with him. He then gave it to the county superintendent, who passed it along "to an unknown yankee doctor, who took it away for a paper weight." Travis soon returned to the mound with a number of men to exhume what was left of the governor's remains. Sifting through shovelfuls of dirt, he and the others carefully picked out the bones of Elbert and his wife and placed them into boxes. "Parts of the marble stone, and metal buttons of his uniform and parts of the coffin were recovered," he told Purcell. They collected all of the remains they could find, and Travis stored them in boxes that he tucked away in his Savannah law office to await a proper burial. Elbert's skull never resurfaced.[39]

---

[37] J. Walker, "Brief History of Ocmulgee Archaeology," 16; Savannah Unit, Georgia Writers' Project, "Rae's Hall Plantation, Part II," 20–21.

[38] *Early County News*, May 4, 1916, 7; Purcell, "Public Career of Samuel Elbert," 105–106.

[39] Purcell, "Public Career of Samuel Elbert," 106; *Early County News*, May 4, 1916, 7.

The boxes holding the remnants of Elbert, his wife, and perhaps others, sat in Travis's office for eight years, even as interested community groups deliberated about what to do with them. The Athens *Banner Herald* reported on October 29, 1923, that citizens in Elbert County expressed a desire to have the general's remains brought there. Their reasoning, of course, was because of their county's name. The Samuel Elbert Chapter of the Daughters of the American Revolution in the county spearheaded the movement. Georgia's Society of the Sons of the American Revolution acted adversely to the request during an annual meeting in Savannah, preferring to keep the governor's remains in the city. Meanwhile, Solomon's Lodge offered to purchase a plot in Savannah's Bonaventure Cemetery for reburial. As the debate raged on, the effects of humidity and exposure to air accelerated the decay of Elbert's fragile bones. One person noted, after seeing them in 1923, that even those exhumed by Travis a few years earlier still intact were crumbling, and Elbert was "now nothing but dust."[40]

Questions about where to rebury Elbert raised more questions, especially regarding funding for purchasing a cemetery plot. A reburial with full military honors, the commissioning of a fitting headstone, and hiring someone to set the marker required additional money. The movement to lay Elbert to rest for a final time was a community effort. By 1924, the Masons had raised a considerable amount to rebury their former grand master. On February 22, the Order of the Cincinnati contributed an additional fifty dollars. All of the interested parties, including Travis, Solomon's Lodge, the Cincinnati, the Georgia chapter of the Sons of the American Revolution, and several chapters of the Daughters of the American Revolution, finally agreed that Savannah's Colonial Cemetery was the most appropriate location to place Elbert's ashes. That too, represented an obstacle since the last person was buried there in 1853, and the city authorities had to grant special permission for another interment, which they did.[41]

Finally, on March 10, 1924, 136 years after his death and first funeral, Elbert was buried a second time, again with full military honors in Savannah's Colonial Cemetery. There, he joined in death many of the people he knew, loved, and respected during his lifetime, such as all three of the Habersham brothers and their wives and father, Lachlan McIntosh, and

---

[40] *Athens Banner Herald*, October 29, 1923, 6; *Jackson Progres-Argos*, November 16, 1923, 3; *Jackson Herald*, February 14, 1924, 4.

[41] *Savannah Morning News*, February 23, 1924; Purcell, "Public Career of Samuel Elbert," 106–107.

Archibald Bulloch. Present at Elbert's second funeral were troops from the United States Army, the United States Navy, and local military units. It was a formal and solemn occasion, replete with gun salutes and speeches extolling the former leader's accomplishments as a military commander and governor.[42] In attendance were some of Savannah's most dignified civic leaders, who joined representatives from Solomon's Lodge, the Cincinnati, the Sons of the American Revolution, the Daughters of the American Revolution, and a host of curious spectators. Elbert's second funeral was much like the first. The only thing missing was the long, mournful procession of family, friends, and grieving citizens of Chatham.

Elbert's grave was not the only thing destroyed in the twentieth century that was dedicated to his memory. Savannah's desire to modernize for automobiles and tourists placed some of the city's historic streets and squares in jeopardy. The great debate about restructuring Savannah's streets to accommodate technological developments in urban transportation began in the late nineteenth century with the coming of streetcars and trolleys. Though many opposed the changes that streetcars would bring to Savannah, the commercial sector ultimately got its way. The arrival of the automobile once again reopened the discussion about modernizing the city's traffic grid, a conversation that began during the 1920s and intensified during the Great Depression. Once again, business interests favored street restructuring to promote commerce and tourism, but they met strong opposition from preservationists who feared the threat that development posed not only to historical structures but also to Savannah's unique atmosphere centered on its squares.[43]

The Depression negatively affected every city in Georgia, and Savannah was no exception. Grueling unemployment caused many of the city's leaders to seek relief through New Deal programs focusing on infrastructure development. Accordingly, Savannah applied for federal funds to improve its transportation networks, and, in 1935, the Bureau of Public Roads appropriated money for highway expansion to bring more tourists, commercial traffic, and heavy trucks into the city. The plan, announced in January 1935 and reported in the *Savannah Evening Press*, was to bring U.S. Highway 17 (the Atlantic Coastal Highway) into the northwestern edge of the city. The route selected for the new expansion went right down historic Montgomery Street and through the middle of Elbert, Liberty,

---

[42] *Savannah Morning News*, February 23, 1924.
[43] N. Walker, "Savannah's Lost Squares," 512–31.

and Franklin Squares.[44]

Engineers chose Montgomery Street for the expansion because of its location, but racism, too, played a role. Many Whites in Savannah considered the squares along Montgomery Street expendable since they formed a general border area between segregated neighborhoods. For example, on Franklin Square, the closest to the river, stood the historic First African Baptist Church (the oldest African American church in the United States), and it represented one of the few places where Blacks and Whites congregated together during the era of segregation. None of that mattered in 1935, however, and the project commenced as planned. A map of Savannah in 1940 showed the impact that the Highway 17 expansion had on the city's historic squares along Montgomery Street. Engineers demolished most of Elbert and Liberty Squares, and, at the project's completion, all that remained of them was a thin strip of grass along the side of the newly expanded road. Franklin Square fared much better, and during the 1980s, it became Savannah's first restored square. "Had some Savannahians in the 1930s not conditioned their respect for such [historical and aesthetic] values on skin color," one expert on the subject observed, "the Montgomery Street squares might not have been lost," and the memorial to Elbert may have still been intact.[45]

Another assault on Elbert's memory also occurred during the Depression, and it involved the fate of what was left of Irene Mound. Increasing development around Pipemaker's Creek created urgency for archaeologists to excavate the ancient structure and preserve its contents before they became irrevocably lost to expansion. A prominent Savannah historian, Dolores Boisfeuillet Floyd, revived interest in the mound, and the Works Progress Administration (WPA) provided archaeologists to oversee the dig and record and retrieve their findings. Work began on the project in 1937 and continued through 1940. By the time they finished, the site became one of the most completely excavated mounds in Georgia. Most of the field excavation crew were African American women, and, at times, their workforce exceeded one hundred people. In the upper layers of the mound, archaeologists found the remains of colonial interments, identified by coffin nails and hinges, buttons, and other fragments of colonial life. Most likely, these artifacts belonged to those buried in the Rae Cemetery. Underneath that layer, archaeologists discovered many Native American

---

[44] Ibid., 522.
[45] Ibid., 525–29; "First African Baptist Church."

burials, stone artifacts, bone awls, gaming disks, and clay vessels and pipes. They concluded that Native Americans occupied the Irene site for five hundred years in the middle to late Mississippian Period (1100–1600). Digging deeper, they discovered below the base of the mound evidence of an earlier Native American village, predating Irene by another five hundred years. This then, represented the buried spirits and historical past that occupied the earth underneath Elbert's grave at Irene. When fieldwork finally concluded, the mound and everything once in it was gone, and the place where it towered for centuries was level with the banks of the Savannah River.[46]

The final assault on Elbert's memory occurred when the Georgia Ports Authority acquired the land formerly making up Rae's Hall and the Irene Mound and turned it into an enormous shipping facility. After World War II, they bulldozed, paved, and developed the whole area, turning most of it into docks and storage areas for shipping containers. Such was the fate of the last remaining physical places associated with Elbert during his life and his death. By the middle of the twentieth century, the destruction of Elbert's memory was almost complete. Few people in the state knew anything much about him beyond professional and local historians. As the twentieth century went on, the state erected a handful of markers at places connected to him during the Revolution. Little else existed to remind Georgians of their Revolutionary War hero except a rural county along the upper stretches of the Savannah River and the little city serving as its seat of government called Elberton.

---

[46] Savannah Unit, Georgia Writers' Project, "Rae's Hall Plantation, Part II," 23–25; Williams, "Irene Mounds."

Chapter 16

"But All Georgia Will Thy Worth Rehearse": The Meaning of Samuel Elbert

Elbert's obituary in the *Gazette* concluded with a sad tributary poem that told the dead leader's immortal spirit, "farewell! *thy weeping friend.*" The short ode suggested that Elbert's name would become immortal, like his spirit. "But all Georgia will thy worth rehearse," proclaimed one line. The little piece concluded that Elbert was worth remembering, not just for his deeds, but also for his "virtue."[1] That is the place to begin unraveling the meaning of Elbert.

The obituary's predictions were accurate. In life, Elbert wanted to appear disinterested and not self-serving as he prided himself on upholding the dual principles of honor and virtue. Historians noticed those aspects of his character, and almost everything written about him since 1788 touched on those values. The first person to write about him was Judge Thomas U. P. Charlton. In 1808, twenty years after Elbert's death, he surmised, "there are few characters, whose lives were spent to greater public advantage and whose deaths were more sincerely regretted," than he; historians could fill "the page with those praises the character of an Elbert deserves." Later in the century, Charles C. Jones wrote that Elbert's virtues placed his "reputation…above reproach." He was, explained Jones, a man of "uncommon virtue and excellence." William Harden, in his history of Savannah and South Georgia, wrote in 1913 that Elbert's character and "record was clean and marked with the strictest integrity." Even Clarice Purcell, more than half a century later, could find nothing in her detailed master's thesis on Elbert in 1951 at the University of Georgia to tarnish his character. Modern historians continued to emphasize the theme of virtue. Elbert was "esteemed," wrote James Cook in his *Governors of Georgia*, "for his integrity," in addition to his patriotism and courage. Summarizing

---

[1] *Georgia State Gazette or Independent Register*, November 8, 1788, 3.

his virtues, newspaper columnist Herbert Wilcox called Elbert in 1971 "one of the most illustrious men of his time."[2]

Certainly, honor, and integrity were hallmarks of Elbert's character. Throughout his career, there were countless examples highlighting those attributes, such as when, on more than one occasion, he denied his own aspirations and refused military promotions that violated the chain of command and respect due to his superiors in rank. He carried himself with honor throughout the Revolution, and, during his one-year term as governor, his administration was free from scandal. He espoused the virtues of an active citizen in a republican form of government. Though he occupied the highest civil and military positions in the state, he never wavered in his devotion to the community where he provided leadership in such organizations as the Masons, the Order of the Cincinnati, the board of trustees for both the University of Georgia and Chatham Academy, and Christ Church. He also attached himself to benevolent societies, and many examples exist where he provided money and other forms of aid to people in need. Measured by his contributions to society, Elbert was the model citizen. Conversely, he shunned those he felt lacked the qualities of virtue and honor that governed his own life. He detested the arrogance, egotism, self-promotion, and boasting that characterized some of the people he knew, like James Wright, Button Gwinnett, and John Ashe.

Unfortunately, Elbert's virtue never extended to society's marginalized groups. When it came to Native Americans, he seemed interested only in how he could benefit from them. As a leader in the fur trade, he made a living on the deerskins and beaver pelts that they provided to his firms. As a commander during the Revolution, his Indian talks and diplomacy were geared toward keeping them neutral or making them allies against the British. He never believed they could possibly have a stake in the war's outcome. After the Revolution, his Indian treaties and talks were motivated by land cessions. The treaties he negotiated, pushed, and defiantly defended contained thousands of acres granted to him by the state in bounties and warrants, and his talks contained exaggerations, mistruths, and empty promises. Nevertheless, Native Americans trusted him and believed, as Elbert claimed, that he always spoke the truth. At times, he expressed sympathy for the plight of Indians and often professed that he was

---

[2] Charlton, "Sketch of the Life of General Elbert," 2; C. C. Jones Jr., *Samuel Elbert*, 39, 42; Cook, *Governors of Georgia*, 57; Harden, *History of Savannah and South Georgia*, 1:257; Wilcox, "Early Governor's 'Lost' Portrait," 38.

their friend, but he never considered them capable of embracing his definitions of honor and virtue. In almost every reference to Native Americans in communications with others, he labeled them "savages" who were incapable of enjoying the virtues of liberty and self-government that he fought for during the Revolution. Extending this observation further, one could argue that his actions and attitudes toward Native Americans pointed to, in the long run, their ultimate removal from the state.

Another marginalized group who never witnessed Elbert's virtue were Loyalists. Again, like the Indians, he denied Loyalists the capacity to be virtuous. It is clear from his orders and letters during the Revolution that one person Elbert most detested was a deserter-turned-traitor, and he placed all Loyalists into that category. He believed, like many of his fellow commanders, that the only proper response to their treason was a death sentence. The great irony in this position, however, was that Elbert was also treasonous because he violated loyalty oaths to King George III and James Wright that he took prior to 1775, in addition to leading a rebellion against their authority. Wright accused him of high treason in the 1781 Act of Attainder, but Elbert refused to appear in the state and answer for the crime. During the Revolution, Elbert afforded Loyalists none of the liberties he professed for himself—including the right to have and voice an alternative opinion about government.

Beginning in 1775, Elbert led the Council of Safety in a ruthless effort to silence, punish, and expel the supporters of the king in his colony, and, although he never participated in acts of torture, like tarring and feathering, he turned a blind eye to those who did. His disdain for Loyalists continued throughout the Revolution as he faced their armies. Even as governor, he nursed Loyalist hatred and promoted their removal and the continued confiscation of their estates, which benefited himself when he obtained Wright's plantation on the Ogeechee. On the other hand, he could also reach deep within himself and forgive those who formerly committed treason, like Andrew McLean, with whom he formed a brief business partnership after the war. However, he never found room in his heart to forgive Wright.

A third marginalized group that never felt the effects of Elbert's virtue were his slaves. Though his obituary called him a "compassionate master," nowhere in his writings or correspondences did he ever accord them the rights and liberties that he espoused for himself.[3] He never considered it.

---

[3] *Georgia State Gazette or Independent Register*, November 8, 1788, 3.

Throughout most of his life, he owned slaves, and one even attended him during his long incarceration in a British prisoner camp. Given Elbert's intelligence, it is astonishing that he never realized or understood that the liberty he felt was worth fighting and dying for was a cherished right of all human beings. To be fair, his attitudes about slavery and freedom represented those of most Whites in his society. Questioning those prevailing attitudes required bravery and deep critical thinking. However, some of his contemporaries, like George Washington, eventually recognized the hypocrisy of professing liberty while owing slaves. He finally freed them in his will. Elbert never arrived at that higher plane of thought.

The meaning of Elbert goes beyond virtue. His story, which began when the trustees ruled Georgia, spanned part of royal Georgia and the entirety of the Revolution and Confederation periods, encompassing most of the eighteenth century. He witnessed many of the events of the Revolution in Georgia firsthand. Though he was a reluctant Revolutionary in the beginning, he became a bold advocate for liberty and independence in 1775, before any of the fighting occurred. "No man in Georgia made a greater contribution to the early movement for independence both in the civil and the military aspects than did Samuel Elbert," wrote Purcell.[4] She was right. From the moment he embraced the Patriot cause, he was present in almost every organization and body that guided and defined the Revolution and at almost every event that defended it. Those bodies included the Committee (or Council) of Safety, the Association, Georgia's Provincial Congresses, and the Grenadier and Unity Lodges, which orchestrated covert movements for independence. He participated in almost every military engagement in Georgia prior to 1780 as a commander, and after each, his rank seemed to increase accordingly, even though his side almost always lost. Those engagements included the Battle of the Rice Boats in 1776; the Battle of Savannah in 1778, which resulted in its capture; and the Battle of Brier Creek in 1779. His victory on the Frederica River in 1778 gave Georgia its only military success in the war, at least until that time. Out of three failed expeditions to Florida, Elbert marched with two and commanded one of them. He also led a brief and largely uneventful western campaign into Georgia's ceded lands. As a prisoner behind British lines, he witnessed the allied siege and failed storming of the Spring Hill Redoubt in 1779. Thus, Elbert had connections to most of the Revolution's major events in Georgia before 1780, and those

---

[4] Purcell, "Public Career of Samuel Elbert," 24–25.

experiences made him unique.

Many have hailed Elbert as a great military commander. In 1971, Wilcox deemed him a "brilliant military man."[5] There was great irony in the statement because even though he became a brigadier general in the Continental Army and a major general over Georgia's militia, he had no formal military training. Elbert was certainly a man of great courage and valor. Never once did he shrink in cowardice or abandon the field without putting up a fight. He also was a strict disciplinarian who emphasized order, soldierly appearances, and strict obedience to his commands. Despite being overbearing at times, he always put the needs of his men before himself. For that, and for his courage, he won the hearts of his soldiers, who both loved and respected him.

Though a model soldier, Elbert's abilities on the battlefield were never tested. During the Revolution, he faced professional British and Loyalist armies twice—during the fall of Savannah and the battle at Brier Creek—and he lost both engagements. Both battles hardly lasted beyond five minutes, and neither highlighted his real strengths at command. Furthermore, the failures at those battles were not due to Elbert or to decisions he made, but rather to the ineptness of his superiors and to circumstances beyond his control. The one military excursion that brought him great recognition and success was his surprise attack on the British fleet in the Frederica River. There, he exhibited his ability to plan and coordinate a daring campaign on his own without interference from his superiors. Had he served for most of the war in Washington's army under more talented commanders, perhaps he could have found better opportunities to display his battlefield abilities and talents.

Elbert was a man of letters, but paradoxically, a person with no formal education. Still, his letters to contemporaries were eloquent and exhibited a masterful command of prose. He knew most of the major players in the Revolution and frequently communicated with them in writing. During his life, he wrote to Benjamin Franklin, Charles Lee, Robert Howe, Benjamin Lincoln, and several others, including some Native American leaders through letters read to them by interpreters. He knew others in person, like Washington, whom he served under as a junior officer at Yorktown. There, he also met Baron von Steuben, Henry Knox, Rochambeau, and Alexander Hamilton. He became intimate friends with Lafayette. In Georgia, he was acquainted with all of the state's revolutionaries, and he

---

[5] Wilcox, "Early Governor's 'Lost' Portrait," 38.

had a deep level of friendship with most of them.

Throughout his life, Elbert exhibited tenacity in the face of adversity. He never gave up during the Revolution when defeat seemed the only outcome. He always held to the glimmer of hope that liberty would eventually prevail over tyranny. As a prisoner enduring some of the most wretched conditions imaginable for well over two years, he never lost faith in his cause. For nearly a decade, he confronted a debilitating and terminal illness that sapped his body of strength, but he continued to serve his community and the people of his state without complaining almost until the day he died. With dogged determination, he clawed his way out of obscurity in the 1760s to become a respected, successful, and established Savannah merchant by the time the Revolution began. Though he lost almost everything connected to his firms during the Revolution, he rebuilt his business career and reestablished himself as one of Savannah's premier merchants, as well as one of its most revered citizens.

While almost everything associated with Elbert's life and the early efforts to memorialize him are gone, at least two of his legacies, the University of Georgia and Independent Masonry, bear more permanence. Other enduring legacies are the county and city that bear his name. Though he has no statues, a few scattered bronze tablets erected around the state mark significant places connected to him. One stands, appropriately, at his grave in the Colonial Cemetery. There are two at the Battle of Brier Creek site. The Masons erected the first in 1954 and the Georgia Historical Commission the other in 1956. At the Frederica River, near the scene of his great victory over a British fleet, stands a third tablet. Even the state of Florida erected a historical marker on Amelia Island in Nassau County discussing Elbert's failed 1777 Florida campaign, and Elberton erected an obelisk in his honor near the old Seaboard Airline depot.

If one visited the Colonial Cemetery in Savannah today and strolled through the winding, grassy paths between the scattered and seemingly endless rows of markers, monuments, and tombstones, they would soon encounter Elbert's grave designated by a rectangular, nearly waist-high stone structure with a capstone. His name is carved on it in big, bold letters. What follows below his name is a brief summary of his life's highlights. Though some of the information is erroneous (it says he was born in South Carolina, for example), the rest tells any visitor that they are standing before a once great and influential leader who was a brigadier general in the Continental Army, a major general in the state's militia, a governor, a past grand master of the Masons, a founder of the Order of the Cincinnati in Georgia, and a former sheriff of Chatham County. The bronze historical marker looming above the sarcophagus adds more details on Elbert's importance, although it, too, duplicates the error carved on the capstone about his birthplace. Other than that, Elbert would be proud of the inscriptions adorning his second grave. It was just how he wanted to be remembered.

Timeline

1733	**February 1**: Sarah Greenfield, Elbert's future mother, arrives in Savannah on board the *Anne* as one of Oglethorpe's original colonists.
1734	William Elbert, Elbert's future father, arrives in Georgia as one of the rangers sent from South Carolina to protect the colony and is stationed at Fort Argyle. **June 22**: William Elbert marries Sarah Greenfield
1740	Samuel Elbert born in Savannah.
1742	Taken to South Carolina with his family as a child, where he lives until 1764
1764	Returns to Savannah in the late summer or early fall
1766	Forms his first business partnership with Samuel Douglass
1769	Opens his first store in Savannah **October 10**: Elected to Commons House of the General Assembly and serves until 1771 **November 29**: Elbert Marries Elizabeth "Betsy" Rae
1771	Justice of the peace for St. George's Parish
1772	**June 20**: Becomes captain of a flank company in 1st Regiment foot militia (Grenadiers), Savannah **December**: John Rae dies
1773	Petitions Grand Lodge in England to constitute Unity Lodge **February 3**: Elbert's grenadiers attempt to incorporate **March 31**: Travels to England **June 1**: Present at New Purchase Treaty in Augusta

1774	Becomes worshipful grand master in Solomon's Lodge
Becomes worshipful grand master in Unity Lodge
Petitions Grand Lodge in England to constitute Grenadier Lodge
April–May: Escorts Creeks with his grenadiers from Savannah to the Ogeechee River border
June 4: Participates with his grenadiers in king's birthday celebration in Savannah and signs Qualification Oath to the King.
October 19: Elbert and grenadiers escort Creek leaders from Ohoopee River through settlements and arrive in Savannah
December 28: On grand jury in Savannah
1775	Becomes worshipful grand master in Grenadier Lodge
January 23: Signs the Continental Association
June 22: Becomes a member of Savannah's Council of Safety
July 4–17: Member of Second Provincial Congress
July 13: Placed on a committee to enforce the Association
July 15: Placed on a committee to assess the state of the militia
July 17: Becomes a member of Georgia's Council of Safety
July 10: Participates in the *Phillipa* affair
August 8: Endorses request to Governor Wright to allow militia soldiers to choose their own leaders
August 9: Marches grenadiers and other militia units from Savannah to Augusta during the Thomas Brown affair
September 15: Elbert elected to the Third Provincial Congress
November: Elected president of the Third Provincial Congress
1776	**January 2:** Promoted by the Council of Safety to the rank of colonel in Georgia's militia
January 17: Elected to Fourth Provincial Congress
January 18: Gave the order in the name of the Council of Safety to arrest Governor James Wright
February 4: Appointed lieutenant colonel in Georgia's 1st Battalion of the Continental Line
February 16: Took loyalty oath to Provincial Congress and Council of Safety
March 2: Elbert's home and business appraised by the Council of Safety as part of the plan to burn Savannah if the British attacked the city.

Timeline

       March 2–3: Participated in the Battle of the Rice Boats
       September 16: Promoted to colonel of the 2nd Battalion of the Continental Line

1777 **January 8:** Sent to temporarily oversee the defenses at Fort Howe and along the Altamaha and Satilla Rivers
       April 16: Took Oath of Fidelity to the United States
       April 26: Given command of the 2nd Florida Campaign
       April 26–May 28: Commanded the failed 2nd Florida campaign
       August–September: Commander of all western armies in ceded lands and participates in a brief western campaign against Indians and Loyalists
       August 14: Gave talk in Augusta to Creek headmen
       October 10: Made commander of all Georgia's Continental battalions

1778 **April 6:** Marches Georgia battalions to Fort Howe and begins third Florida campaign
       April 6–July 14: Participates in the third Florida campaign
       April 19: Captures the *Hinchinbrook*, *Rebecca*, and a prize brig on the Frederica River
       December 29: Commanded Georgia's battalions at the fall of Savannah

1779 **January:** Promoted to brigadier general over Georgia's militia
       March 3: Participates in the Battle of Brier Creek, is captured, and becomes a prisoner of war
       June 19: Signs a formal, written parole as a prisoner of war in Savannah

1781 **June:** Exchanged as a prisoner of war
       September–October Present at the siege of Yorktown and the surrender of Cornwallis and the British army

1783 **January 21:** Put on commission to negotiate with the Cherokee in Augusta
       February 17: Elected by the General Assembly as surveyor for Chatham County
       May 1: Signed Treaty of Augusta with the Cherokee

>
> **November 4:** Promoted to brigadier general in the Continental Army and at the same time promoted to major general over Georgia's militia

1784 **January 21:** Turns down being a delegate to Congress
April 15: Elected as vestryman for Christ Episcopal Church in Savannah

1785 **January 6:** Elected governor of Georgia
December: Elected to the General Assembly for a second term

1786 **January 9:** Elbert's term as governor concludes
December 21: Gives birth to independent Masonry in Georgia

1787 **December 4:** Elected sheriff of Chatham County

1788 **February 13:** Elected to the Chatham Academy Board of Trustees
July 2: Makes a last will and testament
November 1: Elbert dies at Elberton on the Great Ogeechee
November 2: Elbert buried on the "mount" in the Irene Indian mound along Pipemaker's Creek and the Savannah River

1790 **December 10:** Elbert County created

1792 Elizabeth Rae Elbert dies

1801 Elbert Square and Elbert Ward created in Savannah

1803 The town of Elberton incorporated in Elbert County

1916 Elbert's grave exposed and exhumed

1924 **March 10:** Elbert reinterred, Colonial Cemetery, Savannah

Bibliography

PRIMARY SOURCES
Wills and Court Documents
Jury Lists, 1751, Acts #783, 16, Family #115, South Carolina Archives.
Jury Lists, 1751, Acts # 783, 7, Family #86, South Carolina Archives.
Elbert, Hannah. Last Will. November 10, 1766, Wills 11–13, 1767–1771, Charleston, South Carolina, 447–48.
Elbert, Samuel. Last Will. July 2, 1788, Wills Record Book C, 1780–1791, Chatham County, Georgia, Court of the Ordinary, 105–107.
Holcomb, Brent H. *South Carolina Marriages, 1688–1799*. Baltimore: Genealogical Publishing Co., Inc., 1980.
Rae, John, Jr. Last Will. Wills Vol. A–B, 1775–1787, Chatham County, Georgia, Court of the Ordinary, Probate Place.
Rae, Robert. Last Will. October 13, 1779, Wills Vol. A-B, 1775–1787, Chatham County, Georgia, Court of the Ordinary, Probate Place.
Revolutionary War Pension and Bounty-Land Warrant Applications. National Archives and Records Administration (NARA), Case Files of Pension and Bounty-Land Warrant Applications Based on Revolutionary War Service, ca. 1800–ca. 1912, Record Group 15: Records of the Department of Veterans Affairs, 1773–2007, M804.
Baker, Thomas. S15299.
Balthrop, Augustine. W8113.
Collins, James. S1653.
Curtis, Jonathan. S8269.
Elbert, Samuel. File B.L.Wt. 1230–500.
Fergus, James. W25573.
Green, Nathan. S3412.
Gresham, George. W2933.
Hancock, John. R4551.
Hester, Thomas. S6991.
Love, John. R21467.
McElwee, James. W9553.
Newman, John. S1299.
Poplin, William. W10231.
Smith, John. S7540.
Weeks, Francis. W25934
Whitehurst, Simon. W11795.

Somerville, John. Last Will. October 8, 1773, Book AA, Chatham County, Court of Ordinary's Office, Savannah, Georgia, 62–64.

Manuscript Collections
Georgia State Archives, Morrow, Georgia
Georgia Colonial and Headright Plat Index, 1735–1866.
Journal of the Georgia Commissioners Negotiating with the Cherokee Indians at Augusta, including the Treaty of Augusta.
William Few Jr. Collection.

Georgia Historical Society, Savannah, Georgia
Archibald Bulloch Papers
Archibald Campbell Papers
Historic Augusta, Incorporated Collection of Revolutionary and Early Republic Era Manuscripts
James Habersham Papers
John Habersham Papers
John Houstoun Papers
Joseph Vallence Bevan Papers
Lachlan McIntosh Papers
Mordecai Sheftall Papers
Robert Howe Letters
Samuel Elbert Papers
Samuel Huntington Papers
Sir James Wright Papers
Solomon's Lodge F&AM Papers, 1735, 1771, MS 0940
Stanford Brown Collection of Eighteenth Century Papers
Walter Cliffe Papers

Hargrett Rare Book and Manuscript Library, University of Georgia, Athens
"Council Orders, 1772–1773"
Estate Papers of John Rae, July 25, 1773
Telamon Cuyler Collection
Keith Read Collection

Southern Historical Collection, Louis Round Wilson Library, Special Collections, University of North Carolina at Chapel Hill
Preston Davie Collection

Rubenstein Rare Book and Manuscript Library, Durham, North Carolina
Charles C. Jones Papers
Edward Telfair Papers
George Walton Papers

Jared Irwin Papers, 1783–1855
John Twiggs Papers, 1781–1799
John Martin Papers
Lachlan McIntosh Papers
Robert Howe Papers, 1777–1778
Samuel Elbert Papers, account book, 1769–1788

Published Primary Source Collections

Candler, Allen D., ed. *The Colonial Records of the State of Georgia.* 39 vols. Atlanta: Franklin-Turner Company, 1904. Cited as *CRG*.

Candler, Allen D., ed. *The Revolutionary Records of the State of Georgia.* 3 vols. Atlanta: Franklin-Turner Co., 1908. Cited as *RRG*.

Chesnutt, David R., ed. *The Papers of Henry Laurens.* 16 vols. Columbia: University of South Carolina Press, 1985.

Coleman, Kenneth, and Milton Ready, eds. *The Colonial Records of the State of Georgia: Original Papers of Governors Reynolds, Ellis, Wright, and Others, 1757–1763.* Athens: University of Georgia Press, 1976.

Crawford, Michael J., et al., eds. *Naval Documents of the American Revolution.* 13 vols. to date. Washington, D.C.: Naval History and Heritage Command, Department of the Navy, 1964–.

Davies, K. G., ed. *Documents of the American Revolution, 1770–1783.* 20 vols. (Dublin: Irish University Press, 1976).

Hawes, Lilla M., ed. "The Papers of James Jackson." *Collections of the Georgia Historical Society.* Vol. 11. Savannah: Georgia Historical Society, 1955.

Journal of the House of Assembly, August 17, 1781, to February 26, 1784. (Georgia), in Candler, *RRG*.

Journals of the American Congress from 1774 to 1788. 4 vols. Washington: Way and Gideon, 1823.

"Letter Book of Governor Samuel Elbert, from January, 1785, to November, 1785." *Collections of the Georgia Historical Society.* Vol. 5, pt. 2. Savannah: The Morning News Print, 1902. Cited as LBGSE.

"The Letters of Hon. James Habersham, 1756–1775." *Collections of the Georgia Historical Society.* Vol. 6. Savannah: Savannah Morning News Print, 1904.

"Letters from Sir James Wright." *Collections of the Georgia Historical Society.* Vol. 3. Savannah: Morning News Office, 1873. Cited as LSJW.

Marriages of Chatham County, Georgia. Volume 1, 1748–1852. Savannah: Georgia Historical Society, 1993.

McCall, Howard H. *Roster of Revolutionary Soldiers in Georgia.* 3 vols. 1941. Rpt., Baltimore: Geological Publishing Co., Inc., 1996.

McMullan, J. J. *Equity Cases, Argued and Determined in the Court of Appeals of South Carolina I, from November, 1840, to May, 1842, Both Inclusive to which are added Cases Omitted by Former Reporters, from 1827 to 1837.* Columbia, SC: Dubose & Johnston, 1842.

Moore, Frank. *Diary of the American Revolution: From Newspapers and Original Documents.* 2 vols. New York: Charles Scribner, 1860.

"Order Book of Samuel Elbert, Colonel and Brigadier General in the Continental Army, October 1776, to November, 1778." *Collections of the Georgia Historical Society.* Vol. 5, pt 2. Savannah: The Morning News Print, 1902. Cited as OBSE.

"The Proceedings and Minutes of the Governor and Council of Georgia, October 4, 1774 through November 7, 1775." *Collections of the Georgia Historical Society.* Vol. 10. Savannah: Georgia Historical Society, 1952.

"Proceedings of a Court Martial...for the Trial of Major General Howe, December 7, 1781." *Collections of the New York Historical Society for the Year 1879.* Vol. 12. New York: New York Historical Society, 1880. Cited as *CNYHS*.

"Proceedings of the First Georgia Provincial Congress, 1775." *Collections of the Georgia Historical Society.* Vol. 5, pt. 1. Savannah: Braid & Hutton, Printers and Binders, 1901.

"Proceedings of the Georgia Council of Safety, 1775 to 1777." *Collections of the Georgia Historical Society.* Vol. 5, pt. 1. Savannah: Braid & Hutton, Printers and Binders, 1901. Cited as PCS.

Report on American Manuscripts in the Royal Institution of Great Britain. 4 vols. London: Mackie & Co. LD, 1904.

Smith, Paul H., ed. *Letters of Delegates to Congress, 1774–1779.* 26 vols. Washington: Library of Congress, 1987.

Warren, Mary Bondurant, and Jack Moreland Jones. *Georgia Governor and Council Journals, 1772–1773.* Athens: Heritage Press, 2004. Cited as *GGCJ, 1772–1773*.

———. *Georgia Governor and Council Journals, 1774–1777.* Athens: Heritage Papers, 2006. Cited as *GGCJ, 1774–1777*.

White, George. *Historical Collections of Georgia Containing the Most Interesting Facts, Traditions, Biographical Sketches, Anecdotes, Etc.* New York: Pudney & Russell, Publishers, 1855.

Books, Journals, Pamphlets, Memoirs

Campbell, Colin, ed. *Journal of An Expedition against the Rebels of Georgia in North America under the Orders of Archibald Campbell.* Darien, GA: Ashantilly Press, 1981.

Coran, Thomas. *A Brief Account of the Causes That Have Retarded the Progress of the Colony of Georgia, in America.* London: 1743.

Dickinson, John. *Letters from a Farmer, in Pennsylvania, to the Inhabitants of the British Colonies.* Philadelphia: 1774.

Earl of Egmont. *The Journal of the Earl of Egmont: Abstract of the Trustees Proceedings for Establishing the Colony of Georgia, 1732–1738*. Edited with an introduction by Robert G. McPherson. Athens: University of Georgia Press, 1962.

Grimké, John. F. "Journal of the Campaign to the Southward. May 9th to July 14th, 1778." *South Carolina Historical and Genealogical Magazine* 12/2 (April 1911): 60–69.

Johnston, Elizabeth Lichtenstein. *Recollections of a Georgia Loyalist*. New York: Bankside Press, M. F. Mansfield & Company, 1901.

Martyn, Ben. *An Impartial Enquiry into the State and Utility of the Province of Georgia*, London: W. Meadows, 1741.

Moultrie, William. *Memoirs of the American Revolution, so far as it Related to the States of North and South-Carolina, and Georgia*. 2 Vols. New York: David Longworth, 1802. Cited as *MMAR*.

Stephens, William. *The Journal of William Stephens, 1741–1743*. Edited by E. Merton Coulter. Wormsloe Foundation Publications. Athens: University of Georgia Press, 1958.

Tailfer, Patrick, Hugh Anderson, and David Douglas. *A True and Historical Narrative of the Colony of Georgia*. 1741. Reprint, Washington: P. Force, 1835.

Wesley, John. *The Journal of the Rev. John Wesley*. Vol. 1: Journal from October 14, 1735, to November 29, 1745. Grand Rapids: Zondervan Publishing House, 1872.

Zubly, John Joachim. *"The Law of Liberty." A Sermon on American Affairs, Preached at the Opening of the Provincial Congress of Georgia*. Philadelphia: 1775.

NEWSPAPERS
Athens Banner Herald
Early County News (Blakely)
Georgia Gazette (Savannah)
Jackson Herald (Jefferson)
Maryland Journal
Public Intelligencer (Savannah)
Royal Georgia Gazette (Savannah)
Augusta Chronicle and Gazette of the State
Gazette of the State of Georgia (Savannah)
Georgia State Gazette or Independent Register (Savannah)
Jackson Progres-Argos (Jefferson)
Independent Gazetteer (Savannah)
Pennsylvania Packet, and Daily Advertiser (Philadelphia)
Virginia Gazette (Williamsburg)

Other Primary Sources
Articles of Confederation. (1781).
Charlton, Thomas U. P. "A Sketch of the Life of General Elbert." *Public Intelligencer*, October 16, 1807, 2.
Declaration of Independence. (1776).
Cranch, William. *Reports of Cases Argued and Adjudged in the Supreme Court of the United States, in February Term, 1804 and February Term, 1805*. Vol. 2. New York: I. Riley & Co., 1806.
Franklin, Benjamin to Samuel Elbert, December 16, 1787. *Journal of the Society of Architectural Historians* 11/3 (October 1952): 26–27.
Lotter, Tobias Conrad. 1717–1777. A Map of the County of Savannah, 1735/1740. Map hmap174016. Hargrett Rare Book and Manuscript Library. Athens: University of Georgia.
Minutes of the Union Society: Being an Abstract of Existing Records, from 1750 to 1858. Savannah: John M. Cooper & Company, 1860.
Watkins, Robert, and George Watkins. *A Digest of the Laws of the State of Georgia*. Philadelphia: R. Aitken, 1800.
Worchester, J. E. *A Gazetteer of the United States*. Andover: Flagg and Gould, 1818.

SECONDARY SOURCES
Books
Abbot, W. W. *The Royal Governors of Georgia, 1754–1775*. Chapel Hill: University of North Carolina Press, 1959.
Alden, John Richard. *The American Revolution: 1775–1783*. New York: Harper & Row, 1954.
Ambrose, Stephen E. *Undaunted Courage: Meriwether Lewis, Thomas Jefferson, and the Opening of the American West*. New York: Touchstone Books, 1996.
Benedict, David. *A General History of the Baptist Denomination in America, and Other Parts of the World*. 2 vols. Manning & Loring: Boston, 1813.
Bennett, Charles E., and Donald R. Lennon. *A Quest for Glory: Major General Robert Howe and the American Revolution*. Chapel Hill: University of North Carolina Press, 1991.
Borick, Carl P. *Relieve Us of This Burthen: American Prisoners of War in the Revolutionary South, 1780–1782*. Columbia: University of South Carolina Press, 2012.
Braund, Kathryn E. Holland, and Charlotte M. Porter, eds. *Fields of Vision: Essays on the Travels of William Bartram*. Tuscaloosa: University of Alabama Press, 2000.
Braund, Kathryn E. Holland. *Deerskins & Duffels: The Creek Indian Trade with Anglo-Saxon America, 1685–1815*. Lincoln: University of Nebraska Press, 1993.

Bibliography

Cadle, Farris W. *Georgia Land Surveying: History and Law.* Athens: University of Georgia Press, 1991.

Calloway, Colin G. *The American Revolution in Indian Country: Crisis and Diversity in Native American Communities.* Cambridge: Cambridge University Press, 1995.

Carrington, Henry Beebee. *Battles of the American Revolution, 1775–1781.* New York: A. S. Barnes & Co., 1876.

Cashin, Edward J. *Lachlan McGillivray, Indian Trader: The Shaping of the Southern Colonial Frontier.* Athens: University of Georgia Press, 1992.

———. *William Bartram and the American Revolution on the Southern Frontier.* Columbia: University of South Carolina Press, 2000.

———. *The King's Ranger: Thomas Brown and the American Revolution on the Southern Frontier.* New York: Fordham University Press, 1999.

———. "Sowing the Wind: Governor Wright and the Georgia Backcountry on the Eve of the Revolution." In *Forty Years of Diversity: Essays on Colonial Georgia*, edited by Harvey H. Jackson and Phinizy Spalding, 233–50. Athens: University of Georgia Press, 2011.

Cashin, Edward J., and Heard Robertson. *Augusta & the American Revolution: Events in the Georgia Back Country, 1773–1783.* Darien, GA: Ashantilly Press, 1975.

Clarke, William Bordley. *Early and Historic Freemasonry of Georgia: 1733/4–1800.* Savannah: Solomon's Lodge No. 1, F&AM, 1924.

Coleman, Kenneth. *The American Revolution in Georgia: 1763–1789.* Athens: University of Georgia Press, 1958.

———. "Georgia in the American Revolution, 1775–1782," in *A History of Georgia*, edited by Kenneth Coleman, 71–88. Athens: University of Georgia Press, 1977.

———, ed. *A History of Georgia.* Athens: University of Georgia Press, 1977.

Coltrane, Jenn Winslow. *Lineage Book: National Society of the Daughters of the American Revolution.* Vols. 58, 62. Washington D.C., 1922.

Cook, James F. *The Governors of Georgia: 1754–2004.* 3rd ed. Macon: Mercer University Press, 2005.

Coulter, E. Merton, and Albert B. Saye, eds. *A List of the Early Settlers of Georgia.* Athens: University of Georgia Press, 1949.

de Quesada, Alejandro M. *A History of Georgia Forts: Georgia's Lonely Outposts.* Charleston: History Press, 2011.

Dobson, David. *Scottish Emigration to Colonial America, 1607–1785.* Athens: University of Georgia Press, 1994.

Drewien, D. J. *Button Gwinnett: A Historiography of the Georgia Signer of the Declaration of Independence.* Pittsburgh: Rose Dog Books, 2007.

Ethridge, Robbie. *Creek Country: The Creek Indians and their World.* Chapel Hill: University of North Carolina Press, 2003.

Fraser, Walter J., Jr. *Savannah in the Old South.* Athens: University of Georgia Press, 2003.
Gardner, Robert. "Baptists in Georgia, 1733–2010." *Viewpoints: Georgia Baptist History* 22 (2010): 89–107.
Godbold, E. Stanley Jr., and Robert H. Woody. *Christopher Gadsden and the American Revolution.* Knoxville: University of Tennessee Press, 1982.
Granger, Mary, ed. *Savannah River Plantations.* Savannah: Georgia Historical Society, 1947.
Hall, Leslie. *Land and Allegiance in Revolutionary Georgia.* Athens: University of Georgia Press, 2001.
Harden, William. *A History of Savannah and South Georgia.* 2 vols. 1913. Atlanta: Cherokee Publishing Company, 1969.
Harris, Earl Douglas. *Outstanding Georgia Freemasons.* Educational and Historical Commission: Grand Lodge of Georgia Free and Accepted Masons, 2005.
Helsley, Alexia Jones. *Beaufort: A History.* With a foreword by Lawrence S. Rowland. Charleston: History Press, 2005.
Holmes, Yulssus Lynn. *Those Glorious Days: A History of Louisville as Georgia's Capital, 1796–1807.* Macon: Mercer University Press, 1996.
Hünemörder, Markus. *The Society of the Cincinnati: Conspiracy and Distrust in Early America.* New York: Bergham Books, 2016.
Ivers, Larry E. "Rangers, Scouts, and Tythingmen." In *Forty Years of Diversity, Essays on Colonial Georgia*, edited by Harvey H. Jackson and Phinizy Spalding, 152–62. Athens: University of Georgia Press, 1984.
Jackson, Harvey H. *Lachlan McIntosh and the Politics of Revolutionary Georgia.* Athens: University of Georgia Press, 1979.
———. "Georgia Whiggery: The Origins and Effects of a Many-Faceted Movement." In *Forty Years of Diversity, Essays on Colonial Georgia*, edited by Harvey H. Jackson and Phinizy Spalding, 251–73. Athens: University of Georgia Press, 1984, 251–273.
Jameson, J. Franklin. *The American Revolution Considered as a Social Movement.* With an introduction by Frederick B. Tolles. Princeton: Princeton University Press, 1926.
Johnson, James M. *Militiamen, Rangers, and Redcoats: The Military in Georgia, 1754–1776.* Macon: Mercer University Press, 1992.
Johnston, Henry P. *The Yorktown Campaign and the Surrender of Cornwallis, 1781.* 1881. Williamston, Massachusetts: Corner House Publishers, 1975.
Jones, Charles C. Jr. *The Life and Services of the Honorable Maj. Gen. Samuel Elbert of Georgia.* Cambridge: Riverside Press, 1887.
———. *The History of Georgia.* 2 vols. Boston: Houghton, Mifflin and Company, 1883.
———. *History of Savannah, Ga.: From Its Settlement to the Close of the Eighteenth Century.* Syracuse: D. Mason & Co., Publishers, 1890.

Judson, L. Carroll. *The Sages and Heroes of the American Revolution*. 2 vols. Boston: Lee and Shepard, Publishers, 1875.
Juricek, John T. *Colonial Georgia and the Creeks: Anglo-Indian Diplomacy on the Southern Frontier, 1733–1763*. Gainesville: University Press of Florida, 2010.
Knight, Lucian Lamar. *A Standard History of Georgia and Georgians*. 6 vols. Chicago: Lewis Publishing Company, 1917.
———. *Georgia's Landmarks, Memorials and Legends*. 2 vols. Atlanta: Byrd Printing Company, 1914.
———. *Georgia's Roster of the Revolution*. Atlanta: Index Printing Company, 1920.
Leiter, Mary Theresa. *Biographical Sketches of the Generals of the Continental Army of the Revolution*. Cambridge: University Press/John Wilson and Son, 1889.
Levy, B. H. "The Early History of Georgia's Jews." In *Forty Years of Diversity, Essays on Colonial Georgia*, edited by Harvey H. Jackson and Phinizy Spalding, 163–78. Athens: University of Georgia Press, 1984.
Lockley, Timothy James. *Race and Class in Lowcountry Georgia: 1750–1860*. Athens: University of Georgia Press, 2001.
McCall, Hugh. *The History of Georgia: Containing Brief Sketches of the Most Remarkable Events, Up to the Present Day*. 2 vols. Savannah: Seymour & Williams, 1811.
McIlvenna, Noeleen. *The Short Life of Free Georgia: Class and Slavery in the Colonial South*. Chapel Hill: University of North Carolina Press, 2015.
Matter, David. *Benjamin Lincoln and the American Revolution*. Columbia: University of South Carolina Press, 1995.
Mazzagetti, Dominick. *Charles Lee: Self Before Country*. New Brunswick: Rutgers University Press, 2013.
Melton, James Van Horn. *Religion, Community, and Slavery on the Colonial Southern Frontier*. New York: Cambridge University Press, 2015.
Middlekauff, Robert. *The Glorious Cause: The American Revolution, 1763–1789*. New York: Oxford University Press, 1982.
Migliazzo, Arlin C. *To Make This Land Our Own: Community, Identity, and Cultural Adaptation in Purrysburg Township, South Carolina, 1732–1865*. With a foreword by Lawrence S. Rowland. Columbia: University of South Carolina Press, 2007.
Papas, Phillip. *Renegade Revolutionary: The Life of General Charles Lee*. New York: New York University Press, 2014.
Parker, Anthony W. *Scottish Highlanders in Colonial Georgia: The Recruitment, Emigration, and Settlement at Darien, 1735–1748*. Athens: University of Georgia Press, 1997.
Peel, William Lawson, ed. *Historical Collections of the Joseph Habersham Chapter, Daughters of the American Revolution*. 3 vols. Baltimore: Genealogical

Publishing Company, 1967.

Peters, Richard. *The Case of the Cherokee Nation against the State of Georgia*. Philadelphia: John Grigg, 1831.

Piecuch, Jim. *Three Peoples, One King: Loyalists, Indians, and Slaves in the Revolutionary South, 1775–1782*. Columbia: University of South Carolina Press, 2008.

Pressly, Paul M. *On the Rim of the Caribbean: Colonial Georgia and the British Atlantic World* Athens: University of Georgia Press, 2013.

Raab, James W. *Spain, Britain, and the American Revolution in Florida, 1763–1783*. Jefferson, NC: McFarland & Company, Inc., 2008.

Ramsey, William L. *The Yamasee War: A Study of Culture, Economy, and Conflict in the Colonial South*. Lincoln: University of Nebraska Press, 2008.

Reese, Trever R. *Colonial Georgia: A Study in British Imperial Policy in the Eighteenth Century*. Athens: University of Georgia Press, 1963.

Reese, Trever R., ed. *The Clamorous Malcontents: Criticisms & Defenses of the Colony of Georgia, 1741–1743*. Savannah: Beehive Press, 1973.

Roland, Lawrence S., Alexander Moore, and George Rogers Jr. *The History of Beaufort County, South Carolina*. 2 vols. Columbia: University of South Carolina Press, 1996.

Saunt, Claudio. *A New Order of Things: Property, Power, and the Transformation of the Creek Indians, 1733–1816*. New York: Cambridge University Press, 1999.

Saye, Albert Berry. *A Constitutional History of Georgia, 1732–1945*. Athens: University of Georgia Press, 1948.

Searcy, Martha Condray. *The Georgia-Florida Contest in the American Revolution, 1776–1778*. Tuscaloosa: University of Alabama Press, 1985.

Sears, John Randolph. *Anthony Wayne*. New York: D. Appleton and Company, 1903.

Smith, Calvin. "The Habershams: The Merchant Experience in Georgia." In *Forty Years of Diversity, Essays on Colonial Georgia*, edited by Harvey H. Jackson and Phinizy Spalding, 198–216. Athens: University of Georgia Press, 2011.

Smith, Gordon Burns. *History of the Georgia Militia, 1783–1861: Campaigns and Generals*. 2 vols. Milledgeville: Boyd Publishing, 2000.

———. *Morningstars of Liberty: The Revolutionary War in Georgia, 1775–1783*. 4 vols. Milledgeville: Boyd Publishing, 2006.

Spalding, Phinizy. "Colonial Period." In *A History of Georgia*, edited by Kenneth Coleman, 9–67. Athens: University of Georgia Press, 1977.

———. "Oglethorpe, William Stephens, and the Origin of Georgia Politics." In *Oglethorpe in Perspective: Georgia's Founder after Two Hundred Years*, edited by Phinizy Spalding and Harvey H. Jackson, 80–98. Tuscaloosa: University of Alabama Press, 1989.

Spracher, Luciana M. *Images of America: Lost Savannah, Photographs from the Collection of the Georgia Historical Society.* Charleston: Arcadia Publishing, 2002.
Tabbert, Mark A. *American Freemasons: Three Centuries of Building Communities.* New York: New York University Press, 2006.
Temple, Sarah B. Gober, and Kenneth Coleman. *Georgia Journeys: Being an Account of the Lives of Georgia's Original Settlers and Many Other Early Settlers.* Athens: University of Georgia Press, 1961.
Townsend, Leah. *South Carolina Baptists: 1670–1805.* 1935. Reprint, Baltimore: Genealogical Publishing Co., Inc., 1974.
Walker, John W. "A Brief History of Ocmulgee Archaeology." In *Ocmulgee Archaeology, 1936–1986*, edited by David J. Hally, 15–35. Athens: University of Georgia Press, 2009.
Ward, Christopher. *The War of the Revolution.* Edited by John Richard Alden. 2 vols. 1941. Reprint, New York: Skyhorse Publishing, 2011.
Weis, Frederick Lewis. *The Colonial Clergy of Virginia, North Carolina and South Carolina.* 1955. Reprint, Baltimore: Genealogical Publishing Company, 1976.
Wheeler, Frank T. *Images of America: Savannah River Plantations, Photographs from the Collection of the Georgia Historical Society.* Charleston: Arcadia Publishing, 1998.
Wilson, David. *The Southern Strategy: Britain's Conquest of South Carolina and Georgia, 1775–1780.* Columbia: University of South Carolina Press, 2005.
Wilson, Walter E., and Gary L. McKay. *James D. Bulloch: Secret Agent and Mastermind of the Confederate Navy.* Jefferson, NC: McFarland & Company, Inc., 2012.
Wood, Betty. *Slavery in Colonial Georgia, 1730–1775.* Athens: University of Georgia Press, 1984.
Wood, Gordon S. *Revolutionary Characters: What Made the Founders Different.* New York: Penguin Books, 2006.
Wright, Amos J. *The McGillivray and McIntosh Traders on the Old Southwest Frontier, 1716–1815.* With a foreword by Vernon J. Knight. Montgomery, AL: New South Books, 2007.

Journal Articles
Ashmore, Otis, and Charles H. Olmstead. "The Battles of Kettle Creek and Brier Creek." *GHQ* 10/2 (June 1926): 85–125.
Bossy, Denise I. Bossy. "Spiritual Diplomacy, the Yamasees, and the Society for the Propagation of the Gospel: Reinterpreting Prince George's Eighteenth-Century Voyage to England." *Early American Studies* (Spring 2014): 366–401.
Braddock, J. G., Sr. "The Plight of a Georgia Loyalist: William Lyford, Jr." *GHQ* 91/3 (Fall 2007): 247–65.

Brooking, Greg. "'Of Material Importance': Governor James Wright and the Siege of Savannah." *GHQ* 98/4 (Winter 2014): 251–99.

Buker, George E., and Richard Apley Martin. "Governor Tonyn's Brown-Water Navy: East Florida during the American Revolution, 1775–1778." *Florida Historical Quarterly* 58/1 (July 1979): 58–71.

Bullen, Ripley P. Bullen. "Fort Tonyn and the Campaign of 1778." *Florida Historical Quarterly* 29/4 (April 1951): 253–60.

Burnett, Edmund C. "Papers Relating to Bourbon County, Georgia, 1785–1786." Part 1. *American Historical Review* 15/1 (October 1909): 66–111.

———. "Papers Relating to Bourbon County, Georgia, 1785–1786." Part 2. *American Historical Review* 15/2 (January 1910): 297–353.

Cashin, Edward J. "The Trembling Land: Covert Activity in the Georgia Backcountry during the American Revolution." *Proceedings and Papers of the Georgia Association of Historians* 3 (1982): 31–39.

Chandler, Jonathan. "'To become again our brethren': Desertion and Community during the American Revolutionary War, 1775–83." *Historical Research* 90/248 (May 2017): 363–80.

Coleman, Edward M. "Letter from Governor Patrick Tonyn of East Florida to Lord George Germain, Secretary of State for the Colonies, 1776." *Mississippi Valley Historical Review* 33/2 (September 1946): 289–92.

Coulter, E. Merton. "The Birth of a University, a Town, and a County." *GHQ* 46/2 (June 1962): 113–50.

Cox, William E. "Brigadier-General John Ashe's Defeat in the Battle of Brier Creek." *GHQ* 57/2 (Summer 1973): 295–302.

Davis, Robert Scott, Jr. "George Galphin and the Creek Congress of 1777." *Proceedings and Papers of the Georgia Association of Historians* 3 (1982): 13–29.

———. "A Frontier for Pioneer Revolutionaries: John Dooly and the Beginnings of Popular Democracy in Original Wilkes County." *GHQ* 90/3 (Fall 2006): 315–49.

———. "Civil War in the Midst of Revolution: Community Divisions and the Battle of Briar Creek." *GHQ* 100/2 (Summer 2016): 137–59.

Green, E. R. R. "Queensborough Township: Scotch-Irish Emigration and the Expansion of Georgia, 1763–1776." *William and Mary Quarterly* 17/2 (April 1960):183–99.

Jones, George Fenwick. "Portrait of an Irish Entrepreneur in Colonial Augusta: John Rae, 1708–1772." *GHQ* 83/3 (Fall 1999): 427–47.

Hawes, Lilla M., ed. "Letter Book of Lachlan McIntosh, 1776–1777. Part I." *Georgia Historical Quarterly* 38/2 (1954): 148–69. http://www.jstor.org/stable/40577509. Cited as PLM, pt. 1.

———. "The Papers of Lachlan McIntosh, 1774–1799. Part II." *Georgia Historical Quarterly* 38/3 (1954): 253–67. http://www.jstor.org/stable/40577710. Cited as PLM, pt. 2.

———. "The Papers of Lachlan McIntosh, 1774–1799. Part III: Letter Book of Lachlan McIntosh, 1776–1777." *Georgia Historical Quarterly* 38/4 (1954): 356–68. http://www.jstor.org/stable/40577545. Cited as PLM, pt. 3.

———. "The Proceedings and Minutes of the Governor and Council of Georgia, October 4, 1774 through November 7, 1775 and September 6, 1779 through September 20, 1780." Part 5. *GHQ* 35/3 (September 1951): 196–221.

Heidler, David S. "The American Defeat at Briar Creek, 3 March 1779." *GHQ* 66/3 (Fall 1982): 317–31.

Hitz, Alex M. "Georgia Bounty Land Grants." *GHQ* 38/4 (December 1954): 337–48.

Howard, Joshua. "'Things Here Wear a Melancholy Appearance': The American Defeat at Briar Creek." *GHQ* 88/4 (Winter 2004): 477–98.

Hühner, Leon. "The Jews of Georgia from the Outbreak of the American Revolution to the Close of the 18th Century." *Publications of the American Jewish Historical Society* 17 (1909): 89–108.

Jackson, Harvey H. "The Battle of the Riceboats: Georgia Joins the Revolution." *GHQ* 58/2 (Summer 1974): 229–43.

———. "Behind the Lines: Savannah During the War of Jenkins' Ear." *GHQ* 78/3 (Fall 1994): 471–92.

Lambert, Frank. "Father against Son, and Son against Father": The Habershams of Georgia and the American Revolution." *GHQ* 84/1 (Spring 2000): 1–28.

Lamplugh, George R. "'To Check and Discourage the Wicked and Designing': John Weret and the Revolution in Georgia." *GHQ* 61/4 (Winter 1977): 295–307.

Kokomoor, Kevin. "'Burning & Destroying All Before Them': Creeks and Seminoles on Georgia's Revolutionary Frontier." *GHQ* 98/4 (Winter 2014): 300–40.

Little, Thomas J. "The Origins of Southern Evangelicalism: Revivalism in South Carolina, 1700–1740." *Church History* 75/4 (December 2006): 768–808.

Mebane, John. "Joseph Habersham in the Revolutionary War." *GHQ* 47/1 (March 1963): 76–83.

Marcus, Jacob R., ed. "Sheftall Sheftall Describes His Career as a Revolutionary Solder—1777–1783." *American Jewish Archives* 27/2 (November 1975) 139–41.

Miller, Randall M. "The Stamp Act in Colonial Georgia." *GHQ* 56/3 (Fall 1972): 318–31.

Morris, Michael. "George Galphin and John Stuart's America: Parallel Lives and Cross Purposes." *Journal of the Georgia Association of Historians* 31 (2012): 1–53.

Naisawald, L. Van Loan. "Major General Robert Howe's Activities in South

Carolina and Georgia, 1776–1779." *GHQ* 35/1 (March 1951): 23–30.
Nichols, Joel A. Nichols. "A Man True to His Principles: John Joachim Zubly and Calvinism." *Journal of Church and State* 43/2 (Spring 2001): 297–317.
Olson, Gary D. "Loyalist Partisan, and the Revolutionary War in Georgia, 1777–1782. Part I." *GHQ* 54/1 (Spring 1970): 1–19.
Ouzts, Clay. "'A Good Bargain for the Trust': The Ordeal of William and Sarah Elbert." *GHQ* 101/1 (2017): 25–52.
Phillips, Ulrich B. "Some Letters of Joseph Habersham." *GHQ* 10/2 (June 1926): 144–63.
Pressly, Paul M. "Scottish Merchants and the Shaping of Colonial Georgia." *GHQ* 91/2 (Summer 2007): 135–68.
Ranlet, Philip. "Loyalty in the Revolutionary War: General Robert Howe of North Carolina." *Historian* 53/4 (June 1991): 721–42.
Rindfleisch, Bryan. "'Our Lands Are Our Life and Breath': Coweta, Cusseta, and the Struggle for Creek Territory and Sovereignty during the American Revolution." *Ethnohistory* 60/4 (Fall 2013): 581–603.
Robertson, Heard. "Georgia's Banishment and Expulsion Act of September 16, 1777." *GHQ* 55/2 (Summer 1971): 274–82.
———. "The Reverend James Seymour, Frontier Parson, 1771–1783." *Historical Magazine of the Protestant Episcopal Church* 45/2 (June 1976): 145–53.
Robertson, William J. "Rare Button Gwinnett." *GHQ* 30/4 (December 1946): 297–307.
Savannah Unit, Georgia Writers' Project, Work Projects Administration in Georgia. "Rae's Hall Plantation. Part I." *GHQ* 26/3 and 26/4 (1942): 225–48. http://www.jstor.org/stable/40576848.
———. "Rae's Hall Plantation. Part II." *GHQ* 27/1 (March 1943): 1–27.
Schmidt, Jim. "The Reverend John Joachim Zubly's 'The Law of Liberty' Sermon: Calvinist Opposition to the American Revolution." *GHQ* 82/2 (Summer 1998): 350–68.
Siebert, Wilbur H. "East Florida as a Refuge of Southern Loyalists, 1774–1785." *American Antiquarian Society* 37/2 (October 1927): 226–46.
Smith, Gordon. "The Georgia Grenadiers." *GHQ* 64/4 (Winter 1980): 405–15.
Starr, Raymond. "Letters from John Lewis Gervais to Henry Laurens, 1777–1778." *South Carolina Historical Magazine* 66 (1965): 15–37.
Sweet, Julie Anne. "'The natural Advantages of this happy Climate': An Analysis of Georgia's Promotional Literature." *GHQ* 98/1 and 98/2 (Spring/Summer 2014): 1–25.
———. "'An Encourager of Industry': Samuel Eveleigh and His Influence on the Southeastern Trade." *South Carolina Historical Magazine* 112/1 and 112/2 (January–April 2011): 5–25.
Totora, Daniel J. "From Purrysburg to Prosperity on the Southern Frontier: Francis Pelot of South Carolina, 1720–1774." *Swiss-American Historical Society Review* 49/1 (February 2013): 1–19.

Toulmin, Llewellyn M. "Backcountry Warrior: Brig. Gen. Andrew Williamson, The 'Benedict Arnold of South Carolina' and America's First Major Double Agent. Part I." *Journal of Backcountry Studies* 7/1 (Spring 2012): 1–46.

Watson, Alan D. "A Consideration of European Indentured Servitude in Colonial North Carolina." *North Carolina Historical Review* 91/4 (October 2014): 381–406.

———. "The Committees of Safety and the Coming of the American Revolution in North Carolina, 1774–1776." *North Carolina Historical Review* 73/2 (April 1996): 131–55.

Wood, Betty. "A Note on the Georgia Malcontents." *GHQ* 63/2 (Summer 1979): 264–78.

Wood, Virginia Steele. "The Georgia Navy's Dramatic Victory of April 19, 1778." *GHQ* 90/2 (Summer 2006): 165–95.

Theses and Dissertations

Haynes, Joshua Spann. "Patrolling the Border: Theft and Violence on the Creek-Georgia Frontier, 1770–1796." PhD diss., University of Georgia, 2013.

Henry, William. "An Unfortunate Affair: The Battle of Brier Creek and the Aftermath in Georgia." Master's thesis, Georgia Southern University, 2012.

Purcell, Clarice Eulone. "The Public Career of Samuel Elbert." Master's thesis, University of Georgia, 1951.

Other Publications and Sources

Clarke, William B. *Leaves from Georgia Masonry*. Educational and Historical Commission of the Grand Lodge of Georgia, F&AM, 1947.

Elliot, Daniel. "Fort Argyle: Colonial Fort on the Ogeechee." Washington: United States Department of Defense, 2012.

———. "Stirring Up a Hornet's Nest: The Kettle Creek Battlefield Survey." Report 5089. Savannah: LAMAR Institute, Inc., 2008.

Elliot, Daniel T., and Robert Scott Davis Jr. "Captain Robert Carr's Fort and Its Revolutionary War Battlefield, Wilkes County, Georgia." Report 7640. Savannah: LAMAR Institute, Inc., 2014.

Freemason's Chronicle 8/328 (April 9, 1881): 242. Also in vol. 13 of *Freemason's Chronicle*, London: W.W. Morgan, 1880. Accessed November 22, 2021, https://catalog.hathitrust.org/Record/011249120.

"General Samuel Elbert (1740–1788)." State historical marker. Colonial Park Cemetery, Savannah, GA.

"Georgia in the American Revolution." An Exhibition from the Library and Museum Collections of the Society of the Cincinnati. Anderson House, Washington, D.C., October 11, 2003—May 1, 2004.

Johnson, Joseph. "A Biographical Sketch of General Elbert, Life and Services." *The Magazine, and Notes and Queries, Concerning the Antiquities, History and Biography of America.* Volume 4, second series. Morrisania, NY: Henry B. Dawson, 1868.

Lenz, Richard J. *Longstreet Highroad Guide to the Georgia Coast & Okefenokee.* Atlanta: Longstreet Press, Inc., 1999.

"Patriots Day 2005, Marshes of Glynn Chapter Sponsors Patriots Day Activities." *The Hornet's Nest: Newsletter of the Georgia Society Sons of the American Revolution* (January–March 2005). Accessed November 22, 2021. https://gasocietysar.org/wp-content/uploads/2017/04/2005-jan-mar-hornets-nest-low-res.pdf.

St. Helena Parish Register (death record). *South Carolina Historical and Genealogical Magazine* 23/2 (April 1922): 46–71.

Wilcox, Herbert. "Early Governor's 'Lost' Portrait." *Atlanta Journal and Constitution Magazine,* March 14, 1971, 39.

Internet Sources

"About Tondee's." Accessed February 20, 2016. https://tondees.com/historic-notes.

"First African Baptist Church." Accessed December 28, 2019. https://firstafricanbc.com/hist.

Ouzts, Clay. "Elbert County." *New Georgia Encyclopedia.* October 31, 2018. Accessed November 22, 2021. https://www.georgiaencyclopedia.org/articles/counties-cities-neighborhoods/elbert-county/.

———. "Elberton." *New Georgia Encyclopedia.* July 25, 2018. Accessed November 22, 2021. https://www.georgiaencyclopedia.org/articles/counties-cities-neighborhoods/elberton/.

———. "Petersburg." *New Georgia Encyclopedia.* May 31, 2016. Accessed November 22, 2021. https://www.georgiaencyclopedia.org/articles/history-archaeology/petersburg/.

"To George Washington from Major General Benjamin Lincoln, 23 December 1779." Founders Online, National Archives. Accessed December 3, 2021. https://founders.archives.gov/documents/Washington/03-23-02-0536.

"To George Washington from Ezekiel Cornell, 12 February 1782." Founders Online, National Archives. Accessed December 3, 2021. https://founders.archives.gov/documents/Washington/99-01-02-07818.

"To George Washington from Major General Benjamin Lincoln, 7 February 1779." Founders Online, National Archives. Accessed December 3, 2021. https://founders.archives.gov/documents/Washington/03-19-02-0139.

Williams, Mark. "Irene Mounds." *New Georgia Encyclopedia.* September 15, 2014. Accessed November 22, 2021. https://www.georgiaencyclopedia.org/articles/history-archaeology/irene-mounds/.

Index

Act for the Encouragement of Literature and Genius, 374
Act of Attainder, 314, 319
Adams, Sam, 32
Alabama (Upper Creek town), 178
Albercorn (Savannah), 265
Alexander Fiffe & Company, 16
Allen, Rev. W. Moses, 293
Alligator Creek Bridge (Florida battle, 1778), 221
Allison, Alexander, 331
Alston, Philip, 263
Amelia Island (Florida), 162, 164-65, 165, 167, 169, 171
Andrew, Benjamin, 82
Antigua, 299, 310
Armstrong, Deborah (wife of John Rae), 308
Arnold, Benedict, 196
Articles of Confederation, and Indians, 326; and state border disputes, 359
Ashe, John, joins Lincoln at Purrysburg, 263; at Battle of Brier Creek, 277-89; court of inquiry on conduct at Brier Creek, 289; mentioned, 272-73, 276, 278-81, 320, 395
Association (economic boycott), 84, 87-88, 95-98, 105-106, 108
Atkinson, Andrew, 383
Augusta (Georgia), and Thomas Brown incident, 105-108, 113; Brown surrenders, 321-22; shares seat of government with Savannah during Confederation Period, 341-42; conference with Creeks, 116; Creeks held captive (1777), 180, 183, 193; Elbert speaks to Creeks (1777), 183-85; Convention (former General Assembly) convenes (1779), 261-62; fall of (1779), 264-75; Thomas Fee murders Mad Turkey, 73-74; Howe orders evacuation of (1779), 255, 262; and Indian treaties (1783), 324-29; raided by King's Rangers (1777), 178; provisions stored, 230, 235
Baird, James, attack at Fair-Lawn, Savannah (1778), 250-52; gathers intelligence near Savannah (1778), 245; 285-86. *See also* Baird's Corps of Light Infantry.
Baird's Corps of Light Infantry; 228; marches to Augusta, 265; takes unguarded pass at Fair-Lawn, Savannah (1778), 250-51; attacks Walton's militia, Fair-Lawn, 251; attacks Elbert at Fair-Lawn, 252; at Battle of McBean's Swamp (1779), 269; at Battle of Kettle Creek, 279, 283; 271
Baker, John, feud with Elbert, 186; Battle of Thomas Creek, 166, 169, 170-71, 182; 158, 161-63, 165, 345-46
Baker, Thomas, 216, 287
Baldwin, Abraham, Congressional delegate, 350-51
Balthrop, Augustine, 289-93
Banks, Sutton, 355-57
Barclay, Andrew, 119, 128, 130-34, 136
Barnard, Edward, 29, 82
Barnard, Timothy, 332, 340, 366
Bartram, William, 21, 66
Bass, Hardy, 347
Bass, Thomas, 347
Battalions, *see* individual Georgia battalions
Beard's Bluff, 145; attacked by Indians, 146-47; 195, 299, 356, 365-66
Beaufort (battle, South Carolina, 1779), 265-66, 272
Belcher and Ingram (Savannah firm), 348
Belmont Plantation (Savannah), 137
Big Elk (Coweta Creek warrior), 72
Bilbo, John, 193-94
Bloody Marsh (battle of), 10
Booker, Gideon, 193-94
Bosmomworth, Thomas, 20
Boston Massacre, 39-40
Boston Port Act (bill), 76-77
Boston Tea Party; 68-69, 71, 76
Bostwick, Chesley, occupies Beard's Bluff, 147, 150; Augusta smallpox scare, 344
Bounty Land (in Georgia after Revolution), 336-38
Bourbon County (in Mississippi Yazoo

lands), 353-59

Bourquin, Henry, 82

Bowen, Oliver, Act of Attainder, 314; captain in 1st Battalion, 127; council of war on Amelia Island, 168; throws down militia commander commission, 93; committee to supply Georgia with arms and ammunition, 109; Council of Safety member, 108; commands navy in Third Florida Campaign, 208, 219, 224; Disqualifying Act, 309; feud with Houstoun, 224-25; Grenadiers, 92; and John Hopkins, 103; commands *Liberty*, 100-101; as a Mason, 51, 92; commands Georgia navy, 159, 223; Battle of the Rice Boats, 133; Second Provincial Congress, 93; Fourth Provincial Congress, 121; and Hadden Smith, 102

Box, Philip, 82

Boyce, Lott, 347

Boyd, James, organizing Loyalists in the Carolinas, 266; at Battle of Kettle Creek, 274-76; 279

Braddock, John, 209, 216

Bradley, James, 195

Brantley, Brittain, 347

Brewton's Hill (Savannah), 245-46, 248, 258-59

Brier Creek (battle, 1779), 276-89; American losses at, 288-89

British Regiments, James Baird's Corps of Light Infantry (*see* Baird's Corps of Light Infantry), Delancy's Royalist Provincials, 228; Hamilton's Royal North Carolina Regiment, 279; King's Rangers (*see* King's Rangers and Thomas Brown); New York Volunteers, 228, 265; Provincials, 228; 14th Regiment, 161; 16th Regiment, 262; 60th Regiment, 161, 235, 262, 279; 71st Highlander Regiment, 228, 265, 269, 279; 71st Regiment of Foot, 228, 265, 283-85; South Carolina Royalists, 262, 265

Brown, Thomas; Battle of Alligator Creek Bridge, 221; tarred and feathered in Augusta, 105-107, 113, 181; surrenders Augusta, 321-22; flees to St. Augustine, 114; Battle of Burke County jail, 267-68; opinion on Samuel Elbert, 150; raids Georgia (1776), 149; attacks Fort Howe (1778), 208; Indians as allies, 114, 175; pays Indians for scalps of Whigs, 297; creates King's Rangers, 107, 114; attacks Fort McIntosh, 148, 151; raids toward Midway, 235; battle of Midway, 236; evades capture near Fort Tonyn (1778), 220; burns Fort Tonyn, 220; mentioned, 161, 164, 167, 219. *See also* King's Rangers.

Brownsborough, 106

Brown, Rae & Company, 20, 332

Brownson, Nathan, elected governor, 322; 353

Bryan, Jonathan, 33, 35-36, 44; on delegation to confer with Charles Lee, 138

Bryan, William, 278-82, 285

Bulloch, Archibald; 43-45, 55-56; protest to the Coercive Acts, 76-77; conservative Whig, 81; 82; Second Continental Congress delegate but did not attend, 87-88, 97; Second Provincial Congress, 93-95; Council of Safety, 113; death, 151; promotes Florida invasion (1776), 140; Georgia's first president, 115, 135; given dictatorship powers as president, 151; writes Charles Lee about British naval invasion, 139-40; mentioned, 134, 137, 139.

Bull, Stephen, 107, 134

Bugg, Jerimiah, 147, 195

Bunker Hill (battle of), 89, 92

Bunkle, George, 5

Burgoyne, John, 196, 228

Burke County, 216, 261, 266-68, 343, 345, 368, 373, 385

Burke County Jail and Courthouse (battle, 1779), 267-68

Burke, John, 384, 386

Burke, Michael, 384, 386

Burton, Richard, 344

Call, Richard, 340

Calvert, Mary, 1

Calvert, William, 1, 2, 4, 14, 315

Camden County, 345

Cameron, Alexander, 175, 188

Campbell, Archibald, plans to take Augusta (1779), 264-65; marches with troops to take Augusta, 265-70; takes Augusta, 270-71; abandons Augusta, 273-74; expects James Boyd and Loyalists in Augusta, 266; and Fair-Lawn, 250-52; debarks army at Girardeau's Landing, Savannah, 248; allies with Loyalists and Indians to take Savannah, 228-29, 240; loyalty oaths, 264; relieved by Marc Prevost, 276; plans to take Savannah,

Index

239-40; attack plans for Savannah, 246; troops for taking Savannah (1778), 228-29; comments on fleeing citizens in Savannah, 261-62; orders to troops before taking Savannah, 242; outposts around Savannah, 265; on rapid defeat of Patriots in Savannah, 252; prisoners at Savannah, 254, 294-95; on British victory at Savannah, 254; at Battle of Spirit Creek (1779), 269; occupies Treutlen Plantation, 265; sends John Hamilton to Wilkes County, 272; mentioned, 235, 239, 240, 264, 266, 271, 282

Captain Allick (Cusseta Creek *mico*), 74
Carey, John, 47, 57
Carr, Patrick, 333
Carroll, Daniel, 364, 366
Catagee (Creek *mico*), 47
Causton, Thomas, 4, 6-11, 19, 35, 119
Causton's Bluff (Savannah), 118-19
Ceded lands (Wilkes County in 1777), Creek War in (1774), 72-75; and New Purchase, 65-68; Creek war in (1777), 174; 182; *See also* New Purchase.
Chanler, Isaac, 12
Chatham County, 240, 342, 348, 374, 378
Cherhaw King (Lower Creek *mico*), 85
Cherokee Indians, Treaty of Augusta with (1783), 324-28, 332, 336; Cherokee War (1776), 175, 184; talk by Samuel Elbert, 363; talk by Governor Lyman Hall, 327; and New Purchase, 65-67; 161, 187-88
Cherokee Hill (Savannah), 254-55, 262, 265
Chickasaw Indians; desire talk from Elbert, 357; save the life of Thomas Graham, 85-86; 333, 355-56, 358, 368
Choctaw Indians, desire talk from Elbert, 357; 333, 335, 368
Christ Church Coalition (Conservative Whigs), 37-38, 44-45, 54-55, 72, 81
Christ Church (Savannah), 18-19, 53, 101-102, 111, 330, 381
Christ Church Parish, 28, 82, 86
Christmas, Nathaniel, 354, 357-58
Church of England, disestablished, 152, 376
Cincinnatus, Lucius Quinctius, 330-31; *See also* Order of the Cincinnatus.
Clarke, Elijah, wounded at Alligator Creek Bridge battle (Florida, 1778), 221; wounded by Indians on Broad River (1777), 179; Clarke, Elbert & Company, 341, 368; skirmish with Indians in Oconee lands, 373; at Indian treaties in 1783, 325; at Battle of Kettle Creek, 275-76; on Oconee lands, 329; marks boundaries in Oconee lands, 366; mentioned, 267-68, 297, 327-28, 333, 337, 366, 369

Clarke, William, 356, 365
Clay, Joseph, Act of Attainder, 314; as deputy paymaster, 231; Disqualifying Act, 309; on Supreme Executive Council, 298; meeting with Wright (1776), 119-20; 19, 82, 126, 322, 330, 353, 375, 380
Clifton, Charles, 347
Clinton, Henry (British general), sends James Boyd to organize Loyalists in Carolinas, 266; plans to use Indians and Loyalists as allies, 228; plans to capture Savannah, 228-29; 134, 235, 310, 312-13, 315-16;
Cockspur Island (Savannah), 117, 121, 128, 133, 242, 290-91, 293, 299
Coercive Acts (Intolerable Acts), 71-73, 76-77, 84
Collins, James, 283
Colonial Cemetery (Savannah), 390, 399-400
Committee of 31 (response of Georgia to Coercive Acts, 1774), 77
Concord (battle of), 89, 92-93
Conservative Whigs, and dispute over officering 1st Battalion, 122-27; and Constitution of 1777, 151-52; 38, 44-45, 54-55, 72, 81, 92, 301
Constitution of 1777 (Georgia), 151-52
Continental Army Southern Military Department, creation of, 136; commanded by Charles Lee, 136; commanded by Robert Howe, 145
Continental Congress (First), 84-85
Continental Congress (Second), fears Indian war in Georgia (1777), 176; transfers McIntosh to Washington's army (1777); orders Howe to embark on Third Florida Campaign (1778), 207; mentioned, 87, 90, 95-96, 101, 109, 120, 127, 136.
Cook, Shem, 189
Cornwallis, Charles (Lord), 312; 315-17, 323
Council (Committee) of Safety; threatens to burn Savannah (1776), 131-32; and arrest of Wright, 120-21; 90-91, 93-96, 98, 100-111, 113, 115, 117-18, 123,

145, 299, 314, 396
Counties, *See* individual Georgia counties.
Course, Daniel, 384-85
Cowper, Basil, committee to supply Georgia with arms and ammunition, 109
Crawford, Charles, 347
Crawford, David, 337
Creek Indians; Treaty of Augusta (1783), 327-29, 333, 362, 368; border patrols, 177; delegation visits Charleston (1777), 178, 180; Coweta, 114, 174, 176-77, 232; Cusseta, 116, 174, 177-79, 187; Creek War, (1774), 72-75, 79, 114, 181; and murder of John Carey (1771), 47; attacks Samuel Delk's home (1777), 179; Samuel Elbert talk to Creeks in Augusta (1777), 183-85; Governor Elbert talk to, 363-64; attacks Thomas Graham, 85-86; attacks Nail's Fort in Broad River valley, 233; and New Purchase, 65-68, 177; Ockfusky (Ocfuskee), 25, 232; raids into frontier, 177-78, 232-33, 373, 377; reason for fighting in Revolution, 177; Savannah delegation (1774), 74-75, 85; waits on orders from John Stuart, 297; Tallassee Creeks, 334; warfare in Wilkes County, 174-81; 175, 321
Crutchfield, John, 363
Culpepper, Malaciah, 174
Cunningham, John, 179, 185
Curtis, Jonathan, 300
Cusseta King (Creek *mico*), 116, 177
Cuthburt, Seth John; Disqualifying Act, 309; on Supreme Executive Council, 298; 142, 340, 349, 375, 380
Cuyler, Jane, home and June 13 Resolves (1775), 91-92, 95, 97; home and Masonic meetings, 92
Cuyler, Telamon, 91
Darien (Georgia), and Lachlan McIntosh, 126-27; 172, 212, 218
Dartmouth, Earl of (Lord William Legge), 65-67, 78, 84, 86, 89, 93, 101, 110-11, 114-15, 119, 134
Daughters of the American Revolution, x-xi, 389, 390; Samuel Elbert Chapter of the Daughters of the American Revolution, 390
Davenport, William, 354, 356-58
Davis, Jenkins, 353
Declaration of Independence, and Native Americans, 182; celebration of by Order of the Cincinnatus (1787), 376; first reading in Savannah, 139; celebration of in Savannah (1777), 173; 45, 127, 205
Declaratory Act, 31
DeLisle, Roman, 207-208
Delk, Samuel, 179
Deveaux, James, 340, 365-66
Dickenson, John, 32
Disqualifying Act, 309-310, 325
Dobbins, William, 173
Dooly, John; arrest of by Elbert, 193-94; at Battle of Kettle Creek, 275-76; murdered, 296-97; on Supreme Executive Council, 298; mentioned, 80, 283, 185, 198, 267-68
Dooly, Thomas, 179-80; 184-86, 189
Douglass, Samuel, 15, 305, 310
Drayton, Henry, gets Congress to authorize a fourth Florida campaign, 234; 123
East India Tea Company, 68
Ebenezer (Georgia), 260, 264-65, 297, 322
Effingham County, 372
Elbert, Catherine ("Caty," daughter of Samuel Elbert), 49, 196, 331, 380, 384, 386
Elbert County, xiii; created, 385-86; 390
Elbert, Douglass & Company, 15-16
Elbert, Elizabeth (daughter of Samuel Elbert), 49, 196, 331, 380, 384, 386
Elbert, Elizabeth (sister of Samuel Elbert), 10, 13, 49
Elbert, Elizabeth (Betsy) Rae, (wife of Samuel Elbert and daughter of John Rae), death of, 384; miniature, 64; flees Savannah, 244; attempts to purchase White Oak Plantation, 383; mentioned, 23, 27-28, 41, 45, 48, 59-60, 131, 190, 196, 307-308, 331, 380, 382-83, 385, 389-90
Elbert's Grenadiers, Elbert brags on, 136; escorts Creeks to Savannah (1774), 85; at New Purchase conference, 67-68, 74-75; greets Governor Wright (1773), 62; 93; 53-58, 61-70
Elbert, Harriet Ann Jackson, 387
Elbert, Hugh Rae, (son of Samuel Elbert), 49, 332, 380, 387
Elbert, Matthew, (son of Samuel Elbert), 49, 332, 380, 387
Elbert, Samuel, Americanization of, 71-88; opinion on John Ashe, 289, 320, 395; and Association, 88, 92, 96; Act of Attainder, 314; attempts to defend Augusta (1779), 266-70; analysis of

Index

defense of Augusta, 270; recruits Whigs around Augusta (1779), 273; Treaty of Augusta with the Cherokee (1783), 324-27; opinion of John Baker, 186; birth, 8; at Battle of Brier Creek, 278-89; captured at Brier Creek, 288-89; criticizes American position at Brier Creek, 281-82; and Boston Massacre, 80; and Boston Tea Party, 80; described by Thomas Brown, 149; first business partnership, 15-16; first individual business, 16; character and honor, 52, 64, 129, 143, 160, 191-92, 197-98, 382, 394-95; on Chatham Academy Board of Trustees, 380; childhood and early education, 12-14; Order of the Cincinnatus, 330-31, 376-77; Clarke, Elbert & Company, 341, 368; and Coercive Act protests, 78-80; throws down militia commander commission, 93; committee to supply Georgia with arms and ammunition, 108, 116; declines congressional seat, 332; as Conservative Whig, 38, 44-45, 54-55, 72, 81, 92, 122-27, 151, 164; on unruly Continental Light Horse Troop, 186-87, 194; on Council of Safety, 90, 93, 95-96, 98, 101-105, 108, 111; Creeks escorted to Savannah (1774), 74-75, 85, 181; talk to Creeks in Augusta (1777), 183-85, 187; death and burial in Irene Mound, 41-42, 381-82; debts after death, 382-85; exhumation of burial (1916), 289; burial in Colonial Cemetery (Savannah), 390-91; efforts to venerate after death, 285-86; arrest of John Dooly, 193-94; celebrates Declaration of Independence with soldiers in Savannah (1777), 173; on desertion from the army, 169, 189, 194, 198, 229-30; Disqualifying Act, 309; and Elberton (Effingham County), 372-81; in Euhaw Baptist Church, 12; and Expulsion Act, 203-204; father and children, 48-49, 70; finances (1777), 195-96; First Battalion officer controversy, 122-27; fears invasion from Florida (1777), 199; Second Florida Campaign (1777), 161-71; marches troops to Fort Howe after Second Florida Campaign, 174; Third Florida Campaign (1778), 205-26; Frederica River naval engagement, 211-15; report to Howe on Frederica engagement, 214; fur trade, 16-19, 24-25, 67, 94, 181; Georgia Assembly (1769-1771), 27-45; Georgia Assembly (1786), 374; Georgia Assembly sends to Charleston to confer with Howe and Lincoln (1778), 235; refuses command of Georgia Battalions without McIntosh's approval (1777), 191; rebuffs offer to take command of Georgia Battalions from McIntosh, 160-62; assumes command of all Georgia battalions (1777), 192; problems as commander of Georgia's battalions, 192-95, 198, 200-201, 229; on Grand Jury (1774), 86; as governor, 339-71; assessment as governor, 370-71; and Bourbon County, 353-59; governor's talk to Cherokee, 363; governor's talk to the Creeks, 363-64; d'Estang's bounty, 346; elected governor, 339-40; financial problems as governor, 348-52; problems with Florida as governor, 345-46; granting land as governor, 346-47; deals with former Loyalists as governor, 347-49; Indian trade as governor, 341; smallpox scare as governor, 344-45; South Carolina border dispute as governor, 359-62; states' rights as governor, 359-52, 364-71; establishes University of Georgia as governor, 352-53; Grenadiers, 53-58, 61-62, 54-65, 67-70, 74-75; opinion of Gwinnett, 164, 395; on creation of hospitals and regulating doctors, 229, 231-32; sent by McIntosh to Fort Howe, 147-48; marches to Fort Howe (1778), 210; and court martial trial of Robert Howe, 319-21; husbandry of horses, 372-73; fears Indian war (1777), 176; thoughts on Indians, 170, 176-77, 181-85, 262-63, 377-78, 395-96; tells Indians to assassinate British agents, 184; opinion on Marquis de Lafayette, 316; bounty land after Revolution, 336-38, 364, 370; certifies bounty land bounties for former soldiers, 336-37, 347; land grants St. George Parish (1772), 48; land grant in St. Matthew's Parish, 29-30; land grants prior to Revolution, 71; land speculation, 17, 373-74; purchases Wright's former land at Point Plantation, 323-24; writes Charles Lee, 136-37; London trip (1773), 63-64; on Loyalists, 396; Justice of the Peace, St.

425

George Parish, 46-49, 53-54; at Battle of McBean's Swamp (1779), 269; opinion of McIntosh, 164; McLean, Elbert & Company, 334-35; marriage, 23; and Masons (F&AM), 50-53, 58, 69-70, 81-83, 304, 376; Grenadier Masonic Lodge No. 481, 82-83, 91-92; Masonic Grand Master, 82, 111, 304, 376, 382; establishes independent Masonry, 376, 399; Masonic sign at Brier Creek, 285-85; merchant, 16, 52-53, 323-24, 332, 334-335, 373-74; receives express in Charleston about Battle at Midway Church, 236-37; implores Prevost to protect civilians and property in Midway, 238; military (early interests in), 53-54; military commander, 65, 143, 186, 197-98, 201-202, 213, 226, 259, 290, 302, 382, 397-98; committee to improve militia, 97; militia petition to Wright for commissions, 104; promotion to colonel of militia, 117, 121; promotion to brigadier general over militia, 259, 262; promoted to major general over the militia, 329; promotion to lieutenant colonel of 1st Battalion, 127; oath at promotion to lieutenant colonel of 1st Battalion, 129, 155; promoted to colonel of 2nd Battalion, 138, 141, 143; promoted to brigadier general in Continental Army, 329; miniature, 63-64; Moodie Affair, 43-44; at Fort Moore bluff, South Carolina (1779), 266; order book, 141, 159, 313; Qualification Oath (1774), 75, 79, 91; Oath of Fidelity to the United States (1777), 159-60; and Queensborough, 22; scolds paymaster (1777), 195; and patronage, 23; and *Phillipa* Affair, 100-101; comments on by Augustine Prevost, 290; as a prisoner, 290-314; attempts by British to win over while prisoner, 294; business efforts while prisoner, 306-307; prisoner in Charleston, 310-11; civil litigations as prisoner, 304-05, 310, 312, 315, 319; Congress and Elbert's prisoner exchange, 308; exchanged as prisoner, 312-13; finances as prisoner, 305-06; degree of freedom as prisoner, 303; communication with Georgia government while prisoner, 303; attempted murder of by Indians while prisoner, 296-97; Benjamin Lincoln tries to facilitate prisoner exchange for, 303-304, 307; in Maryland after prisoner exchange, 313-15, 319; written prisoner parole, 294-95; on prison ship *Munificence*, 291, 294; Supreme Executive Council attempts to free Elbert as a prisoner, 298-99; Second Provincial Congress, 93-98; Third Provincial Congress, 108; Fourth Provincial Congress, 119, 121; business with John Rae, 23-24; influence of John Rae, 27, 59; returns to Georgia after Revolution, 323; Battle of the Rice Boats (1776), 131-33; impact of Rules and Regulations of 1776 on, 135; celebrates American victory at Saratoga (1777), 196; arrives in Savannah (1764), 14-15, 339; and fall of Savannah (1778), 245-59, 320-21; evaluation of performance at fall of Savannah, 259; troops at Fair-Lawn, Savannah (1778), 249; retreats from Fair-Lawn, 252-53; predicts Girardeau's Landing for British debarkation in Savannah, 246-48; orders to John Smith at Girardeau's Landing, 247; leads men across Musgrove Creek in retreat from Savannah, 253; and siege of Savannah (1779), 299-300; arrives at Zubly's Ferry after Savannah's fall, 256; flees Savannah with family (1742), 10-11; prepares Savannah defenses (1776), 118; renovates Savannah home (1777), 190; chases Scopholites (1778), 210-11; recruiting for Second Battalion, 141-42; parades 2nd Battalion for General Howe, 153; recruiting for Second Battalion, 141-42; parades 2nd Battalion for General Howe, 153; appoints Mordecai Sheftall commissary, 205; sheriff of Chatham County, 378-81; sickness, 293, 307, 313, 320, 332, 377-81; slaves and slavery, 34, 125, 306-07, 319, 324, 396-97; social status (1769), 30; care for soldiers, 153-54, 173-74, 196-98; and court martial trials of soldiers, 156-57, 229-30; drills and clothes soldiers, 135-36, 141, 143, 156, 162; pay of soldiers, 158, 195, 231; and Sons of Liberty, 31, 80; uses spies, 268; at Battle of Spirit Creek (1779), 269; and Stamp Act protest, 31, 80; surveyor of Chatham County, 330; and Edwin Telfair, 314-15; Telfair, Elbert & Company, 335,

Index

341; and Townsend Duties, 33-36, 80; Unity Lodge No. 465, F&AM (1774-1775), 69-70, 82; as a vestryman in Christ Church, 330; opinion on George Washington, 181, 36-18; Western Campaign (1777), 173, 181-192; will of, 49, 380;feelings about Governor James Wright, 33, 44-45, 55, 64-65, 72, 80-81, 309-310, 395-96; arrest of Wright, 120-21; confiscates weapons of civilians (1776), 117; at Yorktown, 316-19; Superintendent of Materials in the Trenches at Yorktown, 316

Elbert, Samuel Emmanuel de la Fayette (son of Samuel Elbert), 49, 332, 380, 386-87

Elbert, Sarah (daughter of Samuel Elbert), 49, 190, 331, 380, 386-87

Elbert, Sarah Greenfield (mother of Samuel Elbert), 1, 4, 5, 8, 10, 13

Elbert Square (Savannah), 392

Elbert Ward (Savannah), 386

Elbert, William (father of Samuel Elbert), flees Savannah (1742), 10-11; influence on son, 26, 83; in South Carolina, 12-13; 2, 4-10, 17, 19, 35, 119, 312

Elliot, Grey, as Provincial Grand Master (F&AM) of Georgia, 51, 83

Elberton (Effingham County), Elbert's death at, 381; 372, 377, 379, 386

Elberton (Elbert County), 386, 393, 399

Ellis, Alexander, 211-12

Ellis, Henry (governor), 20, 51

Ellis, Richard, 355-57

Ellis Square (Savannah), 2

Emistisiguo (Creek *mico* from Little Tallassee), 74, 85, 179

d'Estaing, Comte, and siege of Savannah, 298-300; Georgia bounty to, 336, 346

Euhaw (Prince William Parish, S. C.), 12

Eveleigh, Samuel, 16-17

Ewen, William, 28; background, 35; 37, 39, 42-45; conservative Whig, 81-82; Council of Safety president, 90; in First Provincial Congress, 86; Second Provincial Congress, 93; Fourth Provincial Congress, 121; on Grand Jury with Elbert (1774), 86

Expulsion Act (1777) or Confiscation and Banishment Act, 202-204, 322-23, 329, 348

Fair-Lawn Plantation (Savannah), Howe council of war at, 248; Howe attacked at, 250-53; 246, 257

Farley, Samuel, 28, 82

Fat King (Neha Mico, Creek *mico*), talk at home of James Rae, 328, 333; 328, 334-35, 366-67, 369-70

Fee, Thomas, 73-74

Fergus, James, 280, 288

Few, Benjamin, Act of Attainder, 314; Disqualifying Act, 309; 266-68

Few, William, at Treaty of Augusta with the Cherokee (1783), 325; on Supreme Executive Council, 298; 266-68, 360, 369

First African Baptist Church (Savannah), 392

Florida (*see* Florida campaigns); border problems after Revolution, 345-46; British regiments in, 161; British strength in 1777, 155; British strength in 1778, 210

Florida 1st Campaign, 1776, 138-41

Florida 2nd Campaign, 1777, 153-71

Florida 3rd Campaign, 1778, 205-26

Floyd, Dolores Boisfeuillet, 392

Forest, Monsieur de la, 346

Fort, Arthur, 347

Forts, Argyle; 2, 3; Beard's Bluff (see Beard's Bluff); Carr's, 188-89, 275; Folsom, 188; Frederica, X, 117, 211-13, 240; James, 68; Heard's, 306; Henderson, 269; Howe (*see* Fort Howe); McIntosh (*see* Fort McIntosh); Moore's Bluff (South Carolina), 266, 272-74, 276; Morris, 238-39, 241, 255, 262, 265, 295; Nail's, 233; Captain Phillip's, 188; Joel Phillip's, 188; Tonyn (*see* Fort Tonyn); Wayne, 381; Wells, 188

Fort Howe (Barrington), Elbert commands at, 147-48; attacked and destroyed by Brown (1778), 208-209; opinion of by South Carolina troops (1778), 216-17; wretched conditions (1778), 217; 145-46, 151, 153, 162, 192, 194, 210, 212, 215

Fort McIntosh, attacked, 148-51; impact of loss, 150-51; terms of Fort McIntosh, 150, 170; 145-46

Fort Tonyn (St. Marys River, Florida), 219-25; suffering of American troops in, 221-24

Forts, frontier, 174, 188-89

France, as American ally, 228, 298; at Yorktown, 315-17

Franklin, Benjamin, 51, 378

Franklin County, 336, 346-47, 352
Franklin Square (Savannah), 392
Frederica River Naval Engagement (1778), 211-15, 227, 344, 398
Fullokey, (Creek *mico*), 47
Funded Certificates (Georgia), 348-49
Fuser, Lewis, attack Fort McIntosh, 149-51; takes force toward Sunbury, 235, 238; attacks Fort Morris in Sunbury, 238-39, 240
Gadsden, Christopher, 234
Gage, Thomas, 175
Gaillard, Tacitus, 355-57
Galphin, George, British plot to assassinate, 178, 187,199; Disqualifying Act, 309; fears Indian war, 176-77; talk with Creeks at Old Town (1777), 177-78; escorts Creeks from Charleston, 180; 20, 182, 185, 187-88, 266, 307
Galphintown, 367-69, 377
Gates, Horatio, 196
George III (king of England), birthday celebration in Savannah (1774), 75-76; mentioned, 28, 32, 35, 62, 74, 94, 98, 264, 396
Georgia,
Assembly session (1769-1771), 30-44; Assembly Session (1785), 352-54; Assembly Session (1786), 374-76; Augusta conference with Creeks (1776), 116; boundaries according to 1732 Charter, 359-60; and Bourbon County in Mississippi Yazoo lands, 353-59; limits of governor's powers during Confederation Period, 341; and Confiscated Estates, 348-50; blurred divisions of authority between civil government and Continental Army, 129, 155-56, 174-75, 220, 222-23, 241, 244-45; General Assembly changes name to Convention and meets in Augusta (1779), 261-62; counties created under Constitution of 1777, 152; debt to federal government after Revolution, 348; defenseless in 1777, 146, 200-201; defenseless in 1778, 202, 205-207, 227, 241; economy in 1765, 15;financial problems after Revolution, 348-52; funded certificates, 348-49; sickness in battalions during Third Florida Campaign (1778), 218; impact of Third Florida Campaign on Georgia battalions, 225; desire for Indian land after Revolution, 324-29, 332, 335; Indian trade, 115-16, 188, 332, 335; land distribution after Revolution, 337-38, 346-47; Massachusetts Circular Letter in Georgia, 32-33; Royal government described, 29; fall of Savannah impact on battalions, 263; South Carolina border dispute, 359-362; Stamp Act in colony, 30; states' rights in, 326; Supreme Executive Council replaces Assembly (1779), 298
Georgia Continental Light Horse Troop, 158; 12th Rangers, 180; abandons Fort Howe, 192, 194; unruly, 186-87; 193, 195
Georgia Continental Line, 1st Battalion, occupies Beard's Bluff, 147; created, 109; controversy over officers, 122-27, 135; at first reading of Declaration of Independence in Savannah, 139; battalion flag, 205; John Habersham an officer in, 127, 192; at Fort Howe, 146, 150; reviewed by Charles Lee, 140-41; instructed to build forts by McIntosh, 145; strength late 1776, 142; strength Second Florida Campaign (1777), 158; at fall of Savannah (1778), 253, 263; 92, 293
Georgia Continental Line, 2nd Battalion; marches to Augusta (1777), 181; deserters in the ceded lands, 189; Elbert promoted to colonel of, 138; battalion flag, 205; parades for General Howe (1777), 153; sent to Fort Howe, 153; chases after King's Rangers (1777), 187; recruiting for, 142; strength in Second Florida Campaign (1777), 158; at fall of Savannah (1778), 252; catastrophic losses at fall of Savannah, 254, 263; 192, 337, 340, 347
Georgia Continental Line, 3rd Battalion, commanded by James Screven, 150, 172; John Dooly recruits for, 179; battalion flag, 205; in Third Florida Campaign (1778), 209; shattered at fall of Savannah, 263; 193, 199, 344
Georgia Continental Line, 4th Battalion, authorized, 142; battalion flag, 205; in Third Florida Campaign (1778), 209, 215; shattered at fall of Savannah, 263; 235
Georgia, First Provincial Congress, 78, 86-88
Georgia, Second Provincial Congress,

Index

memorial to the king, 98-99; memorial to Wright, 99; memorial to the citizens of Georgia, 99-100; 90-102, 104
Georgia, Third Provincial Congress, 108
Georgia, Fourth Provincial Congress, organizes 1st Battalion, 122-27; 92, 110, 119, 121
Georgia militia, at Battle of Alligator Bridge (Florida, 1778), 221; First Regiment, 53, 68; marches to Augusta, 105-106; commissions for (1775-1776), 104, 113; preferred by soldiers over Continental Army, 122; in Second Florida Campaign (1777), 161-171; returns to Savannah after 2nd Florida Campaign, 172-73; sickly after 2nd Florida Campaign, 173; at Battle of Thomas Creek (1777), 166-71; 97, 117, 130, 245, 250-51
Georgia navy; birth of in *Phillipa* Affair, 101; congress authorizes, 144; prepares for 2nd Florida Campaign (1777), 154
Georgia Ports Authority, 393
Georgia Society of the Sons of the American Revolution (GSSAR), Elbert County Samuel Elbert Chapter, x; Marshes of Glynn Chapter, x; Edward Telfair Chapter, xi; 389; 390
Gerard, John, 187
Germain, Lord George (Secretary of State for the Colonies), Indians as allies, 175-76, 227-28; 114-15, 178, 290
Germain, Michael, 343
Gervas, John Lewis, 180
Gibbons, Sarah, 240
Gibbons, William, 240-41, 380
Girardeau's Landing (Savannah), 245-46
Glascock, Thomas, 369
Glascock, William, 302, 353
Glen, John, Culyer home meeting of Whigs (June 13, 1775), 91; Second Provincial Congress, 93; 82
Good Child King (Creek *mico*), 366
Gordon, William, 380
Graham, Thomas, shoots Thomas Brown, 149; nearly killed by Ockfusky Creeks, 85-86; 25
Graham, Thomas (James Wright's lieutenant governor), 324
Grant, Daniel, 72
Grant, James, 130, 133
Grass, Admiral de; 316
Green, Nathan, 286

Green, Thomas, 353-55, 357-58
Greene, Nathaniel, 294, 312, 315, 322, 375-77
Greene County, 375
Greensboro (Greene County), 375

Greenfield, Charles, 1
Greenfield, William, 1, 4
Grenadier Lodge No. 481, and *Phillipa* Affair, 100-101; 82-83, 91-92
Gresham, George, 256, 287
Grimké, John F., opinion of Fort Howe (1778), 216-18
Guilford Court House (battle, North Carolina, 1781), 315
Gwinnett, Button, in Assembly, 126; background, 125-26; Declaration of Independence, 127, 205; plans 2nd Florida campaign (1777), 157; temporary president of Georgia; 152; frustrated with Howe, 156; Justice of the Peace for St. John's Parish, 126; feud with Lachlan McIntosh, 141, 152, 154-55, 157-61, 163-64; duel with Lachlan McIntosh, 164, 190, 301; Sunbury headquarters, 157; as a Radical Whig, 123-24; Second Continental Congress, 127; 45, 82
Gwinnett, Samuel, 125
Habersham, James, Sr., dissolves Assembly as acting governor, 56-57; John Carey murder and Creeks, 47-48; and Elbert's Grenadiers, 53-58; feelings about Indians, 57-58; as a Mason, 51, 82; Ann Simpson trial, 58-59, 64; death, 111; 18-19
Habersham, James, Jr. Disqualifying Act, 309; 18, 34, 305, 330, 353
Habersham, John, first lieutenant in 1st Battalion, 127; appointed major in 1st Battalion by Elbert, 192; delegate in Congress, 350-51; captured at fall of Savannah, 254-55; signs written prisoner parole, 295; prisoner in Charleston, 311; mentioned, 18, 236-37, 293, 299-301, 303, 305, 328, 331, 333-34, 349-50, 353, 375, 380
Habersham, Joseph, signs the Association, 88; throws down militia commander commission, 93; commands battery at New Yamacraw, 132-33; on Committee of 31, 77; committee to supply Georgia with arms and ammunition, 108, 116; Council of Safety, 90, 108, 113;

429

Disqualifying Act, 309; in Third Florida Campaign (1778), 219, 222; on Grand Jury with Elbert (1774), Grenadiers, 92; sent to capture Loyalists, 200; and John Hopkins, 103; sent to Fort Howe by McIntosh (1777), 150; steals king's gunpowder, 89-90, 314; commands *Liberty*, 100-101; McIntosh's second in duel with Gwinnett, 164; marriage to Isabella Rae, 81, 132, 137; promoted to major in militia, 117; promoted to major in 1st Battalion, 127; First Provincial Congress, 86; Second Provincial Congress, 93; Fourth Provincial Congress, 121; qualification oath (1774), 75-76, 79, 91; and Hadden Smith, 102; Speaker of the House (1785), 339-40; on Supreme Executive Council, 298; and Whig infighting (1776), 123; enemy of Wright, 111; arrest of Wright, 120-21; mentioned, 18-19, 44, 57-58, 86, 135, 170, 307, 319, 330-32, 380, 384

Haddrell's Point (Charleston, South Carolina), 310-12

Hale, Jacob, 342

Haley, David, 179

Hall, Lyman, Act of Attainder, 314; at Treaty of Augusta with the Cherokee (1783), 325; Declaration of Independence, 127, 205; proclamation to protect Indian land (1783), 327; Indian talks, 326-28; and Liberty Society, 190; sent to confer with Benjamin Lincoln about a fourth Florida campaign, 242; mentioned, 97, 121, 126, 329, 332-33, 354, 371

Hallowing King or Hollowing King (Coweta Creek *mico*), 178, 183

Halsam, William, 239

Hamilton, Alexander, 316

Hamilton, James Inglis, 302, 313

Hamilton, John, at Carr's Fort, 275; sent by Campbell to Wilkes County, 272

Hamilton, Robert, 94

Hancock, John, 154, 156

Hancock, John (North Carolina militiaman), 283, 291, 294

Handley, George, 348

Handsome Man or Handsome Fellow (Creek *mico*), 25, 116, 177-78, 180, 183, 185

Harden, William, 342

Hardy, John, 209

Harris, Francis, sent to capture Loyalists, 200; at fall of Savannah, 253; 169

Hartman, Justice, 343

Hatcher, Archibald, 212

Hawkins, Benjamin, 364, 366, 368

Hawkins, Lieutenant, 268

Heard, Stephen, 297

Henderson, Pleasant, 282

Hessians, 321

Hester, Thomas, 287

Hill, Theophilus, 345

Hillary, Christopher, 347

Hiram Masonic Lodge (Savannah), 376

Holloway, Lewis, 347

Holmes, Adiel, 353

Holmes, David, 175

Holt, Elizabeth (grand-daughter of Elbert), 386-87

Holt, Thomas, 386

Hopkins, John, 102-104

Hookchoie (Upper Creek town), 178

House of Assembly (replaces Supreme Executive Council), 301

Houstoun, John, feud with Oliver Bowen, 224; protest to the Coercive Acts, 76; Second Continental Congress delegate but did not attend, 87-88, 97, 205; on delegation to confer with Charles Lee, 138; granted dictatorship powers as governor (1778), 210; embraces Third Florida Campaign (1778), 205, 207; elected governor, 205; conflict with Howe in Third Florida Campaign, 220, 222-24; calls for a fourth Florida campaign, 241-42; interrogates William Halsam (1778), 239; opinion of Robert Howe, 206-207; report to Congress criticizing Howe, 234; feud with Howe at fall of Savannah (1778), 243-45, 258, 320-21; gives Howe command of militia at Savannah, 245; letter to Benjamin Lincoln on fall of Savannah, 255; fears Indian war (1778), 233; on British treatment of civilians in Savannah 261; criticized by Charles Pinckney, 217; Fourth Provincial Congress, 121; mentioned, 216, 218-19, 226, 231, 298, 335, 339, 345, 350, 353, 371, 380;

Houstoun, Patrick, 67, 75

Houstoun, William, delegate in Congress, 350-52; dispute with the Creeks over Oconee Lands, 364-65; and Georgia

Index

border dispute, 360-61; 332
Howard, Lord Frederick (Earl of Carlisle), 228
Howe, Robert, Congress removes from command, 233-34, 256; court martial trial of, 319-21; on desertion, 218; arrest of John Dooly, 193-94; on Elbert's battalions, 201-202; consolidates Elbert's battalions, 205; opinion of Elbert, 209, 215, 255, 321; opposes 2nd Florida Campaign (1777), 154-56, 162; Third Florida Campaign (1778), 205-26; against Third Florida Campaign, 205-207; ordered to embark on Third Florida Campaign by Congress, 207; frustrations in Third Florida Campaign, 218, 222-24; critique of his Third Florida Campaign, 225-26; reviews Georgia battalions (1777), 153; fears Georgia will be lost (1778), 237-38, 241, 243-45; Fort Howe named for, 145; orders Elbert to Fort Howe (1778), 209; feud with John Houstoun, 205-207, 220-24, 241, 243, 258; fears Indian war (1777), 176; opinion of McIntosh, 155; inspects Fort Morris (1778), 241; and fall of Savannah, 243-59; orders Continental Army to evacuate Savannah after fall, 255; criticized for losing Savannah, 243-44, 257-58; given command of militia at Savannah (1778), 245; criticizes militia in Savannah, 245; council of war at Fair-Lawn, Savannah, 248-49; unguarded passes at Fair-Lawn, 250; letter to Benjamin Lincoln about fall of Savannah, 255; evaluation of performance at fall of Savannah, 258-59; joins Benjamin Lincoln at Purrysburg after Savannah's fall, 256; captures Fort Tonyn (1778), 220; council of war at Fort Tonyn, 224; evacuates Fort Tonyn, 224-25; 139, 157, 170, 199, 201, 209
Howe, William (British general), 119; Indians as allies, 175; 228
Howley, Richard, Act of Attainder, 314; and House of Assembly, 301; elected governor of Georgia, 306; 311
Hudson Ferry (Savannah River), 267, 276-77, 281
Huger, Isaac, arrives with troops in Savannah (1778), 243; 245; disposition of troops at Fair-Lawn, 249; losses at fall of Savannah, 254; joins Howe at Purrysburg after fall of Savannah, 257; 237
Huntington, Samuel, 308, 310
Hutchinson Island, 130-33, 300, 379
Impartial Administration of Justice Act (Jury Act), 76-77
Independent Presbyterian Church (Savannah), 91, 94
Irene Indian Mound (Savannah), appearance of in nineteenth century, 387-88; burial of John Rae, 59; destruction of, 388-89; excavated by WPA, 392-93; 21, 41, 45, 133, 381
Irvine, Garrett, 347
Irwin, Jared, 225, 343
Jackson, James, at Battle of Midway Church, 236; criticizes Robert Howe, 243, 257; and surrender of Savannah, 323; 197, 369, 376
Jackson, James (London merchant), 361
Jay, John, 357
Johnson, Robert, 2
Johnson's Square (Savannah), 22, 305
Johnston, Ann, 106
Jones, James, 134
Jones, Noble, death, 111; 28, 44-45
Jones, William, 304-05
Jones, Noble Wimberly, Act of Attainder, 314; protest to the Coercive Acts, 76-77; Culyer home meeting of Whigs (June 13, 1775), 91; Disqualifying Act, 309; offers command of Georgia Battalions to Elbert (1777), 191; steals king's gunpowder, 89; as a Mason, 51, 54, 82; Second Continental Congress Georgia delegate but did not attend, 87-88, 97; Second Provincial Congress, 93; Fourth Provincial Congress, 121; Speaker of the House controversy with Wright, 55; Speaker of the House controversy with Habersham, 55-58; enemy of Wright, 111; meeting with Wright (1776), 119-20; 28, 84, 320, 323
Jordan, John, 347
Jordan, Thomas, 211, 213-15
Joseph Hull and Company, 388
Kerby, William, 368
Kerr, Catherine (grand-daughter of Elbert), 386-87
Kerr, John, 386
Kershaw, Joseph, 307
Kettle Creek (Battle of, 1779), 275-76
Kialiee (Upper Creek town), 178

King, John, 369
King's Rangers, attacks Augusta, 178; marches to Augusta with Campbell (1779), 265; at Battle of Brier Creek, 279, 283; ordered to Burke County jail, 267; battle at Burke County jail (1779), 267-68; attacks Fort McIntosh, 149-51; at Battle of Thomas Creek, 166; mentioned, 107, 114, 148, 155, 163, 175, 179, 187, 219, 262, 269; *See also* Thomas Brown.
Knox, Henry, 316, 330
Krutman, Edward, 380
Lafayette, Marquis de, 49, 316
Lamar, Zachariah, 375
Lane, Joseph, 262-63
Laurens, Henry, warns Savannah of approaching British fleet, 118; warns Georgia of potential British invasion from New York (1778), 235-36; and Lachlan McIntosh, 190-91; informed about fall of Savannah, 256; mentioned, 107, 180, 202, 207-208, 215, 225, 231-34, 273-74
Lawson, Hugh, 353
Lee, Charles, background, 136; commands Southern Continental Army, 136; Continental Army review in Savannah (1776), 140; defensive river scheme for southern parishes, 144; commands Florida Expedition (1776), 138-41; doubts about Florida Expedition, 140; confers with Georgia delegation, 138; 182
Lee, "Lighthorse" Harry, 321
Letters from a Farmer in Pennsylvania, 32
Lexington (battle of), 89, 92-93
Liberty County, 345, 350
Liberty Society, 190
Lincoln, Benjamin, on fall of Augusta, 270; plans for retaking Augusta, 272; surrenders army at Charleston, 310; given command of Southern Continental Army, 233-34; facilitating prisoner exchange for Elbert, 303-304; opinion of Elbert, 304; expected to lead a fourth Florida campaign, 234-35; worries about Loyalists, 270; arrives near Savannah after fall, 256; informs Henry Laurens about fall of Savannah, 256; collects army at Purrysburg, 263; complains about unruly militia at Purrysburg, 263; dispatches Moultrie's troops to Beaufort to thwart British force, 265-66; on wretched state of American prisoners, 292-93; and siege of Savannah, 242, 249, 254-55; mentioned, 273, 276-77, 282, 287, 298-300; 375;
Lindsay, Reverend, 381
Lisbon (Georgia), 375, 386
Little Tallassee (Creek Indian town), 74
Lloyd, Edward, 342, 348
Long, Nicholas, 354, 357-58
Louisville (Georgia), 22, 374-75
Love, John, 293
Loyalists (Royalists, Tories), on Amelia Island, 167; organized by James Boyd, 266; and Expulsion Act in Georgia, 202-204; plot to kill George Galphin, 178, 187; to use in retaking Georgia (1778-1779), 228-29, 235, 239, 264; raids into Georgia from Florida, 144, 148-49, 177-78, 199-200, 208-209, 235;incite Indians to warfare, 203; at Kettle Creek, 275-76; Scopholites, 209; Wright seeks their help to reconquer Georgia (1778), 227; Whig attitudes toward, 271; attitudes toward Whigs, 273, 296-97; mentioned, 101-107, 111-12, 321-23, 329, 347-49, 355, 395-96
Lucas, John, 331
Lyford, William, 204
Lytle, Archibald, 284-85
MacAlister, Private, murdered by Whigs, 271, 285
McBean Swamp (battle, 1779), 269, 277
McElwee, James, 290
McGillivray, Alexander, opposes Treaty of Augusta (1783), 328-29, 332-33, 362; saves British Indian agents from Georgia Whigs (1777), 188; store clerk for Samuel Elbert, 19; opposes Treaty of Galphinton, 369-71; in Savannah with several Creeks (1779), 297; opposes Treaty of Shoulderbone, 377; collusions with Spain, 333, 354-55, 357; 363-65, 369
McGillivray, Lachlan, 19-20, 188, 329;
McGirth, Daniel, 267-68
McIntosh, George (brother of Lachlan), labeled a Loyalist by Gwinnett, 152
McIntosh, John, captured at Brier Creek, 288; defends Fort Morris in Sunbury fort (1778), 238-39; prisoner in Savannah, 291

Index

McIntosh, Lachlan, Act of Attainder, 314; background, 126-27; on Beard's Bluff attack (1777), 147; promoted to commander of 1st Battalion, 126-27; brigadier general over Georgia's Continental Line, 141; on meaning of the Declaration of Independence, 173; defensive river and fort scheme for southern parishes, 144-45; and disease in the battalions, 173-74; Disqualifying Act, 309; feud with Button Gwinnett, 152, 154-55, 157-61, 163-64; duel with Button Gwinnett, 164, 190, 301; apologizes to Gwinnett's widow, 190; instructions to Elbert at Fort Howe (1777), 147-48; orders Continental horse troop to Fort Howe (1777), 186; fears Indian war (1777), 147, 176; federal commission to the Indians, 366-67; on delegation to confer with Charles Lee, 138; marks boundaries in Oconee lands, 366; Battle of the Rice Boats, 133-34; takes command of militia in Savannah (1776), 129; says Savannah was deserted (1776), 130-31; participates in siege of Savannah (1779), 298; transferred to Washington's army (1777), 191-92; on Wright's escape, 128; wounded (1777), 150; George Walton becomes enemy of, 302; Walton causes Congress to remove McIntosh from command, 302; mentioned, 132, 135, 139, 142, 168-70, 192, 207, 329, 331, 337, 347, 391

McIntosh, William (brother of Lachlan), 152

McIntosh, William (British assistant deputy to the Cherokee), 175, 187-88

McKay, James, 345

McLean, Andrew, 325-26, 334-35, 396

McLean, Elbert & Company, 334, 383

McLeod, Donald, 292-93

McQueen, John, 346

Mad Turkey (Okfuskee Creek *mico*), 72-74, 85

Maitland, John, 269, 299

Malcontents, 7-8, 19, 35

Marbury, Leonard, Disqualifying Act, 309; 186, 276-77, 281, 307, 314, 319, 320, 337

Marchand, Sehoy, 19

Martin, John, elected governor, 322; 304, 325-26, 371

Martin, Joseph, 366

Masonic Lodge of England, (F&AM), 50, 69-70, 91, 376

Masons (F&AM), 50-53, 58, 69-70, 81-83, 91-92, 230, 285-87, 304, 376, 381, 390, 399

Massachusetts Circular Letter, 32-33

Massachusetts Government Act, 76-77

Mathews, George, 371

Middleton, Charles, 181

Midway (Georgia), 209, 235, 293

Midway Church (battle of), 236

Midway Meeting House, 236; burned, 238

Milledge, John, 82

Miller's Long Bridge (Freeman-Miller Bridge) on Brier Creek, 267, 277, 278-81, 284-85, 287

Militia, *see* Georgia militia.

Milton, John, 340

Mingo French Man Stubby (Choctaw *mico*), 357

Miró, Estevan, 355-56, 358

Montgomery Square (Savannah), First African Baptist Church, 392

Moodie, Thomas, 43-44, 81

Moodie Affair, 43-44, 54

Moore, Francis, 181

Moore, Sam, 178, 187, 199

Moravians, 21

Morel, John, Grand Jury with Elbert (1774), 86; as a Mason, 98; First Provincial Congress, 86; 45, 82

Moss, Joshua, 347

Moultrie, William, sent by Lincoln to Beaufort, 265, 272; fears goal of British invasion from New York is Charleston (1778), 238; on Battle of Brier Creek, 288-89; on loss of Fort Morris, 262; criticizes Howe for losing Savannah, 257; on fleeing citizens from Savannah, 261; on wretched state of American prisoners, 292; comments on failed attack at Spring Hill Redoubt, Savannah, 300; mentioned, 216-218, 237, 241, 266, 272, 278, 360

Mowbray, John, 167, 211-12

Mulryne, John, 347-48

Muse, Elizabeth (Elbert's grand-daughter), 386-87

Muse, Louis (Lewis), 386

Natchez, 353-57

Native Americans, Augusta conference with Creeks (1776), 116; Treaty of Augusta with Cherokee (1783), 324-28; Treaty

of Augusta with the Creeks (1783), 327-29; and Articles of Confederation, 326; attack Beard's Bluff, 146-47; meaning of Declaration of Independence for, 182; estimated warriors in Florida (1778), 210; attack Fort McIntosh, 149-50; frontier attitudes toward, 180-81, 362; Georgia and Indian threats (1776), 114-16; Georgia and Indian trade, 115-16, 368; raids into Georgia, 144, 148-50, 232-33; and Irene Mound (Savannah), 392-93; reasons for fighting in American Revolution, 175, 177, 233; purpose of trade after American Revolution, 332; Creek warfare in Wilkes County (1777), 174-88; acts of violence against Chatham County citizens, 297; Wright seeks their help to reconquer Georgia, 227; *See also* individual tribes.
New Imperial Policy, 30
New Purchase, 1773, xiii, 65-68, 71, 110, 174, 177, 181, 375; *See also* ceded lands.
Newman, John, 252
Nichols, Richard, 345
Ninety-Six (South Carolina), and James Boyd's Loyalists, 266; 73, 208
Oakchee Warrior (Creek *mico*), 183
Oconee Lands, 67, 328-29, 332-33, 335-36, 355; 362-70, 373, 375, 378; *See also* Treaty of Augusta with the Creeks.
Odingfell, Sarah, 312
Odom's Ferry (Savannah River), 276
Oglethorpe, James, death of, 362; founds Masonic Lodge in Georgia, 50; 1, 3, 4, 6, 10, 156, 211, 361-62
Old Town (Ogeechee River, Georgia), 177, 367, 374
Oliver, Dionysius, 375, 385
O'Neil, John, 345
Order of the Cincinnatus, 330-31, 376-77, 381, 390
Otis, James, 32
Palachacola Second Man (Creek *mico*), 183
Pannell, Joseph, 193-94
Paris Mill (on Brier Creek), 277, 280-81
Parker, Hyde, fleet arrives at Savannah (1778), 242, 254; 228-29, 240
Patrick, Brown & Company, 20
Pelot, Francis, 12
Perceval, John (Earl of Egmont), 4
Perry, William, 364
Petersburg (Georgia), 375, 385-86

Phillipa Affair, 100-101, 115
Pickens, Andrew, pursues James Boyd in South Carolina, 266; federal commission to the Indians, 266, 368; at Battle of Kettle Creek, 275-76; 321, 327
Pierce, William, 342
Pinckney, Charles C., criticizes John Houstoun, 217; criticizes Fort Howe, 217; describes suffering in Fort Tonyn, 221-22; commentary on breakdown of command at Fort Tonyn, 223; 208, 216, 220
Pinder, William, 348
Point Plantation (Ogeechee River), 323-24, 372
Poplin, William, 290, 294
Porbeck, Colonel von, 321
Porter, Benjamin, 185, 187, 252
Prevost, Augustine, sends diversion force to Beaufort, South Carolina, 265-66, 272; orders Brown's Rangers to Burke County jail, 267; opinion on Elbert, 290; notified about Savannah invasion (1778), 239; occupies Savannah and assumes governorship, 265; during siege of Savannah (1779), 300; mentioned, 219, 228-29, 235, 262, 274, 277, 98-99, 303
Prevost, Marc, at battle of Alligator Creek Bridge, 221; 166; dispatch to Elbert from Amelia Island, 169-70; 182, 220; at Battle of Brier Creek, 277-89; marches forces toward Midway, 235; at battle of Midway, 236, 238-40; takes Fort Morris, 262; sent to relieve Campbell at Odom's Ferry, 276-77; at Battle of Thomas Creek, 166
Prisoners, on British prison ships in Savannah, 290-294; freedoms of prisoners, 303; paroles, 294-95; Sunbury prisoner oath, 295; 310-11;
Proclamation of 1763, 36
Provincial Congress (South Carolina), 107
Pulaski, Casimir, 298, 300;
Pumpkin (Cusseta Creek *mico*), 85
Purrysburg (South Carolina, 256, 262-63, 266, 272, 277, 282, 287
Quamino Dolly, 250
Quartering Act, 76
Quebec Act, 76
Queensborough, 22-23, 30, 46-49, 59
Radical Whigs, dispute over officering 1st Battalion, 122-27; and Constitution of

Index

1777, 151-52; 84, 92, 97, 301
Rae, Catherine (mother of Samuel Elbert's wife, Elizabeth), 49
Rae, Elizabeth "Betsy", *see* Elizabeth Elbert
Rae, Isabella (daughter of John Rae, wife of Joseph Habersham), 81, 132, 137, 219, 384
Rae, Matthew (brother of John Rae), 22, 49
Rae, John, appraisal of property, 1773, 60-61; death, 59-60; murder of Ann Simpson, 58-59; 19-30, 34-35, 37, 41, 43, 45, 46-49, 55-59, 69, 81, 125, 132, 182, 312, 332, 381, 384-85
Rae, James (brother of John Rae), appointed by Elbert as commissary general (1777), 192; Fat King's talk at home of, 328, 333; Second Provincial Congress, 93; Superintendent of Indian Affairs for Georgia, 325; 81, 312, 319, 326
Rae, James (nephew of Robert Rae), 308
Rae, John, Jr. (son of John Rae), in 1st Battalion, 127; death of, 196; will, 49; 59, 61, 81
Rae, Rebecca (wife of Robert Rae), 308, 312
Rae, Robert (half-brother to John Rae), Second Provincial Congress, 93; talk with Creeks at Old Town (1777), 177-78; death of, 307; opinion of Elbert, 307; at naval engagement on Frederica River (1778), mentioned, 24-25, 60, 81-82, 182, 196, 212, 306, 312, 319
Rae, Whitfield & Company, 26, 60, 65-66
Rae's, Elbert & Company, 24-25, 65, 67, 110, 383
Rae's, Elbert & Graham, 25-26, 48, 85, 93-94, 149, 305-306, 312, 315, 319, 383
Rae's Hall, 21-22, 29-30, 41, 59-61, 131-33, 190, 196, 244, 246, 306-308, 319, 331, 384-85; 387-88, 393
Rae & Whitefield, 66
Rae, Whitefield & Company, 110
Reid's Bluff (Altamaha River), 217-19
Reynolds, John (governor), 18, 20
Rice Boats (battle of, Savannah, 1776), 130-35, 299
Richmond County, 261, 266, 337, 383
Roberts, Daniel, 212
Robinson, John, 21
Rochambeau, Comte de, 316-17
Rolland, Henry, 190
Ross, Francis, 280-82
Rules and Regulations of 1776, replaced by Constitution of 1777, 151; 135, 155

Russell, Samuel, 373
Rutledge, John, 178, 180, 187, 264, 292
Rutherford, Griffith, joins Lincoln at Purrysburg, 263; 278, 289
Sack, John, 157
Salagee (Creek *mico*), 47
Saratoga (battle of, 1777), 196, 228, 302
Savannah (Georgia), First African Baptist Church, 392; Creek Indian visit (774), 74-75; shares seat of power with Augusta during Confederation Period, 341-42; British plans to capture (1778), 228-29; Colonial Cemetery, 390; Declaration of Independence celebrations, (1776), 127; Declaration of Independence celebrations (1777), 173; deserted (1776), 130; defenseless in 1778, 243; evacuated by British, 323; expansion of during 1930s, 391; fall of (1778), 242-59; citizens flee after fall, 260-61; fire (1796), 385; founding, 1-4; destruction of historic squares during expansion, 391-92; King's birthday celebration (1774), 75-76; merchants and Townsend Duties, 33-34; provisions stored, 230, 235; siege of Savannah (1779), 298-300, 325; effects of war on, 308-309
Savannah Warehouse & Compress Company, 388
Sawpit Bluff (Nassau River, Florida), 162, 164-66
Scovel, Joseph (or Scophol), 209
Scopholites, 209-11
Screven, James, at Alligator Creek Bridge battle (1778), 221; sent to guard Altamaha forts by McIntosh (1777), 150; Council of Safety, 150; commands 3rd Battalion, 150, 172; sent to capture Loyalists, 199-200; killed at Battle of Midway Church, 236; 192
Sealey, John, 13
Sealey, Hannah, 13-14
Seminoles, raid Georgia, 232; attack Fort Howe (1778), 208, 210; 175
Seven Years' War, 20, 30, 36, 136, 145
Sheftall, Levi, captured at Savannah, 253; on a prison ship, 253; 117
Sheftall, Mordecai, as commissary, 205, 230; Disqualifying Act, 309; as a Mason, 51, 230, 304; merchant, 82; 244; captured at Savannah, 253; on prison ship *Nancy*, 291; signs written prisoner parole, 295;

435

as a prisoner in Antigua, 299, 310; and Union Society, 304; 308, 320
Sheftall, Sheftall, 297, 310
Ships, non-military, *Britannia*, 47; *John*, 379; *Paoli*, 16; *Savannah*, 381
Ships, American naval, *Bulloch*, row galley, 212; *Congress* row galley, 159, 163; *Dolphin* schooner, 159; *Hope* sloop, 159; *Lee* row galley, 159, 209, 212-13; *Liberty*, 100-101; *Polly* transport, 159, 162, 169; *Washington* row galley, 159, 209, 212
Ships, British naval, *Alert*, 242; *Cherokee*, 118, 134, 139; *Galetea*, 211, 214-15; *Granby*, 239; *Hawke*, 167; *Hinchinbrook*, 130-33, 161; *Hinchinbrook* (different from previous and involved in fight on Frederica River), 211-14, 216; *Meredith*, 167; *Neptune*, 239-40; *Phillipa*, 100-101, 115; *Raven*, 119, 134, 139; *St. John*, 131; *Rebecca*, 161, 167, 211-14; *Sandwich Packet*, 118; *Scarborough*, 119, 128, 131, 133-34; *Symmetry*, 130; *Syreen*, 119; *Tamar*, 118; *Vigilant*, 246; *Whitby*, 130; unnamed watering brig, 212, 214
Ships, British prison, *Munificence*, 290-91, 294; *Nancy*, 291; *Whitley*, 291
Shirrell, William, 72
Shirrell Massacre, 72
Simpson, Timothy, 347
Singee (Creek *mico*), 183
Skull Shoals (skirmish with Indians, 1777), 179-80, 185; 365
Silver Bluff (George Galphin's trading post on Savannah River in South Carolina), 185
Simpson, Ann, 58-59
Skee (Creek Indian), 6
Slaves/Slavery, as British allies, 228; British confiscate, 241; use in Third Florida Campaign (1778), 219; 34, 125, 209, 306-07, 324, 331, 342, 378-79, 383, 396-97
Smith, Hadden, 101-102
Smith, John, skirmish with British at Brewton's Hill, 248; 247, 258
Smith, John (North Carolina militia), 291, 293
Solomon's Masonic Lodge (Savannah), F&AM, 50-52, 58, 91, 376, 382, 390
Somerville, Edward (Captain), 22
Somerville, Jane (daughter of John Rae), inherits Rae's Hall, 196; 22, 49, 61, 307-08
Somerville, John (son-in-law of John Rae), 22, 24, 29, 60-61, 384-85
Sons of the American Revolution (*See* Georgia Society of the Sons of the American Revolution)
Sons of Liberty (in Savannah), and John Hopkins, 102; 31, 89
South Carolina Battalions; 1st, in Third Florida Campaign, 208; 139
South Carolina Battalions, 2nd, 139
South Carolina Battalions, 3rd, at Fort Howe, 146; in Third Florida Campaign, 208; at fall of Savannah, 254; 139
South Carolina Battalions, 5th, at fall of Savannah, 254
South Carolina Battalions, 6th, in Third Florida Campaign, 208; 155, 162
South Carolina border dispute with Georgia, 359-62
Spain, as American ally, 228; and Bourbon County controversy, 353-59; 333, 335, 345; 369
Spirit Creek (battle of, 1779), 269
Spring Hill, Savannah, 249, 252
Spring Hill Redoubt (siege of Savannah, 1779), xi, 300, 386
St. Augustine (Florida), Loyalist sanctuary, 114; famine, 148; mentioned, 235; 136-37, 141, 203, 208, 164, 192, 198, 210, 233, 235, 238
St. Catherine's Island, 125, 155, 162-63, 204
St. Jago (Creek *mico*), 74
St. John's Parish, 123-26
Stamp Act, 30-31, 72
Stead, Benjamin, 384-85
Stephens, Thomas, 7, 8, 11, 35
Stephens, William, 5, 8, 11, 19, 35
Stephens, William (different from above), 380
Steuben, Baron von, 316, 319-20
Stevens, John, 82
Stirk, John (probably same as Samuel), takes part of 2nd Battalion to Fort Howe (1777), 153; Disqualifying Act, 309; and arrest of John Dooly, 193-94; 98, 142, 304, 340, 348-49
Stokes, Anthony, 103, 105
Storr & Reid, 305
Story, James, 343
Strong, John, 158, 196

Index

Stuart, John (Southern Superintendent of Indian Affairs), greets Creeks at Savannah (1774), 85; plot to assassinate George Galphin, 178; Indian policy, 114, 116; Indians as allies, 175; Indian trade, 175; encourages Indian raids, 233, 240, 271, 297; at New Purchase conference (1773), 66-67, 72; 179, 188
Sugar Act, 30
Sumter, Thomas, 155, 162
Sunbury (Georgia), attack by Fuser on Fort Morris, 238-39; and surrender of Fort Morris, 262-63; Sunbury prisoner oath and parole, 295; provisions stored, 230, 235; mentioned, 50, 124, 138, 141, 155, 157-59, 209, 215, 218, 297, 299
Supreme Executive Council (replaced Georgia Assembly, 1779), 298-99, 306
Taitt, David, 175, 188, 297
Taliaferro, Benjamin, 353
Tallachea or Talechee (Lower Creek *mico*), 85
Tallassee King (Hoboithle, Creek *mico*), 116, 326, 328, 334-35, 367, 369-70
Tallegee (Creek *mico*), 47
Tallemach, Thomas, 134
Tar and Feathering, 102-103, 111
Tarling, Peter, 343
Taylor, John, 282
Tea Act (1773), 68
Teasdale, Christopher, 345
Telfair, Edwin, Act of Attainder, 314; at Treaty of Augusta with the Cherokee (1783), 325; at Treaty of Augusta with the Creeks (1783), 325; background, 314; committee to supply Georgia with arms and ammunition, 108, 116; Disqualifying Act, 309; recovers debts from Elbert's family, 383; gets Congress to authorize a fourth Florida campaign, 234; steals king's gunpowder, 89-90; 315, 319-20, 332, 335, 337, 358, 362, 369-71, 374
Telfair, Elbert & Company, 335, 341
Ternant, Jean Baptiste de, on unguarded passes at Fair-Lawn, Savannah (1778), 250; 244
Thomas Creek (battle of), 166, 171, 186
Thomas, John, 324
Thompson, Charles, 361
Tondee's Tavern (Savannah), 76-77, 90-91, 93, 120, 139
Tonyn, Patrick (governor East Florida), Indians as allies, 114, 175, 228; offers Loyalists sanctuary, 114; notified about Savannah invasion (1778), 239; 26, 152, 154, 166, 210, 211
Tonyn brown water fleet, 154, 161, 167, 211, 227
Townsend Duties, 30-33, 68
Travis, R. J., 389-90
Treutlen, Frederick, 349-50;
Treutlen, John Adam, opinion of Elbert, 186; chosen governor, 163; term as governor ends, 205; opinion of Indians, 174; 195-96, 199
Treaty of Augusta (Cherokee, 1783), 324-27, 332
Treaty of Augusta (Creeks, 1783), 328-29, 332-34, 362, 364, 368
Treaty of Galphinton, 369-71, 373
Treaty of Paris, 324, 333
Treaty of Shoulderbone, 377;
Treutlen Plantation, occupied by Campbell, 265
Trustees (Georgia), Goals for Georgia, 1-3; 5-11
Trustee Garden, 139
Twiggs, John, at Treaty of Augusta with the Cherokee (1783), 325; at Treaty of Augusta with the Creeks (1783), 325; 267-68, 369, 373
Two Sisters Ferry, 256-57, 265, 272, 277, 287, 298
Tybee Island and lighthouse, Parker's fleet arrives (1778), 242; mentioned, 42, 118; 121, 127, 133-34, 139, 239, 245, 323-24
Tyrrel, John, 218
Tything Decker Ward (Savannah), 2, 315
Union Society, 304
Unity Masonic Lodge No. 465, Savannah (F&AM), 69-70, 82
University of Georgia (Franklin College), 336, 352-53, 399
Vaughn, William, 347
Wallace, Elizabeth, 1
Walton, George; Act of Attainder, 314; Chief Justice of Georgia, 350, 383; protest to the Coercive Acts, 76-77; Council of Safety president, 108, 113; and court martial trial of Robert Howe, 319-21; Declaration of Independence, 127, 205; Disqualifying Act, 309; opinion of Elbert, 209, 311; efforts to get Elbert exchanged as a prisoner, 311-12;

437

thoughts on Frederica River naval engagement, 215; on Third Florida Campaign, 208; opinion of Button Gwinnett, 164; and House of Assembly, 301; elected governor by House of Assembly, 301; wants to enter Indian trade, 374; and Lachlan McIntosh, 190-91, 301-302; commands militia in Savannah (1778), 242-43, 245, 249, 250-51; fears of unguarded passes at Fair-Lawn, 250; criticizes Howe for loss of Savannah, 257-58, 319-21; wounded during fall of Savannah, 251, 320; captured at Savannah, 253; exchanged as prisoner, 300; Second Provincial Congress, 94, 97-98; and Hadden Smith, 102; 306, 328, 333, 340, 360, 362

Walton, John, 29, 82

Ward, Robert, 165, 167

Ward, William, 348

Wardrope, Joseph, 4-5

Washington County, 336-37, 347, 352;

Washington, George, at Yorktown, 315-18; mentioned, 119, 128-29, 133-34, 136, 154, 181, 184, 191-92, 233, 257, 264, 270, 298, 302-304, 308, 311, 330, 340, 381, 397

Watson, Joseph, 6-7, 83

Wayne, Anthony, 316, 322, 325

Weeks, Francis, and Elbert's Masonic sign at Battle of Brier Creek, 287

Wells, George, and House of Assembly, 301-302; 124-26, 176

Wereat, John, Act of Attainder, 314; on Expulsion Act, 204; on Supreme Executive Council, 298; elected by Supreme Executive Council as "president" (1779), 298; demands Wright give himself up for violating parole, 298-99; 207, 244, 301, 306, 320

Wesley, John, 18

West, William, 350

White, John, temporarily put in charge of Georgia battalions (1778), 235; Disqualifying Act, 309; battle of Midway Church, 236; forges letter from Elbert at Midway, 236; informs Elbert in Charleston about Battle of Midway Church, 236-38; 215-16

White, Thomas, 350

White, William, 72

Whitefield, James, 215

Whitefield, George, 18

Whitney, Joseph, 345

Wilkinson, John, 340

Wilkes County, Creek Indian warfare (1777), 174-88; mentioned, 173, 194-95, 261, 267, 271-72, 274-75, 297, 306, 321, 324, 327, 362, 366, 375, 385;

Williams, Andrew, Disqualifying Act, 309; in Third Florida Campaign, 208, 217-18, 223; mentioned, 263, 266, 268, 270, 273-74, 276, 278, 281

Williamson, Littleton, 347

Wilson, Thomas, 320

Winfree, Lieutenant, 167

Winfrey, Joseph, 346

Winn, Bannister, 324

Wood, Joseph, 190

Wood, William, 229

Woodruff, Joseph, as a Mason, 51, 82

Works Progress Administration, excavation of Irene Mound, 392

Wormsloe Plantation, 29

Wright, "Sir" James (Royal Governor of Georgia), Act of Attainder, 314, 319; abandons Georgia (1776), 134; abuse of royal governor powers, 33, 35-37, 43-44, 55, 80-81, 152, 341; address to Whigs from *Scarborough*, 128; arrest by Council of Safety, 120-21; Assembly, 1769, 28-45; dissolves Assembly, 32-33; dismisses Assembly (1771), 44, 46, 55-56; and Assembly controversy about southern parish representation, 36-39, 41, 43; addresses Assembly (January 1775), prorogues Assembly (1775); 88; 87; on Association, 101; baronetized (1773), 62; and Coercive Act protests in Georgia, 77-79; and Creek War (1774), 72-75; criticizes Committee of 31, 77; death of, 362; and Disqualifying Act, 309-310, 325; Elbert land grants, 29-30, 48, 71; sets aside land for the poor, 343; Elbert's Grenadiers, 53-54, 62, 64-65; Elbert purchases his Point Plantation, 323; day of fasting, 95; and Thomas Fee, 73; and John Hopkins, 102-103; Indian trade, 115; Indians as allies, 175, 227; King's birthday celebration, Savannah (1774), 75-76; London trip, 54-55, 65; return from London (1773), 62-63; as a Mason, 51; and Massachusetts Circular Letter in Georgia, 32-33; memorial from Second Provincial Congress, 99; Thomas Moodie

Affair, 43-44; breaks parole, 127-28; New Purchase (1773), 65-69; returns to Georgia as governor during restoration (1779), 297-98; end of Wright's restoration, 321-23; evacuates Georgia after restoration, 323; Battle of the Rice Boats, 134; Royal government eroding, 84, 86, 89, 93, 96, 104-106, 110-11; fears for safety, 93; during siege of Savannah (1779), 300; and Stamp Act, 30-31; mentioned, 14, 16-18, 22, 25, 361, 372, 396

Wrightsborough, 72

Wynn, Richard, 146, 149-50

Unity Lodge No. 465 (F&AM), 69-70, 82, 91

Yamacraw Bluff (Savannah), 1, 3, 6, 300

Yamacraw Indians, 21

Yamasee War, 1, 12

Yazoo Lands (See also Bourbon County), 333, 335, 353-59

Yorktown, Virginia, (siege, 1781), 49, 315-18

Young, George, 212

Young, Isaac, 304-05

Young, Thomas, 385

Young, William, 45, 82

Zubly, John Joachim, Continental Congress delegate but did not attend, 97; Culyer home meeting of Whigs (June 13, 1775), 91; "Law of Liberty" speech, 94-95; memorial to the king, 97-99; minister of Independent Presbyterian Church, 91; Second Provincial Congress, 93-98; 104, 205

Zubley's Ferry, 237, 255-57, 265